Cross-Cultural Dimensions in Conscious Thought

Cross-Cultural Dimensions in Conscious Thought

Narrative Themes in Comparative Context

Psychocultural Research with the Thematic Apperception Test, Volume II

GEORGE A. DE VOS
AND ERIC DE VOS

ROWMAN & LITTLEFIELD PUBLISHERS, INC.
Lanham • Boulder • New York • Toronto • Oxford

ROWMAN & LITTLEFIELD PUBLISHERS, INC.

Published in the United States of America
by Rowman & Littlefield Publishers, Inc.
A wholly owned subsidiary of The Rowman & Littlefield Publishing Group, Inc.
4501 Forbes Boulevard, Suite 200, Lanham, Maryland 20706
www.rowmanlittlefield.com

PO Box 317
Oxford
OX2 9RU, UK

The Interpersonal Concerns Scoring System (ICSS) that is included as an Appendix in this volume is also available as a downloadable .pdf file, in a format suitable for research use. That downloadable file can be found at http://sunsite.berkeley.edu/Anthro/devos/depub_2000.html. At that page, select the button for the decade 2000 and then find the bibliographic listing for the volume's title. You will find the link to the .pdf file there.

British Library Cataloguing in Publication Information Available

Library of Congress Cataloging-in-Publication Data

Library of Congress Control Number: 2003113925

ISBN 0-7425-2674-7 (cloth : alk. paper)

Printed in the United States of America

∞™ The paper used in this publication meets the minimum requirements of American National Standard for Information Sciences—Permanence of Paper for Printed Library Materials, ANSI/NISO Z39.48-1992.

Table of Contents

Volume II
Part III

TAT Research Participants

William Caudill, Ph.D. (Deceased)
Social and Environmental Studies, National Institute of Mental Health, Bethesda, Maryland

Dorsh de Voe, Ph.D.
Visiting Scholar, Anthropology Department, University of California, Berkeley, California

George A. De Vos, Ph.D.
Emeritus Professor of Anthropology, University of California, Berkeley, California

Eric Steven De Vos, Ph.D.
Professor of Psychology, Saginaw Valley State University, University Center, Michigan

David Ephrahim, Ph.D.
Professor of Psychology, National University, Caracas, Venezuela

Emmit B. Evans, Ph.D.
Lecturer, Political Science, California Polytechnic State University, San Luis, Obispo, California

Eun-Young Kim, Ph.D.
Anthropologist

Robert Manlove, Ph.D.
Emeritus Dean, Division of Science, City College of San Francisco, San Francisco, California

Eiji Murakami, Ph.D. (Deceased)
Professor of Psychology, Department of Education, Nagoya National University, Nagoya, Japan

Leslie Rabkin, Ph.D.
Chief Clinical Psychologist, Hawaiian School System, Kona, Hawaii

Nancy Scheper-Hughes, Ph.D.
Professor of Anthropology, University of California, Berkeley, California

Carola Suárez-Orozco, Ph.D.
Co-director, Harvard Immigration Project, Senior Research Associate and Lecturer in Human Development and Psychology at the Harvard Graduate School of Education, Cambridge, Massachusetts

Marcelo Suárez-Orozco, Ph.D.
Victor S. Thomas Professor of Education, Harvard University Graduate School of Education, Cambridge, Massachusetts

Irina Todorova, Ph.D.
Post Doctoral Fellow in Human Development and Psychology at the Harvard Graduate School of Education, Cambridge, Massachusetts

Cicero Emidio Vaz, Ph.D.
Professor of Psychology, Pontifical Catholic University, Rio Grande do sul, Porto Alegré, Brazil

Hiroshi Wagatsuma, Ph.D. (Deceased)
Professor of Anthropology, Tsukuba National University, Tsukuba, Japan

Preface

Volume II:

——This is my quest
To follow that star
no matter how hopeless
no matter how far——

The Impossible Dream

From *Man of La Mancha*
(J. Darein and M. Leigh)

You have in your hands the second volume in a two-volume series. The purposes of the two-volume work are fivefold:

First: In volume I we presented in detail a system of coding categories that enables objective coding of the manifest content of thematic stories, or other verbal or narrative material that depicts both normative and deviant interpersonal concerns, in a manner that enables valid cross-cultural comparative research. The system was initially applied to materials obtained in Japan, 1953–1954. It has subsequently been developed over a period of forty-five years, largely through the efforts of the senior author, George A. De Vos, and colleagues.

The system, which we call the "Interpersonal Concerns Scoring System" (ICSS), has been developed primarily from the analysis of spontaneous narratives given in response to the Thematic Apperception Test (TAT). It has also been used successfully on other types of material produced by methods such as sentence completion tests, problem situation tests, and interviews that evoke various forms of thematic stories or other forms of spontaneous answers.

Second: A major purpose for developing this system is to make possible types of interpretation that are based not only on what individuals actually say (i.e., the manifest content of responses) but also on a group-level assessment of what constitutes normative versus nonnormative responses. In sociological terms, the system is designed to enable quantification of the normative occurrence of collective or social representations within given social groups or cultures. By using this system, one can demonstrate that the TAT or other methods that evoke thematic responses, when quantified properly, can be used with considerable validity in doing systematic cross-cultural comparison of emic descriptions of interpersonal relationships. Some of these comparisons are illustrated in the present volume.

Categorization of data helps us avoid, to some degree, problems of interpretation. Too often, social scientists derive generalized interpretations directly from responses that may not be representative of the group being studied. This may lead to erroneous generalizations and superficial characterizations of a group. This type of direct or unmediated interpretation evades the responsibility for making some normative assessments, whether of within-group or between-group norms. If comparative or cross-cultural work is to be conducted systematically, some form of comparative quantification is necessary. The psychologist as well as the anthropologist or sociologist cannot avoid some commitment to objective assessment of the representative or normative nature of what is elicited from informants. In group research, interpretation should only follow upon some systematic categorization that reveals the normative differences between groups that constitute cultural variability.

Third: This system's sociological and cross-cultural comparative purpose is placed within a developmental-psychodynamic frame of reference that interrelates the coding categories. In developing the system of coding we have made recourse to an explicit psychodynamic approach to human thought and perception. We see, in the existence of culture-based patterning of experience, indications of culturally distinct generational continuities in the development of psychological functioning. We have tried to relate the categories of interpersonal concerns to relevant developmental mechanisms operative in human socialization.

The categories can be seen to reflect a progression of interpersonal concerns from infancy through adulthood that involve the internalization of sociocultural patterns including social or cultural representations of the social world within the individual. This is not simply a list of human concerns. Use of the scoring system can provide an objective basis for more psychodynamically oriented interpretive efforts to relate normative categories of interpersonal concerns to relevant developmental mechanisms and socialization processes.

Fourth: This system attempts to provide a comprehensive system for scoring the full range of manifest content produced by respondents, rather than scoring only those particular aspects of responses related to single-focused issues, be they concerns with achievement, or political issues of interpersonal dominance or control. The major categories of the system reflect psychological universals of interpersonal and self-directed social attitudes. Depending on the group and its broader social context, these attitudes are emphasized differently. But as universal categories of human concern, examples can generally be found in some form in every group studied as is illustrated amply in the present volume.

Fifth: The potentially exhaustive nature of the category system does not mean that it can not be applied to very specific issues of investigation. In the present volume, we shall illustrate in several chapters taken from several selected past studies how the scoring of stories elicited by particular TAT stimuli can shed light on the relative saliency of a variety of specific themes. These themes range from the different status perceptions of husbands by Japanese women from two different villages, through the different perceptions of violence by American and Japanese delinquents, the concerns with competence in particular groups of youth, patterns of alienation characterizing the Korean ethnic minority in Japan, or difficulties of mother-son communication in Canadian students compared with samples of Venezuelans or Brazilians, etc.

The Two Volumes Are Organized in Three Parts

In Part I volume I, "Social Representations in Narrative Expression," we include a brief historical introduction to the use of the Thematic Apperception Test for narrative analysis, a discussion of the experiential self in society, and a preliminary delineation of the universal categories of purpose and emotion found in human experience.

Part II volume I, "The Interpersonal Concerns Scoring System: Expressive and Instrumental Categories," examines each of the expressive, or emotionally oriented, and then the instrumental or purpose-directed categories into which the system is divided. The scorings of these categories are briefly illustrated in each chapter. Note that Japanese and Korean illustrations are used contrastively throughout to highlight issues that are usually treated differently when Western cultures alone are used to generalize about psychological processes.

Part III volume II, "Narrative Analysis: Illustrative Research," contains chapters that are adapted from a number of previously published research reports as well as some unpublished material. These chapters illustrate how the system can help make sense of the human experience of self in relation to others, across a wide range of cultural contexts in Asia, Africa, and the Americas. They also exemplify the type of cross-cultural comparisons that can be made, based on responses to a number of the more commonly utilized Murray TAT cards.

A scoring manual, "Basic Interpersonal Concerns," is included as an appendix in each volume. It comprises the complete ICSS scoring categories and subcategories.

A second appendix, "Illustrations of TAT Cards used in Japan, Kenya, and the Philippines," is also included in each volume. It contains the altered or additional TAT cards used for research in Japan, Kenya, and the Philippines, and should provide the reader with a clear image of various TAT stimuli discussed in the two volumes.

Acknowledgments

Editorial assistance provided by the senior author's wife, Suzanne, has much improved the readability of the manuscript. The senior author also wishes to express special appreciation for the able intellectual advice and editorial assistance provided by his son, Eric, who contributed many helpful suggestions over a period of years, making improvements to the scoring system and its theoretical relevance as it is now being published. Eric ultimately became substantially responsible for editing and co-authoring many portions of both volumes, and is co-author of the entirety of volume I. The senior author is most happy that Eric has chosen to assist as the junior author/editor of these volumes, and that he is now working with his own students to carry this system into the future.

The helpful suggestions of the senior author's students over the years have also been incorporated into versions of the scoring system as it approached its present form. Some of their own innovative work is represented in several of the illustrative chapters in volume II, and their research has informed much of the discussion throughout volume I.

Last, but not least, we want to thank Saun Strobel, technical secretary at Saginaw Valley State University. Her thorough expertise and her inimitable good nature (even while tackling tedious editorial tasks) have contributed greatly to the pleasure with which we are now able to publish this book.

George A. De Vos
Professor Emeritus of Anthropology
University of California at Berkeley

Eric S. De Vos
Professor of Psychology
Saginaw Valley State University

Introduction

Volume II, Part 3: Narrative Research across Cultural Boundaries

For the present volume, we have selected a number of studies, conducted by others as well as by ourselves, to illustrate the wide range of cultural settings and modes of approach that reveal meaningful within-group and between-group differences when the TAT test is used in the context of anthropological investigation. In none of these studies was the TAT test itself the major purpose of their investigation. The authors of these various chapters were concerned with a variety of social issues and found the use of the test facilitative in the task they were pursuing. Space does not permit us to go into full detail about these projects (they are reported elsewhere), but the research contexts of the various authors are sufficiently outlined in each chapter for us to understand their objectives. They illustrate material reflecting not only present family relationships, but also cultural continuities persisting from the past that portend future social and political issues to be faced by an oncoming generation.

Present and Future Uncertainty in Self and Society

In chapter 1, volume II, "Broken Fiddles and Hardened Hearts in Rural Ireland," anthropologist Nancy Scheper-Hughes presents TAT material to illustrate how the TAT aided in the discovery of a number of the psychological themes found to characterize the contemporary rural Irish of the 1970s. The TAT was given to thirty-six typical village adolescents (twenty-two girls and fourteen boys) between the ages of fifteen and eighteen, and to twenty-two psychiatric patients of both sexes from rural County Kerry, ranging in age from fifteen through thirty-six. The frequency with which she found certain types of stories was unique to the Irish sample: stories produced by males in response to Card 1 that involve a broken violin, in the context of narratives describing failure, lack of perseverance, low sense of efficacy, giving up, etc.; and stories produced by young women where there was a refusal to even see the violin as relevant in the stories. Such stories gave powerful reinforcement to the general conclusions of Scheper-Hughes' field research. In her volume *Saints, Scholars, and Schizophrenics: Mental Illness in Rural Ireland* she drew a rather grim portrait of Irish country life. Village social and cultural institutions were in a stage of disintegration, and villagers were suffering from anomic social circumstances leading to high rates of emigration. The religious directives of a severe form of Catholicism reinforced restrictive and inhibiting socialization practices particularly affecting the males. The sexes were locked into isolation and alienation. Deaths and emigrations surpassed marriages and births. Mental illness was rife.

In chapter 2, volume II, "Some Aspects of the Self in a Selfless Society: An Israeli Kibbutz," psychologist Leslie Rabkin reports a piece from his longitudinal study of Israeli-born "sabra" growing up in an Israeli kibbutz founded by their immigrant parents. They were retested almost twenty years after they had previously been tested as part of an intensive anthropological investigation of the Kiryat Yedidim kibbutz by anthropologist Melford Spiro (Spiro, 1970, 1975, 1979). The founders of the kibbutz in question were part of what is known in Israel as the Third Aliyah (immigration), a diverse band of disaffected youth from Austria, Galicia, and Poland, who emigrated to Palestine in the years 1919–1924. Approximately 90 percent of all kibbutz-born children and adults in Kiryat Yedidim were tested, both in 1951 and 1967–1968, with a range of instruments. In 1951, Spiro's adult sample was comprised of five men and four women, ranging in age from twenty-one to twenty-eight. There were, at that juncture in kibbutz history, only twelve kibbutz-reared adults. In 1968, these people were between thirty-seven and forty-five years of age. The most dramatic theme found in their TAT narratives was what he termed a "denigrated self." The sabra self in 1951 emerges from their stories as somewhat insecure, inadequate, and worried about being incompetent (Rabkin and Spiro, 1970, 1975). Spiro (1975) suggested that the sabras' "denigrated self" resulted from a concatenation of forces: their felt incapacity to assume responsibility for kibbutz functioning; their parents' lack of faith in them; and, their basic difficulties in developing an integrated, effective set of ego-adaptive mechanisms for coping with the chronic changes in the caretakers that during their infancy and early childhood had taken the place of more traditional forms of intimate family life (see Rapaport, 1958). Spiro had reported how parental disappointment in their children was endemic among the founders, in great part as the inevitable aftermath of a stage of ideological fervency. A visible parental doubt in their offspring's capacities continues to be salient in the next generation's stories.

Chapter 3, volume II, "Omens of Future Ills: African Youth in Contemporary Kenya" also reflects another form of anomie, but one of frustrated achievement rather than one of inner insufficiency. In 1972, political scientist Emmit Evans obtained responses to three TAT cards from a sample of 699 African secondary school students in Kenya. When coded with the Interpersonal Concerns Scoring System (ICSS) the students' projections revealed a pattern of interpersonal concerns centered around a driving desire to achieve a better way of life for themselves and their families in Kenya's newly independent society. But the data also revealed some disturbing premonitions of the modes of technically illegal adaptation likely to characterize the responses of the students as they left school and found their aspirations and expectations frustrated by the inability of Kenya's polity and economy to deliver the jobs upon which their hopes for a better way of life were built (Evans, 1975, 1977). They exemplify Robert Merton's (1957) discussion of criminal behavior in an anomic society. This chapter also seeks to demonstrate the prognostic value of the TAT through assessing the validity of predictions made on the basis of 1972 data against the record of more recent events in the country.

These three chapters, each considering TAT Card 1 in a different context, dramatically illustrate the utility of the TAT as a quantitative cross-cultural research device, depending on the specific purpose to which it has been put by the investigator. It has proven its usefulness in the highly different social circumstances of contemporary Ireland, Israel, and Africa. In what follows, we shall also demonstrate its value in research on ethnicity, class, and status, using materials from Asia and the Americas, North and South.

Cultural Continuities in Japan and in Japanese Immigrants

Chapters 4 through 7, volume II, present tables demonstrating a variety of statistical comparisons between the groups considered.

Chapter 4, volume II, "Gender Roles, Marital or Sexual Problems: Comparisons of Responses In Two Japanese Villages," illustrates how data obtained from different social strata in the same culture reveal statistical differences in social attitudes in regard to gender roles and responsibilities. As part of our large-scale testing in 1954 we gathered 800 TAT protocols from two cities and three villages. We have previously made a number of separate reports on this research which George De Vos summarized in his volume on the cultural psychology of the Japanese (De Vos, 1973). In studying the inhabitants of an economically marginal fishing village, Sakunoshima, with a number of direct interviews as well as questionnaires, a Japanese research team, of which George De Vos was a part, observed that the social status of the entire village has been traditionally low in contrast to the fairly well-to-do farmers of Niiike where we had interviewed and tested the previous two months. While the overall results on the Rorschach test were in general strikingly similar, on the TAT and on a problem situation test we found consistent differences in attitudes concerning the role behavior and social attitudes expected of women within the primary family in the different villages.

One original effort was to determine whether we could demonstrate the sensitivity of our projective tests to the status differences of the women of different occupations who lived in two rural communities in central or southwestern Japan. Using our system to score various interpersonal categories and subcategories Hiroshi Wagatsuma and De Vos were indeed able to graphically demonstrate differing perceptions about expected social behavior.

In 1959, we turned our research efforts to a nine-year general and specific study of delinquency in Japan. In one phase of this research we used the TAT as well as other projective methods. Chapter 5, volume II, "Violence and Aggression in Fantasy: A Comparison of American and Japanese Lower-Class Youth," reports on research with Eiji Murakami wherein we did a statistical analysis of TAT responses to assess possible differentials in the fantasies of delinquents both from the United States and Japan that we compared with matched samples of lower-class, nondelinquent youth from each country. We thought that if a preoccupation with violence is more characteristic of delinquency-prone youth whether in Japan or the United States, the TAT should reveal systematic differences in story content. Those tested were seventeen to twenty-three-year-old American and Japanese youth specifically of lower-class background. In addition, our American samples gathered at a prison for young adults eighteen to twenty-two years of age were carefully separated into subgroups of African American, Mexican-American, and Americans of various European backgrounds. Quantitative analysis showed some differences between delinquent and nondelinquent youth in both countries that were evident over and above the considerable culturally specific themes apparent in their narratives.

In chapter 6, volume II, "Internalized Achievement: Some Historical Continuities Found in Japanese Social Perception," we present a comparative report of material obtained from Japanese and Japanese Americans by William Caudill, John Connor, Curtis Vaughn, and George De Vos in a number of different research contexts over a period of forty years. The work began in collaboration with Caudill in the late 1940s (Caudill, 1952; Caudill and De Vos, 1956). It proceeded to a large study of Japanese from three villages and two cities, conducted in collaboration with a team at Nagoya National University in the early 1950s (De Vos, 1960, 1973). In this work, George A. De Vos used the TAT very specifically to explore the strong achievement motivation of the Japanese in the United States and Japan. In this chapter we also draw on more recent materials from Japan gathered by John Connor and Curtis Vaughn. Then in later chapters (chapters 8, 9, and 10) we analyze some yet unpublished materials on Japanese Brazilians gathered by Takeyuki Tsuda in Brazil. A comparison of all these studies demonstrates clearly the continuity of internalized preoccupation with self-motivated achievement in groups of Japanese ancestry in Brazil and the United States as well as in Japan itself.

In chapter 7, volume II, "Vitality and Optimism versus Alienation in Ethnic Minorities: The Korean Case," the TAT is used to dramatically demonstrate the sense of personal alienation evident in a good proportion of minority Koreans residing in Japan over four generations (Lee and De Vos, 1981). With Eun-Young Kim, we examined in their TAT protocols the evident alienation expressed by these minority Koreans as compared with the more positive social and family attitudes of Koreans who have in recent years become voluntary migrants to the United States. Koreans in both instances revealed an abiding distrust of official authority.

This study should be seen in the context of a variety of studies which indicate that in the United States there are differential responses of various minority groups to educational adaptation as reflected in school performance and occupational success. On the one hand, a number of the Asian groups are doing relatively well, have taken to the school system in a positive way, and are overrepresented numerically according to population at many of the major American universities. Other groups, such as Mexican-Americans and African Americans, have done relatively poorly in the American setting.

This pattern, however, is not unique to minority members of North American society.[1] The present generation of Korean youth in Japan reflects considerable personal alienation in response to the disparagement and degradation endured since the arrival of their parents or grandparents. Most of these individuals now speak no Korean, and are indeed, culturally, but not socially, assimilated within contemporary Japanese society. We have reported elsewhere (Lee and De Vos, 1981) their very high delinquency rate and many other behavioral symptoms of the alienation, as are symbolized in the psychological material herein presented. Members of the Korean culture demonstrate cultural similarities, but also radical differences in respect to views of future accomplishment. This is not to say that Koreans do not meet some of the discrimination directed toward Asians generally by a white majority culture in the United States. However, compared with the longer history of being a deprecated subgroup that was considered innately inferior (i.e., the experience of Koreans in Japan), Koreans in the United States have gained a level of social acceptance which is totally different from their experience in the Japanese ex-colonial context.

Contrasts in Ethnic Heritage: The Japanese and Other Ethnic Groups in Brazil

Moving our focus from our previous examinations of North American and Japanese multiethnic social climates, we turned to Brazil and Venezuela in South America. Brazil is an ex-colonial society comprised of a great diversity of ethnic groups. The Portuguese and Afro-Brazilians are derivative of an older migration that occurred during the period of colonial slavery that lasted until the 1870s. Since the 1870s,

---

[1]Differences among the recent migrants to western Europe are also being reported. Research in reference to this question is presently under way in a number of countries.

there have been a substantial number of migrants of German, Italian, and East European Jewish background, as well as Japanese, who arrived since the turn of the century. These immigrants, for the most part, settled in the southern areas, from Sao Paulo to the Uruguay border. In the early 1990s, with Cicero Vaz and Takeyuki Tsuda in Brazil and David Ephrahim of Venezuela, we analyzed TAT materials obtained from a number of different South American ethnic groups.

After previously working with George De Vos in Berkeley, in 1987–1988, Professor Cicero Vaz began obtaining TAT samples from various Brazilian ethnic and social groups. In the southern state of Rio Grande do Sul he obtained samples of Brazilians of various origins including Germans, Italians, and East European Jews, as well as Portuguese and Afro-Brazilians from an inner-city Favela slum.

Doctoral work by Takeyuki Tsuda involved a study of Japanese-Brazilians, both in Brazil and in Japan, where many second- and third-generation Japanese-Brazilians have returned as temporary migrant workers (Tsuda, 1997). During this research activity he gathered materials including TAT protocols from Japanese-Brazilians living in both the Sao Paulo area and from Porto Alegré. These protocols gathered by Vaz and Tsuda enabled us to make an examination of how past social attitudes, especially about the primary family and toward authority, as well as internalized attitudes about achievement, are reflected spontaneously in samplings of Brazilian youth that will comprise the coming adult generation.

In chapter 8, volume II, "Heritage of Exploitation: A TAT Report on South Brazilian Youth," we turn first to TAT comparisons of other Brazilian ethnic groups with the Japanese-Brazilians in respect to achievement motivation. We have attempted to demonstrate how, depending on ethnic background, fantasies of present social relations and future occupational possibilities are influenced by past family-social traditions. Our attention has been focused not only positively on the relative appearance of achievement motivation itself, but also on the interference of possibly more salient family problems on goal-oriented fantasy.

In the contrastive use of Japanese-Brazilian protocols we are also demonstrating how traditional Japanese cultural attitudes continue not only in the United States but in the totally different cultural environment of Brazil. One can not fail to note that the Japanese-Brazilians, as true for other samples of Japanese tested elsewhere, remain inwardly concerned with questions of personal competence. As they envision it, however, possible present personal inadequacy can be overcome by hard work. This emphasis on hard work overcoming shortcomings is found also, but to a much lesser extent, in some Italian-Brazilian stories. But in the other groups considered, issues of personal competence or self-confidence give rise to far more pessimistic fantasies.

Chapter 9, volume II, "Brazilian Fantasies of Chastisement, Separation, or Abandonment of Children," reports on specific results comparing responses to Cards 3BM and 16 found in the Brazilian samples. We further note on Cards 3BM and 16 how specific family problems appear in the fantasy of all groups considered, but with different content. Concerns with physical beatings or abandonment are frequent. There are themes about heavy-handed parental dominance or even exploitation. Such themes are totally lacking in Japanese-Brazilians.

In chapter 8, volume II we have already noted how Brazilian stories in all groups are implicitly, if not explicitly, of a more compliant nature than are American stories. In chapter 9, volume II we further illustrate that when there is occasional generational opposition voiced in Brazilian youth, it tends to be thematically portrayed as rebellion rather than as actualizing autonomy. Whereas occasional stories of revolt against parents are forthcoming in Brazil, they do not resemble some American stories in which there is not even a hesitancy about the ability of a youth to defy the wishes of a parent or to negotiate with parents to bend them toward one's own wishes. While there is notable political cynicism about authority in Brazil, one does not note many fancied themes of gaining personal autonomy.

What we also attempt in this chapter and the others covering Brazilian material is to look in great illustrative detail at the actual stories displaying how these concerns can be captured in the scoring categories we utilize. Hence we present not simple numerical comparisons but also extended tables in which the summary content of the stories remains evident to demonstrate the scoring system at work. Just presenting a comparative numerical summary by categories can be misleading, since the details describing the issues experienced between parents and children, for example, can be completely different in tone, despite their being coded into similar major categories. Some further breakdown into subcategories is necessary for meaningful data analysis.

Chapter 10, volume II, "Mentorship or Complicity Between Men: Illustrations from Brazil," reports in extended summary form on stories elicited by presenting a picture depicting an older and a younger man with their heads together (Card 7). In the analysis of this card we see further evidence of how themes of collusion or corruption are easily forthcoming from Brazilian youth. Contrasted with our previous sample of Japanese, both in Japan and the United States, the Japanese in Brazil pay somewhat less attention to social hierarchy, but still manifest a much more positive attitude toward authority relationships than do groups of younger Brazilian of different ethnic backgrounds. In Japanese Brazilians, there were far more narratives that focus on an authority relationship involving mentoring or advice. The Japanese show cultural continuity in their depiction of older authority in a positive light. The Italian group is also occasionally apt to see positive authority. The German Brazilian youth express more ambivalence. Portuguese or Afro-Brazilian youth from a favela do not see many positive anticipations of adult control or any instrumental behavior of a positive nature in their view of the adult world. The exploitative venal tradition derivative of an earlier period of Brazil's history is indirectly still reflected in the stories of some of these present-day Brazilian youth.

Vaz has also obtained samples of indigenous Indians and settlers, mostly of Portuguese background, from the state of Amazonas near the city of Benjamin Constant on the Amazon River. Chapter 12, volume II, "Living on the Amazon:

Tukuna Indians and New Brazilian Settlers" reports on the TAT study that was part of field research first carried out in 1988, in the Amazon region of Brazil. The purpose of the study was to investigate to what extent the process of acculturation influences, if not so much the structure, at least the adaptive reactions of the indigenous Tukuna as they interact with Brazilian settlers from the more technologically advanced areas of Brazil. We compared TAT responses of twenty-six Tukuna Indians and twenty-six Brazilian settlers who had migrated to the same vicinity of the Amazon River. The initial purpose of Vaz was not ethnographic, but psychological. His focus was on personality variables and on the psychological content of communication, not on cultural or behavioral data.

The Tukuna people live on the border of the Javari River and High Solimbes, extending from the boundaries of Brazil, Peru, and Colombia to the town of Beruri in the state of Amazonas. Excerpts from Vaz study illustrate that the TAT can be used on groups who lived in comparatively isolated communities. Using the TAT as a testing instrument, one is able to elicit revealing salient interpersonal concerns. We can aver that there is, today, practically no place on earth so isolated that one is unable to obtain meaningful material characterizing the social and personal concerns of particular social groups.

Problems of anxiety were notably more frequent in the Tukuna sample than in the settlers. On all cards, the Tukuna especially revealed an intrusive abiding fear about becoming victims of violence, hunger, or disease. These concerns were also notably present in the settler group as well. Feelings of sorrow, sickness, death, anger, and problems encountered in sexual and love relationships were very similar for both groups. Although both groups gave relatively few stories concerning self-motivated achievement, the settlers overall showed more interest about possible achievement than did the Tukuna. Missionary activity was directly reflected in a number of their stories. Generally, the Tukuna records suggested a more passive attitudinal stance. Overall, the settlers were somewhat less pessimistic about their social relationships, but gave evidence of worry about drunkenness and physical violence expressed within the family unit.

Some Comparisons of Mother-Son Relationships

In 1993, Professor David Ephrahim, professor of psychology at the University of Venezuela in Caracas, came to Berkeley on a Fulbright grant to work with George De Vos on the projective test material he had been gathering both in Venezuela and in British Columbia, Canada. Ephraim has had available 150 records from various ethnic and class settings in Venezuela. In chapter 11, volume II, "Mother-Son Relationships: Cross-Cultural Contrasts in Interpersonal Perceptions," we utilize forty-nine of these records that we have divided by sex and class background. We have a sample of twenty-four youth from an elite high school in Caracas that is attended by children of at least upper-middle class socioeconomic status. In some instances, these subjects represent families of recent economic success. The second sample of twenty-five is taken from a high school that serves students from a Caracas working class district. The Canadian samples obtained by Ephraim are taken from first- and second-year students attending the arts facility of a west-coast Canadian university. They are of mostly middle class, white, Protestant background. The American sample to which we occasionally refer was obtained by John Connor from the California State University in Sacramento. These students come from a variety of settings. Since they were selected from an ethnically varied student body we have chosen only those considered "Caucasian" in background.

In this chapter, we examine the relative emphases in the interpersonal concerns of small samples of stories produced by both male and female Canadian college students, Venezuelan youth from two different social class strata, the Brazilian high school youth, and the Japanese-Brazilians already reported upon in the previous chapters.

For purposes of focus we report the specific results of only one card, Card 6BM, which is a picture of an older woman turned away from a young man with hat in hand. Comparing even very small samples of age, sex, class, ethnicity, and minority status cross nationally using responses to this TAT card should dispel the often held contention that cross-cultural testing should be considered *a priori* invalid or subject to deep suspicion. There are evident certain human universals in the dimensions of social interaction and social perception that transcend cultural boundaries, and responses to this card make that clear. Though a card such as 6BM appears to be locally limited in its period by specific clothes and racial appearance, the implied mother-adult son relationship is picked up by most individuals presented with the card, regardless of the differing cultural backgrounds. Conversely, there are manifest differences in normative emphasis and the nuances of concerns that also quickly become apparent as soon as one compares groups from different social backgrounds related to age, sex, and national-cultural settings.

Despite the specific range of stories that can be elicited by a card depicting an older woman and a younger man, there are a variety of stories that fall directly into the categories most used in our scoring system. As we illustrate in chapter 11, volume II, within *expressive* stories we can further differentiate whether the depicted issues reflect concerns with affiliative closeness or loss, harmony or discord, dependency or nurture, problems of positive evaluation or shame, or inner emotional states. Variously, problems of pride, esteem, or shame may be at issue. Or the focus may be on family harmony, personal discord, and/or a need for reconciliation.

Stories depicting *instrumental* issues of personal achievement, career concerns, competence, or personal responsibility and potential guilt for negatively perceived behavior may be juxtaposed to interpersonal concerns with control, dominance, or compliance or with mutual instrumental cooperative or competitive activities. In considering Card 6BM comparatively, we illustrate how examples related to all these categories are forthcoming, ranging from a rare appearance to frequent or pervasive appearance within a particular group.

Among instrumental-vertical stories, major concerns about a maternal figure in an authority role were found most often among the Japanese-Brazilians. In this respect, and in other themes, this sample created stories in line with writings previously discussed in various previous reports about Japanese-Americans and Japanese in their homeland.

The Portuguese or Afro-Brazilian youth were less concerned with positive maternal authority than were the Italian and German groups. The forty-eight stories by Portuguese and Afro-Brazilian youth revealed only two stories of a mother as a positive authority figure. There were several stories of wrongdoing on the part of a son. The Afro-Brazilians' stories of wrongdoing were of a somewhat more serious nature. Their expressive stories had the highest proportion of negative or unresolved endings.

There were noticeable overall trends in the Venezuelan sample related to the mother as a dominant figure. Asking for forgiveness was a noticeable theme in both 8 percent of Venezuelan as well as Japanese subjects (four in forty-nine; four in fifty). In the Venezuelan stories, mother is mostly described as a nurturing figure, not a disciplinary one. She can be overprotective. When she scolds the son it is in a protective way. In general, Venezuelan mothers are perceived as refusing to recognize any need for their son to separate from them, for instrumental or expressive purposes; although they may finally accept such separation at the end, it's not a mother's normative expectation.

Contrasted to previous American, Japanese, or Korean samples, instrumental aspirations were of relatively minor concern among this present sample of college-going Canadians. There were only two stories that include a very strong instrumental goal-oriented theme. Only in one Canadian male story is there a successful separation for instrumental purposes. A secondary theme appearing in their stories are themes that suggest a mother needing care. It is the reverse of seeing the mother in an authority or nurturing role with a son. The resolute independence of an older person is emphasized in several stories. A mother or grandmother can be described as very able, in terms of her virtue of endurance. In these Canadian stories one sees a more recent theme depicting the long-term possibility that a son has to take care of an aging mother by placing her away in a nursing home or senior residence. In the Canadian responses to Card 6BM, the most singular feature found unique to them in a variety of contexts is how both male and female students focused so explicitly on the inability of a young man to communicate or to gain satisfactory affiliative closeness with his maternal figure. There appears normatively, in this Protestant sample, a sense of isolation, emotional alienation or an inability to express emotions openly.

Social Esteem in a Philippine Community

We return to an Asian culture in chapter 13, volume II, "Amor Propio and Related Values in the Philippines." Professor Robert Manlove reports how, as part of his fieldwork, he analyzed the TAT and Sentence Completion Test (SCT) results from a random sample of Philippine urbanites. While exploring Philippine urban values in connection with social inequality, Manlove (1990) discovered that many of the consciously described values were not independently defined nor independently operative within the culture. These values include what is locally termed *amor propio* (self-esteem), *hiya* (shame), *pakikisama* (smooth interpersonal relations), *utang na loob* (debt of gratitude), etc. It became clear that there was a definite interrelated structure in their value system. Some values were subsumed by others, and each value took its social significance, i.e., its meaning, by its contrast with the other values in an implicit hierarchy.

Based upon 7400 TAT and SCT responses, Manlove's chapter represents the sensitivity of projective tests to some central core values that define interpersonal relationships within the Philippine culture. He considers this use of projective tests as indispensable in accomplishing the type of emic value exploration he has attempted in his field work. Moreover, he avers that there is a necessary quantification inherent in examining the ideas presented. To handle material from any large or complex community, some statistical approach is necessary. Certainly, without objectively scoring of material elicited with methods like the TAT and SCT, any statistical or quantitative approach would not be possible. While traditional participatory observation is necessary in these explorations, it is not in itself sufficient.

Manlove also considers that there is important work to be done exploring variations in a culturally prevalent value system. It is quite possible that a different emphasis in a system of values will prevail in the villages and towns of the Philippines or in cities of larger size and different function. It is hoped, therefore, that the taxonomy he describes in chapter 13 could be further explored to promote a deepening study of diversity in Philippine culture.

Contemporary Refugees and Migrants

Chapter 14, volume II, "Continuities in Culture Among Tibetan Refugees," examines TAT narratives given by Tibetan refugee youth in India in 1989. Dr. Dorsh de Voe had previously conducted fieldwork with Tibetan refugees in India, from 1980 to 1982, and had collected a small number of TAT narratives from Tibetan refugee youth. In 1989, she collected 468 TAT stories from Tibetan refugee youth between the ages of eight and nineteen years old living in various Tibetan refugee camps and Tibetan children's villages in India. For this particular chapter, Tibetan stories from Card 17BM (the rope card) were scored using the Interpersonal Concerns Scoring System (ICSS). Forty-nine individuals responded to TAT Card 17BM. Their responses corroborate observations from other fieldwork about Tibetan beliefs, motives, and behavior.

The analysis of this collection of TAT narratives demonstrates that projective tests are capable of evoking patterns of response that reveal consistencies in Tibetan culture, even among displaced youth. Themes of nurture and responsibility are dramatically illustrated, and reflect a continuity of traditional Tibetan values and beliefs among refugees. We also see concerns with fate. Perhaps it is not surprising to see the negative hand of fate in narratives produced by Tibetan refugee youth. They are, after all, refugees who feel very strongly the loss of their country. In these stories, there is poverty, deprivation, separation, estrangement, and death. In many narratives, one or two parents were deceased. However, in almost every story, there is recovery and success.

Tibetan youth narratives clearly illustrate that for Tibetans the consequences of loss involve nurturant concerns. Poverty, for example, while causing inordinate suffering, is viewed as an opportunity for achievement, responsibility, nurturance, and for the expression of true sacrifice and love. Suffering and loss can be transcended through virtuous simplicity, spirituality, and diligent industriousness. In Tibetan youth narratives, resolution favors community harmony and family unity, the fulfillment of the child's obligation to his family, and a commitment from the child to protect and provide for his parents. The overwhelming response of Tibetan refugee youth on the rope card is that of fate and nurturance, with usually a harmonious, happy ending. For Tibetan youth, their comprehension of the refugee events in their families' lives and their response to it are grounded in their Buddhist world view. What is most poignant in these narratives is the resilience, the forward-striving efforts to improve not only one's personal circumstances, but also those of others.

Wandering Souls

Similar interpersonal and family concerns have been found in other recent refugee groups, such as the Central American refugees in the United States. Marcelo Suárez-Orozco has documented the violence these refugees experienced prior to flight as well as the fear, deprivation, and loss they experience post-flight, as students in an inner-city school setting in California.[2] As with Tibetan refugee youth in India, family and self-sacrifice appeared as pivotal concerns for Central American refugees. A pattern of mutuality and interdependence emerged that exhibits a basic continuity. As their parents had helped their own old folk, many informants felt it was their turn to help their parents achieve a better future.[3]

As part of her collaborative study with Marcelo Suárez-Orozco, Carola Suárez-Orozco has previously used the TAT in their studies of Latino migration into the United States (Suárez-Orozco and Suárez-Orozco, 1995). In their

---

[2]See Marcelo M. Suárez-Orozco, *Central American Refugees and U.S. High School: A Psychosocial Study of Motivation and Achievement.* Palo Alto: Stanford University Press, 1989.

[3]Ibid., p. 85.

contribution to the present volume, chapter 15, volume II, "Wandering Souls: The Interpersonal Concerns of Adolescent Immigrants," Carola and Marcelo Suárez-Orozco, with Irina Todorova, together examine the experiences of adolescent immigrants and refugees from a variety of contexts: Central America, Mexico, the Dominican Republic, Haiti, and China.

Using the TAT, along with interviews, other projective measures, and ethnographic observations, they find some similar patterns of affiliation and nurture intertwined with achievement concerns. One seeks to accomplish for others, and with the help of others. They also identify several themes that emerge in the context of the upheaval of uprooting and resettlement in the new country. Themes of loss and feelings of inadequacy are preoccupations that run through many of the stories of immigrant youth, regardless of their countries of origin. Their work again illustrates how TAT narratives sensitively capture frequently occurring preoccupations of recent immigrant youth.

Concluding Remarks Regarding Styles of Presentation

Note that each of these chapters treats the presentation of quantified materials somewhat differently. The presentations range from simple or brief notation of the relative number of stories in each of the major categories, through various ways to record subcategories, to an inclusive summary of individual stories listed with each story's scoring. The method of selection chosen to present materials depends on the specific purposes pursued by the authors and the space allotted for presentation. We do not personally advocate any one particular system of numerical presentation. However, we do find that presentations that include unmediated reporting of stories affords dramatic illustrations of nuanced cultural differences in the representation of human relationships and social attitudes.

Notes

Caudill, William. 1952. Japanese-American Personality and Acculturation. *Genetic Psychology Monograph*, **45**: 3–102.

Caudill, William and George A. De Vos. 1956. Achievement, Culture and Personality: The Case of the Japanese Americans. *American Anthropologist*, **58**(6): 1102–1126 (reprinted: 1961; 1966; 1967; 1971).

Connor, John. 1977. *Tradition and Change in Three Generations of Japanese-Americans*. Chicago: Nelson Hall.

Connor, John W. and George A. De Vos. 1989. Cultural Influences on Achievement Motivation and Orientation Toward Work in Japanese and American Youth. In David Stern and Dorothy Eichorn (Eds.), *Adolescence and Work: Influence of Social Structure, Labor Markets, and Culture* (pp. 291–326). Hillsdale, N.J.: Lawrence Erlbaum Associates.

De Vos, George A. 1960. The Relation of Guilt Toward Parents to Achievement and Arranged Marriage among the Japanese. *Psychiatry*, **23**(3): 287–301.

———. 1973. *Socialization for Achievement: Essays on the Cultural Psychology of the Japanese*. Berkeley: University of California Press.

———. 1993. Problems with Achievement, Alienation, and Authority in Korean Minorities in the United States and Japan. In K.K. Lee and Walter Slote (Eds.), *Overseas Koreans in the Global Context* (pp. 145–180). Seoul: Association for the Study of Koreans Abroad.

———. 1997. Heritage of Exploitation: A Brief TAT Report on South Brazilian Youth. In Stanley Renshon and John Duckitt (Eds.), Culture and Cross Cultural Dimensions of Political Psychology. *Political Psychology*, **18**(2): 437–474.

De Vos, George and Kim Eun-Young. 1993. Koreans in Japan: Problems with Achievement, Alienation Authority. In Ivan Light and Parminder Bhachu (Eds.), *California Immigrants in World Perspective*. New Brunswick, N.J.: Transaction Books.

De Vos, George and Lee Kwang-kyu. 1981. Attitude Toward Authority: Dilemma of Ex-colonial Society. In Changsoo Lee (Ed.), *Modernization of Korea and the Impact of the West* (pp. 150–162). Los Angeles: University of Southern California.

De Vos, George and Eiji Murakami. 1974. Violence and Aggression in Fantasy: A Comparison of American and Japanese Lower-Class Youth. In William P. Lebra (Ed.), *Youth, Socialization and Mental Health* (pp. 153–177). Honolulu: University Press of Hawaii.

De Vos, George and Hiroshi Wagatsuma. 1961. Value Attitudes Toward Role Behavior of Women in Two Japanese Villages. *American Anthropologist*, **63**(6): 1204–1230.

Evans, Emmit Bud, Jr. 1975. Secondary Education, Unemployment, and Crime in Kenya. *Journal of Modern African Studies*, **13**(1): 55–66.

———. 1977. Sources of Socio-political Instability in an African State: The Case of Kenya's Educated Unemployed. *African Studies Review*, **XX**(1): 37–52.

Lee, Changsoo and George A. De Vos. 1981. *Koreans in Japan: Ethnic Conflict and Accommodation*. Berkeley: University of California Press.

Lynch, Frank. 1973. Social Acceptance Reconsidered. In *Four Readings on Philippine Values* (rev. ed.). Quezon City: Ateneo de Manila University Press.

Manlove, Robert F. 1990 (unpublished). *Ozamiz: A Case Study in Urban Anthropology*. Ph.D. dissertation. Department of Anthropology, Berkeley: University of California.

Merton, Robert. 1957. *Social Theory and Social Structure*. Glencoe, Ill.: The Free Press.

Rabkin, L.Y. and M.E. Spiro. 1970. The Kibbutz in 1970. In M.E. Spiro (Ed.), *Kibbutz: Venture in Utopia*, (expanded ed.) (pp. 263–292). New York: Schocken.

———. 1975. Postscript: Children of the Kibbutz. In M.E. Spiro (Ed.), *Children of the Kibbutz* (expanded ed.) (pp. 463–499). Cambridge, Mass.: Harvard University Press.

Rapaport, D. 1958. The Study of Kibbutz Education and its Bearing on the Theory of Development. *American Journal of Orthopsychiatry*, **28**: 587–597.

Scheper-Hughes, Nancy. 1979. *Saints, Scholars, and Schizophrenics: Mental Illness in Rural Ireland*. Berkeley: University of California Press.

Spiro, Melford E. 1970. *Kibbutz: Venture in Utopia* (expanded ed.). New York: Schocken.

———. 1975. *Children of the Kibbutz* (expanded ed.). Cambridge, Mass.: Harvard University Press.

———. 1979. *Gender and Culture: Kibbutz Women Revisited*. Durham, N.C.: Duke University Press.

Suárez-Orozco, Carola and Marcelo Suárez Orozco. 1995. *Transformations: Migration, Family Life, and Achievement Motivation among Latino Adolescents*. Stanford, Calif.: Stanford University Press.

Suárez Orozco, Marcelo. 1989. *Central American Refugees and United States High Schools: A Psychosocial Study of Motivation and Achievement.* Stanford, Calif.: Stanford University Press.

Tsuda, Takeyuki. 1997. Ethic Transnationalism and the Channeling of Migrant Flows: The Return Migration of the Japanese Brazilians. In Diane Baxter and Ruth Knolfield (Eds.), *Beyond Boundaries: Selected Papers on Refugees and Immigrants* (volume 5, pp. 35–63). American Anthropological Association.

Vaughn, Curtis. 1988. *Cognitive Independence, Social Independence and Achievement Orientation: A Comparison of Japanese and United States Students.* Dissertation. Department of Education, University of California at Berkeley.

Wagatsuma, Hiroshi and George A. De Vos. 1962. Attitudes Toward Arranged Marriage in Rural Japan. *Human Organization*, **21**(3): 187–200.

Chapter 1

Broken Fiddles and Hardened Hearts in Rural Ireland

Nancy Scheper-Hughes

> (HF1) One day there was a boy out walking near a road and by and by he came across two oak trees. He walked between them and he had a magnificent view. A lovely girl came out to him and she offered him a sweet. But he was very shy. She joined him in walking, and they decided to go home. He took her into his house and his mother was angry. So the girl went home in bad form. The boy forgot to ask her name or address, so he ran back to the same place, but he found the two oak trees glued together and no opening to them. And that's the end. He couldn't get through. [PA-nature FB-shy FA-love DDC-rigid KD-thwart FB-thwart] (A sixteen-year-old female psychiatric patient's reply to TAT Card 16, a blank card.)

In my volume *Saints, Scholars, and Schizophrenics* I drew a rather grim portrait of Irish country life in the 1970s. Village social and cultural institutions were, I contended, in a stage of disintegration, and villagers consequently suffering from anomie. The sexes were locked into isolation and alienation. Deaths and emigrations surpassed marriages and births. Socialization was harsh. Mental illness was rife. These were, I am aware, brutal observations representing one "eyewitness" account.[1] In this chapter, therefore, I wish to introduce data yet unpublished from

[1]In returning to Ballybran in the summer of 1999, twenty-five years after the original ethnographic fieldwork on which this chapter is based, I found many changes, of course. For one, the grimness of lives lived on the margins of a dying rural economy was almost completely transformed for the better following Ireland's successful integration into the European

a more impersonal instrument, that is, through an analysis of the major themes to emerge from the administration of the Thematic Apperception Test (TAT) which was given to thirty-six average village adolescents (twenty-two girls and fourteen boys) between the ages of fifteen to eighteen, and to twenty-two psychiatric patients of both sexes from rural County Kerry, ranging in age from fifteen through thirty-six.

I used the Murray series of standardized pictures which reflect everyday characters in a variety of moods and human situations. I asked the subject to make up a story for each picture with a definite plot and a final outcome. In addition, he or she was encouraged to tell what each character is thinking and feeling. I consider this particular psychological test particularly well adapted to the needs and skills of the anthropologist: it is straightforward, relatively free of cultural bias,[2] and is suited to answering the kinds of broad questions which the anthropologist has in mind regarding the basic cognitive and normative orientations, appropriate role behaviors, and the quality of emotional life, etc., without having to venture into the deeper waters of technical personality assessment or symbolic analysis. In a now

---

Community. In 1974–1975, when the research for this book was being conducted, Ireland was hard hit by the global oil crisis. Inflation, recession, high interest rates, reduced work weeks, lay-offs were commonplace. There were many strikes; dissatisfaction was rife; the cost of living soared. The rural Irish, in particular, felt as though they had been sold down the river, instructed to retire and sell off their idle properties to make way for agricultural capitalism. In 1978 the then Taoiseach (Prime Minister) of Ireland, Jack Lynch, stated that his government did not deserve to be re-elected if it allowed the unemployment level to rise to 100,000, but by the mid-1980s Ireland had to accommodate to a level two and a half times that. In 1993 registered unemployment for the first time surpassed 300,000 or 21 percent of the labor force (Kennedy, 1993). Irish economists descried the devastatingly negative effects of post-colonialist underdevelopment in a country that was frequently described as in the midst of a deep crisis.

Then, suddenly, in the mid-1990s the logjam broke and things began to move very quickly. Employment soared, property values increased, and money, for the first time, became plentiful. An Irish "economic miracle" unleashed the so-called Celtic Tiger as Ireland became the single greatest beneficiary of the European Community (see Sweeny, 1998; Valarasan-Toomey, 1998). Today, Ireland leads all European Community member nations in almost every economic sphere. Irish growth rates, averaging 7.5 percent in the late 1990s, are the highest among EC member states. Over 200,000 new jobs were created in Ireland between 1994 and 1999. National interest rates are low, industrial production is booming, foreign investment has grown considerably, and living standards have grown rapidly (see Sweeny, 1998). With a substantial drop in birthrates, Ireland's living standards will soon exceed those of Britain. Unprecedented prosperity and a self-conscious materialism have followed as Ireland, once the remote and stand-offish "western island," joined the rest of Europe and finally shed its ambivalent economic dependency on Britain (see Gibbons, 1998; O'Toole, 1998).

[2]The original Murray set was perfectly well adapted to rural Ireland with the exception that some young people found difficulty identifying with the "rich" and "well dressed" story characters.

classical review of the multipurpose uses of the Thematic Apperception Test, William Henry (1947:24) stated:

> The TAT gave data on the following points: intellectual capacities, creativity and the use of imagination, social behavior, sexual adjustment, emotional relationship to parents and other people in general, emotionality (in the sense of being generally submissive, passive, or cautious, or aggressive in dealings with other people), presence or absence of anxiety or insecurity, relation to Indian-White culture conflicts, general estimate of personality adjustment, and finally an overall picture of the relationship between the intellectual and emotional aspects of the individual and of these to his overt behavior.

My own purpose in using the test was to obtain data on adolescents' and young adults' perceptions of family relationships, roles, and family dynamics, as well as to tap an internal "emic" view of the socialization process—particularly its effects upon personality differences between the sexes.[3] In addition, by examining the responses of young people who were demonstrating early signs of a basic ability to cope, I hoped to be able to identify some of the social and cultural stumbling blocks which seemed to hinder their adjustment. Ultimately I hoped to isolate those personality predispositions or characteristics which differentiated the vulnerable from the invulnerable with respect to mental illness.

Method of Analysis

The analytic framework used here loosely adheres to the one developed by George De Vos presented in this volume. I coded stories according to ten basic motivational concerns in interpersonal behavior. The fifty-eight young people tested told a total of 835 stories, each characterized by one dominant theme, but often containing from two to five additional subthemes, depending upon length and complexity of the tale. In coding the stories I avoided themes which were implied and relied only on material that was expressly stated. In addition to the thematic coding, I noted the sequences and outcomes of the stories, and paid particular attention to the attitudes expressed towards family figures. Cards 1, 2, 3BM, 4, 5, 6BM, 7BM, 12M, 13MF, and 18GF proved most fruitful for analysis.

---

[3]The particular methodological and theoretical approach to the Thematic Apperception Test used here is both phenomenologial and illustrative rather than explicitly comparative—that is, the responses are used to verify and illuminate what I already know (through participant observation, interviewing, and life history taking) about the meaning of human relationships in rural Ireland. I am aware of the cross-cultural work in the TAT begun by William Henry (1947), continued in the studies of Spindler (1955) and Wallace (1972), and presently being conducted by George De Vos (1973). I consider such work highly valuable and a cross-cultural content analysis of the Irish TAT material will be the subject of a forthcoming article.

In general the Irish records reveal large areas of feeling and motivation locked into conflict. Ambivalence is a dominant psychological mode for all the youth, as village lads vacillate between achievement orientation and anomie, and as village girls and boys debate their responsibility to home and parents vs. their own personal drive for escape from home and village. A sense of shame and incompetence blocks male strivings for achievement and an oppressive guilt often interferes with their need to excel or escape. A certain superficiality in interpersonal relations is expressed in the desire of village and hospitalized males to be affably sociable without the pressures of intimacy. And, throughout all the records runs a strong current of sexual repression and personal asceticism—one that interferes not only with intimacy between the sexes, but with the nurturant and generative aspects of personality as well.

The Sample

The village boys and girls tested represented a large portion of the oldest two grades of the parish secondary school. Most were tested individually, as I transcribed their responses by hand. Tape recorders make me, if not the subjects, nervous. A final sample of eight were tested together—each responding in writing to his or her own copy of the set of pictures. This difference will be noted in the few examples which appear more literary in style. Whenever possible the youth were interviewed following the test on general topics of life history: schooling, family relations, vocational, and other goal orientations. Eight of the fourteen boys tested (ages fifteen to eighteen) were potential, if reluctant, farm heirs, while the remaining six had serious designs for third level education or emigration. By contrast, all but three of the twenty-two girls tested expected to leave the village within "the next few years" in order to pursue a nursing or teaching career or to work abroad. These differences were not selected for, but are a natural reflection of demographic patterns in the area.

The psychiatric patients were selected (two each week) by the director of the county mental hospital, and were tested individually. My only stipulations were that the patients be volunteers for the testing, young, from a rural background, and equally divided by sex. These patients then were decidedly *not* a representative sampling of the county psychiatric hospital population—which is heavily middle aged, elderly, celibate, and more predominantly male than female.[4] Furthermore, the stipulation that the subjects be volunteers (in order to comply with federal regulations for the protection of human subjects, as well as with my own sense of ethics) necessarily resulted in a "natural selection" of the most sociable, outgoing, cooperative, and least disturbed or "sick" patients. In fact, the average length of

[4]See the Irish Psychiatric Hospital Census (1971: 42–46), especially Tables 19, 20, 21 for a complete picture of the County Kerry Hospital Population.

hospitalization for this young sample was short—just under one month, and for the majority it was their first admission into a psychiatric institution. Only the schizophrenic patients (seven of the twenty-two) had had prior hospitalization or were undergoing long-term treatment (usually six months to one year). The age span of the hospitalized group was somewhat greater than that of the average village sample—and this may account in part for the greater preoccupation of the former with sexuality. I have outlined below basic data on the patients; diagnosis was in all cases made by a resident psychiatrist.

Test Taking and Basic Differences between Samples

Because the psychiatric patients were young, cooperative, and several on the point of discharge from the hospital, it should not be altogether surprising that the test results indicate a more significant difference between the sexes of both samples than between the presumably "normal" and the labeled "pathological" samples. Given the separate worlds and social realities occupied by male and female in County Kerry, it is the "culture of sex" and not the "culture of mental illness" that is most distinguishable from the TAT records. Hospitalized young women were consistently more like "average village girls" in their responses than they were like hospitalized young men. The same holds for the average and hospitalized males whose responses generally followed the same trends. The main exception was the schizophrenic patients of both sexes who are immediately recognizable as a distinct subgroup on the basis of their more idiosyncratic stories.

This brings to the fore a major shortcoming in using only a directly quantitative and sociological method of analysis for the TAT. In most systems, in order to code stories according to pre-established categories, not only is much valuable qualitative information lost, but the more bizarre and idiosyncratic are either discarded or somewhat artificially teased to fit. I have opted for qualitative analysis, and scored only the major categories which readily lent themselves to the system. Nonetheless, when the schizophrenic young bachelor, Sean, for example, responds to Card 1: "It's in the mind of the brain he has it; he's asleep on the guitar," some may disagree with my scoring the response "negative achievement," unless perhaps I can demonstrate that this is a not too dissimilar expression of the boredom/disinterest themes given by "average" village males to this card as well. I was pursuing culturally prevalent attitudes, not doing any clinical analysis of the thought patterns of disturbed subjects.

The schizophrenic patients obviously demonstrated more difficulty with the test taking task. They tended to be less at ease, more terse in their replies, and almost always had to be coaxed into giving an outcome or conclusion to their stories. Card 6BM (the mother-son card) aroused some amount of anxiety in two of the schizophrenic males, and one refused to give any story at all to this card. Finally, Card 15 (a gaunt man with clenched hands standing among gravestones) released among psychotic patients of both sexes more magico-religious fantasy than

I had the experience to handle within this method. Despite such shortcomings, however, the exercise proved a valuable tool for exploring the conscious and sometimes unconscious content of feelings, drives, and what Anthony F. C. Wallace (1972:59) might call the "wishes of the soul" of the Kerry youth.

Achievement and Anomie

A major theme in TAT Card 1 (a boy contemplating a violin) told by both average and hospitalized males, but not by girls, illustrates the Irish male's sense of anomie with regard to his life and work.[5] Half the village boys and a quarter of the male

---

[5]In rethinking my analysis of Ballybran, nearly thirty years after the fact, and following a period of return research there in the summer of 1999, I was able to see that not *everything* about life in Ballybran—even then in 1974–1975—was demoralized and anomic. The problem was that the few spaces of vitality, passion, and camaraderie were largely channeled into covert political activities on behalf of the local IRA (the Irish Republican Army). In my "erasure" of this vital feature of local social and political life I joined a long tradition of anthropological ostriches, beginning with Robert Redfield who weathered the Mexican revolution in Tepotzlan without writing a word about it. If he had it would certainly have disrupted his description of a placid, "harmonious" peasant village. Similarly, Conrad Arensberg (1937) failed to address the events of the Easter Rising and the effects of the new Irish Free State on his static portrayal of the timeless "Irish Countrymen" of county Clare. It is a tradition which Orin Starn (1996) has somewhat playfully called anthropologists "missing the revolution."

In this instance, the "missing" was in part intentional—a self-blinding, meant to protect the cover of local activists in the community, some who were operating very close to where we lived. It has taken me more than two decades to confront acts of overt political violence (see Scheper-Hughes, 1996, 1998, 1999) as an anthropological subject which, given my choice of early fieldsites—Ireland in the mid 1970s and Brazil during the military years—must have required a massive dose of denial. While studying the madness of everyday life in Ballybran, and primarily concerned with *interior* spaces and with the small dark psychodramas of scape-goating and labeling within farm households that was driving so many young bachelors to drink and to bouts of depression and rage, I paid scant attention to the mundane activities of a neighbor from whom we rented our cottage and who used our attic to store a small arsenal of guns and explosives that he and a few of his comrades were running to Northern Ireland.

In reviewing the original set of responses to the Thematic Apperception Test (TAT) in preparing the new year 2000 anniversary edition of *Saints, Scholars and Schizophrenics*, I noted an important theme that I had originally overlooked—the many asides and fleeting references to killing, guns, and political violence, as in the following responses [emphasis supplied] to the blameless and innocent card #1—the image of a young boy and a violin:

> "This boy is pondering over a . . . *can it be a gun?* And he's very . . . he's in another world altogether, not really here at all." [girl, age 17]
>
> "This is a little boy and he is trying to play *some kind of a game with a gun.*" [village girl, 15]
>
> "A studious boy who is thinking about all the people who were killed in this way."

mental patients told stories of despondency over a violin or fiddle that was broken or sadly out of tune (see Table 1.1).

Michael, a seventeen-year-old potential farm heir of Ballybran village, told this story:

> (VM3) (normal male) He looks fed up, and his violin is broken. He doesn't know what to do. He's looking at it disgustedly. It might have broken while he was playing with it. Nothing to attract his attention to, only that.
>
> [OD-broken CB-arduous PD-disgust CC-inept]

And, Seamus, a considerably older Irish-speaking bachelor farmer and diagnosed schizophrenic, first imprisoned and then later hospitalized for violent and disorderly conduct at a dance hall, told this story:

> (HM1) (hospitalized male) He feels down and out. (Why?) It's broken, anyway. (What's the future?) He's thinking about his future as a guitarist. (What about it?) There is none.
>
> [PD-depress OD-broken CC-finish]

While to the psychoanalytically oriented the violin is a symbolically phallic instrument, and the broken violin image would be interpreted as an indication of severe castration anxiety among rural Irish males, I believe that the anthropologist can best contribute to the cultural interpretation of projective test material by examining first the manifest content of the images and placing them into the framework of the cultural or social meanings which these images might have on the conscious level. The violin or fiddle, for example, accompanied by the goatskin drum called the badhron and the melodian and tin whistle, is *the* music of the Irish countryside and conjures up strongly patriotic passions in the breasts of villagers at home and abroad. Irish music, like the Irish language itself represents a way of life which the villagers sense is dying. Of their language the old story tellers are wont to say: "the words are broken in my mouth." Of their music, village musicians

---

> village boy, age 16]
>
> "Why, *he is dead in thought.* What's this? A gun? . . . I'm in spirit with him. And what is that article? It has be baffled? *Is that a skull there?* Perhaps *it might be a gun and he sees death or life in it.*" [older village woman]
>
> "I thing this young boy is *thinking about shooting with a gun* or something. Is that a gun? (me—anything you like) Yes, a gun, I think. He will go out and kill some birds." [middle aged bachelor, hospitalized]

And so, I left unexamined the possible links between the political violence in the North and the tortured family dramas in West Kerry that I so carefully documented and which certainly had a violence of their own. But *some*, even passing, reference to those activities—of which some villagers are so very proud—would have modified the unremitting images of rural demoralization and anomie.

can be heard to comment: "My spirit is broken; how can I play when there are none to listen?" This malaise, this cultural demoralization, is expressed and felt most keenly by those young men who must sacrifice so much in remaining loyal to the village and the culture—and who intuitively sense that "things aren't working," necessary relationships are "broken" and "out of tune."

Table 1.1

Selected Achievement-Anomie Themes[6]

Themes/Cards	FEMALES Normal [V]	FEMALES Hospital [H]	FEMALES Total	MALES Normal [V]	MALES Hospital [H]	MALES Total
Card 1 (Boy and violin)	(N=22)	(N=11)	(N=33)	(N=14)	(N=11)	(N=25)
Positive Achievement	14 64%	7 63%	21 64%	6 42%	2 18%	8 32%
Negative Achievement	5 23%	0 —	5 15%	8 57%	5 45%	13 52%
Violin broken or out of tune	2 9%	0 —	7 6%	3 50%	10 27%	13 40%
Violin not seen or misidentified	12 55%	6 55%	18 55%	3 21%	4 36%	7 28%
Card 3BM (Figure huddled on floor)	(N=22)	(N=11)	(N=33)	(N=14)	(N=11)	(N=25)
Tired or boredom	2 9%	1 9%	3 9%	3 21%	2 18%	5 20%

Most of the stories told are characterized by one dominant theme, but often contain from two to four additional subthemes and these are, at times, double-scored.

By contrast, village girls responded to the violin image in an oddly characteristic fashion. More than half the girls in each sample VF 55 percent (village normal); HF 55 percent (hospitalized) told stories which ignored or misidentified the violin. Some referred to it as a gun, a book, a painting, a plane, while others referred directly to the blank sheets of paper beneath the violin, ignoring the instrument itself. Since it has already been established that the fiddle is an important symbol of Irish culture, the failure to notice or recognize it on the part of the girls cannot originate in unfamiliarity. Rather there seems to be an obstinate blocking, denial, or rejection of a possibly threatening instrument. The male phallus? Rural lifestyle? Probably both, I hypothesize.

[6]In this and subsequent tables, the striking differences are marked by underlining.

More than 64 percent of the village girls and hospitalized young women told positive achievement stories to Card 1—themes in which the little boy sets out, often on a path of difficult obstacles, to accomplish set goals. Peg, an eighteen-year-old future nurse, exemplifies this achievement motivation:

> (VF7) A boy has just gotten a new violin. He's sitting down and thinking, "this is a lovely violin; I hope I'll be able to play it well. I really want to learn, but will I be good enough?" And then he thinks, "I am going to do it. Try my best and become successful. I'll be rich and popular and the greatest violinist in the world. Yes, I am going to work hard." I think this boy really will work hard, and who knows, maybe he really could become famous. It all depends upon his determination and spirit.
>
> [OA-own CB-able AA-self OA-wealth ESA-praised CA-test]

So, too, in its own way, does this tentative and disjointed response from a nineteen-year-old depressed female psychiatric patient:

> (HF3) A little boy and a banjo, and he has the . . . he's thinking to . . . he's thinking on how to play the fiddle or whatever it is. He looks content, . . . as if he likes . . . is interested in it. (Outcome?) I'd say he might succeed.
>
> [PA-curious PA-satisfy CA-future]

In rather startling contrast, eight of the fourteen village boys and five of the eleven male psychiatric patients told stories with themes of negative achievement to Card 1—themes in which the main character withdraws from the task at hand, feels bored, sleepy, or otherwise disinterested. The first example is from an average sixteen-year-old boy, the second from a thirty-four-year-old schizophrenic male:

> (VM4, Card 3BM) This one is inclined . . . either he's bored at his work, or he doesn't understand the lesson he's gotten in music, or he might just be giving himself a rest.
>
> [PB-bored CC-inept PA-relief]

> (HM5, Card 3BM) It's in the mind of the brain he has it. He's asleep on the guitar.
>
> [PB-tired]

Sleepy, somnolent boredom was also referred to by young men in other cards—most notably in card 3BM (a figure, in my sample usually a boy, huddled on the floor with his head bowed in his arm): 21 percent of the stories from village lads and in 18 percent of the stories of the disturbed males. And, the man in the sexually suggestive card 13FM was described as feeling "sleepy" in 10 percent of the stories by village boys. It is possible that sleep and boredom may function as defenses for Irish males against realizing their own repressed and threatening drives for achievement as well as for sexuality. Subsequent stories indicate at least two underlying psychological explanations for the low achievement motivation of the boys: feelings of personal inadequacy, and inhibiting and selective guilt from which girls are to a large extent free.

Competence and Inadequacy Themes

Village lads are doubtful of themselves to the extent that 93 percent (thirteen of fourteen) told stories to Card 1 with themes expressing failure, feelings of incompetence, or inadequacy—mediated or resolved by dependency (sometimes hostile) on parents or other authority figures (see Table 1.2).

Example:

> (VM13) He seems to have been a failure so far anyway. (A failure at what?) The violin. His father was a good violin player and they want him to be one too. But he's not a brainy lad from the likes of this picture.
>
> [CA-past CC-inept CD-inferior]

Fiddles are not only broken or "out of tune" in the male stories, but in 25 percent of the cases, the male character cannot fix the instrument without looking for outside help. It is debatable whether or not to code the following poignant story under inadequacy, since the emotion expressed by this psychotic male transcends feelings of incompetence:

> (HM3) I think the young boy is thinking about shooting with a gun or something. Is that a gun? (Anything you like.) Well, a gun then. (What is he thinking of shooting?) Some birds, I think. He will go out and shoot birds. (Outcome?) He could shoot himself by mistake.
>
> [OB-think PA-play CC-inept]

Although village girls are also concerned about their abilities (54 percent of their stories to Card 1 raised the question of competence) they are almost twice as likely (64 percent to 36 percent) as village boys to have the main character resolve his self-doubts and go on to succeed. The same trend towards positive resolution holds for the female psychiatric patients, 36 percent of whom told stories with positive outcomes vs. only 9 percent of the male psychiatric patients.

Table 1.2

Selected Competence-Inadequacy Themes

Themes/Cards	FEMALES *Normal* [V]	*Hospital* [H]	*Total*	MALES *Normal* [V]	*Hospital* [H]	*Total*
Card 1 (Boy and violin)	(N=22)	(N=11)	(N=33)	(N=14)	(N=11)	(N=25)
Competence; Positive avowal of capacity	5 23%	2 18%	7 21%	1 7%	0 —	1 4%
Competence; Negative failure or doubt about capacity	12 54%	3 27%	15 45%	13 93%	4 36%	16 64%
Positive outcome: success theme	14 64%	4 36%	18 55%	5 36%	1 9%	6 24%
Card 2 (Farm scene)	(N=22)	(N=11)	(N=33)	(N=14)	(N=11)	(N=25)
Avowal of capacity regarding emigration	14 64%	4 64%	18 55%	1 7%	5 45%	6 24%
Sense of fate or destiny deciding one's success or failure	0 —	0 —	0 —	4 29%	2 18%	6 24%
Card 6BM (Mother-son)	(N=14)	(N=6)	(N=20)	(N=14)	(N=10)	(N=24)
Failure; incompetence of son motif	4 29%	2 33%	6 30%	5 36%	2 20%	7 29%
Son defends his abilities or opposes his mother	5 36%	1 17%	6 30%	2 14%	1 10%	3 13%

Sexual differences regarding competence also emerged in responses to Cards 2 and 6BM. Card 2 (a country scene in which a young girl carrying books in her arm, stands in front of a man working in the fields while an older woman looks on) evoked emigration themes for all four samples, but where half the average and hospitalized girls told stories in which the girl or boy in the picture decides to give it a try beyond the village, males more often (24 percent) expressed the conviction that "fate" or low aptitude and skills had destined the story figure to life on the farm.

Example:

> (VM4) This family has a small farm. They aren't rich. The girl wants to escape this life through her education. The mother is proud and domineering. The father is simple and hardworking. The son is like the father. He would like to escape, but he has no choice. He'll just be a farmer for the rest of his days.
>
> [OB-compare AA-counter EDC-disdain DDC-rigid AA-persist KD-hopeless]

Card 6BM (an elderly woman standing with her back turned to a tall young man, with his hat in his hands) evoked a number of stories from both male samples (36 percent normals; 20 percent disturbed) in which a mother chastises her son for turning out a failure, or alternatively in which the son apologizes to the mother for being a hopeless incompetent in school, business, or during a brief period of attempted emigration. The first example is from a hospitalized male, the second from a village lad:

> (HM4) He's just after coming home from someplace. He's telling . . . he's just told his mother that he's had bad luck in a job. He's been fired again. She is very disappointed in him. He'd gone away a few thousand miles. He's well dressed. He even has a little money in the bank . . . but not enough to be content with. Now he's come back to live at home again. (How old is he?) Forty-one. (Married?) No, single. (His future?) Not much. He'll be content if he can get some job around home.
>
> [KD-thwart EDB-lessen FC-split FA-mend AB-inactive]

> (VM2) This lady looks like the man's mother. He's after confessing some tragedy, and he's worried all right, but it bothers his mother worse—so much so she looks out the window into nothingness. Is there any hope left? Can he get his job back? Maybe he's failed his exams. She thinks that this is the end—if he failed once, he will always fail in life.
>
> [CB-worry CC-inept EDB-lessen]

Village girls, however, related to Card 6BM in a dramatically different fashion—in more than a third of their stories they told of a son finally gathering up the courage to stand up or assert himself *against* his mother's iron will (VF=36 percent; HF=17 percent; VM=14 percent; HM=10 percent). What is being illustrated here, I believe, is the end result of the differential socialization experience for rural male heirs and their more upwardly and outwardly mobile sisters.[7] Young sons are reared to feel inadequate so as to ensure their loyalty to farm and village, while daughters are encouraged to be socially forward, independent, and even aggressive.

Control: Autonomy vs. Dependency

Attitudes of average and disturbed young people towards the legitimacy of authority, corporal punishment, and parental control come to the surface on several cards—they are important concerns to the Irish youth. As before, the major dichotomy separates the males and females of both samples with the young women

---

[7]See my discussion in Scheper-Hughes, Chapter Six, 1979.

more likely to question and confront authority, and the young men more outwardly conforming. While often locked into silent and seething resentment, some male responses to the card suggest that they are also more likely to direct rage inward. They express both self-destructive motifs and violent fantasies against various displaced symbols of oppression.

Coercion is a dominant theme on Card 1: a quarter of all the responses told of a child forced into study or practice against his will. However, the passivity and conformity of the village boys' responses can be contrasted with the rebelliousness of the village girls, five of whom told stories in which they threw down or broke in anger the violin, or escaped from the tedious lesson (23 percent of the girls' stories vs. none from the boys). There is a vitality to the girls' stories almost totally lacking in that of the boys' (see Table 1.3).

Contrast Anya's story:

> (VF8) (Card 1) He's fed up and feels like breaking the old fiddle now. He's gotten no good out of it, and he throws it down and says, "the hell with it." Then he goes out to have a "crack" with the other lads.
>
> [PB-dislike OC-vandal PA-body FA-friend]

and Peter's story:

> (VM3) (Card 1) It seems to me that this boy was sent to do his violin practice which he doesn't like . . . I don't think he likes music much and he's in a sulk. (Outcome?) He'll get bored and then fall asleep on the violin.
>
> [DSB-obey PB-dislike PB-bored]

Card 3BM (boy huddled against a couch with his head bowed in his arm) conjured up a scene of physical punishment at the hands of teachers or parents for half of the village boys and girls. Psychiatric patients of both sexes, however, tended to identify this picture as one of psychological suffering. Many gave a variation of Brida's theme: "this person is sick in a mental way and unhappy like me." The corporal punishment theme from young villagers is, no doubt, a reflection of the widespread use of "caning" in rural Ireland both in the home and in the schools. A village boy in his last year of secondary school told the following:

> (VM7) (Card 1) A boy being punished for not knowing his Latin lessons. He was slapped in the face at school and when he came home and told his father, he was beaten again and sent to his room to study. But he can't study. He feels sick and angry for having been slapped in front of the whole class.
>
> [DDA-punish CC-inept PB-rage PB-body ESB-shame]

Interestingly, the story character in the above response is not seen as questioning the seemingly unjust beating from the father. Where village girls resolve the physical abuse of the child in their stories with the boy running away from home (41 percent of the themes), or even in a token verbal attack against the punishing parent (18 percent), both normal and disturbed males told stories in which anger or hurt is deflected. Sulking is the most common response to anger at a perceived injustice from an authority figure in male responses to Card 3BM (28 percent normal; 9 percent psychiatric patient stories). The male mental patients are the most intrapunitive, 27 percent of their responses suggest suicide as a possibility. Overall, self-hate and suicide themes were more prevalent in male than female responses to this card (20 percent vs. 6 percent).

When they were not sulking and self-pitying, male stories were twice as likely as female stories to justify or defend parental or other authoritarianism on the basis that severity builds character, while leniency begets moral looseness. In response to Card 3BM a fifteen-year-old boy told this story:

> (VM8) (Card 3BM) The child in the picture has suffered a great personal disappointment. But the child is not calling for its mother. Maybe he has been severely beaten or punished by a parent. . . . The result of the incident will be a further development of the child's character.
>
> [PD-sad DDC-punish RA-reform]

The differential responses of the sexes to parental control is nowhere more dramatic, however, than in the mother-son Card 6BM. Roughly 70 percent of all the stories collected for this card concern a conflict of interest between the generations regarding the son's intended emigration, his choice of a profession, or marriage partner. But where village girls tell stories in which the son asserts himself against the mother (30 percent vs. 14 percent village boys), both village and hospitalized males tended to tell stories in which the son ultimately bends to the mother's wishes or beliefs (64 percent VM; 30 percent HM vs. no such stories for either-female sample).

Contrast Mary's self-assertiveness:

> (VF20) (6BM) This is a widow woman and her son. She had many fine plans for him when he finished the university. He would become a doctor, a very good one, too! But one evening he comes home from school with one thought in mind—how can he tell his mother? He wants to be a priest and not a doctor. In the picture she is taking the news very badly. She refuses to let him become a priest. But the boy insists, and in the end he becomes a priest, and the mother learns to accept it.
>
> [DDA-educate DDC-rigid HB-role HA-mend]

With Johnny's submissiveness:

> (HM4) (6BM) Mother and child problem. He's obviously told her something that upset her. Maybe he wants to marry somebody not to her liking. . . . It might be a difference in the mother's view. Maybe she's not good enough socially or financially. Maybe the mother has a plan for him to marry somebody else. He seems to be fed up now by the expression on his face. He doesn't seem to be determined, rather shy. . . . It could be that the mother could easily influence him,

the domineering type. . . . So, she could decide the whole matter, she could really make up his mind.

[HC-discord EDC-status DDC-rigid DSD-submit]

Table 1.3

Selected Control Themes

Themes/Cards	FEMALES *Normal* [V]	*Hospital* [H]	*Total*	MALES *Normal* [V]	*Hospital* [H]	*Total*
Card 1 (Boy and violin)	(N=22)	(N=11)	(N=33)	(N=14)	(N=11)	(N=25)
Coercion themes	6 27%	1 9%	7 21%	4 28%	2 18%	6 24%
Child rebels against authority figure	5 23%	0 —	5 15%	0 —	0 —	0 —
Card 3BM (Figure huddled against couch)	(N=22)	(N=11)	(N=33)	(N=14)	(N=11)	(N=25)
Punishment themes	10 45%	4 36%	14 42%	7 50%	1 9%	8 32%
Escape from punishment themes	9 41%	0 —	9 27%	0 —	0 —	0 —
Verbal or physical attack against punishing parent	2 9%	0 —	2 6%	0 —	0 —	0 —
Sulking as response to hurt or anger	0 —	0 —	0 —	4 29%	1 9%	5 20%
Self-hate: suicide preoccupation	1 5%	1 9%	2 6%	2 14%	3 27%	5 20%
Card 6BM (Mother-son)	(N=14)	(N=6)	(N=20)	(N=14)	(N=10)	(N=24)
Maternal control themes	9 64%	4 67%	13 65%	11 78%	7 70%	18 75%
Son asserts himself against mother	5 36%	1 17%	6 30%	2 14%	1 10%	3 13%
Son lacks autonomy; gives in to mother	0 —	0 —	0 —	9 64%	3 30%	12 50%
Card 8BM (Surgical scene)	(N=7)	(N=3)	(N=10)	(N=8)	(N=5)	(N=13)
Accidental patricide; death of father	0 —	0 —	0 —	4 50%	3 60%	7 53%

However passive and conforming to authority figures the male stories are on the surface, a certain amount of suppressed rage and rebelliousness does break through in hostile and anti-authoritarian fantasies. Prison breaks and mental hospital escapes are a favorite theme on Card 17BM (man on a rope) for males of both samples (VM 67 percent; HM 100 percent) but not for the females who project an entertainer or athlete theme into this card. IRA revolutionary themes are, in addition, a favored topic for males in Cards 9BM, 8BM, and 7BM. Finally, the death of a father figure (sometimes "accidentally" at the hands of the son) appears in more than half of the male responses (VM 50 percent; HM 60 percent) to Card 8BM (an adolescent boy with a rifle to one side, and a dim surgical scene in the background) (see Table 1.3). This story was given by an eighteen-year-old village youth, a first-born son:

> (VM1) (Card 8BM) The boy is out with a gun . . . (long pause) for fun, and he was playing with it, and he didn't think it was loaded. And he sees his father coming up the road and he fires a gun and there was a bullet in it, and the bullet struck the father in the belly, and now he is just thinking about the doctors operating on his father. (Outcome?) I wouldn't think he'd pull through it.
>
> [PA-play KC-hurt KD-death]

Responsibility-Guilt Themes

If physical punishment were the only form of social control used within the Irish home, one might be led to expect a rather superficial internalization of social responsibility and moral standards among the Irish youth. But such is not the case, for Irish children are not only physically beaten, they are psychologically "walloped" as well by the continual reminder of sin and eternal damnation, as well as through the persistent equation of human motherhood with the divine Motherhood of Mary. As a toddler the Irish child is cautioned, "Don't do that, it will make Holy Mary cry." As an adolescent the child is told, "Don't do that, it will break your poor mother's heart." The powers of folk Catholicism and Irish motherhood feed off each other to the extent that one village mother complained that when Pope John "dethroned" Mary he had abandoned the Irish mother as well.

Indeed, with the Virgin Mary as their model, Irish mothers are artists at the guilt-inducing techniques of moral masochism. The patient, long-suffering, Irish mother is immortalized in national ballads, revolutionary poetry, and Celtic myth, and she emerges in TAT stories as well. Represented in the ubiquitous statue or painting of the Immaculate (and bleeding) Heart of Mary, the Irish mother is, like her, a veritable "mater dolorosa." In village pubs where after rounds of drinking, even when religion and the Holy Father himself can become the subjects of mocking jest, motherhood remains publicly sacrosanct. And, where romantic love is a taboo subject for song or poetry recitation, mother-love is an indulged-upon sentiment, however forced and seemingly artificial. The village at large venerates the ancient, black shawled, holy women who have suffered through the toils and suffering of family life—invariably outliving their husbands and sometimes their children—while no comparable status is reserved for old widowers. The "widow women" are accorded front pews in the chapel, lead the Corpus Christi Procession in Dingle, and can often be seen leaning dramatically and majestically on the arms of one or more sons as they are escorted to and from their homes. The old woman wields control over the lives of her children long after they can be effectively beaten with a cane. The results of this influence can be demonstrated in the Irish youth's overly developed sense of conscience (below) and in their image of the "sainted" and "holy" mother image frequently depicted on Card 2.

Pervasiveness of Guilt

> We do make mountains out of nothing, and I think we do be wasting the priest's time in the box. But we don't know for sure what is a sin, so we do confess it all.
>
> (Old woman's comment while standing in a line for confession)

What is most remarkable throughout the Irish records—particularly in the stories of village males and psychiatric patients of both sexes—is their readily expressed guilt, self blame, idealism, and moral sadism. Although the tendency to guilt feelings is free floating and runs through all the cards, three situations seem to be particularly guilt provoking (see Table 1.4):

1) failing to succeed—i.e., living up to mother's high expectations (as illustrated in the "failure" themes of male responses to 3BM and 6BM, see Tables 1.2 and 1.3, above);

2) negligence towards or disobedience to the "old people," especially in response given to Cards 2 and 6BM;

3) any reference to sexuality: various responses to Cards 4, 5, and especially 13MF (to be discussed later).

Table 1.4

Selected Responsibility-Guilt Themes

	FEMALES			MALES		
Themes/Cards	*Normal* [V]	*Hospital* [H]	*Total*	*Normal* [V]	*Hospital* [H]	*Total*
Card 12M (Man on couch)	(N=22)	(N=12)	(N=34)	(N=14)	(N=10)	(N=24)
Confession motifs	10 45%	5 42%	15 44%	10 <u>71%</u>	2 20%	12 50%
Card 6BM (Mother-son)	(N=14)	(N=6)	(N=20)	(N=14)	(N=10)	(N=24)

Son feels guilty about	4	0	4	6	3	9
leaving home	29%	—	20%	43%	30%	38%
Son leaves home: death	1	0	1	6	1	7
strikes aged parent	7%	—	5%	43%	10%	29%

Guilt and Confession themes are so pronounced in the Irish TATs (especially Card 12M, see Table 1.4) that at one point I considered entitling the book, "The Confessional Conscience." Most pervasively on Card 12M (a young man lying on a couch with an elderly man stretching out his hand above the reclining figure), confessional motifs appeared additionally on Cards 6BM, 7BM, 13MF, 15, the blank card (Card 16). Half of all the themes given on Card 12M were "last confession" motifs—and of these, the greatest number (71 percent of their stories) came from village boys.

Example:

> (VM7) (Card 12M) Paul was only a young man but three months ago he contracted Yellow Fever and from that time on he has been sick in bed. As time went on the doctors began to give up hope, and so the priest was called. As he was performing the "last rites," Paul summoned up his final strength to make a good last confession. As the priest raised his arms to bless him, the young man smiled. He died with all forms of sin cleansed from his soul.
>
> [KD-ill-die HA-rite RA-reform PA-relief]

Paraphrasing Charles Schultz of Peanuts fame, being Irish is having to say "I'm sorry" again and again and again. Here we have the response of a village girl to Card 6BM:

> (VF20) (Card 6BM) This is a man and a woman. They must have been doing something wrong, and now they are before a court. The man is confessing his sin, and he has his head bowed down in shame. The man looks very guilty. The woman seems to be saying something. Maybe she is telling on the man. Or, they both could be in church waiting to confess to the priest.
>
> [RC-wrong HA-rite RA-expiate]

And, a schizophrenic male told this rather weird confessional/guilt story to Card 15 (gaunt man standing among gravestones):

> (HM5) (Card 15) That's a man inside a theater saying Mass. (A theater?) Yes, a cinema theater. He's praying, telling his sins. He seems to be disgusted with himself.
>
> [HA-rite RA-expiate PD-disgust ESD-base]

The double-binding quality of Irish guilt (Scheper-Hughes, 1979) can be further illustrated in the emigration stories given to Cards 2 and 6BM in which the adolescent agonizes over conflictful desires to leave and his obligations to the old people. Parental expectations differ for girls and boys, and although village girls are susceptible to some of the same guilt feelings, it is the village boys who accept the brunt of the burden, and who suffer most under the impossible task of reconciling conflicting role demands. This can be seen in comparing the attitudes of the sexes to the perceived "parting scene" in Card 6BM. Certainly the girls of both samples are less conflicted about choosing between what they want to do and what they feel they *ought* to do than are the village or the hospitalized males. In their stories the boys play out, one after another, the painful departure scene.

Example:

> (VM10) (Card 6BM) Sure it's a somber scene between mother and son. It looks as if he's finally come to tell his mother that he is about to leave. His poor mother is heartbroken by the news and turns away to hide her grief.
>
> [PD-sad <u>FD-parting</u>]

Village girls can imaginatively enact the parting scene with all of its conflicting emotions, and yet still accept the parting as inevitable:

> (VF13) (Card 6BM) This man and his mother must part. She has been a good mother to him, allowing him independence and always being open with him. He is shy with everyone but he manages to reveal his reasons for going to his mother. She is very sad, but she accepts her son as a man, free of her. She doesn't cry because that would only stop him from going, and she knows that what he is doing is right. . . . They will meet again, if his mother doesn't die soon, because he has promised he will return.
>
> [HA-family FA-empathy FA-inform <u>FB-parting</u> FA-happen]

And where "the village girls" stories of emigration all conclude with the son leaving home, half of the male emigration themes have outcomes in which the mother's grief or disapproval deters the son from his decision:

> (VM10) (Card 6BM) I think he, the son in this picture, has been a very special one to his mother. Through the years he has been close to her. Only now he is getting old, and he wants to leave. But now he understands that it is too late. . . . There is really no leaving for this man, because he has waited too long.
>
> [FA-ties AB-torn <u>KD-resign</u>]

Village girls can and do reason that they would have to leave home in any case (marriage as well as emigration) but village boys express through the medium of the TAT that their decision to leave or stay can even determine the life and death of their parents. A common sequence to the average male stories (43 percent) is that of a son who leaves only to receive word that a parent has fallen sick or died during his brief absence.[8] Such stories inevitably conclude with the guilt-stricken son returning home to look after the remaining parent, as in this seventeen-year-old Paddy:

> (VM12) (Card 6BM) Here we see a man and his mother. He is just after coming home from America to find that his father died or said it was from sudden illness while he was gone. The doctor said it was from overwork. Everyone in the village always said his father was a "fright" for work. And now he is dead. The mother turns away from the son to hide her tears. The son feels guilty, because he knows that his father would be alive today if he had been at home to help. He vows never to leave home again.
>
> [KD-death FA-happen KD-death NDA-devote RB-guilt RA-reform]

In the girl's emigration stories, sickness or death often strikes the home parent as well, but the solution is not for the child to return home, but rather for him or her to work harder to send money to the remaining parent. Village and hospitalized girls also tend to justify emigration and leaving parents on the basis of social or economic deprivations suffered at home. On Card 2, the family farm scene, fourteen of the twenty-two village girls and four of the eleven female psychiatric patients told deprivation stories followed by a real or imagined escape from the harsh countryside.

Example:

> (NF21) (Card 2) I think the school girl is not involved, she doesn't fit in—the parents don't seem to accept her. Look, over here by them it is all green and fertile, and over here by her it is all rocky and hard. There is no doubt but that it has been very hard for her up until now. (Outcome?) After she leaves home things will improve.
>
> [FB-unsuited KD-poverty FC-reject KA-recovery]

Where both the average and the "disturbed" girls describe the rural scene in Card 2 as, among other things, "a small bit of mountain end," "a poor farm in the outback," or a "miserable piece of rocky land" (realistic assessments of farming in economically depressed County Kerry), village boys were given to romanticizing the rural scene, calling the farmers "rich and prosperous" or "doing all they can to make their farm a civilized environment." The eleven male psychiatric patients, however, sided with the women and none of these told stories on Card 2 with "pastoral ideal" motifs, and five told social or economic deprivation stories, which were resolved, however, in *resignation* rather than *emigration*.

---

[8]See similar stories about the illness or death of a mother given by Japanese immigrants (Caudill and De Vos, 1956) and Japanese men in Japan (De Vos, 1973). In these stories one can readily interpret the underlying guilt associated with thought of defying or seeking to leave a dominant mother.

Nurturance-Deprivation: Parent Images

The Mother

A mother figure appears on Cards 2, 5, 6BM, 18GF, and one is sometimes written into the script of Cards 1 and 3BM. Here, I will concentrate only on the mother figure as represented by villagers in Cards 2 and 18GF (see Table 1.5).

Of all groups the female psychiatric patients were the most likely to view the mother in a tender, nurturant role, and to perceive her as the patient, long-suffering religious figure, alluded to previously. In response to the family scene in Card 2, hospitalized girls described the older, mother figure as: "holy"; "nun-like"; "so like Our Lady"; "just a farm woman although she looks a bit like St. Teresa"; "the mother is just home from church where she was praying for her family"; "like a Queen."

Card 18GF (a woman with her hands squeezed around the throat of another woman) is generally held by psychological testers to elicit either a perception of violence or nurture. The women in our sample saw only one scene of violence. For the hospitalized young women, whenever this card was seen as two women it was then described in loving, nurturant terms.

(A mother-child relationship in six of ten responses):

> (HF8) (Card 18GF) The girl in the picture was born blind. Her mother is in the picture with her. The girl is going to die, and her mother is holding her in her arms and crying. She will die.
>
> [KD-defect KD-ill-death NDA-comfort PD-sad]

In the two instances where violence was perceived in the picture, the hospitalized girls described the scene as a fight between *two men*. For whatever reasons, the hospitalized girls will not allow themselves to recognize the possibility of violence between mother and child. The only possible negative mother image to emerge from this sample was the occasional reference to the child figure in Card 1 or 3BM as a poor and deprived orphan.

Average village girls were more ambivalent in their characterization of mother figures, although they consistently attempted to overcome intruding negative archetypes with positive and warm outcomes. Nonetheless, in Card 2, the responses are equally divided (5–5) between a perception of the mother as hard-working, self-sacrificing, and holy ("the mother is the soul of fortitude"; "she sacrifices everything to educate her child"; "her worn hands are folded in prayer") and a description of the mother as depriving, mean, selfish, and rejecting (e.g., "the girl has just gotten slaps from her mother"; "the mother takes away the book from her daughter and forces her to work in the fields"). Village girls' responses to Card 18GF are equally divided, with the mother figure seen as nurturant in nine stories ("like Our Lady of Sorrows" offered one adolescent), as violent to a child in one story, and as ambivalent or indifferent to a sick or suffering child in two themes. (The remaining stories are husband-wife or sibling scenes.)

Throughout the village girls' responses—especially in Cards 3BM, 5, and 18GF—there is an attempt by the child to make the mother feel guilty for her punishing or repressive treatment of the son or daughter. A common theme in this regard is that of a daughter forced into running away from home or into self-destruction, after which the mother is portrayed as blaming herself for the trouble. Below are two of the eight stories that fall into this génre:

> (VF16) (Card 18GF) The daughter has just told her mother that she is in serious trouble, she is pregnant. She then throws herself down the stairs and asks God to let her die. Now she is begging her mother to forgive her, because she was young and didn't know better. The mother will blame herself at times for not being a better mother. She will always have doubts about whose fault it was, and who was really responsible.
>
> [RC-sex RA-hurt DSA-forgive RB-guilt RC-duty]

> (VW2) (Card 5) This seems to be a mother coming into a room and she expects to find her child inside, but the child has decided to run away and she probably finds a note on the table. She is heartbroken and thinks what did she do to bring this about? She sends out a party to find her, and when they bring her child back, she explains that her mother had been pushing her too much, wanting her to see and do everything her way. She never seems to understand or trust her. Then the mother realizes that she was wrong and they both try to start off again.
>
> [FC-split DDC-press FB-distrust RA-reform FA-mend]

Of all the samples, village boys were most deeply resentful of, and hostile towards, the mother figure which they describe on Card 2 as: "proud and domineering"; "selfish"; "haughty"; "materialistic"; and, as "a silent type, not really conscious of those around her." Patrick compares the mother figure in this card to the harsh Dingle landscape:

> (VM15) (Card 2) This picture reminds me of "Innisdun." . . . There are parallels here between the older woman and the scenery. The scene is brutal and stony, but has a kind of noble approach not altogether different from the mother.
>
> [DDC-rigid NDC-hard EDA-respect]

Village lads were also given to criticizing the "material, grasping" nature of the mother (and other women figures) as compared to their perception of the simple, humble father figure.

Example:

> (VM2) (Card 2) This is the girl's father and he is just setting off to plow. The mother is haughty and proud, only interested in material things, and how her husband could make more money. . . . The mother is so preoccupied with her husband's work, she doesn't really care about her child at all. . . . This picture

illustrates the difference between humility and pride. The mother is haughty and the husband is . . . well, he isn't totally humble, but he hasn't got the proud features of the mother. The picture also shows a kind of female chauvinism, because the work of the man is going to support the brighter aims of the two females.

[EDC-disdain OC-greed FC-neglect EDC-status DDC-exploit]

Perhaps the most hostile critique of the mother figure in Card 2 was given by this fifteen-year-old village boy:

(VM8) (Card 2) This woman looks bossy and lazy. . . . The mother seems to deprive her of reading, of her education. They live in the countryside, near the sea. The house seems to deprive them of the view of the sea. Her husband seems to be dead and she is taking a view of all the land she now owns. . . . The mother is very lazy. She tells the son that he's spoiled, that he doesn't work hard enough. . . . She tells the daughter that she is too pampered. The mother doesn't really regard them as a family at all, the way she is looking over them into the distance.

[DDC-unfair RC-indulge NDC-deprive KD-deprive DDC-disdain]

And, throughout village boys' responses to Card 18GF runs the same current of ambivalence as in the girls' themes. The mother figure is often characterized as both nurturant and treacherous in the same story. The mother who fondly cradles a dying child, sorrowfully admits that she "had to do it" (i.e., kill her deviant son), while in another motif the mother finds her daughter unconscious at the bottom of the stairs—and then "roughly catches her by the throat and tries to force her to speak."

Hospitalized males were most blocked and, at times, unintelligible when responding to cards with a mother figure. However, like the female psychiatric patients, they tried to ultimately maintain an image of the mother figure as good and holy, particularly in response to Card 2. Sean volunteered that the older woman is "a good Irish peasant lady," while Johnny extols the virtues of a pregnant woman still toiling away for her family. And Ribard, gives the following response to Card 2:

Table 1.5

Selected Nurturance Deprivation Themes

Themes/Cards	Females Normal [V]	Females Hospital [H]	Females Total	Males Normal [V]	Males Hospital [H]	Males Total
Table 1.5a: The Mother						
Card 2 (Farm scene)	(N=22)	(N=11)	(N=33)	(N=14)	(N=11)	(N=25)
Social or economic deprivation	14 64%	4 36%	18 55%	1 7%	5 45%	6 24%
Mother, mean, cruel, or depriving	5 23%	0 —	5 15%	7 50%	0 —	7 28%
Mother kind, holy, or saintly	5 23%	5 43%	10 30%	0 —	2 18%	2 8%
Card 18GF (Woman squeezing throat)	(N=22)	(N=10)	(N=32)	(N=8)	(N=5)	(N=13)
Mother-child nurturing	9 41%	8 80%	23 72%	4 50%	2 40%	6 46%
Mother-child conflict with violence	1 5%	0 —	1 3%	5 63%	3 60%	8 62%
Table 1.5b: The Father						
Card 2 (Farm scene)	(N=22)	(N=11)	(N=33)	(N=14)	(N=11)	(N=25)
Father passive, distant, or uninvolved	2 9%	0 —	2 6%	1 7%	0 —	1 4%
Father kind, hard-working	2 8%	2 18%	4 12%	6 43%	2 18%	8 32%
Card 3BM (Huddled figure)	(N=22)	(N=11)	(N=33)	(N=14)	(N=11)	(N=25)
Punishment	10 45%	4 36%	14 42%	7 50%	1 9%	8 32%
Father profligate, irresponsible, drunk	4 18%	1 10%	5 15%	4 29%	3 27%	7 28%
Card 7BM (Older man, younger man)	(N=14)	(N=5)	(N=19)	(N=14)	(N=10)	(N=24)
Father counsels son	2 14%	2 40%	4 21%	7 50%	5 50%	12 50%
Father corrupts or betrays son	3 21%	0 —	3 16%	4 29%	2 20%	6 25%

(HM11) (Card 2) As you sow, so shall you reap. A mother's place is central, even to the most masculine of chores.

[RA-work (EDA-status)]

Among the schizophrenic males there was a tendency to distance themselves from the family characters in Card 2 by describing the card as intrinsically false, unreal (e.g., "this is a period painting"; "an historical scene"; "just farmer statues working"; "looks like statues in a church") or by concentrating most of their effort on a description of the animal or the background scenery, as in Con's response:

(HM2) (Card 2) This is a period painting of an agricultural scene. There are two ladies and a gentleman, not counting the horse which is an animal. The horse is working very hard. . . . There are some outhouses and some water behind the outhouses, denoting that they live by the sea. Or, at least, that is the artist's impression.

[OB-depict PA-nature Ra-work]

Only in response to Card 18GF (unfortunately only five responses were collected with this card) does any ambivalence or hostility towards the mother figure come through among the sample of disturbed males. In one story the mother strangles her son and after it is over, comments with the characteristic "la belle indifference" of the schizophrenic: "Never mind, my son, let's pick up the pieces and begin anew." And, in the following response of a twenty-four-year-old hospitalized alcoholic with a personality disorder, the mother is presented as an anomalous blend of murderer and lover:

(HM8) (18GF) I think this is a picture of a mother with pity on her face for her son, or possibly she is thinking that she has reared him up to destroy himself. So she thinks that it would be better if she killed him herself with love for him on her face.

[DDC-manage NDB-pity HC-murder]

The Father

Just as the mother is seen by rural youth as filling two possible and conflicting stereotypes—that of the suffering Madonna or that of the mean "stepmother"—the father is described as either the profligate, alcoholic husband or as the self-effacing, hardworking head of household. Sometimes the adolescent can't decide between the two, as in young Maura's response to Card 3BM:

(VF19) (3BM) This is a drunken man who can just barely find his way home. Look, he has dropped his house keys next to the bed. On second thought maybe it is a father praying for his family after a hard day's work.

[RC-abuse RA-work NDA-prayer]

Village males are on the whole more likely to identify the father figure on Card 2 or 7BM as hardworking, kind, and wise (if uneducated and somewhat henpecked by the women in his life), than are the village girls or psychiatric patients of either sex (VM 43 percent; VF 9 percent; HM 18 percent; HF 18 percent). Village and hospitalized girls make less mention of the father figure on Card 2, and when they do he is invariably described by them as an unobtrusive, background figure.

In Card 3BM the brutal and punishing side of the father surfaces for all samples, but especially among the males who also read into this card the image of the irresponsible, alcoholic father (28 percent males vs. 15 percent females).

Example:

> (VM18) (3BM) A man of about forty-eight lying beside a bed. He is probably drunk, too drunk to make it to his bed. He doesn't have a thought for his family, only for himself. Now feeling very sick.
>
> [RC-abuse PB-body]

The Irish stereotype of the child and wife beater comes through strongly in the following two stories, the first from a female psychiatric patient, and the second from an average eighteen-year-old girl:

> (HF5) (3BM) The girl seems to have either seen something that's indecent or seen something that's frightened her. She may have been beaten. Now she seems to be crying as if her heart would break. Maybe she went into her house and saw her father beating her mother. It's not a good home.
>
> [RC-mores HB-fright DDC-punish HC-beat]

> (VF3) (Blank Card 16) Could it be something modern, true to life like? (Certainly.) Well then [her eyes closed] I see a woman having a husband and he is an alcoholic. Well, most of the responsibility for the house and children is left up to her. He's out of work most of the time because he's just drunk mostly. And, if the mother has got six or seven kids at home, she can hardly go out walking. And, he beats the kids and sometimes herself as well. So, she's desperate. And, in Ireland not a lot of help is available to alcoholics and their people. A woman and her children in such a situation is bound to be unhappy. In cases like these, divorce should be available. Also in the cases of battered wives.
>
> [RC-abuse RD-work HC-beat NSD-no help]

While card 7BM (elderly man looking down at a younger man) was successful in revealing various perceptions of masculine role stereotypes (e.g., bachelor buddies; successful but "shady" business partners; priest and penitent; IRA soldiers), it failed to elicit a majority of father-son stories. Villagers and hospitalized patients from rural Kerry had difficulty identifying the well-dressed "gent" as a father figure. Where a father-son relation was perceived on this card, however, village boys generally saw the relationship in a positive "father knows best" light, where village girls told three stories in which the father betrays a son or daughter in order to satisfy his own selfish ends, as in the following:

> (VF13) (Card 7BM) A girl has been friendly with the younger man in the picture. She is serious about it, but he is not. The boy has a bad character. The girl's father knows this but he is very anxious to have his daughter off his hands. He is telling the boy that he is very rich, and that if he marries his daughter he will get a large fortune (i.e., dowry), so it would be worth his while. The father is afraid that she will find out about the boy's character if she knows him any longer, so he gets them married quickly.
>
> [FA-love FC-deceit DDC-unfair]

Affiliation: Intimacy vs. Isolation

In a brief, but extremely perceptive article an Irish psychiatrist and administrator of a southwestern district hospital summed up the "basic" psychological problems he encountered in his practice as follows:

> Emotions which seem to me, and indeed to others, to cause particular problems to many persons presenting as patients in this region are greed, envy, bitterness, frustration, sexual and otherwise, guilt, hatred, anger, a general feeling of lack of love, often associated with a fear of love, a fear of loss, indeed a very high expectancy of and resignation to loss, with consequent fear and avoidance of tenderness and intimacy (Dunne, 1970:23).

Certainly both a fear of, and longing after, intimacy was a central theme on the TAT records of males and females, hospitalized as well as average villagers. This state of lovelessness, lack of tenderness, and consequent feelings of psychological abandonment and loss are, I suggest, part of the basic emotional cast of the "Irish personality." These predispositions are learned early through the experience of a less than satisfactory relationship to the first love object: the mother. The learning continues, however, throughout childhood and up through early adulthood as the orientation towards emotional distance and sexual "flatness'" is reinforced by religious ideology as well as through social patterns which separate the sexes and which, likewise, keep the generations apart.

Between Family Members

Communication failures, or simply absence of communication, between family members appears to be largely responsible for the great sense of personal alienation, loneliness, and isolation which permeate the Irish TATs in all four samples. In the family scene of Card 2, for example (see Table 1.6), half the males (VM 50 percent;

HM 45 percent) and more than a third of the females (VF 41 percent; HF 27 percent) told stories in which one or more of the characters feels isolated, unloved, or alienated from the rest of the family, as in Maure's poignant response:

> (VF22) (Card 2) A girl going away to school. Her mother doesn't say good-bye. Her father is too busy working to look up. . . . They work hard and want their daughter to help out too, but she feels a stranger to them. She doesn't fit in at all, and her parents outcast her and reject her.
>
> [AA-self FB-distant RA-work FC-reject]

Table 1.6

Selected Affiliation or Isolation Themes

Themes/Cards	FEMALES *Normal* [V]	*Hospital* [H]	*Total*	MALES *Normal* [V]	*Hospital* [H]	*Total*
Card 2 (Farm scene)	(N=22)	(N=11)	(N=33)	(N=14)	(N=11)	(N=25)
Affiliation love between family members	3 14%	0 —	3 9%	5 36%	0 —	5 20%
Isolation alienation between family members	9 41%	3 27%	12 36%	7 50%	5 45%	12 48%
Affiliation between the sexes	5 23%	5 45%	10 30%	0 —	3 27%	3 12%
Sibling solidarity	4 18%	0 —	4 12%	6 43%	0 —	6 24%
Card 4 (Man and woman)	(N=22)	(N=10)	(N=32)	(N=14)	(N=11)	(N=25)
Affiliation between a couple	3 14%	2 20%	5 16%	0 —	5 45%	5 20%
Isolation, alienation, indifference	8 36%	4 40%	12 38%	4 29%	1 9%	5 20%
Card 9BM (Men lying on grass)	(N=5)	(N=3)	(N=8)	(N=8)	(N=6)	(N=14)
Male solidarity	2 40%	1 33%	3 38%	6 75%	5 83%	11 79%

In general the story characters tend to be walled off, locked within themselves: sulking, hurting, longing, crying internally, while on the exterior expressing nothing. On Card 3BM, young Mihal says, "the boy feels so hurt and angry he wants to cry" (but he doesn't't); and Grania, a seriously depressed eighteen-year-old from an isolated mountain farm, says:

(HF3) (3BM) The poor creature, she have nobody to talk to. She wants to tell her problems to somebody, but she can't. (Why can't she?) She's the type that keeps to herself like.

[FB-alone FB-isolate]

Returning once again to the family scene of Card 2 (see Table 1.6), villagers and patients of both sexes refer to one or more of the characters as: "a silent type," "doesn't say much," "in a world of her own," or (especially among psychotic patients) describe the figures as lifeless "statues." In this, and subsequent cards, it was characteristic of the Irish west country response style to tell a great deal of what the characters were thinking and sometimes what they were feeling, but to volunteer little dialogue or relate about any interaction between characters.

In Card 6BM, for example, when the son finally gathers up the courage to "confess" to his mother that he wants to leave home or marry or that he has failed her in some way, the mother normally responds with stony or shocked silence, as in the following examples from each of the four groups:

(VM10) "The old women turns pale and stares out the window, speechless."

(VM9) ". . . and as he tells her she looks out the window and tries not to listen to the words."

(VF13) "She doesn't cry or say anything."

(HM2) "It troubles his mother so much that she has to turn away, and stare out the window into nothingness."

(HM9) "His poor mother is heartbroken and turns away to hide her grief."

(HF5) "The woman looks out the window to her environment for comfort."

Or, when she is not totally silent, the mother threatens to withhold love, affection, and ultimately, communication:

(VF16) "The mother refuses to say good-bye or to *give* her blessing to the son who feels very sad."

(VF9) ". . . and the mother says that if he marries this girl, she will never talk to him again."

In the following, the threat is actually carried through:

(VM19) "His mother is so disappointed and angry with him, that when he goes away he never hears from her again."

Lack of communication is not only characteristic of mother-child relationships, but of husband-wife relationships as well,[9] and long-standing feuds between village families rarely erupt into bitter arguments, for contempt and disapproval is expressed in silence: "not giving them the time of day."

Between Peers

Given difficult relationships within the home and between the sexes, friendship ties emerge on the TAT records as a saving grace. A positive dependence upon friends is illustrated in the responses to Card 1 where, for example, Eileen, the boy on the picture as wanting "to throw the old fiddle down and go out to have a 'crack' with the other lads," and where Michael wants to go and find some friends and tell them about his broken fiddle and "then he'll feel better about it."

Themes of camaraderie and male solidarity emerge in 75 percent of the village boys' and 83 percent of the hospitalized males' responses to Card 9BM (four men in overalls lying on the grass). The group of men are described as "soldier buddies," "cowhands," "revolutionaries," "winos," and "farm-hands," and often the story ends with a strong affirmation of friendship, such as:

> (VM4) (Card 9BM) "I bet they're glad not to be alone out there in the wilderness."
>
> (HM5) (Card 9BM) "They are hoping that none of the group gets shot the next day."

Similarly, Card 7BM conjures up a picture for both sexes of two friends at a pub, a football match, a dance hall, or a political rally. However, in this card there intrudes from time to time a nibbling fear of betrayal, and an occasional suspiciousness of the friend (VM 29 percent; HM 14 percent; VF 29 percent; HF 20 percent). This strikes me as a clear reflection of interactional patterns in the village, where both young and old prefer the easy and diluted camaraderie of large groups (e.g., suggested in Card 9BM) rather than the threatening intimacy of particular and individual friendships (e.g., suggested by Card 7BM). In the small, crowded pubs of the village, for example, there is a great effort to keep the conversation "general" and to break up private dialogues.

Sexuality: A Romance with Love and Death

If there is one area of behavior in which the attitudes of the hospitalized and average village most differ it is on the subject of sexuality (including love, marriage, and

---

[9]See Chapter 4, Scheper-Hughes, 1979 (2000).

generativity themes). Throughout the test responses of average village adolescents of both sexes—but most especially in reference to Cards 4 (a woman clutching the shoulders of a man) and 13MF (a man turned away from a partially nude woman in bed)—there is an absence of sexual love or affiliation themes. There is a dearth of romance or marriage stories, and a consistent attempt to defuse or desexualize situations in which the sexes are in proximate contact.

Familism functions as a defense against perceptions of sexual intimacy, and frequently a young man and woman together are described as a brother and sister, or a large age gap is perceived between the two, again removing the threat of sexuality. A few adolescents toy with the idea of a romance or marriage theme in Card 13MF, but then reject it by pronouncing the characters as too young. And the oft-noted Irish fascination with death takes the place of sexuality insofar as almost half of the adolescent villagers described Card 13MF as a scene of suffering, illness, or death (VF 45 percent; VM 43 percent).

Indeed, if American youth can be described, as they often have been, as "in love with love" (in its more superficial manifestations), then the TATs reveal the Irish youth to be "in love with death." It appears to me that the preoccupation and fascination with death (found in responses to Cards 3BM, 12M, 15, and 13MF) functions, like the American preoccupation with sex, as a romantic fantasy. It is in the act of death (rather than in the passion of sex) that the Irish youth imagines his or her moment of final triumph, glory, and fullest appreciation. The following is the response of a sixteen-year-old village lad to Card 16 (the blank card):

> (VM7) (Card 16) John was a little boy whom everyone loved. He was well mannered, good at everything he wanted to be good at, and he got good grades at school. One day his young life was taken when he was knocked down by a motor car. Because everyone liked him, they took this as a great loss to the community, and it was the biggest funeral that there ever was in the parish. As his expensive coffin was lowered into the ground, a great moment of silence came over everyone. Even the dogs seemed to realize that something was wrong and they whined or barked pitifully; even they realized the loss.
>
> [ESA-loved CA-present KD-ac-death HA-rite <u>FD-fate</u>]

Where little physical contact is described between the living, the adolescents tell six stories in which a character wants to hold, for one last time (or, perhaps for the only time), the body of a dead loved one (wife, husband, lover, mother, or father) as in the following examples.

> (VF4) (Card 18GF) This man has fallen down the stairs and he is probably dead. The woman doesn't know what to do with him. I'd say she loves him and wants to keep him forever, not bury him at all. She brings along the priest and explains it to him. Maybe she's a dear friend to the priest, and she asks his advice, about what to do with the man. I'd say the priest tells her to bury him.
>
> [KD-ac-die <u>FD-death</u> CB-help NDA-advice]

(HM7) (Card 3BM) This is a woman trying to open the coffin of a loved one.
[KD-ac-die FD-death]

(VM9) (Card 3BM) A young man has lost his father who was killed in a battle. He kneels beside the grave now, crying and mourning for the father he never realized how much he loved. . . . He feels sad and *empty* as he kneels beside the concrete tomb in which his father lies. He wishes he could open the tomb and take his father's body out and hold it to his breast, just once, as he's always wished he could.
[KD-ac-die FD-death PD-crazed]

(VM8) (Card 15) In a graveyard. An old man with rheumatism is praying over his wife's grave. He looks as if he's come back from a long journey. He's old and worn away, and he's reading the inscription on his wife's tomb. It's taking place at about ten p.m. and he goes away, and tells somebody to return and *close up the grave again.*
[FD-fate PB-body PD-crazed]

The young peoples' "romance with death" also emerged via the administration of a Values Hierarchy Scale which was first developed to investigate value differences between Mexican and American youth (see Diaz-Guerrero, 1963). I requested several grades of village school children (forty-three girls and twenty-four boys between the ages of 10 and 19) to rank order to the following values: career success, knowledge, health, honor, economic security, freedom, friendship, respect, character, love, religious faith, good disposition, humor, wealth, and power. The students protested that certain values—among them good disposition, character, and honor—seemed irrelevant while I had neglected to include the essential values of "happy death" and "self discipline." Given the modified version of the test (Scheper-Hughes, 1979), love just barely outranked happy death, but the latter was considered more important than career success, knowledge, wealth, power, respect, and economic security. (And "what doth it profit a man if he gain the whole world and suffer the loss of his soul?")

In contrast to the average village adolescents, the psychiatric patients—both male and female—told a high proportion of romantic love, sex, and marriage preoccupation stories on the TAT. Male psychiatric patients, for example, were especially given to interpreting the man-woman scene of Card 4 positively (45 percent of their themes, see Table 1.6), and their descriptions include the following: "two lovers who are very sad at parting for a while"; "I suppose these two are in love at any rate"; "they appear to be married, I believe, and quite happy." Village adolescents, however, gave twice as many themes as the hospitalized sample in which either the man or woman is seen as indifferent or lacking in love or warmth, as in the following examples:

(VM1) (Card 4) She's in love with him. But he doesn't take much notice of her. She's saying, "I'm in love with you," and he says, "I don't want to hear about it."

[FB-thwart FC-reject]

(VF3) (Card 4) A husband and a wife. I'd say that he's disinterested in her, and he's determined that his job comes first. . . . The outcome is that he'll go abroad and she'll just get used to being at home alone.

[FB-distant FC-split KD-resign]

A fear of celibacy, isolation, and childlessness pervades the stories of psychiatric patients, the majority of whom were adults in their late twenties or thirties and still single. While village girls tended to tell grandmother stories to Card 12F (young woman with an old woman in a shawl in the background) I got the following two stories from hospitalized girls:

(HF1) (Card 12F) I think that this is a lady when she . . . that's what she'll look like when she gets old. She's thinking about that, displeased with being an old maid.

[OD-body PB-dislike]

(HF4) (Card 12F) I'd say that's a kind of gypsy woman telling her the future, and she finds out that she won't marry the man she's in love with, and that she won't marry at all. And now she's just dreading what will happen. I bet she's sorry for going to that gypsy.

[CB-help CA-magic FB-thwart KD-hopeless]

And Seamus, a malcontent bachelor farmer and hospitalized schizophrenic told this story to Card 3BM:

(HMl) (3BM) He seems to be down and out crying. (Why?) Because he's lonely; he can't get a wife. (Why is that?) He isn't very attractive. (Future?) He haven't much of a future.

[FB-alone ESB-appear]

While themes of guilt, shame, fear, and rejection of sexuality were high for all samples in response to Card 13MF (VF 41 percent; HF 27 percent; VM 36 percent; HM 90 percent) hospitalized males were the most troubled, confused, and preoccupied by sex. And where normal villagers were defensively evasive and digressive in their handling of sexuality, hospitalized males, and somewhat less frequently hospitalized girls, directly confronted the issue at hand as in the following two themes:

(HM3) (13MF) The girl seems to be dead. He's weeping. He reads a lot of books. He's no one to go to, so he buries her himself. (How did she die?) He killed her.

(Why?) Because she wouldn't have the sexual intercourse. (Why not?) She don't like it.

[PD-sad HC-murder FC-reject PD-sex]

(HM2) (13MF) This is a bedroom scene between a husband and wife. The gentleman is just after making love to his wife. This is his first time, and he turns away in disgust, having changed his clothes first, of course. (Why is he disgusted?) He has some kind of guilt complex due to his religion.

[PD-disgust RB-guilt DSD-submit]

Such explicitly sexual stories were absent among normal villagers, who, when they did not immediately identify the card as a sickness or death scene, created far fetched dramas in which a damsel in distress was found washed up on a doorstep during a storm. The nudity of the woman was particularly disturbing to village males who, in four stories, somewhat prudishly attempted to clothe her, as in Brendan's story:

(VM14) (13MF) This woman went swimming in a mountain river where she almost drowns. She gets out of the water alive and then tries to find help. The woman falls unconscious on the doorstep of your man's house. He brings her in, of course, and put her to bed. Then while he waits for the doctor to arrive he takes off her wet clothes, with his eyes closed, and turning away so as not to get bad thoughts, he goes over to the dresser to get her dry ones.

[KB-mishap-o NDA-nurse RB-ideals]

Where average villagers (perhaps in part because of their somewhat younger age than the hospitalized sample) unquestioningly accept sexual repression as right and necessary in their stories, the more rebellious hospitalized sample sometimes ended their stories to Card 13MF with an affirmation of the need for more sexual freedom or understanding, as in the following two excerpts:

(HM4) (13MF) I'd say they probably come to the conclusion that sex is a fact of life, and millions do it. If they're in love, what shame?

[RB-ideals KA-accept PA-relief]

(HM9) (13MF) He has had the sexual intercourse and now he is bitten with pangs of remorse, a thing which shouldn't happen if only we were educated properly to the normality of sexual behavior.

[RC-pre-sex RB-guilt DSD-submit]

A theme of generativity also distinguished the average village adolescents from young psychiatric patients, as the latter frequently made allusions to their largely frustrated urge to nurture, to see living things—crops, animals, and babies—grow, survive, and outlive themselves. Dennis replies to Card 2: "The farmer is setting his rows, planning for the coming winter. He wants to feed his flock." And Seamus says, on the same card, "He's being very patient with his horse." The devotion of bachelors to their farm animals is viewed by married villagers as a somewhat humorous eccentricity of these lonely men.

While hospitalized men and women somewhat shyly and tentatively alluded to the suggested pregnancy of the older woman in Card 2 as "she's that way" or "she could be expecting," not one average villager mentioned or presumably noticed the pregnancy at all. And Card 13MF was described as a birth scene by two "disturbed" young people, and not by any in the "normal" sample. Peter, a twenty-two-year-old tradesman and hospitalized alcoholic given to fits of violence and aggression, told this rather gentle story to 13MF:

> (HM9) (13MF) This is a young girl and she seems to be in great pain, and your man can't bear to look, at her. She could be in labor and having difficulties. You want an ending? O.K. The girl dies, but the baby lives, and the father takes care of it.
>
> [NDB-pity KD-death NDA-nurture]

Following the administration of the TAT, I would at times ask the more outgoing mental patients to consent to the draw-a-person test. Dennis, a thirty-year-old discontented virgin (and diagnosed schizophrenic) drew within a very few minutes a comical but sorry caricature of a man with a huge phallus which, upon second thought, he Xed out of the self-portrait (Scheper-Hughes, 1979). A heavy burden for Dennis, and others like him, this seemingly enormous, bothersome, and superfluous organ. And Seamus, another hospitalized schizophrenic bachelor, summed up in his picture all the longing in lonely souls like himself for growth, creativity, and intimacy. For Seamus Welsh, the bachelor, drew the portrait of a very pregnant woman.

Notes

Caudill, William and George A. De Vos. 1956. Achievement, Culture and Personality: The Case of the Japanese Americans. *American Anthropologist*, **58**(6): 1102–1126.

De Vos, George A. 1973. Socialization for Achievement. Berkeley: University of California Press.

Diaz-Guerrero, Roberto. 1963. Cross Cultural Premises, Attitudes and Cross Cultural Research. Paper presented at the 17th International Congress of Psychology, Washington, D.C.

Dunne, David. 1970. Lose the Heat—Destroy the Head. *The Corridor Echo* Journal of St. Mary's Hospital Castlebar (Feb.) 22–35.

Gibbons, Luke. 1998. *Transformations in Irish Culture*. Notre Dame, Ind.: University of Notre Dame Press.

Haien, Jeanette. 1986. *The All of It: A Novel*. New York: Harper Perennial.

Henry, William. 1947. The Thematic Apperception Test in the Study of Culture-Personality Relations. *Genetic Psychological Monograph*, **35**.

Kennedy, Kieran. 1993. *Facing the Unemployment Crisis in Ireland.* Cork: Cork University Press.

O'Hare, Aileen and Dermot Walsh. 1977, 1978, 1979, 1980, 1981. *Activities of Irish Psychiatric Hospitals and Units*. Dublin: The Medico-Social Research Board.

O'Toole, Fintan. 1998. *The Lie of the Land: Irish Identities*. Dublin: New Island Books.

Scheper-Hughes, Nancy. 2000 (1997, first edition). *Saints, Scholars, and Schizophrenics: Mental Illness in Rural Ireland.* New, expanded and updated 20th anniversary edition. Berkeley and Los Angeles: University of California Press.

———. 1997. Peace-Time Crimes. *Social Identities*, **3**(3): 1–26.

———. 1996. Small Wars and Invisible Genocides. *Social Science & Medicine*, **43**(5): 889–900.

———. 1995. Who's the Killer? Popular Justice and Human Rights in a South African Squatter Camp. *Social Justice*, **22**(3): 143–164.

———. 1985. The Best of Two Worlds, the Worst of Two Worlds: Reflections on Culture and Fieldwork among the Rural Irish and Pueblo Indians. *Comparative Studies in Society and History*, **29**(1 Jan.): 56–75.

Sweeny, Paul. 1998. *The Celtic Tiger: Ireland's Economic Miracle Explained.* Dublin: Oak Tree Press.

Valarasan-Toomey, Mary. 1998. *The Celtic Tiger: From the Outside Looking In*. Dublin.

Waddington, John and A. Hanley Youssef. 1994. Evidence for a Gender-Specific Decline in the Rate of Schizophrenia in Rural Ireland over a 50-Year Period. *British Journal of Psychiatry*, **164**: 171–6.

Wallace, Anthony F.C. 1972. *The Death and Rebirth of the Seneca*. New York: Vintage.

Walsh, Dermot and Kenneth Kendler. 1995. The Prevalence of Schizophrenia in Ireland: Readdressing the Enigma. *Archives of General Psychiatry*, **52**: 509.

Chapter 2

Some Aspects of the Self in a Selfless Society: An Israeli Kibbutz[1]

Leslie Y. Rabkin

"A young boy is contemplating a violin which rests on a table in front of him" (Murray, 1943, p. 18). The purposely flat, laconic prose of Murray's description masks the mysteries and richly textured possibilities of TAT Card 1. Who is this boy? Has he a name? What dreams, desires, thoughts, and feelings engage his fancy behind those downcast eyes? Is he seeking to unravel the latent mysteries of art embodied in the violin? Has he played, and now pauses for a brief respite? Did he play well, and thus rests with satisfaction? Or were his efforts noisome, and his contemplation mired in a sense of failure? If so, did the cause lie in a deficit of ability? A lack of preparation? The knotted complexity of the music?

No, the boy has not played. In fact, he stubbornly refuses to do so. His thoughts are elsewhere—perhaps with the children at play outside, or focused on his fatigue, or a meal which awaits him. He does not want to play those tiresome scales, or even be associated with this "sissy" instrument. He is indignant, sullen. He is contemplating the violin with disgust, apathy, contempt.

---

[1]A version of this paper was presented in February 1987, at the Institute for Personality Assessment and Research, Berkeley, California, as part of a series commemorating the 50th anniversary of the publication of Gordon Allport's *Personality: A Psychological Interpretation.*

Does the boy have a history? Has he long dreamed of playing, of possessing this cherished instrument? or has the violin only lately become part of his landscape? Did he choose this task, or was it thrust upon him by loving parents, or artistically frustrated ones, or those who guiltily feel that a child should be exposed to art? Did the parents, whatever their motive, have to struggle to provide this instrument? Were they cajoled and entreated by their son?

And what of the future? Is there one? Perhaps the boy's contemplation is all, his life in stasis, as if yoked eternally to a condition of longing, or sadness, or bitterness. Can he be about to lift the violin to his chin and continue his—what? conformity to parental demands, a smooth or troubled passage to success, fulfilling his destiny, his dream, or perpetuating his nightmare?

What emotions accompany his contemplation? Is his mood one of sadness or good cheer, of seriousness or frivolity, of anxious expectation or sodden despair, of boldness and surety or timorousness and doubt?

Whatever his personal story, do the contemplative boy and his violin represent something more than a case history? Can he not be construed as Everyboy, indeed as Everyperson facing the arcane challenges of life, particularly the temptations of sex with its triune of thinking, looking, and touching? Does he perhaps embody an Aristotelian dichotomy between the *nous pathetikos* and the *nous poietikos*, the passive, receptive, intellect and the active, form-giving one?

At our instruction, an individual studies Card 1 and produces a text, a document in which he or she chooses some answer to the queries posed above, and, in accord with their inner field of memory, drive, defense, and self-representation, animates the lifeless figure of the contemplative boy. Or, we might say, the story told results from a peregrine interplay of those diverse aspects of personality which Allport (1937) denominated as the proprium—bodily sense, self-identity, self-esteem, self-extension, rational thinking, self-image, propriate strivings, and the function of knowing. And, of course, the text before us is also a product of the interpersonal system created by the storyteller and the auditor. Finally, there will be the mythic dimension of the text, the resonances of supra-individual, cultural, and world-interpretive themes.

The text of the story told to Card 1 is, to appropriate another of Allport's central concepts, an idiographic document. And we, as interpreters of this text, have come full circle. A picture of a contemplative boy was shown to a subject who sat and contemplated the task before him or her. And now we sit and contemplate the story told, our proprium alert to ponder Yeats' (1927) most apposite query:

> O body swayed to music, O brightening glance,
> How can we know the dancer from the dance?

The exegesis of my testing of Israeli kibbutzniks will seek to examine the paradox of Yeats' salient question. But my path will not be true to Allport's way. I will make use of idiographic materials, albeit in a rather discursive manner. What I propose to do is examine the texts of a number of individuals' stories told to Card

I of the TAT, and thereby to illuminate some critical issues within a particular cultural nexus—a specific Israeli kibbutz at two points in its history and that of its children. But first let me briefly relate how these texts were gathered, and the context in which they were created.

For a period of eighteen months, in 1967–1968, under a series of grants from NIMH, I conducted a participant observer study of an Israeli kibbutz, a broad-based examination of personality development and interpersonal functioning in this collective settlement (see, e.g., Rabkin, 1968, 1970a, 1970b, 1975, 1976, 1977, 1986; Rabkin and Rabkin, 1969; Rabkin and M.E. Spiro, 1970; Rabkin and A.G. Spiro, 1975). The kibbutz chosen for my study was the same one which Melford Spiro (1970, 1975) had so incisively analyzed nearly a generation earlier. As a clinical psychologist, much of my focus was on personality functioning as revealed through a wide spectrum of psychological tests—Rorschach, TAT, Rosenzweig Picture-Frustration Test, Figure Drawings, Raven Progressive Matrices, and others. Approximately 90 percent of all kibbutz-born children and adults living in the kibbutz were tested, both in 1951 and 1967–1968, with a range of instruments. For example, Rorschach protocols numbered 85 in 1951 and 173 in 1967–1968.

The kibbutz in question, which Spiro pseudonymously called *Kiryat Yedidim* (Village of Friends), was founded over eighty years ago in a malarial swampland of northeastern Palestine. Its founders were part of what is known in Israel as the Third Aliyah (immigration), a diverse band of disaffected youth from Austria, Galicia, and Poland, who emigrated to Palestine in the years 1919–1924. These young people, predominantly middle-class in background, but impassioned by the tenets of Zionism, Marxism, and ill-digested Freudianism, were charismatic utopians of a secular cast. Their ideological awareness was quite formidable.

The self-conscious mission among the pioneers was to redeem the Land of Israel. They wished to establish a society based on communitarian socialism in which all vestiges of bourgeois family life and social and economic arrangements would he abolished. They sought to create a Gemeinschaft in opposition to the Gesellschaft arrangements of the west, and to achieve personal salvation as midwives to this noble experiment in nature.

What these youth sought, and what by the time of Spiro's 1951 sojourn they had largely achieved, was:

> to create a social system in which science ("reason") rather than religion ("superstition") was to inform its world view; in which cooperation, based on the sentiment of brotherhood, was to be the dominant mode of social relations; in which goods and services were to be produced and distributed according to the guiding principle of "from each according to his ability to each according to his needs"; in which radical egalitarianism, both social and economic, was to be practiced; in which everyone was to be a worker (and hired labor repudiated); in which the means of production (including land), as well as all other capital goods (including housing), were to be publicly owned; in which pure democracy was to be practiced, and to be institutionalized in a manner which would preclude anyone from acquiring power over anyone else; in which children were to be freed from

> the domination of parents and raised with a maximum of freedom in a community of peers; and . . . in which women were to be fully emancipated . . . (through) a radical transformation in the traditional systems of marriage, the family, and sex-role differentiation. (Spiro, 1979, p. 5)

To inculcate these values in their children, the creators of Kiryat Yedidim and their ideological partners developed a program of collective education (*chinuch meshutaf*). This comprehensive process of socialization encompassed the years from birth through age eighteen, during which children lived apart from their biological parents in a peer-group setting of age-graded houses, and were cared for by a succession of caretakers (*metaplot*), educators (*mechanikim*), and teachers (*morim*). This radical system of child-rearing, with some internal changes induced by long experience, still prevailed during the period of my residence in Kiryat Yedidim.

"How can we know the dancer from the dance?" The questions I would pose for clarification are varied. What forms do self representations assume in a communitarian society? From what perspective do these communards view the trajectory of their lives? How is the self constructed out of the disparate figures who constitute their earliest developmental milieu? How does the self find its place in a world in which all one's actions are subject to the scrutiny of the group? How is the inner landscape of the self influenced by societal structure? In what ways are individual value orientations a reflection, repudiation, or conflicted synthesis of those which suffuse their cultural surround? Is there a community of themes which constitute a set of unifying codifications of reality? And how are our traditional forms of parsing psychological functioning manifested in other forms of social arrangements—issues of conformity and rebellion, achievement and failure, efficacy and insufficiency, autonomy and shame or doubt, initiative and guilt, industry and inferiority (Erikson, 1950)?

Not all of these concerns can be fully addressed through an examination of TAT Card 1. But much of importance can be gleaned from this analysis. Card 1 is, after all, the subject's initial foray into the world of fantasy and creativity called for by the instructions of the task. And as the first card, it arouses anxiety, calling for the mobilization of inner resources related to organization, control, and defense. It sets forth a demand and forces one to choose to accede, defy, or form some compromise solution, a reflection of the individual's "first" means of coping and adjustment. Then, as the first card, it requires the subject to determine, on the basis of the real characteristics and inner images of the auditor, what is to be the nature of the interaction sought, fostered, and acted out.

Card 1's representation of a child also harkens back to an earlier period of self-representation or, in the case of a youth, to an identificatory concern with the tasks and feelings of childhood. Its mood of contemplation inspires a similar mood in the subject, inducing the primary imaginal productions and queries of contemplation—Who am I? What am I? What will I be? Card 1 portrays a violin resting on a table before the boy, with all its pregnant implications of action, challenge, and more primitive tool-using.

In what follows, I shall examine these matters through an intensive analysis of a few records excerpted from two sets of data, comprising the stories told in 1951 to Card 1 by Spiro's adult kibbutz-born (sabra) subjects, and the texts produced in my encounter with these same people in 1968. Nine of these stories were told in 1951 and seven by the same subjects in 1968. I will make reference to only a limited number of motifs and themes, focusing my attention on matters related to these individuals' self-presentation and its roots in kibbutz socialization practices.

In 1951, Spiro's adult sample included these five men and four women, ranging in age from twenty-one to twenty-eight. There were, at that juncture in kibbutz history, only twelve kibbutz-reared adults. In 1968, these people were between thirty-seven and forty-five. Their ages and complete stories and their scoring in the De Vos system are as follows:

Sabra TAT Stories, Card 1: 1951 and 1968

(1951 Ilana) (Female, age 21) He obviously received a violin for a present and can't play it. No? He thinks and thinks how to bring tones from that thing. What else? I would return that violin and ask for a present I could use. Too bad it is not in colors, it would be more interesting.

[NSA-reward CC-inept OB-think NSC-refuse]

(1968 Ilana) (Female, age 38) This reminds me of my brother Shlomo, have you seen him? He was sitting opposite the violin and was asking himself: "What did they give me that sort of thing—instead of throwing stones?" The end was that the violin was lying under the wardrobe, until they threw it away. (How does the boy feel?) He is facing a problem he doesn't know how to solve: What is he going to do with that violin anyway? What does he need it for? They gave him an expensive instrument, told him that it was expensive, and yet he isn't interested in it, and he hasn't any need for it.

[NSB-other AD-motive OB-dislike OC-discard]

(1951 Naomi) (Female, age 25) I think he's looking at a picture. No? This boy is quite young, the hour is late, he's tired, ready to go to sleep, eyes almost closed. Not son of rich, son of worker. Half day studies in school, half day plays, and at night he does his lessons and looks at pretty pictures on table. Looks and looks and thinks: "What is drawn here?," and tries to think of a story or picture he sees, and is very tired, but still invents a story about this picture. He has no power to overcome his fatigue. Picture is one of beautiful scenery, and he thinks of all the beautiful places in the world which he will not be able to see. Soon he'll go to sleep.

[PB-tired KD-poverty OB-think CA-create CD-finish PA-nature PD-thwart]

(1968 Naomi) (Female, age 41) A boy has come home from school, and he is sitting and looking at a picture. And he is thinking to himself: "What does this picture say?" Because the teacher at school has told him that he should write a story about the picture. That the story should have a beginning, and should have an end, and should have a middle. It needn't be a long composition. How the boy is sitting there, looking and looking at the picture. A bit hard for him to decode. And he is already very tired, and he is ready to go to sleep, or to play a game, [not play violin]. (What will be?) With the boy? (Yes, in the end) He will write the composition, and he will go to sleep or go out to play.

[OB-think RB-duty PB-tired RA-duty-o PA-play]

(1951 Ruth) (Female, age 27) I think he is a young boy and he began to play the violin. He looks at it and thinks what he'll get from it. His content of life is just pleasure. He thinks it will be the content of his life, and he thinks what future he will have from this violin.

[OB-think PA-aesthetic]

(1951 Shoshana) (Female, age 27) Here before me is a violin, an instrument in which much is treasured. I like it very much, and I think it will be for me everything in life. I hope that I could always be attached to it.

[OA-awe]

(1968 Shoshana) (Female, age 44) The boy is very tired. Yet, in spite of all, he feels that he is obliged to go on playing [play the violin], for he knows that this is very, very important to his parents, especially to his father. He really doesn't want to cause him grief, although he feels that he already can't make it. He is very tired. (What do you think will be in the end?) He won't go on playing because the father will arrive at the conclusion that this is too hard, and that only for his sake has he played. Not on account of the boy's being very musical, not on account of the boy needing it, but it was the father's need. He will stop with this. He will not play (note: as above).

[RA-duty-o NDB-pity CD-inept PB-tired DDA-pardon]

(1951 Shlomo) (Male, age 28) (long time) There are four or five stories I can tell. This boy very much wants to play the violin. He sits now; often practices. He has here music sheets. He is tired. He is a very intelligent boy, according to his look. He sits and thinks about how he can excel in music. I think, according to his look, that he will be a great violinist. He thinks, and has a look of decision. He does not have the look that he has no desire—just the opposite. An interesting picture.

[AB-dream AA-persist PB-tired]

(1951 Shimon) (Male, age 21) A violin. This boy doesn't know how to play the violin. He came to the house, and the violin was on the table, and the boy wanted the violin very much, and to play it. It draws him very much. He's heard concerts, is musical, and has the eyes and mouth of an emotional person. The violin arouses thoughts and desires. He much wants it, and he knows that he can't get the violin. It is not his, and he can only think about it. Although the violin is new—it can be that someone else received it. The boy, since he so much wanted the violin and is musical, since he was so impressed by violin music, when he grew up he got one. Anyone who wants something so much can get it. He was not a great violinist, and played in an average-class orchestra. It is not a long story.

[CB-able OB-want PA-esthetic CD-mediocre]

(1968 Shimon) (Male, age 37) At first—let's suppose that this boy has got a new violin from somebody, a thing he has been dreaming about for a long time, and he is very excited by the present. He has taken it with him alone to see it. And now he is looking at this violin and absorbs it. He is impressed by it, and thinks what he is going to do with it. It's to be supposed that he will play it, and perhaps will be, who knows who, a prodigy. But it may also be that not. At any rate, he has very much wanted the violin and now he has it.

[NSA-reward OB-want CB-able OA-own]

(1951 David) (Male, age 22) He looks at the string which is broken in the violin. He's very sad and thinks where he'll get a new string. (Question) He'll get a new string, so he'll be able to play.

[PD-sad OB-repair CA-future]

(1968 David) (Male, age 38) This is a boy who plays the violin. When he finished playing, he goes to pack up the violin and put it in a box. Apparently something was wrong with him so that he didn't do well at the time of playing. And the boy sits and thinks: "What is it here with the violin?" Why doesn't the playing come out like he wants. He's looking to see how is it possible to get more out of this violin? (How does he feel that it didn't come out so well?) He feels—he sees that it didn't come out so well at the time of playing. I have a violinist son, and I know how he feels when it isn't successful.

[OB-think CB-defect]

(1951 Natan) (Male, age 22) [long time before answering] This boy received a violin as a present after he had asked his parents for a long time, for he liked very much to hear violin music, and his dream was to make music like that. After he receives it, he looks at it but doesn't know how to approach it, as if it was something holy. According to his position, at the end the violin remains closed in the case. He does not know how to play it.

[NSA-reward PA-esthetic OA-awe CD-unable]

(1968 Natan) (Male, age 38) Well, uh, seems to me this boy was crazy about the violin. I remember once seeing a movie about—Dvorak, I believe it was. Since he was very young, he wanted to get a violin, and his parents were crazy about it. I mean, they did not want to have him as a musician. And they were trying to convince him about many other things to do, but he was very insistent and stubborn about it. And I still remember the moment in the movie when he finally got his violin. He was excited. I don't remember what he was doing in the movie, but it reminded me very much of how—maybe you would call it—to term it as shocked he was that he finally got it. He was just motionless for a while, until he could take himself in hand, you know, and start doing something like trying to start and play it, or altogether playing with it. But this picture shows the moment when he just received it, and he put it on the white cloth, as he did not dare to put it on the table, just like a sacred idol for him.

[OB-want DDB-worry NSA-reward OA-awe]

(1951 Zeev) (Male, age 25) Johnny wanted to play the violin from the earliest age. But his parents were poor, and he did not succeed in getting one. After much difficulty, they got him one. He learned a lot, as he was stubborn and diligent, but he had no ability. When that was clear to him, he sat by the table, looked at the violin, and realized that his life ambition was lost—he'll never attain it.

[AA-self KB-poverty NDA-devote CD-inept]

(1968 Zeev) (Male, age 41) Many years the boy dreamt of playing the violin. And his family did not have sufficient means to afford the violin. At last, they got him a violin. The violin had been the desire of the boy for many years, and when he got it he devoted himself to playing with all his heart and soul. He received lessons, and he played and he practiced, was a very conscientious pupil, a very devoted pupil. But after some months it became clear that the boy was lacking musical talent, in spite of his great progress in playing; in fact, in spite of his knowledge of the notes, he did not progress with the violin itself. He did not turn out to be what he had dreamt. He did not turn out to be a real violinist. Neither the family nor the teachers dared to tell him that he really lacked the talent of playing. And, in the course of years, he played and thought and dreamt until he himself came to the conclusion, and it became clear to him that that wasn't that—from the violin doesn't issue the same melody as sounds within himself. And then, at that time when he had the crisis, and he was sitting day after day at the table, looking at the violin and thinking what was going to be with the dream he had been carrying within himself during so many years, and he was disappointed.

[AA-persist KB-poverty NSA-reward NDB-unable CD-inept]

The Denigrated Self among the Israeli Sabra Kibbutzim

The most dramatic theme extracted from these texts is that of the "Denigrated Self." The sabra self in 1951 emerges from these stories as insecure, inadequate, and incompetent—"this boy doesn't know how to play the violin"; "He obviously received a violin for a present and can't play it"; "According to his position, at the end the violin remains closed in the case. He does not know how to play it"; "he sat by the table, looked at the violin, and realized that his life ambition was lost—he'll never attain it"; "He has no power to overcome his fatigue."

In the single text where the hero is presented as someone who "will be a great violinist," the outcome is hedged and rationalized; "methinks he doth protest too much" could be the title here, for the hero's success is framed as: "I think, according to his look, that he will be a great violinist. He thinks and has a look of decision. He does not have the look that he has no desire—just the opposite." The achievement of another is resignedly summed up as: "He was not a great violinist, and played in an average-class orchestra."

It is not the desire to achieve which is wanting: "the boy wanted the violin very much. . . . The violin arouses thoughts and desires;" "his dream was to make music like that"; "he was stubborn and diligent"; "he thinks it will be the content of his life"; "(it is) an instrument in which much is treasured"; "the boy very much wants to play the violin."

Nor, on the surface, is it a lack of facilitative others which undermines the sabras' strivings: "He obviously received a violin for a present"; "This boy received a violin as a present after he had asked his parents for a long time"; "After much difficulty they (his parents) got him (a violin)." Where the other is present, the hero gets what he wants, although this is not an unalloyed good.

Spiro (1975) suggested that these sabras' Denigrated Self was the resultant of a concatenation of forces: their felt incapacity to assume responsibility for kibbutz functioning; their parents' lack of faith in them to do so; a deeper sense of the unreliability of others, due to their early experiences of a long latency between their infantile neediness and its satisfaction by nurse or mother; and their basic difficulties in developing an integrated, effective set of ego adaptive mechanisms for coping with the chronic changes in their caretakers.

The first of these hypotheses, the parental doubt in their offsprings' capacities, is borne out in the resonances of the sabras' stories. The kibbutz "Other," the parental generation, is echoed in the content of their texts: "He's heard concerts . . . the violin . . . is not his, and he can only think about it. Although the violin is new—it can be someone else received it"; "After he receives (the violin), he looks at it but doesn't know how to approach it, as if it is something holy"; "he learned a lot, but he had no ability."

Parental disappointment in their children was endemic among the founders. In great part it stemmed from what Spiro, following Max Weber, denoted as the inevitable aftermath of the stage of ideological fervency, the "routinization of the charisma." Sabra allegiance to the kibbutz, in Spiro's day and more outspokenly in mine, was based not on the affective and exalted, but on the rational and mundane: it was their home, they accepted their parents' inculcated values and were willing to perpetuate the existence of their society, but only from a pragmatic view of its viability and potential for gratification, not one emanating from the eschatological perspective of their parents. This conflict in Weltanschauung imposed a superordinate dimension on the more prosaic conflict of generations.

The second hypothesis, concerning the frustration attendant upon the lag between need and satisfaction, is also present in the sabras' texts: "The violin arouses thoughts and desires, he much wants it, and he knows he can't get the violin"; "He thinks and thinks how to bring tones from that thing"; "He's very sad and thinks where he'll get a new string"; "According to his position, at the end of the violin remains closed in the case"; "he did not succeed in getting (a violin)"; "he thinks of all the beautiful places in the world he will not be able to see"; "this boy very much wants to play the violin."

The attachment issue, and the poignancy, anger, and despair about being unable to maintain the maternal bond, is echoed above and further in the sabras' tales: "He came to the house, and the violin was on the table, and the boy wanted the violin very much and to play it . . . he much wants it, and he knows that he can't get the violin"; "I would return the violin and ask for a present I could use"; "He'll get a new string, so he'll be able to play"; "(he) looks and looks, and thinks, 'what is drawn here,' and tries to think of a story or picture he sees, and is very tired, but still invents a story about this picture"; "he looks at it and thinks what he'll get from it"; "I hope that I could always be attached to it"; "there are 4 or 5 stories I could tell."

The sabra of 1951 has little expectation that he or she can be efficacious. As Bandura (1977) notes, there is a difference between outcome expectancy, a belief that particular behaviors will result in a particular solution, and efficacy expectation, an inner sense that one can successfully perform these behaviors. Low self-efficacy results in lessened persistence, a clear-cut sabra trait.

This brings us to our second major theme, the "Etiolated Self": "I think he's looking at a picture—no? This boy is quite young, the hour is late, he's tired, ready to go to sleep, eyes almost closed. . . . He has no power to overcome his fatigue. . . . Soon he'll go to sleep."

The sabra, as one of Spiro's seven-year-old subjects comments on the boy of Card 1, "thinks and thinks without end." He sits and looks—what is out there? He is tired, overcome by fatigue, and regresses into sleep. "Thoughts and desires" are aroused in him, and these are rife with passive yearnings.

As in the lost dream of art subtheme pervading their stories, the sabras yearn for the unpossessed. But they feel constrained, as if they wish to respond to this yearning but fear doing so: "He looks at it, but doesn't know how to approach it, as if it is something holy." They experience a pervasive helplessness; they will not get what they want, and there is precious little they can do to maintain the presence or constancy of their desired love object when it is there.

In examining the theme of the Denigrated Self, we noted the equation of the violin and the kibbutz, the parental heritage, and the sabras' self-view of being failures, incompetent, and ill-equipped to carry this on. The theme of the Etiolated Self presents us with the equation of the violin and the mother, the object of desire which cannot be obtained or mastered, whose appearances and disappearances throughout the sabras' early life constituted a chronic source of enhanced then shattered hopes, visitations over which they had no control: "He looks at the string which is broken, in the violin. He's very sad, and thinks where he'll get a new string."

Maternal attachment, which collective education so self-consciously undermined, most especially in the wake of the ideological fervor and ambivalent self-abnegation of the founding generation, is the broken string of the sabras' fantasy. But there is a sex difference in their response to this trauma.

Among the women of 1951, the tone of their dealings with the violin is more clearly affective and narcissistic. Their reaction to mother can be seen as one of pure longing, pure sensuality, pure regression, or pure anger and rejection. "He obviously received a violin for a present and can't play it. No? He thinks and thinks how to bring tones from that thing. What else? I would return that violin and ask for a present I could use. Too bad it is not in colors, it would be more interesting"; "I think he's looking at a picture. No? The boy is quite young, the hour is late, he's tired, ready to go to sleep, eyes almost closed. Not son of rich, son of worker. Half day studies in school, half day plays, and at night he does his lessons and looks at pretty pictures on table. Looks and looks and thinks: 'what is drawn here?'" and tries to think of a story or picture he sees, and is very tired, but still invents a story about this picture. "He has no power to overcome his fatigue. Picture is one of beautiful scenery, and he thinks of all the beautiful places in the world which he will not be able to see. Soon he'll go to sleep"; "I think he's a young boy and he began to play the violin. He looks at it and thinks what he'll get from it. His content of life is just pleasure. He thinks it will be the content of his life, and he thinks what future he will have from this violin"; "Here before me is a violin, an instrument in which much is treasured. I like it very much, and I think it will be for me everything in life. I hope that I could always be attached to it."

Ilana, the teller of the first tale, does not perceive maternal "giving" as a gesture of affection, but as a demand to produce something, presumably to love her, the mother, in return. She has failed at this task, but refuses to remain in the position of a "bad child." She returns the gift and turns back the criticism upon the mother. Her inability to get what is wanted from mother is transmuted into a typical sabra defensive posture of *lo ichpatiyut*—"who cares." She appears to be telling mother: "it isn't my fault that I didn't get what I needed, it's yours." Yet, still burdened by a sense of having been responsible for her own deprivation, she adds: "anyway, I wasn't really trying and, anyway, I couldn't care less."

Naomi, whose story ends in a regressive posture of sleep, presents a hero who also does his utmost to avoid the blame attendant upon not receiving narcissistic supplies. Her task is to develop a reaction-formation against any demandingness, to seek maternal love and approval through demonstrating her "goodness" and conformity. Her attempts to instill guilt in mother can be felt in the overblown intensity of her hero's effort to conform and the bittersweet acceptance of deprivation: "all the beautiful places in the world he will not be able to see." The final pathway, in the face of such intense frustration, is that of passivity and withdrawal. For Naomi, one is basically helpless in the face of powerful forces impinging both from within and without.

Ruth, our next expositor, appears to be more optimistic about the possibilities for obtaining pleasure. There is an oral, infantile quality to her need-pleasure expressed here. More importantly, she shifts from active manipulation of the object of desire to a passive stance at some remove, an internalizing gesture, moving from playing to thinking. It is as if Ruth maintains the feeling of maternal gratification through introjection and a narcissistic retreat into fantasy gratification.

Finally, Shoshana, whose hero makes entirely explicit the wish for eternal attachment in what clearly sounds, with its oneiric, infantile tone, to be a return to the womb fantasy. She speaks in a histrionic, theatrical manner, avoiding logical connections, thereby giving her text the quality of a dream. Yet the extremity of her commentary, the overvaluation of the violin, bespeaks a dramatic reaction-formation to an unconscious rejection of mother who is not "treasured," not "everything in life," and to whom there is *no* attachment of a meaningful nature.

For the sabra men, the issue of mother is more straightforward, if no less a cause for grief. "She cannot be played," the string is broken. The connection of the men's heroes with the violin is intense, arousing desires for mastery, achievement, control, and deep attachment. Always and forever they have yearned to make beautiful music with this instrument, but they can never attain their life's ambition; the mother will not respond to their efforts.

Natan makes explicit the mysterious nature of the maternal matrix:

> This boy received a violin for a present after he had asked his parents for a long time, for he liked very much to hear violin music, and his dream was to make music like that. After he receives it, he looks at it, but doesn't know how to approach it, as if it is something holy. According to his position, at the end the violin remains closed in the case. He does not know how to play it.

The mother remains something "holy," untouchable. The men's emphasis on "looking" at the violin, complemented by Shimon's commentary that his hero has "the eyes and mouth of an emotional person," suggests an orphic dimension to the mother-son relationship: they have looked upon the forbidden, thereby forfeiting the chance to possess their love, and sealing their doom.

Even Shlomo, whose hero is alone in achieving success with the violin, is driven to hide his hubris in a welter of obsessive intellectualization and propitiatory detours:

> There are four or five stories I can tell. This boy very much wants to play the violin. He sits now; often practices. He has here music sheets. He is tired. He is a very intelligent boy, according to his look. He sits and thinks about how he can excel in music. I think, according to his look, that he will be a great violinist. He thinks and has a look of decision. He does not have the look that he has no desire—just the opposite. An interesting picture.

The adult sabras of Spiro's 1951 sample are troubled in all those dimensions of personality which define Allport's proprium. The self which emerges from Card 1 is debased and inadequate, plagued by feelings of inefficacy and stasis. It is a self which experiences a profound incapacity to shoulder its kibbutz heritage or to achieve autonomy and succeed at initiative. This self seeks to escape from its shameful exposure through regression and denial. It is a self which has experienced a never-healed disruption of its maternal ties, and is left with unrequited yearnings, feelings of faithlessness, and punitive rage turned back upon itself, expressed through convoluted reaction-formations, or drained and deflected into a state of helplessness.

When we turn to examine the texts of this same group of sabras nearly a generation later, we are immediately struck by the astounding continuity of self-image reflected there. The pervasive air of failure remains; the cycle, reflecting May's (1980) thematic concept, of enhancement/deprivation, continues to mark the males' records; the women remain angry, vaguely mocking, and archly resistant. There is an eerie sense here that nothing—not the passage of time, not maturity, not adult responsibility and achievement, not the changes in kibbutz life and its fortunes, has altered the inner landscape of the sabras.

They appear to be a group of people whose struggles with the issues of competency vs. inadequacy, of pleasure vs. suffering, of activity vs. stasis, have never been resolved or integrated. The persistence of their conflicts is remarkable. They are truly the "children of the desert," the permanently and irremediably damaged sacrifices of a most noble "experiment in nature."

The chilling sameness of their texts can, however, aid us in our quest for understanding the variegated meanings we have attributed to the actions of our contemplative boy of Card 1. For example, in Shoshana's story, we find corroboration of our hypothesis concerning the sabra as the discomforted inheritor of an overwhelming paternal heritage. Even in early middle-age, the image of the demanding father remains all too salient.

> The boy is very tired. Yet, in spite of all, he feels that he is obliged to go on playing, for he knows that this is very, very important to his parents, especially to his father. He really doesn't want to cause him grief, although he feels that he already can't make it. He is very tired. (What do you think will be in the end?) He won't go on playing because the father will arrive at the conclusion that this is too hard, and that only for his sake has he played. Not on account of the boy's being very musical, not on account of the boy needing it, but it was the father's need. He will stop with this. He will not play.

We can read Shoshana's text in this manner: despite one's innermost resistance to the task of perpetuating the paternal dream, one is implacably enjoined to do so. This obligation, this masculine imperative, is central to her theme. We see more clearly limned here what was earlier presented in dream-like disguise—the sacrificial nature of her behavior, the unwilling obeisance paid to the paternal superego, her need to prove herself worthy to be protected against the loss of regard and of love. The hero succeeds in arousing some semblance of guilt in the father, who is forced to recognize his selfish, sadistic demands, and to abate these.

"He really doesn't want to cause him grief." This extreme fabulization of our contemplative boy's feelings masks an opposite attitude—one of anger and revenge. Shoshana's superego appears to demand sacrifice, the relinquishment of personal needs and goals. The paternal image requires frustration, masochistic subjection, and a relinquishment of any form of self-gratification.

Performance is all; the real self must be hidden from view, while a false, conforming self is constantly demonstrated to the "audience." Surcease is achieved only by "pardon" from the paternal superego. By extension, we find the kibbutz is perceived as demanding and controlling, an ambiance which can only be appeased by conformity, in which "love" is allotted in accord with society's own measure of one's willingness to submit to its demands. Anger, rebellion, and despair can only be expressed through fantasy, disguise, and masochistic surrender.

Zeev's new text, infused with an incantatory atmosphere of disappointment, informs our understanding of the seedbed of sabra depression and its relationship to the abrogated mother-child bond.

> Many years the boy dreamt of playing the violin. And his family did not have sufficient means to afford the violin. At last, they got him a violin. The violin had been the desire of the boy for many years, and when he got it he devoted himself to playing with all his heart and soul. He received lessons, and he played and he practiced, was a very conscientious pupil, a very devoted pupil. But after some months, it became clear that the boy was lacking musical talent, in spite of his great progress in playing. In fact, in spite of his knowledge of his notes, he did not progress with the violin itself. He did not turn out to be what he had dreamt. He did not turn out to be a real violinist. Neither the family nor the teachers dared to tell him that he really lacked the talent of playing. And, in the course of years, he played and thought and dreamt until he himself came to the conclusion, and it became clear to him, that that wasn't that—from the violin doesn't issue the same melody as sounds within himself. And then, at the time when he had the crisis, and he was sitting day after day at the table, looking at the violin and thinking what was going to be with the dream he had been carrying within himself during so many years, and he was disappointed.

This tale alerts us as well to the meaning of the lost dream of art subtheme. The intensity of desire to achieve, the love, excitement, and idealization of the violin and its product, appears to be a reparative mechanism, a quasi-magical ritual designed to restore and re-animate the injured object.

"The self-reproaches (of the depressive)," Freud (1917) noted, "are reproaches against a loved object which has been shifted onto the patient's own ego." For Zeev, aggression directed against the abandoning mother has been turned inward; the violin, and its potential for beauty and creation, remains idealized, while the self is felt to be damaged. Natan's exaltation of the violin as a "sacred idol" underscores this split. Thus, good and bad, desired and rejected, yearned for and scorned, love and hate, all remain in split-off, unintegrated form.

Klein's comments are apropos here:

> In some patients who had turned away from their mother, in dislike or hate, or used other mechanisms to get away from her . . . there existed in their minds nevertheless a beautiful picture of the mother, but one who was felt to be unattractive—really an injured, incurable and therefore dreaded person. The beautiful picture had been dislocated from the real object but had never been given up, and played a great part in the specific ways of their sublimation. (Klein, 1937, p. 270)

In its simplest manifestation, the sabra can never achieve a successful synthesis of the kibbutz culture's separation between the frustrating caretaker and the yearned for, gratifying mother.

Coda

Each step in our analysis has raised new and more provocative questions. Our dancers and their dance continually flow into evermore complex configurations. Rapaport's (1958) view that kibbutz society, as do all others, must "pay a price—a necessary sacrifice—in the coin of developmental crises and pathology, for their successes in adapting their successive generations to their ways of life" (p. 597) is true enough. A society, such as the kibbutz, which sought to reconstitute the forms of individual development and human interaction, must be prepared to confront the bedrock of human impulse, needs, and strivings in all their indigenous power.

The founders of the kibbutz, the progenitors of our subjects, embarked on a millenarian quest, empowered by a yearning for Paradise; a wish, though they would never express it thus, to return to a state of blessedness and liberty such as existed before the "fall" of man. Their hubris was punished. Not by the "gods," not even by "God," whose influence they would anyway abjure, but by the apparent inelasticity of human nature. Their children are complex human beings who have suffered from the Promethean excesses the founders' all too admirable desires demanded. The radical system of child rearing practiced in this Kibbutz, as in others, is no longer operative. This generation of children is being raised at home by parents.

I hope that I have succeeded in presenting to you some minimal and fragmentary images of the drama which constitutes the struggle between utopian impulse and human need. And, from another perspective, I hope that I have been able to illumine some of the inspirating potential inherent in an analysis of Murray's TAT Card 1.

> Never trust the artist. Trust the tale. The proper function of a critic is to save the tale from the artist who created it. (Lawrence, 1924, p. 13)

References

Allport, Gordon W. 1937. *Personality: A Psychological Interpretation*. New York: Holt.

Bandura, Albert. 1977. *Social Learning Theory*. Englewood Cliffs, N.J.: Prentice-Hall.

Erikson, Erik H. 1950. *Childhood and Society*. New York: Norton.

Freud, Sigmund. 1917. *Mourning and Melancholia.* Standard Edition, Vol. 17. London: Hogarth Press.

Klein, M. 1937. *Love, Guilt and Reparation*. London: Hogarth Press.

May, R. 1980. *Sex and Fantasy*. New York: Norton.

Murray, Henry A. 1943. *Thematic Apperception Test Manual.* Cambridge, Mass.: Harvard University Press.

Rabkin, Leslie Y. 1968. A Very Special Education: The Israeli Kibbutz. *Journal of Special Education*, **2**: 251–261.

———. 1970a. Some Notes on the Kibbutz. *Voices*, **6**: 20–24.

———. 1970b. Parties and Social Behavior: A Kibbutz Example. *Psychiatry*, **33**: 482–493.

———. 1975. Superego Processes in a Collective Society: The Israeli Kibbutz. *International Journal of Social Psychiatry*, **21**: 79–86.

———. 1976. In Israel's Radical Communes, the Institution of the Family is Alive and Well. *Psychology Today*, **9**: 66–73.

———. 1977. Continuity and Change in the Israeli Kibbutz. *PHP* (Japan), **8**: 2–10.

———. 1986. Longitudinal Continuities in the Personality of a Kibbutznik. *Journal of Psychoanalytic Anthropology*, **9**: 319–338.

Rabkin, Leslie Y. and K. Rabkin. 1969. Children of the Kibbutz. *Psychology Today*, **3**: 40–46.

Rabkin, Leslie Y. and Melford E. Spiro. 1970. The Kibbutz in 1970. In Melford E. Spiro, *Kibbutz: Venture in Utopia* (expanded ed.). New York: Schocken, 263–292.

Rabkin, Leslie Y. and A.G. Spiro. 1975. Postscript: Children of the Kibbutz. In M.E. Spiro, *Children of the Kibbutz* (expanded ed.). Cambridge, Mass.: Harvard University Press, 463–499.

Rapaport, D. 1958. The Study of Kibbutz Education and Its Bearing on the Theory of Development. *American Journal of Orthopsychiatry*, **28**: 587–597.

Spiro, Melford E. 1970. Kibbutz: *Venture in utopia* (expanded ed.). New York: Schocken.

———. 1975. *Children of the Kibbutz* (expanded ed.). Cambridge, Mass.: Harvard University Press.

———. 1979. *Gender and Culture: Kibbutz Women Revisited.* Durham, N.C.: Duke University Press.

Yeats, William B. 1927. Among School Children. In M. L. Rosenthal (ed.), *Selected Poems of William Butler Yeats*. New York: Macmillan, 1962.

Chapter 3

Omens of Future Ills: African Youth in Contemporary Kenya[2]

Emmit Bud Evans, Jr.

In 1972, I obtained responses to three Thematic Apperception Test (TAT) Cards from a sample of 699 African secondary school students in Kenya. When coded with the De Vos Interpersonal Concerns Scoring System (ICSS), the students' projections revealed a pattern of interpersonal concerns centered around a driving desire to achieve a better way of life for themselves and their families in Kenya's newly independent society. The data also revealed some disturbing premonitions of the modes of adaptation likely to characterize the responses of the students as they left school and found their aspirations and expectations frustrated by the inability of Kenya's polity and economy to deliver the jobs upon which their hopes for a better way of life were built.

This chapter revisits the Kenya research after a period of twenty years. Its purpose is to recount the methodology and essential findings of that research as a means of illustrating the utility of the TAT as a quantitative cross-cultural research device; it also seeks to demonstrate the prognostic value of the TAT through assessing the validity of predictions made on the basis of the 1972 data against the record of recent events in the country.

---

[2]The material in this chapter was originally presented as a paper at the XIII Congress International du Rorschach et des Methodes Projectives in Paris, France, on July 26, 1990.

Kenya and the TAT: Background and Methodology

I first became familiar with Kenya in 1969, when I spent a year teaching as a Peace Corps volunteer in an African secondary school north of Nairobi. Several months into that assignment, I became aware of a cruel irony. On the one hand, I was struck by the intensity of the aspirations and expectations that my students held for their future. Following Kenya's political independence from British colonial rule in 1963, a secondary school certificate had become a guaranteed ticket to a job in government service as a combination of departing colonial civil servants and an expanding bureaucracy created a growing demand for government workers with a secondary school education. Most of these new government employees came from Kenya's rural areas, and their education and jobs thus meant a revolutionary transformation in lifestyle from rural poverty and subsistence to an urban utopia replete with such accouterments as an apartment with electricity and running water, a private automobile, and discretionary income to send home and to spend on the luxuries of the "modern" world. In the early years of independence, these demands for civil servants and aspirations for a better way of life merged to spark rapid expansions in schools and enrollments: between 1963 and 1970, the number of secondary schools in Kenya grew from 150 to 783 (a 422 percent increase), and enrollments grew from 27,509 to 122,239 (a 344 percent increase).

On the other hand, I also became aware of the fact that the era of expanding employment opportunities was coming to an abrupt end. By 1969, Kenya's bureaucracies were no longer growing at anywhere near the previous rate, and most of the posts in the civil service had been both Africanized and filled by relatively young workers. I was astonished to learn that up to 90 percent of the students I was teaching had *no* prospect of employment after graduation, either in government service or in any other sector of the country's economy. Structures of neocolonialism, more subtle, but no less debilitating than the formal structures of direct colonial rule, continued patterns of foreign domination that allowed few jobs for Kenyan citizens.

I was teaching in Kenya while on leave of absence from graduate study in political science at the University of California at Berkeley. From that perspective, the social and political implications of the incongruity between my students' hopes and the likelihood of unemployment seemed a fertile ground for study. Even with the dramatic increases in school enrollments noted above, Kenya's schools only had places for the brightest and most capable 10 percent of its secondary school age population. What were the prospects for social and political instability in a country where the best and brightest youth were being driven into circumstances seemingly certain to result in high levels of disenchantment and alienation? Those implications seemed especially relevant to Kenya's prospects for development—how could such a process succeed in the context of the instability that seemed likely to result? And, given the parallels between Kenya's post-independence experiences and those of other newly independent countries in Africa and Asia, what might be learned of value for understanding similar obstacles to development in other areas of the Third

World? I returned to graduate school in 1970, and began designing a research project that would enable me to pursue these questions and concerns in detail.

The Thematic Apperception Test

The research strategy that began to emerge led me first to the TAT. I was acquainted with David McClelland's *The Achieving Society*, and had been impressed by the proportion of my students in Kenya who seemed to exhibit the characteristics of individuals with a high need for achievement. I had also been studying under George De Vos, and knew both of the ability of certain TAT Cards to reveal levels of concern with achievement and of the ability of the ICSS to identify and categorize such motivations within the framework of overall patterns of concerns. An assessment of the nature of achievement motivation among Kenya's secondary school students seemed a good place to start my research on the logic that the negative social and political implications of unemployment among school leavers should vary directly with the level, sources, and objects of their achievement motivation—the frustration of self-motivated high achievers seeking self-defined and self-valued interpersonal goals would seem to constitute a much greater threat to social and political order than the frustration of, for example, low achievers driven to pursue goals primarily defined and valued by their parents.

My first research priority became the administration of a set of TAT Cards to a sample of Kenya secondary school students. In contrast to the qualitative analysis of individual personality that motivated the original developers of the TAT, my interest was, of course, that of a quantitative social scientist seeking quantitative data. My goal was to use the ICSS as the basis for a content analysis of TAT responses from a relatively large sample of students, aggregating those responses to obtain an understanding of the traits and characteristics of the group as a whole.

I first chose Cards Numbers 1 and 17BM [see Appendix B, Kenyan Cards, Figures 1 and 2] for the project because of their ability to reveal concerns with achievement, and to define the nature of achievement within the broader social context of the forces and factors giving rise and definition to achievement motivation. With respect to the contextual elements elicited by these cards, William E. Henry (1956) describes what he terms the "latent stimulus demand" of each in the following terms:

> *Card 1:* This picture appears to be one dealing with the general issue of impulse versus control, or the question of the relationship of personal demands to those of outside cultural agents (p. 240) . . . it seems most readily to elicit feelings and stories dealing with authority, with the reactions to authority, and with the degree of initiative and self-directed control which the subject can maintain (pp. 47–48).
>
> *Card 17BM:* This is an extremely useful picture because it reflects the subject's concept of the relation of the individual to his environment and the images of his

> prowess or vulnerability to environmental forces. Narcissistic, exhibitionistic, and competitive ideas are readily aroused here as are notions of fear and escape (p. 261).

I later added Card Number 2 [see Kenyan Cards, Figure 3] to the research battery because of its particular relevance to the circumstances of Kenya's rural secondary students leaving their homes and farms to attend school. Henry describes the latent stimulus demand of this card as follows:

> *Card 2:* The contrast between the new and the old, as represented by the story of a girl going off for education as opposed to the farm folks. In this respect it is a useful picture in activating attitudes toward personal mobility and ambition and the extent to which the individual sees the traditional as valuable or as inhibiting (p. 242).

With these TAT Cards selected, I then turned to a search for other research devices that might both confirm the validity of the TAT data and provide further insight into the aspirations and expectations of Kenya's secondary school students. That search led me to the Self-Anchoring Striving Scale.

The Self-Anchoring Striving Scale (SASS)

The SASS is designed to obtain open-ended, self-defined statements of hopes and fears for one's personal future and the future of one's country. It is termed "self-anchoring" because of the manner in which it requires that the respondent define the extremes (or anchoring points) of the spectrum of his hopes and fears in terms of his own past experiences, assumptions, goals, and values. The measure taps an individual's "reality world," a concept which the developers of the scale describe as "the pattern of assumptions that a person builds up by means of which he interprets the natural and social world around him" (Cantril and Free, 1962, p. 8). Their argument is that every individual, because of a unique set of purposes and past experiences, perceives the world differently; since an individual's behavior is based upon his "reality world," that world must be taken into account in attempting to understand human behavior. They characterize their approach "as adopting the first-person point of view, as opposed to the third-person point of view which assumes an objectively definable reality which, except for error, is the same for all" (Kilpatrick and Cantril, 1960, p. 158).

In administering the SASS, open-ended, self-defined statements of the respondent's personal hopes and fears are first obtained through asking the following questions:

> All of us want certain things out of life. When you think about what really matters in your own life, what are your wishes and hopes for the future? In other words, if

you imagine your future in the *best* possible light, what would your life look like then, if you are to be happy?

Now, taking the other side of the picture, what are your fears and worries about the future? In other words, if you image your future in the *worst* possible light, what would your life look like then?

These statements are then used to form the end-points, or anchoring-points, of a scale of personal hopes and fears, and the respondent is asked to establish his past, present, and expected future positions on that scale at various time intervals through the following procedure:

Here is a picture of a ladder. Suppose we say that the top of the ladder represents the best possible life for you, as you have just described it; and the bottom represents the worst possible life for you.

On which step of the ladder do you feel you personally stand *at the present time*?

Where on the ladder would you say you stood *five years ago*?

Just as your best guess, on which step of the ladder do you think you will be *five years from now*?

SASS Ladder
10
9
8
7
6
5
4
3
2
1
0

The same procedure is then completed with reference to hopes and fears for the respondent's country:

Now, what are your wishes and hopes for the future of your country? If you picture the future of your country in the *best* possible light, how would things look, let us say, ten years from now?

And what about your fears and worries for the future of your country? If you picture the future of your country in the *worst* possible light, how would things look about ten years from now?

> Now, looking at the ladder again, suppose your greatest hopes for your country are at the top, your worst fears at the bottom.
>
> Where would you put your country on the ladder *at the present time*?
>
> Where did your country stand *five years ago*?
>
> Just as your best guess, where do you think your country will be on the ladder *five years from now*?

In designing my research, I had been particularly sensitive to the tendency of the research instrument most commonly used in my discipline, the attitude-opinion questionnaire, to force the centrality of particular issues upon respondents. The TAT and the SASS, each characterized by low stimulus demand, provided an effective solution to that problem. For example, with respect to the SASS, Cantril writes that

> an accurate appraisal of an individual's reality world can never be obtained if he is forced to make choices or selections between categories, alternative, symbols, or situations as these are posed in the usual type of questionnaire (Cantril, 1965, pp. 21–22).

Cantril and Free note that the SASS elicits the current preoccupations of the respondent, cutting away "those things that are so taken for granted or so far from the forefront of the mind that they are not matters of concern" (Cantril and Free, 1962, p. 11).

Although directed at a lower level of consciousness, the TAT works in much the same manner. When faced with an ambiguous TAT picture and instructed to "tell what has led up to the event shown in the picture; describe what is happening at the moment, what the characters are feeling and thinking; and then give the outcome," the subject unconsciously interprets the situation as one arising in his own "reality world" and explains it by drawing upon that dominant set of personal attitudes, values, motivations, and past experiences that regularly guide and characterize his response to his environment. The type of response elicited by the TAT is based on

> the tendency of people to interpret an ambiguous situation in conformity with their past experiences and present wants, and the similar tendency of those who write stories to draw on the fund of their experiences and express their sentiments and needs, whether conscious or unconscious (Thompson, 1949, p. 7).

The TAT and the SASS promised, in short, an open-ended, self-defined picture of the dominant preoccupations, hopes, fears, attitudes, values, and motivations of my intended sample of Kenyan secondary school students, a picture largely uncontaminated by artificially and arbitrarily imposed expectations and categories. It was anticipated that such a picture would provide an invaluable base for considering the levels of frustration likely to be experienced by the students as they found their aspirations and expectations unfulfilled, and for considering the implications of those frustrations for Kenyan stability and development. In this connection it is significant to note the broader, nonmethodological goals of the developers of the SASS:

> Yet increasingly in today's world, no matter what its nature, we may assume that any system must go a certain way toward meeting the complex, varied, and subtle requirements members of a society expect or demand of it if the system is to be effective and viable over the long haul. A system must appear to those living under it to be in general accord with, or at least not athwart of, the satisfaction of their needs, desires and aspirations. . . . [Our interests] . . . are now concentrated in discovering the aspirations, fears and preoccupations of individuals, peoples and elites that are related to the demands they make on the socio-economic and political systems under which they live (Cantril and Free, 1962, p. 7).

Sample and Procedure

The TAT and the SASS formed the core of a research program that was funded by a Fulbright-Hays Dissertation Research Abroad grant and conducted in Kenya in 1972. The research battery was first pre-tested with 120 students at two different schools, then administered to a final sample of 699 students from six different schools between the dates of January 31 and May 25. The sample was carefully structured to represent the most socially, politically, and economically important groups in Kenyan society, and to facilitate comparisons between and among those groups. Of the forty-two different ethnic groups in the country, three were most significantly involved in national affairs. The largest, the Kikuyu, comprised 20.1 percent of the country's total population and controlled Kenya's post-independent political and economic systems; the Luo, who comprised 13.9 percent of the population, were actively challenging the dominance of the Kikuyu through at times violent confrontations; and the Kamba, who comprised 10.9 percent of the population, made up most of the ranks of Kenya's police and military services. My sample was drawn equally from members of each of these ethnic groups. Within each group, an equal number of students was drawn from each of the four years (or Forms) of Kenya's secondary education system.

The sample was also constructed to focus on those groups who made up especially large segments of Kenya's secondary education system, and whose frustrations seemed likely to be especially acute and sociopolitically significant. Only rural students were included, both because they comprised 70.8 percent of secondary school enrollments and because their frustrations seemed likely to run especially high as they joined the ranks of the growing body of rural migrants to Kenya's cities, competing for scarce jobs against their elite urban counterparts in an unfamiliar urban world. Similarly, only males were included, both because they comprised 71.0 percent of secondary school enrollments and because the actions and reactions of unemployed male school leavers seemed likely to have the most direct implications for social and political stability.

The six different schools from which the sample was drawn were selected on the basis of the way in which they represented different types of rural male secondary schools. At each school, I completed four one-hour research sessions with groups of approximately thirty students at a time. The first hour consisted of a brief introduction and completion of a background questionnaire; during the second hour, each student was provided with an 8½ by 11 inch copy of the three TAT cards, and written responses were obtained to each; the SASS was completed during the third hour; and an attitude-opinion questionnaire focused on expectations and aspirations for the future was completed during the fourth.

Content analysis procedures were used to categorize the content of the students' TAT stories and SASS responses. The coding of the SASS responses was quite straightforward, given the specific focus of the SASS questions ("what are your hopes and fears?") and the availability of a published code book for the content analysis of SASS responses (Cantril and Free, 1962). The analysis of the TAT stories was somewhat more complex, but made manageable and systematic by the ICSS.

The first step in coding a TAT response using the procedure that I followed involved identifying the themes that described the activities and relationships explicitly stated in the story. Each story contained anywhere from zero to four or five such themes. Each of the themes identified was then successively classified through four different levels of categorization.

At the *first level*, each of the themes identified was categorized as being: Instrumental (goal oriented); Expressive (dealing with human relationships); Motivated by External Forces, Circumstances or Objects.

At the *second level*, themes which fell into the *Instrumental* category were then further classified into subcategories that included: Achievement; Competence; Responsibility; Control; Mutual Purpose.

Themes which fell into the *Expressive* category were further classified into subcategories that included: Harmony; Affiliation; Nurturance; Esteem; Pleasure.

At the *third level*, the nature of each theme was then classified as: positive-active; positive-passive, unresolved, inactive, or indeterminate; negative-active; or negative-passive.[3]

The *fourth level* of categorization made it possible to specifically classify each theme in considerable detail. For example, a theme dealing with an Instrumental concern with positive-active Achievement could be placed in subcategories which included:

---

[3]In the present chapter, the distinction is made between positive-passive, unresolved, inactive, or indeterminate concerns. This distinction is not required by the present ICSS, where these are all grouped together as B category concerns. Nevertheless, as is indicated in the present chapter, this distinction may be useful, and can always be made where it is so desired.

self-initiated activities towards the attainment of a goal,
parent-initiated activities towards the attainment of a goal,
peer group-initiated activities towards the attainment of a goal,
achievement for nurturance,
inspired or idealized achievement,
compensatory achievement,
achievement to escape, or
general, unspecified achievement activities.

Patterns of Achievement and Frustration

Table 3.1 shows the percentages of stories containing themes from various coding categories for the three TAT Cards (Numbers 1, 2, and 17BM) that were included because of their ability to reveal concerns with Achievement. The picture that emerges is of a group of individuals strongly concerned with Achievement, and with the Pleasure of demonstrating their Competence and Adequacy in overcoming challenges posed by External Events.

The table also shows that Achievement was also an important concern in the responses to Card Number 2, which was included because of the relevance of the farm scene to the students' circumstances. The Card Number 2 responses reveal more of the social context giving definition to the concerns with Achievement. The Pleasure themes were almost equally divided between positive-active expressions and negative-active and negative-passive expressions, indicating an understandable ambivalence about farm life from a group caught in the middle between the attractions of the modern world and the security and familiarity of the traditional. The concerns with Nurturance on Card 2 reveal a strong sense of desire to take care of parents and siblings, and of a feeling of responsibility to do so.

Table 3.2 shows the manner in which the Achievement themes found in the responses to all three cards were predominantly positive-active in nature. And Table 3.3 shows the remarkable degree to which these concerns with positive-active Achievement were self-initiated.

Note the way these themes of positive-active, self-initiated Achievement run through the following sample stories written in response to Card Number 1:

> (KY Card 1) Johnson liked music so very much that he could forget about eating when he heard music somewhere. He had been going to dance at different theaters in which different bands were playing music. He had a hope of becoming a member of a playing group.
>
> [PA-aesthetic AA-self MTA-task]

Table 3.1

Themes by Frequency Expressed

(all themes recorded; totals do not equal 100%)

	Card 1	*Card 17BM*	*Card 2*
Achievement	62.5%	78.5%	25.5%
Competence	25.5	31.2	12.6
Mutuality	0.7	15.5	4.7
Control	4.7	8.8	7.9
Responsibility	9.3	9.1	6.8
Harmony	7.4	8.5	24.7
Nurturance	9.4	10.4	28.6
Affiliation	6.7	2.1	18.2
Esteem	8.3	11.9	3.9
Pleasure	61.3	28.2	31.7
External Events	41.0	37.0	28.8

Table 3.2

Achievement Themes

	Card 1	*Card 17BM*	*Card 2*
Positive Active	58.1%	79.2%	78.8%
Positive Passive	26.9	4.6	12.3
Unresolved	2.5	0.4	0.0
Negative Active	6.8	13.3	1.7
Negative Passive	5.7	2.6	7.3
Totals	100.0%	100.1%	100.1%

Table 3.3

Positive Active Achievement

	Card 1	*Card 17BM*	*Card 2*
Self-Initiated	87.8%	68.7%	46.8%
Parent-Initiated	0.0	0.2	11.3
Peer-Initiated	0.4	0.2	0.7
For Nurturance	2.0	4.1	10.6
To Escape	0.4	15.9	0.0
Other	9.4	10.8	30.5
Totals	100.0%	99.9%	99.9%

(KY Card 1) One day he sat on a chair with his guitar on the table and started thinking how he could practice or become a guitarist. After a long time of thinking, the only decision he had was, first to learn a little of physics—about sound, and in this way he could improve little by little. So he joined a school where physics was taught. After eight months he has mastered how to play a guitar. Now he is one of the famous men in music.

[AA-self CA-expert AA-persist ESA-fame]

(KY Card 1) Then at last he joined one of the outstanding bands, and in fact, everyone was amazed. His character stressed the general saying, "Practice, Practice, makes Perfect."

[MTA-task ESA-praised AA-persist]

(KY Card 1) This man was educated, but wasn't given enough education. He was probably given fees but didn't use his time in school quite well or he wasn't provided for with money for his education and thus he did not hope for a good future time. He didn't have enough education so as to be employed.

[AD-lack RB-omit NSD-lack KD-poverty]

(KY Card 1) "But there is always something to do if a person is prepared," he thought. "I can be a musician, and in that way I can earn myself a living and probably others, too." He thus planned to form a band and composed songs and thus through his singing, he earned a lot of money; enough for him and his friends.

[AA-self MTA-task NDA-means]

(KY Card 1) If this he can do, then he can provide for his needs even though he hadn't enough education.

[NSD-lack CA-present AA-self]

Achievement, in short, was the dominant concern characterizing the TAT records of the students. Findings from the SASS provide a valuable complimentary understanding of the goals toward which that concern with Achievement was directed. Table 3.4 summarizes the responses provided to the first section of the SASS which asked the students to describe their wishes and hopes for the future:

Note the way in which these various hopes of Table 3.4 are woven together in the following sample responses:

(KY SASS) If all turns out to be possible in my future life, I first think of employment. When I get a job of probably over 85 Pounds a month salary, I will first build my background. By this I mean I will buy a plot and build a house where I and my wife will live in our old days. After I do that I will marry and then the money which will be remaining after our expense I will keep in the bank. This will be for me and my family. I will educate my children.

(KY SASS) In order for my future to be in the best possible light, my wishes and hopes are mainly concerned with getting a good education as the first thing. When I feel that I am in a good position and I am getting a good salary, and my parents

> are also well off, I shall then think of a wife. In my opinion, I would like to have about four children.

The most frequently expressed object of the students' drive for Achievement was employment. With unemployment likely for 90 percent of Kenya's school leavers, the dimensions of the alienation and frustration likely to be experienced begin to come into focus. The social and political implications of that frustration are multiplied, however, when one considers the pattern of related themes and concerns that are part of the drive for employment. The data presented above reveal the manner in which employment was viewed as the instrument for attaining other more expressively valued goals of family happiness, well-being, and security.

Employment, and the education thought necessary to make employment possible, was viewed as a means of breaking out of the poverty and hardship experienced by the bulk of Kenya's rural population, and integrally linked to desires to take care of one's parents and brothers and sisters, and to establish and provide for one's own family. The data made it clear that, when considering the social and political implications of the frustration likely to be experienced by the students, one had to also consider the implications of the related frustration likely to be experienced by the parents, siblings, and, ultimately, wives and children whose lives were to have been made easier and better by the students' education, employment, and income.

An appreciation of the nature of that frustration was first provided in responses to the second part of the SASS, where the students were asked to describe their fears for the future. Table 3.5 summarizes the dominant fears expressed.

Note the way in which the themes summarized in Table 3.5 are woven into the following sample SASS Personal Fears responses:

> (KY SASS) On the contrary, if I fail in my exams I will lead the poorest life. I will not get a job, i.e., a good job with a good salary. Probably I will be employed by some rich people to be working in their gardens. My policy is if I do not do well in my exams and I fail to get a good job I will not have a wife. Even if I am employed whereby I earn about 25 Pounds I will not marry. I will lead a miserable life because my parents look forward to see me do well so that I will carry the heavy load of paying school fees for my younger brothers and sisters.

> (KY SASS) My fears are based on financial problems. I might miss money to enable me to continue in school, and as other intellectuals left at home, I would seek a job in other people's shambas [farms]. This is something I don't even like to imagine, working in a person's shamba or house, which is little better than being enslaved. I won't like my wife, for instance, to work in people's shambas so that she can acquire food. This would not make me at ease and I would rather die than lead this kind of life.

Table 3.4

SASS Personal Hopes

(expressed by over 20 percent of sample)

Employment—a good job; independence in choice of occupation; interesting job or work situation; chance of advancement	58.9%
Self-development or improvement—opportunity for independence of thought and action, for following through with own interests; further study; education in general; pass exams; fame	53.2
Improved or decent standard of living for self or family—sufficient money to live better or to live decently; freedom from debt; make ends meet; relief from poverty; not suffer want, hunger, etc.	40.8
Happy family life—happy marriage; pleasant home; love within family; have a (good) husband or wife; have children	34.6
Relatives—concern for spouse, children, parents, or other relatives; be close to them; keep them together or get them together again; help or take care of them; live up to their expectations	29.8
Desire to be useful to others—ability and opportunity to serve the people; community, nation, world; or to hold public office	22.9

Table 3.5

SASS Personal Fears

(expressed by over 20 percent of sample)

Deterioration in or inadequate standard of living for self or family—not sufficient money to live better or to live decently; debt; poverty; suffer want, hunger, etc.	49.5%
Unemployment—no steady work; inability to find or hold a job; a poor job	41.7
No self-development or improvement—no opportunity for following through with own interests; no further study	25.0
Unable to care for or live up to the expectations of parents, wife, children, etc.	21.7

Similar fears were manifest in responses to the National Fears section of the SASS, where 54.1 percent of the students expressed a fear for their country of "no improvement in or inadequate standard of living" and 30.2 percent a fear of "unemployment" in terms such as these:

> (KY SASS) If my country of Kenya were not to undergo development in ten years from now there will be severe problems of unemployment, hunger and people will starve because of many things.

> (KY SASS) The worst thing is unemployment which is increasing at a very big pace and if nothing is done about it, in ten years from now the situation would be at its worst.

The following samples of TAT stories, which were written in response to Cards Number 1 and 17BM, provides an especially poignant and comprehensive statement of these fears of poverty and unemployment:

Card 1

> (KY ID 2320 Card 1) From this picture I think the young man was in need of being educated from his childhood, but his parents lacked enough money both for feeding and educating him—the young man. When he grows up to an adolescence age, he sees his friends of his age group are well led by their parents and are now working in offices and elsewhere, receiving enough cash. The young man then decides not to leave a quiet life. So he remembers that melodious voice God gave him and so worked hard to buy a guitar. Remember he works casually for he has no education. After this he tries hard to attract people and asking them to give him some coins to sing to them. All is in vain for to be a musician, one has to be educated first, and so this man gets no advantage. He has no money to pay for his music lessons. The outcome is that the young man tries to think very hard, unable to eat well, unable to play music, and he is having a lot of problems, e.g., marriage, suiting himself in clothing, and so many other things. I think he would decide to die rather than live such a poor life.
>
> [KD-poverty NDD-means AA-counter KD-poverty AD-lack PD-despair]

> (KYID 4412 Card 1) The boy was brought from a poor family, he was taken to primary school, the school fees of which the parents could still afford. Reaching his sixth year the parents happened to die, how I can't tell, perhaps in an accident. The boy had two younger brothers who by that time had not started schooling. When the parents had died they were left with nothing to spend on their living. Because when the parents were still alive they could dig a small shamba nearby and get their food, or sometimes they did beg in the streets. The boy experiencing such tragic future managed to leave school and it happened that there was a certain group of boys who were having a band for music. The boy knew that since there

was no job in the town to do that could enable him to survive with his two younger brothers, he joined the band thinking that he could earn his living. The amount they got from there, they spent with prostitutes in the town and his two younger brothers were suffering very miserably. At last the boy realized and started to think of his parents that if they would have been living he would have not had such a miserable life with his two younger brothers even though they were poor.

[KD-poverty NDA-means KD-ac-die MTA-task RC-sex RB-indulge RB-regret]

(KYID 3323 Card 1) This man shown in the picture has been playing banjo. He has been entertaining people in social centers collecting some money. But then some people came up called missionaries preaching about playing banjo, that it is sinful. So the man one day sat down and thought over it and he realized that he had been doing wrong. So he left playing banjo. These days, this man has got no income because maybe that there are no jobs available for those who did not go to school. This man will begin to find a way by which he can get some money because perhaps he is too lazy to work in shambas. He will form a gang with other follows under the same sphere and begin robbing business people, banks, etc. So by telling people not to do what they can to get money is just but to increase robbery in the state.

[OB-money RC-mores RA-reform RC-indulge MTC-allied AC-gang]

(KYID 5413 Card 1) It seems as if this man's parents did not have any money to send him to school or they had a little money which they could educate up to the Standard Seven level. After primary education probably he left school due to financial circumstances. This caused him to change his mind and he joined a group of guitarists hoping to get rich. As the guitarists continued with their work, probably another better group of guitarists rose up which caused many people to follow them and a decline of the first group followed. The first group was left without any support and this character was agitating what he would do next. At last, he considered to join a group of robbers probably in Nairobi. He joined it and after a few days they were put in prison, and sentenced to seven years of imprisonment.

[NDD-means MTA-task OA-wealth MTA-task AC-gang MVD-quit MTC-crime NDA-police]

(KYID 5304 Card 1) A man has been playing a musical instrument for a long time actually to refresh his mind, probably after a piece of hard work. He doesn't perhaps have some money to go and buy some drink in the shop. Thus does this lead to playing his musical instrument. He plays and plays and plays his instrument, singing as well, following the rhythm of the instrument. He begins to sweat, froth coming out of his mouth, then exhausted a thought suddenly creates in his mind. "I have no money! Therefore no drink! No job! Oh! What the hell am I coming to!?" He will continue thinking until he probably becomes psychologically ill as a result of which he will either go and steal some money or go to search for a job. Maybe even sell his musical instrument rather than die without food.

[PA-relief OB-money KD-poverty PD-crazed AC-crime OD-loss]

(KYID 3305 Card 1) The story is about a man who used to play guitar for his living. This man used to play a guitar which was made of wood and a few strings. He used to play his guitar in the evening when he is from a garden or after looking after his cattle. While playing he used to sing some pleasant songs and people used to gather where he was. One day he went to market place and played his guitar in the market and a very large crowd of people came to see him. It happened that the Chief of Police wanted people for a meeting but people just ran away to where the man was. So the Chief of Police wanted to arrest the man, but he ran away. When he reached home he kept the money that he got from the market and he left his guitar in the house and then ran away. When the man returned he found that his guitar had been destroyed by the Chief of Police and this is what is looking at on the table in front of him. He is seriously thinking of how he will get another guitar. He will earn his living by playing.

[OA-job ESA-approve DSA-assert DDC-punish AA-persist]

Card 17BM

(KYID 5305 Card 17BM) Ah! Poor man. He had no money, no job, yet a lot of children. He went to a big city intending to look for a job. But wherever he went a notice board, written in red capital letters, said "HAKUNA KAZI," i.e., "No Work." In the town he even experienced difficulties in feeding and clothing himself. Then he went back to his home without anything to give his children. He was rebuked seriously by his wife. Now he is seen having decided to hang himself without any clothes at all. He has said he would rather die than live in this cruel world without anything to help himself with. Not even a single cent in his pockets. The result will be that his children and wife will still suffer the most. Some of them might become thieves, big robbers. Others villains and so on. His wife might probably be in the streets or worse still hang herself because she cannot endure it any more.

[KD-poverty NDD-unable NSC-suicide AC-crime
ESD-defiled NSC-suicide]

(KYID 2328 Card 17BM) A Narrow Escape: The man in the picture is a thief as I may tend to imagine. The cause of his theft is poverty and obedience. The man was left by his parents by the time he was a small boy. He became very poor and he could not get any money in order to buy food to eat. Once he thought of getting money through theft in the cashier's box in the 8th floor upstairs. He tied a rope from the 8th upstairs. He climbed and went there in and stole the whole box full of red notes. He dropped it down to his comrades who took it and ran away. Accidentally before reaching down he was seen, the rope was cut and by the time he was eight feet above the floor. He fell down and ran as quick as he could. He survived because he was very strong with very good formed muscles. In the picture the rope is cut and by now his is dropping down. So what I can say is that his people or comrades are feeling very well because he had stolen the money enough to feed a tribe for three years. What I can conclude is that even if you are strong and you have seen how I wrote, don't even try to steal not even a pin, brother. I am only describing the picture through imagination. Therefore be justice and don't be a lazy boy. Work for your living and don't attempt stealing. O.K. Thanks. "Natoweka sasa."

[RC-illegal NSD-deserted KD-poverty MTC-crime DSC-escape CA-body NDA-social RA-work]

(KYID 5310 Card 17BM) This man was born in a poor family and when he grew up he hadn't any means of getting money and his parents were giving him little help. He thought of stealing to get rich. He practiced stealing small things and then became a professional thief.

Now one day his neighbor who was richer than anybody else went to visit his friend with his whole family; this thief was watching till he saw that they had gone. Then he came to their house and found that it was well locked. He thought of breaking the windows but he didn't do that since the owner will know. He decided to climb to the roof and pretend that he was repairing, to anybody who passed there. He took a rope and threw it to a branch of a tree while he was near the roof of the house where he could break in. When he tied the rope, he started climbing, but before he got up the owner of the house came and he pretended that he was mad by making amusements and twisting around with the rope, and also putting away his clothes. After that he was taken to jail.

[KD-poverty NDD-unable AC-crime KD-mishap NDA-police]

(KYID 3329) The gentleman, as a result of his father's death, who of course had not enough earnings was undecided as to what to do next. There she was, his mother, with a few young brothers to feed. The gentleman not only being pocketless, was still too young to toil for the family. Now what to do next? The only decision was to get the easiest job to do in order to get the family going smoothly. So the poor gentleman decided to go and do some thieving. He went to one of the rich men's house and with a rope in hand decided to throw it high in the storey building so that after the rope had been firmly fixed in the upper window he would try his luck by climbing up the wall. Fortunately enough rope was firmly fixed, but on the other hand, a bad fortune was also in his trial in that his interference was noticed by the house-servant who was then in the house. The servant cut the rope with the boy half way up the storey. The boy fell down and was very badly injured on his back-bone. And at last he died.

[KD-death NDD-unable AC-crime KD-mishap KD-ac-die]

(KYID 5302 Card 17BM) This man was well fed, grew into a muscular man and did not prove any good in education. When he was old enough as to look after himself, he had nothing of his own. What could he do? Now he thinks to himself, "What else is there for me to do except to go and steal money for my food? I'm hungry and I need clothes." He plans to attack a rich man's house which is surrounded by a high wall. He climbs over the wall with the aid of a rope and goes on with his plans. He is then seen and caught and taken to jail. There he will be beaten and will do hard labour for years. But had he not been involved in such evil thoughts of stealing and indulged in better work, he would not have got into such troubles.

[CC-mental RC-indulge OB-money OB-clothes AC-crime]

> (KYID 6404 Card 17BM) It happened that this man lived a life of poverty. One day he met a beautiful girl who he talked to and she told him unless you get some money you can't marry me. When this man came to his home he tried to get any possible means to get money, working, stealing, borrowing. His mind brought him to stealing a bank, but he could see the danger ahead of him, but he was blocked by love. He violated the bank by night with a very thin and long rope, and used it to get in the bank. When he was about 50 feet above the ground almost at the point this rope broke and sent him to the ground, and fell heavily. He said death has brought to him by money to buy love. These were his last words.
>
> [KD-poverty FB-thwart AC-crime OB-money KD-mishaps KD-death]

> (KYID 5415 Card 17BM) This may represent two things to me, i.e., an actor or a robber. If the person may represent a robber he has might have seen some day some where there were things which he wanted to steal and thought of means of climbing there, resulting with the rope as the simple means which he could do without being noticed. And therefore this time he is climbing very carefully and watchful so that he is not going to be noticed and caught, before he takes what he wanted to take. This may have ended up with the man being noticed and caught ending with being taken to jail or he might have taken what he wanted.
>
> [RC-illegal AC-crime NDA-police]

> If then the person is an actor he might have been in a theatre where he was showing people some of the expertness on certain fields which included climbing up a rope. He is now therefore performing his duty, i.e., climbing up the rope. This may end up with the person finishing his work successfully or he may get tired when up at the top of the place where the rope is attached and end up with falling down resulting in injury or death.
>
> [ESA-approve RA-work CD-finish KD-death]

Modes of Adaptation and Response

The first objective of my research had been to establish that Kenya's secondary school leavers were in fact likely to experience high levels of alienation and frustration as they attempted to find places in Kenya's economy. The combination of TAT and SASS responses summarized above left no doubt about that conclusion: the data described in rich detail a group of self-motivated high achievers who aspired to employment as the key to realization of an array of strongly held interpersonal goals and responsibilities, and who were about to enter a job market that had no place for them. With that fact established, my attention turned to an effort to understand the implications of the situation for Kenya's society, polity, and economy. Robert K. Merton's (1964) theories on social structure and *anomie* took me directly to the heart of the issues involved.

Merton begins his argument by distinguishing between two different elements of social and cultural structure that exist in any society. The first consists of those culturally defined goals and purposes that are held out as legitimate objects of achievement for the members of a given society. These goals and purposes define the frame of aspirational reference, or the "things worth striving for" in that society. The second consists of the institutionalized regulatory norms that define and control the means of pursuing those values; these norms form the legitimate avenues open to the members of that society for the pursuit of culturally defined aspirations.

Merton finds that there is often an imbalance between these patterns of goals and means. The Kenya case provides an example of an acute disjunction between the two, in which the avenues leading to the achievement of the goals which the country's secondary school students were socialized to expect were rapidly becoming closed. In Merton's terminology, the dominant success goals of Kenya's school leavers were becoming widely separated from the institutionalized avenues available for seeking them. In circumstances such as this, Merton writes that individuals tend to adapt and respond in ways that include ritualism, retreatism, rebellion, and innovation. These categories of adaptation provided a valuable theoretical framework for considering the likely responses of Kenya's secondary school leavers to their predicament.

Ritualism

Ritualism involves a mode of adaptive behavior in which the individual, unable to achieve the goals set by his culture, responds by significantly lowering his level of aspiration while at the same time clinging almost compulsively to the institutional norms of his society. This is the response of the social ritualist, the individual intent on "not sticking your neck out," on "playing safe," and "being satisfied with what you have." The dangers and frustrations inherent in the competition for highly valued cultural goals are avoided through the abandonment of those goals, while a sense of security is maintained through close conformance to safe routines and institutional norms. In the Kenyan situation, ritualistic behavior might involve spending month after month, year after year going through the routines of job seeking, filling out endless forms, and standing in endless employment lines, but never really expecting success. It did not seem likely that ritualistic behavior would characterize the adaptations of very many of Kenya's secondary school leavers. On the one hand, this personality type is in sharp contrast to the type of high achievers revealed by the TAT records; on the other, ritualism is a response dependent upon some means of support and livelihood, and therefore not a response that significant numbers of unemployed from poor families could maintain for very long.

Retreatism

Retreatism involves the substantial abandoning of both major cultural goals and the institutionalized practices customarily pursued for the attainment of those goals. Merton writes that retreatism

> is most likely to occur when *both* the cultural goals and the institutionalized practices have been thoroughly assimilated by the individual and imbued with affect and high value, but accessible institutional avenues are not productive of success (p. 153).

Retreatism is especially likely to occur, he adds, when it appears that a condition of hopelessness, anxiety, and social isolation will continue indefinitely (p. 188). The social conditions which Merton describes as giving rise to retreatism were remarkably similar to the conditions experienced by, and to be experienced by, Kenya's secondary students, and it seemed likely that this mode of adaptation would come to characterize the responses of many school leavers, at considerable costs. In psychological terms, individuals forced into this mode of adaptation are characterized by defeatism, quietism, resignation, and high levels of apathy, indifference, cynicism, and moral fatigue; in social terms, retreatist behavior characterizes the adaptive activities of chronic drunkards, drug addicts, vagrants, tramps, psychotics, and autists (p. 153).

Rebellion

When the institutional system of a society becomes regarded as a barrier to the achievement of culturally legitimized goals, the stage is set for rebellion as a mode of adaptive response. Here the individual becomes alienated from both the dominant goals and norms of his society—the structures of authority that govern that society have become, for him, illegitimate, and he has come to envisage and seek a new social structure embodying and facilitating a more equitable and just correspondence between individual effort and social and economic success. If confined to relatively small and powerless elements of a society, this mode of adaptation is likely to manifest itself in the formation of subgroups alienated from the rest of the society, thereby creating a social problem, but having limited political impact. If rebellion becomes widespread in a substantial portion of the society, however, a potential for revolution, aimed at restructuring the society and establishing new goals and new patterns of means for achieving those goals, is created.

Merton's ideas indicated that political rebellion among unemployed school leavers was one of the logical consequences of the growing gap between the culturally valued goals of Kenyan society and the avenues open for the pursuit of those goals. A solid body of other social science theory reinforced that conclusion.

In Smelser's terms, for example, the problem of unemployment among school leavers can be viewed as one resulting from discontinuities between processes of differentiation and integration: differentiated educational institutions had worked to socialize students into the "modern" socioeconomic sector, but that sector was unable to integrate them successfully into its new institutions. Smelser (1968, p. 127) notes that the consequences of such discontinuities are often social disturbances that, collectivized, crystallize into social movements that may take various forms ranging from peaceful agitation to political violence, underground subversion, and revolution.

Theories of status inconsistency provided another perspective. Lenski (1966, pp. 87–88) observes that individuals who feel status inconsistency are prone to react against the existing social and political order, and are more likely to support radical movements designed to alter the political status quo than are persons of consistent status. And Merton (1964, p. 157) finds that it is typically members of a rising, or aspiring, class, rather than the most depressed strata of a society, who organize the resentful and the rebellious into revolutionary groups. Here special emphasis must be given to the students' literacy when considering their likely involvement in movements of political protest and agitation. Huntington finds, for example, that "participation by literates is much more likely to snowball with potentially disastrous effects on political stability" (1965, p. 420). Lenski (1966, p. 88) notes that the importance of the educated unemployed in radical political movements is out of proportion to their numbers. And Callaway writes that

> politicians are keenly sensitive to the threat of jobless literate youth to stability, particularly at a time when many African countries are going through a period of intense political re-alignment. Thousands of idle young men, aware of the widening gap in incomes between the highly paid and the less fortunate, might well rally around a self-appointed leader to press for a radical change in the established order. And in an age of rapid communications, political agitation can erupt quickly among young discontented literates (1963, p. 371).

Within this context, it was easy to understand the concern of a member of Kenya's parliament when he warned that

> the people are unemployed everywhere, and this is material for disgruntled politicians. Today we have revolutions in Africa because of disgruntled millions, and as long as ours is not yet disgruntled we should try to see how best we can remedy the poverty which is in our country (Muliro, 1968).

Similarly, a particularly strong critic of Kenya's political regime wrote that

> school-leavers become the unemployed and the unemployed become the bitter men of the streets. The jobless, the frustrated, the peasants starving on the land, will endure much hardship, but how much more and for how long? (Odinga, 1967, 314–315).

It seemed likely that rebellion in a form capable of significantly affecting Kenya's political stability could easily result if the intense frustration likely to be experienced by Kenya's unemployed school leavers were combined with a consciousness, or awareness, of the links between government policy and the country's economic conditions *and* if organizations came into being through which political discontent could be collectively and strategically channeled. Data summarized from the SASS National Fears indicated that an awareness of the links between government policy and the country's social, political, and economic conditions was understood by a significant number of the students:

Political instability, civil war, chaos	33.5 percent
Tribalism, national disunity	28.2 percent
Dishonest government, corruption, nepotism	14.4 percent
Social injustice, discrimination	12.0 percent

Such fears were expressed in terms illustrated by the following sample SASS National Fears responses:

> Things will be really bad, the dreams of getting a job because you are educated will fade away to nothing, for nepotism and tribalism will increase at a very high rate. The president will not be ruling, and there will be tribal warfare for each tribe will want its candidate to be accepted as the rightful president. Since agriculture will be abandoned because of these politics, there will be famine.

> In Kenya there is something badly being practiced, and its name is tribalism. Since we have one ruling tribe at present, by name Kikuyu, we find that all the big posts in the country are filled by them, while other tribes produce men, some of whom have got higher education than some of the Kikuyus, and yet you find that some of the Kikuyu with their low education are their bosses. . . . When I picture all this I find that in ten years time when these things shall still be going on there shall be a lot of disorganization, corruption and frequent civil wars in the country.

> If things continue as they are, Kenya will be in a devastating state ten years from now. The rich will have grown richer and richer and the poor, poorer and poorer. The result will be much resentment among the poor class.

Innovation

Merton's category of innovation includes the adaptive behavior of individuals who continue to seek the goals established as important by their society, but respond to obstacles in their way through creating new avenues through which to pursue those goals. Considering the high level of achievement motivation found among Kenya's secondary school students, innovation would seem a likely mode of adaptation for many.

Innovation in the form of entrepreneurship seemed an especially likely, and promising, alternative. McClelland's (1961) description of the characteristics of successful entrepreneurs—independence, initiative, creativity, adventurousness, a willingness to take risks, aggressive competition, dedication, and hard work—seemed in fact to be a description of Kenya's students. And entrepreneurship would seemed to offer much to both the students, in terms of income, and to their country: one could easily envision a dynamic entrepreneurial class driving a process of economic development. The structure of Kenya's neocolonial economy, however, severely restricts opportunities for small entrepreneurs. Lacking is both government support for indigenous entrepreneurship and a domestic cash economy capable of generating enough income for many of Kenya's citizens to purchase the products and services of small entrepreneurs. The limited nature of legitimate employment and income opportunities in Kenya's economy meant that another form of innovation seemed more likely to characterize the adaptive behavior of Kenya's unemployed school leavers.

The new avenues created by innovators to pursue society's goals may be either legitimate, in terms of conforming to established norms (e.g., entrepreneurship), or illegitimate, in terms of not conforming to those norms. One of the most distressing findings of the research was that one particular form of illegitimate innovation—crime—seemed likely to characterize the responses of large numbers of Kenya's educated unemployed. When looking toward their future, a significant number of the students in my sample displayed a concern with being forced into a life of crime, not just as a means of obtaining wealth, but as a means of simple survival.

I first became aware of this concern with crime while coding the stories written in response to TAT Card Number 17BM. Quite unexpectedly, I found that 15.6 percent of the students had produced stories dealing with people engaged in criminal activities. Following are examples of the terms in which this theme was expressed:

> This man in the picture is having no job. So in order to help himself he begins to rob. . . . Perhaps in this picture he is trying to get on top of a house in order to get into the house and take some things, e.g., money from banks and other business places. . . . The outcome of his man is that his life is not promising because he may be caught and imprisoned or killed. . . . The man in this picture thought that he would earn his mainstay by finding a way of doing exercises and he would also gain prestige. . . . And also he thought that doing such exercises would enable him to learn better methods of getting into others' houses. . . . This sort of game is not all that good as robbery is concerned. To earn one's living by breaking into houses is the worst game to practice. . . . Anyway it is not his own will, this is brought about by lack of employment. . . . The outcome of the game may be death or to be put to jail forever. . . . So government should try as much as it could in order to fix any fit person to a position in order to earn one's living.

I discovered the same concern with crime as I turned to the coding of the Personal Fears section of the SASS. Here, 18.7 percent of the students stated a fear of becoming a thief or taking to crime. Note the way in which this fear is linked to problems of poverty and unemployment in the following sample responses:

> If I finish my school course and I get no employment I fear that I would fall into troubles. Such troubles may lead me to do a great loss to the country, such as robbing and killing the rich people for my bread (though it is not my wish at all even if I am in whatever poor conditions I might be).

> After completing Form 4 I am uncertain whether I shall get any job in Kenya because it is very hard to get jobs in Kenya. I shall then go back to my home and think what to do next. Since my father has got no money or good shambas, I shall be in a very decimated predicament. I shall start loitering about finding what to eat and sometimes steal other people's property in my village. I think I shall be in the worst life which no human being has ever faced in this world.

> This is realized after failing the Ordinary Level Examination. After failing this exam I will be the victim of all that is experienced by the jobless. Being in a state of going from door to door asking for employment is a problem. There will be no good food. After failing to get employed I would turn into a beggar. I would be scorched by the sun while begging in the streets and my food would be the refuse deposited in the dustbins. Failing to get this would make me indulge myself into robbery with or without violence.

Similar concerns were expressed in response to the National Fears section of the SASS, where 20.5 percent of the sample stated a fear of "no law and order; increase in crime; failure to maintain public peace" in terms such as these:

> At the present moment I fear very much for my country in that the population is increasing at a high rate and there are no jobs for them. Towns are filled with job seekers. Most of them are school leavers. This is why theft and robbery is very common in the country. Now if in any case no steps are taken to eliminate these robberies then in about ten years' time the whole country would be full of criminals because they don't have any way of supporting themselves.

> In my opinion the most dangerous thing in this country is lack of industries and if government is not going to take steps in this calamity and fix educated youngsters in jobs it is clear that in ten years the country will be called a country of robbers, because Secondary Schools are very many, including Harambee, Private Schools and the production of forms 4 and 6 are many in the towns; and if the number is not reduced as I said above even the government will fall into depression because tourists will stop coming to Kenya because of robbers in the country. Therefore, jobs = peace, no jobs = no peace.

In pursuing an analysis of the students' concern with crime, I identified those respondents who had given a crime response on two or all of the three measures cited above so that their crime responses were counted only once. That exercise left me with the statistic that 42.5 percent of the sample had stated a concern with crime in responding to research measures in which they themselves defined the content of their concerns. As the students looked towards their own, and their country's future, they clearly perceived crime as one of the major problems that they, and their countrymen, would face.

The manner in which crime themes were expressed, as illustrated by the sample responses reproduced above, provides excellent support for Merton's central hypothesis that deviant or nonconforming behavior in a society is not generally the result of weaknesses and shortcomings in morals or character, but the logical outcome of a dissociation between culturally prescribed aspirations and the socially provided avenues available for their achievement (Merton, 1964, p. 134). It appeared that many of Kenya's unemployed school leavers were likely to become involved in criminal activities not as a result of an inability to control deviant impulses, but as a result of innovative behavior driven by the simple necessities of their circumstances. The crime themes found in the responses to TAT Card Number 17BM are especially helpful in demonstrating this point. Themes of criminal activity can be coded into two different categories in the ICSS. When unsanctioned action is expressed as only a means of achieving a particular goal, it is scored as "Negative Active Achievement"; when it is expressed in normative terms as an immoral and irresponsible act, it is scored as "Negative Active Responsibility." Such themes depicted on Card 17BM themes fell predominantly into the former category by a two to one ratio: Negative Active Achievement: 68.0 percent: Negative Active Responsibility: 32.0 percent.

The manner in which much of crime in any society derives from imbalances in social structure, rather than from psychological deviancies and moral shortcomings in individuals, is of special importance in appreciating the links between crime and politics. Politics is commonly defined as the process through which the scarce values of a society are authoritatively allocated (Easton), or the process that determines who gets what, when, and how (Lasswell). In his dialogue with Socrates, reported by Plato in *The Republic,* the Greek sophist Thrasymachus is one of the first Western political observers to describe how this determination is usually made through the strong taking command of the institutions of force and authority and writing and enforcing laws that justify their taking more than their equal share of the benefits that society has to offer (see Cornford, 1941, pp. xx, xxi, 15, 18, and 30). In this context, Might makes Right, or, as Pascal wryly observes, "Not being able to make that which is just strong, man has made that which is strong just" (see Lenski, 1966, p. 43). Similarly, Marshall (1970, p. 53) writes that "government" comes into being when a group, or class, is "strong enough to secure or to preserve those institutions that favor its activities."

Crime, in short, is largely what those in power say it is. Most of the legal systems of the world are based on such definitions of positive law (as contrasted with normative law that holds that there are natural laws that apply universally to all men in all societies at all times). Much of what is called property crime is in fact just one aspect of the political allocation process that determines who gets what—it is conveniently labeled "immoral" by those in power because it challenges the particular distribution of property that has been established for their benefit; it ignores the immorality of the process that determined how the powerful came to control most of the property in society at the expense of the weak in the first place.

This "dual standard" derives from a process described by Thrasymachus as one in which the politically powerful use

> force or fraud to plunder the goods of others, public or private, sacred or profane . . . in a wholesale way. If you are caught committing any one of these crimes on a small scale, you are punished and disgraced; they call it sacrilege, kidnaping, burglary, theft, and brigandage. But if, beside taking their property, you turn all your countrymen into slaves, you will hear no more of those ugly names; your countrymen themselves will call you the happiest of men and bless your name, and so will everyone who hears of such a complete triumph of injustice (Cornford, 1941, pp. 25–26).

Machiavelli later echoes Thrasymachus' analysis in *The Prince* (see Donno, 1981, p. 62), where he describes how those political leaders who are the most successful in holding their power maintain a balance between "force and fraud" through adopting the traits of the lion (force) and the fox (fraud). Those who are especially successful are especially cunning in creating public appearances that mask their "wholesale plunder" while enforcing laws that control "crime on a small scale."

The preponderance of Negative Active Achievement themes in the Kenyan students' crime stories and the SASS National Fears of tribalism, corruption, nepotism, and social injustice described on page 90 indicate that many of the students were little fooled by this dual standard, even at the preconscious and unselfconscious levels tapped by the TAT. This does not seem surprising in Kenya where criminal activity is validated by widespread crime in high places that is obvious and well known to the public. Kenya's political leaders are better lions than they are foxes—they have not been very successful in concealing the commonplace political corruption, or use of public office for private gain, that characterizes their rule.

Omens of Future Ills

The combination of data and theory summarized in the preceding pages provided the basis for predictions that high levels of unemployment among secondary school leavers in Kenya were likely to result in increasing levels of crime and other forms of sociopolitical instability in the years to come, severely undermining prospects for development (see Evans, 1975, 1977). Forecasts of direct challenges to Kenya's institutions of political authority were noted as contingent on the formation of organizations of political dissidents capable of effectively concentrating and directing political discontent. Forecasts of indirect challenges in the form of rising crime rates driven by innovative adaptations to the obstacles blocking access to the culturally valued goals of Kenyan society were made in much more certain terms.

Over the past two decades, the Kenyan government has been largely successful in repressing direct challenges to its authority. While a variety of political opposition groups, both peaceful and violent, have formed and continue to operate on a small scale, the country's political elites have so far been able to effectively control and contain such overt threats. The international human rights organization Africa Watch notes the government's use of fear to control dissent, and reports the persistent torture of political dissidents and the widespread use of security forces to "spy on almost every aspect of normal life" (Press, 1991, p. 4).

The government has not, however, been successful in controlling and containing crime. In the summer of 1990, I reviewed a year of issues of Kenya's leading national newspaper, *The East African Standard.* Daily reports of widespread instances of various kinds of crime immediately brought to mind the SASS national fear quoted on page 90 above that "in about ten years time the whole country would be full of criminals because they don't have any way of supporting themselves." Petty crime is commonplace, in fact so commonplace that it has contributed to a severe overcrowding of Kenya's prisons. In the September 20, 1989, *East African Standard* (p. 2), the Commissioner of Prisons disclosed that 38,000 prisoners were being held in facilities capable of accommodating 16,000, and that diseases like meningitis and AIDS were posing "a serious threat to prisoners." On the following day, an *East African Standard* editorial (p. 6) reported that forty-seven deaths in Kenya's prisons over the last month could "be attributed to overcrowding and declining standards of health as a result of a large number of inmates," and urged that prison overcrowding should be avoided by "reducing the number of inmates by offering outside jail terms to petty offenders who constitute the majority of inmates." In the following month, President Moi freed 10,274 prisoners serving terms of up to ten months when faced with an outbreak of meningitis (*East African Standard*, October 11, 1989, p. 1).

More serious threats to Kenya's citizens, and visitors, are presented by violent gangs. Almost daily reports in the *East African Standard* tell of gangs composed of from five to fifteen members armed with weapons ranging from knives to automatic weapons roaming throughout the country holding up banks, entire marketplaces, other businesses, and private homes in broad daylight, breaking into businesses and homes at night, and terrorizing the population; one story told of a village whose "residents were sleeping in the bushes for fear of bandits who were molesting them in their homes" (*East African Standard,* May 21, 1990, 11). It is reported that the citizens are responding through an increase in vigilantism (*East African Standard,* October 31, 1989). The government has responded with the

Hanging Act, which orders hanging for anyone convicted of committing robbery with violence.

Violent gangs operating in Kenya's game parks have presented special problems, both through the poaching of endangered wildlife species and threats posed to tourists visiting the parks. In 1989, four tourists (two French, one American, and one British) were murdered in game parks. Also murdered that year was George Adamson of *Born Free* fame, killed in Kenya's Kora National Reserve by gunmen apparently bent, according to police reports, on robbery in the National Reserve. In describing Adamson's murder, Richard Leakey, Kenya's director of wildlife, commented that "The gangs that were operating have no gainful employment. They don't know where to go" (see Manegold, 1989, p. 32).

One of the SASS National Fears responses quoted above predicts that, if steps are not taken

> to fix educated youngsters in jobs it is clear that in ten years the country will be called a country of robbers . . . even the government will fall into depression because tourists will stop coming to Kenya because of robbers in the country. Therefore, jobs = peace, no jobs = no peace.

Following the 1989 game park incidents described above, the United States State Department and several European governments issued travel advisories warning about the dangers of travel in Kenya's game parks and of street crime in Kenya's capital city of Nairobi. Given the fact that tourism is Kenya's leading earner of foreign exchange (surpassing exports of coffee and tea), President Moi responded with the rather extraordinary act of directing his "security forces to shoot on sight people found loitering inside the country's national parks" (*East African Standard,* August 27, 1989, p. 1). The *East African Standard* lauded the president's action the following day in an editorial titled "A Timely Directive" (p. 6), and followed with another editorial on September 12, 1989, which observed that

> recent acts of banditry and murder may have tended to portray the country's national parks as unsafe . . . [while the situation is not, as some of the international media had described it, a "security crisis"] no self-respecting country would be expected to leave vital sectors of its economy exposed willy-nilly to saboteurs, be they poachers or armed bandits (p. 6).

The Prognostic Value of the TAT

The concerns with crime projected by the students in their TAT stories and expressed in their SASS fears for their and their country's future provide remarkably accurate descriptions of the nature and widespread extent of crime in Kenya today. The validity of the predictions made from the data twenty years ago appears to be well substantiated.

From a humane perspective, it is difficult to find much satisfaction in the substantiation of the predictions when one considers the resulting plight of many of Kenya's citizens. Our social and political affairs do not seem to have changed much since Thrasymachus wrote more than 2,000 years ago—human self-interest and greed still drive political processes in which might still makes right, the strong still take a disproportionate share of the benefits that society has to offer, and systemic conflict and instability continues to result as those who find obstacles blocking their pursuit of societies' values respond and adapt.

It is not difficult, however, to find satisfaction from a methodological perspective. The substantiation of the predictions provides a solid demonstration of the prognostic value of the TAT and the SASS. That value was realized in the Kenya research in two different ways. The first made use of the measures in conjunction with social theory. Here the instruments were valuable in revealing patterns and levels of motivation and aspiration that, when contrasted with actual opportunities, indicated the likelihood of severe social imbalances and disjunctions; social theory then indicated the likely responses and adaptations of individuals in such a situation. The second made direct use of the content of the students' projections and responses, with a value independent of the application of any theory or logic. Here the measures allowed us to see directly into the preconscious and unselfconscious (TAT) and conscious (SASS) fears and concerns of the students.

The manner in which the modes of adaptation and response predicted by social theory correspond to the direct fears and concerns revealed by the students provides a check on the reliability of each approach. The correspondence between the findings drawn from the TAT and from the SASS provides a similar check on the reliability of each of the research measures. This point is especially important in the context of the consideration of the TAT that is the focus of this volume. The preceding retrospective examination demonstrates the high degree of confidence with which we can utilize the TAT as a valid and reliable quantitative cross-cultural research instrument capable of effectively revealing the dominant patterns of interpersonal concerns that characterize a given group or society, and of predicting future patterns of social change and stress.

The TAT has special epistemological value as a quantitative social science research instrument. That value stems from the manner in which the TAT taps the preconscious and unselfconscious levels of the mind where the foundations of the attitudes and values that motivate human behavior are found, and from the low stimulus demand intrinsic to the measure which lessens the bias which often results from measures that impose rigid categories of response based on assumptions about what is or is not important and significant to one's respondents.

The TAT also has a more practical, heuristic value to those concerned with ways in which our political institutions might be made more responsive to the needs of more of the world's citizens. As we enter the twenty-first century we seem to be living in a time marked by a convergence of crises in human and environmental systems that threatens to overwhelm the political power structures that have for so long dominated our social, economic, and political affairs. In an update of Plato's plea from *The Republic,* Schumacher (1973, pp. 293-294) writes that

> there has never been a time, in any society in any part of the world, without its sages and teachers to challenge materialism and plead for a different order of priorities. . . . Today, however, this message reaches us not solely from the sages and saints but from the actual course of physical events. It speaks to us in the language of terrorism, genocide, breakdown, pollution, exhaustion.

Toffler (1990) argues that we are at one of the greatest turning points in history as such breakdown and exhaustion converge to challenge the power structures that control our societies.

As political elites attempt to maintain their positions in the face of mass demands that their needs be better met, it seems possible that political decision makers will increasingly turn to science for valid and reliable knowledge upon which they can accurately and rationally assess the effects of various courses of political action. With the epistemological strengths noted above, the TAT could contribute much to efforts to understand the needs of the world's peoples as the basis for the design of new political institutions capable of better serving humankind.

References

Callaway, Archibald. 1963. Unemployment Among African School Leavers. *Journal of Modern African Studies,* **I**(3) (September): 351–371.

Cantril, Hadley. 1965. *The Pattern of Human Concerns.* New Brunswick, N.J.: Rutgers University Press.

Cantril, Hadley and A. Lloyd. 1962. Hopes and Fears for Self and Country: The Self-Anchoring Striving Scale in Cross-Cultural Research. Supplement to *The American Behavioral Scientist,* **VI**(2), Supplement (October).

Cornford, Francis MacDonald. 1941. *The Republic of Plato.* New York: Oxford University Press.

Donno, Daniel. 1966. *The Prince by Niccolo Machiavelli.* New York: Bantam Books.

East African Standard, various dates.

Evans, Emmit Bud, Jr. 1975. Secondary Education, Unemployment, and Crime in Kenya. *Journal of Modern African Studies,* **13**(1) (March): 55–66.

———. 1977. Sources of Socio-Political Instability in an African State: The Case of Kenya's Educated Unemployed. *African Studies Review,* **XX**(1) (April): 37–52.

Henry, William E. 1956. *The Analysis of Fantasy: The Thematic Apperception Technique in the Study of Personality.* New York: John Wiley and Sons.

Kilpatrick, Franklin P. and Hadley Cantril. 1960. Self-Anchoring Scaling: A Measure of Individuals' Unique Reality Worlds. *Journal of Individual Psychology,* **XVI**(2) (November): 158–173.

Lenski, Gerhard E. 1966. *Power and Privilege: A Theory of Social Stratification.* New York: McGraw-Hill Book Company.

Manegold, C.S. 1989. Death in the African Bush. *Newsweek* (September 4), 32.

Marshall, Thomas H. 1970. The Nature of Class Conflict. In Eric A. Nordlinger (Ed.), *Politics and Society: Studies in Comparative Political Sociology.* Englewood Cliffs, N.J.: Prentice-Hall, Inc.

McClelland, David C. 1961. *The Achieving Society.* New York: The Free Press.

Merton, Robert C. 1964. *Social Theory and Social Structure.* (Revised Edition). London: Free Press of Glencoe.

Muliro, Masinde. 1968. Statement in *National Assembly Debates,* vol. xvi, Sixth Session, September 3, cols. 98–99. Nairobi: Government Printer.

Odinga, Oginga. 1967. *Not Yet Uhuru.* Nairobi: Heinemann.

Press, Robert M. 1991. Behind Kenya's Push for Multiparty Reform. *Christian Science Monitor* (August 14), 4.

Schumacher, Ernst F. 1973. *Small is Beautiful: A Study of Economics as if People Mattered.* New York: Harper and Row.

Toffler, Alvin. 1990. *Powershift: Knowledge, Wealth, and Violence at the Edge of the 21st Century.* New York: Bantam Books.

Chapter 4

Gender Roles, Marital or Sexual Problems: Comparisons of Responses in Two Japanese Villages

George A. De Vos
Hiroshi Wagatsuma

In this and the following chapter we draw on field research completed in Japan in 1954 that illustrates how the TAT can be used to reveal within-group differences between social segments of a particular culture such as the Japanese. In this chapter we draw on a previous report first published in 1962 in which Hiroshi Wagatsuma and George De Vos (1962) illustrated how individuals from different social strata in the same culture can reveal differences in social attitudes in regard to gender roles and responsibilities. We then illustrated how various interpersonal categories and subcategories demonstrate the different perceptions about expected social behavior we found in a lower-status Japanese fishing village compared with a middle-class farming village visited in 1954.

This material draws principally on material from TAT Cards 4, J9, 13, and 18GF. Among those cards George De Vos has most frequently used in his research with the TAT are Murray Cards 4 and 13, which very frequently elicit stories of marital or love relationships and their vicissitudes. Card 18GF most frequently brings forth situations of conflict or nurture. In the United States, themes on this latter card occur between women as well as in a child-parent relationship. In Japan, the second figure in many stories can be depicted as a husband or son. Card J9 (see Appendix B) constructed in Japan depicts a Japanese family scene featuring a young man in the foreground and three women looking toward him in the immediate background.

Attitudes toward the Role Behavior of Women in Two Japanese Villages

Using a number of direct interviews, questionnaires, and psychological tests, the Japanese research team, of which George De Vos was a part, contacted the inhabitants of Sakunoshima, an economically marginal fishing village located on the coast between Tokyo and Nagoya. We observed that the social status of the entire village has been traditionally low, in marked contrast to the fairly well-to-do farmers of Niiike, a village close to the Inland Sea, near Okayama, where we had interviewed and tested the previous two months.

Our original immediate effort was to determine whether we could demonstrate the sensitivity of attitudes obtained in our projective tests to the observed status differences of women in these two rural communities. The overall results on the Rorschach test were, in general, strikingly similar. Yet on the TAT and on a Problem Situation Test we could find consistent differences in attitudes concerning role behavior, especially the social comportment expected of women within the primary family. In this effort we were successful. The results reflected the different specific occupations of these two villages located in what is described generally by Japanese social scientists as central or southwestern Japan.

Historical Diversity in Family Relationships in Rural Japan

The accumulation of intensive data on Japanese rural culture has revealed many regional differences in Japanese values and attitudes. Scholars concerned with Japanese culture generally have also been aware that they must distinguish between what is broadly characteristic of the society as a whole and what is specific to smaller segments. Such differences are historical in origin and still reflect differences in social status that obtained in the premodern past. Japanese scholars[1] characterize premodern rural social organization as having two principal forms: a "Northeastern" pattern emphasizing behavior regulated by kinship and pseudo-kinship relations,[2] and a "Southwestern" pattern giving a greater role to functionally directed communal organizations not based on kinship.

---

[1]For example, see K. Ariga, "A Study of Social Organization in Japanese Farming Villages" (1940 in Japanese), and Ariga, Nakano, and Morioka "The Japanese Family," *Transactions of the Second World Congress of Sociology*, 1954.

[2]See Y. Okada, "Kinship Organization in Japan," *Journal of Education Sociology* (1952 in Japanese).

Although attitudes and values concerning the social position of women varied greatly within the Northeastern pattern, they emphasized a relatively lower position for females within a hierarchically organized patriarchal family structure. In the Southwestern area, the status of women was considered to be somewhat higher; there was a greater tendency toward bilateral kinship, and familial and other relationships were less strongly hierarchical. Within the range of these broad regional variations, anthropologists have further described many local differences in status and social values related to specific occupational groups.

Throughout Japan, as in the southwest areas we investigated, it is recognized that the relative status of women tended to be higher in fishing villages than in farming villages. It is obvious that socioeconomic factors operated to differentiate fishing communities from others. The occupations of men and women in fishing communities were such that the wife tended to assume more day-by-day authority in the household. Her relationship to her own parents was better maintained, and unilateral patrilineal ties did not tend to develop as strongly as they did in farming communities. The relative poverty and isolation of fisherfolk did not allow them to give much heed to possibilities of bettering their social status by emulating the samurai-Confucian patterns governing the relationship of the sexes. Communities therefore historically differed in the degree to which they had been influenced by inculcating the Confucian values of the socially superior samurai class. In some communities for example, arranged marriages did not appear until the turn of the century. Women's sexual behavior was freer, and the test of desirability of a woman for marriage was her strength and possible fertility, not her virginity.

In villages in the 1950s, before the subsequent general movement into urban areas, the grandparents and grandchildren had attitudes toward sexual behavior more similar to those of one another than to those held by their thirty-five- to fifty-year-old parents. The "modern" changes that were occurring in some lower-status villages were in actuality a reversion to older, looser patterns. Women in fishing villages, like women we have studied subsequently in a working-class area of Tokyo in the 1960s, showed very little evidence of the deferential behavior expected of women emulating the samurai tradition, such as was apparent among the higher status families of Niiike in 1954.

After being temporarily infatuated by Western thought, the leaders of the new Meiji state redirected Japanese governmental ideology back toward the traditional samurai values as standards of conduct for the nation as a whole. These values, including the assignment of women to a social position much inferior to that of males, became an integral part of the moral education imparted to all rural and urban commoners through the newly established compulsory education system.

The "democratization" of Japan with modernization in the Meiji period after 1868 in effect lowered the relative status of women in much of the rural areas including the Southwestern area where we did our fieldwork. For the first time rural folk were to be taught "proper" social behavior which emphasized the relative status of the head of the family and all males vis-à-vis women. This teaching seemingly had less effect on the lower-status fisherfolk than on the better-placed farmers, who in a sense could more readily aspire to higher status mobility.

The samurai values also served as a foundation for the new Japanese civil code. Rural Japan had previously had little direct contact with government except through the local feudal lords. With increased communication, the rural areas were permeated with new ideas. Rural modes of marriage selection were altered by samurai ideas as to what was proper and fitting. Arranged marriage, characteristic of the samurai, not previously practiced in many villages, became widely adopted.

As the tempo of communication increased, long-established local marriage practices tended to disappear. Despite government pressure at the turn of the century, the industrialized urban areas began to show the effect of increasing contact with Western ideas of individualism. One can safely say, however, that for most individuals, attitudes toward family relationships did not change radically or abruptly.

It was not until after World War II that any number of Japanese showed clearly observable evidence of radical changes in their concept of the family. Changes in the relation between the sexes can now be observed in prevailing urban and remaining rural areas. But the rural life we observed in 1954 tended to remain more conservative than urban life because the individuals most seeking change were migrating to the urban centers. At this time the more conservative elements remained in their rural homes, and the rural communities were thus able to maintain more traditional forms of economic and social stability. What we found in our research results from three villages obtained in 1954 was essentially village attitudes that were still traditional. In Niiike and Sakunoshima, and in Nagura Mura a forestry village in the mountains of Nagano prefecture, the differences found were in their traditions, and did not as yet reflect differences in postwar change of attitudes.

The Communities Compared

Niiike was a representative, relatively well-off, farming community as we have described elsewhere.[3] It revealed noticeable differences from Sakunoshima. The villagers of Sakunoshima were living on an island at the entrance of Mikawa Bay in Aichi Prefecture. In 1954, there were two hamlets; the eastern one, where we located our study, had a population of 618 individuals in 138 households. From some time in the thirteenth century until the end of the Tokugawa period (1868), the island of Sakunoshima was on a central route of water transportation connecting Edo (Tokyo) in the east, and Kyoto and Osaka in the west.

The subsequent development of land transportation and the use of larger steamships diminished the usefulness of this small island as a stopping-off place.

[3]See Hall and Beardsley (1959).

In 1954, the inhabitants of Sakunoshima were making a poor living by fishing or small-scale farming. Some of the younger individuals spent a number of years working on the mainland nearby or traveling as far as the Keihan district of Osaka or to Kyoto and Kobe seeking menial work. The fields were small and inadequate for raising rice. Only wheat, potatoes, and some vegetables were grown.

Self-sufficiency in food was impossible, and therefore fishing was indispensable as a supplementary industry. In 1954, about 68 percent of the total households were engaged in some form of fishing in addition to farming. Earning a living usually required the combined efforts of the whole family; the men worked on fishing boats or in the cities, some of the younger women worked in nearby industries on the mainland, and the married women worked in the field and at home.

As observed in 1954, the two communities of Niiike and Sakunoshima differed considerably in how they viewed themselves in contact with the world outside their immediate communities. The farming community self-consciously traced its founding to impoverished samurai, and this historical view of origin probably contributes heavily to coloring the status pretensions of the villagers. The fishing people had no such tradition. They maintained relationships with certain family members who at various times migrated to port cities such as Yokohama or Osaka, and these ties were maintained bilaterally, with occasional visiting.

The attitudes expressed in the farming community of Niiike exemplified what has been said by Beardsley and many others concerning the centrality of the concept of the family or "household," that is, as the cornerstone of rural social life and the concept of clearly defined social role found in the Japanese family.[4]

In contrast, the fishing community studies on Sakunoshima showed much less evidence of samurai-Confucian attitudes in family relationships. The social status of fishermen has always been low. Women did not assume a significantly deferential role. Relationships within the village seemed more relaxed than in Niiike. There was evidence of considerable drinking, to excess, by some of the men, in contrast to the relative absence of drinking in Niiike.

Analysis of TAT Materials: The Nature of the Sample

Differences in attitudes about social roles of women between the inhabitants of Niiike and Sakunoshima appear throughout the projective test material. We have selected, for illustration, four areas from the TAT that point up certain noteworthy differences: (1) attitudes toward an arranged marriage and a love marriage; (2) attitudes toward sexual relationships; (3) fantasies of self-assertion and the expression of violence in conflicts involving women; and (4) concern over conflict between the wife and her husband's mother.

---

[4]See Hall and Beardsley, *Village Japan* (1959).

The records we are considering in this report include 807 TAT stories from eighty individuals in Niiike and 385 stories to the same cards from thirty-five matched individuals from among those tested in Sakunoshima. In Niiike approximately two-thirds of the inhabitants were sampled. In Sakunoshima less than one-fifth of the population was sampled. We were successful, however, in seeing that the age and sex distribution of the total village was proportionately represented.

Attitudes toward a Love Marriage versus a Family-Initiated Marriage

In attitude surveys conducted in the 1950s, such as that conducted by Stoetzel (1955), a surprising number of young Japanese—close to 50 percent—stated in answer to a direct question that marriage is an individual affair. This was true in both urban and rural areas. One would presume from such results that individually initiated marriages are on the increase. Steiner (1950) quoted statistics from areas near Tokyo that supported this supposition. Later surveys in the subsequent years into the 1980s, however, attest to the continuance of arranged marriages as the predominant form.

As previously indicated (De Vos, 1960), according to material from Niiike, there was a tendency to accept the idea of marriage for love in response to direct presentation of problem situation items requiring a direct answer, but the TAT test stories, given more spontaneously by the same villagers, did not tend to support such a positive acceptance of a love marriage. Rather, when subjects constructed stories of love marriage, they tended to view such marriages as ending in some form of failure. In the Problem Situation Test responses, the emphasis was not on how the marriage subsequently turned out but on the "right" to enter into such a marriage on the part of individuals. This emphasis on individual rights by 1954 had become part of the conscious value system—whether it could be emotionally or behaviorally implemented or not.

Rather negative underlying attitudes in Niiike toward love marriage contrasted with the more relaxed and freer attitudes in Sakunoshima toward love and marriage as indicated by the ethnographic data as well as the projective instruments. Our TAT evidence substantiated the impressions gained informally by observations and interviews in both villages.

In our 807 TAT stories obtained from eighty individuals in Niiike, there were forty-two explicit spontaneous references to the circumstances of marriage (see Table 4.1). (Note that none of the cards used necessarily suggested the theme of marriage circumstances per se.) Thirteen explicit references were made to some form of arranged or family-type marriage, and twenty-four references were to love marriage or to an individual-type marriage. Only three of the stories mentioning arranged marriage showed tensions existing between individuals, whereas in only two of the twenty-four stories mentioning a love marriage was there absence of tension. Most frequently (ten stories) a love marriage was depicted as ending in some form of failure. (It should be noted that the percentages of stories giving the explicit circumstance of marriage are similar in both communities (5.2 percent for Niiike; 4.9 percent for Sakunoshima).)

In Sakunoshima the evidence is of a different nature. Of 385 stories to the same cards obtained from thirty-five individuals, nineteen made some mention of marriage, and there is no difference in distribution of tension stories and stories without tension with respect to love marriage or to arranged marriage. A qualitative examination of differences in the stories strongly suggests the nature of the differences in attitudes in the two villages.

For example, in Sakunoshima we find the following stories given to Card 4:

> (SakuW, age 19) (Card J4) They are dancing together. They will live together. They will marry, in the future they will get along all right.
>
> [PA-play FA-love PA-joy HA-harmony]

> (SakuW, age 55) (Card J4) Two of them; they are looking at something. This is a well-drawn picture. They are looking at something passing by outside from the window. Looking at their lives (what are they thinking?). They are thinking of marrying and living happily, as the people they are looking at. Both of them are working laborers. They came to love each other. They will marry, live happily, work together, I suppose.
>
> [AA-purpose FA-love RA-work]

There is marked contrast between these stories and those given in Niiike. The following two stories were given to Card J13 in Niiike:

> (M, age 35–49) (Card J13) A young man regrets his love marriage with a maid of a bar who cajoled (seduced) him. He regrets his marriage when he sees her slovenly attitude.
>
> [RB-regret EB-status FD-seduced RC-indulge]

> (M, age 35–49) (Card J13) A husband is addicted to drinking and comes back home to his slovenly wife, who is sleeping. He had married her as a result of a love relationship. They are divorced, they each go on to terrible ways—the woman becoming a procuress, the man contracting an infectious disease. He goes to prison and eventually kills himself on the railroad tracks.
>
> [RC-abuse RC-indulge FA-love RC-messy FD-separate AC-illicit RC-result PD-suicide]

Table 4.1

Expression of Tension in TAT Stories in Which Circumstances of Marriage Are Explicitly Mentioned

	NIIKE			SAKUNOSHIMA		
	Male	*Female*	*Totals*	*Male*	*Female*	*Totals*
Total Respondents	36	44	80	17	18	35
Total Stories			807			385
Stories giving marriage circumstances	22	20	42	7	12	19
Arranged Marriage Totals	3	10	13	2	7	9
No tension	3	6	9*	1	4	5
Tension	0	3	3*	1	3	4
Indefinite	0	1	1	0	0	0
Love Marriage Totals	15	9	24	4	5	9
No tension	1	1	2*	0	4	4
Tension	14	8	22*	4	1	5
Eventual conformity to family pressure	2	0	2	1	0	1
Conflict without outcome	4	3	7	2	0	2
Successful persistence	3	0	3	1	1	2
Eventual marriage failure	5	5	10	0	0	0
Other	4	1	5	1	0	1

It should be noted that the percentage of stories giving the circumstances marriage are similar in both communities (5.2 percent for Niiike; 4.9 percent for Sakunoshima).
*Chi-square, Yates Cor. P < .001.

These stories are extreme, indicating by their moralistic tone and graphic depiction the terrible end that can result from going contrary to an arranged marriage. No such stories appear in Sakunoshima; instead, positive stories of love marriage appear proportionately more frequently. It must be noted, however, that arranged marriages also are represented in the Sakunoshima stories. It cannot be said, therefore, that one village subscribes to arranged marriages as proper and the other to love marriages; but the residents of the fishing village place less emphasis on arranged marriage and are more optimistic as to the outcome of love marriages. Both villages show the presence of traditional Japanese core values about arranged marriage.

Comparison of General Attitudes toward Sexual Relationships in Niiike and Sakunoshima

There are numerous stories from both villages in which the principal concern is some form of heterosexual relationship. These stories again demonstrate consistent differences between the two villages in viewing problems in heterosexual love relationships. There are thirty-one stories in Niiike depicting nonmarital love relationships between young individuals. Fourteen of these stories involve conflict between a child and a parent, most of them with no resolution (see Table 4.2).

Negative stories appear on a variety of Cards in Niiike:

> (NK M, age 25–34) (Card J6M) A mother scolds her son on account of his indulgence in female company. The son is antagonistic toward his mother.
> [NDA-scold RC-pre-sex HC-discord]

> (NK W, age 12–17) (Card J18) A parent and son quarrel over son's love affair and the parent strangles the son to death.
> [HC-discord RC-pre-sex HC-murder]

> (NK W, age 35) (Card J9) A son was scolded by his father about his love affair. Finally he will leave home.
> [NDA-scold RC-pre-sex FD-split]

There were no comparable stories in the Sakunoshima sample. There were seventeen stories in Niiike of various other tensions in a love relationship. In twelve of these, a woman is rejected by her lover in one way or another. Only one story of this kind appears in Sakunoshima. The remaining stories in Niiike depict an act of violence of a man toward a woman or a separation.

There was no notable difference between the two villages in the manner of depicting nonmarital triangular relationships, in which, characteristically, two men quarrel over a woman. The principal concerns in the stories from Sakunoshima were extramarital triangular affairs involving a husband (father), or transient sexual relationships of various kinds.

> (Saku M, age 50–64) (Card J11) The mother looks sad over something. This is her son—I see the hat and the briefcase of her husband but she looks very sad—I guess she is sad because her husband's conduct is not good. The child is sorry for the mother and is worried too. They were happy in the past. They were well off and had a child, but now the husband's conduct is not good, and the wife is sad and the son is worried. If the husband reforms himself, the son and the wife will be happy.
> [FC-betray FB-aware HA-harmony KA-wealth RC-ex-sex RA-reform PA-joy]

In the Niiike sample, seduction is depicted as leading to an unhappy marriage and regret. In Sakunoshima, seduction or casual sexual contact is seen as leading to regret or to some personal demoralization of the individual concerned but not to marriage (Table 4.2).

> (Niiike M, age 23) (Card J13) This does not look like too good a place. This young man was seduced by a prostitute, a woman taking the initiative. They did bad play in such a place, I suppose. This young man had never done such a thing before, I think. From now on . . . he will become interested in such things and will become a delinquent . . . well, I think that's all that it is. The woman is urging him to sleep with her and he is at a loss, not knowing what to do, I guess. He becomes a delinquent but then, reforms himself again. He will become a serious person again.
> [FD-seduced RC-mores RC-control RA-reform]

In all but two of the extramarital relationships depicted, one in each village, it was a man who goes to a mistress or has an affair, causing unhappiness at home. Characteristic throughout these stories in both villages was a moralizing attitude of the teller about the consequences of this sexual behavior on the future of the individual.

In summary, in spite of certain overall similarities, the differences in the stories were sufficient to indicate marked differences in what is the concern of the two villages toward sexual behavior. In Niiike the focus was on the effects of going against the moral code requiring arranged marriage and obedience to parental figures. Tension between parents and children over sexual behavior is not a theme in Sakunoshima. The villagers are more concerned with the potential evil outcome of the infidelity of the father and of transience and irresponsibility in sex. These results were clearly in line with the other attitudinal differences in the two villages toward aspects of the Confucian ethical code concerning marriage.

Perception of Women as Capable of Violence or Aggression

The traditional Japanese ethical ideal was that women were, under no condition, to express a violent or aggressive attitude toward their husbands. However, under the stress of extreme circumstances violence could be turned toward the self in the form of suicide to preserve one's honor, or toward one's children if the greater honor of the family or some overriding obligation made it necessary. By examining in some detail two of the TAT cards calling forth stories of violence or aggression between individuals, one can readily document differences between the two villages in the underlying attitudes toward a woman's capacity for aggression or violence. The two cards most suited for this analysis are Card J18, which depicts a female figure readily interpreted as choking either another woman or a man, and Card J13, often interpreted, by the Japanese at least, as a situation of quarreling or discord between husband and wife.

Table 4.2

Heterosexual Relationships in Stories Given to Ten TAT Cards in Sakunoshima and Niiike

	Niike			Sakunoshima			
	M	*F*	*Totals*	*M*	*F*	*Totals*	*Significance*
Total stories (10 cards)	257	273	530	170	180	350	
Total heterosexual relationships*	31	24	55	18	11	29	Not sig.
% of total stories*			10.4%**			7%	
Nonmarital love (marriage not an outcome)							
Essentially involving							
Parental-conflict	7	7	14	0	0	0	p < .001
Aggression-violence	2	1	3	0	1	1	
Separation	1	1	2	1	0	1	
Rejection of woman	5	7	12	0	2	2	P < .01
Totals	15	16	31	1	3	4	P < .01
Nonmarital triangular							
man-two women	1	0	1	1	1	2	
two men-woman	8	5	13	3	2	5	
Totals	9	5	14	4	3	7	Not sig.
Extramarital triangular							
husband's affair	4	2	6	7	3	10	
wife's affair	1	0	1	0	1	1	
Totals	5	2	7	7	4	11	P < .05
Transient sex leading to							
regret or reform	1	1	2	4	0	4	
demoralization or suicide	1	0	1	2	1	3	
Totals	2	1	3	6	1	7	P < .05

^The 10 cards are: J2, M3M, U3F, J4, J6M, JM7M, J9, J11, J13, J18, J22

*Excluding circumstances of marriage stories shown in Table 4.1.

**Significant differences in proportion of stories on heterosexual relationships between Niiike and Sakunoshima.

Situations of Violence on Card J18

Stories to Card J18 involve either themes of violence, on the one hand, or some form of affiliative concern, such as illness or the reunion with a beloved, on the other. The stories from Niiike emphasize the mother's intensity of feeling about raising her son to become a responsible adult in the traditional culture. Such feelings, although not absent in Sakunoshima, are proportionately less frequently expressed.

There was little difference between the total percentage of stories of violence given to this card in the two villages (48 percent in Niiike to 46 percent Sakunoshima), but in Niiike there were markedly more stories involving the chastisement of an errant son. Four stories given in response to J18 follow; the first two are from Niiike and the second two from Sakunoshima.

> (NK M, age 12–17) (Card J18) A mother strangles to death her prodigal son and she will be imprisoned.
>
> [RC-wrong HC-murder RA-injure NDA-police]

> (NKM, age 18–24) (Card J18) A mother chastises severely her son who played a trick on a child next door.
>
> [RC-mores NDA-scold]

> (SakuM, age 34) (Card J18) A mother scolded her son—the son always asked for money and played all the time. He did not want to work. She could not stand to see the attitude of her son any longer and chastised her son very severely. Though she did, the son did not change his mind. But, I think, he will reform himself later, perhaps when the mother gets sick or he loses his mother. He has no father. The father died when he was small.
>
> [RC-indulge NDA-scold OC-deceit KD-death KD-ill-die RA-reform]

> (SakuM, age 12–17) (Card J18) There was a parent and her child. The child became a delinquent and was doing bad things every day. The mother was told about her child by somebody and chastised her son very severely. The mother looked at her son's face and shed tears. She said, "Why do you like to make trouble around here?" The mother began chastising her son frequently.
>
> [RC-wrong NDA-scold NDB-pity RA-injure]

From these examples it was clear that men see a woman capable of violence in disciplining her child. The chastisement was not depicted as the expression of an uncontrollable anger or of fury, but as arising from the deep sense of responsibility to society for the behavior of one's child (see discussion of *Responsibility* in chapter 11, volume I). The bad behavior of a child, especially when it is directed against societal norms, might threaten the reputation of his parents or violate their sense of responsibility to society. In the traditional Confucian pattern, the parents and their children were emotionally tied together and are not altogether differentiated out of the psychological unity of the family. Therefore, what children do may have a direct emotional effect upon their parents. Parents may experience what their children do almost as if a part of their own ego were responsible. Accordingly, when their children's behavior is negative and threatens their own ego-ideal, they may react by chastisement, which may primarily express their resentment against the uncontrollable part of themselves. Parents may even want to kill their children, which actually means punishing themselves, in order to be faithful to their ego-ideal and to maintain their psychological security. (The stories of chastisement in Niiike have a more severe tone than those in Sakunoshima.) Parents expect their children's behavior to support the parental aspirations for their children's success and to brighten the reputation or honor of their parents and the lineage. Thus, all that is required of children may be phrased in terms of fulfillment of the parents' sense of duty and responsibility to their family and society. Parents may not know how to cope with a situation in which a child goes so against the expectations of the parents as to make them fail in their responsibility. One reaction would be to disown the child; the response in the extreme situation, in fantasy at least, would be to kill the child who has failed in his duty.

In the traditional pattern, parental pressure, expectation, or control is exerted more strongly on a son than on a daughter because important social status and roles were usually limited to men and much more social responsibility was required of men. One may also point out that when children act against parental expectation, it is more often their mother who is exposed to a strong sense of failure. The mother, coming as an outsider into the family, has to demonstrate her capacity by being responsible for the correct upbringing of her children.

In Niiike an interesting contrast between the attitudes of mother toward daughter compared with those of mother toward son is to be noted throughout the TAT material. In responses to Card J18, in stories of affection or concern over illness where the sex of the figure is explicitly noted, the mother is most often seen as concerned over the health or well-being of her daughter. This is true throughout the remainder of the Niiike TAT material. There are fewer stories of such affectionate concern over the health of a son.

Throughout the remainder of the Niiike TAT material, the mother-daughter relationship is almost invariably idealized as one in which the mother is lovingly concerned with the health and well-being of her daughter. When a negative mother-daughter relationship appears, it is most often attributed to a stepmother or a mother-in-law. On the other hand, the mother is more often seen in a disciplinary role toward her son. Responses in Niiike to Card J18 show that a mother's desire to see her son grow up properly can lead to violence on her part. In Sakunoshima stories such a difference between the mother's behavior toward the son and that toward her daughter is not evident.

Chastisement of a son by a mother was not exhibited in the stories from Sakunoshima; there was as much aggression expressed by a woman toward a daughter or another adult as toward a son. Whereas Card J18 evoked several stories of aggression between adult married individuals in Sakunoshima, in Niiike no such stories were elicited. In three of the Sakunoshima stories a wife is actually described as choking her errant husband.

If we examine more specifically the stories of violence between adults, we note that, even in these stories, certain differences between Niiike and Sakunoshima are apparent. In Niiike when a woman is seen as violent or aggressive toward other adults, she is depicted as being either insane or a widow (unusual social statuses in which role expectations are more relaxed). The following stories are from Niiike:

> (NKM, age 18–24) (Card J18) A mother strangles to death a woman who tempted her innocent son. Mother becomes insane and dies. The son begs his mother's forgiveness.
>
> [HC-murder FC-seduce PD-mad RA-apology]

> (NKW, age 12–17) (Card J18) A woman and a man fight. The woman is insane and does not know what she is doing.
>
> [HC-injury PD-mad]

> (NKM, age 65 or over) (Card J18) A mother strangles to death her small child because she is bound to some giri (obligation) and has no other solution. She will commit suicide.
>
> [HC-murder RB-role RA-hurts HC-suicide]

> (NKM, age 18–24) (Card J18) A widow strangles another widow in their quarrel over money.
>
> [HC-murder OC-wealth]

In contrast, in the following stories told to Card J18 by Sakunoshima villagers, a woman kills both herself and her child because her husband is poor, which can be considered as violence directed toward her husband; a woman fights with another woman; and in two stories a wife is directly aggressive toward her husband. No comparable stories of a wife's aggression toward her husband appear in the entire Niiike TAT sample.

> (SakuW, age 50–64) (Card J18) Because of the poverty or the idleness of her husband this woman is going to kill her child and commit double suicide. Both will die.
>
> [KD-poverty RC-indulge RA-injury HC-suicide]

> (SakuM, age 18–24) (Card J18) Its terrible. The hands are not normally shaped—a parent?—well, I don't know. In their past, this woman bore that woman ill will and now she is trying to vent her spite. A love affair—a rivalry, I mean. She cannot live happily because of her ill will toward this woman.
>
> [KD-defect HC-injury HC-hostile FC-triangle]

(SakuW, age 23) (Card J18) They are married. The husband was playing the prodigal—drinking all the time and gambling, playing with his mistress. So the wife tries to grip his throat. He will change his mind and become a good husband.
[HA-depict RC-abuse RC-ex-sex HC-injury RA-reform]

(SakuM, age 24) (Card J18) Well, trying to kill somebody? Oh—they are a married couple. The husband deceived his wife. This is the husband who deceived his wife and he is going to be killed by his wife.
[HA-depict HC-murder FC-deceit]

Themes of Discord on Card J13: Perception of Active and Passive Attitudes in Heterosexual Relationships

The stories given in response to Card J13 (which depicts a woman in the background lying on bedding with her breasts exposed and a man standing in the foreground with his arm thrown before his eyes), when considered solely from the standpoint of the aggressive or passive behavior of the principal figures, show a striking difference between the two villages (see Table 4.3).

In the stories from Niiike, in a domestic quarrel or in other situations as well, a man is much more likely to be depicted as active, even violent or aggressive, toward a woman. In Sakunoshima, there is a greater tendency to depict a woman as sexually aggressive and, in a story of a quarrel between husband and wife, the man may be pictured as helpless or passive in relation to the woman. In only one story from Niiike is the woman depicted as scolding or dominant in any respect, whereas the husband is pictured by a number of men as regretting his marriage and initiating divorce as a consequence. In Sakunoshima, in eight out of ten stories, the wife asserts herself, or the husband is depicted as weak or helpless in the quarrel. The following example is from Niiike:

(NKM, age 35–49) (Card J13) I don't know—how shall I think. I want to do this later. [Rejects card; card is given to him again after he finishes the sequence.] A young salaried man lives with his young wife. His wife is an extravagant woman, so he cannot support them with his salary. One day the young man came back home late at night. His wife became sulky and did not speak to him, showed contempt in her attitude. Her husband was really angered and began to feel miserable. He thought in his anger that his marriage was a failure, and he cried with mortification. He is at a loss whether he should start a new life or continue to live with her. He is afraid that if he divorces her, he will miss her, but he will divorce her just the same.
[RC-waste EDC-disdain HB-anger HD-hurt FB-longing FD-split]

Table 4.3

Comparison of Principal Themes in Niiike and Sakunoshima on Card J13

A. Distribution of Major Thematic Categories

	NIIIKE			SAKUNOSHIMA		
	Male	*Female*	*Totals*	*Male*	*Female*	*Totals*
Total responses	20	22	42	17	18	35
Main emphasis in the stories:						
Concern over death and illness						
of wife	4	9	13	2	5	7
of mother	1	5	6	2	3	5
Totals	5	14	19	4	8	12
Emphasis on aggression or violence						
husband to wife	0	2	2	0	0	0
man to woman	2	1	3	0	0	0
Totals	2	3	5	0	0	0
Sexual aggressiveness						
man to woman	1	0	1	1	0	1
woman to man	2	0	2	2	1	3
Totals	3	0	3	3	1	4
Quarrel or discord						
Wife dominant Subtotal	0	1	1*	5	3	8*
wife scolds	0	1	1	(2)	0	2
wife ignores	0	0	0	(2)	0	2
husband apologizes or reforms	0	0	0	0	1	1
husband defeated or helpless	0	0	0	1	2	3
Husband boss Subtotal	7	2	9*	1	1	2*
husband scolds	1	0	1	0	0	0
regrets marriage	2	0	2	0	0	0
husband divorces	4	0	4	0	0	0
wife apologizes or reforms	0	0	0	1	0	2
mutual reconciliation	0	2	2	0	0	0
Totals	7	3	10	6	4	10
Other	3	2	5	4	5	9

B. Total Stories of Aggression, Discord, and Illness, by Protagonist Depicting Relative Activity or Passivity in the Relationship

	Male	*Female*	*Totals*	*Male*	*Female*	*Totals*
Man active	8	3	11	1	0	1
Man passive	2	0	2	3	4	7
Woman active**	2	1	3**	4	1	5**
Woman passive or sick**	5	14	19**	5	8	13**
Mutual	0	2	2	0	0	0
Other	3	2	5	4	5	9

*Fischer's Exact Test, P < .01.
**Chi-square, P < .05.

In contrast we find the following four examples in Sakunoshima:

(SakuW, age 40) (Card J18) The husband had been drinking, that's all. He will apologize to his wife for having come home drunk. Yes, he will apologize.

[RC-abuse RA-apology]

(SakuM, age 34–50) (Card J13) A husband and a wife quarreled. They are still young. The husband is working in an office. Sometimes he drinks a little sake on the way back, and his wife complained about it. It is not a serious quarrel at all, and they will be on good terms again. They will live as ordinary people. He is now excited and wishes he could go out somewhere again, but he cannot do it. He is thinking, "Why cannot she act a little more gently toward me."

[HC-discord RC-abuse FA-mend NSB-help]

(SakuM, age 50–64) (Card J13) This must be a husband and wife. Looks like a petticoat-government situation (kaka-denka). Therefore, they always quarrel. They cannot have a good child that way. The woman is sleeping, you see. They have often quarreled like this. This is not a good family. Anyway, this wife is egocentric (wagamama). They will come to no good in the future. The husband has come back from the office.

[DDC-control HC-discord RD-control NDC-selfish HD-decay]

(SakuW, age 25–35) (Card J13) In this family a husband came home later than usual. The wife had gone to bed alone and is crying.

[RC-mores FB-accord]

It is noteworthy, in regard to the question of initiative between men and women, that whereas five individuals in Niiike saw a man or husband in picture J13 acting violently toward a woman, there is no single person in Sakunoshima who saw a man in this picture as violent in the same manner. Following are three examples from Niiike of stories of the man as violent or aggressive.

(NKW, age 12–17) (Card J13) A husband killed his wife because the wife complained too much about his low salary. He regrets it very much.

[HC-verbal HC-murder RB-regret]

(NKM, age 23–40) (Card J13) A man kills a woman who is a dancer and entertainer because she rejects him when he makes advances toward her. He runs away.

[HC-murder EDC-status FC-reject RD-wrong]

(NKM, age 12–17) (Card J13) A man who is rather licentious carries a woman to his room and perspires because it is hot. He forced her to come, bewitched by her sexual charm.

[PA-sensual RC-ex-sex OB-body HC-force]

The results of Card J13 strongly indicate that in a heterosexual relationship in Niiike the man is expected to take the initiative. In contrast, in Sakunoshima there are numerous stories indicating a dominant attitude on the part of a woman. Both groups give stories to this card depicting the wife as ill or dead, but such stories are much more evident in Niiike and most Niiike women give such a response. This evidence is in line with that previously cited and emphasizes the different perceptions of role relationships in the two villages.

Concern over the Mother-in-Law Relationship

In viewing their traditional family system self-consciously, the Japanese were well aware that the point of greatest difficulty between family members is in the relationship of a young bride to her mother-in-law. There are many accounts of conflict between a mother-in-law and her daughter-in-law or bride. A mother-in-law was seen as prone to torment or maltreat her daughter-in-law, who comes from another family and who must therefore be indoctrinated into the different ways of living in her new home. Numerous instances of tension in this relationship were found in Japanese novels, family court cases, and everyday life in the 1950s.

The phenomenon of a mother whose emotional attachment to her son tends to make her jealous of her son's bride, whom she sees as possibly taking her son away from her, is not peculiar to the Japanese. However, this tendency seems to be accentuated by many factors peculiar to the traditional hierarchical pattern of the Japanese family. A woman was bound to be dutiful to her new parents-in-law. The mother-in-law in her turn has come to realize status in the family through her son, whom she has reared to take over the family responsibilities. Once an outsider herself, she becomes the most vigilant of all in protecting the family's interests. A son became for her a means of self-realization, and it was only with difficulty that she allows him to be detached from her as a primary object of love. In a traditional family a young bride was in no position to alienate her husband from his mother, because the marital bond was not conceived as a primary relationship between a husband and his wife, but as a family contract. The mother, however, was well aware of the potential intimacy between the new couple, which may act as a wedge between her and her son. In effect, the wife's role is defined very much as is that of the mother, in terms of maternal solicitude and emphasis on the nurturant relationship to the husband. These factors combined to make an older woman feel that her role, her position, her self-assertion through her son were all threatened and endangered by the young bride.

The Nichiren Buddhist priest who was the head of the parish in which Niiike was located clearly saw this particular conflict as the main problem of his parishioners. He informed us that more than 90 percent of the individuals who came to see him were either mothers-in-law concerned with the new brides of their sons, or new brides coming to complain bitterly against unnecessary harassment by the mother-in-law.

In Niiike, we originally included a TAT card depicting an older and younger woman figure. The responses to this card were so consistently stories of a mother-in-law harassing a young bride that we deleted the card from the series given in the fishing village. It is therefore impossible to compare the two villages in regard to the stories on this card; however, spontaneous stories of a mother-in-law tended to be stimulated by other cards in the series given in both Niiike and Sakunoshima. Such stories appeared to a much greater extent in Niiike than in Sakunoshima.

In Niiike there were eleven stories in which there was explicit mention of a mother-in-law, whereas in Sakunoshima there were only two such comparable. In Niiike a number of responses were given in which the mother-in-law was introduced into the story although no such figure actually appeared on the card; although absent, she was deeply involved in the story of what was happening between the two principal characters.

In Sakunoshima the two stories that explicitly mention a mother-in-law were in response to Card J9, picturing a family scene in which one of the individuals depicted might be identified as a mother-in-law. In only one of these two stories in Sakunoshima is there actual conflict between a man's mother and his wife. In the other story, on the contrary, the mother is seen in a conciliatory role in a conflict between man and wife:

> (SakuM, age 23–34) (Card J9) They are the members of a family and the elder brother made some mistake and his mother and sisters are worried. I guess he made some mistake concerning his wife. Well—after all, the relationship between his wife and his mother is not good. If I look at the face of the mother I feel that this family is not harmonious and the young sisters are sorry for their elder brother and they are worried, too. Future? Thanks to the sisters, the mother's anger will be calmed down, the elder brother's anger will be calmed down, and they will not be worried any longer. The elder brother is sad, not knowing which side he should take, his mother's or his wife's.
>
> [RC-wrong <u>HC-discord</u> FB-aware HA-pacify FB-commit]

> (SakuM, age 25–34) (Card J9) A husband and a wife quarreled and, well—his mother came out and is calming them down. This is their young daughter crying, embraced by the wife. The quarrel will be solved happily—the man is a prodigal and his wife was about to leave the house taking their child and the quarrel started.
>
> [<u>HC-discord</u> HA-pacify NDA-comfort RC-wrong FA-mend]

In Niiike the mother-in-law was described directly as an aggressive scolding person in most of the stories. In four stories from Niiike the mother-in-law scolds her son's wife or is aggressive toward her. For example:

> (NKW, age 18–24) (Card 3BM) She was scolded by her mother-in-law; she cannot talk to her husband, leaves him, and cries but eventually comes back.
>
> [<u>DDC-unfair</u> FB-thwart FC-gone HA-mend]

> (NKW, age 25–34) (Card J3F) A mother-in-law is not satisfied with her daughter-in-law. The daughter-in-law will leave home and tell the story to her own family.
> [DDC-unfair FC-gone NS A-comfort]

When a conflict takes place with a mother-in-law in the traditional setting, there is no guarantee that the husband will attempt to protect his wife. He is most likely to remain inactive, although he may take his mother's side against his wife when his emotional attachment to his mother and his loyalty to the family is greater than any feeling of affection he may have toward his wife. Many Japanese women knew of this possibility in the event of a conflict. In a story told by a woman under thirty-four in Niiike, there is an implicit expression of the wish that a husband would be assertive against his mother and take the part of his wife.

> (NKW, age 12–17) (Card J4) A husband is feeling violent against his mother who is jealous of the couple, and his wife tries to stop him; she talks to his mother. The couple decide to live separately from his mother.
> [HB-inhibit FB-jealousy HA-pacify DSA-free]

Actually, it would be highly unlikely in a rural village that a man would move away from his mother and live separately with his wife. Finally, two fanciful stories were told in Niiike demonstrating rather extreme attitudes toward the yomé-shutomé (mother-in-law vs. bride) conflict.

> (NKW, age 18–24) (Card J3F) Ghost of a dead bride come back to haunt a severe mother-in-law.
> [DDC-unfair HC-revenge]

> (NKM, age 64) (Card J6M) A mother and a son are going to visit the grave of her dead daughter-in-law (his dead wife). The family relations will become better than they were before.
> [HA-rite HA-mend]

In the first of these stories the dead bride can get back at her mother-in-law only by haunting her after her death. In the second story the interpretation that because a son and mother visit the grave of a daughter-in-law the family relationships become better suggests that the daughter-in-law was a cause of alienation between mother and son. The evidence from the TAT stories would strongly support what was suggested by observation, namely that in the fishing village the role for the mother-in-law was not one of a guardian of family custom as it was in Niiike. In Sakunoshima, with the relationship between husband and wife considered primary, the mother-in-law had no unusual authority over the wife, who tended to be autonomous in her own home to a degree not realized in the farming village.

Conclusions

Starting with the hypothesis that differences in social status and role of women would be reflected in projective psychological materials, we compared TAT stories told by people of two Japanese rural villages: one, a farming village in which it was obvious from other behavioral evidence that traditional samurai-influenced values were still held with considerable firmness; the other, a fishing village that appeared ethnographically to be relatively free from emphasis on these values. The major findings of the TAT material support the hypothesis well.

In each instance the evidence is consistent with the picture of greater emphasis on lineage and hierarchical relationships in defining role relationships between the sexes in the farming village as compared with the fishing village. The fishing village shows much more emphasis on more freely conceived and less structured relationships in family role relationships. In the fishing village there is more willingness to perceive love and aggression expressed between individuals, regardless of specified traditional sex or family roles.

It is suggested that these differences between the two villages represent different value emphases related to functional differences in social organization found in various occupations as well as in various regions in Japan. In certain areas and in certain segments of the population, the position of women has been higher, and less emphasis has been put on formal social roles, status, and lineage. The pattern most often considered traditionally Japanese by certain authors writing in the 1950s was by no means as universally dominant as they would have led us to infer.

References

Ariga, K. 1948. *Nihon Konin Shiron.* (Essay on the History of Marriage in Japan.) Tokyo: Nikko Shoin.

Ariga, K., T. Nakano, and K. Morioka. 1954. The Japanese Family. *Transactions of the Second World Congress of Sociology*, **4**: 215–221.

De Vos, George. 1960. The Relation of Guilt Toward Parents to Achievement and Arranged Marriage Among the Japanese. *Psychiatry*, **4**(3): 287–301.

Hall, John, and Richard Beardsley. 1959. *Village Japan.* Chicago: U. of Chicago Press.

Okada, Yuzuro. 1952. Kinship Organization in Japan. *Journal of Educational Sociology*, **26**: 27–31.

Steiner, Kurt. 1950. Postwar Changes in Japanese Civil Codes. *Washington Law Revue*, **25**: 286–312.

Stoetzel, Jean. 1955. Without the Chrysanthemum and the Sword: A Study of the Attitudes of Youth in Post-War Japan, UNESCO. New York: Columbia University Press.

Wagatsuma, Hiroshi and George A. De Vos. 1962. Attitudes Toward Arranged Marriage in Rural Japan. *Human Organization*, **21**(3): 187–200.

Chapter 5

Violence and Aggression in Fantasy: A Comparison of American and Japanese Lower-Class Youth[1]

George A. De Vos
Eiji Murakami

Problem

Preoccupation with violence and aggression is acknowledged to be a characteristic trait of delinquents by specialists of widely divergent theoretical positions (Bandura and Walters, 1959; Aichhorn, 1935; Bennet, 1960; Redl and Wineman, 1957). It is also generally presumed that internal fantasy about violence will in some measure, at least, be related to deviant behavior or neurotic incapacitation. From a behavioral research standpoint, it is crucial to find methods to tap such internal preoccupation by controlled means. Toward that end, we attempted more than thirty-nine years ago, in 1960, to elicit spontaneous stories including any violent

[1]The research reported here was sponsored by NIMH Grant SROI MH 0487 07 for comparative research on delinquency at the Institute of Human Development, University of California, Berkeley (1959–1968). Work was also facilitated by the Social Science Research Institute of the University of Hawaii. The material in this chapter is modified slightly from the article that appeared in De Vos and Murakami (1974).

fantasies from delinquents, both in the United States and in Japan, stimulated by the standard Murray set of TAT and a Japanese set we had developed at Nagoya.[2]

By analyzing the responses to the constant stimuli of TAT pictures, we hoped to assess possible violence differentials in the vaguely structured fantasies of delinquents that we then compared with matched samples of lower-class non-delinquent youth both in the United States and Japan. We thought that if a preoccupation with violence is more characteristic of delinquency-prone youth whether in Japan or the United States, the TAT should reveal systematic differences in story content.

While a number of attempts to delineate the patterns found in delinquency had already been made using this instrument, they had generally failed to produce definitive findings because of what we came to consider somewhat questionable assumptions, and to some inherent limitations in the approaches taken. As we shall indicate in the discussion of our results below, many of the unsatisfactory results obtained with the TAT reflect inadequate research design in respect to sufficient consideration of age, cultural, ethnic, and class variables (Buss, 1961). In our study, therefore, we have attempted to delimit the characteristics of our subjects as much as possible. Those tested were seventeen- to twenty-three-year-old American and Japanese youth specifically of lower-class background. In addition, our American samples were carefully separated into subgroups of African American, Mexican-American, and Americans of various European backgrounds.

We started out with two basic questions. First, how do delinquent and non-delinquent groups in lower-class populations differ in respect to relative number and content of fantasies of violence and aggression? Previous studies had indicated that such differences exist. The second question was cross cultural: whether differences in fantasies of violence and aggression found in lower-class American youth would resemble those found in lower-class Japanese subjects. Would there be characteristic fantasies related to delinquency in both cultures, or would the cultural differences between the two countries be more important than any similarities specific to the delinquent groups?

[2]In the original research in Japan, we used a number of projective instruments as well as intensive interviews to assess personality characteristics, social attitudes and perceptions, and primary family influences related to delinquency formation. We were trying to understand better what social institutions or settings, as well as what psychological factors, might help give rise to delinquency. Other results were reported elsewhere. (De Vos, 1967, 1969; De Vos, 1980; De Vos and Borders, 1979; De Vos and Wagatsuma, 1969, 1972; Mizushima and De Vos, 1967). See especially Wagatsuma and De Vos (1984).

Procedure

The American delinquent subjects in our study were obtained from the Duell Vocational Institution in Tracy, California. They included thirty African Americans, thirty Mexican Americans, sometimes then called "Chicanos," and thirty lower-class whites of European background. These subjects were also used in systematic research being conducted by others at this institution at the time of our study. The subjects were all eighteen to twenty-two years of age. We took care to eliminate any individuals who might be of middle-class background, limiting our selection to those of obvious working-class origin and orientation. We matched the delinquent sample to a sample of non-delinquent youth drawn from various lower-class urban neighborhoods in the San Francisco Bay area and from a number of U.S. Army draftees available in nearby army facilities. Our non-delinquent sample of fifty was not evenly matched for ethnicity—the final group included twenty-nine majority whites, seven Mexican Americans, and fourteen African Americans.

We cannot stress enough the difficulty of preventing systematic biases from entering the collection of data from lower-class American youth. It quickly became clear to us why so few studies have been done on young adults, eighteen to twenty-two years old, of lower-class origin who are not presently engaged in formal education. The difficulties inherent in collecting such samples on a non biased basis are considerable.

The Japanese subjects, who ranged from seventeen to twenty-three years of age, were obtained from various sources. Three institutions provided samples of delinquents: the Gifu Juvenile Classification Center near Nagoya, the Kurihama Reformatory near Yokohama, and the Nakano Prison in Tokyo. Our matched non-delinquent controls in Japan were obtained from a previous large-scale interdisciplinary research project done at Nagoya University. From this source we could select both rural and urban subjects, aged eighteen to twenty-three. In addition, we obtained another sample of working-class non-delinquent youth of the same age range and of rural and urban background from the Nihon Steel Mills, located near Tokyo.

There are some minor deficiencies in the matching. We were not certain that all individuals in our control group from the Nagoya rural sample were properly classified as of lower-class background. Although the individuals may come from poverty-stricken families, the traditional social orientation of the Japanese farmer is middle-class. The Nagoya urban sample may also contain a few subjects who should be classified lower-middle class rather than lower class. We were more certain of the class status of the Kurihama and Nakano Prison samples than we were of the Gifu sample. Generally speaking, however, we could aver that the Japanese samples were predominantly lower class.

To standardize administration, the senior author supervised the testing of all the samples, both in the United States and Japan. The American prison subjects were gathered with the assistance of a professional staff of social workers and psychologists who were instructed in our administrative procedures. The non-delinquent control sample in the United States was tested with the help of graduate students attending the School of Social Welfare at the University of California, Berkeley, who had received special instructions in administration. The senior author helped train the professional psychologists and psychology majors who tested all the Japanese delinquent and non-delinquent samples except those from Gifu. The Gifu testers, who were students majoring in psychology, were trained by Dr. Fumio Marui, a Japanese psychiatrist on the interdisciplinary research projects being conducted at Nagoya.

For comparative purposes, we had available twelve cards to use with the Japanese subjects and ten or eleven cards to use with the American subjects. We are reporting the results obtained on the nine cards that are directly comparable cross-culturally. The Japanese TATs that we used is a standard set that the senior author helped adapt from the Murray TAT Harvard edition, in his collaboration in Japan with Fumio Marui. The features and physical background were modified to be appropriate to the Japanese cultural scene. The cards were adequately pretested in a large-scale study done in Japan (De Vos, 1973). However, our results showed only one minor discrepancy between the Japanese and American test sets that affected the results. We will point it out in our discussion.

We divided the TAT cards into two groups: Group A, from which we expected to only rarely elicit stories of violence and aggression. Group A included Cards 1, 2, 6BM, 7BM, and their Japanese versions (J6 and J7). Group B, included cards from we expected to elicit stories with violent themes more frequently. This set consisted of Cards 3BM, 4, 8BM, 13MF, and 18GF (J4, J8, J13, J18).[3]

In determining the presence of violence and aggression, we considered only stories in which there is direct mention of physical contact of a violent nature or in which there is mention of possible injury caused by physical assault. What is sometimes called "verbal aggression" in interpreting TAT stories we included in a separate general category that we termed "discord or disharmony" (see chapter 7, volume I). In line with the scoring system presented in this volume, our operational definition of "violence" in scoring TAT protocols embraced both active and passive forms. Included is explicit mention of physical assault, or injuries inflicted or incurred by the central character of the story or through some act of nature or an accident. The "hero" or protagonist of the story could be the subject of violence by others, or he or she might inflict self injury or take one's own life. Among the stories of violence, we further differentiated out stories of deliberate violence from those of accidental violence, or injury which we considered in another category (see chapter 13, volume I). We also compare the incidence of stories in which there are dreams involving violence, or the protagonist is a nonparticipant witness to violent acts (see chapter 3, volume I).

---

[3]See cards illustrated in Appendix B.

Results

In general, greater differences in violence stories are found cross-culturally between lower-class Americans and Japanese than between delinquents and non-delinquents. Some notable differences in the content of fantasy are apparent.

We noticed first that, in addition to stories of discord and violence, the cards frequently evoked stories depicting a figure in an unusual physiological state—dead or dying, suffering from illness, or under the influence of alcohol or drugs. Therefore, we used as a supplementary related differentiation a category of "unusual physiological states" in our comparison (see Table 5.1). These were combined in arriving at a total score of categories.

The American non-delinquent sample gives the *fewest* number of total stories of both categories (48 percent). The Japanese non-delinquents, in contrast, have the highest proportion of stories of both discord/violence or unusual physiological states (57 percent). The Japanese delinquents and American delinquents are intermediate, with almost identical percentages (54 percent). This larger contrast between the Japanese and American non-delinquents reaches significance on a chi-square test of significance.

Americans generally show less concern with unusual physiological or bodily states than do the Japanese. The American delinquents differ from the other samples significantly in giving the *fewest* stories of unusual physiological states.

The Americans generally gave more stories of discord or violence than did the Japanese. Thus, in general, the Japanese find it easier to depict someone as drunk, sick, or exhausted than as involved in interpersonal discord or violence. The largest differences were found between the Japanese and American delinquents. The Japanese delinquents give the *lowest* percentage of stories of discord or violence, and are significantly lower than the American delinquents in this regard. Though there are some significant statistical differences in emphasis when both of these categories are considered together, there are nevertheless remarkable cross-cultural correspondences in the type of stories given.

Table 5.2 demonstrates some interesting differences in content. The Japanese non-delinquent group was more apt to give stories of interpersonal disharmony without violence. They give almost no stories of accidental violence.

The Japanese delinquent group, compared with the Japanese non-delinquent group, shows a non-significant trend to give fewer stories of disharmony without violence and more stories of accidental violence in which no one is responsible for the mishap. The Americans as a whole, compared with the Japanese, show a significant tendency to see violent stories in the "A" group of cards that rarely elicit violent themes. Americans also see more violent stories on the cards that more readily elicit violence, so the overall tendency to give more violent stories cuts across all the TAT cards. The American groups as a whole also place greater emphasis on accidental violence.

Table 5.1

Subjects Classified by Themes of Violence or Unusual Physiological State in TAT Stories

Sample	*N*	*Total TAT Stories*	*Discord or Violence*				*Unusual Physiology State*		*Total Both Categories*	
			A Cards	*B Cards*	*Total*					
			%	%	%	N	%	N	%	N
Japanese										
non-delinq. (JN)	70	600*	9.6	55.7	34.8	209	21.8	181	56.7^	340
delinquent (JD)	82	738	7.9	51.5	32.2	236	22.6	167	53.5	403
American non-delinq. (AN)	50	450	11.0	64.0	40.2	181	11.6	52	48.2^	216
delinquent (AD)	90	772**	17.8	60.6	40.7	314	16.9	131	53.6	414
Significance (X_2)			A>J<.01 AD>JD<.05				J>A<.001 JD>AD<.01 JN>AN<.01 AD>AN<.05		AN>JN<.01	

Group A: Cards 1, 2, 6BM, 7BM (violent themes rare)
Group B: Cards 3BM, 4, 8BM, 13MF, 18GF (occasional themes of violence)
*3 stories missing on Cards 2, 3, 6, 7; 18 stories missing on Card 18
**38 stories missing on Card 8

Table 5.2

Emphasis on Discord without Violence, Compared with Deliberate Violence, and Accidental Violence in TAT Stories to A and B Cards*

	A	*B*	*Total*		*Significance (X2)*
			INTERPERSONAL DISCORD WITHOUT VIOLENCE		
Sample	%	%	%	N	A Cards JN>AN<.05
JN	7.8	13.7	11.0	66	AD>AN<.05
JD	6.4	9.0	7.9	58	
AN	4.5	9.6	7.3	33	
AD	9.7	9.9	9.8	76	
			VIOLENCE DELIBERATE		
	A	*B*	*Total*		*Total*
	%	%	%	N	A>J<.01
JN	1.8	41.3	23.5	143	AN>JN<.01 AD>JD<.05
JD	1.5	40.0	22.9	168	*A:*
AN	6.5	45.6	28.2	131	A>J<.01 AN>JN<.05
AD	7.8	43.2	26.7	207	AD>JD<.05
			ACCIDENTAL		
	A	*B*	*Total*		*Total*
	%	%	%	N	A>J<.05
JN	—	0.7	1.3	2	AN>JN<.05
JD	—	2.5	1.4	11	*B:* A>J<.01
AN	—	6.5	4.9	18	AN>JN<.01
AD	0.3	7.5	4.0	31	AD>JD<.05
			TOTAL		
	A	*B*	*Total*		*Total*
	%	%	%	N	A>J<.001 AN>AN<.001
JN	1.8	42.0	23.8	143	AD>AD<.001
JD	1.5	42.5	24.3	179	*A:* A>J<.01
AN	6.5	54.4	33.1	149	AN>JN<.01
AD	8.1	50.7	30.7	238	AD>JD<.01 *B:*
					A>J<.01 AN>JN<.01 AD>JD<.01

*Classified by Cards: Rarely Eliciting Violent Themes (A Group)
Occasionally Eliciting Violent Themes (B Group)

Table 5.3

Comparative Distribution of TAT Stories on A and B Cards Expressing Concern with Death, Illness, Drinking, and Drugs

DEATH AND ILLNESS

Sample	*A*	*B*	*Total*		*Significance (X_2)*
	%	%	%	N	
JN	4.0	10.4	7.5	45	**Total:**
JD	5.5	12.7	9.5	70	n s; **A:**
AN	11.9	31.2	.8	35	n s; **B:**
AD	7.5	11.6	9.7	75	n s

EXHAUSTION

	A	*B*	*Total*		
	%	%	%	N	**Total:** J>A<.001
JN	7.7	9.2	8.5	51	JN>AN<.001; JD>AD<.01
JD	6.1	6.8	6.5	48	**A:** J>A<.001
AN	0.5	3.6	2.2	10	JN vs AN<.01; D vs AD<.01
AD	1.1	5.8	3.6	28	**B:** J>A>.01; JN>AN>.05

DRINKING AND DRUGS

	A	*B*	*Total*		
	%	%	%	N	**Total:**
JN	1.5	9.4	5.8	35	J>A<.01
JD	0.3	11.7	6.6	49	JN>AN<.05; **B:**
AN	—	2.8	1.6	7	J>A<.001; JN>AN<.01
AD	1.7	5.3	3.6	28	JD<AD<.01

TOTAL UNUSUAL PHYSIOLOGICAL STATES

	A	*B*	*Total*		
	%	%	%	N	**Total:** J>A<.001
JN	13.2	29.0	21.8	131	JN>AN<.001; JA>AD<.001; AN>AD<.05
JD	11.9	31.2	22.6	167	**A:** JN>AN<.05
AN	8.5	14.0	11.6	52	**B:** J>A<.001
AD	10.3	22.7	16.9	131	JN>AN<.001; JD>AD<.001; JD>AD<.01

In an internal comparison of the American non-delinquent with the American delinquent there is only one significant difference. The American delinquents gave the highest number of stories of interpersonal disharmony on "A"-group cards.

This result may indicate that the delinquents are more concerned with difficulties in interpersonal relationships than their non-delinquent controls. No such difference appears in the Japanese are groups. On the contrary, it looks as if the Japanese delinquents are somewhat consciously inhibited compared with non-delinquents in that they avoid giving stories of interpersonal discord on the B-group cards that more readily elicit such stories. (The meaning of the results on Table 5.2 will be clarified when we compare the content of individual cards on subsequent tables.)

Comparing the American and Japanese groups on stories of unusual physiological states (see Table 5.3), the American non-delinquent sample, as already indicated, is lowest in all respects. The Japanese samples are especially high in stories depicting figures in a state of physical exhaustion from overwork. They are also higher than the American samples in seeing individuals under the influence of alcohol. There are very few stories about drugs (eleven stories), but they invariably appear in either the Japanese delinquent (seven stories) or American delinquent samples (three stories). The death and illness stories overall are lowest among the American non-delinquents, whereas the American delinquent resembles both Japanese samples in this respect.

On A-group cards, Japanese see significantly more exhaustion stories; in contrast, Americans are slightly more prone to see death and illness on these cards. Generalizing, one might say that Japanese are particularly likely to see figures as extremely tired or exhausted. The work ethic makes this posture an easily elicited response. On one particular picture (Card 4), which we will discuss shortly, Japanese are more apt to see individuals as belligerently drunk.

Modes of Violence

Looking in specific detail at the content of the stories of violence (see Table 5.4), we separated the plots into those where the hero is in a passive relationship to the violence depicted; those where the hero himself is the perpetrator of violence; and stories in which the violence is directed at the self or is suicidal.

Although the number of stories in each of these categories is very small, we found notable cross-cultural differences on certain cards. There was a non-significant tendency for the Japanese to see a passive hero as a victim of deliberate violence, whereas the Americans tended to see the passive hero as a victim of accidental violence. In Card 8BM, the Americans tend to see more scenes of accidental shooting whereas the Japanese see the shooting on the card as being witnessed in a dream or deliberately inflicted on a passive prone figure. However, a further part of this observed difference is shown by Card 18, in which the

Americans frequently see a person accidentally falling down the stairs. (Unfortunately, in adapting this card to Japanese houses, the stairway was taken out of the picture. We believe, therefore, that this difference in results is due to a lack of true comparability between the Cards 18GF and J18.)

There is a significant trend for the Japanese to see more suicide. The major difference between the two groups in this regard occurs because the Japanese delinquents see suicide on Card 18 much more than do the other groups. These are suicides usually of a *distraught but responsible mother with a delinquent child*. The Japanese non-delinquents tend to see suicide of women on Cards 3 and 13, sometimes due to rejection by a lover, sometimes due to illness or to some act of self-sacrifice—all Japanese themes. The Americans in 16 instances see suicide on Card 3 resulting from being rejected by a lover. This is a higher total than noticed in other American samples.

Looking at other differences, card by card, we note that the American groups on Card 3 show a significant tendency to see an individual who has just committed *an impulsive act of violence* or is contemplating such an act. On Card 4, in contrast, the Japanese groups tend to give slightly more violent stories. The Japanese samples differ significantly from the Americans in seeing a hero who initiates violence, very often in response to a personal insult. In Card 8, while there is no overall difference, we have already noted a non-significant tendency for the Japanese to depict a victim of deliberate violence, while the Americans see accidental violence. On Card 13 there is a very great difference between the American and Japanese stories. The Americans are much more apt to see this card, which is often depicted as a sexual scene, as involving not only sex, but violence. The Japanese non-delinquents, in contrast, often see a woman committing suicide on this card.

Table 5.4
Distribution of the Incidence and Modes of Violence in Group B TAT Cards

Card	**3BM**				**4**				**8BM**			
Sample	*JN*	*JD*	*AN*	*AD*	*JN*	*JD*	*AN*	*AD*	*JN*	*JD*	*AN*	*AD*
Total N	70	82	50	90	70	82	50	90	52	82	50	90
Non-Violent Stories	59	31	82	70	63	34	53	44	16	18	35	20
Total Violence	15	11	19	31	26	29	16	27	32	47	32	30
%	*21*	*13*	*38*	*34*	*37*	*35*	*32*	*30*	*61*	*57*	*64*	*70*
Passive Hero												
Deliberate	2	—	—	—	3	—	—	—	8	6	3	6
Accidental	5	—	—	2	—	1	—	1	—	3	5	5
Dreamed	3	2	—	—	5	—	—	—	6	8	1	4
Witnessed	6	—	—	—	2	2	—	1	2	8	6	6
Active Hero												
Accidental	—	—	—	—	—	—	—	—	2	6	4	6
Dreamed or imagined	—	—	—	—	—	—	—	—	3	2	2	1
Deliberate	1	1	8	15	23	27	11	22	11	14	11	8
Self-Directed												
Suicide	12	3	6	10	—	—	—	—	—	—	—	—
Card	**13(MF-J13)**				**18(GF-J18)**				**Total**			
Sample	*JN*	*JD*	*AN*	*AD*	*JN*	*JD*	*AN*	*AD*	*JN*	*JD*	*AN*	*AD*
Total N	70	82	50	90	67	82	50	90	328	410	250	412
Non-Violent Stories	47	60	16	49	25	17	15	16	190	236	114	203
Total Violence	23	22	34	41	42	65	35	74	138	174	136	209
%	*33*	*27*	*68*	*45*	*68*	*79*	*70*	*82*	*42*	*43*	*54*	*51*
Passive Hero												
Deliberate	2	—	—	—	3	—	—	—	8	6	3	6
Accidental	5	—	—	2	—	1	—	1	—	3	5	5
Dreamed	3	2	—	—	5	—	—	—	6	8	1	4
Witnessed	6	—	—	—	2	2	—	1	2	8	6	6
Active Hero												
Accidental	—	—	—	—	—	—	—	—	2	6	4	6
Dreamed or imagined	—	—	—	—	—	—	—	—	3	2	2	1
Deliberate	1	1	8	15	23	27	11	22	11	14	11	8
Self-Directed												
Suicide	11	3	—	3	1	15	2	—	24	21	8	13
%									*7.4*	*5*	*3.2*	*3.1*

Overall: Significance trends: accidental A>J; deliberate J>A

Active Hero:	C18 J>A<.001; C3 A>J>.001; C13 A>J>.001; C4 J>A .05
Total Active:	A>J<.001; JN>AN<.05
Self-Directed:	C18 JD>JN<.01; C3 JN>JD>.05; C13 JN>JD>.05
Tot. Self-Directed:	J>A<.001; JN>AN<.01; JD>AD<.05
Passive Hero:	C18 J>A<.001
Tot. Violence:	C18 D>N<.05; C3 A>J<.001; C13 A>J<.001 C3 AD>JD<.05; C13 AN>JN<.05; C13 AN>AD<.05

On Card 18 we find a very significant internal difference between the Japanese delinquents and non-delinquents. The Japanese delinquents almost exclusively see either an act of choking (often the choking of a child) followed by suicide, whereas the Japanese non-delinquents are apt to see this card as an affectionate relationship (we infer this to indicate the Japanese delinquent's readiness to perceive a responsible distraught mother, and the presence of some guilt toward a mother on the part of the delinquent). This is one of the most notable differences between delinquent and non-delinquent groups in the results.

The American delinquents also see a higher incidence of committing suicide because of illness or sexual rejection, and the Japanese delinquents are more apt to see the suicide of a distraught mother. In general, the Japanese non-delinquents are more apt to see women committing suicide because of illness of sexual rejection, and the delinquents are more apt to see the suicide of a distraught mother.

Of the American subjects, the American delinquents more often depict Card 18 as a situation of deliberate aggression. This card does show overall differences between delinquent and non-delinquent samples. Non-delinquents are more apt to see affection in this card, whereas delinquents, whether Japanese or Americans, are more apt to see aggression.

In summary, generally, in comparing American delinquents and non delinquents, there is less likely to be any differences on the four other cards that ordinarily elicit scenes of violence. Rather, as far as sensitivity to aggression is concerned, we see that the American delinquents are more apt to see aggression on cards that rarely elicit such themes: a boy with a violin (Card 1), a farm scene (Card 2), a mother-son (Card 6), or father-son (Card 7) situation. However, the delinquent sample is not apt to see Card 18, a figure with hands on the throat of another, as an affectionate interchange between a mother and daughter.

Interpersonal Relationships Depicted in the Context of Violence

Cross-cultural differences are quite apparent when one compares the interpersonal roles of those seen in stories of violence (see Table 5.5). The Americans, in contrast to the Japanese, tend to give significantly more stories of extra-familial relationships, whereas the Japanese, especially the Japanese delinquents, depict parental relationships or peer-group and friend relationships in the five B cards.

Almost one-half of all the stories given by the Japanese delinquents depict some act of violence inflicted by a parent upon a child. Most often such acts result from a child's "bad" behavior. The most notable difference in respect to parental relationships is found on Card 18. Almost one-fourth of the stories of violence by the Japanese delinquents are seen as occurring between a mother and child. Also, almost unique to the Japanese delinquents are scenes of a father violently castigating a child.

It is also only the lower-class Japanese youth who see a wife strangling or otherwise violently attacking her husband. Such stories are not given by Americans.

On Card 18 jealousy is a frequent theme. Japanese see two women in a scene of violence, very often produced by sexual jealousy over a man. In American delinquents this is the theme given in almost half of their stories contrasted with American non-delinquents among whom the theme appears in less than a third of their stories.

On Card 4 and on Card 13, the Americans are very apt to see a man attacking a woman with whom he has a sexual relationship. The Japanese are much less apt to see violence on Card 13. On Card 4, when Japanese suggest violence it is between two men rather than between a man and a woman. Interestingly enough, some stories in the Japanese sample see a woman inflicting violence on a man and then committing suicide. Such stories are nonexistent in the American samples. Uniquely prominent among the Japanese delinquents are stories of peer-group or gang violence. These appear on both Cards 4 and 8.

In sum, on interpersonal cards the context of violence for the Japanese tends to be familial, marital, peer or gang, while for the Americans violence tends to be between a husband and wife or an unrelated man and woman. The Japanese concern with violence, especially in the delinquent groups, sees the parent capable of violent chastisement of an unruly or wayward child. This is seen as an extreme act of responsibility on the part of the distraught parent. A wife is also depicted as capable of choking a wayward husband. This is a class-related theme in Japan. In our previous normative studies on the Japanese such themes occurred only in a lower-status fishing village and did not appear among middle-class farmers (see chapter 4, volume II, above). Japanese women are not as apt to be depicted as mild or self-sacrificing among these lower-class youth, either delinquent or non-delinquent. But the delinquent youth emphatically see the mother of a bad child as potentially distraught, angry, and possibly violent.

Motives Depicted as Underlying Expressions of Violence and Aggression

In about 80 percent of their stories the Japanese showed specific concern with motives prior to the acts of violence depicted. This contrasts with the finding that in less than two-thirds of the American stories are any motives specified for the violence depicted. (See Table 5.6 for the distribution of the motives cited.) The Americans are more apt to give stories of accidental violence.

Table 5.5
Interpersonal Relationships Depicted in the Context of Violence in Group B TAT Cards

Sample	*JN*	*JD*	*AN*	*AD*	*JN*	*JD*	*AN*	*AD*	*JN*	*JD*	*AN*	*AD*
Parental	**3BM**				**4**				**8BM-J8**			
Mo to Dau	—	—	1	—	—	—	—	—	—	—	—	—
Mo to Son	—	—	—	—	—	—	—	—	—	—	—	—
Fa to child	—	1	3	4	—	—	—	4	—	1	8	7
Total	—	1	4	4	—	—	—	4	—	1	8	7
	13MF-J13				**18GF-J18**				**X2**			
Mo to Dau	—	—	—	—	15	22	11	15	Total:		J<A<.01	JD>AD<.001
Mo to Son	—	—	—	—	7	8	—	2	C8:Fa-child			J>A<.001
Fa to child	—	—	—	—	1	9	—	1	C18:Mo-son			J>A<.001
									C18:Fa-son			JD>AD<.01
Total	—	—	—	—	23	39	11	18	C18:Fa-son			JN>JD<.01
Marital	**3BM**				**4**				**8BM-J8**			
Husb to wife	—	—	—	—	—	1	5	6	—	—	1	—
Wife to Husb	2	2	2	5	—	—	—	—	—	—	—	—
Total	2	2	2	5	—	1	5	6	—	—	1	—
	13MF-J13				**18GF-J18**				**X2**			
Husb to wife	1	3	7	6	—	—	—	1	C4:hus-wife			J>A<.001
Wife to Husb	—	—	—	—	6	9	1	2	C8:Hus-wife			J>A<.001
									C18:wife-hus			J>A<.05
Total	1	3	7	6	6	9	1	3				
Extramarital, Unrelated	**3BM**				**4**				**8BM-J8**			
Man to wo	—	—	1	—	—	—	6	18	1	1	—	—
Wo to Man	7	4	3	2	—	—	4	1	—	—	—	—
Man to man	—	—	—	1	20	15	1	1	7	4	13	16
Wo to wo	—	—	—	—	—	—	—	—	—	—	—	—
Total	7	4	4	3	20	15	11	20	8	5	13	16
	13MF-J13				**18GF-J18**				**X2**			
Man to wo	8	16	27	34	—	1	1	1	Total:			J>A<.001
												JN>AN<.001
Wo to man	—	—	—	—	—	2	4	5				JD>AD<.001
Man to man	—	—	—	—	—	—	1	—	Cards 4 and 13:			
Wo to wo	—	—	—	—	10	7	15	44			man to wo	J>A<.001
									C3:wo to man			J>A<.001
Total	8	16	27	35	10	10	21	50	C18:wo to wo			J>A<.001
Peers and others	**3BM**				**4**				**8BM-J8**			
Friends	—	—	—	—	—	—	—	—	1	8	—	2
Gang	—	—	—	—	—	—	—	—	5	8	1	3
Other	6	4	—	—	6	5	—	1	18	25	9	8
	13MF-J13				**18GF-J18**				**X2**			
Friends	—	—	—	—	—	—	—	—	Total:			J>A<.001
Gang	—	—	—	—	—	1	—	—	Cards 4 and 8:			J>A<.001
Other	14	3	—	—	2	7	1	3				JN>JD<.05

Table 5.6

Motives Depicted as Underlying the Expressions of Violence and Aggression

Card	**3BM**				**4**				**8BM**			
Sample	*JN*	*JD*	*AN*	*AD*	*JN*	*JD*	*AN*	*AD*	*JN*	*JD*	*AN*	*AD*
Total N	70	82	50	90	70	82	50	90	52	82	50	90
Economic	3	2	—	—	—	1	2	2	—	5	1	1
Loss of love object	5	3	2	2	—	—	—	2	—	2	—	—
Jealousy	1	1	—	1	7	6	3	2	—	—	1	—
Revenge	—	—	—	—	7	4	2	4	1	6	1	2
Discord and impulse	2	2	3	2	8	11	5	2	4	6	1	2
Parent authority	1	1	1	5	—	—	—	—	2	1	1	2
Self defense	—	—	—	—	—	—	—	2	—	—	—	3
Madness	—	—	—	1	—	1	—	2	2	1	—	—
Accident (include war)	—	2	—	—	—	1	—	2	—	1	11	19
Unspecified	3	2	11	20	4	5	4	9	19	17	13	14
Card	**13**				**18**				**Total %**			
Sample	*JN*	*JD*	*AN*	*AD*	*JN*	*JD*	*AN*	*AD*	*JN*	*JD*	*AN*	*AD*
Total N	70	82	50	90	70	82	50	90	52	82	50	90
Economic	3	1	—	—	2	11	1	7	5.8	11.4	2.9	4.8*
Loss of love object	7	11	11	16	—	—	1	—	8.7	9.7	9.6	9.6
Jealousy	3	5	5	—	5	5	7	17	11.6	9.7	11.8	9.6
Revenge	1	—	—	—	1	3	2	3	7.3	7.5	3.7	4.3
Discord and impulse	1	1	2	5	3	4	1	10	13.0	13.7	8.8	10.0
Parent authority	2	—	—	—	21	30	3	5	19.0	18.0	3.7	5.7
Self defense	—	—	—	—	1	1	—	1	.7	.5	—	2.9
Madness	—	—	—	3	7	6	2	—	6.5	4.6	1.5	2.9
Accident (include war)	—	—	—	—	—	—	—	—	2.9	5.8	20.6	15.8
Unspecified	6	3	15	17	2	3	8	13	24.7	18.8	37.4	34.4

X2				
Economic	Total:	J>A<.05		
Jealousy			**Card 18**: A>J<.05	
Interpersonal	Total:	J>A<.05	**Cards 4 and 8**: J>A<.05, JD>AD<.05 **Card 18**: AD>AN	
Parental Control	Total:	J>A<.001	**Card 18**: J>A<.001	
Madness	Total:	J>A<.05	**Card 8**: A>J<.01	
Accident	Total:	A>J<.001		
Unspecified	Total:	A>J<.001	**Card 18**: A>J<.01	**Card 3**: A>J<.01

The Japanese, especially the Japanese delinquents, are apt to see economic distress as a motive for violence. This is characteristic of the stories given to Cards 8 and 18 by the Japanese delinquents. Loss of a love object as a reason for violence does not differentiate among any of the groups; however, jealousy is a particularly sensitive motive for the American delinquents, especially on Card 18. Revenge is somewhat more apt to be seen as a motive by Japanese than by Americans, but the trends do not reach significance. Unplanned, impulsive violence resulting from previous interpersonal tension is more characteristic of the Japanese than of the American stories. Such stories appear most frequently on Cards 4 and 8. As we have already indicated, tensions over parental control and authority resulting in violence are a very strong differentiation between the Japanese and American samples. On Card 18 the Japanese are also more apt than Americans to see a mentally distraught situation leading to violence.

Consequences or Aftermath of Violence

Not only are the Japanese more prone to be concerned with the prior motives of violence, they are also more concerned with the aftermath or consequences of violence (see Table 5.7). The Japanese, especially the Japanese delinquents, more often show what can be called a superego reaction to violence. They depict some form of guilt, self-punishment, mental derangement, or summoning outside authority after a violent act. The greatest difference between Japanese and Americans in this regard is found in Cards 8 and 18GF. The Japanese delinquents on Card 18GF are more apt than any other group to indicate a future reconciliation after violence. American delinquents are more apt than non-delinquents to see reconciliation or separation as an interpersonal result of violence. Our impression, prior to the testing, that the Japanese more often than Americans would summon authority or would see arrest following violence was not substantiated by our findings. No significant differences occurred in this regard. In general, comparing both the motives for aggression and the aftermath of aggression, we note a greater sense of past, present, and future in the Japanese stories of violence than in the American stories, which are more apt to concentrate solely on the violence itself rather than on its motives or its consequences.

Table 5.7
Consequences or Aftermath of Violence Depicted in Group B TAT Cards

Sample	*JN*	*JD*	*AN*	*AD*	*JN*	*JD*	*AN*	*AD*	*JN*	*JD*	*AN*	*AD*
Card	**3BM**				**4**				**8**			
N	70	82	50	90	70	82	50	90	70	82	50	90
Card	**13**				**18**				**Total**			
N	70	82	50	90	67	82	50	90	347	410	250	450
Super Ego Reactions												
Card	**3BM**				**4**				**8**			
Guilt	4	5	2	5	2	2	—	—	7	9	3	3
Self punishment	—	2	1	1	—	—	—	—	—	—	1	—
Mentally deranged	1	—	—	1	—	—	—	—	1	—	1	—
Authority summoned	—	2	—	—	—	2	—	—	1	4	1	1
Total	5	9	3	7	2	4	—	—	9	13	6	4
Card	**13**				**18**				**Total %**			
Guilt	5	6	7	11	7	3	—	—				
Self punishment	1	2	—	2	4	13	1	—				
Mentally deranged	5	3	—	—	1	3	2	—				
Authority summoned	5	7	6	5	1	3	2	1				
Total	16	18	13	18	13	22	5	1	32.6	37.8	19.8	14.4
X2	Total: J>A<.001; JD>AD<.001; JN>AN<.01 Guilt and self punishment: JD>AD<.01; JN>JD<.05								Card 18: J>A<.01			
Reactions Related to Others												
Card	**3BM**				**4**				**8**			
Reconciliation	—	—	1	3	—	7	5	3	—	1	1	2
Separation	1	—	1	1	1		—	1	—	—	—	1
Escape authority	1	—	4	1	1	—	—	1	2	1	—	2
Arrest by authority	—	—	—	5	—	1	2	5	3	7	4	2
Total	2	—	6	10	2	8	7	10	5	9	5	7
Card	**13**				**18**				**Total %**			
Reconciliation	—	—	—	3								
Separation	—	—	—	1								
Escape authority	1	1	4	1								
Arrest by authority	—	—	7	5								
Total	1	1	11	10					16.6	20.5	25	27.2
X2	Related to others: J>A<.05				Card 13 Arrest by authority: J>A<.01							
Other, Unspecified												
Card	**3BM**				**4**				**8**			
N	8	2	10	14	8	17	9	19	18	25	21	25
Card	**13**				**18**				**Total**			
N	6	3	10	10	18	25	25	54	58	72	75	122
Total Violent Stories												
Card	**3BM**				**4**				**8**			
N	15	11	19	31	26	29	16	27	32	47	32	36
Card	**13**				**18**				**Total**			
N	23	22	34	41	42	65	35	74	138	174	136	209

Discussion and Conclusions

To summarize our results, comparing the four samples we note that the greatest differences occur cross-culturally. Different cultural factors differentiate American delinquents from Japanese delinquents in their responses. Card 18 consistently acts as the best differentiation of delinquent and non-delinquent groups.

While we noted a number of differentiating trends with respect to delinquents vs. non-delinquents, in no instance did we find the very strong dissimilarities that have been reported in previous American TAT tests of institutionalized delinquents and non-delinquent controls. We conclude that social-class dissimilarities are far more overriding than has been acknowledged in much of the previous research using the TAT.

At the time we were completing our own work Arnold Buss (1961) had already attempted a systematic review of the use of the TAT in the study of aggression. There is no need to recapitulate here except to indicate certain impressions of some of the studies he considered as they related to our particular findings.

Researchers attempting to identify violent propensities by means of the TAT have disagreed over whether one should use special cards or the standard TAT cards. We chose in 1960 to use the standard cards, but we had already obtained normative sample of Japanese with the cards used and we could make a more direct comparison between various groups already tested. Clinically, the Murray set had been regularly applied by clinical psychologists in psycho-diagnostic work. As for the particular cards used, it became apparent that there were, indeed, particular instances where the production of a story of violence was diagnostically significant. For example, for Card 1, only in the American delinquent group were there, at this time, stories of someone trying to break the violin.[4] A story that stood out as a clear indicator of a delinquent's special concern with violence was the story for Card 1 in which the face of the boy was interpreted as having been smashed in. Such extremely subjective themes are rare and cannot be treated in any statistically meaningful way in comparing groups.

In spite of such individual findings, our work generally has not sustained many of the conclusions of previous studies reported in the literature. Our concern with cultural background factors has made us particularly question studies that have been done without control samples drawn from the very same population and background. A number of studies have made no systematic attempt to consider the social class and environment of the control sample as carefully as the delinquent sample. Illustrative of the types of conclusions that we were unable to confirm are those reported by F. M. Young (1956). He states that the delinquents he tested were

[4]It is disconcerting to have reported to me that the deliberate breaking of the violin is appearing in some responses of normative tests being taken in American elementary and secondary school samples of the 1990s.

unduly concerned with death or injury or accident to the father in two-thirds of the stories for given cards of the standard TAT. In our own sample we found no such sharp differentiation between delinquents and non-delinquents in regard to stories on any cards, nor did such themes appear with the frequency reported by Young. Secondly, he reports that delinquents were concerned with an undesirable environment, economic stress, and other problems. Again we find no differentiation between delinquents and non-delinquent Americans from comparable lower-class backgrounds. We find further (anticipating future reports) that achievement themes and themes of adequacy and inadequacy do not markedly differentiate the delinquent from the non-delinquent, nor are delinquents particularly apt to give more unhappy endings than non-delinquents. It is our impression that what is attributed to a supposed specifically delinquent subculture is often an aspect of a more general lower-class subculture that produces a large number of delinquents.

Careful examination of the control samples used by certain studies reveals severe weaknesses in comparability. For example, there is the study by S. Fujita (1959), of thirty delinquent Japanese boys aged fifteen to nineteen in a juvenile detention home, by means of the TAT. As controls, Fujita used students in an in-service class for internal revenue clerks, no doubt a very select group of lower-status in individuals and not really comparable in background with his delinquent subjects. True, many of the TAT stories reported by Fujita did resemble stories found in our own delinquent Japanese sample, but their supposed significant uniqueness is not borne out in comparing them with our lower-class control sample. Especially questionable are such statements as "The delinquents have an inferior self-image." Our data do not distinguish between delinquent and non-delinquent samples in self-image.

Another difficulty in comparing studies is that studies differ in the ages of their subjects. In our normative work with TAT samples we find marked differences in results with different age-groups. The Rorschach test gives fairly consistent results for Japanese samples beyond the age of twenty (De Vos and Boyer, 1989). But the TAT, in a normative Japanese sample of over 800 subjects that we tested, produced stories that varied, in content and identification of the subject with particular figures in the story, for each age group.

The follow-up longitudinal study of Symonds and Jensen (1958) reports differences in the stories of adults as compared with their earlier testing thirteen years before, when they were adolescents. They found that individuals who showed aggressive themes in adolescence were frequently inhibited behaviorally. However, by more than chance frequency at a later stage of development, they manifested overt aggression in various ways. Their results suggest that in certain cases the thematic expressions of aggression have tapped latent aggressive trends that could only come to the level of social behavior with opportunity at a later date.

Such a finding counters the theoretical point of view that the relation between thematic and behavioral aggression is an inverse one rather than a direct one. This theory has been stated in some studies that use what is termed a "drainage" theory of fantasy.

The aggressive themes found in the non-delinquent cultural samples in our study may point to the presence of a latent but greater potential for future overt aggression in lower-class than in middle-class youth. There is considerable evidence in other research that there is greater expression of manifest aggression in lower-class individuals than in middle-class individuals. We might cite as an example of this class differential the reports of Jurgen Ruesch (1950), which demonstrate that lower-class people have a much higher proportion of physical accidents, injuries from fights, etc., than middle-class individuals. Many of these accidents and injuries, however, are not officially adjudicated, so the individual does not acquire a criminal record. One must remember, in comparing delinquents and non-delinquents from particular populations, that our classification is limited by the fact that there is an adjudication record in some cases but not in others. This does not imply any difference in the expression of aggression, just that violence can occur without anyone getting into trouble. In our society, the middle-class person is subject to more severe social sanctions by peers for the direct expression of violence than are lower-class individuals. Expectations related to class status differentiate what is condoned and not condoned. Individuals of working-class origin to whom mobility toward higher status becomes important tend to move toward greater inhibition of aggression.

One of the most systematic, well-controlled studies relating delinquent aggressive behavior to family variables is that of Bandura and Walters (1959). Their sample consisted of lower-middle-class whites, intact families living in areas with low rates of delinquency. They demonstrated that aggressive behavior is selectively related to certain developmental experiences within the primary family. However, careful as this study was, one cannot generalize from it to lower-class groups who, for example, form at least 85 percent of the institutionalized delinquents in the state of California. A number of professionals working with delinquents have expressed the view that the middle-class delinquents found in a prison tend to have more noticeable emotional disturbances than the much larger population of lower-class delinquents similarly institutionalized. We therefore believe that whatever one finds in the way of systematic differences between the expression of aggression or of the relation of aggression to delinquency in middle-class subjects could not be directly applied to the lower class.

Purcell's study (1956) shows the limitations of a study that does not control class difference between delinquent and non-delinquent groups. We could find no substantiation in our results for his finding that the proportion of internal punishment to fantasy aggression is much larger for his non-antisocial group by $p < .0001$. Another hypothesis that he believed was supported by his data was that the anticipation of internal punishment is a more potent deterrent to anti-social behavior than is the anticipation of external punishment. Again, this is not confirmed in our study when we hold class constant. Purcell's incidental finding that the antisocial subjects were more direct in their expression of fantasy aggression than controls is contradicted by our data: our delinquents gave slightly fewer stories of direct violence on the part of the hero of the story. That we found a higher incidence of aggression and witnessed violence on cards not usually used for aggressive themes suggests that the delinquent, preoccupied with feelings of violence within, seeks to deflect from himself the responsibility for initiating violent behavior. In some instances the delinquent seems to have a paranoid type of defense, blaming the hostile outer environment for his behavior, or he perceives the external environment as filled with hostility, rationalizing his behavior as a defensive adjustment to a hostile world.

But according to our data such a generalization cannot be limited to the delinquent sample; rather, it probably applies to all lower-class youth. There is some suggestion of less realistically induced hostile or violent responses to cards that suggest it. Thus, rather than distance or remoteness from aggression being a criterion, it seems more likely that realistic answers to aggressive stimuli are counter-diagnostic to delinquency, while the use of inappropriate stimuli to project hostile or violent behavior is more positively diagnostic. The fact that such reversals occur only in a minority of the subjects tested does not lessen the potential for diagnostic significance. Purcell (1956) correctly points out that in interviews there is a marked tendency for antisocial subjects to justify their aggressive reactions by pointing to the harsh treatment imposed upon them by others. He states, "If the antisocial individuals can prove that the world is against them, there is no need to recognize any obligations to others. The very fact that they so frequently find it necessary to resort to this projection technique argues that the delinquent ego is busily engaged in disposing of still existing remnants of guilt." Purcell further correctly suggests that "one of the implications of this state of affairs is that general policy of retaliation only reinforces this defensive maneuver and makes it easier for the delinquent to pursue his antisocial course on a guilt-free basis.

It seems that such contentions may be valid, but it is hard to demonstrate radical differences between lower-class delinquent and non-delinquent youth to support them. Our comparison of delinquent and non-delinquent subjects showed no essential difference in the tendency to internalize. It seems more likely that there are certain constituents of behavioral control, not directly reflected in projective materials, that differentiate the delinquent and the non-delinquent. We must remember that lower-class social circumstances and one's individual history help determine why one person becomes delinquent and another does not. Certain individuals live in an environment that is more inducing of social attitudes leading to delinquency as a more probable outcome of an internal state of tension, whereas other individuals, due to situational supports, are spared the stresses that induce some to delinquency. The same caveat applies to testing for the incidence of mental illness with diagnostic techniques in a normal population. It is obvious that some individuals suffering no manifest breakdown do not differ in personality or in strength of internal controls from individuals who have manifested a psychotic relapse. One must distinguish between a potential for ego disruption and situational social circumstances either causing stress or helping an individual surmount internal weaknesses of adjustive structure.

Our results from our comparative study indicate that, holding other things constant, we would presume that in the lower class there are more stories of aggression and aggressive behavior than in the middle class. It is quite another matter to attempt to differentiate within the lower class itself, between those who are "delinquent" to the degree of being in an institution, and those who have no such adjudicated record of delinquency.

Finally, one may ask what we have gained by a cross-cultural comparison of Japanese and American lower-class youth? It should be apparent, first that cross cultural comparisons of emic interpersonal concerns can be conducted on groups that demonstrate differences in nuances that are culturally relevant. The problem is to find a method of scoring and categorization that can capture these differences in an objective manner that remains true to what is verbally expressed by the subjects being compared.

Specifically, judging from fantasies of violence, the Japanese show somewhat less overall concern about violence than do Americans, but there are not the great dissimilarities that some people would imagine. The most striking differences are ones that have already emerged in our previous research on Japanese culture: for example, even lower-class Japanese youth compared with other cultural groups are concerned with behavior and its consequences, over a longer time span. Past causality and future consequences appear more often in Japanese stories, whether they are causal patterns explaining stories of violence and their consequences, or what eventuates in other social circumstances.

Lower-class Japanese, more than Americans, see the context of their problems within either parental or peer role relationships. Americans are more concerned with violence, at least in heterosexual situations. Some of the further cultural nuances found in these stories cannot be captured in a chapter geared more to quantitative demonstration. We would therefore say as a final note that quantification creates objectivity but it does not permit as direct an experience of cultural differences as does an actual reading of the content of fantasies, as demonstrated in other chapters of this volume. Culturally nuanced content can be related specifically to negative concerns such as violence, or as we have discussed in the previous chapters, to positively considered achievement or self-fulfillment viewed from within the total context of a cultural ethos such as the Japanese.

References

Aichhorn, August. 1935. *Wayward Youth*. New York: Viking Press.

Bandura, Albert and Richard Walters. 1959. *Adolescent Aggression*. New York: Ronald Press.

Bennet, Ivy Lee. 1960. *Delinquent and Neurotic Children*. New York: Basic Books.

Buss, Arnold H. 1961. *The Psychology of Aggression*. New York: John Wiley and Sons.

De Vos, George A. 1967. The Japanese Adolescent Delinquent in a Period of Social Change. *East West Center Review*. University of Hawaii, **4**(2): 35–53.

———. 1969. Parental Interaction and Delinquency Formation. . . . Some Perspectives from Japan. *The Young Adult.* Des Plaines, Ill.: Forest Hospital Guest Lecture Series. pp. 47–72.

———. 1973. *Socialization for Achievement: Essays on the Cultural Psychology of the Japanese.* Berkeley, Calif.: University of California Press.

———. 1980. Delinquency and Minority Status: A Psychocultural Perspective (Chapter 6). In Graeme Newman (Ed.), *Crime and Deviancy: A Comparative Perspective* (pp. 130–180). Beverly Hills, Calif.: Sage Publications.

De Vos, George A. and Orin Borders. 1979. A Rorschach Comparison of Delinquent and Non-Delinquent Japanese Family Members. *Journal of Psychological Anthropology*, **2**(4): 425–442.

De Vos, George A. and L. Bryce Boyer. 1989. *Symbolic Analysis Cross-Culturally: The Rorschach Test.* Berkeley, Calif.: University of California Press.

De Vos, George A. and Eiji Murakami. 1974. Chapter 12: Violence and Aggression in Fantasy: A Comparison of American and Japanese Lower-Class Youth. In William Lebra (Ed.), *Youth, Socialization and Mental Health.* Honolulu: U. of Hawaii Press.

De Vos, George A. and Hiroshi Wagatsuma. 1969. Minority Status and Delinquency in Japan. In William Caudill and Tsung-yi-Lin (Eds.), *Mental Health Research in Asia and the Pacific* (pp. 342–357). Honolulu: East-West Center Press.

———. 1972. Family Life and Delinquency: Some Perspectives from Japanese Research. In William P. Lebra (Ed.), *Trans-cultural Research in Mental Health* (pp. 59–87). Honolulu: University of Hawaii Press.

Fujita, S. 1959. TAT with Delinquents. *Psychological Diagnosis Series*, 3, 255–267. Tokyo: Nakayama Books [in Japanese].

Mizushima, Keiichi and George De Vos. 1967. An Application of the California Psychological Inventory in a Study of Japanese Delinquency. *Journal of Social Psychology*, **71**: 45–51.

Purcell, K. 1956. The TAT and Anti-Social Behavior. *Journal of Consulting Psychology*, **20**: 448–456.

Redl, Fritz and David Wineman. 1957. *The Aggressive Child.* Glencoe, Ill.: Free Press.

Ruesch, J. 1950. Social Technique, Social Status, and Social Change in Illness. In Clyde Kluckhohn and Henry A. Murray (Eds.), *Personality in Nature, Society, and Culture.* New York: Alfred A. Knopf.

Symonds, P.M., and A.R. Jensen. 1958. The Predictive Significance of Fantasy. *American Journal of Orthopsychiatry*, **28**: 73–84.

Wagatsuma, Hiroshi and George A. De Vos. 1984. *Heritage of Endurance: Family Patterns and Delinquency Formation in Urban Japan.* Berkeley: University of California Press.

Young, F.M. 1956. Responses of Juvenile Delinquents to the TAT. *Journal of General Psychology*, **88**: 251–259.

Chapter 6

Internalized Achievement: Some Historical Continuities Found in Japanese Social Perception

George A. De Vos

Generational Changes: TAT Research in the 1980s with Japanese and Japanese Americans

As noted in volume I, George De Vos started research with psychological tests of the Japanese working with Caudill in the late 1940s (De Vos, 1951; Caudill, 1952; Caudill and De Vos, 1956). In 1953, he initiated a large-scale sample of Japanese from three villages and two cities obtained in Japan in the collaborative work with a team at Nagoya National University (De Vos, 1960, 1973) he continued further comparative work focusing on delinquency formation in the 1960s (Wagatsuma and De Vos, 1984). It has therefore been possible to do some historical comparison of TAT protocols over a period of some forty years. What is interesting to examine in these various materials are some normative continuities and changes that occur in social perception in youthful members of the society of Japan itself, and in Japanese migrants who become ethnic minorities in North and South America.

In exploring many possible themes, we have been most involved with using the TAT for better understanding the achievement motivation of youthful Japanese living both in the United States and Japan. In the present chapter we draw most upon the work of two sets of more recent research materials obtained by John

Connor and Curtis Vaughn gathered as part of their comparative research in Japan and the United States in the 1970s and 1980s.

Herein we shall examine in a comparative context the results on Card 1 presented on the tables of Connor and Vaughn to illustrate how the scoring system and a more detailed examination of content bring out further significant cultural differences between groups and subgroups related to ethnic background. A comparison of our studies demonstrates clearly the continuity of internalized preoccupation with self-motivated achievement in groups of Japanese ancestry in the United States as well as in Japan itself. Our TAT material reflects not only cultural continuity, but also some change in social attitudes that can occur with time in a particular society such as the Japanese. The work in Brazil in the 1990s, reported below in chapter 8, volume II further supports how self-initiated achievement persists generationally among the Japanese migrants to Brazil.

A Comparison of Continuity and Change in Samples of Japanese and American Youth by John Connor

Table 6.1 briefly summarizes the responses to TAT Card 1, "The Boy with the Violin," obtained by John Connor from 127 American college students, forty-five Japanese-American college students, and eighty-three Japanese college students. The data on American college students were collected in the fall of 1983 and in the spring and fall of 1984, on the American high school students in the fall of 1984, on the Japanese Americans over a five-year period from the late 1970s to 1984, and on the Japanese students at Gakuin University and Kyushu University in 1981. In analyzing the hundreds of stories told to Card 1, Connor found that they could be classified into two major categories: *achievement-non-achievement* and *authority-rebellion* concerns in response to parental pressure.

The principle themes he differentiated were: Positive self-initiated achievement, Achievement to please others, Reluctant achievement, Escape into fantasy, Authority and rebellion, and "Other." Positive achievement refers to those stories which describe the boy practicing the violin largely because of his own volition and possibly dreaming of becoming a great violinist some day. Included in this category, but not separated out by Connor, as we shall discuss below, are a number of nuanced stories involving doubts about present or future competence or ability. "Escape into fantasy" refers to those inactive themes in which there is neither active achieving nor rebelling, but some form of day-dreaming about a future.

Table 6.1

Responses to TAT Card 1 in American and Japanese College Students

College Students	American			Japanese American			Kyushu Japanese		
Tot. Responses	*M*	*F*	*Total*	*M*	*F*	*Total*	*M*	*F*	*Total*
	65	62	127	15	30	45	36	47	83
Principal themes:									
Positive Achievement (sometimes despite concerns with competence)	11	2	13 (10%)	2	5	7 (15%)	10	8	18 (22%)
Motives Questioned or Reluctant Achievement	21	17	38 (30%)	5	8	13 (29%)	6	9	15 (18%)
Inactivity or Daydreaming Fantasy	7	9	16 (13%)	1	3	4 (9%)	1	2	3 (7%)
Authority or parental presence in the stories:									
Compliance: Achievement to Please Others	8	6	14 (11%)	3	9	12 (27%)	4	13	17 (20%)
Rebellion	17	22	39 (31%)	4	5	9 (20%)	9	8	17 (20%)
Other	1	6	7 (4%)	0	0	0	7	6	13 (16%)

A glance at Connor's Table 6.1 discloses that the American and Japanese styles of achievement concerns numerically can be clustered into two major areas. In the American sample per se, they saw self-initiated positive achievement in 10 percent of the stories and reluctant resolutions toward achievement in 30 percent of their stories. Achievement, initially compliant to please others accounted for 11 percent, while rebellion themes were reported by 30 percent. Of the remaining two categories, "Escape into Fantasy" accounted for 12.5 percent, and "Other" accounted for 5 percent of the total. There are 52 percent of themes in which achievement is involved positively or negatively This was in marked contrast to only 24 percent achievement themes Connor (1977) recorded among college students at California State University at Sacramento in the early 1970s.

The Japanese-American sample was comprised of some fifteen male and thirty female third generation or "Sansei " who were administered the TAT over a five-year period. Table 6.1 discloses that 15 percent reported positive achievement themes, 29 percent noted reluctant achievement themes, 27 percent stated that they would practice to please someone else, 20 percent gave themes of rebellion, and 9 percent gave inactive themes of fantasy or dreaming about achievement. All in all, positive or negative instrumental achievement concerns were apparent in 71 percent of the Japanese American responses.

In this generation of Japanese college students gathered from the southern main island of Kyushu by Connor, maternal pressure is appearing in more stories than in our previous samples. Connor's Japanese college students gave responses indicating 22 percent positive achievement; 18 percent reluctant achievement; 20 percent achievement to please others; 20 percent rebellion; five percent dreaming or fantasy; and 16 percent "other" responses. While 20 percent reported themes that directly stated that the child practiced to please others, it must be stressed that there are references to outside pressure and other's expectations of some the other themes as well. In the United States, records reluctance to initiate achievement to please others had also become a theme in American-born *Nisei* responses, but was relatively lacking in the immigrant *Issei* generation as first reported by Caudill and De Vos (1956) in their study of the first- and second-generation Japanese Americans in the Chicago area after World War II. In the responses of this Issei generation, self-initiated behavior was of paramount concern. However, considerable worry or concern was expressed about one's ability or about one's capacity to take on the task. In the Japanese samples taken in the 1950s, such worries were most frequently resolved by stressing the necessity for hard work and diligence.

In American records there was more expressed reluctance to assume or commit to the task at hand. In contrast to the self-motivated behavior and concern with competence of the immigrant Issei or Japanese samples, reluctant achievement was a major category registering hesitation or internal conflict about personal motivation. This remains a motivational dilemma appearing characteristically among all Americans taking the TAT. In my subsequent comparative samples of the 1950s, Americans saw unresolved or difficult to resolve problems over wanting to commit oneself to the task of learning the violin or not, whereas Japanese in Japan, more characteristically, saw problems about present or future adequacy. Parental press as a theme was relatively absent in the 1950s. In both American and Japanese American records, the mother, not the father, was often depicted as playing the decisive role in getting the child to practice. Parental pressure appeared as a significant theme in Nisei, American-born Japanese in Caudill's sample in contrast to the relative absence of this theme in the older immigrant Issei and in the native rural and urban Japanese in the 1950s.

Parental presence appeared characteristically in many American protocols from the first results reported by Caudill (Caudill and De Vos, 1956) on testing conducted in the late 1940s. A later study by Connor (1977) reported that in a sample gathered in the 1970s, rebellion against parental pressure had notably increased. As reported by Caudill, reluctance to practice more typically ended with compliance to parental pressure in middle class subjects in the past, but in Connor's

American group tested in the 1970s there was considerably more refusal or rebellion depicted, to a degree Caudill had found only in his lower class American controls. Connor's report in the later 1980s (Connor and De Vos, 1989) manifests some diminution of the rebellion themes but out of a total of 127 records thirty-nine end in resistance to parental pressure, a full 30 percent of the American records.

What we see in Connor's sample of Japanese college youth is representation of a greater amount of parental pressure and less appearance of self-initiated, positive themes compared with a previous generation. However, as we shall point out below in considering Vaughn's high school subjects, Connor's results are less positive or optimistic than what is reported for more youthful Japanese subjects who still reveal the older previously reported pattern. Parental pressure is much less evident in Vaughn's large sample of 900 Japanese subjects when compared with his American controls, who manifest similar results to those reported for Americans by Connor.

Illustrative Differences in Connor's Stories

In Connor's more recent sample, stories in which the child is depicted as ultimately resisting parental pressure result in no disciplinary retaliation or little resultant regret. The themes of outright rebellion are easy to determine, they inevitably end with the boy refusing to practice. There are varying degrees of hostility or resentment over being controlled expressed as a reaction to parental pressure. Illustrating compliance one twenty-one-year-old American female stated:

> (AaConf 2) A young boy who is forced to take violin lessons would rather be outside playing, but his mother told him he has to practice. Violin wasn't his choice but his parents want him to be "cultured." He knows he should practice but he wants to be out with his friends. Right now he resents the practice but someday he'll look back and be thankful he learned such a skill.
>
> [NDA-family PA-play RA-duty-o FA-friend <u>HB-control</u> <u>DSB-obey</u> NSA-grateful]

In analyzing his more recent series in comparison with those of the early 1970s, Connor was impressed by the change in tone. Overt hostility was increased. A not untypical response by a male, age twenty, in 1974 was as follows:

> (AbConm 1) The boy has never liked playing the violin, and his parents have always insisted that he learn how. His father was an excellent violin player and was determined to pass on the tradition. Tired of being told what he should do, the boy stares at the violin lying on the table. "I hate this violin," the boy cried. "Why do I have to play it?" With that the boy crushed the violin violently against the ground.
>
> [NDA-family EDA-family HC-contempt <u>DSC-family</u> <u>HC-injury</u>]

In today's students of Connor's sample such stories, openly expressive of even violent revolt were again more submerged. There was still some overt resentment against being forced to practice, but in the late 1980s more than a few students of this sample saw pressure and frustration as being for their own good. For example, a female, age twenty-four responded:

> (AcConf 4) The boy's parents bought the child a violin. He is being forced to practice. At this moment, he is contemplating all of his friends outside playing without him. He would rather be with them. He does not wish to practice. He is not motivated. He is bored. Eventually he will practice since his mother will insist, forcing him to practice before he can play.
>
> [NDA-reward NDA-family FA-friend AD-motive PB-bored DSB-obey PA-play]

Another persistent theme that was seldom seen in the early 1970s was that of failure followed by ultimate triumph as in the following response from a male student, who refers to Isaac Stern as a symbol of success:

> (AcConm 3) Eighteen months of practice and for nothing. The recital went badly, my string broke, my bow creaked, I scratched when I should have sung. Eighteen months ago I was given this violin. I practiced hard. I know my pieces but when it came time to go through with it—it all went wrong. Maybe I should quit! This was Isaac Stern, seven years of age.
>
> [CC-failure KD-accident NDA-reward AB-decide AA-persist]

Still, as Hsu (1972: 317–319) has pointed out, rebellion from parental authority has been a recurrent theme in American culture, one that has remained strong over the years. When Hsu administered the TAT to his students at Northwestern University in 1961—a time in the post-Sputnik period when achievement was still high—he found overall achievement themes of 53 percent as compared with 40 percent on those obtained from Hong Kong students.

Some Japanese Americans share this general American unresolved problems with parental (maternal) authority, but the proportion of positive compliance is higher. A (Sansei) third-generation Japanese American female, age twenty, notes as follows:

> (AJcConf 52) The boy's mother had just told the little boy the he has to practice the violin before he goes out to play. In this picture he is sulking because he doesn't want to practice. Ultimately he practices because he wants to go outside to play.
>
> [NDA-family PB-sulk DSB-obey PB-defer]

Another response by a twenty-one-year-old Sansei male is as follows:

(AJcConm 51) The boy is frustrated that he cannot play his instrument properly. He probably would rather not play it at all. His mom probably is making him play it, but he would rather be doing something else.

[CB-difficult AD-motive NDA-family AB-torn]

An additional response by a seventeen-year-old Sansei (third generation) female recalls the theme of achievement through expiation that De Vos (1973: 71) found so typical of many of the Japanese responses:

(AJcConf 54) It looks as though the boy wants to play it. He wishes he had the skill to play it. I guess that he will learn to play it because his father has died and left him this violin. And loving his father deeply he decides to play it.

[AA-self CB-worry AA-inspire FA-love]

Another response by a twenty-two-year-old Sansei female discloses that perhaps some of the pressure to practice is to carry on the reputation for achievement that was so typical of their parents and grandparents (Caudill and De Vos, 1956):

(AJcConf 56) The boy is looking at the violin that he doesn't want to play, but is forced to by his mother. He doesn't like playing the violin specifically, but his mom makes him because her dad played it so well and she wants to keep up the tradition.

[AD-motive NDA-family DSB-obey EDA-family]

The Japanese-Americans do indeed continue to play the violin well. A report released by the Bureau of the Census indicates that in the 1980 census 81 percent of Japanese Americans compared with 51 percent of majority Americans were in school in California at age eighteen. At age twenty-one, 66 percent, at age twenty-three, 45 percent of Japanese Americans were attending school compared with 34 percent and 22 percent, of majority Americans at comparable ages.[5] Japanese Americans continue to place a high value on academic achievement. This is the continuation of a trend that was first noted in their parents and grandparents over fifty years ago (Strong, 1934).

Among the college students tested in Kyushu, Connor found many references to outside pressure and the expectations of others throughout the TAT and other projective test material. For example, a twenty-one-year-old college male responded:

---

[5]Source: Connor and De Vos (1989), 1980 Census of the Population. General Social and Economic Characteristics: California Section 1 of 2 United States Department of Commerce, Bureau of the Census, July 1983. Tables 75 and 93.

(JJConm 101) The boy practicing the violin is suffering very much because he doesn't like to play it. His mother forces him to practice. The practicing is very hard on him. What should he do later?

[PD-suffer AD-motive DDC-pressure AB-decide]

Another by a Japanese college female, age twenty, is as follows:

(JJConf 102) The boy is suffering in front of the violin because he doesn't want to play it. His parents force him to practice but he doesn't improve, and his teacher scolds him as well. There is no way to quit without trouble.

[PD-suffer AD-motive DDC-pressure NDA-educate CC-failure DSB-control]

An additional example by a twenty-one-year-old college male contains a destructive rebellion theme:

(JJConm 101) All he can think of is playing outside, but his mother, who is eager for him to study, doesn't allow him to play and forces him to practice. He is suffering and thinks ill of her. He is thinking that he might stick the violin bow in his mother's throat.

[PA-play DDB-rigid PD-suffer HB-control]

It must be stressed that the above rebellion theme, as with those reported by 20 percent of the students, are totally at variance with the responses recorded in the 1950s and 1960s (De Vos, 1973). In the earlier protocols there were very few themes of rebellion associated with TAT Card 1. Where rebellion themes did occur they were, more often than not, elicited by other cards and in only one-fifth of such responses was the child successful in his opposition to parental wishes (De Vos, 1973: 98). Indeed, the majority of the earlier rebellion themes ended in punishment or misfortune.

One theme of continuity that links these earlier TAT responses with those more recently gathered by Connor is that *hard work* is necessary, even sometimes to the point of moral masochism or abasement. There is still present a belief that one must accept blame or feel guilty when things go wrong, or that personal pain and misery suffered does more good than harm. Persistence (AA-persist) is a theme in a majority of those TAT responses where the boy is encountering difficulty: A boy who has been practicing the violin has just received the music which he is to play at the next performance. It is a little difficult and he is suffering. But he practices and practices and will do well at the concert.

Connor notes a possible trend in the category of reluctant achievement which was given by 18 percent of these students. Are they some early indication of a possible change in the nature of Japanese achievement motivation in the future? This entering wedge of lowering achievement is apparent in the following response by a college female, age twenty-one:

(JJConf 104) Every member of his family is a musician and he is practicing since he was a small child. He likes to play baseball much more than the violin, but he will continue to play the violin reluctantly.

[EDA-family P-play AB-torn DSB-obey]

Another response by a college female, also age twenty-one:

(JJConf 106) I don't like to play the violin. My mother said to me, "You must continue to practice the violin today too." But I do not like to play the violin. I put the violin on my desk and pray: Let me play it well and let me enjoy it. But is has no effect at all. Let us resign ourselves to playing the violin. When I am a father someday, I'll never insist on my son playing the violin.

[AD-motive DDC-rigid RB-resign NDA-free]

United States and Japan High School Comparisons in Achievement Motivation by Curtis Vaughn

As a school psychologist, Curtis Vaughn has been conducting ongoing comparative research of school functioning and both cognitive and non-intellectual features of school adaptation—what contributes to or what interferes with relative school success. He has conducted comparative research in six Japanese high schools located in five different cities and three U.S. high schools located in a San Francisco Bay area county. As part of his study, Vaughn used measures of cognitive independence, various subscales (socialization and achievement subscales of the California Psychological Inventory, and a selection of cards from the standard Murray Thematic Apperception Test; Vaughn, 1988). Using the TAT, he collected test responses from 969 Japanese high school students and 453 U.S. students (1988). The U.S. sample, which has been collected from high schools in a San Francisco Bay area county, reflects considerable diversity in ethnicity (e.g., black, Caucasian, Hispanic, and Southeast Asian participants). In addition, based on California Assessment Program test scores, the schools attended by the students represent three distinct levels of academic achievement (Vaughn, 1988).

The two Japanese schools used illustratively herein are relatively highly ranked among the six schools investigated. Nevertheless, the material processed statistically, when informally considered, shows no radical differences in content from that of the other Japanese schools. Similarly, the one school selected from the American samples was a school rated among the top ten in the California school system. Again, similarly, the themes obtained from that school showed no radical differences from the total data now being processed.

We note how a number of the culturally induced attitudes described in *Heritage of Endurance* (Wagatsuma and De Vos, 1984) are again demonstrably present in the Japanese high school students. The positive economic momentum which has focused so much world attention on Japan in recent years remains partially a function of the intra-family dynamics and educational programs instilling internalized vocational motivation within a Japanese culture. But, while continuities between past and present are apparent, there are also stories that reflect new concerns which are to be reported on by Vaughn.

Students from the three high schools which we are reporting on in Table 6.3 were primarily seniors, seventeen to eighteen years of age. For purposes of reporting, the U.S. school is referred to as Vista High while the Japanese schools are designated as Haruna, in Tokyo, and Toné which is located in Takasaki. While at their respective schools, all of the subjects received group administrations of the Thematic Apperception Test, as well as a measure of cognitive field independence (Witkin, 1967) and various scales from Gough's California Psychological Inventory (Gough, 1957; rev. ed. 1964). On the measure of field independence Haruna and Toné scored significantly higher than Vista, whose students in turn significantly outperformed students from the other two U.S. schools. Descriptive statistics computed on the cumulative grade point averages of 123 participating seniors from Vista High reveal a normal distribution of scores, and grade point average significantly correlated with cognitive independence (Vaughn, 1988).

In selecting TAT cards for coding, random number tables have been used for obtaining a sample of the students who participated at each of the high schools. Presented in Table 6.2 are eighty-five students from Toné and Haruna and eighty-five Vista subjects. Although the present selection does not examine possible male and female differences in coded responses, an attempt has been made to obtain a fairly balanced proportion of male and female Card 1 responses. It is important to note that Toné High School is a public all-male facility while Haruna and Vista high schools are both public and coeducational.

Self-Initiated Achievement: Results on Card 1

Four Thematic Apperception Test cards, including Card 1 from the Standard Murray set were employed in the group administration procedure. The Card 1 illustrative responses selected for presentation below were chosen because they are illustrative of themes which are more typically reflective of a Japanese or a U.S. achievement orientation. In the process of determining which Card 1 responses are representative of particular aspects of either a Japanese or U.S. achievement orientation, the researcher looked for the presence of similar themes in both the Japanese and U.S. data.

Similar to the results of the 1950s, "Questions of motivation and competence" independently emerged as the dominant concern for the Haruna and Toné students. Seventy-five percent of the Japanese student responses fell into the motivation and competence category exhibited in Table 6.2. For the American Vista students, again the results were similar to previous samples in respect to a prevailing concern with parental pressure. Of the Card 1 responses, 60 percent were categorized in the areas pertaining to "Questions of parental pressure," compared to only 14 percent for the

Japanese sample. It is evident that in comparing the two student groups noted above, in terms of interpersonal orientation, Japanese student perceptions of self are revealed as being less contrastive with parents than the perception of self for U.S. students.

Americans by and large are highly resistant to internalizing social expectations. The Vista stories on Card 1, with their emphasis on the assertion of individual choice in decision making, often are in conflict with perceptions of parent-initiated or -sanctioned achievement goals, reflecting a sometimes contentious separation of self from others. The consequences are left unresolved or are seen as negative in forty-four out of the total of eighty-five American stories. There is compliance in only seven stories. Individuality and independence in social orientation are stressed far more than is evident in the Japanese materials.

Personal feelings and concerns in the Japanese stories are subordinated without question to an internalized achievement orientation which often assimilates externally defined obligations without their appearance in the surface of stories as a conscious concern. These results differ from the more conscious resistance evident in the Kyushu college sample reported by Connor, above.

Following Parental Expectations

In Vaughn's Japanese Card 1 responses there is more congruence between parent-initiated and student-initiated achievement related goals. The following response to Card 1 illustrates how the theme of self-initiated achievement is sometimes put consciously into the context of past emotional dependence. Among the Japanese Card 1 responses, one discovers this particular theme, or a similar one, which highlights a social orientation placing emphasis on inspiration as a reason for internalization.

> (JJVf 7) Looking at the violin, the boy is in deep sorrow. This boy's late mother left this violin as a memento. He is recalling memories of his mother when she was alive. He wishes she could be brought back to life. He will live successfully, holding his mother's memory. He will become an internationally famous violinist.
>
> [PD-sad PA-memory NDA-reward FB-longing AA-inspire]

Themes of adequacy or competence as well as hard work can be mentioned in the context of a character who is described as being dependent upon his mother for advice.

Table 6.2
Comparison of Card 1: Japanese and U.S. High School Students*

Groups	*Japanese*	*United States*
Total Cases	85	85
1. Questions of Motivation and Competence	**64**	**27**
Percentage of Total Sample	75%	32%
Positive direction	45 (70%)	15 (56%)
succeeds—or studies hard	29	6
studying in process	4	4
concern with ability but succeeds	6	0
concern with broken object, fixes it, succeeds	1	0
receives violin, will learn to play well	1	0
supernatural or magical competence	4	2
succeeds with little effort, talented	0	3
Negative or unresolved	19 (30%)	12 (44%)
ambivalent about motives, unresolved or quits	4	3
concern with ability, unresolved	9	4
no ability, gives up	2	3
not concentrated, falls asleep	1	1
supernatural or magical competence	3	0
daydreams about achievement	0	1
2. Questions of Parental Pressure	**12**	**51**
Percentage of Total Sample	14%	60%
Positive	6	7
complies and continues positively	6	7
Unresolved	5 (50%)	44 (86%)
forced, results not indicated	4	26
Negative	1	
complies but results no good	1	4
complies only temporarily or refuses to study	0	4
Other	**9**	**7**
Percentage of Total Sample	11%	8%
Resolved	4 (44%)	4 (57%)
curiosity, discovery, emotional pleasure, joy	4	4
Unresolved	5 (56%)	2 (29%)
scolded by father or teacher, accident trouble	2	0
affiliation (frustrated, lonely)	3	1
desire for an object	0	1
Negative (loss of parent)	0 (0%)	1 (14%)
Total unresolved and negative results	35%	69%

*Vaughn's Summary 1988.

(JJVf 50) The boy is said to be a musical genius. He has been practicing late and has a headache. He is massaging his temple. His headache has not disappeared. Recalling his mother's advice not to work too hard, he will take some medication and go to bed.

[CA-present AA-persist KD-illness NDA-advice NDA-means]

Japanese fathers are also mentioned in a context of self-initiated achievement and positive active nurturance. In the following response to Card 1 the character expresses feelings of gratitude. Also expressed is a theme of deference toward the father.

(JJVm 683) The boy's father was a famous musician and every time the boy looks at this violin, which his father cherished he recalls his warm and strict father. But, he died in an unfortunate accident. The boy picked up the violin and played it, but not as well as his father. After many desperate struggles to play the violin well he always recalls his father; and he is becoming a greater musician than his father.

[EDA-fame PA-memory KD-ac-die CB-inferior AA-persist MVA-profess]

In a number of responses by the Japanese subjects one also finds themes of inspired achievement, and the spirit of an ancestor can be mentioned. By communicating with the spirit of a deceased relative, the character in the following response to Card 1 is able to attain a sense of inner strength in pursuing a difficult aim.

(JJVm 603) He is looking at the violin which is a memento from his grandfather. He is thinking about his grandfather, and talking to his spirit. He will practice and will succeed greatly as a violinist.

[NDA-reward AA-inspire AA-persist]

A more dependent social orientation does not preclude the internalization of self-initiated achievement motivation. One can be sensitive to the needs and concerns of others in the achievement context while assuming self-oriented responsibility for carrying out goals and obligations. The following story reflects the internal struggle associated with self-initiated achievement which accompanies resignation to the role expected by others.

(JJVf 39) He has been taking violin lessons. Because he can't play well, the teacher gets angry and leaves the boy saying, "Practice yourself." Left alone, the boy wishes he could stop his violin lessons. Thinking of his parents' expectations he can't. So, he will pull himself together; and, with renewed energy, start playing one note after another.

[CC-failure AB-waver RA-duty-o AA-persist]

In the following story the concern over competence is expressed. Competence themes, often reflecting worry regarding adequacy in achieving a goal, appear with a relatively high degree of frequency, in comparison with American Card 1 responses. This Japanese story, like the one above, also conveys the element of endurance as part of an achievement orientation.

> (JJVf 42) He is a little discouraged that the lesson has not gone smoothly. He had become interested in playing the violin after watching someone play on TV. He then asked his parents to buy him one. Even though he would like to quit, because of these circumstances, he cannot say this to his parents. So, he will pull himself together and later become a world famous violinist.
>
> [CB-arduous NSA-means RA-duty-s <u>AA-duty</u> EDA-fame]

Even though the achievement is self-initiated, the character in the story does not want to show his disappointment because he is the one who asked to play. Under these circumstances he cannot say he wants to quit, even though it was his idea to pursue the goal of playing the violin.

Issues of Control and Noncompliance with Authority

The following stories from a U.S. sample reflect a different orientation. Among the Vista High Card 1 responses, a frequently expressed interpersonal theme is the concern over individuality and self-expression, in a context often emphasizing reluctant obedience or resistance to parent-initiated achievement goals. There are parent-initiated achievement themes among the Japanese responses, but typically not represented in the context of interpersonal values expressed in the sample of U.S. stories illustrated in the following responses.

In the negative or unresolved categories under "questions of parental pressure" twenty-six of the responses fall in the "forced, results not indicated" subcategory while eleven of the dominant Card 1 themes have been placed in the "refuses to study" category. A dominant theme depicting the application of parental "force" is found in those stories in which the central character is portrayed as being subjected to the operation of circumstances which permit no alternative to compliance. From the recipient position the character is occasionally described as suffering or being bored in response to circumstances beyond his control.

> (AVm 1083) "I hate school. It's so boring," thought the boy. Another music lesson. "Why does mommy make me take violin lessons? I can't play as well as the teacher wants me to. . . . He couldn't stand the long, cold halls of the school. The unfriendly teachers always berating him for this or that. But mommy wouldn't listen to his pleas, so he returned each day.
>
> [PB-boring DDC-rigid ESC-disappoint NDA-censure OB-body <u>DSB-obey</u>]

> (AVm 1091) Andrew hates to play the violin. Only his mother makes him and is always nagging him to practice. He'd rather be outside with the other boys and girls. . . . Andrew is a sneaky boy and is trying to figure out a way to avoid this

torture. He sneaks out the door only to find his mother who stepped outside briefly. He learns that there is no escaping, he will have to put up with practicing the violin.

[PB-work DDC-rigid FA-friend RC-evade DSB-obey]

(AVm 1099) In the picture, we have a boy named Ed. It appears that he is reluctantly doing his studies. He was supposed to eat dinner but wasn't allowed up from the table until he finished his plate, so his mother brought his homework to him at the table. Ed came home from school that day with an "F" on a test, and his mother is clamping down on him. He doesn't want to study at all and is very sad. Actually, he really isn't studying. He's just going through the motions. He's really thinking about the ball game he's going to on Saturday. However, his mother will think he's studying and will be satisfied for the week, after which things will return to normal.

[DSB-obey CC-failure AD-motive RC-evade]

(AVf 1046) "Mom never gives up, push, push, push," exclaimed Joey as he sighed and glanced at the violin on his lap. "Why do I have to play with this . . . this piece of wood? I hate it!! If she wants me to play with a piece of wood, why don't I play with a fishing pole instead! After all it is just another piece of wood." Joey began to fumble with the strings of the violin and let his mind wander to the thoughts of using a fishing pole instead. "Doesn't mom want me to be happy? How can such a small object cause such misery?" As Joey finished saying this he looked up to see before his face mother looking down upon him from the doorway. "Joey, why didn't you tell me you didn't like the violin. You don't have to play it if you don't want to. Besides I have a surprise for you." Joey looked up as she pulled from behind her back a beautiful red fishing pole. Joey's eyes lit up like candles in the dark. "Thanks, mom," he said, and walked to her placing his hand on her shoulder. "I love you," he said and ran out the door with his fishing pole ready to catch a big fish at the lake nearby.

[DDC-press AD-motive DDA-free NDA-reward FA-love PA-play OC-debase OA-own]

Unlike the Japanese responses to Card 1, the characters in the U.S. stories from Vista High reflect less internalization of an achievement motive that incorporates the wishes and concerns of adult authority. Achievement is more of a negotiable issue for the characters in the Vista stories, and parents are more often portrayed in a role of trying to persuade or induce the child to achieve. A frequently mentioned consideration is the child's "happiness," as it conflicts with the parent's expectation toward achievement. Unlike the Japanese stories, such conflict is resolved in terms of the child asserting his needs and wishes over those of the parent, which appear to be less salient.

(AVf 1038) The boy is looking at the violin. His mom and teacher want him to play and practice for his big recital which is coming up next week. He doesn't like playing and just got in a fight with his mom about it. He's gonna talk to his dad about whether or not he still has to play it. He wants to join a baseball team with

all his friends. If he joins the team his parents know he'll never have time to play the violin but they know he doesn't like playing it and they want him to be happy.
[PB-dislike NDA-family NDA-educate HC-discord FA-mend DDA-free FA-friend PA-play]

Resistance to family pressure is expressed as a positive virtue in a number of the Vista stories. In several instances the stories have a moralistic tone. The character's persistence against family pressure portrays exemplary conduct, reflecting a perception of right and wrong behavior.

(AVm 1119) Johnny has just received a present from his wealthy and affluent parents. They expect him to be a virtuoso and play beautiful music as they had done when they were kids. Johnny, however, does not appreciate the instrument. He would rather have a baseball bat to hit balls with. The result of Johnny's displeasure is that he will not obey the music instructor and thus he will be sent to his room. This strong attitude of Johnny's not to succumb to his parents' will, will create a strong and successful personality for him in the future.
[KA-means NDA-reward PB-dislike PA-play DSC-disobey NDA-punish DSA-assert CA-future]

(AVf 1052) There is only one thing in the whole world that Arthur hates, and that's the violin. "Practice, Practice, Practice!" Arthur thinks to himself. . . . Every time he had to practice he would think of ways to avoid it. "There had to be a way out of playing the violin for good he thought." . . . What Arthur liked best and was best at was the drums. "THE DRUMS!!!" Arthur's mother exclaimed when she came home that day. Arthur told her that he played this instrument best and that she should let him play what *he* wanted and not what *she* wants. So, Arthur's mother gave in and thanked Arthur for teaching her a lesson. He taught her that every person is an individual and should be treated that way. If he/she wanted to dress strange with blue hair then that is their choice. Just like Arthur wanted to play the drums and not the violin.
[PB-dislike RC-evade DSA-assert DDA-free NSA-edified]

In the Vista stories affiliative concerns about friends are often mentioned. The characters are portrayed in a context in which the pull of peer-related influences are incompatible with parent-initiated achievement goals. In the Japanese achievement context there is more congruence between perceptions of parent-initiated or -sanctioned achievement goals and those valued by peers. Effort toward completion of a task also receives less emphasis in the Vista stories. The obvious attribution on ability as the reason for success, and underemphasis on hard work in the following story, mirrors some of the achievement-related concerns of U.S. students noted by other researchers (Covington and Omelich, 1979; Holloway, 1988).

(AVm 1100) Bobby returned home from school in a happy manner. Nothing special had happened that day but he was just glad to be out of school. When he arrived at home, his mother seeing the smile on his face, offered him a glass of milk and some cookies. He accepted them with a "Thank you" and sat down to eat. As he was eating, a thought came to his mind. He remembered that he had a violin recital that night and that he hadn't practiced at all that week. He hurriedly ate the rest of his cookies and gulped down the rest of his milk. He then ran upstairs to his room. He dug through his closet, through all his comic books, and found the violin. He then remembered that he forgot his music sheet. Sitting down, he put his hands against the sides of his head and tried to remember how to play the music. Unbelievably, he grabbed the violin and started to play. It was a miracle! He played so well that his mother came up and applauded at the end. That night, he went to the recital and played his heart out. He got a standing ovation and felt very proud. However, his instructor came over and told him that it was the wrong music that he played. The music he had played was for the last recital. "Oh, well," he said, and took a bow.

[PA-relief NDA-food RB-omission CA-comic ESA-approve ESA-self AC-illicit]

Implications: Social Orientation and Achievement

In the Vaughn material, the preponderance of Vista High Card 1 responses relating to "questions of parental pressure," particularly in the negative or unresolved categories, is reflective of an emphasis on the perceived significance of idealized striving toward *individualistic* interests in the context of attitudes toward achievement in the United States. In the Japanese there is a high number of those concerned with internalized achievement motivation. In Vaughn's material not presented here but discussed in his dissertation (Vaughn, 1988), the Japanese youth's motives are seen consonant with family and community purposes. On Card 1, the parent does not appear characteristically putting pressure on the child that meets with obvious resistance as in the case of the American records.

For the Americans, family interactions often center on conflictual concerns revolving around the character's attempt to ultimately assert one's autonomy or independence. The final obligation is to one's self, not one's group. This result is in line with De Vos' contentions with regard to cultural differences in the social expression of cognitive field independence (De Vos, 1992). In the American context, individualistic self-motivation can be antagonistic to group purposes and takes priority over social harmony (Wagatsuma and De Vos, 1984; Madsen, 1967; Madsen and Shapira, 1973).

The Japanese score higher than Americans on cognitive field independence; hence, according to American research presuppositions they should manifest individualistic behavior in the schools. Observation of school behavior finds no such evidence. In the Japanese context, we conclude, the individual may be cognitively independent but the self-perception of goals is such that their realization is constrained to take place within a socially non-conflictful context. The individual must limit his or her overt behavior to that permitted within a non-contending group context (De Vos and Suárez-Orozco, 1986). Cognitively, the *self* experiences independent thought, but this independence of thought is not to be exhibited in individualistic behavior. In the American context, the cognitively independent self *is* exhibited in individualistic behavior which may be at odds with parental directives as well as disputatious within peer group relations.

One must note that there are, in effect, two analytical levels (structural and experiential) on which to examine social attitudes related to group dependence ("field dependence") in the context of an experiencing self. On one level, dependence is a socially conscious attitude. Such dependence is to be distinguished from what occurs on a structural-cognitive level. These two levels tend to be fused, if not confused, in American research literature (Witkin and Berry, 1975; Witkin and Goodenough, 1977; Witkin et al., 1974) in understanding the relationship between the *cognitive* dependence term, which limits behavior within one's cognitive capacities, and the *social* dependence term in which behavior is constrained by a conscious need to continue to conform to one's social group.

In some group studies, such as those of Mexican Americans compared with Anglo-Americans, a clear, systematic difference is found for both domains (Madsen, 1967; Madsen et al., 1973). The field-independent child also tends to give less regard to social conformity.

Examining Vaughn's results comparing American and Japanese youth to the previous studies of field dependence versus field independence in the United States has led us to conclude that the Japanese are characteristically more field-independent than are Americans on a cognitive level. In contrast, the Americans are still struggling toward some self-realization that liberates them from parental pressures. The Japanese manifest continuing social need for interdependence in relation to peers. Nevertheless, they are internally more concerned with personal competence and self-initiated achievement. We must note, therefore, that we are examining group consciousness, as well as structural levels of personality, in looking at concepts of dependency, cognitive or social. For the Japanese, social dependency continues into adulthood and is socially reinforced, although an internalization of norms and an identification with parental directives have occurred earlier in childhood. This is well in evidence in the highly internalized achievement motivation of the Japanese which exceeds that found even in the more privileged segments of American society represented in the elite California high school sampled in this study.

Japanese have a highly internalized sense of social responsibility and a high susceptibility to severe guilt feelings, should there be failure to perform adequately in accordance with social expectations (De Vos, 1960, 1973). Vaughn's sample taken in 1985–1986 is startlingly similar to the Japanese samples of 1953–1955 and 1960–1963. The Japanese continue to be preoccupied by worries over a capacity for mastery as a central concern of the social self.

This concern with adequacy and the need for achievement appeared earlier in Caudill's samples of Japanese immigrants and their children and are appearing interestingly in the more recent samples of Korean immigrants into the United States (De Vos, 1993; De Vos and Kim, 1993, see chapter 7, volume II, below). There are striking similarities in the internalization of a need for achievement within Japanese and Koreans which one can attribute, partially at least, to the role of the mother as educator within a Confucian family. What is evident is that there is a resolution toward family responsibility in Koreans as well as Japanese.

In both cultures, mutual interdependence in hierarchical structures is a strong, expressive need. Compliance in authority relationships is age-graded—the younger depend on the older. However, the age-grading is much more in evidence in the Japanese and there is more concern with the dubious legitimacy of authority in Koreans that attests to past and present political difficulties which is only beginning to appear in very recent Japanese records.

In the Japanese, there is belief in a promised continuation of nurture and mentorship. The high school sample remained especially selectively permeable to individuals perceived as authority figures. They are not defensive, nor resistive to taking advice from such mentors. Japanese are socialized normatively to endure the sufferings of the moment and situational frustrations in order to realize ultimate, social goals. These psychological traits are the very opposite of those listed as characteristic of the "field-dependent" person in Witkin's psychological formulations.

In Vaughn's study, the Japanese students of the Haruna and Toné generation are but a step or so away in terms of lineal distance from the previous subjects who have been administered similar projective instruments forty years past. The objective of the present discussion has been to note some emerging continuities between previously and more recently collected fantasy materials. The Japanese material is receiving further analysis by Vaughn in respect to school differences in frequencies of particular themes (e.g., vocational versus nonvocational Japanese schools).

The Japanese in Brazil

In later chapters we shall do further comparison of recent Japanese samples, this time from Brazil. Again we shall note the cultural continuity of themes to The TAT cards. For example, in the Japanese Brazilian samples, on Card 1 there were concerns about achievement or competence without the presence of any parental or authority figure in 72 percent of the stories. This approximates the results obtained by Vaughn in Japan (75 percent) in contrast to only 32 percent such stories occurring in his American high school sample. Japanese Brazilians gave 13 percent stories with parental pressure (with only four such stories, 5 percent in the remaining Brazilian samples). This compared with the 14 percent of Japanese and the 60 percent of Americans tested by Vaughn.

As shall be discussed below in more detail in chapter 10, volume II, parents or teachers, when represented by Brazilian Japanese, are still seen positively in a mentor role in contrast to far fewer such stories in Brazilians of other ethnic backgrounds.

References

Caudill, William. 1952. Japanese-American Personality and Acculturation. *Genetic Psychology Monograph*, **45**: 3–102.

Caudill, William and George A. De Vos. 1956. Achievement, Culture and Personality: The Case of the Japanese Americans. *American Anthropologist*, **58**(6): 1102–1126 (reprinted: 1961; 1966; 1967; 1971).

Connor, John. 1977. *Tradition and Change in Three Generations of Japanese Americans*. Chicago: Nelson Hall.

Connor, John W. and George A. De Vos. 1989. Cultural Influences on Achievement Motivation and Orientation Toward Work in Japanese and American Youth. In David Stern and Dorothy Eichorn (Eds.), *Adolescence and Work: Influence of Social Structure, Labor Markets, and Culture* (pp. 291–326). Hillsdale, N.J.: Lawrence Erlbaum Associates.

Covington, Martin V. and C. L. Omelich. 1979. It's Best to Be Able and Virtuous Too: Student and Teacher Evaluative Responses to Successful Effort. *Journal of Educational Psychology*, **71**: 688–700.

De Vos, George A. 1951. *Acculturation and Personality Structure: A Rorschach Study of Japanese-Americans*. Dissertation: Dept. of Psychology, University of Chicago.

———. 1960. The Relation of Guilt Toward Parents to Achievement and Arranged Marriage Among the Japanese. *Psychiatry*, **23**(3): 287–301.

———. 1973. *Socialization for Achievement: Essays on the Cultural Psychology of the Japanese*. Berkeley: University of California Press.

———. 1992. *Social Cohesion and Alienation: Minorities in the United States and Japan*. Boulder, Colo.: Westview Press.

———. 1993. Problems with Achievement, Alienation, and Authority in Korean Minorities in the United States and Japan. In Kwang Kyu Lee and Walter Slote (Eds.), *Overseas Koreans in the Global Context* (pp. 145–180). Seoul: Association for the Study of Koreans Abroad.

De Vos, George A. and L. Bryce Boyer. 1989. *Symbolic Analysis Cross-Culturally: The Rorschach Test*. Berkeley: University of California Press.

De Vos, George A. and Eun-Young Kim. 1993. Koreans in Japan: Problems with Achievement, Alienation Authority. In Ivan Light and Parminder Bhachu (Eds.), *California Immigrants in World Perspective*. New Brunswick, N.J.: Transaction Books.

De Vos, George A. and Marcelo M. Suárez-Orozco. 1986. Child Development in Japan and the United States: Prospectives of Cross-Cultural Comparison. In Harold Stevenson, Hiroshi Azuma, and Kenji Hakuta (Eds.), *Child Development and Education in Japan* (pp. 289–298). New York: Freeman.

———. 1990. *Status Inequality: The Self in Culture*. Newbury Park, Calif.: Sage Publications.

De Vos, George A. and Cicero Vaz. n.d. *A TAT Report on Portuguese and Afro-Brazilian Adolescents from an Lower Socio-Economic Urban District in South Brazil*.

Gough, Harrison. 1957 (rev. ed. 1964). *Manual for the California Psychological Inventory*. Palo Alto, Calif.: Consulting Psychologists Press.

Holloway, Susan. 1988. Concepts of Ability and Effort in Japan and the United States. *Review of Educational Research*, **58**(3333): 327–345.

Hsu, Francis L.K. and B. Waltrous. 1972. An Experiment with TAT. In Francis L.K. Hsu (Ed.), *Psychological Anthropology*. Cambridge, Mass.: Harvard University Press.

Kagan, Spencer and Millard Madsen. 1971. Cooperation and Competition of Mexican, Mexican-American, and Anglo-American Children of Two Ages under Four Instructional Sets. *Developmental Psychology*, **5**: 32–39.

Madsen, Millard. 1967. Cooperative and Competitive Motivation of Children in Three Mexican Subcultures. *Psychological Reports*, **20**: 1307–1320.

Madsen, Millard and A. Shapira. 1973. Cooperative and Competitive Behavior of Urban Afro-American, Anglo-American, and Mexican Village Children. *Developmental Psychology*, **9**: 16–20.

Martinez, Joe Jr. 1977. *Chicano Psychology*. New York: Academic Press.

Mebane, D. and D.L.A. Johnson. 1970. Comparison of the Performance of Mexican Boys and Girls on Witkin's Cognitive Tasks. *Inter-American Journal of Psychology*, **4**: 227–239.

Ramirez, M. and Douglass Price-Williams. 1974. Cognitive Styles of Children of Three Ethnic Groups in the United States. *Journal of Cross-Cultural Psychology*, **5**: 212–219.

Strong, Edward K. 1934. *The Second Generation Japanese Problem*. Stanford: Stanford University Press.

Vaughn, Curtis. 1988. *Cognitive Independence, Social Independence and Achievement Orientation: A Comparison of Japanese and United States Students*. Dissertation. Dept. of Education, University of California at Berkeley.

Wagatsuma, Hiroshi and George A. De Vos. 1984. *Heritage of Endurance: Family Patterns and Delinquency Formation in Urban Japan*. Berkeley: University of California Press.

Witkin, Herman A. 1967. Cognitive Styles Across Cultures. *International Journal of Psychology*, **2**: 233–250.

———. 1969. Social Influences in the Development of Cognitive Style. In David A. Goslin (Ed.), *Handbook of Socialization Theory and Research*. Chicago: Rand McNally.

Witkin, Herman A. and J.W. Berry. 1975. Psychological Differentiation in Cross-Cultural Perspective. *Journal of Cross-Cultural Psychology*, **6**: 4–87.

Witkin, Herman A. and Donald Goodenough. 1977. Field Dependence and Interpersonal Behavior. *Psychological Bulletin*, **84**: 661–689.

Witkin, Herman A., Douglass Price-Williams, M. Bertini, B. Christiansen, P.K. Oltman, M. Ramirez, and J. Van Meel. 1974. Social Conformity and Psychological Differentiation. *International Journal of Psychology*, **9**: 11–29.

Chapter 7

Vitality and Optimism versus Problems with Achievement, Alienation, and Authority in Ethnic Minorities: The Korean Case

George A. De Vos
Eun-Young Kim

In the United States, there are differential responses of various minority groups to educational adaptation in schools and in occupational success. On the one hand, a number of the Asian groups are doing relatively well, have taken to the school system in a positive way, and are overrepresented numerically according to population at many of the American major undergraduate and graduate institutions of advanced learning. Other groups, such as Mexican Americans and African Americans, have done relatively poorly in the American setting. What is the situation elsewhere in respect to the adaptation of ethnic minorities with particular histories of discrimination within a majority dominated school system? Research in reference to this question has been initiated in a number of countries.[1]

In studying ethnic minorities in the Japanese islands one also notes differences in the adaptation of Japanese minorities (De Vos and Wagatsuma, 1969; Lee and De Vos, 1981). Let us consider the case of the Koreans in Japan. The present

[1]Anthropologists and other social scientists in Europe are beginning studies of the children of migrants in North European industrial states. See, for example, Roosens (1988).

generation of Korean youth in Japan reflects considerable personal alienation in response to the disparagement and degradation endured since the arrival of their parents or grandparents. Most of these individuals speak no Korean, are indeed, culturally, but not socially, assimilated within contemporary Japanese society. De Vos (1973) has reported elsewhere their very high delinquency rate and many other behavioral symptoms of the alienation symbolized in the psychological material herein presented.

Colonial History: The Degradation and Exploitation of Koreans in Japan

When Japan formally colonized Korea in 1910, it subjected the Korean population to programs of forceful Japanization as well as social attitudes of derogation and depreciation. It was the intention of many Japanese, throughout the thirty-five year history of direct colonization, to eradicate, not only any desire for Korean political autonomy, but also any continuity of a sense of separate ethnic and cultural identity. A coercive governmental policy periodically attempted to force them to become Japanese culturally without offering full social acceptance as true Japanese. Defeat of the Japanese in World War II allowed the Korean state to reestablish itself in 1945. Since that time Korea has made remarkable progress toward modernization and industrialization on its own terms.

During the colonial period, many Koreans had been brought to Japan first coerced by grinding poverty, then later by military necessity, to replace the troops used on the continent against the Chinese. After the surrender of the Japanese at the end of World War II approximately two-thirds to three-fourths of the Koreans eventually repatriated (Lee and De Vos, 1981). Close to a million remained, some now "passing" as Japanese.

Changsoo Lee and I have attempted to tell the sad history of the minority status of these Koreans remaining in Japan. The four generations of Koreans in Japan go back to the importation of unskilled and unlettered poor farmers and rural folk to take on unskilled jobs during the industrial development of Japan in the late 1920s and 1930s. Then, with the increasing manpower demands of the Japanese incursion into China in the 1930s they replaced most of the remaining Japanese unskilled and semi-skilled labor being drafted into the increasing war effort. The effects of disparaged status have been most strongly felt by the remaining close to a million Koreans who did not repatriate at the end of World War II.

Continuing Social Dissension

Socially, Koreans in Japan, past as well as present, generally find their need for harmony dissipated by deep and abiding distrust, discord, inherited hostilities, and traditions of divisiveness. Political groups manifest long-standing splits between North and South; between pro-government and anti-government groupings; between Christian and non-Christian. Whereas many Koreans with considerable justification blamed these cleavages on the fact that they are pawns in a power game in which the chief players were the Soviet Union, China, the United States, and Japan, they must face the fact that discordant factionalism continued to be caused by intragroup, factional animosities on the part of particular Koreans which remain generationally active.

The usually most expedient group mechanism for achieving internal harmony is to find some means of deflecting socially disruptive behavior or attitudes onto outside individuals or groups. This is a well-researched mechanism in social psychology. Displacement of internal tensions onto an outside enemy is basic to ethnocentrism wherever it operates. But it is indeed an unfortunate destiny of many minority groups to embody in their subordinate social traditions forms of discord that are more internally expressed than externally displaced.

Unfortunately, for many Koreans the "outgroup" is often another faction of Koreans. For example, in Japan, the North Korean-oriented groups in their schools, and elsewhere, have sought to further their internal group solidarity by expressing discord toward "less virtuous" factions of the Korean community.

Koreans today, both at home and in Japan, to attain internal harmony often have recourse to labeling the Japanese collectively as the enemy. It is easier to deflect hatred onto all Japanese rather than to distinguish those who are indeed prejudiced from those who are accepting and potentially helpful. Hence Koreans sometimes behave with anger and hostility toward all Japanese, irrespective of their personal guilt or innocence. This reciprocal stereotypic attitude of hatred contributes to acts of animosity on both sides.

Most Korean groups exercise particularly heavy sanctions against group members who take Japanese citizenship. Since the Japanese also reject them, naturalized citizens of Korean origin have set up their own group, the Seiwa Club, a name that can be roughly translated as "the realization of harmony." In this group, naturalization is a form of avoiding passing by openly acknowledging one's Korean background and at the same time asserting one's Japanese citizenship. Finding themselves in a fairly precarious position and generally isolated, naturalized Korean-Japanese hope to make their position more acceptable or tolerated by others.

Problems in Family Cohesiveness

Perhaps the greatest problem that we have noted is how disruptive the circumstances of discrimination have been to the harmonious functioning of the Korean family. The destruction of the male's occupational prowess, the wounding of his sense of dignity, results in spasmodic acts of compensatory masculinity at home. It also results in disparagement of the husband by his wife within the home setting.

Confucianist values, in which the wife ideally plays a subordinate role to the head of the house and sees to it that the children are obedient to those in authority, are not well exercised in many Korean homes. This leads to a sense of worthlessness about their family on the part of growing children. The family relationships themselves become bonds of aggressive displacement, of mute frustration, and of inescapable ignominy. The family is not a haven but a place of alienation. As noted above in respect to achievement motivation, many youths express their feelings in some form of delinquent behavior that eventuates in a criminal career.

Attitudes toward Authority and Group Loyalty

Korean Japanese children seem to do relatively poorly in school for similar reasons found to operate in some American minorities, such as among African-Americans or Mexican-Americans (De Vos, 1980). Individuals do not identify or internalize standards and expectations set for them by members of the external majority. Instead, the peer group becomes the principal source of affiliative gratification, discouraging acquiescence and conformity to the school as an institution. The peer group also becomes the arena for demonstration of prowess and competence, the source of appreciative judgment from other youth.

We must also note impressionistically that Korean-Japanese youth in many instances are stronger in their disregard of family or adult authority simply because there is less gratification to be gained from interdependent family relationships. Affiliation is sought from peer group relationships that are frequently delinquency oriented and antagonistic toward social authorities, including teachers and others functioning in Japanese administrative agencies. These attitudes of protective association and antagonism toward the outside are sometimes perpetuated into adulthood.

Affiliative Concerns

Korean-Japanese seem to seek out individual affiliations in marriage. Although their Confucian tradition emphasizes the authority of family role patterns rather than intimate companionship, they seem today less prone to concern themselves with family considerations. One notes that among younger Koreans, just as among younger Japanese, there is a greater desire for closeness and intimacy in the marital bond. Indeed, romantic love today in some few instances transcends the social barriers set up between Koreans and lower status Japanese. Such marriages can compound problems of identity on the part of the Korean partner. He or she is faced with the necessity to affirm or deny Korean affiliations outside of marriage and at the same time to maintain solidarity with his or her mate.

There are numerous instances of difficulties arising in mixed marriages owing to external pressures of family or internal problems of divided loyalty. In turn, mixed marriages produce children who have their own identity problems, who must decide on their principal allegiances and the principal groups from which they will seek out companions.

The Maintenance of a Korean Identity in Japan

The present generation of Korean youth in Japan reflect considerable personal alienation in response to the disparagement and degradation endured since the arrival of their parents or grandparents. Most of these individuals speak no Korean, and are indeed, culturally but not socially, assimilated within contemporary Japanese society. De Vos (1973) has reported elsewhere their very high delinquency rate and many other behavioral symptoms of the alienation symbolized in the psychological material herein presented. The Korean minority in Japan examined psychoculturally are presented with a numbers of dilemmas in resolving who they are, and to whom they owe their loyalty and whom in authority do they find worthy of respect.

Dilemmas of Achievement Motivation in Minority Koreans[2]

The Korean minority in Japan examined psychoculturally are presented with a number of dilemmas in resolving who they are, to whom they owe their loyalty, and which authority figures they find worthy of respect. Frustration of a need for achievement within any contemporary society including Japan has had five predictable results involving different forms of alienation or individuation. *First*, there is *political dissidence,* some of it illegal and violent. In our volume (Lee and De Vos, 1981) we discuss the history of social protest, including violent political radicalism, past and present. Koreans have been motivated to take a wide variety of means to redress their social plight. *Second*, there are various forms of *innovative social behavior,* some of it leading to individualistically achieved professional and even business success in minority Koreans within the heavily group-oriented Japanese society. *Third*, there is goal-oriented *criminal activity*. The Japanese criminal underworld contains many relatively successful Koreans, but even here, there is a great deal of disguise and passing practiced. *Fourth*, many Koreans, especially the youth, manifest unresolved difficulties in applying themselves to future plans. They act out deviantly in one way or another against both family and outer social expectations. The rate of *delinquency* among Korean youth is seven times that found among ordinary Japanese. *Fifth*, one notes cases of social and psychological *alienated withdrawal*.

---

[2]The following discussion draws directly on material discussed more fully in De Vos, *Social Cohesion and Alienation: The United States and Japan,* Chapter 4, 1992.

Operative among the dilemmas faced is whether or not to "pass," and pretend to the casual outsider to be ordinary Japanese. "Passing," a term first used by light-skinned American blacks, is a universal phenomenon found in any hierarchical setting in which background may disadvantage the individual. This is practiced in any social setting in which some form of escape from community surveillance is possible. The complex urban environment makes some form of passing possible in modern societies. The problem however is more difficult in a caste-like setting accorded Koreans in Japan in which intermarriage is vigilantly interdicted.

Instrumentally based definitions of social, occupational, economic, and political success or achievement are found in every society. In any pluralistic society that emphasizes the ascendancy of one group, the achievement of social success may well require one to disguise one's minority class or ethnic status origins. In our volume (Lee and De Vos, 1981, Chapter 12), we note examples of why and how some Koreans have changed behavior and disguised their background to obtain success, especially in the less carefully monitored world of entertainment. In passing from one class or caste to another in a rigidly controlled society the individual is continually subject to exposure. Sometimes a linguistic usage or an inadvertent form of behavior betrays past affiliations.[3]

To be known as of Korean background today is still to court failure through ostracism. Intermarriage is extremely rare with other than Burakumin outcastes. Even an entertainer of Korean background remains an anomaly. Some Koreans naturally find it expedient to attempt to maintain a disguised background, but here expressive needs become counterpoised; they cannot maintain affectional ties with family or friends from the Korean community. Among those Koreans who choose not to pass there is continual ambivalence toward those who attempt it. There is sometimes some insistence on covert contacts or signs of allegiance. Whatever the circumstances, an individual is conduced toward a sense of personal alienation. Most Koreans choose not to attempt to pass.

In our volume (Lee and De Vos, 1981) we discuss the history of social protest, including violent political radicalism, past and present. Koreans have been motivated to take a wide variety of means to redress their social plight. It must be noted, however, that religious sects still vie with political groups as a basis for ultimate ideological commitment. From the Japanese perspective, Koreans have been and continue to be feared as a source of potential political and social violence.

However, looked at psychologically as well as socially, the social protest of Koreans in Japan displays a broad spectrum of social adaptive and psychologically adjustive reaction patterns. These patterns range all the way from infantile destructiveness rationalized as social purpose, to mature espousal of a political cause deriving from a sense of common humanity and compassion. In our empirical work in the field of delinquency in Japan (De Vos and Wagatsuma, 1969; De Vos,

---

[3]In yet rigidly maintained class segments of British or French societies, for example, certain individuals delight in exposing upwardly mobile pretenders.

1980; Wagatsuma and De Vos, 1984) not only did we document the uncommonly high rate of delinquency among Korean youth, but also the sad background of many discontented or broken families resulting from the oppressive atmosphere of social degradation experienced by many Koreans living in marginal slums.

The indirect as well as direct effects of social disparagement have generational consequences for family life. Delinquent behavior is not simply a reaction to outside discrimination, but comes to reflect damaged parental authority often due to alcoholism and family disorganization experienced from early childhood on. There is much evidence of personal self disparagement and lack of confidence in one's abilities. There is a sense of *emotional* as well as *economic* deprivation. What is evident is that the Korean family in Japan has become generationally *vulnerable* to social disparagement. School failure is very high. The choice among these modes of reaction are not dissimilar to those practiced by African-Americans in the United States.

In reference to poor school performance, youth do not identify or internalize standards and expectations set for them by members of the external majority. Their peer group becomes the principal source of affiliative gratification. The peer group also becomes the arena for demonstration of prowess and competence, the source of appreciative judgment from other youth. Nevertheless, Koreans in Japan find it difficult to use their group identity as a means of countering moments of individual doubt about ability. Frequently the minority individual cannot depend on a sense of confidence drawn from past group experience. In a form of self hate, he or she comes instead to introject some of the prejudice directed at one's group.

The Postwar Period in Korea

Defeat of the Japanese in World War II allowed the Korean state to reestablish itself in 1945. Since that time there has been remarkable progress toward modernization and industrialization on its own terms. The Korean postwar success has come as a surprise to Japanese generally. There still remain problems about authority, some directly due to how to establish legitimate authority after being colonized and subordinated to an alien governmental structure. Attitudinal problems concerning the exercise of authority and its recognition by subordinates are found within the individual Korean, especially during youth, as well as being evident in the distrust manifest in the political arena, or in social factions as we shall presently demonstrate in very brief form.

A Contrastive American Experience

Contrasting with this history of Koreans in Japan has been the recent history of Korean immigration from an independent Korea to the United States. Since 1965, we have had an influx of over 1,000,000 Koreans. The history of this group has been phenomenal. Their capacity for educational adaptation and economic betterment is exceptional among immigrants. This is not to say that Koreans do not meet some of the discrimination directed toward Asians generally by a white majority culture in the United States; however, compared with the longer history of being a deprecated subgroup considered innately inferior which was the experience of Koreans in Japan, Koreans in the United States have gained a level of social acceptance that is totally different from their experience in the Japanese colonial context. What we must point out is that the younger Koreans coming to the United States already evidence the effects of a sustained focus on education in the newly independent postwar Korean state.

The situation for Koreans is different in the United States from that experienced in Japan. Their Korean Confucian heritage and its emphasis on social hierarchy within the family are better practiced in the United States than it has been in the Japanese context. We note, however, that these immigrants share the suspicion about legitimate authority found in their homeland or in Japan.

Those coming to the United States as immigrants do so voluntarily-seeking the promises of personal and family advancement. The families are intact. There is here no history of specific degradation and unemployment. One must quickly note class variables are also involved. Members of the families of those coming in have in many instances already achieved some form of professional occupation. Although many must work at occupations beneath their specific training, they do so with the conviction that their children, through mounting the educational ladder, will succeed better. The present statistics demonstrate they are doing so. Koreans are overrepresented in the major American universities.

A Comparison of Minority Korean Attitudes in the United States and Japan

To buttress some of the above observational impressions, let us report to you on our study using a projective test, the TAT. The results obtained are highly corroborative of the differential reaction of a minority group to a different pattern of relative acceptance or discrimination in two host societies. Youth of Korean ancestry *are* adapting differently in Japan and the United States. Underneath these patterns of adaptation are attitudinal differences revealed in our test results. In effect, the observed behavioral differences demonstrate the validity of the TAT results. Underlying attitudes are indeed captured in different cultural settings, demonstrating that projective tests can be used cross culturally, despite the opinions held to the contrary by many social scientists skeptical about the possible validity of such tests when used cross-culturally.

This present generation of arriving Koreans resembles on psychological tests the Japanese immigrants two generations past. What is particularly clear in comparing responses to the Thematic Apperception Test in small samples taken in Japan with those obtained in Korea and in the United States, to be discussed below, is the difference in future time orientation. The Japanese sample of Korean youth tested show little future time orientation. They avoid projecting into the future with any optimism. In contrast, the new Korean-Americans see future potentials in vital, positive terms.

From the TAT results it is obvious that youth are adapting differently in Japan and the United States.[4] The Korean cultural background of both samples is identical. However, their recent history going back some three or four generations has been very different.

Presented here is a small sampling of the present generation of Korean youth in Japan as they reflect personal alienation in response to the disparagement and degradation endured since the arrival of their parents or grandparents. As noted, most of these individuals speak no Korean and are indeed culturally, but not socially, assimilated within contemporary Japanese society. Characteristic of this group is a very high delinquency rate (De Vos, 1973) and many other behavioral symptoms of the alienation symbolized in the psychological material herein presented.

In this report we shall consider only the partial results obtained by a brief analysis of three cards as they reveal attitudes related to questions of achievement and alienation, and a fourth card dealing with attitudes toward authority. What we report is only one small part of the results we are obtaining by systematic comparisons of a samples of 100 records from Korea with a small sample of thirty-one from the cities of Kyoto and Osaka in Japan and a sample of fifty Koreans from Los Angeles. A previous publication (De Vos, 1983) reports in detail the findings on the Korean sample compared with previous samples of immigrant Japanese done by William Caudill in 1947 (Caudill and De Vos, 1956). What was remarkable in comparing these samples was the similarity in attitudes and concerns about achievement reflected in the thematic fantasy of both the Korean and Japanese samples (De Vos, 1973).

Card 1: The Boy with the Violin

Card 1, the boy with the violin, has proven to be extremely useful in comparative studies. In each instance the card elicits a concern with self-motivated ambition in a percentage of those tested. Such stories, by and large, have a future time orientation which depicts either a lack of resolution or a resolution in fantasy of the possibilities of successful achievement.

---

[4]The same Murray set of TAT cards was used with a sample of immigrant Koreans tested in Los Angeles and another located in the Kyoto Osaka area in Japan. For comparative purposes the original set was used as identical stimuli with several different cultural groups.

There is a striking contrast in the comparison of the stories given by the Korean samples in respect to any future time orientation. Card 1 evokes, for most samples, some percentage of stories related to achievement motivation projected into the future. Illustrative material can be more telling than the simple noting of statistics; hence, the following stories reveal more graphically what the tables demonstrate. The sample of Koreans from Japan suggest much less incentive to resolve stories toward a self-motivated positive view of the future. Of the fifty sampled in Los Angeles, twenty-five gave stories of eventual success in contrast with the sample from Kyoto and Osaka of thirty-one who gave *only two* such stories. Parental pressure appears as an element in the stories comprising 42 percent of the Japanese sample. In only two of these thirteen stories was there a positive compliance. Parental pressure also appeared in 32 percent of Los Angeles sample, in which five of sixteen were resolved positively. Overall, 87 percent of the Osaka-Kyoto sample gave stories with no resolution or with negative outcomes compared with 36 percent among the American Koreans. The Koreans in Japan do not give stories like the majority Japanese who worry about incompetence but persist. Yet the Koreans coming directly from Korea to the United States give stories similar to those of the majority Japanese. For example, in the Los Angeles sample we obtained such stories:

> (L.A. Female age 22) The boy hopes to be a good violinist. Today he played the violin badly before his violin teacher. He would practice the violin harder. He will eventually be a good violinist.
>
> [AA-self CC-artist ESB-shame AA-persist]

> (L.A. Male, 25) A pupil who learns to play the violin. He practiced the violin concerto several times but his performance was not very good. He thinks now how he will be able to master the tune. He will practice very hard and he will eventually master this concerto.
>
> [AA-self CC-artist AA-persist]

Concern with competence in thirteen of the stories results in overcoming incompetence and eventual mastery—in all but four of the Los Angeles stories. Competence is the single most prevalent theme dealing with personal motivation. In brief, the fantasies elicited on Card 1 give evidence that the Korean immigrants, by and large, maintain a very positive attitude about the possibilities of achievement.

They seem very aware of a necessity to have a strong will to overcome individual weaknesses and disabilities in attaining a long range goal. Contrast this with these illustrative stories from the Koreans in Japan.

> (J.K. Male, 25) He was bought and given a violin. But he does not know how to play the violin, so he is watching the instrument. He is worrying if he will become a violinist. I wonder if he has a toothache. That's all.
>
> [NSA-reward CB-able KB-illness]

Table 7.1

Comparison of Card 1: Los Angeles Koreans and Korean Japanese

Groups	*Los Angeles*	*Japan*
Total Cases	50	31
Themes		
1. Questions of Motivation and Competence	**29**	**14**
Percentage of Total Sample	58%	45%
Positive direction	25	2
succeeds—or studies hard	5	0
studying in process	2	0
concern with ability but succeeds	9	1
blind man studying to improve his attitude	1	0
concern with broken object, fixes it, succeeds	2	0
receives violin, will learn to play well	3	1
ambivalent about motives resolved positively	3	0
Negative or unresolved	4	12
receives violin—unresolved (physical complaint)	0	2
ambivalent about motives, unresolved or quits	1	6
concern with ability, unresolved	0	4
no ability, gives up	2	0
not concentrated, falls asleep	1	0
2. Questions of Parental Pressure	**16**	**13**
Percentage of Total Sample	32%	42%
Positive	5	2
complies and continues positively	4	2
changes task and succeeds	1	0
Unresolved or negative results	6	3
forced, results not indicated	5	3
complies but results no good	1	0
Refusal	5	8
complies only temporarily	2	3
refuses to study	3	5
3. Other	**5**	**4**
Percentage of Total Sample	10%	13%
Resolved	2	0
instructs the feeble minded	1	0
receives toy, throws it away	1	0
Unresolved	3	4
sad son seeking mother	1	0
scolded by father or teacher	1	1
cripple studying instrument to assist himself	1	0
accident trouble	0	3
Total unresolved and negative results	36%	87%

(J.K. Female, 25) He is bemused by an accident that has no relation to this violin. If this scene were after his violin practice, the accident might be related to the violin.

[KD-accident]

(J.K. Male, 26) He was receiving the lesson of the violin from a tutor. As he could not make a good sound however, he was annoyed, and then, . . . that is all.

[NSA-means CC-Failure PB-anger]

(J.K. Male, 22) Troublesome indeed. Past and future of this man? In this kind of era there is nothing special to say about the past. Nothing about present. Well, a violin and a child. They may separate in future. That's all.

[PB-trouble OD-loss]

(J.K. Female, 21) He is sunk in thought about how to play the violin better because he could not play well at his lesson. (refuses to end story)

[CB-defect]

The next large category of stories are those in which there is some mention of parental insistence on learning the violin. Both groups give stories of compliance wherein results are not depicted or are negative in tone. However, among the Japanese Koreans, eight of thirty-one total stories (compared with five of fifty of the L.A. group) depict a boy complying only temporarily, or outright rejecting parental insistence. This result is in the direction of the past results reported by William Caudill with a lower-class American sample where the rate of refusal was even higher. To illustrate:

(J.K. Male, 23) Parents had hoped this boy would have a lot of musical skill. But now he is thinking he should do otherwise. He will probably quit music although I can't guess what he will do. I don't know what he will do next but now he is being lazy.

[AA-parent AD-withdraw RD-work AB-decide]

(J.K. Female, 25) He was scolded by his mother once because he quit playing it. He feels gloomy because he has to go practice again. He will *not* be a violinist.

[NDA-scold PB-work DSC-family]

What differs from previous American samples generally is that among Japanese or Koreans there are very rarely stories of wishing to go out to play as is often the case with either lower-class, from the 1950s on, or present day middle-class American youth. Such individualistic interests in play are not readily depicted by youth from a Confucian family tradition. However, the Korean youth in Japan are resistive to parental pressure. They do not comply to an imposed task.

Card 17: A Man on a Rope

Let us turn now to Card 17 which is another symbolic measure of achievement concerns. There is a kinesthetic response to this card that results in the individual on the rope either being perceived as climbing up, resting, or climbing down. This card can be used as an indication of a relative amount of spontaneous vitality and upward surge projected spontaneously by particular individuals. The content elicited is also symbolic of attitudes of self confidence, the awareness of performance before an audience or concern in some instances with possible illegal or sexual activities.

Expressions of confidence and vitality betoken interest in active accomplishment. By and large the Korean American stories are highly imaginative compared to some other samples that have been studied. Out of the fifty stories, most of those sampled in Los Angeles see activity of an active energetic nature. Their stories are more positively toned than those gathered from Koreans in Japan.

> (KLAm, 21) He is an acrobat. He climbs up the rope. He seems to be an old man but he is healthy. He is a veteran acrobat. He is full of confidence in climbing on the rope. He is looking at somebody. He has a slight feeling of repugnance for his job but he will climb to the end of the rope.
>
> [OB-body CA-able CA-test PB-dislike]

> (KLAf, 29) He climbs the rope. He must be climbing up a mountain. Maybe he will go to the top of the mountain easily. He is a person who enjoys mountaineering. He enjoys rock climbing.
>
> [CA-test AA-self PA-nature]

> (KLAf, 21) This man is a circus performer. He wants to demonstrate his talents to his friends so he goes up a castle wall. He will climb to the top of the castle.
>
> [CA-present ESA-praised CA-test]

> (KLAf, 22) He is a naive country person but he wants to get a job in a circus troupe. He is now showing his talent to others. He will become a circus performer and will succeed well in such a job.
>
> [AA-self CA-present ESA-approve]

There is direct contrast between the L.A. and the Japanese group in the tone of the stories dealing with these stories of performance or sportlike activity. In contrast to the American Koreans with a very vital positive tone, the Japanese Koreans give stories in which the performer is malformed, or is clownish in a depreciated way.

(KJm, 25) Should I look at picture lengthwise or crosswise? He is playing a fool. His face is playing a fool. He is playing as a show, for a show booth. He is masculine. This is more cheerful one than the other pictures. I don't mind if he is naked or not. This is the most masculine and cheerful picture.

[ESC-detract-s ESA-approve OB-body PA-joy]

(KJf, 20) This reminds me of a hunchback of Notre Dame. He may be a clown in a circus. Is he naked? He may wear a tight wear. He is very masculine. He seems to be opposed against the law of gravity. This is the poorest picture that I've seen.

[KD-defect ESC-detract-s OB-body CA-defect]

(KJm, 31) This is . . . (laughing). . . . The present is that he is practicing a circus performance. He is coming down. He is an acrobat of the swing show. But he looks pretty old. So in the past . . . let' s see, he is an orphan and has lived in a circus. This is because I have a prejudice regarding circus life. He has been brought up there as an orphan, or a child of a refugee. He joined the circus group and was taught acrobatic skills. Well, the present is that he is practicing it and well, the future is that he will live as a circus man as he lived, and lives, because this is the only way for him to live.

[CA-able NSD-means NSD-comfort AA-counter]

However, among the American Koreans it must also be noted that in eight of the active stories, the climbing is done positively but for illegal or unsanctioned activity. Here are examples of vigor being put to questionable purposes.

(KLAm, 25) The man is an inquisitive person and he likes to see games. He is climbing on a rope to see a game free. He will enjoy seeing the game and will satisfy his risky attempt.

[PA-curious AC-illicit]

(KLAm, 31) The place is a public bath. On the other side of a window is the woman's bath. This fellow tries to climb on the rope because he wants to look. He satisfies himself looking at many naked women's bodies. He will then come down on the rope without any accident. He is not a sincere man, but may be someone like a bad drunk.

[PA-curious RC-pr-sex RC-abuse]

Both groups have a number of reactions to the seeming nudity of the performer. A small number—four in the American and one in the Japanese group—see the figure as insane or demented. In the negative stories given by the Kyoto-Osaka group there is a tone of despair and degradation found in none of the American sample. There is alcoholic abuse mentioned. This is unique to the Koreans in Japan.

(KJm, 23) This is a monotonous wall, isn't it? (past) Probably he might have been a hero of a circus but he was once discouraged by a physical accident like breaking a bone or by a mental shock. Then he become afraid of going up high, was kicked out of the circus and indulged in drinking heavily. (present) This could be a prison. Anyway he is trying again, recalling his past. (future) He will not be able to go back to the colorful world that he was in before. Like in this picture, he will fall low. And probably he will *find no release from his drinking*. His face is gloomy. He has a recollection of the past, but reality is coming upon him . . . least he should do so.

[CA-past KD-accident RC-abuse CD-finish]

Both groups give a number of escape stories, but the American Koreans are more apt to see an escapee from prison apprehended by the police. Negative scenes of escape, climbing down, or some form of failure occur in 26 percent of the American Korean stories as opposed in the past samples of Caudill to 30 percent among the Issei and 22 percent of the American Nisei Japanese. This contrasts with 37 percent among Koreans in Japan.

Two of the Japanese Korean stories refer to a short story by Akutagawa evoking the sad plight of an alienated man doomed to hell. The Buddha, glancing down a well, sees him. Compassionately he has a spider send down a filament to allow the sufferer to climb. In his anxiety to prevent others from following up the delicate strand he kicks at his fellow suffers causing the thread to break, dooming him to hell once more.

(KJf, 23) This one reminds me of the "Thread of a Spider" by Akutagawa. And this man is the first one climbing, and there are some others following him, and he is telling them to stop, Well, so the story goes, a spider's thread is coming down . . . and when he says something, it is cut suddenly. . . . The thread is cut suddenly, and he will return to hell. . . . This picture reminds me of that story. But if so, his body. . . . His masculine body bothers me . . . the rope. He is not climbing a tree. But he may be competing in a rope climbing contest.

[CC-failure KD-accident OB-body MVA-game]

Many of the LA sample responses involved an audience and a confident performer.

(KLAf, 30) This picture is a circus performance. The man is climbing on the rope. He is prideful before an audience. He is satisfied with his occupation in the circus. He will continue in this job.

[CA-present ESA-status PA-satisfy]

This was true for only three of the Korean Japanese cases. Instead, they gave such stories:

(KJf, 25) He is not a primitive man because he has a long hair. He may *begin something after getting drunk*. After getting drunk, he said, "I can do everything." He was unclothed and began climbing up the wall.

[OB-body RC-abuse RC-wrong]

Table 7.2

Comparison of Card 17: Los Angeles Koreans and Korean Japanese

Groups	*Los Angeles*	*Japan*
Total Cases	50	27
Themes		
1. Climbing	**27**	**14**
Percentage of Total Sample	54%	52%
Climbing positive tone	20 (74%)	3 (21%)
going to the top (mountains, sportsman, etc.)	4	0
competing in contest	0	1
circus expert performing well	11	1
practicing, exercise	4	1
escape (very positively toned)	1	1
Climbing, performing, ambiguous tone	5 (19%)	5 (36%)
searching, watching, dreaming	1	2
escape from danger	4	1
performing (flat tone)		2
Performing, but with negative tone	2 (7%)	6 (43%)
performing, but with despair	0	1
refugee or orphan must earn living in circus	0	1
playing a fool, clown (hunchback 2)	0	3
drunk	0	1
just a blue collar worker, not so good	2	0
2. Climbing for unsanctioned activity	**8**	**2**
Percentage of Total Sample	16%	8%
mischievous	3	0
sexual	4	2
thief	1	0
3. Escaping, climbing down or falling	**13**	**10**
Percentage of Total Sample	26%	37%
escaping from prison, etc.	2	4
unsuccessful escape (recapture by police, etc.)	5	0
falls in escape from hell	0	2
running away, mad	4	1
accident, falls into alcoholism	0	1
falls to death (in circus 1)	2	1
self destruction in elevator shaft	0	1
4. Other	**2**	**0**
Percentage of Total Sample	4%	0%

(KJ.K.f, 25) I wonder if he is going upwards or downwards. Maybe he is going upwards. He is searching for something desperately. This does not let me feel anything but fear. I don't know.

[PB-anxiety]

In sum, even when symbolically climbing the Koreans in Japan give negative or self-disparaging stories compared with the L.A. Korean sample. The incidence of alcoholism among Koreans in Japan is high. Koreans drink in Los Angeles too, but debilitative alcoholism is not evident as it is in Japan.

Card 2: The Farm Scene

Card 2 of the Murray series shows a man working with a horse. It is generally interpreted as a representation of rural life everywhere. Although a horse is not used for plowing in Japan, out of hundreds of records De Vos has examined, only one or two comments to this effect have appeared. Generally speaking, people accept the card and project willingly into it according to their attitudes. The girl with the book in the foreground represents for many a concern for social change or achievement. Responses to this card typically either put emphasis on internal family dynamics and the need for work on the farm, a rural context, or on the future concerns of the young woman with the books. Results on this card can be rather complex to analyze since themes can vary considerably. There are cross cutting themes of family harmony and disharmony as well as themes of personal ambition that conflict with a concern about the fulfillment of obligations or other social roles.

Among the Japanese Issei in Caudill's sample, 43 percent of the stories emphasized negative feelings about the poverty inherent in farm life and compensatory activities toward self and family betterment. These themes harken back to the fact that the Issei who came to the United States in the early 1900s were indeed escaping the poor economic circumstances of farm life in Japan at that time. However, the second most prevalent theme among them (38 percent) was concern with ambition.

To summarize our present results comparing minority Koreans in Japan with L.A. Koreans: disharmony and alienation characterize the stories of Japanese Koreans while immigrant Koreans in America emphasize family obligation and ambition.

In the L.A. Korean sample, stories focus on problems of family harmony. The story content varies however and no particular issues become paramount. In other stories, a daughter is seen leaving to realize personal ambition. Out of nine such stories, five depict a returning to help the parents revealing a concern with a daughter's obligation to her family. In other stories, Koreans depict sexual triangular situations which cause conflict between two women. Such stories were totally absent in the Japanese but present in the Korean American samples.

Some stories among the recently arrived American Koreans depict situations in which the man is usually forced to make a choice between one or another woman. In the Korean stories, it is the young woman who invariably loses out to a wife. These stories symbolically illustrate the traditional duties of the man to his wife, whatever may be his straying sexual interest. This underscores continuing Confucian emphases on propriety and legitimacy which are still very explicitly discussed as moral imperatives among Koreans.

A second unusual theme found in the Korean sample, not to be found in some other groups, can be explained by the self-consciousness of Koreans about missionary work in their rural villages. In our sample of fifty there are nine stories mentioning missionary work as the activity of the protagonist. The missionary is represented by the woman with the books. The mission work is seen, in effect, as another form of achievement theme. Farmers initially resistive to her missionary efforts ultimately succumb to her persistence.

> (KLAf 22) This is a country in a pioneer stage. The woman with the books did missionary work in rural villages. Many rural people did not listen to her but the woman must have succeeded finally in her mission work.
>
> [NDA-teach NSC-refuse AA-persist]

The stories attest to the fact that Christians have played an important part in Korean modernization. This is acknowledged by Christian and non-Christian Koreans alike. They played and continue to play a forceful role in contemporary Korean society. There is more consciousness in the Koreans than in the previous Japanese sample to the girl as playing a woman's role rather than representing an abstract concept of individual achievement. The Koreans see more self-consciously a necessity to continue the woman's role than did the Japanese immigrants from Japan, and the young girl suggests problems of how to marry as well as problems of what to study. Any conflict between the two is resolved in the direction of maintaining the woman's role. In effect, Koreans are more Confucian in this respect than the Japanese.

> (KLAm 19) They are parents with their daughter. The daughter goes to school and the parents are peasants in the countryside. The parents want to be helped in their agricultural work by their daughter. The daughter cannot assist them. She is conflicted in her mind. What shall I choose between studying and farming. Sometime later she will assist her parents farming.
>
> [NSB-help AB-decide NDB-means RA-duty-o NDA-active]

> (KLAm 25) The young woman student on the left is in deep thought. In the past she was eager to study in school. Now she goes to school, she thinks, "If I did not study hard, I will have to work hard on the garden like those others. If I marry somebody, I will also be pregnant like that woman. After marriage, I will be a good wife and good mother."
>
> [AB-decide AA-counter FA-sex RA-duty-o]

We note how this respondent, throughout his story, makes the girl self-conscious of the alternative decisions to be made by young women. It is to be noted that more of these stories of roles are given by men than by women in our sample. In the stories given by the Korean Japanese, there was less concern with the specific dimension of women's roles:

> (JKf 25) What's this? (As if she received an unexpected picture.) It seems to be a scene of a farm. I can't explain it. I want to do this afterwards. Is it all right? The right woman seems to be angry, but absorbed to meditate. No. After all, she looks like angry. This person (left) seems to be daughter. She wants to talk to mother, but can't make an opportunity. There seems to be a split between them. That is all. I don't know any more.
>
> [HC-discord HB-split]

> (JKf 17) It is not a pleasant picture. The past . . . I cannot think too much about it. The past is nothing special. But, they may have been poor. This girl is not very attractive. She was inflexible. . . . I don't feel anything about the other two. From this scene I don't think they having been eating good food. This woman seems to be pregnant. She will have a baby and will continue to lead the same life. I don't feel anything.
>
> [NSD-means OC-display <u>OD-body</u> OB body FD-Affect]

> (JKm 22) I've seen this picture before . . . the past . . . May I say it in a word? There is no past, present, or future. It exists without time or feeling.
>
> <u>[PD-denial]</u>

> (JKm 22) Ah well. . . . Is it right just to give my impression? from this picture? [It] is a farm scene somewhere in a foreign country. . . . How to express it . . . well . . . it is not a prosperous farm. That's all.
>
> <u>[KD-means]</u>

Among the Koreans in Japan, their sense of alienation is represented by their withdrawal from the family implications of this card. The American Koreans depict family life in forty-three of their stories. They directly depict both harmony (fifteen) and discord (sixteen) in their stories. In other stories a girl is depicted as torn between personal ambition and family continuity. In sharp contrast, the Japanese Koreans in more than half of their stories see unrelated people, often in some state of personal dissatisfaction. The subjects withdrew from this card evasively by giving some form of card description. There is at best in some stories a resignation to circumstances.

> (JKm 16) A fantastic picture. It is a scene that appears in someone's dream This one (left) seems too sad. He (center) is cultivating a field. What is this woman? (right) She seems worried about something. This picture is fantastic as well as realistic.
>
> [PD-sorrow CB-worry <u>PD-unreal</u>]

(JKm 23) What is this? Naked man is disagreeable! I feel as if I have come to a world of different era. (past) (and present) This is a society that male is tortured and female can go to school and have more opportunity than male. A man is required to engage in physical work and woman is not required to do anything. (future) But it became a male-centered world after all in the result of males showing their ability.

[OC-display DDC-unfair CA-future]

(JKm 20) This woman (left) is waiting for somebody like a man or lover. But he has not appeared yet. She is thinking what to do if he did not come.

[FB-wait]

(JKm 31) Which one shall I talk about? I don't get a clear image. Well, the presence of a woman leaning against the tree is that she is pregnant, isn't she? So her future is that she is going to have a baby. I don't know her past. . . . The person in the middle looks like a Caucasian. But what does it mean that he is pulling his horse? He looks like a manual laborer. In the future, he will continue to work (laugh). The past, I don't know. The woman with the book here does not have much expression. She is a student, and in the future she will have a mediocre marriage. Her present and past are mediocre. . . . That's all.

[OB-body RB-resign]

Table 7.3

Comparison of Card 2: Los Angeles Koreans and Korean Japanese

	Groups	*Los Angeles*	*Japan*
Total Cases		50	31
Themes			
1.	Mission or social welfare work (% of Total)	**5**	**1**
	Percentage of Total Sample	10%	3%
	succeeds	5	0
	failure	0	1
2.	Harmony emphasized	**15**	**4**
	Percentage of Total Sample	30%	13%
	family role	5	2
	pioneering	4	1
	improve conditions	1	0
	guilty about school	1	0
	ambitious, returns (help to parents, etc.)	4	0
	unresolved about farm or school	0	1

Table 7.3

Comparison of Card 2: Los Angeles Koreans and Korean Japanese

	Groups	*Los Angeles*	*Japan*
3.	Leaves farm without discord	**7**	**3**
	Percentage of Total Sample	14%	10%
	parental sacrifice	0	1
	likes city or study more	1	1
	does not return from city, marries	2	0
	ambition but does not return (guilty)	1	0
	returns, but dislikes farm	0	1
	dislikes farm life	3	0
4.	Interpersonal difficulty	**17**	**6**
	Percentage of Total Sample	34%	19%
Loneliness		1	2
Sexual involvements			
	waiting for lover	0	1
	return to native land	1	0
	(triangularity)-responsibility	4	0
	triangularity/competition	4	1
Discord			
	discord resolution	2	0
	dislike farm/discord/leaves	1	0
	discord separation	3	0
	discord religion	1	0
	discord, no resolution	0	2
5.	Other	**6**	**17**
	Percentage of Total Sample	12%	55%
Neutral tone			
	unrelated activities or motives	5	3
	passer-by or observer	1	4
	picture description	0	3
	dream	0	1
Negative tone			
	exploitation of workers	0	1
	dissatisfied life	0	4
	male lack of opportunity	0	1

Table 7.4

Comparison of Card 7: Los Angeles Koreans and Korean Japanese

Groups	*Los Angeles*	*Japan*
Total Cases	50	31
Themes		
1. Younger-older: Cooperate, advice, comfort	**12**	**4**
Percentage of Total Sample	24%	13%
Positive older younger relationship	3	2
son's acceptance of father's advice or comfort	3	2
son's acceptance of a scolding	1	0
son succeeds father's business, but son doesn't give good impression	1	0
discord resolved in eventual harmony	3	0
son does not follow father's advice	1	0
2. Mutual cooperation and conflict	**10**	**8**
Percentage of Total Sample	20%	26%
No status diff.		
cooperative or positive exchanges	8	4
dispute or negative exchange	2	4
3. Conspiracy: Evil or negative activity	**13**	**1**
Percentage of Total Sample	26%	3%
Status diff. (older-younger)		
evil advice	0	1
businessmen conspiring (age diff. secondary)	7	0
older and younger conspire	2	0
older man deceives younger man	1	0
debauched son does not correct behavior	1	0
father bends to strong willed son	2	0
4. Conspiracy and evil activity	**11**	**16**
Percentage of Total Sample	22%	52%
No status differences		
friends together in a plot	2	2
two conspire against another	0	1
politicians conspiring	4	3
businessmen conspiring	3	6
evil thing going on nonspecific	0	1
lawyer and criminal	0	1
Mafioso types	1	1
hired to kill for money	1	0
5. Other	**3**	**2**
Percentage of Total Sample	6%	6%
lawyer advises client	1	0
man pressured to become son-in-law	1	0
"discussing"—no elaboration	0	2

Attitudes toward Authority: Card 7

A second set of attitudes which influence adult adaptation in minorities differently have to do with authority relationships seen in responses to Card 7, a picture depicting an older and a younger man in some form of conversation. In the Japanese this picture is most often interpreted as some form of mentorship, an older man such as a company president advising or encouraging a younger man. Among the Koreans there is, in contrast, many stories of conspiracy and plotting (48 percent in the L.A. group and 55 percent in Japanese Koreans). Compared with majority Japanese, relatively less attention is given to the age and status differential of the two figures. In Japanese Issei immigrants (De Vos, 1983b), 94 percent depicted compliant attitudes as did 68 percent of Nisei. In 28 percent of the Nisei, however, there was rebellion, assertion of autonomy, or status equivalent relationships. Only one Issei gave such a story. In majority Japanese in Japan, age disparity also remained central to the story (De Vos, 1973).

In the L.A. Koreans, a age-status differential still appears in 50 percent of their stories. However, in strong contrast, in the present sample of contemporary Koreans in Japan only in 16 percent is respect for age or differential status a consideration expressed in the story themes. In contrast to the L.A. sample who see positive younger-older situations in 24 percent of all their stories, the Japanese sample gave only four such stories (13 percent). One notes that overall, the Koreans in Japan are much less mindful of status differentials than are the Koreans in L.A. The Koreans in Japan are more negatively tuned than any previous sample collected. Only eight of their thirty-one stories (25 percent) have any positive quality.

In respect to conspiratorial situations, distrust is normative in both Korean groups. In L.A., in half of these older-younger situations (thirteen), there are thoughts of possible conspiracy. In eleven of the remaining stories without attention to age, there are other negative themes, either about politicians, business men, criminals, or simply friends, a total of 48 percent of their stories. One must conclude that the propensity to be politically or socially distrustful is heavily present in both samples. Being so inordinately high among those in minority status in Japan reveals further evidence of their sense of alienation. The problems of distrust toward authority, even evident in those coming to the United States, is compounded in Japanese Koreans by a bleak conviction that the future holds no hope. There is hope for success only if you curry favor with someone who is corrupt, as is suggested in the following:

> (KJf 25) They seem to be doing something evil. They are directors of a company or politicians. This older man is saying, "How is that business going? You have to manage successfully by using a bribe." So, younger one answers, "Yes, sir. I'll do it skillfully." This older man is talking calmly, this younger man (points to the right) is carefully listening to him. He is trying desperately to gain his favor.
>
> [MTC-plot DSA-soothe]

Contrast these stories with the more positive tone of the L.A. stories:

> (KLAf 23) They are discussing business. The person on the left is the other man's boss. The topic they are discussing is about the sales strategy of the company. The plan which will be produced from their discussion will be successful because they seem to be very bright men.
>
> [NDA-author MTA-task CA-present AA-peer]

> (KLAm 25) The man on the left is a professor and the man on the right is his assistant. They are waiting for the results of their experiments to test their hypothesis. Their hypothesis will be proven right and they will become famous scientists.
>
> [NDA-author MTA-task AA-peer EDA-fame]

Conclusions

In each of the cards utilized, the themes of the Koreans in Japan show a sense of alienation and lack of resolution toward either future accomplishment or a future positive destiny in interpersonal relationships. We have tapped themes of deep personal alienation which are pervasive and characterize many of the Koreans in Japan. This material gives indirect evidence of a contention that we have raised generally about the effect of degradation over several generations on a minority population. We do not posit that the Koreans remaining in Japan are genetically inferior or in any other way inferior to the sample that we obtained from new immigrants in the United States. We must see, therefore, that their social history and the vicissitudes of the Japanese effects on a minority population are to be read in the sense of personal alienation in youth pervading the sample obtained from Japan. Central to the negative influence of minority status in Japan is the pervading sense of personal alienation and negative self reference, which is in very obvious contrast to the attitudes found among voluntary immigrants to the United States, who move with the intention of bettering themselves and their families in their new setting.

This effect of minority degradation and disparagement is a general process whether it appears among Koreans in Japan or, in the American instance, groups subjected to caste like status for several generations (De Vos, 1982). Unemployment, resort to alcohol, family desertion, and other forms of alienated behavior is common among adult males.

A theme we shall further consider in a Brazilian context in chapter 10, volume II, below, is how some groups come to look with suspicion toward those involved in the political process. They see the functioning of politicians in a very critical perspective. Governmental or professional corruption are more readily elicited themes either from those suffering a degraded social status or experiencing economic destitution.

References

Covington, Martin V. and C.L. Omelich. 1979. It's Best to Be Able and Virtuous Too: Student and Teacher Evaluative Responses to Successful Effort. *Journal of Educational Psychology*, **71**: 688–700.

De Vos, George A. 1960. The Relation of Guilt Toward Parents to Achievement and Arranged Marriage Among the Japanese. *Psychiatry*, **23**(3): 287–301.

———. 1973. *Socialization for Achievement: Essays on the Cultural Psychology of Japan.* Berkeley: University of California Press.

———. 1978. Selective Permeability and Reference Groups Sanctioning: Psychocultural Continuities in Role Degradation. In Milton Yinger and Stephen Cutler (Eds.), *Major Social Issues—A Multi-Community View.* New York: Free Press.

———. 1980. Identity Problems of Immigrant Minorities: A Psychocultural Comparative Approach Applied to Korean Japanese, (Chapter 31). In Roy Simon Bryce-Laporte (Ed.), *Sourcebook in the New Immigration: Implications for the United States and the International Community* (pp. 321–328). New Brunswick, N.J.: Transaction Books.

———. 1982. Adaptive Strategies in American Minorities. In Enrico E. Jones and Sheldon Korchin (Eds.), *Minority Mental Health* (pp. 74–117). New York: Praeger.

———. 1983a. Achievement Motivation and Intra-Family Attitudes in Immigrant Koreans. *The Journal of Psychoanalytic Anthropology*, **6**(2): 125–162.

———. 1983b. Adaptive Conflict and Adjustive Coping. In Theordore Sarbin and Karl Scheib (Eds.), *Psychocultural Approaches to Ethnic Identity* (pp. 204–230). New York: Praeger.

———. 1992. *Social Cohesion and Alienation: Minorities in the United States and Japan.* Boulder, Colo.: Westview Press.

De Vos, George and Eun-Young Kim. 1993. Koreans in Japan: Problems with Achievement, Alienation Authority. In Ivan Light and Parminder Bhachu (Eds.), *California Immigrants in World Perspective.* New Brunswick, N.J.: Transaction Books.

———. 1993. Problems with Achievement, Alienation, and Authority in Korean Minorities in the United States and Japan. In Kwang Kyu Lee and Walter Slote (Eds.), *Overseas Koreans in the Global Context* (pp. 145–180). Seoul: Association for the Study of Koreans Abroad.

De Vos, George A. and Marcelo Suárez-Orozco. 1986. Child Development in Japan and the United States: Prospectives of Cross-Cultural Comparison. In Harold Stevenson, Hiroshi Azuma, and Kenji Hakuta (Eds.), *Child Development and Education in Japan.* New York: W.H. Freeman and Company.

———. 1990. *Status Inequality: The Self in Culture.* Newbury Park, Calif.: Sage Publications.

De Vos, George A. and Hiroshi Wagatsuma. 1969. Minority Status and Delinquency in Japan. In William Caudill and Tsung-yi-Lin (Eds.), *Mental Health Research in Asia and the Pacific* (pp. 342–357). Honolulu: East-West Center Press.

Henry, William E. 1956. *The Analysis of Fantasy.* New York: John Wiley and Sons.

Holloway, Susan. 1988. Concepts of Ability and Effort in Japan and the United States. *Review of Educational Research,* **58**(3): 327–345.

Kernberg, Otto. 1975. *Borderline Conditions and Pathological Narcissism.* New York: Jason Aronson.

Lee, Changsoo and George De Vos. 1980. Identity Problems of Immigrant Minorities: A Psychocultural Comparative Approach Applied to Korean Japanese (Chapter 31). In Roy Simon Bryce-Laporte (Ed.), *Sourcebook in the New Immigration: Implications for the United States and the International Community* (pp. 321–328). New Brunswick, N.J.: Transaction Books.

———. 1981. *Koreans in Japan: Ethnic Conflict and Accommodation*. Berkeley: University of California Press.

Roosens, Eugeen. 1985. Migration and Caste Formation in Europe: The Belgian Case. *Ethnic and Racial Studies*, **II**(2): 207–217.

Spindler, Louise. 1962. Menominee Women and Culture Change. *Memoir of the American Anthropological Association*, no. 91.

———. 1978. Researching the Psychology of Culture Change and Urbanization. In George Spindler (Ed.), *The Making of Psychological Anthropology*. Berkeley: University of California Press.

Wagatsuma, Hiroshi and George A. De Vos. 1984. *Heritage of Endurance: Family Patterns and Delinquency Formation in Urban Japan*. Berkeley: University of California Press.

Witkin, Herman A., Douglass Price-Williams, M. Bertini, B. Christiansen, P.K. Oltman, M. Ramirez, and J. Van Meel. 1974. Social Conformity and Psychological Differentiation. *International Journal of Psychology*, **9**: 11–29.

Chapter 8

Heritage of Exploitation: A TAT Report on South Brazilian Youth[5]

George A. De Vos

From 1991, we have been conducting research with the TAT in Brazil, for the most part with Professor Cicero Vaz in the southern state of Rio Grande do Sul. The samples used here were gathered as part of this research. Professor Cicero Vaz had obtained samples of Brazilians of various ethnic origins including Germans, Italians, and East European Jews, as well as Portuguese and Afro-Brazilians from the state of Rio Grande do Sul in southern Brazil. He had also obtained samples of indigenous Indians and settlers, mostly of Portuguese background, from the state of Amazonas near the city of Benjamin Constant on the Amazon River (see chapter 12, volume II). The Portuguese and Afro-Brazilian ethnic groups are derivative of an older migration that occurred during the period of colonial slavery that lasted until the 1870s. Since the 1870s, there have been migrants of German, Italian, and East European Jewish background, as well as Japanese, arriving since the turn of the century, for the most part settling in the southern areas, from São Paulo to the Uruguay border.

---

[5]Adapted from George A. De Vos (1997), "Heritage of Exploitation: A Brief TAT Report on South Brazilian Youth." *Political Psychology*, 18(2), 439–481. Also, George A. De Vos (1996), "Internalized Achievement or External Authority: Some Cultural Comparison of Responses to TAT Card 1." In Irving B. Weiner (Ed.), *Rorschachiana XXI Yearbook of the International Rorschach Society*. Göttingen: Hogrefe & Huber.

What we have been interested in during our initial comparative endeavors with the use of the TAT in Brazil has been to examine how social attitudes, especially about the primary family and toward authority as well as internalized attitudes about achievement, are reflected spontaneously in samplings of youth that will comprise the coming adult generation. How much is their view of social relations and future possibilities influenced by recent changes or by past family-social traditions?

Many Brazilians are mixtures of Portuguese with African or indigenous Indians. Most overtly claim either more Portuguese or Afro-Brazilian background. Fewer directly claim now to be "mixed" with one parent predominantly Afro-Brazilian and the other Portuguese.

Additionally, to Vaz's samples we have utilized the TAT materials of Takeyuki Tsuda who completed his doctoral work with a study of Japanese Brazilians both in Brazil and in Japan where many second and third generation Japanese Brazilians have returned as migrant workers (Tsuda, 1997). While in Brazil, he gathered Japanese materials including TAT protocols from both the São Paulo area and from Porto Alegré.[6]

Ethnic Differences in Brazil

There are many that consider that there are two "Brazils." Northern Brazil was initially marked by the political and economic traditions of a Portuguese colonial past with African slaves (ended only in the 1870s) and continuing profound problems of social exploitation reminiscent of the history of the agricultural American south. Until recently, north Brazilian traditions of exploitation continued without interference on large elite land holdings with impoverished labor, ethnically Portuguese, African, Amer-Indian, in various mixtures. However, it is to be noted that caste attitudes per se were not in force. Unlike in a true caste society, marriage as well as concubinage could readily occur across racial lines in Brazil. Individuals included in the elite Portuguese group could evidence some "mixed" ancestry without loss of status. A few individuals with dark skin who managed to gain wealth found that "money lightens."

In Brazil, the family as an institution became itself marked internally by exploitative social traditions. This was especially apparent in the treatment of women, except some among the élite. There were less puritanical Protestant religious influences than found in the American society. Sexual exploitation was more overt, less hypocritical, and less guided by rigid racial definitions or attempted prohibitions. Still today, lower status women, regardless of their African, Portuguese, or other mixture, continue to be exploited for their labor as well as their

---

[6]There were no observable differences between these two sets of Japanese Brazilians.

brief sexual attractiveness in youth. Traditions of individual social advancement through education for either sex were not developed until very recently.

In contrast, the south, including the territory up to and including São Paulo, is for the most part a relatively prosperous part of Brazil. Rio Grande do Sul, where we located our study, is largely an immigrant state populated by Europeans arriving toward the end of the last century. The city of Porto Alegré is its capital. It has about 1,300,000 inhabitants. Porto Alegré is one of the cities of Brazil which has the best overall level of housing and living. There are other smaller cities and towns in the more mountainous hinterlands with Brazilians of various ethnic origins. Most notable are large settlements of Germans and Italians who first arrived in waves from 1875 on. Japanese first arrived at the turn of the century. Their immigration continued into the 1930s. A few immigrants continued to arrive until World War II.

After 1945, there has been continuous immigration into southern Brazil, but on a smaller scale. But as elsewhere, it has large pockets of both urban and rural poverty, most notable in the cities.

Of the Afro-Brazilian and Portuguese records from Porto Alegré, 59 percent were taken from schools servicing "Favela" areas. The other 41 percent tested were from other urban schools. A *favela* is a neighborhood consisting of the poorest Brazilians, often without inside running water, sewers, or sanitation facilities. They are built up unofficially by incoming families from the hinterlands. Dwellings can be rudely constructed of cast-off materials. Living quarters are severely crowded, and criminal and delinquent behavior is frequent, more often outside rather than within the community. Some become recognized and gradually upgraded into becoming an officially recognized area of the city.

The sample of Italian Brazilians included in this report were taken from a small Italian city from the center of the Brazilian wine industry in southernmost Brazil. The Japanese sample of individuals herein selected was obtained by Tsuda from urban areas in the state of São Paulo and from Porto Alegré. They are not strictly comparable to our high school samples. Tsuda's records were not taken from any high school but are representative of the adult population. We selected thirty of his youngest records. There are twenty-one individuals in their twenties, and nine in their thirties. (Trends toward more positive achievement orientation appear in these older records.)

Poverty separates the class levels of Brazilian society. According to data from the Brazilian Institute of Geography and Statistics, there are approximately 46,018 inhabitants over ten years of age who earn no more than half of a minimum monthly salary (about US$50), 182,791 who earn less than one minimum monthly salary (US$100 monthly), and 332,791 habitants earning double the minimum monthly salary. Families and individuals on this economic level live for the most part in Favela neighborhoods peripheral to the city. The number of families with both parents unemployed is large in these areas. This is where we obtained 59 percent of our Portuguese and Afro-Brazilian groups. In these poorer neighborhoods of metropolitan Porto Alegré, there are very few of German or Italian origin. One doesn't find any one of Jewish or Japanese origin.

Although many Brazilians are of mixed origin, there is some categorization into "Portuguese" and other categories of European origin versus those categorized directly as "Afro-Brazilian" or of mixed Indian-European background. In our sample, there were four youth directly categorized as having a "Portuguese" and Afro-Brazilian parentage. While first separated out as AB, for simplicity, we finally included them on the tables with the Afro-Brazilians, since their responses tend to resemble other Afro-Brazilians more than the Portuguese.

Over all, the largest change apparent in all segments of recent Brazilian society in the last twenty-five years is a notable increase in the level of education found throughout the country. One sees that a significant difference is now occurring in the education of youth. It is a historical irony that a conservative government dominated by military figures came to support secondary and university education by allotting considerable finances to the public educational systems and to the sending abroad of graduate students not only in technical fields, but in all subjects. There has been a shift in youthful formal instruction from about 2 percent of the population thirty years ago receiving advanced education to close to 25 percent of college age youth at the present time.

This has resulted in a better-educated populace, more effectively vocal and directly critical of the traditions of corruption that characterized elite politics in Brazil. This development of a more educated electorate has been a strong factor in the political changes going on in national politics at the present time. Even optimists doubted they could help oust a corrupt president, which was, however, actually accomplished at the time of my visit. A dynamic change is apparently at work in Brazilian society. We are not familiar enough with present circumstances to know whether this change is equally apparent in all sections of Brazil. What we observed, albeit briefly, and had described to us, was a continuing difference between the north and south of Brazil in social attitudes.

In the areas south of São Paulo, attitudes toward work and the internal dynamics of the family are more derived from immigrant cultural traditions brought in by more recent waves of immigrants from the end of the nineteenth century on, mostly from Europe, but some from Asia. For example, large settlements of Italians from the Po valley were coming in around the time of the abolition of slavery. Contrary to the American pattern that brought immigrant workers to the northern United States, the southern immigration into Brazil was not due to massive industrialization; rather, there was emphasis on progressive agricultural and livestock raising traditions, and at best, relatively small-scale industries.

Some members of these ethnic groups, especially Italian, Germans, East European Jews, and Japanese, settling in the south, have been more prone to seek out for their youth new careers through advanced education. As a whole, in recent years, this area has become more progressive economically. They see themselves as more hard-working and productive than the northerners. They see northern Brazilians as lazy and backward. There has even appeared a political movement to separate the three southern states from the north. It considers that taxes imposed on the south have been much too supporting of "less deserving" northern regions of the country.

In our research, attention has been focused not only positively on achievement motivation but also on possible problems of delinquency, violence, and destructiveness. The reported incidence of such problems is much greater among the adolescents of Afro-Brazilian and Portuguese origin than in any other ethnic group. As we shall document, the TAT results reveal a great deal of concern about family disruption and fear of abandonment in youth as well as other worries that we shall presently discuss.

After consulting with representatives of the Department of Education of the State of Rio Grande do Sul we obtained permission to initiate our research in state schools. In Brazil, the education system is divided into primary grades, "Primeiro Grau," which reaches from first to eighth grade (elementary or primary school, usually with children seven to fourteen years of age), and "Segundo Grau" (three or more years of secondary school, with students, usually aged fifteen to seventeen years old). The schools selected as experimental samples were located in three of the economically poorest neighborhoods on the outer limits of the city of Porto Alegré. Utilizing school records we made a selection according to birth certificates and general information about family structure of sixty-five students between thirteen and eighteen years old. These subjects had no obvious problems of a psychiatric nature. These sixty-five students were given an explanation of our purposes. They were told that they would be subjected to an interview and a psychological test. Thirty-nine students, twenty boys and nineteen girls, agreed to the process. Sixteen were Portuguese with both parents ethnically Portuguese. Seventeen had Afro-Brazilian parents. Four were of mixed origin with one parent Afro-Brazilian and one Portuguese. Two were of German origin. There was no notable skewing of the distribution of acceptees between male and female or Afro-Brazilian versus Portuguese from those that constituted the original sample. Similar procedures were used in obtaining the other ethnic samples. Some Japanese and East European Jews were also obtained from Porto Alegré. The Italian and German youth were tested in smaller cities in the mountainous interior where large settlements of these ethnic constituencies were located.[7]

Results

The Murray TAT Cards given to each subject were: 1, 2, 3BM, 4, 6BM, 7BM, 8BM, 13MF, 16, 17BM, and 18GF. Given the limitations of the present volume, we shall discuss here in chapter 8, volume II, attitudes centering around achieve-

---

[7]Unfortunately, prior to De Vos' involvement, the Murray instructions to use different cards for males and females makes comparison of the female German and Italian subjects impossible on some of the cards.

ment, and alternative concerns obtained on Cards 1, 2, and 17. Then, in chapter 9, volume II we start with views about loneliness, peer group or parental interaction as elicited by Cards 3 and 16. The detailed results on parental or authority relationships obtained from Cards 7BM and 6BM follow in chapters 10 and 11. These chapters in each instance follow up our comparisons between the Japanese Brazilians and other ethnic groups. To allow for some discussion of cross-cultural comparison, some incidental references shall be made to our previous publications on studies of American, Japanese, and Korean groups.

Note, again, that in our approach we did not take the total results of individuals and then compare them. We were not focused on personality patterns of individuals that comprise a social group. Rather, we simply analyzed the results elicited by each card. We are concerned with the normative distribution of given themes in a population.

Children from Broken Families: No Appreciable Findings

One specific concern we wished to test was whether negative fantasies of alienation, or illegal or violent behavior in thematic stories given to the TAT would be of higher frequency in adolescents from single-parent families as compared with those from families with two parents. Any such possible differences in the records were *not* borne out in our results; we could find no possibly significant trends. Overall, we could not find any significant differences between those from technically intact families with two parents compared with those from broken families. Only on one card (Card 16) did the tendencies to give more negative stories show any really appreciable difference.

Rather, we found that a general awareness of Brazilian social problems were present in the stories of Favela youth generally. And although statistically less frequent, stories of drug use and corrupt politicians appeared also in lesser numbers among the youth of other ethnic groups. Overall, the relative frequency of negative stories about a delinquent use of drugs, running away from home, poor school performance, the frequent beating of children by cruel parents, and the drunken behavior of a father was not significantly more present in those suffering actual family separation compared with those from intact families.

The General Awareness of Negative Social Circumstances

Our preliminary work with a group of ethnic Italian, German, and Japanese origin seems to indicate that concerns with abandoned or abused children or the use of alcohol or drugs by parents as well as youths themselves are not only of direct concern to those living in poor circumstances. To a lesser degree, they may be of some general conscious concern throughout Brazilian youth, and less apparent, but not missing, among the Japanese as well. Such concerns must be considered as a reflection of a charged social atmosphere in which such occurrences are on the minds of those who actually experience such behavior as well as some who are aware of it occurring among others not in their immediate environment, but elsewhere in their society. Economic concerns, including a sense of political mismanagement, appear periodically in the stories to a degree we have not encountered in other samples. Shared mass media may stir consciousness of negative potentials in their society in all Brazilians regardless of the relative differences in depicting goals of achievement and success.

Overall, our striking results with all the cards used in an urban favela do suggest, *per se*, a general characteristic neighborhood experience of economic deprivation witnessed by Afro-Brazilian and Portuguese children living in a socially exploitative environment. However, such themes are not absent entirely from groups living at some distance from urban poverty.

Attitudes toward the Future: Cards 1, 2, and 17

There were positive stories about self-motivated achievement given by some of our subjects, but with the exception of the Japanese Brazilians, they did not come close to the larger proportionate numbers of positive stories we have been finding true for ethnic groups and subgroups we have examined prior to working in Brazil. For example, previous research with Japanese American and Japanese and samples of recent Korean immigrants to the United States as reported in the previous chapters.[8]

On Card 1, depicting a boy looking at a violin, in the Brazilian stories processed so far, there were fewer projections into a distant adult future, although these were not entirely missing. While Portuguese youth from the favela give some optimistic themes, this Brazilian urban sample also gives stories in which there are occasionally expressed a sense of social helplessness, concern about deep personal inadequacy, concerns with poverty, lack of opportunity, family dissension, and tentatively hopeful needs for facilitative mentorship or financial assistance and emotional support. Girls in both the poorer city groups and among the Italians are more apt to see personal incapacity and project future negative outcomes than are boys.

On Card 2, a farm scene, Brazilians examined so far show some similarity to the family concerns with family harmony, support, help, and assistance shown in Mexican American and Central American records obtained by Suárez-Orozco (1989). In these records, contrasted with non-Hispanic American youth, the Mexican samples taken in Mexico and from Mexican immigrant youth in the United

---

[8]See also the Immigrant Central American records obtained by Suárez-Orozco (1989), and Mexican youth from a good high school in St. Miguel, Mexico (Suárez-Orozco and Suárez-Orozco, 1995). Both show much higher proportions of stories with self-initiated achievement motivation than do the Brazil Portuguese and Afro-Brazilians.

States (Suárez-Orozco and Suárez-Orozco, 1995), there is a general dependence on the assistance of older relatives or benevolent mentors for financial assistance. Such fantasies are not found in more individualistically oriented non-Hispanic, American youth (Connor and De Vos, 1989; Vaughn, 1988; Suárez-Orozco and Suárez-Orozco, 1995).

On Card 2, in both the Hispanic and Brazilian groups, for example, there is more concern with expressive relationships in the family than in personal ambition to study and leave home for a better life. While the farm scene evokes in some a sense of poverty to be transcended, in other Brazilians there is also more emphasis on positive family life in which support and nurture among the family members is envisioned in a positive way.

Card 17, depicting a man on a rope going either up or down, picks up some themes of vitality and exercise in Brazilian youth. There are proportionately fewer stories of an achievement type challenge to ascend a mountain or to strive for athletic success than found in immigrant Korean groups to the United States (see chapter 7, volume II).

Brazilian Responses to Card 1

The preponderance of Brazilian responses are about *instrumental* concerns. These can, for the most part, be classified into some of the subcategories related to concerns with Achievement (A) and/or Competence (C), as we shall illustrate in some detail. Secondarily, there are occasional concerns with Control (D), most often exercised by parental figures. Concern with an internalized sense of Responsibility (R) and the Mutual Purpose (M) category of competition or cooperation appeared relatively infrequently.

In the *expressive* realm there were a number of positive and negative stories in the Pleasure (P) category focused on feelings of joy or sadness. Dependency stories and stories of facilitation, reward, or deprivation categorized under Nurturance (N) appeared occasionally. Esteem (E) in stories concerned with shame or appreciation appeared in some stories with a group context. There were two negative stories of discord or violence scored under the Harmony (H) category. There was one story in which a positive need for harmonious group participation occurred as an expressive need. Affiliation (F) as a *positive* peer group theme did not appear in the present sample. Occasionally stories of peer group friendship activities appear in other samples as Vaughn and Connor reported in their American samples discussed above. However, negative affiliation themes of loneliness and isolation as well as separation through death appeared in a small number of stories.

Concern with material Objects (O) was occasionally represented in a preoccupation with the violin as a desired object, or the evocation of concerns with lack of material resources due to poverty. Fate or Kismet (K) categories were rarely elicited. There was a secondary concern with death or illness in only a few stories.[9]

The evidence of some cultural continuity in respect to achievement motivation in Japanese is strongly supported in material from Brazil. It is in line with our other research reports. Examined in quantitative detail, in the Brazilian samples on Card 1, there were concerns about achievement or competence *without the presence of any parental or authority figure* in 72 percent of the stories. This was very close to Vaughn's (1988) sample reported from Japan, 75 percent in the same categories in contrast to only 32 percent such stories occurring in his American high school samples (see chapter 6 above). However, more of the stories of Japanese Brazilians were left unresolved rather than ending positively. The results were closer to those of Connor's Japanese college sample (Connor and De Vos, 1989).

All Japanese samples showed some sensitivity to parental pressures toward accomplishment. There were questions of parental pressure in 14 percent of Vaughn's Japanese, compared with the Brazilian sample. While Japanese Brazilians gave five stories (17 percent) with parental pressure, there were only four of eighty-two (5 percent) such stories appearing in the remaining Brazilian samples. This contrasts with the Japanese Americans reported in Connor's more recent samples. As reported in chapter 6, above, the American culture is generally very high in eliciting stories of conflict between parental directives or expectation and personal interest on Card 1. The opposite seems to be the case in Brazil. The Brazilians do not see the parents pressuring their children against their will in this respect. In other Brazilian stories of parental pressure on some other cards, there periodically appears a pressure for a child to go to work rather than go to school. In effect, parental pressure is an American concern, not a Brazilian one.

As we shall discuss below in more detail, parents or teachers, when represented by Brazilians other than the Japanese, are seen as helping in 16 or 19 percent of the stories, or, in a not infrequent negative context, in some disruptive family situation.

In citing problems over questionable ability, the Brazilian stories were more pessimistic; in ten out of twelve (14 percent of the overall story total) such stories ended in failure. Ambivalence about motives occurred with some frequency among the Japanese (17 percent), more rarely in the other Brazilian samples (9 percent).

The "Negative Emotional States" and "Other" categories contain a few significant themes of parental abandonment in five of the stories. Such stories find no representation in either the Japanese or American samples of Vaughn. In another six stories, the boy is depressed or lonely, a theme found only very occasionally in American and Japanese records.

Among the Brazilians, the thirty younger Japanese we selected gave the highest proportion of positive, self-initiated achievement themes, with no other

---

[9]Stories of concern with illness were not infrequent on TAT Card 1 in the sample administered by Cicero Vaz to Amazonian Indians (see chapter 13, volume II).

individuals represented in the stories (37 percent). They also gave the most records of an unresolved or inconclusive nature related to concerns with inability (20 percent) or ambivalent motives (13 percent). Concerns were for the most part internally directed. They did not show the concern with poverty or other negative circumstances that appeared occasionally in the other Brazilian samples.

In sum, there is an observable downward gradation in achievement concerns from the Japanese on one end to the Afro-Brazilians on the other. The Italians are certainly median. There is also, with the exception of the Japanese, a sex difference in the distribution of positive and negative stories, with the girls showing more pessimism or helplessness about competence or achievement throughout the cards.

Table 8.1 is a detailed categorization of all the responses. We are representing various steps in the tabular representation of results. For most purposes such detail may not be necessary. We are also illustrating in detail the various types of stories elicited to serve as examples for those attempting to learn the subcategories as well as the more general categories we utilized. The underlined scoring we consider salient to classifying the story in any chart or table.

Some Specific Illustrations

The Japanese Brazilians

Returning to compare Japanese protocols with their fellow Brazilians as well as Japanese from the United States or Japan, we do find a cultural continuity of stories internally preoccupied with achievement or competence, rather than stories set in a more interactive context as found in the other Brazilian samples.

> (JBf17) (Card 1) A boy is thinking and looking at the violin. He wants to learn the violin and will become a famous violinist in the future.
>
> [AA-self ESA-status]

> (JBm19) (Card 1) A house with a boy thinking, studying music. He is looking and thinking. He will eventually be able to play the violin. As a boy of his age, he will be able to play the violin. If he is thinking about working hard, he will be able to do it.
>
> [AA-self CA-future]

Overall, as we have indicated, the positive achievement themes of the Brazilian groups, excluding the Japanese, occurred more in social situations (twenty-six of thirty-six stories or 72 percent). In sixteen stories (45 percent), external assistance was needed to become successful. There were *no* such Japanese stories of outside facilitation.

In many Japanese stories, the individual, to succeed, must overcome doubts about ability. In the present sample it occurs in 20 percent of the stories.

> (BJf 18) (Card 1) When I look at this picture, I see a boy who wants to learn the violin. But by his face, the way he is looking at the violin, he is having difficulties. All instruments are difficult to learn because they are all so different. I used to take piano lessons too, but it was very difficult because of the notes, technique, rhythm, etc. Why is he having difficulties? Because he is still a youth, and at his age, all that is different is difficult, but with time, it will become easier for him. In the future, I perceive that he will eventually be able to play this violin—it is simply a matter of time. It is hard at first, but becomes more easier later.
>
> [AA-self CB-arduous AA-persist CA-future]

When problems with personal ability were seen as the central issue, in five of six (20 percent) of these Japanese stories the issue might not be resolved with any certainty, but persistence is emphasized.

> (BJf 33) (Card 1) Practicing the violin, but it is not going well. Thinking and realizes he must try harder from now on.
>
> [CB-arduous AA-persist]

Only in two of their stories is there even any mention of any desire to be taught by someone, and it is in the context of having to persist by oneself despite the difficulties with *Competence*. In these stories the focus may be more on issues of competence than on a will to succeed, which may be taken for granted.

> (BJf 3) (Card 1) Is it broken? No. Had a father who was a musician. Father was one of most famous in São Paulo. Father became sick and could not longer teach him, but he really wanted to learn. One day, looking at the violin of his father . . . very sad and is thinking . . . much better if he could play the violin.
>
> [OB-break EDA-fame KD-illness NDD-unable CD-unable PD-sad]

In the Brazilian sample there is more “thinking” and less “doing” than in the previous Japanese samples. The more typical theme found previously is to mention hard work rather than emphasizing inactive thinking or present incapacity.

> (BJm 10) (Card 1) Maybe received a present from his father, who used to be a violinist. Imagining whether could be as good as his father, or could follow in his footsteps. Maybe will become able, but currently sad because he can’t. Sees it’s difficult to become like his father.
>
> [NDA-reward AA-inspire CB-hope CB-arduous PD-sad]

> (BJm 44) (Card 1) Gazing . . . listened, but cannot play. Wants to, but doesn’t know how.
>
> [AB-inactive CD-unable]

Even though there is less activity mentioned in our present Brazilian samples, ten out of thirty of the Japanese stories were straightforward concerns with achievement. There is expressed curiosity about the functioning of the instrument and a desire to know. There is direct attention called to a "will" to learn.

> (BJm 26) (Card 1) Thinking about playing, whether he could hear how it sounds, curious to know who invented it, and how one gets sound out of the instrument. He wants play and to know how the violin functions. Intends to learn his music.
>
> [AB-think PA-curious CA-future]

> (BJm 4) (Card 1) Wants to learn. Will eventually learn because he has a way of being studious.
>
> [AB-think RA-duty-s CA-future]

Four of the 30 stories of the Japanese Brazilians bring in ambivalent motivation.

> (BJm 13) (Card 1) Child is practicing the violin and is learning how to play, but is bored. Can't play well although he has practiced, therefore bored. Attitude is expressed in the position of his hands.
>
> [AA-persist PB-bored CB-arduous]

But only one is outright rejection.

> (BJf 1) (Card 1) Thinking and saying thank you for being able to study the violin. Has tried hard to play but too difficult for him. Looking at the violin. He will not become a violinist. Does not want to study.
>
> [NSA-grateful CD-finish AD-motive]

In Brazil, in the stories so far scored, the pattern of parental pressure toward learning is uniquely Japanese.[10] Five of the Japanese stories are about feeling constrained to play the violin. In one instance it is the father, in another, parents, but in three stories the source of the pressure is not named. The prevailing attitude is resistance to this pressure. Of the nine stories about resistance to parental pressure or dubious motivation, seven are given by women (about 40 percent of the female responses). In studying Nisei in the United States a resistive trend was more noted in Nisei women than in men. There may be a proneness in some to reject the traditional expectations directed toward women.

> (BJf 25) (Card 1) He does not like the violin, but will play it. By his manner, children act like this, they do not have lots of persistence. He has difficulties now, but will eventually be able to play. His parents will force him to do so.
>
> [PB-dislike AD-endure RA-duty-o DSA-comply CA-future DDC-press]

---

[10]We have not yet processed a sample of Jews of East European origin living in Porto Alegré. Some stories of parental pressure will be forthcoming from them.

(BJf 47) (Card 1) Poor fellow . . . father forced him . . . because father likes classical music. Boy doesn't want to play. Future, he will become good, but will not become extremely successful or famous.

[DDC-press AD-motive DSA-comply CA-future ESB-status]

(BJf 2) (Card 1) Made to study the violin but is not able.

[DDA-educate CD-unable]

In the "Other" category there is only one story given by the Japanese sample of a troubled youth playing the violin as distraction. As we shall show, stories of inner stress are more often elicited in the other groups.

(BJf 46) (Card 1) Thinking and troubled . . . can't think of a solution. So he decided to play the violin for relief.

[PB-trouble CD-finish PA-relief]

The systematic presentation of these stories from the different ethnic groups in Brazil should well illustrate that the differences found in the nuances of the stories can be brought out by using an objective scoring system applied to the manifest content of the stories. The Japanese in Brazil continue to express self-motivated achievement.

Table 8.1
Detailed Comparative Responses to Card 1
The Boy with the Violin: Brazilian Ethnic Samples

Total	**112** (male 57; female 55)
Portuguese	29 (15 m; 14 f)
Afro-Brazilian (4 mixed)	29 (17 m; 12f)
Italian	24 (11 m; 13 f)
Japanese	30 (12 m; 18f)

1. Concerns with Motivation and/or Competence (A), (C)							
	m 40	f 41	total **81**	P 24	AB 18	I 16	J 23
% of Total Sample	72%	71%	72%	83%	62%	67%	77%
Achievement Concerns (AA) (Positive Endings)		(31%)	[46]	18	9	8	11
	m 24	f 22					
Self-Initiated Achievement Themes			[18]	6	2	1	10
	m 10	f 7					
with eventual success				m,f	-	m	5m,4f
with inspiration				f	-	-	f
against poverty				m,f	m	-	-
against loneliness				m	-	-	-
Ambivalence Overcome			[2]	2	0	0	0
	m 2	f 0		2m	-	-	-

Table 8.1

Concern with Ability Overcome			[4]	1	0	2	1
	m 2	f 2		m	-	2f	m
Success in a Group Context			[6]	3	1	2	0
	m 4	f 2					
emphasis on competition				m	-	m	-
official appreciation				m,f	f	m	-
Achievement or acquired competence due to gift, assistance, or direction			[16]	6	7	3	0
	m 6	f 10					
given violin				2f	m,2f	-	-
assisted or taught				m,2f	2m	2m,f	-
directed				f	2f	-	-
Thinking or Dreaming (AB)		(4%)	[4]	0	2	0	2
	m 3	f 1		-	-	2m	m,f
Competence Problems (C)		(16%)	[18]	3	5	4	6
	m 7	f 11					
Willing motives: but inconclusive due to ability problem				f	f	-	3f,3m
Failure or negative ending				m,f	2m,2f	m,3f	-
Negative or Unresolved Motives (A)		(11%)	[12]	3	2	3	4
	m 5	f 7					
Inconclusive or Negative Outcome				2m,f	m,f	m,2f	m,3f
2. Authority or Parental Pressure (D)							
	m 3	f 6	total 9	P 1	AB 2	I 1	J 5
% of Total Sample	7.5%	15%	(11%)	3%	7%	4%	17%
Compliance with Authority			[3]	1	0	1	1
	m 1	f 2		f	-	m	f
Rejection or Unresolved Problems			[6]	0	2	0	4
	m 2	f 4		-	m,f	-	m,3f
3. Negative Emotional States (P), (F), (H)							
	m 6	f 5	total 11	P 3	AB 4	I 2	J 1
% of Total Sample	15%	12%	(14%)	10%	14%	8%	3%
Troubled, Depressed, Lonely (P), (F)			[7]	2	1	0	1
	m 4	f 2		2m	m	2m,f	f
Family Problems, Abandonment (H), (F)			[4]	1	1	1	2
	m 1	f 3		f	f	m	2f
4. Other							
	m 8	f 5	total 13	P 1	AB 5	I 5	J 2
% of Total Sample	20%	12%	(16%)	3%	17%	18%	7%
Concern with the Nature of the Objects (O)			[5]	0	0	3	2
	m 3	f 2		-	-	2m,f	m,f
Concern with Pleasure or Possession of Violin (P), (O)			[8]	1	5	2	0
	m 5	f 3		f	4m,f	m,f	-

Italian Brazilians

The stories of the Italian youth from a provincial town reveal another directed social orientation and awareness. Seventeen of the twenty-four Italian records are concerned with achievement, motivation, or competence. These stories are often related externally to a schoolroom situation in which positive performance is anticipated or to facilitative mentorship. They generally indicate a compliant attitude toward authority. Only three, however, have positive outcomes in self-preoccupied situations concerned with ambition or questions of ability.

Facilitation occurs, as it does in all the other Brazilian records, with the exception of the Japanese. The boy is given lessons and becomes great. In another, receiving a violin from his father, he studies and succeeds. In a third, he needs the opportunity given to enter a seminary and becomes a violinist as well as a good priest. Two instrumental stories are of a boy studying to get a good grade and another complying to a school assignment. In seven stories, however, there are negative or unresolved situations related to doubtful motivation (three) and frustrations over inability (four). Five of these negative stories are given by Italian girls.

Parents, teachers, and a priest appear, as do fellow students. Throughout, one gains an impression of an awareness sense of social context, with no individualistic challenge of any authority figure. There is, however, a story of a father injured due to the son's inability to rescue him, which of course deserves symbolic interpretation.

In the remaining stories, there is one theme of an abandoned child. Three are preoccupied by the nature of the instrument, and two give rather extraneous stories.

It must be noted in contrast to the Japanese, an internally oriented story of self-initiated achievement appears in fewer stories. One is of self-motivated achievement.

> (BIm 1) (Card 1) A child wanted to learn to play violin. He began to take lessons When the child grew up, he or she became a great violinist. The child worked hard and made it.
>
> [AA-persist CA-future]

Five stories are similar to the Japanese in which the boy overcomes problems of competence and succeeds (20 percent). For example:

> (BIf 7) (Card 1) A boy went to a violin lesson. When he arrived there he did not know how to begin. He found this instrument difficult. He began to wonder whether taking lessons was good or not. After a long time he decided that in life everything is difficult, but not impossible. He went to the lessons and learned to play violin.
>
> [CB-arduous DDA-educate AA-persist]

In several stories, facilitation, opportunity, or competence are direct conscious issues.

(BIf 13) (Card 1) One day a certain boy received a present from his father, and he was worried because he did not know how to use the present, which was a violin. He asked his father for some lessons in order to know how to play it. He receives the lessons and learns to play.

[NDA-reward CB-arduous DDA-educate <u>AA-parent</u>]

Opportunity appears in one story through the facilitation of the Catholic church. The church appears implicitly as a means of social advancement for some youth.

(BIm 23) (Card 1) It is a boy who liked violins. His dream was to learn to play it. His parents could not afford it. One day a priest came and invited him to enter a seminary, and there people learned to play various instruments, among which were violins. He learned to play, becoming a good priest.

[AB-dream NDD-means DDA-educate <u>AA-parent</u> RA-duty-o]

The positive assistance or intervention of some mentoring figure appears in two stories. For example:

(BIm 6) (Card 1) It seems to be a boy who was given a violin a long time ago and who is not able to learn. He takes lessons but he does not manage to learn. His mother says he should learn; the father gives the impression that he does not like it. He tries to learn and is not able to. He looks sad. He sits and remains thinking of why he cannot learn. The father changes his mind and encourages him; he becomes more enthusiastic and works hard; he manages to learn.

[NDA-reward CD-unable NDA-comfort <u>AA-parent</u>]

Doubtful motivation or negative competence appears in seven stories. Five of these negative stories are given by girls. For example:

(BIf 3) (Card 1) The boy is studying because he needs to get a good grade, but he does not feel like studying, he is sleepy. He did not study and he won't do well at the test. He thinks that it is a notebook or a violin. He feels bad about it because he wanted to do well, but he was sleepy because he had to help his father and didn't sleep at night.

[ESA-approved <u>AD-motive</u> PB-tired RD-work RB-regret RA-duty-o]

(BIf 10) (Card 1) It was a boy who tried to play violin. Maybe he was not able to do it for various reasons: for knowing not how to play or for having not learned right. He quit playing and became very frustrated. He felt incapable of accomplishing something. This shows everybody's fight, the profits or the frustration that the person's day had. He quit playing the instrument because a person who feels incapable once does not try to do it again.

[AA-self AD-endure CD-chagrin CD-weak]

In the remaining seven stories (30 percent), the concerns have nothing to do with motivation. There is one theme of an abandoned child, another of a boy who doesn't know how to shoot a gun to protect his father from a wild beast. Three stories are boys preoccupied by the nature of the instrument, and two with rather extraneous stories. There is in some a respect for authority or a need of help.

(BIm 16) (Card 1) There is a boy who arrived at home and saw a strange thing. And he kept thinking. In the beginning he thought it was a support, but he soon discarded the idea. As he did not know, he went straight to ask his parents The father said it was a sound instrument.

[CB-help NSA-assist NSA-edified]

The Portuguese Sample

Overall, the Portuguese gave the highest number of optimistic responses of any of the Brazilian subgroups including the Japanese. Nine (31 percent) of their positive stories were achievement themes. In three of these stories achievement overcomes poverty or loneliness. In 21 percent of their stories (six), their positive achievement is assisted by parental or educational authorities. In another three stories there is appreciation or successful competition depicted. Some self-initiated achievement stories (AA-self) were concerned with future competence (CA-future) and hard work (AA-persist). Here are some excerpts from the full stories:

(BPf 12) (Card 1) Studying hard to become a capable lawyer.

[AA-self CA-future AA-persist]

One demonstrates a sense of responsibility:

(BPm 54) (Card 1) Studying for something important. For a test. Dutifully studious. Will continue studying.

[AA-self RA-duty-s AA-persist]

Achievement may be inspired (AA-inspire) by a past figure, usually a father or family member. In one particular story the father's fame is a direct concern evoking use of an evaluative category (EDA-fame). A fateful accident (KD-ac-die) caused the father's death.

(BPm 62) (Card 1) Father's violin. His name was known almost all over . . . car accident. Sad, and kept father's violin would look at the violin and decided would be just like father. Try to be as great. In 10 years managed to make dream come true.

[EDA-fame AA-inspire ESA-fame AA-persist]

Compensatory achievement usually occurred in situations of poverty (KD-poverty) or to overcome some social malaise such as loneliness (FB-alone), or some unspecified sadness (PD-sorrow). Becoming famous (ESA-fame) is a possible outcome.

(BPm 05) (Card 1) The lonely boy. Once the boy named Rafael decided to make a story which talked about our world. He locked himself in the bedroom and began his story. His mother said that it is nonsense, since he is yet too young to make stories. But the boy insisted on his story and went to his bedroom and there he shut himself. He spent hours and hours upon his text until, at a time, he finished the text. Soon after that he went downstairs, to the living room, and called his mother: "Mom come to see the story I made." Then the mother read her son's story and found it great, for she had never thought that the boy had evolved that much. Rafael became so cheerful that he went again to the room to write new stories. The days passed and the boy grew. At the school the boy was already a great student. At 15 years old he started to make his own book and so he wrote more books and became famous.

[FB-alone AA-counter ESA-approved PA-relief ESA-fame]

As part of one's instrumental purposes in compensatory achievement, an expressive theme of helping others can be introduced in the story as a need to nurture (NDA-charity). This is most often seen on Card 2 in stories where there is a repayment for the sacrifice of parents (NDA-family) (see below).

(BPm 09) (Card 1) A boy is deciding what he is going to do in order to study, but he was turned out of the school. He thinks of how he is going to get a job. Then I think, will I have to work as a garbage collector? Working as a garbage collector is too much running! But one day I went to a school and they accepted me, but the headmistress said that if I made one single disorder or difficulty I would be turned out again. Then I studied as hard as I could and passed from year to year. I reached college and wanted to be a lawyer, and thought: "Lawyer is a very good function and I'll have a family to celebrate this joy."

[KD-thwart PB-work CA-present DDA-censure AA-counter AA-nurture NDA-family]

Stories can introduce other complex issues of how to overcome economic duress, sadness, as well as frailty.

(BPf 53) (Card 1) Fair, small, thin boy, sad expression, wanted to learn to play instrument at home, but couldn't afford a single lesson. decided to work and got a job. What he earned wasn't enough. Finally dutifully worked for teacher in exchange for lessons. Succeeds.

[OB-body PD-sorrow KD-poverty AA-counter RA-work]

In this Portuguese sample, two stories of motivational problems are overcome. In such stories there are usually unresolved problems over possible motivation to whether or not to commit oneself to a task and give up other possible pleasurable activities (AB-waver) such as play (PA-play) or activities with friends (FA-friend). In many of these stories there is an achievement motivation that triumphs. In others considered below there is not. Resolutions toward seeking to accomplish as an *inner* decision are to be distinguished from the interpersonal stories considered below wherein *parental pressure* became a central issue.

In the present stories when a sense of duty arises, it is self-imposed (RA-duty-s) not imposed by others (RA-duty-o).

> (BPm 11) (Card 1) He is ambivalent about having fun or being studious. He dutifully studies and finishes school.
>
> [AB-waver PA-play RA-duty-s AA-persist]

Receiving the gift of a violin (NDA-reward) can raise the issue of motivation. A decision to take on the task may not be expressed in terms of obligation or duty, but rather by becoming self-motivated.

> (BPm 59) (Card 1) Given a violin for birthday. He didn't like it much. Then he decided to take violin classes and now is a violinist.
>
> [NDA-reward PB-dislike AA-persist]

Some stories express need for assistance (NSB-help) when capacity is in doubt. One story in which a question of ability arose is successfully resolved, even though there is no help (NSD-no-help) or someone is unable to help (NDD-unable). One eventually learned despite a lack of help.

> (BPm 08) (Card 1) Once upon a time there was a boy who liked very much playing violin, beautiful, but he didn't know how to do it. As his grandfather was already too old he could not teach him to play violin. Then the boy grew and learned to play, and became a great violin player.
>
> [PA-esthetic CB-able NDD-unable AA-persist]

Concerns with competence or other instrumental activities often take place in the presence of peers. In a few there can be a sense of instrumental competition which is overtly expressed as successful in academic endeavor (MVA-profess), in games (MVA-game), or as some act of being smarter than someone else (MVA-smart).

> (BPm 57) (Card 1) Studying for a math test. Serious. He is the last student to leave school. Nervous. Very surprised. Received highest grade in his class. became the first student of his class.
>
> [RA-duty-s AA-persist CB-able MVA-profess]

In other group contexts it is expressive needs for satisfactory appreciation or recognition that are of salient concern (ESA-approved) (ESA-praised), (ESA-fame). A concern with shame (ESB-shamed) may be expressed. There can also be expressed a social need to participate as part of a group. Such stories are classified in the Harmony category (HA-group). Need for social appreciation appeared in five stories. For example:

(BPf 14) (Card 1) Does well on test. Is appreciated by his teacher.
[CA-present ESA-approved]

(BPm 15) (Card 1) Wants to be in orchestra. Shameful about ability, afraid of error. Watches how friends do it. Finds too, he is able. Becomes recognized as great.
[HA-group ESB-shamed CB-able CA-model AA-self EDA-fame]

Six stories (five by females), see success due to some facilitation by parents or mentors: providing a boy with a desired violin (NDA-reward) or having received a violin as a gift (NSA-reward); teaching or advising him (NDA-advice); transporting him to a teacher (NDA-active); or a mother's efforts to support him (NDA-means) and enroll him in a class (NDA-active). For example:

(BPf 01) (Card 1) Marcos was a boy who had a dream of learning to play violin. But he did not understand how to use it. He used to spend all the time looking at the violin. He would like to learn with someone. One morning, Mr. Pedro, an old man who knew how to play violin decided to teach Marcos how to play violin. As time passed, with good lessons, Marcos became a violinist.
[AB-dream CB-help NDA-advice AA-persist]

(BPf 07) (Card 1) Dreamt of one day being a great violin player, but his dream couldn't come true: his parents couldn't afford lessons. Until his aunt got an old, second-hand violin, and he fixed it up with damaged things; and so played and nowadays he is a great violin player.
[AB-dream KD-poverty NDD-means NDA-reward CA-defect AA-persist]

(BPf 61) (Card 1) Willing to learn to play violin . . . thinking to learn should first study and examine all of its parts. Then he looked for someone to teach him. He found someone and learned.
[AA-self PA-curious NDA-assist CA-present]

Some themes show following direction or advice to succeed or compete.

(BABf 17) (Card 1) Follows parents' advice to compete successfully.
[NSA-edified MVA-profess]

(BABf 79) (Card 1) Difficulties in mathematics. Looked for orientation and was ordered to study and now he is studying hard and does well at the test, probably. Managed to do well.

[CB-arduous DDA-author AA-persist CA-present]

The Portuguese have only one story with any possible authority pressure. It merely depicts a boy complying with a teacher's task.

(BPf 16) (Card 1) Writes lesson given as an assignment.

[DSA-author]

There are six stories about problems of ability intermixed with insufficient motivation, in the Portuguese sample. In two there is resultant failure.

(BPm 51) (Card 1) Wondering whether he would play it or not, whether continue course or not. Keeps looking and thinking. The boy has fair hair. The color of his eyes, green or blue.

[AB-decide OB-depict]

(BPf 55) (Card 1) Given violin as present. But doesn't know how. Will have to take lessons. But remains sad because he can't learn.

[NSA-reward CC-inept PD-sad]

In the "Other" category, one story is simply about the pleasure of playing the violin.

(BPf 13) (Card 1) He has pleasure in playing a violin.

[PA-satisfy]

A final three stories have emotional distress. In one the boy is depressed (PD-depress). One lost his parents in an accident (KD-ac-die FD-death). Another is of a boy who can't concentrate due to the discord between his parents (HC-discord).

(BPm 10) (Card 1) The sad boy is reading; depressed.

[PD-sad]

(BPm 63) (Card 1) He is looking at a picture of himself, his father and his mother, because there had been an accident with him and his parents, and both died and he survived. In the future he would like to have his parents back.

[KD-ac-die FD-death FB-alone]

(BPf 04) (Card 1) Parents are separating; miserable, isn't able to concentrate.

[FC-split PD-suffer CD-unable]

Afro-Brazilians

Afro-Brazilian results contrast significantly from those of Portuguese youth sampled from the same schools. While Afro-Brazilians have 31 percent positive achievement stories, in seven of nine of these stories, they were given assistance or direction. In contrast to the other groups, they were less goal oriented and more focused on expressive themes of a positive or negative nature. They had seventeen stories with negative endings (58 percent). Four out of five stories with instrumental concerns about ability end in failure. Their stories with some desire for competence or achievement have a plaintive quality with expressive needs for help or direction as well as an abiding sense of economic deprivation than cannot easily be overcome. Throughout the stories there is a symbolic concern about receiving, possessing, or caring for the violin. One can readily interpret this concern with possession of the violin as some pervading sense of general economic want or deprivation. The question is *why* is it not equally appearing among Portuguese youth living in equally economically straitened or deprived circumstances?

The only successful self-initiated story by a male from a single family household was about the compensatory active achievement of a son overcoming illness and want.

> (BABm 19) (Card 1) The boy was sick and had a dream of learning to play violin, but his father was very poor and could not afford the course. Boy started working and saving money and put the money in the safe. Time passed, and the dream came true.
>
> [KD-illness AB-dream <u>NDD-means</u> RA-work <u>AA-persist</u>]

One other positive achievement story involved worry about performance, but ended with successful accomplishment and social recognition.

> (BABm 82) (Card 1) Once upon a time a boy who liked very much reading. Then, one day chosen to read a text for his classmates. He spent many days reading and reading same text, in order that there would be no mistakes in his presentation. The great day came and he was ready; beside him were two girls ready to read too. The first read her text with enthusiasm, but the text was huge. Then, the whole class thought that she had read badly, for she read one line and skipped three. The second didn't want much to read because she wasn't prepared. Finally there came the boy's time and he read his text with much inspiration, for he knew that his grade was ten!
>
> [<u>AA-self</u> ESB-shamed <u>MVA-profess</u>]

The other achievement-motivated stories (seven) all emphasize a need for outside support or assistance. For example:

(BABf 16) (Card 1) Given violin as present—didn't know what to do with it—tried to find some use; asks his parents for lessons. Mother went and enrolled him. Started . . . intends to continue studying until he becomes a good violinist.
[NSA-reward CB-able NSB-help NDA-active AA-persist]

(BABm 85) (Card 1) It's a boy. His dream was to learn to play violin or music. But he couldn't afford a violin. One day a neighbor who was a music teacher asked him a favor; he did it and in exchange he was given a violin. With the help of a manual, he learned to play it. Now he is studying, he's beginning to study the violin. He used to practice every day. With time he became a great musician.
[AB-dream KD-poverty NDA-social NDA-reward AA-persist]

(BABf 77) (Card 1) Sad. Liked playing. Violin got broken. Parents no money. Spent hours fondling it. Father felt sorry. Took extra work for repair wanted to see son smiling and playing again. Father had it repaired. Boy improved. Becoming great violinist.
[PD-sad OD-broken NDD-means NDA-devote CA-improve AA-persist]

Two of the other positive male Afro-Brazilian stories are of dreaming rather than actual activity.

(BABm 18) (Card 1) He is thinking of what he is doing in making a little house. He is deciding whether he shall make a house, a building or a church.
[AB-decide PA-create]

(BABm 29) (Card 1) Once upon a time there was a boy who liked to play violin. Always enchanted about playing violin. Always dreamt of success, of being the best violin player. [no ending]
[PA-esthetic AB-dream MVA-work]

Of the five stories about doubtful competence, four end in failure.

(BABf 33) (Card 1) A boy is sad. He is seated, looking at the guitar. He wants to play but he can't; he goes ahead, but he is very sad.
[PD-sad CD-finish]

(BABf 35) (Card 1) Sad, looking at his violin. He can't play. I think he wants to, but he can't.
[PD-sad CD-unable]

(BABm 75) (Card 1) Broke his father's violin. Kept wondering how to fix it, a very noble instrument. Pictured himself playing in a grand symphonic orchestra just like his father. Wouldn't be able to fix and finally left it for father.
[CC-break OA-awe AB-dream CD-unable RD-personal]

(BABm 25) (Card 1) Marcos is learning how to draw, but he was in doubt about his drawings. And the teacher counseled him to enter a drawing school, for his drawings were good. Marcos liked the idea and entered the school downtown. Marcos learned how to draw, as you can see. Marcos is there with a good profession, but he didn't find anyone who would help him; therefore, there he is now as a plaza sketched [drawing on the sidewalk].

[AA-self CB-able NDA-advice NSD-no-help CD-mediocre]

In the Afro-Brazilians, eleven of their twenty-nine stories to this card were expressive in nature, a higher proportion than any other group. There are also two stories about boredom or sleepiness.

(BABf 27) (Card 1) Once upon a time there was a boy called Rafael who had violin classes on Mondays, Wednesdays, and Fridays, but he didn't like the classes very much, for they were too boring.

[PB-bored AD-motive]

Five stories are concerns about the pleasurable possession of a violin, in two of these there is gratification in receiving (OB-own NSA-reward), one depicts sadness about not receiving (PD-sad OB-want), one envy about a brother's violin (OC-envy) another concern about the violin being broken (OD-broken).

(BABm 26) (Card 1) Some time ago there was a boy who liked very much playing violin but he had no violin. He thought that the violin was cheap and started saving money. And when he discovered that the violin was very expensive—knew that he couldn't buy it—he became very sad. Till one day a rich old man decided to give him a violin. Became very happy and went playing violin down the street.

[AA-self PA-esthetic NSD-means PD-sad NSA-reward OA-own PA-joy]

(BABm 80) (Card 1) There is a boy seated. He was thinking of a violin that he would get. Then, he would not be given the violin anymore; he became very sad and in the end he wasn't given the violin.

[PD-sad OB-want NSD-means]

(BABf 30) (Card 1) Deciding if he would take his brother's violin to play it or not.

[OB-torn OC-envy]

(BABm 28) (Card 1) Before, he had a violin. After, his violin was broken. Then he had to buy another one.

[OC-destroy OB-want]

Another three stories were direct expressions of loneliness and depression.

(BABm 20) (Card 1) The boy is thinking and staring, staring, staring in order to understand what was inside his imagination and that is now appearing before him. He looked in order to understand what it was, the strange object which he wasn't able to decipher. He thought, thought, and understood that this strange object was his depression materializing itself.

[CB-arduous PD-depress OB-think]

(BABf 21) (Card 1) Marcelo was a very sad boy; he had neither friends to play with, nor brothers or sisters. He was alone. But one day Marcelo intended to study and made his mother put him in the school. Marcelo began to study. He learned new things so that he can teach them to other people. Now Marcelo wants to leave school, for he thinks he already knows everything, but deep inside he knows nothing. This is Marcelo's story.

[PD-sad FB-alone AA-nurture AD-withdraw]

A final story was about quarreling with family.

(BABm 40) (Card 1) He quarreled with his parents, then he became sad and went to his room in order to think. Then he thought and decided to talk to his parents.

[HC-discord PD-sad FA-mend]

In contrast to the Italian and the Portuguese ethnic youth who did see some concern with achievement, albeit in situations of need or helplessness, the twenty-one Afro-Brazilians and mixed Afro-Brazilian are even more focused on *expressive* emotional themes of a positive and negative nature, rather than instrumental future goal-oriented stories. In those few stories that are instrumental, the girls are more concerned negatively with incompetence and failure. Only one of the male stories is about compensatory active achievement, overcoming the poverty of one's father, saving money in order to realize dreams of advancement as we mentioned above (BABm 19).

Two of the other positive male Afro-Brazilian stories depict daydreaming rather than any activity itself. One male gave a story of abject failure due to the absence of anyone to help. One girl envisions the boy succeeding with the active help of parents, another eventually learns to sing a song and thereby becomes appreciated. Another four stories by girls have a negative outcome due to basic inability that cannot be overcome.

The remaining eleven stories were all expressive in nature. One is about boredom. Four stories were about gaining actual possession of a violin, in two of these there is gratification in receiving a violin as in BABm 23 quoted above.

One story is about envy of a brother's violin, and in another is about having to replace a broken violin, it is not difficult to interpret the abiding sense of material deprivation guiding such thoughts. Four other stories were simple direct expressions of loneliness and depression.

The final two stories were about internal family dissension or a family dealing in drugs. Concern with drugs appears throughout the TAT but including such a story to Card 1, testifies to the saliency of such thoughts.

(BABm 32) (Card 1) He quarreled with his parents, then he became sad and went to his room in order to think. Then he thought and decided to talk to his parents.

[HA-pacify]

(BABf 34) (Card 1) Boy was seated on the chair in a room. He opened the book and began to think. Suddenly he started reading a comic strip. This story told about a family who was very interested about people. Suddenly this family started smuggling drugs with these people. Some of these people used to drug themselves very much, but they didn't know what they were doing. Then appeared a friend, and he said: "Don't you see that this family is cornering you?" And the other said: "Now there is no more way to get out, for I should have realized this before I started."

[AC-illicit RC-abuse CD-chagrin]

Card 2: A Farm Scene

Card 2 of the Murray series depicts a rural scene. There is a young woman with books in the foreground. The background shows some farm buildings. At center in the distance is a figure of a man behind a horse, working the field. On one side leaning against a tree is a woman in work garb, who in a minor proportion of stories is seen as possibly pregnant.

On this card we compared sixteen Portuguese and sixteen Afro-Brazilians from our original Favela sample, and twenty-four stories from the Italian community. We compared these groups with fifty Japanese Brazilians divided into a younger and older sample.

The farm scene calls up for some ideas of labor in a more exploitative past, for others, a difficult present or a hopeful future. The Japanese Brazilians gave the most responses with purposeful stories of an achievement nature (64 percent). The Italian sample produced nine out of twenty-four such stories, or 37 percent. The Portuguese produced three achievement stories, or 19 percent, and the Afro-Brazilians produced only one such story or 6 percent.

What is relatively absent in all the Brazilian samples compared with some previous findings are the occasional more sexualized themes of liaisons, triangular relationships, or jealousy between women found in American lower class samples (Caudill and De Vos, 1956) or recent samples of youth generally in the United States (Vaughn, 1988; Suárez-Orozco and Suárez-Orozco, 1995).

What is notable in the distribution of stories, even those involved with achievement, or an even larger number concerned with the nurture and care of a farm family, is the difference of context in which either achievement or expressive concerns are educed.

In Table 8.2 we have summarized in detail the Brazilian stories given to Card 2. This allows us to illustrate how in categorizing these stories with our scoring system one may extract in brief the phrases that are most salient in the stories. We are presenting here this process in more detail as an example of how one might structure the data in the process of analysis.

Table 8.2
Story Summaries about a Farm Scene

Total	156 (male 57; female 55)				
Portuguese	16 (7 m; 9 f)				
Afro-Brazilian (4 mixed)	16 (10 m; 6 f)				
Italian	24 (12 m; 12 f)				
Japanese younger	50 (29 m; 21 f)				
Japanese older	50 (25 m; 25 f)				
Instrumental Concerns					
Positive Achievement through Study [46]	**P 3**	**AB 1**	**I 9**	**Jy 13**	**Jo 19**
Self-initiated toward future		AB 1	I 2		Jo 1
Thinking about life and about what she wants to do.					ABm
Each accomplishes. Girl graduates. Plower makes garden.					If
Girl will be teacher. Fa and bro work fields.					If
Going to school as a teacher, parents are working on the farm.					Jom
Studying			I 2		Jo 9
Carrying out their duties. Student leaves to study.					Im
Studying is diff from farm work. Nothing is impossible.					If
Workers on farm; woman, who is studying.					Jom
Student in studying. Fa working hard. Mo brings her lunch.					Jom
Has come to study from the countryside.					Jom
From the countryside. Going to the city to study.					Jof
Studying. I don't know what she is thinking.					Jom
Daughter student in city studying. Returned fat working hard. Mo bringing her lunch.					Jom
She has come to study from the countryside.					Jom
Going to school as a teacher. Parents are working on the farm.					Jom
She is from the countryside, going to the city to study.					Jof
From the countryside, going to the city to study					Jof
Assisted study or opportunity	P 1		I 1	Jy 3	
Can't afford to go to school. Rich lady provides.					Pf
Girl graduates from convent as sister. Earns own money. Mo didn't help. Fa did.					If
Opportunity					
Daughter has money, so she is studying.					Jyf
Difference in opportunities, determined to enjoy a better level of existence					Jym
Guilty for opportunity					

Table 8.2

Parents work hard at the farm. Goes to school, feeling a little guilty toward her parents				Jyf
Compensatory achievement			Jy 5	Jo 2
Wants to study so that does not working on the farm				Jyf
Teacher looking at an agricultural family, a hard life. Sad/does not want to become like that.				Jym
Value of education—much higher in level than the work of the fazenda				Jym
Wants more. Others only conform to the environment. Will work hard/overcome.				Jyf
Fazenda, family works daughter will work leave and become a professor. Parents want it.				Jom
Feeling bad about farming. Studying and wants to do more than just farm				Jof
Ambitious. Wants more from life, does not know what is good for her, conforming, not happy. Marry later and become happy.				Jyf
Compensatory achievement/nurturant acts	P 2	I 4	Jy 3	Jo 4
Ambitious. Didn't like to see her parents living in poverty.				Pf
Dedicated to study for future to help family and all children of Brazil.				Pf
Studies hard to be a teacher. Also takes care of mo. (preg) and bro.				Im
Teacher helped farmers or prepared lessons for pupils.				If
Can help better the world by studying and working.				Im
Tasks tough. Studied. Helped bro, sis and parents.				Im
Bros, working, suffers, helping mo. Studies not to live same life.				Jyf
Study for better life. Will remove mo from farm mo sacrifices self				Jof
Trying to imagine a better future—also better life for her family				Jym
Wife wants education. Worried about children's future mo-in-law and husb. Diff mentality.				Jom
Feels pity for the parents. Will get a better life parents sacrificing for her. She will succeed.				Jom
Wanted daughter to study. Worked hard to allow education dau. Studies hard for sake of parents.				Jyf
Man thinking make a nice farm. Woman worked hard and made a nice farm. Daughter grateful				Jom
Achievement vs parental opposition				Jo 2
Conflict. Mo, fa is contrary and irritated at plans. But she thinks of future. Dedicated to study.				Jom

Table 8.2

Is going to city to help parents. To become a professor. The parents not satisfied with her attitude.						Jym
Negative Achievement Stories [2]				**Jy 1**	**Jo 1**	
No opportunity						
Land is bad. Always worrying about crop failure. As a result, daughter cannot go to the university.						Jom
Parental pressure						
Fa very rigid obliges her to study. Girl rebellious and will not.						Jyf
Competence and Improvement [3]	**P 2**	**AB 1**				
Back from school. Learning how to garden.						ABm
Worried about exam.						Pm
Improves. Works with machines to make task easier.						Pm
Collective Work (positive or neutral attitude) [20]	**P 1**	**AB 4**	**I 6**	**Jy 5**	**Jo 4**	
Positive outcome						
Poor area. Build school room for teacher happy gathering						ABm
Farms food for family.						Im
Reap fruit, read books.						ABf
Taking a break wife is looking with much satisfaction. Friend visits.						Jom
Daily work						
Daily work.						Pm ABf 5 I (3m, 2f)
Planting and reaping together in an ancient age.						ABm
Instrumental concerns						
A well organized fazenda. The woman imports/hires workers						Jom
Life of the family. Woman pregnant while the man works. Girl giving classes in the rural zone						Jym
Daughter student, and the parents are working in agriculture.						Jym
Fazenda planting. Sister, goes to the school. Pregnant. Beautiful place.						Jym
Wife wishing for a good harvest						Jom
Fa a farmer. Mo works at home. Daughter is receiving education.						Jyf
Teacher explaining a picture on wall teaching students about agriculture						Jom
In Italy, woman is a teacher, dau and parents working in agriculture.						Jym
Work with Status Differences Emphasized [11]			**I 2**	**Jy 4**	**Jo 5**	
Slavery						
Woman observes slaves on plantation.						Im
Slaves rebelled against exploitation.						Im

Table 8.2

Epoch of slavery. A senhora is with her slave worker.						Jom
Low status workers						
Diff between student and rural worker. Wearing clothes of a different class.						Jof
Agriculture/farming. Women in general don't work as much. Pregnant. Other not of the family.						Jof
Teacher						
Workers in a rural area. Girl is a professor						Jyf
Professor not part of family. Diff mode of life in contrast with city life.						Jyf
Prof giving classes. In rural school. Not an advanced girl from city.						Jom
She is a teacher in the countryside.						Jyf
Teacher. Looks at farmers; observes hardships. Returned to teach.						Jom
Agriculture. Student has returned to home village became teacher.						Jym
Negative Responsibility [1]		**AB 1**				
Too hot. Horse won't work. Sister didn't help. Mo gives up.						ABf
Description or Just Observing [3]		**AB 1**	**I 1**		**Jo 1**	
Observing woman. (No story; card description)						If
Watching man taming horse. (Description)						ABf
Farm family. Dau going to school and worried about something						Jof
Expressive Concerns [30]						
	P 9	**AB 9**	**I 8**	**Jy 2**	**Jo 2**	
Beauty		AB 2				
Observing the beauty of nature.						ABf
Surprised at beauty of farm.						ABf
Affiliation Concerns [10]	**P 4**	**AB 2**	**I 2**	**Jy 1**	**Jo 1**	
Positive						
Invited in for some coffee.						Pf
Disapproval of mother about talking to a boy.						ABm
Family scene (no action).						Pm
Nostalgia-Home sick						
Homesick, melancholy. Thinks about life, when there were children.						Jyf
Used to work farm. Now too mechanized. Used to be relaxed life longing/for past good age.						Jom
Negative: Betrayal and abandonment						
Betrayed by married man.						ABm
Triangular Love Relationship						
Girl loves already married farmer						Im
Women's Role						

Table 8.2

	P	AB	I	Jy	Jo	
Once women could do men's work. Wo not to envy one another.						If
Sadness and Isolation						
No one to talk to.						Pf
Sad girl and a pregnant woman.						Pf
Care, Security [13]	**P 5**	**AB 4**	**I 4**			
Religious intervention						
Praying for rain.						ABm
Prayed to God. Having a good harvest.						ABm
Work to nurture						
Worked to bring food for peasants.						Pm
Writer helps by writing the story of a sad Brazil						Pf
Comfort and care						
Worried about pregnant mother.						Pf
Wants to comfort poor people (pregnant woman)						ABf
Teacher worried about people (preg woman) she was observing.						If
Sad girl, bro died but fought to take care of two others.						Pm
Worried about husb's health.						If
Security						
Fortunate to live in a place without robberies.						Pf
Pity and Social Conscience [5]		**AB 1**	**I 2**	**Jy 1**	**Jo 1**	
Prevents man maltreating of horse.						ABm
Princess Isabel. Story of liberation of slaves.						If
Slaves beaten until liberated.						Im
Pity for farm laborers—images of slavery. Melancholy with their sacrificial work, but she won't do anything about it.						Jof
Passing by wondering, why woman by tree not helping out.						Jym
Card Rejection [3]						
	Pm 1	ABm 1		Jyf 1		

Japanese Brazilians

Older Japanese most characteristically give simple stories emphasizing purposeful study (nine stories).

> (JBfo 51) (Card 2) She is from the countryside. She is going to the city to study. [AA-self]

(JBmo 7) (Card 2) This is a family in a farm. The daughter is a student in the city and is studying to succeed. She has now returned from the school to the farm where the father is working hard. The mother is bringing her lunch.

[AA-self NDA-nurture]

Younger Japanese give stories of compensatory achievement, overcoming present difficulties of poverty (eight stories).

(JBf y 3) (Card 2) One day—a day with lots of sun, Maria, a professor, was thinking about her brothers, who are working in the fazenda and suffering. She struggles (*lutar*) a lot with her studies as she learns in the school in order not to live the life that her brothers have. The mother is struggling with an illness and therefore, they are experiencing lots of difficulties in this period. As to the absence of the mother, the father needs more labor. The brother, George, worked in both rain and sun each day, and helped contribute to the house because of the mother's sickness.

[NDB-goods PD-suffer AA-counter KD-illness NDA-family]

Some of these stories by both younger and older Japanese emphasize nurturant repayment for parental sacrifice (seven stories).

(JBfy 5) (Card 2) She is looking at her mother, with deep thoughts. One day, the mother will be able to sell the farm and work in the city for a better life. The daughter is studying now for a better life. She will graduate and remove the mother from the farm where she sacrifices herself in labor.

[NDB-welfare AA-counter NDA-devote NDA-family]

(JBmo34) (Card 2) There are three pictures here—three people and three different thoughts. The man is thinking that even with a rocky mountain like this, one can make a nice farm, depending on how one thinks about it. The old woman feels that even with such rocky/uneven (*dekoboko*) terrain, they have worked hard and made a nice farm. She is happy. The daughter feels that because of her parents, she went to a good school and is living a good life. She is grateful towards her parents.

[AA-purpose NSA-grateful]

Parents are facilitative:

(JBmo 26) (Card 2) This here is a fazenda, a plantation in Belo Horizonte. The family works the farm and is thinking now whether it will rain. The girl is a student, the daughter of the couple. In the future, she will work so that she will no longer have to work on the farm and will leave the fazenda and become a professor. There is no conflict here because the parents want her to do this too—it is better for her; all parents want education for their children.

[HA-depict AA-counter NDB-welfare NDA-family]

Finding some opportunity to study, for someone coming from a poor rural family becomes the central issue in some other stories (four).

(JBfy 37) (Card 2) This is old Brazil. These are farmers. There is a daughter and a slave/worker and the wife. The family is working hard. The daughter has money, so she is studying.

[RA-work DDC-exploit KA-wealth AA-self]

(JBmy 41) (Card 2) This is about the difference in culture and ways of thinking between the agriculturist and the modern person. The difference is in the opportunities, and the will (determination/desire) and other external circumstances. They enjoy a better level of existence.

[FB-distant KA-social AA-self]

(JBmo 39) (Card 2) This is a country farm that makes soybeans. However, the land is bad. The area is small and they are using horse power to plow the land. Because of this, there are limits to their thoughts/expectations. They are always worrying that the crop will not go well like last year. As a result, the eldest daughter cannot go to the university. They are thinking about how they could improve the situation.

[KD-poverty KB-want NSD-means CB-arduous]

A daughter can become guilty for her special opportunity, as in this single story.

(JBfy 46) (Card 2) This is a country girl and her parents. She goes to school, but her parents work hard at the farm. So as she goes to school, she looks over her shoulder and is feeling a little bad (guilty) toward her parents.

[RA-work KA-luck RB-guilt]

The Japanese stories show concern with status differences as the central issue in nine of their stories. In one, the slavery past of Brazil is recalled. In others there is a distance between those who have the opportunity for learning and those without.

(JBm 14) (Card 2) This is during the epoch of slavery at a scene of a campo/field. A senhora is with her slave worker.

[DDC-exploit]

(JBf 12) (Card 2) This picture shows the different between the student and the rural worker and the owner/woman of the house (*Dona da casa*). I can tell because of the scenery in the picture and because the student's clothing is different from the rural workers. The Dona is also wearing clothes of a different class from the rural workers.

[EDB-status OB-clothes]

In ten stories (20 percent), nine by men, the work and responsibility of farm life is the central theme elicited by Card 2.

(JBmy16) (Card 2) This would be a family on the farm, this picture is showing the life of the family. The woman leaning against the tree is pregnant while the man works. The girl in the foreground is going to school in the rural zone. In fact, she is not taking classes, but giving classes to children in the rural zone.

[HA-depict NDA-active]

(Jbfy36) (Card 2) This is the countryside. The father is a farmer. The mother works at home. The daughter is receiving an education. She is either learning or teaching.

[HA-depict]

Although expressive concern with the care of parents, etc. appears in a number of the stories in the context of achievement motivation, essentially emotional, or expressive concerns by themselves appear only in four stories. This contrasts with the other Brazil groups.

Two stories depict nostalgia for a past life, and two others depict worry about giving or receiving necessary help when it is needed.

(JBmo 8) (Card 2) I remember how I used to work in a farm too. Currently, agriculture is mechanized and of a much bigger scale. It was an age without machines, when everything was done with human power. It was a very relaxed life back then at a low tempo. It was not the fast, mechanized life of today. I feel a certain longing/homesickness for that time. It was a good age.

[RA-work HA-depict FB-longing]

(JBfo 28) (Card 2) I think differently (with this card). There are two workers (empregados). She could be a professor. She feels pity for them (the farm laborers), but she will not change anything for them. I reminded of lots of images of slavery. This professor does not teach the workers or has taught them in the past. She is melancholy with their sacrificial work, but she won't do anything about it.

[NDB-pity DDC-exploit NDD-unable]

The instrumental identification with the hard life on the Brazilian farm found in these stories reflects the past experience of the relatively successful Japanese immigrants. Their eventual betterment through education has also been well demonstrated by the next, Brazilian born generations. Brazilian born Japanese have well used educational opportunities and have gone into professions. They have demonstrated the highest rate of education of any Brazilian ethnic group.

Italians

The Italians show work-oriented instrumental concerns in fifteen (63 percent) of their twenty-four responses to this card. In seven stories (29 percent) the responsibilities of daily work are central. Some stories are simply descriptive.

> (BIm 2) (Card 2) The man is looking at the plantation he had plowed with his horse. The daughter is going to school. His wife is by his side. He'll plant corn. Harvest will be good.
>
> [HA-depict KA-luck]

> (BIm 19) (Card 2) There was a couple. The husband plowed the field with his oxen. His wife was a teacher, she was coming back from school. The wife was at school and is going home. The husband is preparing the oxen for a long journey of work, and after he's going home.
>
> [HA-depict RA-work]

In nine achievement stories (38 percent) studying is depicted in matter of fact tone as taking place in a family context wherein each member is doing their expected tasks.

> (BIm 20) (Card 2) These are people who are working in the field. The man is plowing the soil, the woman observes the landscape and the girl is going to school. They are people from the hinterlands who are doing their jobs and carrying out their duties. The student leaves the hinterlands in order to study.
>
> [HA-depict RA-work FB-separate]

In one story the girl studies at a convent, implying she will become a sister. The others are concerned with their daily tasks. The man looking forward to cultivating a satisfactory garden.

> (BIf 9) (Card 2) There is a person working, plowing the soil; the horse is pulling the plow. There is another person who is thinking, looking out somewhere. There is a girl who is going to school, or who is going to study at a friend's. This person who is plowing thinks this will be a nice kitchen garden to cultivate. The woman is thinking that someday she will go to that place. The girl is studying and, to be somebody, goes to take liturgy at the Church. They will try to get what they want. She will graduate. She will go to that place. He will be lucky. The man who cultivates the kitchen garden is central. The three people are making what they want to do. They take pleasure in good order.
>
> [HA-family RA-work PA-order AA-self]

In four others there is achievement to help nurture others, similar to the themes found in the Japanese.

> (BIm 6) (Card 2) This woman looks like a teacher. She was a student who wanted to be a teacher. She is young, she is not even 20 years old. She studies hard in order to be a teacher and at the same time she cannot work because she has to take care of her mother, who is sick and pregnant. The brother who is beside her works always. She has to postpone her wish. The baby is born and the mother dies. She stays looking after of the baby of her mother. She finishes her studies and tries to pass a public contest. She passes. She has to go to classes with her brother. She

works hard and manages to do both things: studying and looking after her brother. Two, three years passed and the boy grew up, and she earns more money and hires a baby-sitter. She marries a guy and takes care of her brother as if he were her son. She feels revolted and happy at the same time.

[AA-persist RA-duty-o KB-crisis RA-work KD-death NDA-family FA-love]

In nine expressive stories, no one living in the relatively rural farm area where we obtained our Italian sample sees the beauty of surrounding nature. There is one triangular story of a girl in love with a married farmer. One story questions a woman's role in labor and would discourage envy between women. There is a more intellectual tone to the remaining six stories about nurture and pity. Only two involve other family members, rather, there are four stories about exploitative slavery. In two there is direct reference to the liberation of the slaves by Queen Isabella.

(BIm 17) (Card 2) This is slavery time, when Negroes had to work for the white people receiving nothing in turn. They lived in slave quarters; whenever they tried to escape they were caught and tied to a post and beat. Till one day Princess Isabel signed the Lei Aurea (Golden Law), [figure with books] the Princess. She might be 30. They were working. They'll be set free.

[DDC-exploit DDC-punish RA-work NDA-rescue DDA-create DDA-free]

One presumes this story reflects the teaching of history in the Brazilian schools. One can surmise among the Italians a matter of factness about family duties. There is less direct internal family concern related to hardship and physical illness and more awareness through the school program of the history of exploitation in nineteenth-century Brazil. These results on Card 2 as on Card 1, parallel their lesser concern with deprivation in Italians compared with the urban favela sample.

Portuguese

Of the sixteen Portuguese favela records only three are concerned with a direct achievement theme. In one there is facilitated achievement provided by a rich lady.

(PBf 1) (Card 2) It was in a little house where lived Elisabete, a very poor girl. She would like to go to school but her father couldn't afford the enrollment. A lady decided to pay the enrollment, for she was very sorry for the girl. When she arrived at home her father asked why she was so cheerful. She answered that a very rich lady had decided to pay her enrollment. In turn, she should visit her every morning.

[KD-poverty NDD-unable NDA-active NDB-pity PA-joy RA-duty-o]

The other two are achievement to help others: one's parents in one, and all the children of Brazil in another.

(PBf 12) (Card 2) This is a very studious girl. She is very dedicated to her studies. She intends to study in order to have a good future, so that she can help her family and have a good profession. She intends to be a teacher in order to help all the children of Brazil.

[RA-duty-s AA-duty AA-nurture]

Two more instrumental stories are concerned with personal adequacy: one is concerned with improvement and other with passing an exam. Among nine expressive themes (56 percent), there is one story of simple friendliness providing coffee as hospitality. There are two stories of sadness and isolation.

The prevailing expressive concern elicited by this card among the Portuguese youth is nurture. It appears in seven or 43 percent of their stories. In addition to the two achievement for nurture themes are five others in which in response to social or family issues there is a need for security or care of others.

(PBm 9) (Card 2) The girl from the country was sad because her brother had died and there was only her 8-year-old son. But even so she fought in order to maintain herself and her son.

[KD-death AA-nurture]

A writer to help improve conditions tells all the story of sad Brazil. A boy works to feed poor peasants.

(PBm 6) (Card 2) It was a boy who worked and brought food for the peasants of the hut. He works in order to bring food for the peasants.

[RA-work NDA-active]

Two are concerned for one's pregnant mother or after a death, for one's brothers. For the urban young Favela woman giving the story wistfully the farm area is fancied as a haven from crime.

(PBf 2) (Card 2) The teacher was coming from school and stopped in order to watch the man who is plowing and sowing, and the other woman is looking at the city where she lives. The woman looks at the city and thinks that her city is better than some other ones, for in those there are too many robberies, and children on the streets. Her city is better for living because it is small, and there is no robbery.

[HA-depict HB-unrest HB-f-attack NSA-secure]

In three, the card elicits no affect or suggests avoidance: there is one scene of daily work and in another a simple description of a farm family. One rejects the card.

Afro-Brazilians

There is only one story with what may be a predominant self-motivated achievement theme in the sixteen Afro-Brazilians. It is an existential questioning of what life is about and what to do.

> (BABm 20) (Card 2) It is a woman thinking about life and about everything which already happened to her, about what is happening and about what she hopes will happen. She thinks about everything she has already done and about what she wants to do, for she looks like having the idea that life is short and one must seize the day.
>
> [AA-purpose]

Among possibly instrumental themes, one Afro-Brazilian is concerned with capacity to learn, another with work and a love for books. There are also three stories of collective work together. In one there is collective labor to build a school house.

> (BABm 26) (Card 2) This is the farmer's teacher. Some time ago there was a teacher in a farm which had no classroom. Then they had a meeting and decided that they had to make a classroom for the teacher to give classes. Everybody began to help building the classroom. The teacher became very happy and on the first day of classes they made a party. Everybody ate and drank, and the students became very happy, for they had got a classroom to study in. And so the teacher could give her pupils classes.
>
> [MTA-task NDA-social HA-rite PA-joy HA-depict]

But another is a negative story about farm work as onerous responsibility.

> (BABf 21) (Card 2) It was a very sunny day. Dona Luiza looked at her son Paulo. He was working, trying to pull a plow, but as it was too hot, the horse didn't want to walk. His sister Bete didn't care about helping them. She was only concerned about books which told about love, happiness and other things. Paulo was already giving up pulling the plow. His mother yelled very much at him. He made his best in order to pull, but the horse didn't pull it. The horse didn't want to go ahead because the sun was too hot and the sand began to burn its hoofs. Paulo's mother began to give up. She told Paulo to leave the field and to go away. His sister wanted to interfere, but they didn't listen to her. At the end the horse was at the same place, while Paulo and his mother went away.
>
> [KD-thwart NDC-succor RC-indulge DDC-press AD-withdraw]

Twelve records are about various expressive concerns. One sees the help of parents. Two stories are pity for a pregnant woman, another stops the abuse of a maltreated horse. Two more are about praying for rain to assure good crops. Three of these stories are positive expressions of the beauty of nature. One see a happy family with a pregnant woman. For the urban dweller of a poor neighborhood farm life can be idealized. One gives simple description, another rejects the card. Two have vaguely sexual themes, a girl is first distrustful of a friendly greeting. Another is a girl betrayed by a married man.

> (BABm 19) (Card 2) The woman was a student and she made a trip. During the trip she met a guy and with the passing time she ended up liking him. The guy was married, but she didn't know that. Every day her friends told her so but she never believed. One day she got tired of it and decided to follow him and then discovered that he was married and had two children. She went back to her city and there she stayed.
>
> [FA-love FC-triangle <u>FC-deceit</u> FD-retreat]

The different emphasis given to this card by the different ethnic groups is quite apparent. The family concerns among the Japanese are placed in the context of instrumental activities. Among Italian youth there is a matter-of-fact attitude toward work. Study is another expected form of work. Simple self-motivated achievement appeared only in one Portuguese story. Concern with nurture was paramount. Expressive interpersonal themes were the most prominent found among the Afro-Brazilians.

Card 17: A Man on a Rope

This card depicts a man seen in tights (or possibly naked) with his hands on a rope stretch vertically on the picture his feet are free in the air. No ground is visible. Card 17 allows for an ascendant climbing of a rope as a task or as a challenge with enjoyment or as an exercise or exhibition of prowess to an audience. It may be someone working in a circus. The opposite possible stories emphasize slipping or going down. It may stimulate seeing a scene of an escape—either legitimate or criminal in nature. In a symbolic psychological sense this card gives opportunity to create a positive upbeat story emphasizing an energetic sense of going up, versus negative themes of failure or escape. This card was not given to the Italian sample.

Japanese Brazilians

The upward endeavor or display of prowess themes found in American groups of immigrant Japanese and Koreans (see chapter 7, volume II) were not in as much evidence in the present Japanese sample. Achievement (A), Competence (C), or goal-oriented stories comprise only seventeen of their fifty stories (34 percent).

Among the achievement stories three responses directly use the card as symbolizing achievement.

(BJm 10) (Card 17) A picture of a type one sees in Brazil. He is trying to climb the cord to rise, financially. The picture is a metaphor in this sense.

[AA-self AA-purpose]

An expression of positive competence is found in five stories. Training is necessary to attain competence in one's career as an acrobat.

(BJf 5) (Card 17) Someone is training to be an athlete or for an athletic event, for a circus. He is doing exercises with the cord/rope; going up and down.

[AA-persist CA-test]

A competitive effort is the theme of two stories. A sense of challenge is met positively.

(BJm 39) (Card 17) He is a banker responsible for accounting. Everyday, he calculates people's money and has been doing this for many years. Today, he went to a friend's house and drank a lot. Each person was required to do a trick/stunt. So as not to be outdone by the previous stunts, he is trying to cross on a rope, but luckily, the rope broke, and so he was able to do this funny pose.

[RA-work MVA-game]

Some stories (four) depict escape from accidents or a rescue effort.

(BJf 3) (Card 17) In a road near my house, a building caught fire and a desperate woman was caught in the building as a prisoner and was struggling for her life. This man got sufficient cord/rope to save the woman and started climbing the rope immediate in order to try and save the woman.

[KD-mishap NSB-help NDA-active]

Performing before an audience is found in five stories.

(BJf 32) (Card 17) He is a ordinary person showing off his ability and strength.

[ESB-praised CA-present]

The figure is seen as possibly naked suggesting abnormality or a crazed condition in five stories.

(BJm 44) (Card 17) He is naked. If he were going down the rope to help someone, this would be strange. He is not doing some act/trick either, nor is he trying to show off. It is not a circus, because then, he would be dressed differently. This is a strange, crazy, person.

[OB-body NDA-active EDC-disdain PC-crazed]

Six women give stories of escape wherein there is an ambiguity in respect to the legitimacy of the act (four women) or the act is an escape from improper imprisonment (two women).

(BJf 33) (Card 17) He was imprisoned because he did something bad, but I don't think he is a bad person, so he wants to escape. He tied a rope together and is trying to escape. He will probably be able to leave.

[DDA-police DSC-escape]

(BJf 25) (Card 17) This is a fugitive from a prison. Things will become better for him after he flees because he has no guilt. In fact, he is not a criminal, but a victim. From his face, he seems a little crazy.

[DSC-escape DDC-unfair PC-crazed]

Five men and two women see the escape as from prison or legitimate authority.

(BJf 37) (Card 17) This is a Brazilian thief. He was discovered and now he is running away by climbing down the rope.

[DSC-escape]

Table 8.3
Empirically Derived Categorization: Comparison of 17BM, the Man on a Rope

N Favela 37	Female 39	Male 49	Portuguese 18	Afro-Brazilians 21	Japanese 50
Achievement, competence, competition					
	10 f	21 m	4 P	9 AB	18 J
Achievement symbolized		2			2
Goal-oriented	2	3		2	3
Enjoyment	2	3	1	3	1
Exhibiting competence	2	6	1	1	6
Training or striving	3	4	2	1	4
Positive competition	1	3		2	2
Escape from difficulty or rescue					
	8 f	4 m	4 P	2 AB	6 J
Rescue	2	2	2	1	1
Getting out of difficulty	6	2	2	1	5
Negative endings or failure					
	3 f	6 m	4 P	4 AB	1 J
Activity ambiguous as to legitimacy					
	7 f	3 m	2 P	1 AB	7 J
Unsanctioned activities					
	9 f	7 m	4 P	2 AB	10 J
Burglary	4 f		2	1	1
Escape from hospital	2 f		1	1	
Escapes prison	1 f	5 m	1		5 J

Illicit sexuality		2 m			2 J
Unspecified "bad" activity	2 f				2 J
Abnormal person		4 m			4 J
Other	1 f	1 m			2 J
Rejection	1 f	3 m		2 AB	2 J

Portuguese

The subsample of boys showed relatively more positive stories. In sixteen stories, this card elicits a possible positive challenge in four of seven Portuguese boys, stories of athletic challenges, rescues, or ambition to become a fireman; but in three other stories there is failure. More negative stories are given by Portuguese girls than boys (seven of nine).

Afro-Brazilian

Six of the eleven male records were negatively toned. There are two rejections (one male, one female).

Negative stories were given by more Afro-Brazilian girls (seven of ten). In total, fourteen of nineteen responses were negatively toned in girls. One may presume there is relatively more confidence toward tasks envisioned as physical in nature by the boys. There was also lack of confidence more in evidence in a task that is considered drawing on a capacity for study or sustained application to a task (see above).

In all, less than 50 percent of the stories of Afro-Brazilians were positive or neutral in tone (41 percent), whereas 48 percent were stories with negative endings, unsuccessful escapes, etc. These results resemble most the stories we obtained from Koreans in Japan which were in direct contrast to the Korean sample from Los Angeles (see chapter 7, volume II). Out of their fifty stories given to this card, most of the Koreans sampled in Los Angeles saw positive activity of an active energetic nature in 30 or 60 percent of their stories. Additionally they saw activity of a mischievous or sexual nature in another eight (16 percent). Of the remaining, 26 percent do see unsuccessful escapes or other negatively toned material. In contrast, the Koreans in Japan saw only 14 percent of the positive type stories while in 37 percent of their stories they picture a futile escape or such accidents as falling down. Moreover, most strikingly in an additional 22 percent of their stories of performance, they pictured the performer as deformed, playing the fool, drunk, or despondent.

As reported in a previous chapter, the minority Koreans in Japan when compared with other Korean samples, directly manifest throughout their test results on the TAT, as well as in direct interviews, severe problems with achievement and various forms of active alienation in acts of delinquency, as well as forms of passive withdrawal and alienation. Our Brazilian favela results, in contrast to minority Japanese, are also in a negative direction. But as also suggested on other cards there is a striking sexual difference with women more pessimistic about both present and future capacities. The results on this card certainly indirectly symbolize optimism or pessimism about the future in different groups. The Afro-Brazilian youth are the least optimistic of our Brazilian samples.

Brief Discussion

There are fewer signs of encouraging independence as a mark of individuation in the Brazilian record; rather there are periodic depictions of excessive domination by a parent, or uncertain family integrity and dissension between parents. This dissension is in some circumstances seen related to excessive use of alcohol and sometimes other drugs. Governmental authority is periodically directly depicted as insufficient or possibly corrupt. In the following two chapters we examine TAT cards that further illustrate some of the contrastive spontaneous concerns of Brazilian teenagers from different ethnic backgrounds in regard to parental or civil authority and family functioning as well as the present and future economic stresses faced by youth.

In the first three cards we have examined we have been able to illustrate that what is internalized as part of the self does distort how one sees the future. McClelland's perception of how achievement motivation works is correct in stressing that some individuated self concerns directed toward future purpose will result, in a statistical sense, in a higher rate of accomplishment than that possible for those who see more readily a negative economic or social destiny, or are internally preoccupied with a sense of deprivation or neglect. Private projections of either a positive or negative nature are both selective, hence can be seen as distortions influenced by internalized personal inclinations. These inclinations result in different forms of social behavior.

The ICSS enables us to make distinctions between themes that are not differentiated by the scoring system used by McClelland and his associates (Smith, 1992). There are differences in the groups we have here considered as to the nature of spontaneous instrumental fantasy directed inwardly in activity fancied as acts of personal volition or self-will directed toward future goals, which we score as an internalized need for "Achievement," versus a positive sense of mastery, or questions of inner incapacity, which we score under the category of "Competence." This category does not exist in the McClelland scoring system. In the results described above one notes how the Japanese Brazilians, as other samples of Japanese tested elsewhere, are inwardly concerned with questions of personal competence which, however, they envision can be overcome by hard work. This emphasis on hard work overcoming inadequacy is found to a much lesser extent in some Italian stories, but contrasts in other groups where issues of personal competence or self confidence lead to more pessimistic results. (Instrumental issues of "Mutual Purpose" [competition or cooperation] which McClelland also does not distinguish from self-oriented achievement motivation are not sufficiently elicited as instrumental concerns by the particular cards used in the present research to concern us here.)

Another important instrumental distinction is that between what we score under "Responsibility" as contrasted with "Control." The former are themes related to self-control or potentials for guilt that are internalized. These can be differentiated from the latter themes that focus on issues of power or control between self and authority, whether within the family of in relation to other social institutions. In this respect, the North American stories considered in some of the following chapters (including Japanese-American) differ from the Brazilian stories (including the Japanese Brazilian). In the American responses to Card 1, for example, one finds a clash of wills. There are proportionately many more stories about questionable personal motivation and unresolved parental pressure and uncertainty about whether parental pressure will be met by defiance or self-will directed toward pleasure or interests other than those envisioned by the parents. In contrast, the Brazilian stories in all groups are implicitly, if not explicitly, of a more compliant nature.

These various patterns can be seen as evidence of each group's unique legacy as they have adapted to Brazil's cultural, social, and historical context. Evidence of these varied legacies can also be seen in the variety of concerns expressed about the legitimacy of authority. We find that the Brazilian narratives reveal a lesser degree of noncompliance than do narratives produced by North Americans. Where occasional stories of revolt are forthcoming in the Brazilian sample, they differ from the North American stories. Rather than an expression of personal autonomy, some of the narratives indicate concern with dominance or exploitation, and also with physical beatings or abandonment. Nevertheless, although there is notable cynicism in Brazil, one does not note themes of personal autonomy that ultimately question the exercise of dominance or exploitation within the family or outside of it. From the perspective of the social scientist, these are underlying themes that merit much further direct exploration, since they are at the heart of personal attitudes toward the political as well as interpersonal processes that constitute a society's future.

We consider expressive concerns to be essential components of a group's adaptive pattern. In the area of expressive concerns, however, McClelland's system does not differentiate various forms of Harmony or discord, Evaluative concerns with pride or shame, or feelings about Nurture or dependency. It deals only with a need for Affiliation. For example, when working with material from Brazil one sees the need for a scoring system that attends to concerns with economic deprivation, as they are central to the narrative in a number of Brazilian stories. While there is no doubt that economic disparity marks the Brazilian society, we have noted that it appears in a different guise in the different groups we have considered. Instrumental and expressive themes are differently intertwined in different groups. One would expect that there will be a difference in actual behavior between those whose internalized sense of self spontaneously envisions self-determination and a will to succeed against outer odds or inner incapacity, and those who must imagine some outside succor as necessary to escape economic want, or who feel they will need outside help to reach future goals. Some forms of internalization of initiative are more self-empowering, even where the odds of realizing success may objectively be small.

References

Caudill, William and George A. De Vos. 1956. Achievement, Culture and Personality: The Case of the Japanese Americans. *American Anthropologist*, **58**(6): 1102-1126 (reprinted: 1961; 1966; 1967; 1971).

Connor, John W. and George A. De Vos. 1989. Cultural Influences on Achievement Motivation and Orientation Toward Work in Japanese and American Youth. In David Stern and Dorothy Eichorn (Eds.), *Adolescence and Work: Influence of Social Structure, Labor Markets, and Culture* (pp. 291–326). Hillsdale, N.J.: Lawrence Erlbaum Associates.

De Vos, George A. 1962. Deviancy and Social Change: A Psychocultural Evaluation of Trends in Japanese Delinquency and Suicide. In Robert Smith and Richard Beardsley (Eds.), *Japanese Culture: Its Development and Characteristics* (pp. 153–170). Chicago: Aldine Publishing Co.

———. 1993. Problems with Achievement, Alienation, and Authority in Korean Minorities in the United States and Japan. In Kwang Kyu Lee and Walter Slote (Eds.), *Overseas Koreans in the Global Context* (pp. 145–180). Seoul: Association for the Study of Koreans Abroad.

———. 1996. Internalized Achievement or External Authority: Some Cultural Comparisons of Responses to TAT Card 1. In Irving B. Weiner (Ed.), *Rorschachiana XXI Yearbook of the International Rorschach Society*. Göttingen: Hogrefe & Huber.

———. 1997. Heritage of Exploitation: A Brief TAT Report on South Brazilian Youth. *Political Psychology*, **18**(2): 439–481.

De Vos, George A. and Kwang-Kyu Lee. 1981. Attitude Toward Authority: Dilemma of Ex-Colonial Society. In Changsoo Lee (Ed.), *Modernization of Korea and the Impact of the West* (pp. 150–162). Los Angeles: University of Southern California.

Smith, Charles P. 1992. *Motivation and Personality: Handbook of Thematic Content Analysis*. Cambridge and New York: Cambridge University Press.

Suárez-Orozco, Carola and Marcelo Suárez-Orozco. 1995. *Transitions: Migration, Family Life and Achievement Motivation Among Latino Adolescents*. Palo Alto, Calif.: Stanford University Press.

Suárez-Orozco, Marcelo. 1989. *Central American Refugees and United States High Schools*. Palo Alto, Calif.: Stanford University Press.

Tsuda, Takeyuki. 1997. Ethnic Transnationalism and the Channeling of Migrant Flows: The Return Migration of the Japanese-Brazilians. In Diane Baxter and Ruth Krulfeld (Eds.), *Beyond Boundaries: Selected Papers on Refugees and Immigrants*, Volume 5 (pp. 35–63). American Anthropological Association.

Vaughn, Curtis. 1988. *Cognitive Independence, Social Independence, and Achievement Orientation: A Comparison of Japanese and United States Students*. Dissertation. University of California, Berkeley.

Chapter 9

Brazilian Fantasies of Chastisement, Separation, or Abandonment of Children

George A. De Vos

Responses to Cards 3 and 16 in Japanese Brazilians Compared with Samples of Brazilian Youth

As we have discussed elsewhere in this volume, the way in which the various concerns are combined into patterns of experience reveal much about a group's responses to the complex interaction of their cultural, social, and historical circumstances. The previous chapter has demonstrated our use of the scoring system to categorize responses elicited by Cards 1, 2, and 17. The method has revealed ethnic-group differences in the apperception of acts of personal volition directed toward future goals. Whereas some groups emphasize hard work and overcoming inadequacy in pursuit of goals, other groups appear more pessimistic about Achievement and Competence.

Although such themes are revealed in responses to Cards 1, 2, and 17, the various cards differ in their stimulus values. Different cards evoke different apperceptions and different narrative emphases, such that they reveal additional nuances of the ways in which concerns with authority are patterned. In what follows, we shall use responses to Cards 3BM and 16 to further illustrate how instrumental themes of Control (D) and Responsibility (R), as well as expressive themes of Harmony (H), Nurture (N), and Affiliation (F) are experienced in a variety of ways by different groups in Brazil.

The stark economic disparity and the legacy of exploitation that marks the Brazilian society can also be demonstrated as a substantial theme in the narratives of all the groups we studied as they respond to Cards 3BM and 16. What we attempt in the present chapter is to look in great detail at how these concerns can be captured in the scoring categories we utilize. Hence we present not simply numerical comparisons but tables which retain abbreviated content of the stories. This can demonstrate the scoring system at work. Numerical comparisons alone can be misleading, since the content of the problems experienced between parents and children, for example, can be completely different in tone from one group to the next.

Card 3BM: A Youth Slumped against a Bench

Card 3BM depicts an indeterminate figure slumped against a bench. Used in a number of previous studies, it draws forth a number of disparate themes. They range variously from a figure depicted as tired from working or unhappy due to a broken love relationship or a quarrel. Some stories depict a youth chastised by parents for some specified or unspecified wrongdoing. The figure can be seen as either male or female. In my experience the figure in recent years is most often depicted as female. There is an indistinct object in the foreground that is ignored in most stories. When utilized, it is usually a pair of scissors or a gun.

The variety elicited among fifty Japanese Brazilian stories resembles some of our Japanese samples obtained in previous research. Perhaps there are proportionately fewer expressive stories of being tired (four), sick (three), a broken love relationship (four), and scolding by parents (four), than in some previous results. The number of stories of quarreling (five), unresolved problems (four), and sadness not specified as to content (eight), a severe depression, even suicide (eight), are similar.

Stories of possible suicide were found in other Japanese research, but are very rare in any other samples. What is most notable compared with previous samples of Japanese elsewhere are three stories centering on drug use and three stories of economic despair that together comprise 12 percent of the present Japanese Brazilian sample. As anticipated in previous work with this card, there are stories given by all groups about sickness, tiredness, accident, or disability. There are stories about separation, desertion, or death of a beloved. These latter categories are found in many other samples. Throughout, in the present sample, however, as we shall illustrate in detail, these stories also show a difference in themes between the sexes and between the groups considered.

Table 9.1. Story Summaries
3BM: The Figure Slumped by a Bench

Groups	Portuguese	Afro Brazilian	Italian	Jyoung	Jold
Total N 110 (m 58, f 52)	**16**	**21**	**24**	**25**	**25**
[33] a. Instrumentally Focused					
	12	8	7	3	6
[1] Competence (C)	0	0	0	0	1
[20] Parental Authority (D)	8	5	3	0	4
[12] Wrongdoing (R)	1	3	4	3	1
[77] b. Expressive Categories					
[18] Need for Nurture (N)	4	3	4	5	2
[13] Love or Affiliation (F)	0	2	7	2	2
[14] Quarrel and Dissent (H)	2	1	6	4	1
[1] Esteem (E)	0	0	0	1	0
[27] Internal Affectivity (P)	1	2	0	11	13
[3] Fate: accident (K)	0	1	0	0	0
[1] Reject	0	1	0	0	0

[33] a. Instrumentally Focused

[1] Competence (C) — 0 P — 0 AB — 0 I — 0 Jy — 1 Jo

Tired of fighting, dispirited. Family problem mixed with a professional failure. Will continue fighting. In future, continue to live a simple life without big achievements. — Jo

PB-trouble CC-failure HC-discord AA-persist CD-mediocre

[20] Parental Authority (D) — 8 P — 5 A — 3 I — 0 Jy — 4 Jo

[10] Legitimate behavior (DDA)

Authority Sanction, Parental Assistance

Lies about drugs. Smuggled goods. Picked up by police. Parents help him give up drugs. — ABm

RC-abuse FC-deceit AC-crime DDA-police NDA-advice

Scolded by Parents

Crying about what she did. Failed test for university and was scolded, crying. — Jo

PD-sad CC-failure DDA-scold

Troubled after scolded by her parents. Realizes she did bad. Doesn't know what to do. — Jo

PB-trouble RC-wrong DDA-scold

Sick or was scolded, crying. Scissors on floor. Trying to construct something with them. — Jo

PD-sad KD-sick CC-failure DDA-scold

Beating (legitimate)

Did wrong. Father swore. Relatives beat. Questions herself. Decides parents' decision right. They know best. Pm

RC-wrong DSB-torn DDA-punish

Annoying child. Spoiled something. Fa beats. To avoid embarrassment goes to room. Im

RC-mores DDA-punish ESB-shame

Abandoned as Punishment

Boy drinks alcohol. Sent away sleeps on park bench. Pm

RC-abuse DDA-punish NSD-deserted

Violence on the streets. Sniff glue. Smoke and do dope. Don't want to work. Sent away. Pm

HB-f-fury RC-abuse RD-work NDC-desert KD-hopeless

Bad influence of friends. Didn't want to work parents sent her away. Pm

DSD-peer RD-work DDA-punish NSD-deserted

Thief. Turned out from home. Mistakenly picked up for glue sniffing by police. ABm

RC-propriety DDA-punish NSD-deserted RC-abuse DDC-unfair

---

[3] Ambivalent about authority (DSB)

Crying. Mother didn't let him go out. ABm

PD-sad DSB-torn DSB-obey

Big sister hadn't let her go out to play. ABf

DSB-torn PA-play

Wailing over misfortune. Wrongdoing and/or beating. Im

PD-suffer RC-wrong DSB-torn

---

[6] Beatings, excessive or abusive (DDC)

Studies hard, becomes very tired. Yet, her fa tells her not enough and scolds her. Not to trouble her parents she suicides. Jmo

PB-tired AA-persist DDC-press HC-suicide HA-pacify

Beaten by fa, wanted him to work; but grfa played with him; mo protected him, play allowed. Pf

DDC-punish RD-work PA-play NDA-protect

Mo used to beat her. One ran away from home. Returned, more beatings like an animal. Pm

DDC-punish FC-flee HC-cruel

Violence from her parents. Scars, burns, etc. We must do something to evil doers. ABm

HC-cruel HD-injury DDC-punish

Beat constantly by his parent. Didn't dislike them. But now abandoned. Im

DDC-punish HC-cruel NSD-deserted

Brazil! Drugs and child abuse. Parent's lack of education or lack of love? Or self—one by child? Pf

RC-evade DDC-punish RC-abuse FC-neglect

[1] Ineffective authority (DDD)

Son a glue-sniffer. She didn't know what to do. — Pf
DDD-helpless RC-abuse

[17] Wrongdoing (RD, RC, RD)	*1 P*	*3 AB*	*4 I*	*3 Jy*	*1 Jo*

Regret

Tired. Doesn't manage to do his homework. Has to work. Forgets work. Loses grade. — Pm
PB-tired RD-work DDA-punish

Regretted killed a bird. — ABf
HC-murder RB-regret

She hurt a person. Crying. — ABf
PD-sad HC-injury RB-regret

Something bad happened. Guilty. Cannot be repaired. — ABm
RB-guilt KD-hopeless

Disliked husband. Wished death. Accident. Guilty. Devote life to children. — Im
FB-dislike HC-magic KC-accident RB-guilt

Wrong doing. Reform. — If
RC-wrong RA-reform

Sad: not satisfied with her job. Starves. Sad and disheartened. Seeks job again. — If
RB-torn PD-suffer RA-work

In regret, has become self-incriminating. How got she this wrong attitude? — Jmo
RB-regret DSC-disobey

Drugs

Rich girl takes to drugs. Fa rescues. Hospital cure. — Im
KA-wealth RC-abuse KC-luck NDA-goods

Sad because she is drugged out with what is lying on the floor there. — Jmy
PD-sad RC-abuse

Took drugs, cocaine. Revolted parents are good, but she unsatisfied with her life—no future. Die early. — Jfy
RC-abuse DSC-family PD-satisfy KD-death

Drugged out discarded container. Woman, too well-dressed to be a beggar. — Jmy
RC-abuse

2. Expressive Categories

[18] Need of Nurture, Help (N)	*4 P*	*3 AB*	*4 I*	*5 Jy*	*2 Jo*

[6] Needs emotional help (NSB, NSD)

She is crying. Someone will come to help her. — Jmo
PD-sorrow NDA-comfort

Disabled boy needs help. — Pf
CD-weak NSB-helps

Sad for not receiving studies. Still hopeful. — Pf
PD-sad NSD-no-help NSB-help

With a problem. Parents do not listen locked up alone. Parents will not help her and she will have to find the help of others. 2) If she believes in herself and the positive side of life, she will be able to resolve her own problem. Jfy
NDC-comfort NSA-s-help

Pain very difficult problem about herself or another, e.g., what happened in her family. Can't count on external help, needs to resolve the problem—to wait for the situation to pass. Thinking about suicide. Depression. Jmy
PB-trouble CB-arduous <u>NSD-no-help</u> <u>PD-depress</u> <u>PD-suicide</u>

Adolescent, searching, confused. Does not know what she would do will not be able to help herself. Poor. What to do? Jmy
<u>NSB-help</u> <u>KD-poor</u> <u>NSD-sustain</u>

---

[4] Needs economic assistance (NSD)

Poor miserable person I don't know what she is doing. Jmo
<u>KD-poor</u>

Health system in Brasil. Those without money, the government pays. But must wait long time. Hours. Or weeks. Jfy
KD-poor <u>DDD-inept</u> KD-poor

She is living in Brasil and facing the difficulties brought day by day in the Third World. Jfy
KD-poor <u>NSD-goods</u>

Beggar—nothing to eat. Found purse. Rewarded. Opens an orphanage with the money. Pm
KD-poor NSD-goods KA-luck RA-other <u>NDA-charity</u>

---

[8] Abandoned, homeless or run away (NSD)

Abandoned child. No shelter. Nobody wanted to help. Suffers. ABf
<u>NSD-deserted</u> OD-body NDC-succor PD-suffer NSD-no-help

Many in Brazil. Homeless. Become outcasts. Gov should build facilities. Im
<u>NSD-parent</u> ESD-defiled DDD-neglect

Doesn't have parents, or he ran away from home. Pm
<u>NSD-parent</u> <u>DSC-family</u>

Homeless. No place to sleep begs for food. Decides to go an orphanage. ABm
<u>NSD-parent</u> OD-parent PD-sad NSB-no help RB-torn NSA-assist

Violent city, children live on street; asked for alms, night and day. Stole things. Taken to orphanage by police. Educated. ABf
<u>NSD-parent</u> NSD-goods RC-propriety DDA-police NDA-edify

Homeless and starving. Waiting for help. Im
<u>NSD-parent</u> NBS-help

Hungry, cold. No family. Im
<u>NSD-parent</u> PD-suffer

Without parents. Hungry. Become criminal. Im
<u>NSD-parent</u> PD-suffer AC-crime

[13]	*Love or Affiliation Issues (F)*	*0 P*	*2 AB*	*7 I*	*2 Jy*	*2 Jo*

[3] Undefined or Fearful (FB)

Troubled and crying. Does not know what to do, not economic issue, but human relationships. Jfy
FB-problem

Afraid to be hurt. Shuts out the world. If
FB-distrust

Sad over problems to be faced (possibly over friendship or financial problems). Im
PD-sad FB-problem KB-poverty

[4] Loss through broken affair . . . desertion (FD)

She is exhausted with a problem. Maybe she picked up a boyfriend and was dumped. Jmo
PB-tired FD-rejected

Broken love affair. She is able to mollify. ABm
FC-split HC-discord HA-pacify

Husband ran away. If
FD-reject NSD-deserted

Regrets someone's departure. If
FD-rejected

Loss Through Death

Lost his mother severely depressed ABm
FD-death PD-depress

Son killed in fight. Go to God's home. Im
KD-death FD-fate HC-murder NSA-god

Poor town. Lost son in holdup. Husb joins her. If
KD-poor FD-fate HC-murder

Lost son. How to live? If
FD-death NSD-sustain

Relative died; about to cry. Worn out and does not know what will happen. Jmy
KD-death FD-fate CB-worry

Crying, an accident occurred. Someone died. She is wondering, what should I do from now on? Jmo
KD-accident KD-death FD-fate CB-worry

[14]	*Quarrel and Dissension (H)*	*2 P*	*1 AB*	*6 I*	*4 Jy*	*1 Jo*

Quarrel

Very sad and dejected. Someone quarreled. Pf
PD-sad HC-discord

Running and fighting. Hurt. Im
HC-fight HD-injured

Girl friend beat her.

HD-injured — If

Quarreled with somebody. Reestablishes friendship.

HC-discord FA-mend — If

Economy of Brazil. Or fight with man. Trying to calm herself. Will be able to resolve the problem.

KD-poverty HC-discord CA-s-help — Jmy

She is crying after fighting with her boy friend on the phone.

HC-discord — Jfy

Someone crying because he/she fought with someone. Or perhaps, she drank too much and is sleeping.

HC-discord RC-abuse — Jfy

Serious mental problem. This is after a fight.

PD-crazed HC-discord — Jmo

Maladjusted, depressed after fighting with parents. Started drinking and is currently thinking about suicide.

HC-discord RC-abuse PD-suicide — Jfy

Family Disorder

Drugs and family problems, is abandoned.

CB-worry NSD-deserted HB-family RC-abuse — Pf

Parents quarreled. Poor, couldn't afford studies decided to work. Happy.

HC-discord KD-poor NDD-unable HB-family RA-duty-o PA-joy — ABf

Husband drinks. She sadly leaves. Unhappy quits drinking. She with other man. Husband now left alone, suffering.

RC-abuse HC-injury FC-split RA-reform FD-rejected PD-suffer — If

Beat by husband. Looks for better life. He improves.

HD-injured FB-unmet RA-reform FA-mend — If

Argues with husband. Leaves. Comes back to try again.

HC-discord FC-split FA-mend — If

[1]	*Esteem (E)*	*0 P*	*0 AB*	*0 I*	*1 Jy*	*0 Jo*

Worried with a problem. Has been rejected by a show.

PD-sad ESC-lessen — Jmy

[27]	*Internal Affective States (P)*	*1 P*	*2 AB0*	*0 I*	*11 Jy*	*13 Jo*

Sadness (not specified) (PD)

Sad man (reasons not specified)

PD-sorrow — ABf

Adolescent. After crying, she is sleeping, and sleeping well.

PD-sorrow — Jfo

Suffering/in pain and is sad. Perhaps, drunk. Suffering is important to polish the soul and built up personality.

PD-suffer RC-abuse RA-stoic — Jmo

Devastated and sad. Need to know what is on the floor to understand what is happening in this scene. Jmo
PD-shock PD-sorrow

Sad person, because of the position she is in. Crying. Devastated. Jfo
PD-sorrow

Sadness. I can tell because of the position of the girl's hand. Jmy
PD-sorrow

Crying. A grave motive. Jmo
PD-sorrow

Crying and sad, as if under a shadow. She didn't expect this to happen. Jfy
PD-shock PD-sorrow

Pistol on floor? Sad (*kanashii*). I've never seen what a pistol looks like up close. Jfo
PD-sorrow (suicide)

Severely Depressed

This is person who is depressed. Why? I don't know. Jfy
PD-depress

Crying. No one knows why. One side of her that is trying to commit suicide but she used to try to cut her wrists. Jfy
PD-sorrow PD-suicide CD-decide

Sick and has problems. Having emotional problems and is depressed. Doesn't have the psychological conditions to try. Jmy
KD-illness KB-crisis PD-depress PD-crazed

Like a rock—hard. Feels she can end her life here—life will end like a rock. Things can't be this way. Therefore, crying. Jmo
PD-depress

She is tired and depressed with life. Jfy
PD-depress

Tired of work and life and does not know what will happen. She is pessimistic. Jmo
PD-depress

Mental Condition

Depressed with mental problem. Needs attention and wants someone to care for her. Like a mental patient. Jfy
PD-depress PD-crazed NSB-help

Crisis of depression. Psychological help will not help this condition. No external origin. Jfy
PD-depress PD-crazed NSB-help

Tired or Sleeping

Sleeping. Pf
PB-tired

Tired and slept. ABf
PB-tired

Resting.

PB-tired Jmy

Parents have gone out. Tired of waiting and fallen asleep.

PB-tired Jmo

Tired or resting something happened.

PB-tired Jfy

Unresolved Problem

Desperate, crying very grave. All have problems, if one does not rise and resolve it will be bad for that person. Jfy

PB-trouble CB-arduous

There is a problem and she is wondering what she should do from now on. Jfo

PB-trouble CB-arduous

She is crying because she is troubled. It is because of some kind of personal problem. Jfo

PB-trouble CB-arduous

Out of hope. Weak person life is worthless but shouldn't think this way. To be desperate is wrong. Jfo

PD-depress NSB-help CD-weak ESD-worth AD-withdraw

Dispirited because of alcohol. Her problem is either economic or family. Dependence on drink and even up to suicide. Jmo

PD-depress RC-control KD-poor HB-family HC-discord PD-suicide

[3]	*Fate: Sickness or Accident (K)*	*0 P*	*3 AB*	*0 I*	*0 Jy*	*0 Jo*

Had an accident needs help.

KC-accident ABm

May have fallen down, then she got hurt and cried.

KD-accident ABm

She is sick like a disabled child.

KD-illness CD-weak ABf

[1]	*Reject*	*0 P*	*1 AB*	*0 I*	*0 Jy*	*0 Jo*

Instrumental Categories

Achievement or Competence Stories

Unlike Card 1, Card 3BM only rarely picks up a story of concern with frustrated achievement, incompetence or failure with some direct emphasis on dispirited affect. There is just one such story found in the present samples, given by an older Japanese male. This problem with competence is an educational one. This theme is a typically Japanese concern:

> (J27mo) (3BM) The woman is tired of fighting, and dispirited. It is a family problem mixed with a professional level. She is having problems with education, and of a certain age, she will continue fighting. In the future, she will continue to live a simple life without big achievements.
>
> [PB-trouble CC-failure HC-discord AA-persist CD-mediocre]

Control and Responsibility: Authority or Wrongdoing

In the Brazilian ethnic youth generally, there is an *instrumental* focus on the behavioral *Control* exercised by parents as they affect a child. Of the total sixty stories in our sample, eighteen are directly concerned with parental authority either legitimately or excessively exercised (29 percent). (We illustrate many, but not all of these stories.) This is a much greater specific preoccupation with beatings (nine or 14 percent) and/or abandonment (eight or 13 percent) as punishment than in any other sample with which I am familiar. It suggests a widespread fear of punitive parents for many children in Brazil. Such forms of discipline or coercion are not found in the fantasies of Americans, Japanese, or Koreans.

In all the Brazilian stories the father is depicted more as the proper or improper disciplinarian in contrast to American records, wherein the mother is usually the disciplinary or demanding figure. An additional six stories (10 percent) of the Brazilian stories are about internal family breakdown, parental disorder, and discord. Such stories are most rare in Asian samples obtained on this or any card.

The possible wrongdoing of children scored under the *Responsibility* category suggests a pervasive concern with youthful drug use throughout Brazil, regardless of the group considered. This use of drugs is sometimes related to the parental abandonment of children who become homeless living on the street. In 16 percent (ten stories), there are themes of homeless, abandoned, or needful children. Another ten stories are of personal wrongdoing or quarreling.

Two of the four Japanese stories of parental scolding have to do with school problems. Such strong parental pressure to do well in school does not appear in the other groups.

(J31mo) (3BM) She is inside the house crying about something she did. She failed a test for the university and was scolded and is crying.

[PD-sad CC-failure NDA-scold]

One story depicts excessive parental pressure leading to suicide.

(J39mo) (3BM) This is a school student in Japan like those I told you who were sleeping on the JR line (train system). Everyday, she wakes up early to go to school. At night, she becomes very tired and returns late. Yet, her father tells her that she does not study enough and scolds her. However, she cannot do any better no matter how hard she tries within her abilities. Because she does not want to bother/trouble her parents, she decides to leave this world. This is a pistol, isn't it?

[PB-tired AA-persist DDC-press HC-suicide HA-pacify PD-suicide]

The Japanese see only four stories of wrongdoing (8 percent) compared with fourteen such stories (22 percent) among the other groups. The general Brazilian concern with drugs appears in three of these four stories of a slumped figure.

(J47fy) (3BM) Slumped because she took drugs, maybe something like cocaine. She is a youth who revolted (*revoltado contra o mundo*) against the world. The parents are good, simple, and normal, but she is revolting because she is unsatisfied with her life—about who she is, what she wants, and where she wishes to go. In the future—well she has no future. She will die early.

[RC-abuse DSC-family PD-satisfy KD-death]

In stories involving authority themes or wrongdoing there are fifteen males and ten females. In contrast to the Japanese Brazilians the parental discipline depicted in the other groups is more severe than simple verbal scolding.

Only in two stories, one by an Afro-Brazilian and one by an Italian is parental intervention positive in a nurturing way. In both instances it is a story of a youth on drugs. Characteristically, in the Italian story it is a father who is the concerned parent. In the Afro-Brazilian it is more characteristically the mother.

(AB19 m) (3BM) The boy used drugs, but his parents never learned about that. He was the only child. He asked his mother permission to make a trip and lied to her, saying that he would study far away. In his trip he used to smuggle goods. Then the police discovered it and caught him, and his mother never heard that he was in prison. Family friends told her so, and she made a trip. She then heard that her son used drugs. She took him out of the prison and sent him for a trip with her parents. As time passed, little by little they helped him to abandon drugs.

[RC-abuse FC-deceit AC-crime DDA-police NDA-advice]

(I 6m) (3BM) It is a woman who was happy; she had everything she wanted, she was rich. She begins to go out along with bad fellows and her friends use drugs; she tries it and becomes addicted. In the beginning nothing happened because she had money. Her father went broke and they became poor overnight. She doesn't have any more money and is not able to buy drugs any longer. She gets worse and worse. She is thrown to a corner. Her father finds out her addiction and takes her to a hospital for a recuperation. She makes the treatment and gets better.

[KA-wealth RC-abuse KC-luck NDA-goods]

The stories about beating as discipline separate into those wherein beating is seen as legitimate, and those in which it is seen as excessive. In two stories of males, the father is seen as acting appropriately in beating his son for wrongdoing.

(I 16m) Paulo, a kid who annoys a good deal, spoiled something at home again. His father, very angry, beat him. In order not to be embarrassed before his neighbors, Paulo went to the living room.

[RC-wrong DSB-torn DDA-punish]

As in the story given by a Portuguese young man, beating can be seen as administered by other than parents.

(I 6m) (3BM) It is a girl who is crying and who perhaps did something wrong, which she shouldn't have done, and hence her father swore at her and her relatives beat her. She is thinking about her life. She thinks of the reason why she did it. She shouldn't have done it. Or was her parents' attitude unfair? Deep inside she likes her parents and knows that they, being parents, made the right decision. Because parents know what is the best for their children and they try to be most devoted to their children.

[RC-mores DDA-punish ESB-shame]

Excessive beating appears in the stories of three Portuguese, one Afro-Brazilian, and one Italian.

There are many children on the streets in urban Brazil. These children usually are not orphans. They may be escaping family brutality. Awareness of this situation is spontaneously expressed in this story by a Portuguese youth:

(P 5m) (3BM) The girl had a very bad mother. When she arrived late from school, her mother used to beat her. Then, one day the girl ran away from home, but soon the mother put an advertisement on the newspaper, saying that whoever saw the girl should please inform. But soon the mother found the girl, and the girl goes home being beaten, just like an animal. And so the girl remained at a corner, crying.

[DDC-punish FC-flee HC-cruel]

A young Afro-Brazilian male uses Card 3BM to directly, and self-consciously, express his feelings about family violence in Brazil:

(AB 29m) (3BM) The Violence. Many children are beaten by their parents without having a reason. Nowadays, parents are understanding. They don't expect us to make anything wrong. They yell; they beat and maltreat them in order to hurt, to give serious wounds such as scars, burns, etc. Thus, it is necessary to put an end to this controversy about these parents who want to see their children dead. Many times, a child suffers violence from her parents, stepmothers and aunts since she is 2 years old. And from her mother's friend. So we have to do away with it, for it is unfair. It is necessary to do something with these evil doers.

[HC-cruel HD-injury DDC-punish]

As in the following story by a Portuguese youth the beating is sometimes to force a youth to work. For many Brazilians work comes to mean exploitation, not a self-motivated desire for achievement:

(P 1f) (3BM) Alex was a boy who was beaten by his family, who wanted him to work as a carpenter. But Alex felt more like playing with some boys from the village. The only person who understood him was his grandfather Pedro, who was teaching him how to play a game. His mother, Maria, was making a trip. As she came back, she asked her husband where her son was. He answered that he was somewhere around. She went out, looking for the boy, and found him on a chair, crying. He explained that his father used to beat him very much. She said that she wouldn't let him beat him any more and that he could play ball with his friends. He shouldn't work with his father. He agreed with his mother's idea.

[DDC-punish RD-work PA-play NDA-protect]

An errant child is sent from home, abandoned in stories created by two Portuguese and one Afro-Brazilian male and one Portuguese female.

(P 8m) (3BM) The violence on the streets starts by the abandoned kids who begin to sniff glue, to smoke and to dope themselves. It happens because their mothers send them away from home, for they don't want to work. And it will be very hard to do away with this violence.

[RC abuse RD-work DDA-punish NSD-deserted]

(P 2f) (3BM) It is a woman who has no house to live and who sleeps on a street bench. Instead of thinking about working, she followed the ideas of her friends, who made her throw her life away. Instead of helping her parents, she didn't want to; she is influenced by her friends, and her parents sent her away from home. As she doesn't have a place to live, she went to the street bench.

[DSD-peer RD-work DDA-punish NSD-deserted]

(AB 24m) (3BM) The Little Thief. At a certain occasion, the boy who had been turned out from home had nowhere to go. He had only one thing to do: sleeping on the street. He was sleeping when he heard some shots and the police, pursuing the boys who were near him on the street. They were sniffing glue, smoking marijuana, intoxicating themselves. And a policeman said: "What happened to that boy? Let's take him to the police station." They held Silvio and took him as if he was a thief, a street child. When he asked a policeman what he was doing there, the policeman said: "You are here because you were on the street and near the guys who were sniffing and making other things." Then Silvio said: "You mean that nobody can

remain on the street, near bad people? You take everyone without knowing why they are here. That's why these drugs will never end."
[RC-property DDA-punish NSD-deserted RC-abuse DDC-unfair]

(P 6m) (3BM) It is a boy who used to drink alcohol. His parents didn't like that. At a certain night, when he had drunk too much, his parents quarreled with him and sent him away. He began to sleep on the park bench.
[RC-abuse DDA-punish NSD-deserted]

There are seven additional stories of inadvertent wrongdoing, such as killing a bird, that do not involve parents (two male, five female).

Expressive Stories

Themes of Nurturant Need

There are eighteen stories that do not explicitly concern themselves with either parental punitive acts or wrongdoing on the part of a child that forward themes of homelessness and a need for nurture.

Seven Japanese stories of nurturant needs emphasize economic duress. These stories also give evidence of a concern with being self-reliant or being able to solve ones' own problems.

(J16my) (3BM) This is an adolescent, searching, confused. A lost child, but not a mendigo (beggar). She does not know what she would do—in this way (jeito) she will not be able to help herself. To make matters worse, she is poor. She really does not know what to do in the future.
[NSB-help KD-poor NSD-sustain]

(J26my) (3BM) This here is a person dispirited/discouraged. It can be because of alcohol—it depends on the drink. Her problem is either economic or it could be a family problem also. Today, financial problems influence the family a lot. If she does not resolve the economic problem, the situation is bad. Her tendency is dependence on drink (alcoholic beverages) and even up to suicide.
[PD-depress RC-control KD-poor HB-family HC-discord PD-suicide]

(J32fy) (3BM) Someone like this must have a problem. This is her last gasp/she is out of hope. She is sort of a weak needy person if she is like this. She feels life is worthless and useless, but she shouldn't think this way. To become this desperate is wrong. If she didn't think like this about life, it would not be this way for her.
[PD-depress NSB-help CD-weak ESD-worth AD-withdraw]

Three of the stories directly reflect on governmental inadequacy.

(Jmy 22) (3BM) What she is crying would be the economy of Brazil, something about the family—how to pay the bills. Or it is a fight between a man and woman, like this. She is not feeling good, is passing through a bad state and is trying to calm herself. It is hard to tell whether the situation will improve because I can't see her face and eyes. It all depends. She is reflecting, but it is true that she will be able to resolve the problem. She needs to have a dialogue, to cry, to be loosened/freed, then she will be able to.

[DDD-inept KD-poor HC-discord NSA-s-help PA-relief]

(Jfy 37) (3BM) This is the health system in Brazil. You go to the doctor and for those without money, the Brazilian government pays. But to meet the doctor, you must wait for a long time. It may be hours—eight hours. Or even two or three weeks.

[DDD-inept KD-illness KD-poor]

(Jmy 41) (3BM) She is living in Brazil and facing the difficulties brought on day by day in the Third World.

[DDD-inept KD-poor]

While economic need is also found as a background in the stories of the other samples, more up front are concerns with abandoned, homeless, or runaway children. These situations are seen by four Italian, three Afro-Brazilians, and four Portuguese. There are two additional stories by Portuguese females of unmet needs on the part of a disabled boy or a hapless student.

(AB 21f) (3BM) An abandoned child. It was a chilly night. Everybody who walked on that street was wearing heavy clothes. They paid no attention to that person who was just like them, a human being, but who had nobody who would shelter him. It was a boy who was shrunk in a corner, suffering from cold, hunger and sleep. But nobody wanted to help him. Days passed by. He thought that some guardian angel would help him, but nobody appeared in order to take him out of that cold, dirt street, where he felt hunger.

[NSD-deserted OD-body NDC-succor PD-suffer NSD-no-help]

(AB 26m) (3BM) A Street Boy. There was a boy who didn't have a house to live. He didn't have a place to stay in, then he started sleeping in the open air. And during the day he asked for food. He was always sad, because he had nowhere to sleep, and nowhere to live. On the street he could only become a thief. So one day he decided by himself to go to an orphanage.

[NSD-parent OD-parent PD-sad NSB-no help RB-torn NSA-assist]

Some of these stories are less immediate and more intellectualized as if seen at a distance from the teller.

(P8m) (3BM) The violence on the streets starts by the abandoned kids who begin to sniff glue, to smoke and to dope themselves. It happens because their mothers send them away from home, for they don't want to work. And it will be very hard to do away with this violence.

[HB-f-fury RC-abuse NDC-desert RD-work KD-hopeless]

(P7f) (3BM) Here we see how our Brazil is. What do drugs and children abuse do? What do this boy's parents do? Was it a lack of education or lack of love? Or was it his own choice, to get involved with drugs and have such a sad life?
[RC-abuse CC-mental NDC-comfort RC-result]

(I 15m) (3BM) In Brazil there are many children who do not have a home and who sleep in street benches and even on sidewalks. Many of these needy people who don't have a place go to the outside limits of the cities, where they are likely to become outcasts. In order that this does not happen, it is necessary that the President and his staff build dwellings where there be infrastructure for these people to live carefree.
[NSD-parent KD-poor ESD-defiled NDA-active]

In summarizing, Italian youth when they deal with the theme of homelessness tend to assume missing parents, whereas Portuguese and Afro-Brazilians are more apt to see children being driven out of the home for some reason by parents.

Affiliation

In twelve affiliative stories, the nature of the card suggests the major concern is loss through desertion or rejection in four stories. Three affiliative stories of desertion or rejection are told by Italian teenagers (one male and two females) There were no such stories among the Japanese or Portuguese. Only one Afro-Brazilian gives such a story:

(I 11f) (3BM) It is a person crying because her husband ran away and she doesn't know why. She keeps expecting news from him, but she doesn't receive news.
[FD-reject NSD-deserted]

In six stories there is an affiliative loss through death. In two Japanese stories loss prompts thoughts of the future.

(J13my) (3BM) A relative of her died and by her attitude, it looks like she is about to cry. She is worn out and does not know what will happen.
[KD-death FD-fate CB-worry]

(J49Mo) (3BM) She is crying because an accident has just occurred. She has learned that someone has died. She is wondering, what should I do from now on?
[KD-accident KD-death FD-fate CB-worry]

Among the Italians, in two of three stories the loss is due to violence.

(I 13f) (3BM) In a poor town, several people experience sad moments. The case of a lady who lost her son at a holdup. The lady received this news when she saw someone knocking at her house's door, informing her of the tragic happening.
[KD-poor FD-fate HC-murder]

(I 2m) (3BM) The woman is crying because they killed her son. Her son was at a ball, and he was killed during a fight. Afterwards she gets up and thinks that there is no use in crying, for one day all of us will go to God's home.

[HD-death FD-fate HC-murder NSA-god]

Esteem

On this card in this sample there is only one story (Japanese) in which self-esteem is involve as a major concern. An individual is rejected as a performer in a show. The story does not elaborate if it is a question of competence or not; but the emotion experienced is social rejection.

(J44my) (3BM) She came home, dropped her keys on the floor, and is now leaning against the sofa crying without even removing her shoes. Disgracefully she has been rejected by a show.

[PD-sad ESC-lessen]

Quarrel and Discord

Quarrel and discord stories are given by five Japanese and eight others. The Japanese depict a mentally unstable person in two of their conflict stories.

(J14mo) (3BM) This is a scene with a person with a serious mental problem. This is after a fight.

[PD-crazed HC-discord]

(J25fy) (3BM) A woman is in desperation because she drank too much. She is maladjusted and very depressed after fighting with her parents. She has started drinking and has arrived in this state and is currently thinking about suicide.

[HC-discord RC-abuse PC-suicide]

It is five girls (three Italian, one Portuguese, one Afro-Brazilian) who give themes of drunkenness and quarreling in parents. In one of these, given by an Afro-Brazilian, the child submitting to work solves the family tension. Again, note that in the Afro-Brazilians the economic pressure to work is of more immediate concern than any possible fantasy of self-actualizing achievement.

(AB17 f) (3BM) Janaina, along with her deep sorrow, sat on the floor with her head leaning against the sofa. She was crying because her parents quarreled too much, because they were poor and couldn't afford her studies. Janaina stood up, wiped her tears and asked her parents to stop quarreling. They sat together in the living room in order to hear what Janaina had decided: "Dad, Mom, I have thought a lot and made a decision. I am 14 and in spite of everything I can read and write. So I decided to work." Her parents became happy for her having made this decision. Finally all of them became happy.

[HC-discord KD-poor NDD-unable HB-family RA-duty-o PA-joy]

In two of the family quarrel stories of the Italians, it is the woman who is physically beaten in a quarrel. Drinking on the part of the husband is involved. In these youthful stories the future remains optimistic.

> (I 3f) (3BM) This is a woman who is suffering because her husband drinks. He arrived drunk and beat her. She left sadly because she liked him. Then he began to notice her virtues; he saw he was unhappy and quit drinking. He went to fetch her, and she was with another man. He remained alone, suffering, just as he had made her suffer.
>
> [RC-abuse HC-injury FC-split RA-reform FD-rejected PD-suffer]

> (I 5f) (3BM) A woman lived with a man who beat her a lot, and she left by the back door crying and complaining about the kind of life she has. She is longing for a better life. She will get a better life. He will understand her in order that they live happily.
>
> [HD-injured FB-unmet RA-reform FA-mend]

Three stories of peer quarrel and dissension are told by Italians (one male and two females).

> (I 8m) (3BM) It is a guy seated on the floor with his head on the sofa; he is sleeping. He was running and fighting. He is a little hurt. He'll get up, wash himself and go to bed. He is 17 or 18 years old.
>
> [HC-fight HD-injured]

We note comparatively throughout these cards that the Italian group is most apt to see physically aggressive acts, whether as abusiveness, animosity, or punishment.

Internal Affective States

It is notable that one of the most significant differences distinguishing the Japanese from other Brazilians is the proportion of individuals who give stories that focus on an internal affective state that does not directly involve mentioning others. The condition is to be resolved internally. The cause of sorrow or depression is not specified in many stories. The degree of despair experienced may even lead to suicide in some of the stories. In general stories of suicide as a result of inner tension is very seldom depicted on this or other cards in most samples of TAT stories. In our experience, they are more apt to be elicited from Japanese. The difference between groups is dramatic. In other than the Japanese, there are only three such stories, two of which are simple stories depicting a "tired " or sleeping figure, another describing someone as "sad." The Japanese stories suggest that it is a sign of internal weakness not to be able to resolve difficulties internally.

> (J26mo) (3BM) This here is a person dispirited/discouraged. It can be because of alcohol—it depends on the drink. Her problem is either economic or it could be a

family problem also. Today, financial problems influence the family a lot. If she does not resolve the economic problem, the situation is bad. Her tendency is dependence on drink (alcoholic beverages) and even up to suicide.

[PD-depress RC-control KD-poor HC-discord PD-suicide]

(J35fy) (3BM) Someone like this must have a problem. This is her last gasp. She is out of hope. She is sort of a weak person if she is like this. She feels life is worthless and useless, but she shouldn't think this way. To become this desperate is wrong. If she didn't think like this about life, it would not be this way for her.

[CD-weak PD-depress RC-control]

Severe forms of depression are described in eight Japanese stories.

(J3fy) (3BM) In a room, a girl was crying. No one knows why. There is one side of her that is trying to commit suicide but she could not completely succumb to this side of herself, but there was always this threat. She used to try to cut her wrists.

[PD-sorrow PC-suicide CB-decide]

(J10my) (3BM) Maybe she is a person who is sick and has problems. She received a big shock and is having emotional problems and is depressed. She doesn't have the psychological capacities to try to leave this state.

[KD-illness KB-crisis PD-depress CD-weak]

(J34mo) (3BM) The girl is like a person carrying a rock. She feels that she is like a rock—hard. She feels she can end her life here—that life will end like a rock. But she feels that things can't be this way. Therefore, she is crying.

[PC-suicide PD-suffer CB-decide]

Fateful Events

Illness can be the central reason for the position of a slumped figure. In these samples only three stories focused simply on physical concerns, illness, or accident were given by Afro-Brazilians.

(AB28) (3BM) One day a woman was walking by the house, when she slipped, fell down on the floor and fainted over the sofa. And there she remained until someone would appear.

[KD-accident]

In considering Card 3BM overall it depicts considerable infra-family difficulties and concern with exercising a proper discipline other than physical beating or even abandonment driving children out of the house as punishment. We may presume that there is a widespread attention to the reality of children in the streets and the use of drugs by youth in contemporary Brazil. In the Portuguese, AfroBrazilian, and Italian groups, there are thirteen such stories, over 20 percent of the stories. Beatings, legitimate or otherwise, appear in fourteen stories in some form; again, this is in over 20 percent of the stories, another notable theme. Alcohol and drug abuse in either parents or children is mentioned in eight stories, or over 11 percent of the cases. Adult desertion is another recurring theme appearing in five stories. Contrastively, these themes are almost absent in the Japanese Brazilians. They are extremely rare in any previous sample with which I am familiar. Some of these contrastive concerns are supported by the evidence of Card 16.

Card 16: A Blank Card

Administering a blank card permitting totally free interpretation toward the end of a series of more definable pictures allows us to score and interpret what spontaneously comes to mind. What resulted as themes among the Brazilian samples? The results indicate how this card allows for abstractions about the human condition, from general existential comments to concrete interpersonal fantasies.

On this card we again found the most dramatic differences between the Japanese sampled and the other Brazilian groups. The Japanese approach to this card ranged the farthest, from a highly specific, concrete use of imagination, to a highly abstract detached commentary.

The forty-six available Japanese records suggest they felt very challenged by Card 16. Twenty-six (57 percent) of the stories elicited were of a highly symbolic nature. These included using the color white to symbolize musing about life purpose (six),"the end" (two) "eternity" (one), peace and purity (eleven). Conversely, there were nine rejections, or 20 percent of those tested. Additionally, seven Japanese simply gave forms of card description. It seems that responding to a difficult stimulus the Japanese can resort to symbolic, even poetic explanations or reject the task.

These results were reminiscent of the Japanese approach to the Rorschach Test I witnessed in several samples (De Vos and Boyer, 1989). In work with Japanese samples in the United States and Japan we elicited some very imaginative symbolic integration of what they perceived as the complexity of some of the ink blots. For example, Card IX, a colored card, difficult to organize, could be interpreted as an abstraction depicting the "gaiety of a Mexican fiesta." Alternatively, when considered too complex, Card IX also elicited a relative high proportion of card rejections. There was what we consider as "quality ambition." It was a characteristic to resolve the task as one demanding a symbolic explanation, since the design was not amenable to a more concrete solution.

Among the sixty Portuguese, Afro-Brazilians, and Italians, card description or rejection appeared only in two Afro-Brazilians. The Italian youth gave generally optimistic stories. Of these twenty-four Italian stories, there were five of an existential symbolic nature (21 percent). Two questioned the meaning of life; in one of these there is wonder about God; in the other, each person composes his or her own life. In the other three, one expressed the concern that humans are destroying their own environment. Another worries about world peace. The last suggests directly that the blank card should be painted in with a picture of a richer, less corrupt Brazil.

These ethnic groups most characteristically gave stories focused either on parents or on peer group relationships. Expressive or esthetic concerns with plants or animals appeared in other stories. Achievement or competence concerns appeared in seven stories. In a negative direction, there were economic worries in several stories and fateful events or accidents depicted in several others.

This was one card that picked up some notable trends between those from intact families compared with those from single parent situations. Those from single parent families were most prone to give proportionally more stories of economic concerns or worries about accidents. Moreover, four from single parent situations gave very negatively toned views of parental behavior. Three Afro-Brazilians from single families give stories of rowdy or unruly classroom behavior on the part of students.

There were definite gender emphasis to be found among these stories. Of the seventeen stories given about parental relationships, thirteen were given by young women. Nine of thirteen stories of economic concerns and accidents, most of a physical nature, were given by males.

Table 9.2
Card 16: A Blank Card

Groups	Port	Afro-B	Ital	Jyoung	Jold
Total N 110	**16**	**20**	**24**	**25**	**25**
[37] 1. Instrumental Stories					
	9	7	13	4	4
[8] Musing about Purpose (A)	0	0	2	2	4
[7] Achievement or Competence Themes (A, C)	1	2	4	0	0
[7] Parental Relationship (D)	4	1	2	0	0
[3] Mutual Purpose (M)	2	0	1	0	0
[12] Responsibility (R)	2	4	4	2	0
[53] 2. Expressive Stories					
	7	12	12	12	10
[4] Pleasure-Pain (P)	0	0	0	3	1
[10] Affiliation (F)	1	4	2	3	0
[7] Nurture (N)	1	2	3	1	0
[17] Harmony (H)	0	3	3	4	7
[2] Esteem: peer appreciation (E)	0	0	2	0	0
[12] Kismet-Fate (K)	4	3	2	1	2
[1] Concern with Objects (O)	1	0	0	0	0
[7] Card Description	0	0	0	4	3

[9]	Rejection	0	2	0	2	5
[6]	Missing	0	0	0	3	3
	1. Instrumental Stories					
[8]	*Existential Musing about Purpose (AA)*	*0 P*	*0 AB*	*2 I*	*2 Jy*	*4 Jo*
	Studying but nothing interests him. Wonders about god. Wasteful quest. Lives in present. AB-purpose HB-god AA-purpose					Im
	Life is a blank page on which we write. Each decides on one's own life. AA-purpose					If
	This is an idea about a way/or a free, open road (*estrada*). Imagining a person who is walking. It is a long road (*estrada comprido*). He is walking straight . . . I don't know where he is going. The person should know. AA-purpose					Jfy
	I am like this white paper. I was born where I couldn't see anything. To write on this white paper is like growing up. One must think hard, or others will laugh at you. One must think hard before one writes. AA-purpose ESB-shame					Jmo
	Life is like this paper. You write something and throw it out and repeat this over and over again. This is how life continues. AA-purpose PA-endure					Jmo
	We can design our dreams and imagination on this paper and according to imagination, creativity. We can create on paper. AA-purpose PA-create					Jmo
	Should not forget past. Make a white sheet first, then, decide what is important one by one. This is hard when you are confused. But one must forget things to a certain extent and then start ordering them from what is most important. AA-purpose					Jmo
	I see myself returning to Japan after my dekasegi experience, re-adapting to this country. I am homesick from my stay in Japan, but am trying to construct my life anew again in Brazil—a better life. AA-purpose					Jmy
[7]	*Achievement or Competence Themes (AA)*	*1 P*	*2 AB*	*4 I*	*0 Jy*	*0 Jo*
	Dreams of being an artist. Succeeds. AB-dream AA-inspire					Pf
	Planting trees to pick fruit. AA-self PA-nature					ABm
	Avoid rowdy crowd. Transfers classroom to study. RC-mores AA-self FC-split AA-persist					ABm
	Poor. Likes school much, survives difficulties, has girl friend. KD-fate AA-self PA-curious FA-love AA-counter CA-present					Im

Ancient times. Colonist to Brazil. Did not receive what promised. Will succeed. Im

KB-survive FD-fate NSB-distrust NSD-goods AA-persist

Try hard at science classes, but bad grades. Does best to be approved. If

CB-able AA-persist ESB-praise

Facilitated Achievement

Priest makes opportunity. Mo says goodbye to son going to seminary. Im

FB-parting NDA-active AA-parent

[7]	*Parental Relationship (D)*	*4 P*	*1 AB*	*2 I*	*0 Jy*	*0 Jo*

Good

Fa counsels son out of association with criminals. Pf

DDA-advice RA-reform HA-family

Girl gets dirty playing with cats. Mo scolds her. If

RC-messy DDA-scold

Negative and Improper Parental Behavior

Father doesn't accept pregnancy. Daughter defiant. Pf

RC-pr-sex DDA-scold EDC-moral DSC-disobey

Mo forces son to sleep on her lap. Pm

DDC-press DSA-comply

Parents refuse marriage plans of lovers. Pf

FA-love DDC-press DSB-torn PD-sad

Son helps. Father angry at mistake. Mo won't allow beating. School, but afraid of father. Im

CC-failure DDC-punish NDA-secure HB-f-anger

Drunk father forces children into car. Kills other child by car. Dies in drunken accident. ABm

RC-abuse DDC-press NDC-succor RC-result

[3]	*Mutual Purpose (M)*	*2 P*	*0 AB*	*1 I*	*0 Jy*	*0 Jo*

Jaguar used to frighten little animals. Panda prepare a joke with little animals. Jaguar very angry, decided time away. Pf

HB-f-attack MTA-defense FC-split

Competition or Cooperation-Appreciation

Match won. Didn't score goal. Teammates reassure. Pm

MVA-game CB-able FA-friend EDA-praise

Famous driver. Car race. Fun. Accident. Disappoints fans. Not his fault. Im

ESA-fame MVA-game KD-accident ESC-lessen ESA-praise

[12]	*Responsibility (R)*	*2 P*	*4 AB*	*4 I*	*2 Jy*	*0 Jo*

Daily Responsibility and Work

Going to school. If

RA-work

Works to buy uniform to go to soccer school. Pm

KD-poor RA-duty-s AA-self

Working, suffers a lot. Arrived here, but suffering more, believes people betrayed her. But will not lose hope. PD-suffer RA-stoic MTC-betray	Jfy
Personal Irresponsibility	
New teacher. Rowdy students threatened with expulsion. EDC-brash RC-mores DDA-author RA-reform	ABm
Student suspended for poor behavior. Quits. RC-mores DDA-author RD-wrong	ABf
Imprudent act causes the death of two friends. RC-control KD-accident RB-regret	Im
Governmental Corruption or General Irresponsibility	
Ecological concerns with planet. PA-play PA-nature KB-crisis PD-suffer	ABm
Future will be different. Man destroying what he creates. Solution is to become aware. RD-ignorant CA-aware	If
Blank to be painted in with a richer and fairer Brazil. Less corruption. RC-duty KB-hope KA-social	Im
Government discrimination and corruption. Why not give food to people? DDC-unfair KD-poor RC-duty EDC-exploit NDC-goods	Pf
God sad. Not enough police. Too many thieves. NSB-god AC-crime DDD-helpless	ABf
Lots of poverty in the whole world, barbarity, of races and ethnic groups fighting each other, of all against all. Brazil has to improve its system of health, of life, of education. If we had a better life here, we would have more pride towards Brazil, would have more patriotism towards this country. There should be more pride as Brazilians. KD-poor HD-decay EDB-lessen ESB-shame	Jmy

2. Expressive Stories

[4]	*Pleasure-Pain (P)*	*0 P*	*0 AB*	*0 I*	*3 Jy*	*1 Jo*

Happiness (Symbolized)	
I want cards (TAT) that are more brighter/cheerful. PA-joy	Jfy
Result of previous stories. Each has happiness and suffering, light and dark, joy and sadness—especially fun. Human life is like living in the way of the stories just written. PA-joy PD-suffer	Jmo
Surprise	
Someone has just come in. I wonder who it is. PB-surprise	Jfy

Unhappiness

	Based on the previous cards. Not happy scenes, but miserable and sad. At end, one is unsatisfied. PD-sorrow	Jmy

[10]	*Affiliation (F)* *1 P* *4 AB* *2 I* *3 Jy*	*0 Jo*
	Volleyball with friends during recess. FA-share PA-play	ABm
	Group with counselor-excursion FA-share PA-play	If
	Children find member lost in the woods. FB-apart NDA-secure	Pf
	Triangular love relations. Remain friends. FC-triangle FB-thwart FA-friend	ABf
	He only wants friendship not love. Avoids. Girl frustrated. Needs to give to a young man. FC-flee PD-suffer FB-thwart	Abf
	Positive anticipation of the arrival of a considerate lover. FA-empathy	If
	Girl friend studying. Goes to movie with friends. PA-play RD-duty FA-friend	ABm
	A white card . . . is us. Exchange of words between us, the exchange of ideas, definitions, doubts that we are searching for in order to understand each other and to become friends. FA-friend	Jmy
	Loneliness	
	A blank wall is too lonely, so you paint. You fill it up. Normally, on a wall, you put pictures or clocks, etc. on it. FB-alone	Jfy
	Dreaming	
	Street vendor tired asleep and started dreaming a different world animated/upbeat. Pursue life. Happy. One plays, and knows lots of people. Suddenly, wakes up and sees that being together is not reality. KD-poor PA-play FA-empathy	Jfy

[7]	*Nurture (N)* *1 P* *2 AB* *3 I* *1 Jy*	*0 Jo*
	Animals help lost children. Next time listen better to parents. PA-play NDA-charity FA-love DSA-comply	ABm
	Rescue of beautiful bird shot by hunter. PA-esthete HC-cruel HD-hurt NDB-pity NDA-charity	If
	Girls saw mental defective. Mo called asylum. PA-play KD-defect DDA-author NDA-active	ABf
	Grandpa rescues boy from drowning. CA-present KC-accident NDA-rescue	Pf

	Girl breaks doll's leg. Cries. Mother fixes it. Learns to take better care. CD-break NDA-nurture RA-reform	If
	I want a grandchild to care for/watch out for. My children married five years, but they had two miscarriages. NDB-thwart KD-accident	Jfy
	Needy child. Lady denied help. Adopted by wealthy foreigners. Graduate of computer science. NSD-goods NDD-goods NDA-active AA-counter	Im
[17]	*Harmony (H)* *0 P* *3 AB* *3 I* *4 Jy*	*7 Jo*
	Positive	
	World should have *peace*. God said to love one another and not to become delinquents. HA-symbol HA-peace DSA-god FA-love RA-duty	Im
	Happy family in garden. HA-family PA-play	ABf
	Happy family in the field, with children—trees, grass. HA-family PA-nature	Jfy
	World must be one—like white dove, let it fly. Diff languages and feelings become united as one. War. Will not happen. HA-symbol HA-pacify	Jfy
	White is purity—it means that there are no differences, no racism, that all is equal. PA-purity HA-symbol	Jfy
	Hope, and health and harmony between people and cordiality as well. HA-rite HA-family	Jmy
	White is a peace symbol—a peace symbol flying. It is the hope of all. HA-symbol KB-hope	Jmo
	All that is white is all peace. It is all good. I feel this peace too. A clean thing, a pure thing. HA-symbol PA-purity	Jmo
	White is peace, purity. All parents and children hope to live in peace with each other. All want this because there is lots of violence, malice, bad things. We therefore ask God to let us live in peace. HA-symbol PA-purity RA-resp-o KB-hope HB-unrest HA-god	Jmo
	Like that my sons will have a better world. Lots of hope for a better world without dissension/discord. KB-hope HA-group	Jfo
	White. Family commemorating Christmas, with everyone united, with peace, love, I want the world to become more peaceful. HA-symbol HA-rite HA-group	Jfo
	Stories a mixture of us family and sentimental side. Conflict among couples as well as help between people. Hope for each. HA-group	Jmo

A good place. Brazil is a country with problems, but no unsolvable. We all live healthy and happily here. The future is bright. Good harmonious social organizations. Jmo

AA-counter CB-arduous KA-health NSA-grateful KA-wealth HA-group

Discord

Parents quarrel. May separate. Bad teacher replaced. She does better. Parents happy. Im

HC-discord FB-apart

No more quarrels. If

DSB-rebel DDA-educate MVA-profess HA-pacify

Father absent. Mo quarrels with eldest son, but it is resolved. ABf

FC-split HC-discord HA-mend

Quarrelsome parents father left home girl wants reunion. ABf

HC-discord FC-split HB-family

[2]	*Esteem: peer appreciation (E)*	*0 P*	*0 AB*	*2 I*	*0 Jy*	*0 Jo*

Boy who quit violin, but later, plays for friends who applaud him. Im

CC-failure ESA-praise

Concern with money causes breakup of son's acceptance of poor girl by rich family. If

FA-love OB-compare ESB-status FD-split

[12]	*Kismet-Fate (K)*	*4 P*	*3 AB*	*2 I*	*1 Jy*	*2 Jo*

Positive

The earth. Born, had nothing when I die, have noting as well, just like this blank sheet. This is how human life is. Jmo

KA-accept

Human life. Can't worry too much about it, even if poor, sad, etc. a matter of destiny. Jyo

KA-accept

[refers to previous stories] Father will return financially well. Sick daughter's problems solved. Family able to obtain education for the children to raise the level of living. Jmy

KA-recovery

Wins lottery. Pm

KA-luck PA-joy

Robbed. Lucky lost only ID card. ABm

HD-rob OD-loss KA-luck

Illness, Accidents, and Injuries

Two years to live. New diagnosis. Not to die. ABf

PA-joy KD-ill FC-flee KA-recover

Runs out of gas. Fills up. ABm

KC-luck CA-repair

Bumped by car on bicycle, gets better. Pm

PA-play KD-accident CA-defect

	Aged lady killed by car driver not caught. KD-ac-die DSC-escape HB-revenge					Pf
	Skating accident. Friends counsels. PA-play FA-friend KC-hurt-s CC-failure					Pm
	Fishing boat burned. Lucky to be out of it. KC-accident KA-luck					Im
	Something happened to family. Sad girl seeks solace. KC-ac-die NSB-help					If
[1]	*Concern with Objects (O)*	*1 P*	*0 AB*	*0 I*	*0 Jy*	*0 Jo*
	Family vacation, sell home buy in new place. PA-play OA-own					Pf
[7]	*Card Description*	*0 P*	*0 AB*	*0 I*	*4 Jy*	*3 Jo*
	Blank Symbolizes End or Infinity					
	I see a "the end." Description Abstraction					Jfo
	Conclusion of an episode. A second between episodes the blank is between. Description Abstraction					Jmo
	Many stories, white card. Extensive or suggestive. In pure white, infinity. More abstract than a story with a figure. Description Abstraction					Jfy
	Was dreaming and woke up. Don't remember anything—only up to a certain point. The rest is forgotten. Description					Jfy
	I see a white line on this card down the middle. It is like a river and on both sides is a café fazenda—farmland. Description					Jmy
	White. It is empty. Description					Jmo
	I passed through the tunnel of strawberries in Japan, it was all white at the end of the tunnel. Description					Jfy

Stories of Individual or Social Purpose: Instrumental Activities

Existential Musings about Purpose (eight stories)

For the Japanese, in six stories, the white blank sheet represented finding purpose and meaning in one's life trajectory

> (47fy) (Card 16) (blank) This is an idea about a way/path or a free, open road. Imagining a person who is walking. It is a long road. He is walking straight . . . I don't know where he is going. The person should know.
>
> [AA-purpose]

(J34mo) (Card 16) (blank) I am like this white paper. I was born where I couldn't see anything. To write on this white paper is like growing up. One must think hard, or others will laugh at you. One must think hard before one writes.

[AA-purpose EB-shame]

(J40mo) (Card 16) (blank) Life is like this paper. You write something and throw it out and repeat this over and over again. This is how life continues.

[AA-purpose PA-endure]

(J41mo) (Card 16) (blank) We can draw/design our dreams and imaginations on this paper and do according to our imagination and creativity. We can create this on paper.

[AA-purpose PA-create]

(J41mo) (Card 16) (blank) Should not forget the past. Make a white sheet first, then, decide what is important one by one. This is hard when you are confused. But one must forget things to a certain extent and then start ordering them from what is most important.

[AA-purpose]

(J17my) (Card 16) (blank) I see myself returning to Japan after my dekasegi experience, re-adapting to this country. I am homesick from my stay in Japan, but am trying to construct my life anew again in Brazil—a better life.

[AA-purpose]

Two Italians give similar stories of purpose; one evokes questions about the existence of God:

(I 6m) (Card 16) (blank) It is a guy who had a nice childhood, who grew up and who is now studying to enter college. He doesn't know what he wants because there is nothing that interests him. It is a guy who thinks about life, who wonders why he is in the world and how he is in the world. He wonders if he believes in God, and asks himself if there is really a God and what God is. In order not to keep wasting time with these questions, he decided to live life in the present time.

[AB-purpose HB-god AA-purpose]

(I 10f) (Card 16) (blank) Our life is a blank letter. Only one writer can write on it, and this is we. In this letter we decide what we will write, what we will do, how we're going to fill the book. Nobody can judge or write but for ourselves, for each person decides how he or she will be. There is no law fairer than this: each person makes his or her own life.

[AA-purpose]

Achievement or Competence (seven stories)

The Italians give four of seven stories centering around fantasies about *Achievement* and *Competence*. Their themes include compensatory achievement fantasies of a poor boy who survives difficulties through kind assistance. In another story centered even more upon nurture, a poor lad is adopted by wealthy foreigners and graduates in computer science.

> (I 15m) (Card 16) (blank) Once upon a time there was a needy child who had asked a lady for help but she had denied help. The boy grew up with the alms he got in the street. Seeing that, the youth court adopted him to a family of foreigners. He grew up and nowadays he is graduating in computer sciences.
>
> [NSD-goods NDC-goods NDA-active AA-counter]

In a story of facilitated achievement told by a male, a boy departs home to enter a Catholic seminary. We note throughout on several cards occasional Italian stories that suggest that the Catholic church is viewed as an important social influence.

> (I 2m) (Card 16) (blank) The mother is saying good-bye to her son, who is going to the seminary. A priest came to their house and invited the son to go to the seminary. The son accepted and went on to study.
>
> [FB-parting NDA-active AA-parent]

One achievement theme is found in a long story of endurance, of broken promises of facilitation—how in ancient times colonists survived the broken promises of the Brazilian government and managed to succeed.

> (I 20m) (Card 16) (blank) The life of . . . a man of ancient times who came from Europe to Brazil, leaving, therefore, his family. He had to sail on one of these ancient ships, impelled by wind. He was afraid of seeing his relatives dead on board and of being hunted at the sea. He was afraid of arriving in Brazil and receiving not from Don Pedro what he had promised. Here he had seen that there wasn't anything of what had been promised. Even not receiving what had been promised, they will fight and will make it.
>
> [KB-survive FD-fate NSB-distrust NSD-goods AA-persist]

Another story is one of persistence in both affiliative and compensatory achievement motives.

> (I 16m) (Card 16) It was a very poor boy who began to study at the age of 8. As he didn't even imagine what school was, he liked it very much and went on studying. His first love was at the age of 10, with a girl from the school. His best grade was 9, during the time of the elementary school. With lots of difficulties, he came to Santo Antonio School. Today he is at the eighth class, with a new love and with good grades.
>
> [KD-fate AA-self PA-curious FA-love AA-counter CA-present]

One story of questionable competence, by a young female, expresses direct concern with persistence to attain good performance for acceptance at school. Themes of an evaluative audience observing performance are not frequent in our present samples except where they are appear as anticipated in response to Card 17.

> (I 4f) (Card 16) It is me at the physics and chemistry test. I keep looking at my watch, I am bad in this subjects. And I calculate and calculate again, until it works, but most of it doesn't work. It is hard! I try, but always get a bad grade. I'll try to do my best in order to be approved.
>
> [CB-able AA-persist ESB-praise]

There is only one achievement story given by a Portuguese. It is given by a young woman who depicts a boy who dreams about becoming an artist.

> (P 12f) (Card 16) The boy dreams of being an artist, and he loves to watch television in order to learn how to be a good artist some day. And he is able to make his dream come true, and nowadays he is one of the best artists in the world.
>
> [AB-dream AA-inspire]

In two achievement stories by Afro-Brazilians, one is of a good student seeking to avoid the distractions of his rebellious peer group:

> (AB 19m) (Card 16) At the school, there was a rowdy group. There was also a hardworking boy who wanted to pass, to study, but he used to seat near some who didn't want to study. For him to pass, he had to leave this group. He asked for a transfer to other classroom, but there was no vacancy; he couldn't go, but with effort he managed to pass.
>
> [RC-mores AA-self FC-split AA-persist]

The second Afro-Brazilian achievement theme is a positive fantasy of purpose in reaping the fruits of nature. A young woman plants a fruit tree so that in future she may be able to eat the fruit. A wishful fantasy of a giving, idyllic nature by someone living in an urban favela.

> (AB 28m) (Card 16) It is a person. Today she is planting a tree. This tree has grown and she is picking the fruits today.
>
> [AA-self PA-nature]

Control Fantasies (seven stories)

There are no fantasies of parental control elicited from any of the Japanese. There are eight such stories in the other groups: four by Portuguese, one by an Afro-Brazilian, and three by Italians.

Among the Portuguese stories, a positive exercise of authority is depicted in only one of the four stories involving parental authority.

(P 3f) (Card 16) A man is seated on a sofa, talking to his son. He is talking about life. He said to his son that life is not so easy. The son, seated on the sofa, is listening to him, seeing that the father is right. He is too young to keep mixing with crooks. So his father and his mother became happy, and they had a calm life.

[DDA-advice RA-reform HA-family]

In another, a father does not accept the pregnancy of an unwed daughter.

(P 4f) (Card 16) (blank) It was a girl who was five months pregnant and didn't know how to tell her parents that, for they wouldn't accept the fact of having a daughter who would be a single mother. But one day she had to tell them, for there was no way of hiding it any longer: her belly was very prominent. Her father was the most revolted for he kept silent without talking to her. But she didn't care about it, for she would have her child, and nothing else interested her. Thus she remained at home.

[RC-pr-sex DDA-scold EDC-moral DSC-disobey]

Parents refuse the marriage plans of lovers.

(P 13f) (Card 16) (blank) A couple of lovers, who love each other very much, wants to get married in the future. But they are still too young. They are kissing each other. Their parents don't want neither marriage nor the date. Therefore, they are very sad.

[FA-love DDC-press DSB-torn PD-sad]

A mother forces a son to sleep on her lap.

(P 10 m) (Card 16) (blank) This an aged woman with her son; she is making him sleep on her lap. He didn't want to sleep. The mother made him sleep on her lap.

[DDC-press DSA-comply]

The one fantasy of an Afro-Brazilian is of a drunken father acting brutally.

(AB 26m) (Card 16) (blank) The drunk driver! Once a man drank very much, and forced his children into the car and went for a ride. But he came to a bar and started to drink even more. Then he, almost without balance, took the car and started to drive very fast, not paying attention to signals, until a certain moment, when the traffic lights were indicating STOP, he decided to cross it very fast. He bumped a child and didn't even stop in order to help her, and later he crashed against a truck, which caused his death.

[RC-abuse DDC-press NDC-succor RC-result]

In the Italian group there are two parental themes split between positive and negative concerns. In one, a mother scolds a daughter for getting her dress dirty. In a more negative direction one story depicts a mother preventing a father from beating his son who remains afraid of the father.

(I 8m) (Card 16) One day I was at the field with my father, and I was seven years old. We went to put fertilizer in it. I climbed the tractor and loosened it into a gully. My father was mad at me. He removed the tractor with the help of the neighbor's one. He wanted to beat me, but Mom didn't let him do it. I went to school and came back. I didn't eat. I went to sleep, afraid of my father. Dad didn't beat me, he forgets.

[CC-failure DDC-punish NDA-secure HB-f-anger]

Mutual Purpose (three stories)

There are no Japanese stories suggesting mutual purpose. Two Portuguese, and one Italian give stories of mutual cooperation or competition. One is a childlike animal story by a Portuguese female:

(P 1f) (Card 16) Little panda bear had built his little house. But a jaguar used to frighten all the little animals. Panda decided to prepare a joke with some little animals. They threw a net. The jaguar became very angry and decided to spend a long time away.

[HB-f-attack MTA-defense FC-split]

Two males see sports competition. These stories combine instrumental competition and concern with the esteem of peers.

(P 9m) (Card 16) (blank) The boy was cheerful, for he won the soccer match, and his mates too. Only one of them was sad, for he hadn't scored any goal. But his mates said: "My friend, it wasn't only you who didn't score a goal." And the boy believed his mates and participated cheerfully.

[MVA-game CB-able FA-friend EDA-praise]

(I 1m) (Card 16) This is a car race and a favorite pilot of the race. He has a lot of fans who cheer for him, most people. He takes off in the pole position. In the middle of the contest there is an accident with the late-comer he was passing, and he gets involved in the accident and disappoints many people. He doesn't win. He stopped because he crashed his car. But it wasn't his fault. People are disappointed, but later they admit that it wasn't his fault.

[ESA-fame MVA-game KD-accident ESC-lessen ESA-praised]

Responsibility (twelve stories)

In addition to stories of positive responsibility (two) or personal wrongdoing (three), there is concern in six stories with a questionable Brazilian government which come out in stories given to the blank cards. Two additional stories are of human irresponsibility in respect to ecological dangers. Using this blank card to represent the problems found in present-day Brazilian society suggests the degree of general popular concern with governmental irresponsibility in solving problems of social welfare.

Ecological concerns are expressed by both an Afro-Brazilian and an Italian youth:

(AB 20m) (Card 16) (blank) These are many people, having fun at the place where they are, close to nature, field or forest. Those people worry about the environment very much, and they are so strongly linked to nature that they suffer deeply when they see what is happening to the planet.

[PA-play PA-nature KB-crisis PD-suffer]

(I 21f) (Card 16) (blank) In the future, things won't be like they're now. Man is destroying everything he created. I think that there is a solution, if he becomes aware of the situation.

[RD-ignorant CA-aware]

Some stories symbolize the blank card to represent a lack of proper responsibility taken by the government of the country. One waits for change or states what should be done:

(J16my) (Card 16) This could be a formula for what is already ending. There is lots of poverty in the whole world, barbarity, of races and ethnic groups fighting each other, of all against all. Brazil has to improve its system of health, of life, of education, so that we will not have to go back to Japan. If we had a better life here, we would have more pride towards Brazil. We would feel more patriotism towards this country. There should be more pride in us as Brazilians.

[KD-poor HD-decay EDB-lessen ESB-shame]

(I 24m) (Card 16) It is a blank picture waiting to be worked on and painted. It is imagining that one waits to draw a richer and fairer Brazil, with less corrupt people than now.

[RC-duty KB-hope KA-social]

(P7) (Card 16) (blank) What to do with so much discrimination? To call the police? It doesn't work. They are so confident about what they're doing that they don't even fear the police anymore. Innocent people, with children in their arms, living under the bridge. What kind of government is this? They waste money in restaurants, luxurious cars, and let these people, who could be helping them to move Brazil forwards, thrown on the streets. Robbery; unnecessary streets, unnecessary buildings are raised; they set up factories and hospitals, and let the machines be thrown on a corner. Why not giving that money in food to these people?

[DDC-unfair KD-poor RC-duty EDC-exploit NDC-goods]

(AB 35m) (Card 16) The sky (god) was very sad up there because there were too many thieves and not many policemen down here, and he didn't know how to help.

[NSB-god AC-crime DDD-helpless]

Three stories are concerned with work or school responsibilities.

(If 12) (Card 16) A student is leaving home to go to school. He is having lunch. He arrives at school and attends classes.

[RA-work]

(P 6m) (Card 16) (blank) It is a boy who wanted to join a soccer school, but he had neither money nor uniform in order to join it. Then he had to walk and look for a job in order to pay the school and buy the uniform. After almost a year of work, he was able to join the school.

[KD-poor RA-duty-s AA-self]

(J fy 25) (Card 16) (blank) A person was working, a person that suffers a lot. So she arrived here, but is suffering more than when she was working there because she believes that certain people betrayed her. But she will not lose hope.

[PD-suffer RA-stoic MTC-betray]

In addition to an Afro-Brazilian story of unruly peers cited above, there are two other stories by male Afro-Brazilians that focus on rowdy classroom behavior. Ambivalence about the teacher's authority is evident. This is an unusual theme to bring up in three of their twenty stories on a blank card.

(AB 24m) (Card 16) (blank) Once upon a time, at Benedito de Moraes School, there was a teacher who had just arrived at the school. She was new, but when the students had the first gym class with her, they started to give her nicknames, without her knowing about that. But the teacher didn't care. Some time passed, she started to teach volleyball to the 6th level and had four students who were very rowdy. They used to disturb the classes. One day the teacher asked them to make an only-boys team. Those 4 boys started to kick the ball with their feet. The teacher asked them to stop, and then she went to the headmistress and asked her to talk to them. The headmistress said that if they didn't stop and didn't obey the teacher, they would be turned out of the school. After this talk with the headmistress, the students behaved better.

[DSB-torn EDC-brash RC-propriety NDA-author RA-reform]

(AB 27f) (Card 16) (blank) In a classroom there was a very annoying student. No teacher could bear seeing his face any longer. At a certain day, the History teacher asked him to leave the room. He said "I won't." She: "I'll take you to the office." She took him to the office and gave him a 20 days suspension, and when he'd return, he should come with his parents. Twenty days passed, and he never came back again.

[RC-mores DDA-author RD-wrong]

Pleasure and Pain (four stories)

Four Japanese stories symbolically represent positive and negative internal states:

(Jfy) Someone has just come in. I wonder who it is.

[PB-surprise]

(J35mo) (Card 16) I want cards (TAT) that are more brighter/cheerful.

[PA-joy]

(J39mo) (Card 16) (blank) The result of previous stories. Each has happiness and suffering, light and dark, joy and sadness—especially fun. Human life is like living in the way of the stories just written.

[PA-joy PD-suffer]

(J 52my) (Card 16) (blank) This is based on the previous cards. They are not happy scenes, but miserable and sad. At the end, one is unfulfilled/unsatisfied. This is the conclusion.

[PD-sorrow]

Overall, the seventeen Afro-Brazilians, more than in any of the other groups on this card turned to scenes of nature for expressing a sense of pleasure as part of their stories (23 percent). For example, a story of purposeful tree planting by AB28m illustrated above, and by AB22m, of idyllic pleasure in the context of Harmony (H), illustrated below.

Affiliative Concerns (ten stories)

There are ten expressive stories of Affiliative relationships given to the blank card. We had anticipated that Brazilian youth would give more positive peer stories than we elicited on this card. Of those given, eight are positively toned.

The sole Affiliative category story given by a Portuguese youth sees a peer group finding a lost member:

(P 14f) (Card 16) Once a group of children had gone for a walk in a wood. There was a lot of animals. And one of the children got lost in the middle of the wood. Everybody started to look for this child. Hours after they were able to find the child, and afterwards they came back home.

[FB-apart NDA-secure]

One Italian youth sees a group excursion of her class with a counselor. Another anticipates the arrival of a peer in what may become a love relationship. Three stories by Afro-Brazilian young women envision love relationships.

(AB 17f) Eliana and Fernanda used to fight for the same boy. He wasn't handsome, but what we liked most in him is that he is beautiful inside. Eliana, confused, said they should calm down. She talked to Sergio and asked him who he liked more. Sergio, confused, answered: "I like both." Eliana and Fernanda answered: "Sergio, you can't like both at the same time. For one you may have friendship, for the other you may have love." Then Sergio thought. "You both give me some time. Tomorrow morning I'll give you the answer." Eliana and Fernanda, nervous, were already arguing before he arrived. When he arrived, he said:

"Fernanda, I want to be your friend, but I like Eliana." Fernanda became a little sad and accepted, but under one condition: that both remained her friends.

[FC-triangle FB-thwart FA-friend]

(AB 21f) Paula liked a young man, but she didn't want to say it to him. He didn't care about her, he only wanted to be her friend. But she didn't want friendship, she wanted more. On Sunday, when Paula left home for a walk, she saw her love with another girl. Paula came back home in despair, crying in the middle of the street. When she arrived home she locked herself in the bedroom. She didn't want to talk to anybody, she only wanted to think about the love she could give him.

[FC-flee PD-suffer FB-thwart]

Two of the three given by Japanese, however, symbolically suggest possible loneliness or friendship.

(J22my) A white card . . . is us. Exchange of words between us, the exchange of ideas, definitions, doubts that we are searching for in order to understand each other and to become friends.

[FA-friend]

(J50my) For example, there is a white wall, and you are painting something. A blank wall is too lonely, so you have to paint. You fill it up with stuff. Normally, when you have a wall, you put frames (pictures) or clocks, etc. on it.

[FB-alone]

(J3fy) (Card 16) There was a time, a vendor of matches. He was in a street in a city and was tired because he couldn't sell anything. Suddenly, he fell asleep and started dreaming that he was in a completely different world where everything is animated/upbeat and one can pursue life and all is happy when one arrives in this country. One plays, and knows lots of people. Suddenly, he wakes up and sees that being together is not reality.

[KD-poor PA-play FA-empathy]

Nurture (seven stories)

Six cards depicted a variety of nurturing themes of rescue or concern with a needy animal or child.

(I 14f) (Card 16) There was in the sky a beautiful white bird flying happily. But it was suddenly shot by a hunter, and it fell and fell until it came to the ground. It was very hurt. The hunter didn't find it. There was a happy boy who was walking until he found the pigeon. As he felt sorry for her, he decided to take her home and bandage her. Many days passed. The pigeon began to fly again.

[PA-esthete HC-cruel HD-hurt NDB-pity NDA-charity]

(30 ABf) Cristina and Paula were at the park, when they saw a mentally defective person. They ran home and talked to their mother, and their mother called the asylum to help. Then the girls came back to the park.

[PA-play KD-defect NDA-author NDA-active]

(P16f) He was a boy! He could swim, but he almost drowned, for there wasn't anybody near him. Then I ran to call my grandpa, for him to take him out of there. Then Grandpa ran and took him out of there.

[CA-present KC-accident NDA-rescue]

Harmony/Discord or Peace (seventeen stories)

The Japanese in Brazil still reveal spontaneous Confucian-like concerns. They use the blank card to depict symbolically in eleven of their thirty-seven stories (30 percent) a wish for social peace and harmony as most highly desired. They also mention in several of their stories a sense of purity and cleanliness in the context of peace. This sense of purity is part of old Shinto religious concerns with purity and pollution. While no longer evident in direct religious consciousness peace and purity are still linked in the mind.

(J24fy) White is purity—its means that there are no differences, no racism, that all is equal.

[PA-purity HA-symbol]

(J33fy) The world must be one—all as one, like a white dove, and I want to let it fly. That is, where different languages and feelings become united as one and where war and bad things will not happen.

[HA-symbol HA-pacify]

(J11mo) White is a peace symbol—a peace symbol flying. It is the hope of all.

[HA-symbol KB-hope]

(J7mo) All that is white is all peace. It is all good.

[HA-symbol PA-purity]

As well as peace and purity, the future of one's family and society is a major concern in some Japanese stories.

(J19mo) I think white is peace, purity. It shows all that I want for my children. All parents hope to live in peace with their children and the children hope to live in peace with the parents. I am trying to . . . perceive peace. It is difficult to raise children now, but I want a future of peace for all, with everything, but especially with our own life. All people want this because there is lots of violence, malice, bad things. We therefore ask God to let us live in peace. Everyday, I see this.

[HA-symbol PA-purity RA-resp-o KB-hope HB-unrest HA-god]

(J5fo) I would like that my sons will have a better world. Lots of hope for a better world without dissension/discord.

[HA-group KB-hope]

(J20my) White. I will create a positive and optimistic story, a good thing. All the cards here are bad situations—I didn't like any of these situations. There are good

> and bad moments in life, but one has to make a balance, to create a positive story, with lots of care, love, *festa* (entertainment, festivities), peace, hope, and harmony in the family. I would create a situation, a story of a family commemorating Christmas, with everyone united, with lots of peace, love, hope, and health and harmony between people and cordiality as well. People with lots of this type of feeling, with warm hearts, disseminating (*esbanjando*) and transporting this happiness to others. This hope should exist not just right now, but is necessary during everyday of life and one must always look well at things, without criticizing anyone, or complaining about things, or without opposing/protesting/complaining in situations.
>
> [HA-rite HA-symbol <u>HA-group</u>]

One story is a true paradigm of traditional Japanese social thought. It summarized the compensatory achievement motivation overcoming a poor past that brought many Japanese to Brazil. There is concern with Brazilian social problems, but optimism about realizing a harmonious future and a underlying sense of gratitude which remains a deep part of sensibility in many Japanese.

> (J42mo) These are my thoughts in general. I came here 38 years ago, leaving behind the brutal natural environment of *Hokkaido* (northern Japan). I felt comfortable/carefree/without worries (*anraku*). It is good that I immigrated—I am full of feeling. The surrounding environment is the most important for human life—not just the natural environment, but the social environment, for instance in Brazil. This is a good place. Brazil is a country with problems, but they are not unlovable. Brazil will not remain behind the times (*jidai hazure*) forever. It will get better. I am really grateful that I could come here. We (my family) all live healthy and happily here. And this goes for Japanese associations here as well. We all live healthy and happy lives. The future is bright.
>
> [AA-counter <u>HA-group</u> CB-arduous KA-wealth <u>NSA-grateful</u> KA-health]

The other Brazilian groups give more concrete and immediate fancies of either harmony (three) or discord or violence (three). The one exception is an Italian respondent who brings in the presence of God in a global fantasy of peace.

> (Im 23) The picture shows us that in the whole world there should be only peace. When God put us on the Earth, he said "Love each other," and not that we should become delinquents.
>
> [<u>HA-symbol</u> HA-peace DSA-god FA-love RA-duty]

The Afro-Brazilian give four stories depicting parental relationships. One wistfully depicts an idyllic scene, again in nature, of a family playing happily together in a garden.

> (ABf 22) Here there is a happy family. Everybody is in a garden with the children, playing, and the parents are happy.
>
> [PA-nature <u>HA-family</u>]

But three others depict tension and discord. There is fear of parents separating. A young woman from a single parent Afro-Brazilian family creates a story of a mother quarreling with her children in a house where the father is absent. There is positive resolution in the fantasy.

> (AB 33f) It is a family that has a woman and 3 children. The father doesn't live with them. The mother gets on better with the elder son. They quarrel sometimes, but they always set things up at the end.
>
> [FC-split HC-discord HA-mend]

In another story there is a hope for reunion of the parents, but the situation remains unresolved.

> (AB37f) It is a girl whose parents used to quarrel all the time. The father left home, and the mother stayed with the children: 3 girls and a boy. The second oldest girl wanted the father's return. The mother didn't, but she wanted them to get together again.
>
> [HC-discord FC-split HB-family]

In another story with a more hopeful ending, told by an Italian female, a girl's behavior at school improves, and by so improving her behavior she, helps alleviate the quarrels and possible separation of parents.

> (I 9 f) A girl had difficulties at home: her parents used to quarrel a lot. She was worried, wondering whether her parents would separate or not. She has problems with teachers. The Chemistry teacher was boring; he didn't like the students, who acted against him. He left, and another one came: Mauro. He was sweet to the students. The girl's parents said that he was very nice. In the elections of the children's club, their (her) slate won. Her parents were glad, and they kept together. She could go to the field because she passed at school and won the elections. They remained together forever. Her parents didn't quarrel anymore. The father saw that it was wrong to quarrel with his wife and they stayed together.
>
> [HC-discord FB-apart DSB-rebel NDA-educate MVA-profess HA-pacify]

Esteem: Appreciation of Peers or Others (two stories)

We found surprisingly few stories of peer evaluation or concern with peer observation of one's activities. In records of Israeli youth that I was shown some time past by Martin Wolens, such stories were much more in evidence. There were only two evaluative stories given to the blank card. These two were by Italian youth:

One is a simple story of a boy who doubts his ability but is encouraged to play the violin by the approval and appreciation of his peers.

> (I 22f) Story of the boy who quit playing violin. Not good. A little later he took the violin and played it for his friends. It was so good that his friends clapped for him!
>
> [CC-failure ESA-praise]

Family and peer attitudes about the unacceptability of someone too poor break up a love relationship.

> (I 3f) In a birthday party, a boy and a girl met, and they liked each other. But there was a problem: the boy was rich and the girl was poor. His family didn't know that she was poor. They went on dating, but one day his family found it out. They wanted him to break down with her. But he liked her. They said she only wanted the money and they tried to convince him. Everybody was against him, all his friends. He quit liking her because of his friends and relatives. He just pretended that he liked her. Without understanding what was happening, the girl went away and married another guy, even still liking him. And so did he too.
>
> [FA-love OB-compare ESB-status FD-split]

Kismet-Fateful Events (twelve stories)

Japanese give two symbolic stories of destiny and one positive fantasy of overcoming illness. The other groups give eleven stories; eight of them are negative fantasies of accidents and possible death. Good fortune is winning the lottery in one story, or having only one's ID card stolen in another. Three of the negative stories are by youth of single parent families.

Japanese symbolically discuss how one must accept destiny and fate.

> (J48mo) This is true for both Japanese and all Brazilians. Humans are born from and return to the earth. When I was born, I had nothing and when I die, I will have nothing as well, just like this blank sheet. This is how human life is fated.
>
> [KA-accept]

> (J32) This will be based on my impressions of the previous cards. Human life is just as it is. You just can't worry too much about it, even if you are poor, sad, etc. It is a matter of destiny. You should not become stressed or impatient because it will simply become time lost. One can't do anything about it.
>
> [KA-accept]

One can have a fantasy of good luck.

> (P 5m) The draw. There was a draw in the lottery; then a young man decided to bet on the numbers he had dreamed of. On the next day he had the result, and he won the maximum prize. The young man became very cheerful, for he said something: "It is very good to dream," and lived his life very happily.
>
> [KA-luck PA-joy]

One can with good fortune recovery from serious illness.

> (AB 31) On a certain day, a very beautiful and healthy girl was born. While growing up, she was a very cheerful and happy child. When she was 16, she heard her father and her mother saying that she had only two more years of life. She

became very sad and stopped being that cheerful, happy girl. Her life, for her, had finished at that very moment. She didn't want to talk to anyone, and she also didn't want to go out to the street. She only wanted to weep and to become angry with everybody. After one year, she decided to go to a doctor in order to make a check-up. She found out that she wouldn't die anymore, and with that news she became cheerful again.

[PA-joy KD-ill FC-flee KA-recover]

One can inadvertently run out of gas and overcome it by filling the tank.

(AB18m) The driver was driving the car, and in the middle of the road the gas was used up. He had to push the car up to the gas station. When he arrived there, the owner of the gas station put gasoline and he went out very cheerfully.

[KC-luck CA-repair]

Accidents are used as themes used imaginatively by three Portuguese youth. Three stories are about fateful events happening to the individual. Recovery is imagined in two of the three stories.

(P 2f) I saw an aged lady crossing the street with traffic light closed for pedestrians. A car came and bumped her. The car escaped and the other people who saw it called the police and took her to the hospital. It did not work, for she was already dead. They tried to identify her, for she had no documents. She appeared on TV and her relatives recognized her. They went to the hospital in order to wake and bury her. They tried to prosecute the guy who had bumped her, but they couldn't, because he wasn't seen anymore.

[KC-ac-die DSC-escape HB-revenge]

(P 8m) Once upon a time there was a boy who liked very much riding a bike. But one day a tragedy happened: he was riding his bike, when a car bumped him. His mother was desperate, for the doctor had said he would never be able to ride a bike again. But with some time he got better, and again he was riding a bike.

[PA-play KD-accident CA-defect]

(P15m) The boy was skating on the sidewalk. His friends were behind him. He was paying attention only to his friends and suddenly, when he saw the curb of the sidewalk, he fell down and got hurt a little. His friends asked him to be more careful when he skated.

[PA-play FA-friend KC-hurt-s CC-failure]

Italians see two more fateful stories.

(I 17m) They are fishing. They put the motor boat in the water and they will try it. They run a lot and when they come back they leave it still in the bank of the river, and when everybody got out of it, it burned. After the fire, we laughed because we were lucky for not being in the boat.

[KC-accident KA-luck]

(I 18f) It is a sad person, crying for something that happened to her and to her family. She leaves in order to talk to someone. A relative died.

[KC-ac-die NSB-help]

Comment

The present chapter allowed us to detail the stories in such a way that the method of scoring could be well illustrated. The detailed scoring of the stories on extended tables with summarized stories also gave us much more nuanced material revealing differences that would be lost in simple comparisons of numerical differences.

There were very pronounced ethnic and age differences revealed in the groups considered. The Japanese continued to manifest approaches to the test situation that set them apart from other Brazilians. These differences replicated the findings of our previous research. What was particularly noteworthy was how the approach to a blank card elicited their major, traditional central concern with social harmony. Beyond this, the nuances of the stories again, in many indirect ways, suggested strong internalization of self-motivated achievement and a strong sense of social responsibility. The often-expressed view that Japanese are highly motivated by shame as a social sanction has been no more forthcoming in the present stories than in previous research with the TAT.

More than any other evidence obtained from the TAT, Card 16, a blank card displayed inner attitudes. Some Italians, as many more Japanese, show some propensity to distance themselves from the immediate social environment with some objectivity and detachment. One saw more optimism in the Italians and, especially in the Japanese, than appeared in the Favela subjects. But in all groups, for some, personal optimism is well tempered by a skepticism or concern about the future of Brazil. There is a profound, spontaneously shared evoked awareness of mismanagement and so far failed opportunity as a nation. There is also a haunting concern with homeless or abused children as a major social issue.

Reference

De Vos, George A. and L. Bryce Boyer. 1989. *Symbolic Analysis Cross-Culturally: The Rorschach Test*. Ruth M. Boyer and Horace Miner, Contributors. Berkeley: University of California Press.

Chapter 10

Mentorship or Complicity between Men: Illustrations from Brazil

George A. De Vos

Social Continuities in Attitudes toward Authority or Mutual Purpose: Card 7BM

In this chapter, in order to further illustrate some themes of instrumental purpose, authority, or mentorship, we look in detail at stories scored in our system taken from a specific card, Card 7BM. It presents a scene suggesting a discussion between an older and younger man. We shall again use Japanese Brazilians as well as a variety of Brazilian youth for illustrative purposes.

As we have noted in our prior studies with majority Japanese in Japan, this picture is most often interpreted as some form of vertical status mentorship, an older man, such as a company president, advising or encouraging a younger man. In the Japanese, the age disparity found depicted in our research samples taken in the early 1950s (De Vos, 1973) remains central to the story in the sample taken by Vaughn in the late 1980s (Vaughn, 1988). In Japanese Issei immigrants taken by Caudill about 1950, 94 percent depicted compliant attitudes as did 68 percent of Nisei (Caudill and De Vos, 1956). In 28 percent of the Nisei, however, there was rebellion or assertion of legitimate autonomy.

Korean samples taken in the 1980s have given contrastive themes of questionable activities by politicians or businessmen. We have written elsewhere (De Vos and Lee, 1981) that there has been a dilemma especially noticeable in Korean youth about respecting legitimate authority. This attitude is related to the past colonial occupation of Korea by the Japanese for thirty-five years ending with the Japanese defeat in World War II. In chapter 7, volume II above, we discussed very briefly the differences we found in Korean minorities in Japan and Los Angeles (De Vos and Kim, 1993). We noted how on responses to TAT Card 7BM, compared with majority Japanese, Koreans were more distrustful of the two figures seen interacting. They gave many stories of conspiracy and plotting. Such stories comprised 48 percent of the stories given by the fifty Los Angeles group of immigrants compared with 55 percent of the thirty-one Korean Japanese. The difference in the two groups was that only one Japanese Korean noted the status difference between the two figures, whereas the status difference was important in thirteen (26 percent) of the conspiracy stories given by fifty Los Angeles Koreans. The immigrants to the United States were more Confucian in respecting age than were the more alienated minority Koreans of Japan.

Overall, compared with majority Japanese, however, Koreans have given relatively less attention to the age and status differential of the two figures. As illustrated in chapter 7, volume II above, in the more optimistic Los Angeles Koreans, a status differential still appears in 52 percent of the stories, but only in 16 percent of minority Koreans in Japan is age or differential status a significant consideration of the story themes. In many socially disparaged Korean families in Japan, there has been an internal loss of patriarchal status and respect as well as continuous disparagement coming from the Japanese majority. Unemployment, resort to alcohol, family desertion, and other forms of alienated behavior had become common among adult males.

In themes given to Card 7BM, as on other cards, the Koreans in Japan reveal their sense of alienation and lack of resolution toward either future accomplishment or a future positive destiny in interpersonal relationships. As reported in chapter 7, volume II, we have tapped themes of deep personal alienation which are pervasive and characterize many of this Korean minority.

In Brazil, what is discussed by two men with their faces together in conversation? What proportion attend to an age differential? What will a comparison of Brazilian ethnic groups reveal about attitudes of trust or respect accorded authority figures? What will youthful high school age Brazilians and the Japanese Brazilians of two older age categories reveal in their social attitudes? Let us examine our representative sample of Japanese Brazilians and compare them with our small available samples of Italian and German youth from towns located in the hinterland of Provincial Rio Grande do Sul and youth from the favelas of the city of Porto Alegré.

Contrasted with our previous sample of Japanese, both in Japan and the United States, the Japanese in Brazil pay somewhat less attention to social hierarchy, but still manifest a much more positive attitude toward authority relationships than do groups of younger Brazilian of different ethnic backgrounds. In the twenty-nine male and twenty-one female Japanese Brazilians, there are a total of eighteen (36 percent) of the records that focus on an authority relationship involving mentoring or advice. This is similar to our recent sample of Korean immigrants in the United States. Only in four of these stories is the authority figure depicted in any dubious light. Of eleven younger men, six (55 percent), and of fourteen younger women, six (43 percent), see vertical relationships. In effect those of the younger women are slightly less prone to see proper authority while five of seven (71 percent) older women stress the status position of the older male.

Table 10.1 is a complete listing of the Brazilian stories. It is illustrative of a stage of analysis in organizing stories once they are scored for the manifest content. We consider this a necessary step in attempting any interpretation and generalization. The summary of the story permits the reader to see the method used in first grouping the stories into major categories, then into more specific subcategories. One can note that it is somewhat arbitrary in complex stories to group the stories under one given category. The grouping does bring together related stories of a given nuance, revealing that some are more prevalent for one group than for another.

Table 10.1
Card 7BM: An Older and a Younger Man in a Discussion

Code:

Portuguese	*P*	*Afro-Brazilian*	*AB*
Italian	*I*	*German*	*G*
Younger Japanese	*Jy*	*Older Japanese*	*Jo*
Male	*m*	*Female*	*f*

Total 110	**Favela 37**		**Towns 23**		**City Japanese 50**	
	P 16	**AB 21**	**I 12**	**G 11**	**Jy 25**	**Jo 25**
Male-Female (m 69, f 41)	m 7, f 9	m 11, f 10	m 12	m 11	m 10, f 15	m 18, f 7
Instrumental Issues Paramount Total 69	**P 5**	**AB 10**	**I 9**	**G 5**	**Jy 20**	**Jo 20**
(m 44, f 25)	m 2, f 3	m 5, f 5	m 9	m 5	m 9, f 11	m 14, f 6
Autonomy [D] Total 3	**P 0**	**AB 0**	**I 1**	**G 1**	**Jy 0**	**Jo 1**
(m3, f0)			m 1	m 1		m 1

Father trusts son and tells he believes in him. Father saying son can do what he wants—giving him permission. Jo 60m

DDA-free FA-trust

Father tries to convince son not to follow his choice of job, but one which father wants. Son does not accept this and revolts against the father. Before, he studied and the father always told him what to do. The son does what he wants. I 17m
DDA-control DSA-assert

Businessmen. Father and son. Giving son advice. Son doesn't agree; will try his way and succeed. Father will be proud. G 10m
DDA-advice DSA-assert ESA-pride

Control, Direction Advice, Mentorship [D] Total 26	**P 1**	**AB 1**	**I 4**	**G 3**	**Jy 8**	**Jo 9**
(m 19, f 7)	m 1	f 1	m 4	m 3	m 4, f 4	m 7, f 2

Positive Control directives
(m 3)

I 3

Father won't let the son wanted to go to the ball. Son argues but he listens to the father. I 2m
DDA-control DSB-obey DSA-comply

Aged man giving his son explanations. Son thinking. Man was giving directions for life. The son follows advice. I 8m
DDA-educate DSA-comply

This is the father saying to the son that it is time for him to start to work. I 22m
DDA-control RA-work

Advice
(m 14, f 5)

P 1 *AB 1* *I 1* *G 1* *Jy 8* *Jo 7*

It is a father talking to his son and indicating him what to do about his problems at his job. He'll follow his father's advice. I 24m
DDA-advice DSA-comply

Father gives son advice. Study to become great engineer. P 15m
DDA-advice NDA-teach AA-inspire

Father is giving son advice so he doesn't get lost in life. Son listens with great attention. Is experienced, knows life well. G 14m
DDA-advice CA-past AB-purpose

The elder is giving his impressions and opinions to the younger. Jy 1f
DDA-advice

The uncle is talking with the youth. They are thinking about something. Older man is giving the youth advice and counsel. Jy 9f
DDA-advice

This is a father giving counsel to the son. About what? I don't know. Jo 14m
DDA-advice

Receiving advice. He is listening to elders. What are the elders talking about? It is hard to tell. Jy 15m

DDA-advice DSA-comply

Not necessary for generation conflict but counsel from the old to youth. Necessity for youth to listen to guidance of the elder. Jy 16m

DDA-advice DSA-comply

Professor or a father and son. Is talking and explaining to son about life in general. The son will obey. Difficult for son this age to listen to mother's counsel. Jo 19m

DDA-advice DSA-comply

Father is trying to explain about life. How to live, study, work, and better the family. Son listens and learns elders are valid. Jo 26m

DDA-advice CA-past DSA-comply

Father and rebellious son. Giving counsel about life. Younger one rebels not just against father, but against life in general. Adolescents always rebellious by nature. So the father counsels the youth. Jo 28f

DDA-advice DSB-rebel

One who has lots of experience with life is teaching the youth. There is some problem. Jy 55f

DDA-advice CA-past

Father counseling son. Son is in trouble—girl friend or work. He is working and the father is counseling. Jo 51m

DDA-advice CB-difficult

Youth and his elder (a director, friend, or counselor). The youth is listening and agreeing. Jy 64m

DDA-advice DSA-comply

He is talking about an issue with his social superior. Jo 65

CB-help DDA-author

There is a problem. The father is teaching the son many things or is giving advice or discussing the problem with his son. Jy 66f

DDA-advice

Like Einstein. Youth being lectured thoroughly. Explaining his experiences. Youth listening and is understanding. Jy 72m

DDA-educate CA-past DSA-comply

Father who has lots of patience with the son. But in fact, he has educated the son badly and not able to get respect deserved. The son does not understand in some ways that all the father wants is good for him. Jo 23m

DDD-inept ESD-unfair NSD-intake

Counseling about Responsibility
(m 1, f 1)

Father counsels not to do wrong son listens. AB 37f

DDA-advice RA-duty-o DSA-comply

Father talking to son. Telling son to become a good man. Think carefully and not go astray. Father's wish become respectable and splendid. Jo 54m

DDA-advice RA-duty-o ESA-praised

Negative or inadequate use of authority
(m 4)

G 2 *Jo 2*

Employee comes to his boss and tries to change the way of working, but boss doesn't allow change. He won't change. G 7m

DSA-permit DDC-rigid

Dad was mad at me, thinking that I had broken the glasses and plates. Said not I. He didn't believe. Aunt came, said it had been she. I told Dad never more to accuse without proof. G 12m

DDC-unfair DSA-assert-s

Chief of big company. Bad mood. Things are not going well. Complaining to younger worker—to work harder. President does not have any good ideas and is asking if the youth has a good opinion. Jo 59m

DDC-press CC-inept CB-help

Planning in a very low voice. Made an arrangement. Will succeed in carrying out the plan. He is boss of other one. G 23m

MTB-secret DDA-lead

Inept government authority
(m 1)

m 1

Mayor wants to help with economic needs, but he doesn't know how. AB 29m

DDD-inept NDB-comfort CD-unable

Responsibility or Wrongdoing Issues [R] Total 5	P 1	AB 1	I 2	G 0	Jy 0	Jo 1

Legal Concern
(m 2)

I 1 Jo 1

Trial. Lawyer giving orientation. Instructing young man to defend himself from the accuser's lawyers. Problem controversial. I 20m

DDA-advice DSB-punish CB-arduous

Younger having problem with the police and he is talking and discussing the issue with his lawyer. Jo 68m

DSB-punish NSB-help

Younger Figure Wrongdoing
(m 1, f 1)

AB 1 I 1

Committed crime. Confesses to priest. Advised to surrender to police. Receives commuted punishment. AB 17f

RC-illegal NSB-help RA-reform

Drunkard has wife and children. Wife separated. Kidnaped his son. Told his father went to his wife and confessed. Father took him to the hospital. Cured and went to visit his son with love and care. — I 6m

RC-abuse RC-illegal FC-reject NDA-active RA-reform

Negative Parental Activities (f 1) — P 1

Heads of the families involved with gangs, drugs, smuggling. Negative education of children. — P 7f

RC-abuse RC-illegal DDC-corrupt RD-control

Achievement [A] Total 1	**AB 1**

Son wants to emulate father. Becomes a police officer. — AB 28m

AA-inspire DDA-police

Mutual Purpose Total 32	**P 3**	**AB 6**	**I 2**	**G 1**	**Jy 12**	**Jo 8**
Competitive (m 1, f 1)	P 1	AB 1				

Negotiating on price of a house. — P 16f

OB-want KD-poor MVA-deal

Listening to the president. Against him. Praying that he won't win the election. — AB 18m

MVA-faction

Cooperative (m 7, f 5)	P 1	AB 1	I 1		Jy 5	Jo 4

Father and son, together, owned an industry. Face new problem together. — AB 34f

OA-own MTA-task

Father and son. Build an ark. Took it to the sea. Accident? Disappeared at sea. — P 5m

MTA-task KD-luck

Senators were discussing parliamentary system. Preparing for f work. Afterwards go home to families. Find solution. — I 19m

MTA-task HA-family CA-present

Father and son, commenting on something. Meeting in a theater. Speaking of what is restoring around. Or jury, listening. Lawyer and judge to understand whether accused be condemned or acquitted. Serious topic stern, not good business. — Jy 22m

MTA-task MTA-interest

Political meeting of two people. It is like the ministers here in Brazil. It is about power and its execution. — Jy 25f

MTA-task MTC-plot (DDA or DDC)

Relationship between father and son. Trying to do something and are discussing. — Jy 61m

MTA-task

This is a meeting and they are discussing something. Jo 63m
MTA-task

Father and son are discussing an important problem. Jy 70f
MTA-task

Commenting, whispering, a subject that interests only them. Sharing their ideas commenting on, judging others around. Jy 20m
MTA-interest EDB-evaluate

Father and youth talking together about a social problem. The youth is listening. Jo 52f
MTA-interest DSA-comply

Father and son. Talking about something important. Jo 71f
MTA-interest

There is an exchange of ideas between the two. A conversation of a problem, a problem that is controversial. Jo 11m
MTA-task MTB-differ

Ineptitude AB 1 Jy 1
(m 1, f 1)

Ill advised economic plan. Young man agrees. AB 20m
CD-inept MTC-plot

Dentists. Should not have worked on tooth because he has diploma. Dental errors, everything has ended for him. Jy 3f
NDA-pity HB-f-anger CC-failure

Secretive: Purpose not defined as passive or negative Jy 4 Jo 5
(m 4, f 5)

They are whispering during a meeting. Jy 2f
MTB-secret

They are talking about something so that others can't hear. Jy 4m
MTB-secret

Father-son in confidence about a secret. Important thing for son. Father revealing something guarded. Jo 5f
MTB-secret

This is a lawyer talking confidentially to his client. Something dangerous is going on. Jo 6m
MTB-secret CB-worry

These are two men in a type of meeting between people. There exists here a confidential comment about a topic that can't be revealed to others. Confidential. An exchange of ideas. Jo 7m
MTB-secret

This is a secret conversation. Jy 56f
MTB-secret

This is a secret meeting at a company. — Jo 69m
MTB-secret

They are talking in secret (*naisho*). They are not friends. They are looking at something and are talking at a seminar. — Jy 57f
MTB-secret

Doesn't look like he is scolding. He is receiving some secret message from the social superior. — Jo 58f
MTB-secret

Plots or corrupt activities (m 3, f 4)	P 1	AB 3	I 1		Jy 2	

Managers of some bank. They have to fire older workers. Cheaper to use younger ones. — P 2f
MTC-ethic

Did something wrong. Going to do another wrong thing. — AB 22f
RC-wrong MTC-plot

Congressmen voted against a law good for the people. — AB 23m
MTC-false

Congressman tells friend, a city father about the wrong things he said at the assembly. — AB 27f
MTC-false

Penitentiary plotting to escape. Some manage to escape, others will be arrested. Police prevent. Older dies. Younger escapes. — I 1m
RC-group DDC-corrupt DSC-escape DDA-police HD-death RD-wrong

Problem typical of Brazil. Two politicians talking about how to gain more money. Only for their own benefit and are trying to strengthen their political and economic positions. — Jy 10m
MTC-selfish

Not good to talk secretly like this. It's better to talk openly in front of all the people. — Jy 53f
MTC-false

Expressive Concerns Central Total 39	**P 11**	**AB 10**	**I 3**	**G 6**	**Jy 4**	**Jo 5**
(m 22, f 17)	m 4, f 7	m 5, f 5	m 3	m 6	m 0, f 4	m 4, f 1
Affiliative Themes Total [F] (m 7, f 8)	**P 4**	**AB 2**	**I 1**	**G 1**	**Jy 2**	**Jo 4**
Friendly Interaction (m 3, f 5)	P 2	AB 1	I 1		Jy 2	Jo 2

Father and son talking of thinking. — P 10m
FA-empathy

Talking about their families. Even listen to their wives. P 3f
FA-friend

Brothers are friends talk about families. AB 33f
FA-friend HA-family KB-chance

Rich man involved with poor woman, got pregnant. Discovered later had a son. Boy upset father hadn't looked for him before. Explanations. Get along; work for father. I 23m
RC-ex-sex KD-means HB-resent FA-mend MTA-family

I see here the fraternity between the husband and son. Jo 12f
FA-friend

Uncle or another relative. Good friend speaking with him about his girlfriend because relationship problem. Lots of life experiences, knows a lot so he is helping youth. They are good friends. Jy 67f
FA-friend CA-expert FB-problem NDA-advice

Friendship between two people giving counsel each other in close proximity. Type of exchange of confidence between close friends, like between fathers and sons. About work, about life, about how to do things, how to be. Jy 18f
FA-friend NDA-active MTA-interest

Father and son friendly and agreeable; about women. There is no conflict. Jo 21m
FA-friend

Loss
(m 2, f 2) P 2 AB 1 G 1

Two brothers helped each other. Family activities. Shared loss. AB 26m
FA-share HA-family FD-fate KD-death

Loss of wife. Father and son share sorrow and return to happy moments. P 1f
FD-fate FA-share

Saw friend at a restaurant. Left never met again. P 14f
FA-friend FC-split

Friends since childhood, liked the same woman. Married the older one, never more talked. Now together because woman died. Despite sadness a little happiness because they had met again. G 17m
FA-friend FC-triangle HC-discord FD-fate FA-mend

Lack of Communication
(m 2) Jo 2

Parents raise children and work with them, but thinking is different. Jo 8m
NDA-nurture HA-family FB-distant

Father and son talking to each other, but thinking is different and they do not agree. Jo 62m
MVB-elders

Nurturant Themes Total 14 [N] (m 9, f 2)	**P 5**	**AB 6**	**I 1**	**G 1**	**Jy 0**	**Jo 1**
Positive Context (m 7, f 3)	P 4	AB 3	I 1	G 1		Jo 1
Advice of older friend. NDA-advice						P 11m
Man sad, other man is comforting him. He will be very happy. PA-sorrow NDA-comfort PA-joy						P 13f
Father wants son to succeed. To have a good job give his own children good studies, and good family life. DDA-advice NDA-family						P 12f
Father a judge. Son soccer player. Both rich. Both give half their wealth to poor. KA-wealth KA-social NDA-charity PA-joy						P 9m
Peevish man turned out of his house. Neighbor takes him in. He's grateful. FC-reject NSD-goods NDA-rescue NSA-grateful						AB 35f
Son gives much desired picture to his father. PA-esthete OB-want KD-poverty NDA-reward NSA-grateful						AB 24m
Rich colleague give means to poor friend to succeed with violin. Reaches friend's social class. NSD-means AA-self NDA-means MTA-task EDA-status						AB 19m
Father and son talking about a play. Son said very beautiful. Father said would take him again. In order to reward father, son decided to stage play with family, to show to his father. FA-share PA-esthete NDA-reward						I 15m
Funeral. Father had son for greatest comfort, now wife lost. Father accepted this loss with resignation. Life is not happiness only. FD-fate NDA-comfort KA-accept						G 2m
Elder is comforting son. Son has lost wife and discouraged. Will overcome this state. All go through this phase. NDA-comfort KD-death FD-fate PA-relief						Jo 27m
Negative Behavior in Respect to Need (m 2, f 2)	P 1	AB 3				
Brothers; without money drinking and begging. KD-poverty RC-abuse NSB-help						P 6m
Father is ill and drinks. Sons attempt to help. Doesn't work. RC-abuse NDB-thwart						AB 36m
Abandoned by true mother. Father reluctant to reveal her identity because she deserted her child. NDC-desert FB-reach						AB 21f

Friends drink together. Drunken one asks other for money. Refused. FA-friend <u>RC-abuse</u> NSB-help NDA-rescue							AB 31f
Quarrel **Total 8** (m 4, f 4)	**[H]**	**P 1**	**AB 1**	**I 1**	**G 3**	**Jy 2**	**Jo 0**
Father dislikes son. Quarrel. No resolution. Revolt continues. <u>HC-discord</u> <u>FB-dislike</u> DSC-disobey							P 8f
Arguing about taking over another man's wife. <u>HC-discord</u> FC-triangle							AB 30f
Old acquaintance. Bad-tempered, he turned his face and went away. He doesn't come back. Didn't answer because old enemy. <u>HC-discord</u> FD-split							I 16m
Parliament member listening to speech of another saying bad things. Went and punched him. Process was not solved yet. Will never be solved. This is still Brazil. <u>EDC-calumny</u> HC-injury RD-social							G 3m
Brothers united since little. Started to quarrel. Left. Both went in search of one another. Met again and became good friends. HC-discord FC-split <u>FA-mend</u>							G 11m
Father and son argued. Became half-enemies. Missed each other and apologized. Became friends again. <u>HC-discord</u> FC-split HA-pacify FA-mend							G 22m
Father talking to son, trying to counsel. Youth looks aggressive; but not about a fight between them, but normal conversation. <u>HC-discord</u> DDA-advice							Jy 17f
Young man angry or jealous. Older man is trying to teach him what is right. But the youth has lots of remorse. <u>HC-discord</u> HB-resent FB-jealous DDA-scold RB-regret							Jy 24f
Problems of Social Acceptability **Total 3** (m 2, f 1)	**[E]**	**P 1**	**AB 1**	**I 0**	**G 1**	**Jy 0**	**Jo 0**
Man and young man talking about the wedding of his daughter. Saying that daughter had married a rich man. FA-friend <u>EDA-status</u> KA-wealth							AB 32m
Uncomfortable Secrets							
Father reveals true mother. Had threatened to expose father. Son doesn't want to know her. Spoils ambition. FB-reveal ESD-disgrace FC-flee <u>AC-asocial</u>							P 4f

Boss called the employee and told him that he would be fired, but employee had conditions of getting another job. DDA-censure EDC-expect KA-recovery			G 16m
Reject	AB 25m		
Missing		Jy 13m	

Vertical and Horizontal Instrumental and Expressive Stories Instrumental Stories

Control Directives Paramount Stories of Authoritative Direction, Advice, Counsel Mentorship Thirty Stories

Italian and German Brazilian Groups

Italian and German subsamples are apt to see the father or boss in a strict authority role in over 50 percent of their stories (seven of twelve Italian and six of eleven German), compared with youth from a favela who give only four out of thirty-five such stories. The Italian and German Brazilian groups come close to the Japanese emphasis on parental advice and authority, but the nuances in the stories are very different; in the German youth, they are of a more negative nature.

There are three stories emphasizing autonomy. In the Japanese story, note that it is the father who gives autonomy to the son.

An Italian and a German give a story of autonomy or self-assertion.

> (Gm 10) Two businessmen. A father and son. The father is giving the son advice, and the son doesn't agree. He will try to do it his way and will succeed. And the father will be proud of him.
>
> [DDA-advice DSA-disobey ESA-authority]

> (Im 17) A father tries to convince his son not to follow the career he wants, but the one father wants. Son does not accept and revolts against the father. The son does what he wants.
>
> [DDC-pressure DSC-resists AA-self]

The Italian youth see the father acting properly in four control or advice responses (33 percent).

> (Im 02) The son wants to leave, but the father won't let him out; he says it is too dangerous. Before they were arguing because the son wanted to go to the ball, but the father didn't want him to. The son doesn't go to the ball, he listens to the father.
>
> [DDA-control DSB-obey DSA-comply]

> (Im 22) This is the father saying to the son that it is time for him to start to work.
>
> [DDA-advice]

(Im 08) An aged man giving his son some explanations. The son is thinking. The man was reading and son was out. He came back. The man giving his son directions for life. The son follows his father's advice.

[DDA-advice DSA-comply]

(Im 24) A father talking to his son and indicating to him what to do about his problems at his job. He'll follow his father's advice.

[DDA-advice DSA-comply]

In a few stories positive instrumental counsel or mentorship is given in situations involving possible wrongdoing on the part of the younger figure. These appear in two Italian stories.

(Im 20) A trial lawyer is giving him an orientation so that his accuser doesn't speak any nonsense. He is instructing the young man to defend himself from the other accuser's lawyers.

[MVA-smart NDA-edify]

(Im 06) A drunkard [younger figure] used to go home drunk. One day his wife separated. Both wanted a son. They fought in court. He drinks in order to relieve the expectation. The judge's decision came and he lost. He kidnaped his son. He told his father what he had done, who convinced him to bring son back. The wife lodged a complaint in the police. He went to his wife and confessed that he had done it and apologized. She forgave him. They kept separated. His father took him to the hospital to treatment in order to stop drinking. later he was cured and went to visit his son with love and care. He had been a drunk since he got married.

[RC-abuse HC-discord RC-illegal NSB-help DDA-advice RA-apology NDA-active NDA-love]

Only one German youth gives such a response emphasizing positive direction.

(Gm 14) Father and son are talking. His father is giving the son advice so that he doesn't get lost in life. The son listens with great attention. His father is experienced and knows life well.

[DDA-advice DSA-comply]

There may be problems with an authority figure acting too rigidly or unfairly. The German youth in four of their twelve stories give such a story.

(Gm 07) The employee comes to his boss and tries to speak to him to try to change the way of working, but his boss doesn't allow him to change his way of working. He was working before. He won't change.

[DDC-rigid]

(Gm 16) One day the boss called the employee and told him that he would be fired, but the employee had possibility of getting another job.

[DDC-result KA-recovery]

(Gm 12) Dad was mad at me, thinking that I had broken the glasses and plates. I said that it hadn't been I who broke it. He didn't believe. My aunt came, said that it had been she who did it. I told Dad never more to accuse me without having proof.

[DDC-unfair DSA-assert-s]

For one German youth, the two men may be cooperating on a mutual task, but a status difference is noted, one man is boss. Their use of low voice suggests conspiracy or negative activity.

(Gm 23 14) Two men are planning something in a very low voice. They had made an arrangement and are going to make what they have arranged. They will succeed in carrying out the plan. The one with a moustache; he is the boss of the other one.

[MTB-secret DDC-corrupt]

Brazilian Favela Groups: Portuguese (sixteen), Afro-Brazilian (seventeen), German (two)

Only four stories in the favela group of thirty-five see positive authority. Two Portuguese males, one female, and one Afro Brazilian female youth, depict good instrumental advice or the father as a good role model.

(Pm 15) Father gives son advice. He should study to become great engineer and have a future. He should study in order to have a position.

[NDA-edify DDA-educate AA-parent]

(ABm 28) A Father and son. Before he was small and wanted to be just like his father. Now he has grown up and is a police officer.

[EDA-respect RA-example AA-inspire ESA-self]

The Portuguese and Afro Brazilians give only one advice story apiece. One Portuguese girl sees both instrumental advice and nurture from a father.

(Pf 12) A father wants his son to succeed in life. He would like his son to have a good job give his own children good studies and a good life to his family.

[AA-parent NDA-edify NDA-family]

In one story, instrumental counsel or mentorship of a priest is given in a situation involving wrongdoing.

(ABf 17) Pedro committed a crime last night. Desperate, he decided to go immediately to the Church in order to confess and to ask the priest for advice. He said, "Priest, help me, I committed a crime. If the police knows about it, I'll spend the rest of my life in prison. Priest, I can't stay in prison. I have my wife and two children to support." The priest was very sad and said: "Son, surrender yourself. This is the best thing you've got to do, for if you don't surrender, they'll catch you." Then Pedro followed his advice and surrendered himself. He explained

> everything to the police. The police officer, sad but in anger at the same time, because he had a wife and two children to support, let him free. He only could not leave the country.
>
> [RC-illegal RA-apology DDA-advice RA-expiate DDA-pardon]

To recapitulate: among the vertical stories, one notes that the Italian male youth had the highest percentage seven of twelve stories (58 percent) of vertically ordered story with the older figure in an authority position. The German males were next (six of eleven) with more depicting a more rigid form of authority or need for autonomy (four stories). The Portuguese had four of twenty-two stories (15 percent), whereas the Afro-Brazilians had only one such story.

The Japanese Brazilians

In contrast to the other Brazilian groups, positive advice is a prevailing story among Japanese. It is central in sixteen out of fifty stories. Compared with our previous sample of Japanese, both in Japan and the United States, the Japanese in Brazil pay somewhat less attention to social hierarchy, but still manifest a much more positive attitude toward authority relationships than do groups of younger Brazilians of different ethnic backgrounds. In the twenty-nine male and twenty-one female Japanese Brazilians, there are a total of eighteen (36 percent) of the records that focus on an authority relationship involving mentoring or advice. This is similar to our recent sample of Korean immigrants in the United States. Only in four of these stories is the authority figure depicted in any dubious light. Of eleven younger men, six (55 percent), and of fourteen younger women, six (43 percent), see vertical relationships. In effect, those of the younger women are slightly less prone to see proper authority while fifty-seven (71 percent) older women stress the status position of the older male. In administrating the F scale of the authoritarian personal study in Japan in the early 1950s we found that rural older women tended to be the most authoritarian of the various age and sex and residence samples tested (De Vos, 1973).

The following stories show the implicit respect for the advice that can be received from the elderly. It also shows how the older person expects to give counsel and advice, and in a Japanese cultural context expects compliance rather than opposition. In general, instrumental mentoring is done with an implicit, if not explicit, nurturant attitude. Patience, wisdom, and understanding come with patriarchy, Japanese style.

Younger and Older Japanese

Examining our grouping of story summaries we note that, among the Japanese, one older male sees that there is permission given to assume autonomy.

> (Jms 60.61) A father trusts his son and tells him he believes in him. The father is saying son can do what he wants—he is giving him permission as well as expressing his confidence/trust in his son.
>
> [FA-trust DDA-free]

Individuals can talk things over with an elder.

(Jmy 64.31) This is a youth and his elder (a director, friend, or counselor). The youth is listening and agreeing.

[DDA-advice]

(Jfs 65.56) He is talking about an issue with his social superior.

[NSA-advice DDA-advice]

(Jmy 15.24) He is listening to an elder. What they are talking about is hard to tell.

[NSA-advice DDA-advice]

One story is about present advice.

(Jms 14.53) A father is giving counsel to the son.

[DDA-advice]

Some stories are about long-range advice.

(Jms 19) A professor or a father and son. He is talking and explaining to the son. About life in general . . . the son will obey. . . . It is difficult for a son of this age to listen to a mother's counsel.

[DDA-advice NDA-edify DSA-comply]

(Jmy 13.27) They are discussing and examining their own experience. The older man is talking about the characteristics of life and is giving advice, like a parent.

[FA-empathy NDA-edify DDA-advice]

(Jms 54.67) A father talking to his son. Telling the son that he has become a good man, so he should think and not go astray. Father's wish that son will become respectable.

[EDA-praise RA-duty-s DDA-advice]

How life experience capacitates an elder is stressed in several stories.

(Jmy 72.30) The older man looks like Einstein. Youth is being lectured/scolded through and through/completely. As a person with experience the older is telling the youth what it's like, explaining experiences. Youth is listening quietly and is agreeing/understanding.

[DDA-advice CA-expert DSA-comply]

(Jfy J1.20) He (the elder) is giving his impressions and opinions to the younger. The older is instructing him about life, about how to behave and survive. The youth is nervous, uncertain and the older person is explaining as someone with more experience about life.

[DDA-advice CA-expert CB-worry]

(Jmy 16.32) A father and son. There is a necessity for the youth to listen to the counsel of an elder. He has to choose between options and is listening to advice. Therefore, this is different from the previous card where there was generation conflict.

[CB-help DSA-comply (elders)]

(Jfy 24.21) A young man here appears to be angry or jealous. The older man is sheltering him and trying to teach what is right. But the youth has lots of remorse.

[HB-resent FB-jealous NDA-edify DDA-advice RB-regret]

(Jms 26.37) A father and son again. The father is trying to explain the situation to the son, about life. He is counseling him about how to live, to study, to work, and to better the family. The son listens to the father and learns from him. The opinions of older people are always valid.

[DDA-advice NSA-advice NDA-family CA-expert EDA-praise]

In these stories the younger man's problem can be about work or some relationship. Sometimes the problem is not specified. Although, there are occasional tense situations that arise, it is noteworthy that unlike in the mother-son relationship depicted on Card 6BM (see chapter 11, volume II) ineptitude or incompetence does not seem to arise as readily as part of an issue in paternal mentorship. Questionable activities of ineptness or irresponsibility on the part of the young man do not reach the dramatic severity found in the other Brazilian samples we shall presently examine.

(Jms 51.60) A father talking to his son. He is counseling. The son is in trouble—various reasons such as a girlfriend or work. He is listening and the father is counseling.

[DDA-advice CB-help]

(Jfs 52.54) A father and a youth talking about a social problem. The youth is listening.

[DDA-advice CB-help]

(Jfy 55.21) This is the opposite situation [from his story given to Card 6BM]. One who has lots of experience with life is teaching his child. There is some problem.

[CA-expert DDA-educate CB-help]

(Jfy 66.24) A problem. The father is teaching the son many things or is giving advice or discussing the problem with his son.

[CB-help DDA-educate]

A father can be seen as practicing patience with a rebellious son.

(Jfs 28.37) A father and a rebellious son. He is giving counsel about life. The younger one rebels not just against the father, but against life in general. Adolescents are always rebellious by nature. So the father counsels the youth.
[DSC-resist DDA-advice DDA-patience]

Generational differences can cause difficulties for parents.

(Jmy 17.29) A father talking to his son, trying to pass on counsel. The youth is antagonistic by the expression on his face. However, it is not about a fight between the father and son, but a normal disagreement conversation with the father and son.
[DDA-advice DSC-resist MVB-elder MTB-differ]

(Jsm 8) The same as the last card (he saw Card 6BM as representing generational difficulties . . .). The direct interaction between generations is small and exists in few families. . . . The values and ways of thinking between parent and son are different. The parents raise the children and work with them but their thinking is different.
[DDA-advice MVB-elder MTB-differ DSA-free]

Even a father who has failed to educate his son well is seen by the giver of the story as having good intentions. The attitude of the storyteller is that a son should show more respect for the status of his father regardless of failure to perform well in the past.

(Jms 23.38) A son and father. The father has patience with son. But has educated the son badly and is not able to get respect. Son does not really treat him like a father. He should not have such a expression. Should have a better attitude but the father did not get him a good education and son did not want such an education. The son does not understand that all the father wants is good.
[DDA-patient DDC-result EDC-disdain FC-selfish NDB-welfare]

One story by an older male suggests some dubious authority, but a willingness of a boss to seek instrumental advice from a subordinate. This is practiced frequently in a Japanese business hierarchy. It does not alter the status relationship to gain the advice of a subordinate.

(Jms 59.74) The head of a big company. Bad mood and not pleased . . . things not going well due to modern economy, complaining to a younger worker—he wants and asks them to work harder. Youth organizes information and is trying, with current recession, can't work to satisfy the president. President does not have any good ideas and is asking if he (the youth) has a good opinion.
[PB-work KD-poor DDC-press CB-help]

Two older Japanese women see an authority figure in a somewhat dubious secretive giving of secret information. Most of the conspiratorial stories we shall presently consider below do not so expressly distinguish the different status of the figures.

> (Jfs 58.65) It doesn't look like he is scolding him (the younger one). He is receiving some secret message from a social superior.
>
> [DDA-scold RC-illegal]

> (Jfs 5.42) The father is taking his son under his confidence about a certain secret. It is an important thing for the son. He is revealing something protected/guarded.
>
> [DDA-give FA-trust]

One vertical story given by an older male is of an expressive nature. It depicts a father comforting a discouraged sorrowful son. This emphasizes a vertical expressive nurture.

> (Jms 27. 39) This is a "senor" of greater age and a youth. The elder is comforting. As his son lost his wife and he is discouraged/exhausted. The other is comforting him. He will overcome this state. He is journeying though a transitional, temporary stage. All people go through this phase.
>
> [NDA-comfort KD-death PD-depress PA-endure]

Horizontal Stories of an Instrumental Nature

The Japanese. There are few straightforward stories of mutual enterprise. The pattern of distrust general to Brazil is also found in the Japanese, but to a lesser degree than in the other groups. When two individuals have their heads together, questionable activities are suggested to a number of the Japanese Brazilians as well as among the samples of Brazilian youth. Even some stories that are not directly conspiratorial have an aura of danger or controversy. Cynicism is higher in the younger group. Overall, six of eleven younger men (55 percent), six of fourteen younger women (43 percent) but only five of eighteen older men (28 percent) and one of seven women (14 percent), a total of eighteen, or 36 percent, saw mutual instrumental stories.

Some mutual tasks in five of these stories have no negative implications.

> (Jmy 61.24) Relationship between the father and son. They are trying to do something together and are discussing it.
>
> [MTA-task]

> (Jms 63.52) This is a meeting and they are discussing something.
>
> [MTA-task]

> (Jfy 70.24) A father and son are discussing an important problem.
>
> [MTA-task]

(Jfs 71.38) A father and son. Talking about something important.

[MTA-task]

(Jmy 20) Here, there are two who are commenting, whispering, talking low about a subject that interests only them. They are talking to each other and sharing their ideas with each other, or one of them is commenting on the others around them who, at this moment, are not interested in these two people. Their conversation stays within.

[MTA-task]

Another suggests controversy.

(Jmy 11.39) There is an exchange of ideas between the two. A conversation of a problem, a problem that is controversial.

[MTA-task CB-arduous]

Placed in a courtroom or in a legal situation, three stories suggest more negative situations.

(Jms 6.73) This is a lawyer talking confidentially to his client. Something dangerous is going on.

[MTA-task CB-worry]

(Jmy 22.32) A father and son, commenting. They are meeting in a theater or cinema speaking of what is happening around them. Or a jury, listening lawyer and judge is saying something to each other. Using easy words to understand whether the accused should be condemned or acquitted. It is a serious topic because the young man appears closed/stern. It is not good business.

[MTA-task RC-wrong]

(Jms 68.54) He (the younger one) is having a difficult problem with the police and he is talking and discussing the issue with his lawyer.

[MTA-task RC-wrong]

Secretiveness is suggested in five stories. However, there is no elaboration of a negative nature.

(Jms 7.42) These are two men in a type of meeting between people. There exists here a confidential comment about a topic that can't be revealed to others. It is confidential. An exchange of ideas.

[MTA-task]

(Jfy 2.24) They are whispering during a meeting.

[MTA-task MTC-plot]

(Jmy 4.32) They are talking about something so that others can't hear.

[MTA-task MTC-plot]

(Jfy 56.26) This is a secret conversation.

[MTA-task MTC-plot]

(Jms 69.52) This is a secret meeting at a company.

[MTA-task MTC-plot]

Compared with the other samples below there is less definite negative material. Nevertheless, plots or corrupt activities are more directly suggested in four stories. The political arena is mentioned in only two records, but again suggest politicians are interested in power or money not public good.

(Jfy 25.27) This is a political meeting. Like the ministers here in Brazil. It is about power and its execution.

[MTA-task MTC-plot]

(Jmy 10.24) A problem typical of Brazil. Two politicians are intriguing to gain more money. It is only for their own benefit to strengthen their political and economic positions.

[MTA-task MTC-plot]

(Jfy 53.29) A meeting. It is not good to talk secretly like this. It's better to talk openly in front of all.

[MTA-task MTC-plot]

(Jfy 57.29) They are talking in secret. They are not friends. They are looking at something and are talking at a seminar.

[MTA-task MTC-plot]

Only six of the eighteen stories of mutual interaction on a horizontal level are positive in content. Japanese Brazilians go only slightly in the direction of the general Brazilian distrust of public figures or instrumental mutual activities engaged in for any purpose.

Italian and German Groups. There are three Italian of instrumental interaction. (One German story mentioned as vertical above stressed a status difference.) Their remaining stories are in categories of affective interchange.

Only one Italian story depicting public figures ends on a positive note.

(Im 19) Two senators were discussing the problems of the Brazilian parliamentary system. Preparing themselves for a long journey of work. They go home with their families. They find a solution.

[MTA-task]

Another story deals with re-establishment of a positive instrumental relationship after previous exploitative wrong doing by a rich man.

> (Im 23) A long time ago a very rich man had got involved with a poor woman, and she got pregnant. After a long time he discovered that she had had a son of his. Then the boy became upset because his father hadn't looked for him before. The father gave him many explanations. They got along with each other and the son began to work with his father.
>
> [KA-means RC-ex-sex HA-mend MTA-family]

The third depicts convicts working together plotting their escape.

> (Im 01) Two men at a penitentiary talking, arranging the last details of their escape. They are leaders of the penitentiary, they're the ones who decide when the escape will take place and how it will restore. They will go along with the other prisoners. Some manage, others will be arrested. When police try to prevent escaping, the older one dies and the younger one escapes.
>
> [RD-wrong MTC-plot DDA-lead DSC-escape CD-fail]

Favela Subjects. Negative themes of mutual interaction are especially noted among both groups. Only the Portuguese see one positive cooperative story. It depicts a mutual instrumental theme very briefly.

> (Pm 10) A father and son talking or thinking together.
>
> [MTA-task FB-empathy]

One is of a competitive negotiation involving lack of money.

> (Pf 16) There is a man talking to his neighbor, because he won't be able to pay the price of the house. Then he asked the neighbor to lower the price a little. Then the neighbor said he would think about it.
>
> [OB-want MVA-deal KD-poor]

Another Portuguese story of positive mutual activities between a father and son ends on a dubious note.

> (Pm 5) Joel was a great young man, and he had his father by his side. Once both decided to build an ark. Then they gathered all the money they had and bought wood. Days passed by and both went on building, till one day it was ready. They took it to the sea and there they used it for the first time. As everything went all right, they decided to travel around the world. But nobody heard about them anymore. They disappeared suddenly. They were considered as definitely disappeared.
>
> [MTA-task KD-luck]

Two Afro Brazilians suggest ineptness or questionable plans.

(ABm 20) According to their facial expression, the older man is asking the younger one to do something which has to do with economic interests, money. According to this man's facial expression, he shows not to be economically very capable, and he accepts the proposal of the other man.

[MTA-task CC-mental]

(ABm 29) The Mayors! This is M. Olivio Dutra, who is always increasing bus fares. He only wants to help, but he doesn't know how. For example: he could improve the vehicles, and build more plazas, houses, free places, etc. Now he is trying to turn out people who are set on green areas which don't belong to them. But these people do not have a place to go. He said he will turn out people who are on the green area, and that he won't set them in a better place.

[CD-finish DDC-result]

There are seven stories of a mutual conspiracy or corrupt government officials: four are given by Afro Brazilians, two by Portuguese, one by a youth of German ancestry living in the favela.

(ABf 22) They did something wrong. They are going to do another wrong thing.

[RC-illegal MTC-plot]

(BPf 2) Managers of some bank. They have to fire older workers. It is cheaper to use younger ones.

[MCT-injury MTC-plot]

The negative example of parents is a conscious theme given by one Favela youth.

(BPf 7) The lack of seriousness of these days is reaching even the heads of the families. They involve themselves with gangs, drugs, smuggling. They think it is a better way to support their families. But what kind of education are they giving to their children, who are growing up and learning how to fight against these horrible things which are happening nowadays? Do they love their families?

[MTC-plot RC-abuse AC-crime RC-result RC-example]

Corruption in government and in government figures is represented in three Afro-Brazilians and one Favela German:

(BABm 23) In a political parliament, a 38-year-old congressman and a 50-year-old one voted against a law which the government had imposed. But it didn't make difference. The law was good for the people, who had increased the hope for a better life. This law concerns the increase of the minimum wage. After the increase, the congressmen became annoyed, and decided not to take part in the next voting.

[MTC-false]

(BABf 27) It is a congressman, talking to his friend, who is a city father. He is talking about the wrong things he had said in the last meeting, at the assembly, in the presence of the audience.

[MTC-false]

(BGFm 38) Corruption in Government! Gesiel was a city father who had been elected in 1990, with the help of his uncle, the congressman Jarbas Vasconcellos. As time passed by, Gesiel started to see the corruption in government. He quit the post.

[MTA-family MTC-false RA-injury]

(BABm 18) The President is saying that he will win the election in 1993, and he is listening to what the President is saying, but he is praying that he won't win the election.

[DDC-manage MTC-false HB-resent NSA-pray]

In brief, the stories of authorities or elders in a situation of mutual interchange evoke a good proportion of cynical stories by the Favela youth.

Horizontal Stories of an Expressive Nature

In the Japanese Brazilian samples, there are only six remaining stories of an expressive nature. There are only a few stories wherein the nurturance is explicitly more important than the underlying status differential between young and older.

The following shows this status leveling toward friendship very explicitly.

(BJfy 67. 26) Not the father, but an uncle or another relative. He is a good friend of the younger man and is speaking with him about his girl friend because he has a relationship problem. The elder has lots of life experiences and knows a lot and so he is helping the youth. They are good friends.

[FA-friend FB-problem CA-expert NDA-edify]

There are two stories of friendly interaction.

(BJfs 12) I see here the fraternity between the husband and son.

[FA-friend]

(BJms 21) This is contrary to the previous story where there was conflict between the mother and son. Here, it's more agreeable and friendly (amigável). The father and son are talking to each other in a manner that is friendly and agreeable (amigavelmente) about women. There is no conflict.

[FA-friend NC-discord]

There are two stories of nurturant consolation and mutual support.

(BJfy 3) Louis was thinking in a room. He is in the room doing business. No, I will change the story. Gumersindo is sad with his son, Manuel because he is suffering about a patient who brought a lawsuit against him. This is about treatment, about what a dentist should do. They are dentists. This should not have occurred because Manuel has a diploma. For Manuel, to be a dentist was always his life. Due to having committed dental errors, everything has ended for him.

[NDA-comfort HB-f-anger CC-failure]

(BJfy 18) Here is a picture of the friendship between two people giving counsel to each other in close proximity. This is a type of exchange of confidence between close friends, just like between fathers and sons. The counsel is about work, about life, about how to do things, how to be.

[FA-friend MTA-task]

There is only one story of direct discord. The tone is more resigned than combative. It is a question of basic generational disagreement

(BJms 62) This is the same as the previous card, except it is a father and son this time. They are talking to each other, but their thinking is different and they do not agree.

[MVB-elders HC-discord]

For the Japanese the prevailing themes aroused are of an instrumental nature. They do not see the internal family problems more evident in the other Brazilian groups. Several stories depict generational differences in an objective way without seeming to take sides. Given that they are over twenty years of age they have a different perspective than the youth who run from fourteen to eighteen years of age.

The Italians and Germans. Their remaining stories see both friendship and quarreling between father and son as well as between friends. The German youth see quarreling in four of their total of eleven stories. This is the highest proportion of discord expressed by any group.

For the Italians, friendship can be a source of nurturant support and advice. Despite differences in age there is no status difference in the relationship.

(BPm 11) It is a young man who is talking to an older friend. He is in doubt about a matter and he is asking for the opinion of an older person, who has more life experience. This person is giving him advice, he is giving him his opinion about what he should or should not do, and the young man is listening very closely to what his friend is saying to him, for it can be exactly what he needs to hear.

[NSA-assist NDA-advice]

(BPm) This depicts the advice given by an older friend.

[NDA-edify]

There is an affiliative story of mutual loss.

(BPF 01) Jose had an only child who would come to live with him for some time. He arrived at a certain morning. It seems that it wasn't very good for both to meet each other again. His father had lost his wife. He explained that he didn't send him a telegram only because he had no time. His son asked him to take his mother's picture to his bedroom, so that he doesn't remember sad recollections anymore, but only happy moments they experienced together.

[FD-loss FA-share]

There is a nurturant undercurrent in one of the Italian stories of positive affiliation.

(BIm 15) Father and son were talking about a play they had seen. The father asked the son how he liked it. His son said that he had found it very beautiful. And his father told him that he would take him again to see plays, and to other places too. Then in order to reward his father, the son himself decided to stage a play, to show to his father and family.

[FA-friend PA-esthete NDA-edify NDA-reward]

There is one German story of mutual loss and mutual comfort.

(BGm 02) It's a funeral. The son was comforting the father. And the father had in his son his greatest comfort, now especially that he had lost his wife. The father accepted this loss with resignation, understanding that life is not happiness only.

[KD-death NDA-comfort KA-accept]

Three quarrel stories given by German youth end in the re-establishment of a friendship.

(BGm 11) These are brothers who were very united since they were little children. Later they started to quarrel. However, both went in search of one another. One day they met again and became very good friends.

[FA-friend HC-discord FA-mend]

(BGm 22) Father and son had argued. They became half-enemies. Later they missed each other and apologized to each other. They became friends again.

[HC-discord HA-pacify FA-mend]

(BGm 17) They were friends since childhood. They were torn apart because both liked the same woman. She married the older one, and he never more talked to the other. Now together because the woman had died. Despite this sadness there was still a little happiness because they had met again.

[FA-friend FC-triangle HC-discord KD-death FA-mend]

There are two stories of enduring personal animosity.

(BIm 16) An old rascal saw his old acquaintance and asked him: "How is your business?" he said, "Fine, why did you ask?" The old man, without an answer, changed the subject and said: "How are your children going?" Bad-tempered, he turned his face and went away. Doesn't come back. He didn't answer because he was an old enemy.

[HC-discord]

(BGm 03) It's a parliament member from Brasilia. He was listening to the speech of another who was saying bad things about him. Then an older politician came to him and said: Go ahead, hit him! He went there and punched him. And until today he was already reelected for three times, and the process was not solved yet. The process will never be solved. This is still Brazil.

[EDC-calumny-HC-injury MVC-slander]

A Favela German youth gives a dramatic story of suicide.

(BGm 39) They were happy together. The father was a governor. The son wants to be mayor. The mother dies and the son suicides.

[FA-friend MTA-family FD-loss HC-suicide]

The Favela Groups. There is friendly interaction in four stories, two Portuguese, two Afro-Brazilian.

(BPf 3) These are two people together, talking about their families and about their wives. They talk and even listen to their wives.

[FA-friend]

(BPf 14) It's difficult. A man went to a restaurant, saw his friend sat there. He asked to sit beside him. The friend agreed. They started to talk. The man said he had to leave. He left and they never saw each other again.

[FA-friend FC-split]

(BABm 33) These are two brothers, two friends, talking about their families. The family of one of them is all right, and the other one's family isn't very well, they say. But they go on living anyway; in the world there is always something which isn't all right.

[FA-friend HA-family FDD-loss]

(BABf 32) A man and a young man were talking about the wedding of his daughter. He was saying that his daughter had married a rich man.

[FA-friend KA-wealth]

There is mutual wrongdoing in the form of alcohol abuse. Desire for money can be involved and requests rejected.

(BABf 31) Once two men decided to go out in order to drink. They arrived at the bar and drank a lot. After having drunk a good deal, one of them was already without balance. But he wanted to drink more, and asked his friend, who wasn't very drunk, for money. But he didn't give it to him.

[FA-friend RC-abuse NBS-help NDC-deprive]

(BPm 6) Two unemployed brothers, without a place to live and without money, had nowhere to go. They remained in the streets, drinking and asking for money.

[KC-means RC-abuse NBS-help]

There are uncomfortable secrets and deceit depicted in two stories.

(BPf 4) It is a young man, an adopted child. One day his father decided to tell him the whole truth, for his true mother had discovered where her son was, and had threatened his father: if he didn't tell him the truth she would tell him. But as the boy was very ambitious. He didn't want to know whether it was true or not, for his mother was a poor woman, and he didn't accept this fact.

[FC-flee RD-person AC-asocial]

(BABf 21) He was abandoned by his true mother. The father is reluctant to reveal her identity.

[NDC-desert FB-reach]

There are four stories of giving and receiving. One must note how the two Afro-Brazilian stories develop an elaborate fantasy that involves the need for money. One Portuguese story suggests how success in sports is a fantasized way to be able to help others in need.

(BPm 9) The son is a soccer player; the father is judge at the court, and both are very rich. They thought of giving half of their wealth to the poor people. And they, with half of their money, became happy, because the poor people weren't in need any longer.

[KA-wealth KA-social NDA-charity PA-joy]

(BPm 13) A man who is sad, the other is comforting him. Will be very happy.

[PD-sad NDA-comfort]

(BABm 24) Mr. Ari liked very much American and Brazilian pictures and sculptures. He didn't do anything other than going to museums in order to see pictures and things from the past, for it had to do with him. His son Carlos also liked the things his father talked about. But Mr. Ari was very poor, and had no money to go to the museum in order to see the pictures. But once his son Carlos, who had saved some money, made his father a surprise by giving him two pictures, an American and a Brazilian picture. One of the pictures looked like Mr. Ari and Carlos. Mr. Ari was delighted when his son came with the picture. The son had made a dream come true, a dream he wanted to make coming true for a long time: to have at home both pictures, the American and the Brazilian one. He said to his son thank you very much.

[PA-esthete OB-want KD-poor NDA-reward NSA-grateful]

(BABm 19) Both were colleagues at work, but one was rich and the other was poor. The poor one used to play violin in nightclubs. The rich one was a model. Once the poor one wanted to go to New York in order to play in nightclubs there, for he was told that they paid well there. Then he wanted to get the ticket to NY by all means, and sold almost all of his furniture. The rich friend heard that he was needing money. He looked for him and gave him the ticket and the name of the nightclubs. He helped him and traveled along with him. He helped him to succeed in life, to grow. And after some time he reached his friend's social class, and they started to work together.

[NSD-means AA-self NDA-means MTA-task]

Mutual dislike and quarreling appear in only two stories.

(BPf 8) A long time ago there was an altercation between a father and a son. They used to quarrel, and the father didn't like the son very much. Everybody thought that time would cure this revolt between both. But they were very wrong; this revolt remained for many years.

[HC-discord FB-dislike DSC-disobey]

(BABf 32) Anderson and Claudio were arguing because Anderson wanted to marry Claudio's wife. Because Claudio would separate from his wife. Then his friend wanted to take her for him.

[HC-discord FC-triangle RC-ex-sex]

In sum, there were proportionately more expressively oriented stories in the Portuguese and Afro-Brazilian than in the Italian or German subgroups. Their stories reflect more worries about money and internal family problems with drink than they do issues of helpful mentorship or proper paternal discipline.

The small German sample showed the most affective ambivalence. Their vertical or horizontal stories suggest potential dissension. In the vertical stories with an authority figure there is resistance. In the expressive stories there were more expressions of quarreling than in any other group, although such situations often resulted in the re-establishment of a positive relationship.

The Afro-Brazilians had the most negative stories with wrongdoing, plotting or quarreling. There were ten of fifteen in a negative direction. Two males see ineptitude in officials. Four see corrupt officials. Wrong doing includes alcohol (two) sexual behavior (one), and abandonment of a child (one). These negative stories were countered by five more positive stories emphasizing giving (two), inspiration to be like the father (one), and mutual friendship (two). Note there is no positive mutual instrumental behavior depicted in any of their stories.

The Portuguese were varied. Of their seventeen stories there is one story of mutual instrumental negotiation. There are three stories of positive friendship. There are three stories of nurture. There were four stories of positive advice; one of these was in a situation of a son's wrongdoing. Mutual activity in one story ends dubiously. There is plotting in another (one). In three there is present or past wrong doing as part of mutual activities. There is mutual dislike in one story.

The Japanese continue a culture continuity of seeing older authority in a positive light. The Italian group is also apt to see positive authority, the German youth express ambivalence. The Favela youth do not see many positive anticipations of adult control or instrumental behavior of a positive nature in their view of the adult world. The exploitative venal tradition of an older Brazil is indirectly reflect in the stories of present-day youth.

Discussion

This detailed examination of a series of stories again gives direct evidence of how ethnic groups can differ remarkably in concepts of paternal authority and political leadership.

The TAT is a form of documentation that when coupled with other evidence such as interviews or ethnographic observation deepens our respect for the persistence of distinct ethnic patterns in some populations.

Oscar Lewis forcefully challenged us to consider as semi-autonomous the diverse ethnic family continuities that continue both positive and negative traditions from one generation to the next. In discussing what he termed a "culture" of poverty, he documented by intensive interviews such patterns operative among the ex-peons of Mexico (1961) and the Puerto Rican immigrants in New York (1969). In this specific study one notes that negative patterns concerning patriarchy or mentorship continue adverse attitudes from one generation to the next. We can argue semantically whether any social segment by itself can constitute an independently operative "culture." But we cannot dismiss, as has been done glibly by many, the force of generational continuities that deform the perceptions and anticipations of the life course of those trapped in an underclass or those that continue, without direct consciousness, a tradition such as Confucian ethics and morality.

What we have done in the presentation of this and the other related chapters is to give a small sample of empirical results from the social context of a region of present-day Brazil. It should be evident how fantasy, even that of high school adolescents, reflects not only personal issues but continuities in more general social attitudes and subsequent behavior. The past, in some deformation, lives on in the present. That is the nature of "cultural" continuity. In this instant we examined attitudes of various ethnic segments of Brazilian society about elders, authority, mentorship, and possible political corruption.

"Social change" is a change in present institutions. There may occur changes in economic or political institutions, but such change by itself is not congruent with "culture change."[1] For a "culture" to change, the specific institutions directly concerned with the basic socialization of the next generation, the intimate family, and youthful peer interaction must be altered. Mao was accurate in calling what he attempted in China a "cultural" revolution. To change Chinese ways of thinking he knew it was necessary to change the internal dynamics of the family itself. Family patterning as an institution resists to some degree at least, and for some considerable time, changes in technology or political institutions. There is what I term a psychological lag between what occurs in the outer society and what persists in the family matrix and the immediate social community.

It is through the birth family and the intimate face-to-face community and peer group that social experiences, seemingly shared by all in a modern state, can be reflected quite variously through the prisms of selves formed differently by ethnic or class belonging and the heritage into which one is born. The norms for different groups continue to be different.

References

Caudill, William. 1976. Social Change and Cultural Continuity in Japan. In George De Vos (Ed.), *Responses to Change: Society, Culture and Personality*. New York: D. Van Nostrand Company.

Caudill, William and George De Vos. 1956. Achievement, Culture and Personality: The Case of the Japanese Americans. *American Anthropologist*, **58**(6): 1102–1126 (reprinted: 1961; 1966; 1967; 1971).

De Vos, George. 1973. *Socialization for Achievement: Essays on the Cultural Psychology of the Japanese.* Berkeley: University of California Press.

——— (Ed.). 1976. *Responses to Change: Society, Culture and Personality*. New York: D. Van Nostrand Company.

———. 1993. Problems with Achievement, Alienation, and Authority in Korean Minorities in the United States and Japan. In Kwang Kyu Lee and Walter Slote (Eds.), *Overseas Koreans in the Global Context* (pp. 145–180). Seoul: Association for the Study of Koreans Abroad.

De Vos, George and Eun-Young Kim. 1993. Koreans in Japan: Problems with Achievement, Alienation Authority. In Ivan Light and Parminder Bhachu (Eds.), *California Immigrants in World Perspective.* New Brunswick, N.J.: Transaction Books.

De Vos, George and Kwang-kyu Lee. 1981. Attitude Toward Authority: Dilemma of Ex-Colonial Society. In Changsoo Lee (Ed.), *Modernization of Korea and the Impact of the West* (pp. 150–162). Los Angeles: University of Southern California.

Lee, Changsoo and George A. De Vos. 1981. *Koreans in Japan: Ethnic Conflict and Accommodation.* Berkeley: University of California Press.

Lewis, Oscar. 1961. *Children of Sánchez: Autobiography of a Mexican Family.* New York: Random House.

---

[1]See W. Caudill's discussion in Chapter 1 of "Social Change and Cultural Continuity in Japan," in De Vos (1976).

———. 1966. *La Vida; A Puerto Rican Family in the Culture of Poverty—San Juan and New York*. New York: Random House.

Vaughn, Curtis. 1988. *Cognitive Independence, Social Independence and Achievement Orientation: A Comparison of Japanese and United States Students.* Dissertation. Dept. of Education, University of California at Berkeley.

Chapter 11

Mother-Son Relationships: Cross-cultural Contrasts in Interpersonal Perceptions

George A. De Vos
David Ephrahim

A comparison of stories elicited by Murray Thematic Apperception Test Card 6BM from a number of different national-cultural settings afforded David Ephrahim and myself some opportunity to examine together some of the underlying attitudes about the expected roles assumed by an aging maternal figure in present-day youth. Worldwide, is there some diminution of the authority role of parents and some desire to shift emotional relationships toward closer horizontal-affiliative bonds while attaining greater autonomy and personal independence from the older generation? How is this trend reflected in the present samples from a number of different societies we or our colleagues have tested?

In the present chapter we shall compare samples from Canada and Venezuela, gathered by David Ephrahim, and the California and Brazil samples already utilized in previous chapters. We examine herein how relationships between an older woman and a younger man are interpreted by subjects in their responses to Card 6BM. As we shall demonstrate, our method of scoring the manifest content of Card 6BM permits us to compare these normative groups more objectively by scoring in detail the nuances found in interpersonal concerns that focus on an older maternal figure.

There are some general categories of responses to the TAT cards that are elicited regardless of the cultural or social setting in which they are used. But, again, what is also quickly noticeable, when comparisons are made with categories and subcategories, is that there are very notable salient responses that distinguish one group from another.

In what follows we shall examine the relative emphases in the interpersonal concerns of small samples of male and female stories of Canadian college students, Venezuelan youth from two different social class strata, Brazilian high school youth from different socioeconomic and ethnic groups, and Japanese Brazilians of varying ages.

Comparing these very small samples of age, sex, class, ethnicity, and minority status crossnationally on the TAT should dispel the often held contention that cross-cultural testing should be considered *a priori* invalid, or subject to deep suspicion. There are certain human universals in the dimensions of social interaction and social perception that transcend cultural boundaries. Conversely, there are manifest differences in normative emphasis and the nuances of concerns quickly apparent as soon as one compares these groups from different social backgrounds.

In our present samples, we again use the Japanese Brazilians obtained by Takeyuki Tsuda in Sao Paolo and Porto Alegré. The fifty records we selected have an age distribution from early twenties to late sixties. As before we have subdivided them at age thirty-five into a younger and an older group. The remainder of the Brazilian samples, obtained by Cicero Vaz, were taken from various high schools both in the city of Porto Alegré and from nearby ethnic communities in the German and Italian regions of Rio Grande do Sul. Unfortunately we have only the samples of male subjects from the Italian and German groups, since the females had been given another card.

David Ephrahim has available 150 records from various settings in Venezuela. In the present sample we utilize only forty-nine of these records. We have chosen a sample of twenty-four male and female youth from an elite high school in Caracas, representing families of at least upper middle class socioeconomic status. In some instances, these subjects represent families of recent economic success. The second sample was taken from a high school servicing students from a Caracas working class district.

The Canadians, a bit older, were obtained by Ephrahim from among first and second-year students attending the arts faculty of a Canadian west coast university. They are of mostly middle class white Protestant background. The American sample to which we occasionally refer comparatively was obtained by John Connor from an inland California state university. These students come from a variety of settings. Selected from an ethnically varied student body we herein are reporting on only those considered "Caucasian" in background.

Given the variety of groups considered, the within-group numbers are small, and could be amplified by later substantiation. Our purpose herein was to show the dramatic cultural differences in the issues depicted in the elicited stories, given even the small numbers considered. We shall note that in the responses to this particular card, there are several universals considered by subjects regardless of their age, sex, or background. For example, is the status relationship with the older woman depicted more as a vertical-unequal or horizontal-reciprocal nature? A second major overall differentiation we note in our scoring is whether the relationships depicted are primarily of an emotional, expressive nature, or whether they are instrumentally goal-directed issues in which the story figures are involved.

Despite the specific range of stories that can be elicited by a card depicting an older woman and a younger man, there are a variety of stories that fall into the categories used in our scoring system. As we shall illustrate, within *expressive* stories we can further differentiate whether the issues depicted represent affiliative closeness or loss, depict harmony or discord, involve dependency or nurture, show problems of positive evaluation or shame, or focus on inner emotional states. Variously problems of pride, esteem, or shame may be at issue. Or the focus may be on family harmony, personal discord, and/or a need for reconciliation.

Stories depicting *instrumental* issues of personal achievement, career concerns, competence, or personal responsibility and potential guilt for negatively perceived behavior may be juxtaposed to other interpersonal instrumental concerns with control, dominance or compliance, or mutual instrumental cooperative or competitive activities. In considering Card 6BM comparatively in what follows we shall illustrate how examples related to all these categories are forthcoming, ranging from a rare appearance to a numerically pervasive concern appearing within a particular group.

Instrumental and Expressive Themes Expected on Card 6BM

The nature of the card, a woman with her back turned and a young man with hat in hand, limits the Instrumental concerns we can expect from this card. Nevertheless, one theme depicted, with some frequency in American records, has been a young man reluctantly leaving home to seek a career or to make a separate life with a wife. This is usually an achievement theme and is scored either primarily or secondarily in the Achievement (A) category. It may be entwined with expressions about gaining autonomy from home. Such Autonomy themes stressing independence in decision making are scored under the Control (D) category. Frequently both scores are necessary.

Other elicited stories involve some consideration of ineptness or wrongdoing. When it is a question of instrumental inadequacy in performing a task, it is scored within the Competence (C) category. When the wrongdoing is related to duty, morality, or social expectations, it is scored under the Responsibility (R) category. In either case if the mother is seen as an authority figure it is double scored with Control. Either Control or Responsibility, for example, can be the primary category, and the other category scored as a secondary concern. Rarely are there stories of Cooperation or Competition (M) depicted on this card. Such stories are more frequently given to the Card 7BM, which depicts an older man and a younger man with their heads together, sometimes resolving a mutual task or objective.

The most frequent Expressive stories expected in response to this card are Affiliative (F) stories. They can be positive depiction of a reunion after absence or stories of separation due to necessity, or due to career or marriage decisions of a son that can be either resolved positively or remain unresolved. There are also negative stories of mutual loss of a father or other loved one. Concerns with dependent or Nurturance (N) needs are also frequently depicted. Breaches of Harmony (H), such as quarrels over marriage choice, are not infrequent. Stories of Esteem (E) related to family pride or shameful behavior are occasionally elicited. The concern expressed directly concerned with Pleasure or suffering (P) is usually embedded in the context of other issues rather than being a central issue evoked by the picture. Concerns with illness (Fate K) are related to aging in a number of stories

Overall Results: Instrumental or Expressive Concerns; Horizontal or Vertical Status Relationships

Overall, the main divisions in the distribution of stories in the samples considered here (215 responses) are divided between eighty-seven stories (40 percent) with a vertical status differential depicted between the younger and older figure and 126 situations (58 percent) of the stories in which there is no attention to vertical differential status between mother and son (see Table 11.1).

In seventy-four instrumental stories (34 percent) we find various vertical control (D) or authority relationships depicted between mother and son. Some are related to acts of advice or admonishment on the part of the mother (fifteen stories in which only one is depicted in any negative sense). There are an additional eleven stories where the son is seeking or exercising autonomy or seeking freedom from the mother. Four of these are depicted as rebellious acts of which three have negative consequences (see Table 11.2).

There are twelve stories wherein the mother is in a superordinate position concerned with a son's incompetence (C); five of these note that the mother's help is needed. Another thirty-three stories suggest wrongdoing on the part of a son that is the concern of his mother or grandmother (see Table 11.2).

Situations of nurture, or lack thereof (N), are found in thirteen (6 percent) of the vertical stories considered primarily expressive in thematic content. In most of these the son is in the superordinate position dealing with the needs of a dependent older person (see Table 11.3).

In the stories wherein no status differences are depicted between mother and son (Horizontal relationships) only a few (sixteen or 7 percent) are of an instrumental nature. There are three stories of mutual cooperation (M) or responsibility (R) (see Table 11.3). The other thirteen depict the son's achievement (A) or independence (N) needs as more salient or stronger than any continuing expressive relationship with the mother.

This percentage of Achievement (A) cases in our present samples is far below previous percentages reported for middle-class American samples that focused more frequently on an achievement need in conflict with maternal attachment (Henry, 1956; Caudill, 1956; Vaughn, 1988; Connor, 1977). William Henry (1956) in his pioneering work with the TAT did a study comparing relatively successful with relatively unsuccessful American executives. He noted that successful executives saw the young man leaving home in situations wherein their personal need to achieve was greater than a regretful parting with a mother. Unresolved stories, or stories wherein the young man does not leave, were found more characteristic in the less successful group. In a sample of college age Euro-Americans obtained by Connor (1977), 42 percent saw such a theme of possibly leaving home. Of these one-third saw the son not being able to leave.

In our present samples, 104 stories (48 percent of the total across groups) depict some form of expressive interaction, without any status considerations (see Table 11.3). The most numerous of these (forty-nine or 23 percent) are a variety of responses to fateful events such as death or bad news (K). The remaining are first, affiliative concerns (F) (thirty-six, 17 percent): (a) a concern with separation due to a loss or a situational necessity (thirteen or 6 percent); (b) affiliative concerns suggesting either positive forms of closeness or coming together (ten or 5 percent); (c) thirteen stories (6 percent) of negative affiliation or unresolved difficulties in establishing closeness and communication. Second, there are situations depicting some form of antagonism or mutual discord (H) that are found in eighteen or 8 percent of the stories. There are a few stories in which evaluative considerations (E) (five) and nurture (N) (two) are included as expressive categories.

What we can now examine is how the various ethnic samples included in our samples differ significantly in the distribution of stories in these categories. And as we shall illustrate, there are manifest cultural differences in the nuances of interaction depicted as occurring between a mother and son.

Table 11.1
Card 6BM: Vertical and Horizontal Relationships

Code: Total Number [215]

Portuguese	*P [22]*	*Jap-Brazilian ≤ 35*	*Jy [25]*
Afro-Brazilian	*AB [26]*	*Jap-Brazilian >35*	*Jo [25]*
Italian	*I [12]*	*Canadian*	*C [45]*
German	*G [12]*	*Venezuelan Status high*	*Vh [24]*
		Venezuelan Status low	*Vl [25]*

Basically Vertical Status Relationships (40%)

	P	Ab	I	G	Jy	Jo	C	Vh	Vl
87	9	8	6	5	10	12	12	7	15
Instrumental issues (34%)									
74	5	4	6	5	9	12	9	7	14
Expressive situations (6%)									
13	4	4	0	0	1	0	3	0	1

Basically Horizontal Status Relationships (58%)

	P	Ab	I	G	Jy	Jo	C	Vh	Vl
125	13	16	6	7	14	12	30	16	10
Instrumental issues									
16	0	1	2	1	2	3	3	4	0
(7%)	(0%)	(4%)	(17%)	(8%)	(8%)	(12%)	(7%)	(17%)	(0%)
Expressive situations or fateful events									
109	13	15	4	6	12	9	28	12	10
Other (including card descriptions and rejection)									
5	0	2	0	0	1	1	3	1	0

Dominant Concerns of Vertical and Horizontal Categories

Appearing in the vertical stories:
Instrumental concerns: (74) Control [30]; Competence [12]; Responsibility [32]
Expressive situations: (13) Affiliation [2]; Nurture [11]

Appearing in the horizontal stories:
Instrumental concerns: (15) Achievement [12]; Cooperation [3]
Expressive situations: (60) Nurture [2]; Affiliation [36]; Discord [18]; Evaluation [4]

Fateful events (49—double scored with interpersonal categories):
Instrumental concerns: (6) Responsibility [1]; Competence [1]; Endurance, Self reliance [4]
Expressive situations: (40) Emotional State [9]; Nurture [8]; Affiliation [23]
Without affect: Descriptive [3]

Table 11.2
Card 6BM: Vertical Relationships
Basically Vertical Status Relationships N=87 (39%) of 215

	P	Ab	I	G	Jy	Jo	C	Vh	Vl
87	9	8	6	5	10	12	12	7	15
	(41%)	(31%)	(50%)	(42%)	(40%)	(48%)	(27%)	(29%)	(60%)
Instrumental issues									
74	5	4	6	5	9	12	9	7	14
Expressive situations									
13	4	4	0	0	1	0	3	0	1
a. Instrumental Concerns: Related to Control, Competence, or Responsibility N=74 (34%)									
	5	4	6	5	9	12	9	7	14
Authority/Autonomy									
14 Proper authority									
	2	0	2	0	3	6	0	1	0
1 Negative authority									
	0	0	0	0	0	0	0	1	0
7 Autonomy									
(4) successful									
	1	0	0	1	0	0	0	0	2
(2) negative consequences									
	0	0	0	0	0	0	2	0	1
4 Revolt									
(1) successful									
	0	0	0	0	0	0	0	0	1
(3) negative consequences									
	0	1	0	0	0	0	0	1	1
Incompetence/Wrongdoing									
12 Son's incompetence									
(7) general									
	0	0	0	0	0	3	2	0	2
(5) needs help									
	0	1	0	1	0	0	0	1	2
33 Wrongdoing									
(22 general									
	2	3	3	3	4	1	2	1	3
(11) seeks forgiveness or apology									
	0	0	0	0	2	2	3	2	2
b. Expressive Concerns: Related to Nurture N=13 (6%)									
	4	4	0	0	1	0	3	0	1
Nurture									
10 Positive care									
	3	2	0	1	0	3	0	0	1
3 Unresolved or negative									
	1	2	0	0	0	0	0	0	0

Table 11.3
Horizontal Stories Expressive Concerns and Reactions to Fate
Basically Horizontal Status Relationship N=126 (59%) of 215

		P	Ab	I	G	Jy	Jo	C	Vh	Vl
		13	16	6	7	14	12	30	16	10
		(59%)	(62%)	(50%)	(58%)	(56%)	(48%)	(67%)	(67%)	(40%)
a. Horizontal Instrumental Concerns N=22 (10%)										
	22	1	2	2	1	2	3	3	8	0
Mutual Cooperation or Responsibility	*3*	0	0	1	0	1	0	1	0	0
Autonomy or achievement in conflict with expressive needs (separation)	*13*	0	1	1	1	1	3	2	4	0
Instrumental Reactions to Fate										
Endurance (self-reliance)	*4*	0	0	0	0	0	0	0	4	0
Instrumental concern	*2*	1	1	0	0	0	0	0	0	0
b. Horizontal Expressive Concerns N=104										
	104	12	14	4	6	12	9	26	12	10
Affiliation										
Separation	*13*	1	3	1	2	2	3	0	2	0
Positive communication	*10*	2	3	0	1	0	0	4	0	0
Negative affiliation (includes sadness or inability to be close or communicate)	*13*	3	2	1	0	1	3	3	0	0
Nurture										
Pity	*2*	0	1	0	0	0	0	0	0	1
Evaluation or Esteem										
Disappointment	*1*	0	0	0	0	0	0	1	0	0
Discomforting revelation about family	*4*	0	0	0	0	0	0	3	0	1
Harmony-Discord										
Dissension discord	*15*	3	1	2	0	4	2	0	2	1
Over marriage choice	*3*	0	0	0	0	1	0	0	0	2
Expressive Reactions to Fate Bad News, Death										
Pity or nurture	*8*	0	1	0	0	1	0	0	4	2
Affiliative resolved	*6*	0	1	0	0	2	0	1	1	1

Table 11.3

17	Affiliative (unresolved/negative)								
	1	0	0	0	0	0	14	1	1
9	Emotional state								
	2	1	0	1	1	1	0	2	1
3	Neutral								
	2	1	0	0	0	0	0	0	0

Some Themes Illustrated: Mother as Authority

The Japanese

Among instrumental-vertical stories, major concerns about a maternal figure in an authority role were found most often among the Japanese Brazilians (see Table 11.2). Of twenty-nine stories given by both younger and older men, eighteen (62 percent) saw a mother in a dominant role, whereas six of twenty-two women (29 percent) gave similar stories. There was also a notable age difference. The older group above thirty-five years of age saw more positive advice and admonishment (55 percent of all stories); the younger group saw more wrongdoing in a son (four stories), that, in half the cases, led to maternal rejection. In one story a son begs forgiveness for having to leave home against the mother's wishes (one). Examining the Japanese as a whole, as we shall illustrate later, there were also further gender differences. Younger women were varied in their fifteen stories. However, four (27 percent) saw direct dissension or discord occurring between mother and son, the highest number of stories of discord of any subgroup in our comparative samples.

This sample created stories in line with those previously discussed in various previous writings about Japanese Americans, and Japanese in their homeland. Among older Japanese men (eight of eighteen records, 44 percent) and younger men (three of eleven records, 27 percent), the mother figure depicted is one commanding respect and one maintaining pressure on one's children to succeed in the instrumental goals toward which they have been directed. In some a mother's assistance is needed. She can be consulted. The mother continues to be concerned with the future of her son. She does not reject the son with the finality that occurred in some previously gathered Japanese and Japanese American stories.

> (Jmy 15) This scene shows the respect that youth should have towards elders.
> [DSA-family EDA-awe]

In the older Japanese the mother is a proper authority in 50 percent or twelve of their stories. There are six stories of advice or admonishment.

(Jmo 54) This is a mother and her son. The mother is gray haired and is at the end of her life. She does not know when she will die. She is telling her son to become a respectable and splendid (*rippa*) person like his father. This is her wish.

[KB-survive EDA-status DDA-educate]

(Jmo 19) This appears to be a mother and son. The son is telling her about a problem about something that happened. What problem? It is a problem about his work. This is a situation that shows lots of worry. When a son consults a mother, it is because he wants the mother to help him and the mother's advice is always good.

[CB-arduous NSB-help DDA-advice]

In the older records, acts of wrongdoing receive admonishment or scolding.

(Jfo 65) He is listening to the mother. He is being admonished.

[DDA-scold DSA-family]

(Jmo 68) This is a mother and son. There is a difficult problem at hand. They are discussing it or the mother is scolding the son. Probably, they are discussing.???

[CB-arduous DDA-scold MTA-task]

Incompetence may or may not be the cause of a son's failure. Three older men suggest a mother cannot always resolve the difficulty.

(Jmo 27) He appears sad at this moment. Apparently this is his mother. They are sad about some fact that occurred in the family. He is sadder than she. The problem is with him. He lost his job or has trouble with some woman. The problem is some factor with him, not only about family problems.

[PD-sad CC-failure FB-problem]

(Jmo 51) A son returns very disappointed and discouraged. His mother is very disappointed. His work did not go well. Or it might have been about his university entrance test if he is younger. But since he looks older, it is probably about work. He didn't do well, or otherwise he was kicked out (fired). He tells his mother about it.

[CC-failure]

The mother can remain critical despite all efforts.

(Jmo 59) A mother and son. Everyday, the son goes to the work hard and tries his best. World economic recession is affecting his company, he can't earn enough to pay rent. His mother waits with expectation for the son and prepares food. When he sees her, his face is sad and eyes downward. Thinking something. . . . He must work more and harder. In the current situation, he cannot satisfy/please his mother. What should he do?

[KD-poor CB-arduous NDA-food DDC-press]

It is the younger group that shows more concern with wrongdoing (seven of twenty-five *young*; compared with three of twenty-five *old*). Note that is the younger males who in 4 of 11 stories (36 percent), give stories of wrongdoing. This is the highest of any male group.

> (Jmy 20) A mother and son. It is a bad situation—not happy—a situation in crisis. The mother or grandmother is giving a sermon and he is listening, but there is no agreement There is a problem between the two, for instance, something that he did that she thinks is wrong. He is listening properly to what she is saying. Another possibility is a situation in which she is surprised (she looks surprised) at something that is happening at that immediate moment. One can tell by her eyes that something happened—it is a difficult moment. But is it more possible that he is listening to the mother.
>
> [DDA-scold RC-wrong DSA-family]

> (Jmy 72) His mother's troubled face. She lectured and *scolded*, but she is not angry—staring out. Her son is troubled, but mother does not feel troubled. The youth did something bad and the mother is looking like it was expected.
>
> [RC-wrong DDA-scold EDC-expect]

In previous samples, a son was not to leave home simply for individualistic reasons. Should he do so the mother can be unforgiving (Caudill and De Vos, 1956; De Vos, 1973). Such stories do not appear in the present Japanese Brazilian sample. Wrongdoing can hurt the mother; solutions are sought with propriety.

> (Jmy 61) The son did something wrong. There is a difference between them and the mother has become sad and upset.
>
> [RC-wrong HC-discord PD-sad]

> (Jfo 5) The son is taking leave of the mother. He did something that hurt the mother and is apologizing and asking her for forgiveness. He doesn't know what to do, but he will find a way to better the situation.
>
> [RC-wrong DSA-appease RA-reform]

> (Jmy 4) He is coming to ask forgiveness from his mother. He has come to say he is sorry.
>
> [DSA-appease RA-apology]

The Italians and Germans

The Italian and German males in Brazil, younger in age than the Japanese Brazilian subjects, saw mother in an authority role in close to half of their stories (six or 50 percent of the Italians; five or 42 percent of the Germans). In the Italian youth the mother in two of their stories gives advice which is followed.

(Im 16) His mother, looking outside, addressed her son and said: "Son, it's time for you to have a direction in your life." The son follows her advice.

[DDA-advice DSA-comply]

Maturation brings back respect for parental advice.

(Im 19) Aged couple older son, when younger, used to obey parents' advice. Now grown up he doesn't listen to parents' advice. But he learns to be conscientious, listening to his parent's advice.

[DSC-resist DSA-comply]

In another story, her advice is sought.

(Im 24) This is a son along with his mother discussing his problems and trying to solve them. He asked for his mother's opinion and they solve the problems.

[CB-help MTA-task]

The issue depicted in three instances is some form of wrongdoing. Two Italians specify sexual acting out as the problem. In another, drugs becomes an issue. In all their stories there are attempts at compliance to the mother's pressure. A mother does not accept improper behavior.

(Im 15) The lady is his mother. He made some wrong and tries to explain it to her, but she doesn't want to demonstrate attention. He got a woman pregnant without being married to her. She didn't accept it, but she liked the idea of having a grandchild. They talk, she demands that they get married and they do it.

[RC-pr-sex FC-reject HA-family RA-reform]

(Im 14) A 52-year-old lady found out that her son used drugs. She told him to get out of her house. He said he wouldn't do it anymore. He finally went to a clinic specialized in drug addicts. He used drugs because he was discontented with the world.

[RC-abuse PD-thwart FC-reject RA-reform]

Bad character may make reform hopeless.

(Im 16) This guy is a gigolo; he dates one woman in one night, and in the next night with another woman. He betrays all of them. One night he does not take care and gets a woman pregnant. He tells everything to his mother. His mother forces him to marry the woman. He marries her and the child is born. He keeps betraying her. Without her knowing it. Because he is a gigolo he cannot quit the addiction he has.

[RC-ex-sex FC-betray DDA-family DSA-family CD-weak]

The Germans are more oriented toward autonomy or wrongdoing rather than seeking advice.

(Gm 12) Grandma Nilce didn't want to allow Diago to go out. They argued a lot. Then Grandma saw that she shouldn't mind Diago's business. Grandma Nilce regretted because she didn't let Diago live his own life.

[DDC-rigid HC-discord DDA-free]

Autonomy may lead to bad results.

(Gm 17) When a son leaves home, his mother stays normally alone, and she doesn't want it to happen. This was the case in that house. The son was leaving the house and his mother was astonished, but he did it anyway, leaving her alone and without knowing that, because of this, she would die 2 months later.

[DDA-free FB-neglect FD-death]

Afro-Brazilians and Portuguese

The Portuguese or Afro-Brazilian youth were less concerned with positive maternal authority than were the Italian and German groups. The forty-eight stories by Portuguese and Afro-Brazilian youth revealed very few stories of mother as a positive authority figure (two). There were however five stories of wrongdoing. In the Afro-Brazilians, stories of wrongdoing were of a somewhat more serious nature.

(ABm 19) A mother brought up her son not to be a smuggler. But he used drugs, it was hidden. The family's friends knew but nobody would tell. He forgot cocaine on the table. She saw it and asked him why. But he lied to her, saying that he had been forced to use it. She discovered the lie and sent him away from home.

[RC-abuse FC-betray DDA-punish FC-reject]

(ABm72) In a very simple house there was a woman who loved her grandson very much. She spent days explaining to him that one shouldn't try drugs. But the grandson, already a grown up man, didn't obey his grandmother. He began to get involved with certain individuals and from then on his worst nightmare took place. The grandmother who liked her grandson very much went in search of him, but she couldn't find him. He went to many places, until she found him dead on his own bed.

[NDA-teach DSC-resist FB-peer FD-death]

As we shall presently illustrate, the Portuguese Brazilians had the most expressive-horizontal concerns with issues of affiliation (F) (44 percent) or nurture (N) primary (25 percent). The male stories throughout were somewhat more positive in tone than those given by females. The Afro-Brazilians had only three out of twenty-six (12 percent) instrumental stories. Their expressive stories had the highest proportion of negative or unresolved endings. We shall illustrate these differences below.

Venezuelan Samples

There are noticeable overall trends in the Venezuelan sample related to the mother as a dominant figure. Asking for forgiveness is a theme in 8 percent of Venezuelan subjects as well as the Japanese on Card 6BM, (four in forty-nine; four in fifty). In the Venezuelan stories, the mother is mostly described as a nurturing figure, not a disciplinary one. She can be overprotective. No one says she is "stubborn," as in three Canadians stories (see below). When she scolds the son it is in a protective way.

In general, mothers are perceived as refusing to recognize any need for their son to separate from them, for instrumental or expressive purposes; although they may finally accept such separation at the end, it's not a mother's normative expectation. They remain very openly concerned with a nurturing need. But underneath, they are also dependent on the son. These excerpts illustrate this.

> (Vhf 53) She overprotects him. She is frustrated because she does not understand that her son wants to leave.
>
> [NDC-indulge FB-thwart]

> (Vhf 45 y) Mother does not understand. She thinks that she is feeling bad, that she does not want her son to leave her by herself.
>
> [FB-thwart FD-autonomy]

> (Vhm 57) He wants to go abroad for studying but his mother does not agree because she protects him and does not want to have her son far away.
>
> [NSA-free HC-discord NDC-indulge]

In some stories it is evident that the son will behave well, not due to an internalized sense of what is right or what is wrong, but in order not to inflict any pain on his mother. The important thing at the end seems to restore closeness, not the act committed. A mother can control her son's behavior with her pain. The act committed is not judged severely from the perspective of the narrator of the story; rather, repentance and a disposition to conform are emphasized. In such stories there is a clear verticality. Mother is in a superior position, from where she has the power to forgive her son.

Our Venezuelan samples showed sex and class differences in how a mother was depicted in an authority role and how a son was depicted in respect to autonomy. Based on previous experience, stories of a son leaving home for instrumental purposes were less than anticipated in the several ethnic samples we are considering. Only in the upper-status Venezuelans were there four of twenty-four stories depicted with this theme. It is part of contemporary reality that higher status youth go abroad for advanced education in a number of professions.

(Vhm 50) The mother was surprised. She didn't expect it. She cannot believe it. He is telling her he is leaving home because he is going to study somewhere else.

[AA-self PB-surprise FB-split]

(Vhf 53) Widow works hard, including Sundays—so her son has everything. She overprotects. He has to leave their small town. She is frustrated, doesn't understand why son wants to leave. He always send her letters. Thanks to his absence she found a new mate.

[NDA-active NDC-indulge DSA-free NDB-thwart FD-empathyFA-distant FA-love]

(Vhf 45) He is telling her he is leaving to study or for another reason. She is sad, touched by news. He has already made a decision. He leaves. She is alone. He does not like leaving mother alone, but has to rise in the world, to study. Mother doesn't understand. She is feeling bad, doesn't want to be by herself. Her son leaves, studies, graduates. Mother finally understands (comes back).

[AA-status FB-split FD-autonomy CA-able FA-empathy]

(Vhm 57) He is discussing, having argument with his mother. He wants to go abroad for studying. His mother doesn't agree. She protects him and doesn't want to have him far away. He is angry and he tells her that he wants to do something different and live alone. His father died. It cost very much to convince but she agrees finally. She is very sad at the beginning, but she knows that it is the best for his son.

[HC-discord AA-self NDC-indulge FB-apart FD-death KA-resign]

Only one other higher status Venezuelan saw a direct issue of autonomy, which was depicted more as an unsuccessful revolt.

(Vhm 63) He came back from a trip and is talking with mother. Being relatively young, 16 or 17 years old, he wanted to travel around the world but mother forbade him to go. He left home and after some time came back, when he felt nostalgic, and reconciled with mother. Later on, mother dies, she might be very old, and he thinks it is his fault, that he should not have gone and should have stayed because his mother needed him more.

[DSC-family DDA-family PA-curious FA-mend KD-death NDC-desert RB-guilt]

The higher status Venezuelan males in 50 percent of their stories were depicted in a subordinate relationship to their mothers, both in positive and negative ways.

Two saw improper pressure on the part of a mother.

(Vhm 46) A woman *complaining* or angry about something. He lowers his head, listening all that she says wondering if his mother is right or wrong, but the fact is that he *has* to listen to her, even if she is wrong.

[DDA-scold DSB-advice]

(Vhm 65) High class family. He is pressured without choice to go to a university but he failed graduation. Mother is more conventional, concerned about opinions and family status, and possible ridicule. Therefore he is uninterested in school. But now he is thinking he is doing harm to his mother and family.

[CD-fail DSC-resist EDA-status CC-failure ESB-shame RC-result RB-guilt]

Wrongdoing requires apology.

(Vhm 52) His mother said something that struck the man's conscience. He is *remorseful* about what he said before, came to to ask for *forgiveness*. The women tells him that it does not matter, and he will go to sleep.

[RC-improper RB-regret DDA-pardon]

(Vhm 56) She was very depressed and *disappointed* in him. He is repentful and depressed. ??? Why did I do that? (He fought with his brother), repentful, she is going to *forgive* him.

[ESC-lessen RC-improper RB-regret HC-discord DDA-pardon]

Incompetence requires help.

(Vhm 64) It's hard for her to tell her son something that leaves him thinking on what he is going to do. I imagine that they solved problem. *He is needing to receive a lot of support from her* in order to face and overcome the problem.

[DDB-waver FB-thwart CB-help NSB-help]

Higher status females, in their thirteen responses, saw only two authority situations illustrated above: in one there is wrongdoing, in the other the mother is simply giving good advice.

The lower status males in three stories of twelve stories also saw unresolved problems of asserting autonomy against the wishes of the mother in respect to career or marriage. In one story, as in some American lower class stories, interest in sports is greater than in learning an occupation.

(Vlm 13) The woman wanted that he studies medicine and he says no, that he wants sports. He does not know anymore what to do with his mother. That makes him feel guilty and bad, because she is very disappointed in him, but he will do what he wants.

[DDA-educate DSC-family PA-play RB-guilt ESC-lessen DSA-assert]

In two stories, marriage choice leads to discord and dissension that is not easily resolved. Marriage related to status is of conscious concern among the Venezuelans.

(Vlm 24) A man who talks to his mother. He announces to her that he is going to marry and she feels bad with the news, because she thinks that he didn't choose well his wife. She doesn't support him because she wanted him to marry with another woman. They will solve those differences, but in the future. Right now it will not be possible.

[FA-love DDC-press HC-discord EDD-withhold DSA-assert FA-mend]

(Vlm 15) A mother complains. He didn't obey her by marrying at an early age, but he searched for his happiness with the women that is his wife today. She wanted him to marry with a professional like himself, but she didn't have that dream accomplished. He wanted to make his own life, and they were discordant for a long time. He is asking for forgiveness. The woman complies. She tells him that she always wanted him to be happy and so now she stays calm.

[DDA-scold FA-love EDD-withhold DSA-free HC-discord HA-forgive]

The lower status females were most negative in how they depicted the son's behavior. In seven of their total of twelve stories (58 percent) the young man is either inept or wrongdoing (six instances) or unsuccessful in seeking autonomy.

(Vlf 19) The mother's face suggests a problem, not a grave one. She is indignant. He's guilty. He was a useful man and she was proud; now there is no father . He presently did something that she is *complaining* about [poor judgment], but without violence. There will be a positive future. An understanding woman and he loves her. No problems anymore. He tells her he will never do hurt to her.

[DDA-scold RB-omission CC-failure EDB-lessen FA-empathy HC-discord]

These are themes of a son needing help, possible incompetence, or wrongdoing in which the mother is depicted as giving emotional as well as instrumental support. A son is someone who depends on his mother to solve the problems. She has the capacity that he lacks. Some of the stories of forgiveness are more related to ineptitude or incompetence than to irresponsibility as such. The important suggestion here is the *lack of confidence in themselves* in the instrumental sphere.

(Vlf 10) The young man has a problem, he is *feeling bad* . . . he goes to his mother who supports him and gives him advice, but he still feels bad. but eventually with her *help*, he will experience no more difficulties.

[CB-help RB-omit RB-regret DSB-advice CA-future]

This story is very useful in defining a condition of wrongdoing in the culture. The son did not make any transgression, but failed in terms of his competence. The condition for getting mother's love is not, as for the Venezuelans, being close or remaining dependent, but being competent or successful instrumentally. This would be a story of instrumentalized nurturance.

(Vlf 1) *Scolding* her son. He is repentant asking for *forgiveness*. He is old enough to have to know what is good and bad. She is not going to be after him all his life, telling him do this, don't do that. They will talk and solve the problem. (Son was an entrepreneur who bought some things seen as a business solution but she sees that as a poor judgment problem.)

[DDA-scold RB-omit CC-failure DSA-forgive RA-apology MT-task]

Seeking autonomy can lead to negative consequences. There is one story of successful autonomy achieved by a young man who opposes a mother's concern with social position in a marriage choice. He prevails, but the teller suggests unresolved guilt by having the new wife die at the end.

(Vlf14) This is a fellow that was studying in the military academy. He graduates with honors and come back home. Tells his mother how happy he is, and mother was also happy until he tells her that he is going to marry. His mother asks if she has a social position, if she has money. He says that no but that it doesn't matter to him. She gets angry and says that she is not going to let that wedding happen, that they have a social position to respect. He says no. At the end mother accept and he marries and well . . . they live happy until the muchacha dies. [hidden guilt]

[AA-self CA-present PA-joy EDC-status HC-discord DSA-free KD-death]

In another story a mother finally recognizes times have changed in respect to parental authority.

(Vlf 9) A (señora) talking to her son. He is angry because women of her age don't understand that the world has changed. . . . And she believes that he should behave as in her times, that he could tell her when he is coming late, because this day he came late. [Future?] She is going to understand that he is an adult and he can do it. She will feel calm and happy.

[DDC-rigid HC-discord DSC-disobey DSA-free FA-mend]

Canadians

Contrasted to previous Japanese, Korean, or American samples, instrumental aspirations were of relatively minor concern among this present sample of college-going Canadians. There are only two stories that include a very strong instrumental theme depicting horizontal relationships. Only in one Canadian male story is there successful separation for instrumental purposes. The resolute independence of an older person is emphasized as well as the achievement of a grandson.

(Cm 44) It's a sunny day. This is a grandson and his grandmother. They are in his room in the house, and the grandson is leaving for a job in another country. He's a very well educated man, probably a doctor. His grandma is also very intelligent and wise, and although upset about him leaving, she has a great sense of pride about him leaving. His parents were divorced, it was her son and she longs for having a family together again. And he, the grandson, understand this and will hopefully return one day with his own family. She is a very strong woman and will wait for him.

[AA-self CA-present EDA-praise FB-longing FB-wait CA endure]

The grandson is described as very competent; the grandmother is also described as very able, in terms of her virtue of endurance. On the other hand it is very centered in what is happening inside the selves; it is more self-oriented than relational. Even in such a positive story, there is an affiliative failure mentioned in the background; the parents got divorced.

In another positive story given by a female student, a son appeals to get recognition for his marrying plans. Although there is an initial disagreement, they reach an agreement through discussion that gains the support of the mother. This story given by a female student is more interrelational than the previous one.

(Cf27) This is mother and son. The mother is worried, concerned about a situation that the son is discussing with her. The son is frustrated, but I sense there is a strong bond between them. He is appealing to her to get recognition for a future plan, is something he wants her support for. I have a feeling he has a girl friend, wants to get married and the mother is concerned about his decision, concerned about his well being. The possible outcome would be that they resolve the conflict. The mother, through discussion will understand her son's point of view and they will reach an agreement.

[FB-thwart FA-love ESB-accept NSB-bless FA-empathy]

A very important aspect of these stories, the only two positive ones on this theme, is that they are clearly horizontal. The following also horizontal in tone, has irony to hide the necessary hurt inflicted.

(CfF 35) Looks like Perry Mason. His parents died so his grandmother raised him. He has come to tell her he is getting married, so he is leaving the farm. She is really upset because she will be left all alone once he is gone, but she will have her 50 million cats to keep her company. He is upset because he doesn't want to hurt her, but he wants to have his own life and his own family.

[KD-death NDA-active FB-apart FA-empathy RB-regret DSA-free]

The vertical stories of this type are unresolved or negative. Self-conscious concern with seeking autonomy appeared in three other stories. In two male stories, autonomy can end in injury or death.

(Cm 38) He leaves to go to war against his mother's wishes. He gets injured and has to go home. Both feel relieved. They are happy to see each other.

[DSA-assert KC-hurt-s FA-happen]

(Cm 7) Her son is working at this place to raise money to go to school or move out of town. He has not told his mom this. . . . Eventually, she finds out, the son was hinting to her. She is disappointed because she thought he would stay and help her out. She was dependent on him, but felt he needed his independence and to go on his own. She knew he wanted to move out and experience life. She becomes jealous of his new decision. She feels she will be isolated and won't cope with life anymore. So she tries to prove that his job now is good and that he knows this town and is familiar with this town. He says: But it's too familiar and he needs more friends and experiences. . . . She still can't believe in his decisions. Thinks he should at last stay for his mom, because he owes it to her for all she's done . . . he doesn't agree with his mom and goes off. The mom is depressed, feel there is no hope and no one to lean on, and she ignores attempts by other people to support her. So eventually she lives in isolation and dies of old age and malnourishment.

[AA-self FB-apart NSB-help FA-empathy FB-jealous FB-alone DDA-advice PA-curious RB-duty DSA-assert NSD-no-help PD-depress NSC-refuse KD-death]

The recurring thought in a number of their vertical stories is an expressive *evaluative* concern with disappointing the mother. In fact in some of these stories the evaluative concern outweighs the instrumental aspects of the story. In some instances Mother's instrument of control seems to be through a manipulation of self-esteem, a possible rejection of worth. She doesn't punish; her evaluation is her sanction. It is clear in this story of leaving home.

(Cf 41) This is a mother and a son. . . . The son has come to visit his mother after being gone a long time. The son is feeling nervous because he knows his mother disapproves of him. She is angry with him for leaving her and moving so far away. He will spend his visit trying to befriend his mom, and will end up leaving, feeling as he had disappointed her again.

[FB-close ESB-accept HB-resent HA-pacify ESC-lessen]

Again in the following, the mother is primarily seen as an inflexible authority figure.

(Cf 47) This is a mother and her son. He has said something to disappoint mother. When he goes to talk to his mother, she refuses to speak to him and stares out the window. He is quite hurt with her action, so he just holds his hat, staring at the floor. And he is trying to think of a way to make up for what he has done. But after many attempts at trying to talk to his mom, he finally gives up and leaves because his mother is so stubborn.

[ESC-disappoint FC-reject FD-reject HA-pacify DDC-rigid FD-retreat]

Within the Canadian group, disappointment, or individual or family shame appear in several of their stories.

(Cf 52) This mother is *disappointed* with her son for going out and buying an expensive car and not thinking about his family. She is letting him know how *disappointed* she is and that she didn't raise him to spend money so frivolously. He feels really guilty, so he takes the car back to make his mother happy.

[RC-waste ESC-lessen DDA-scold RB-guilt RA-reform]

> (Cf 17) He has hurt his mother. He is regretful for having been fired. She pulled a few strings to get him the job. He is very *ashamed*; not self-confident. He is like a little boy again. His mother has given up on him. He leaves. She is resigned: "Although he's my son, there is only so much we can do."
>
> [CC-loss RB-regret ESB-shame CB-able NDD-unable]

Evaluative concerns are found related to shameful family secrets.

> (Cm 72) An unknown half-brother is discovered at the father's funeral. He didn't always lives a *respectable* life. A very personal story.
>
> [ESB-expose]

> (Cf 9) He is having difficulty believing what his father may have done.
>
> [ESC-disgrace]

As in our other samples, Canadian males also saw stories of wrongdoing with some frequency (three of twenty-three or 13 percent).

> (Cm 64) A mother and son. Both are sad. He did something done wrong. She is rejecting him, turned away *ashamed*. He broke the law. Trying to please and help. Forged a check to give her money. She will eventually forgive him. He feels very hurt and wants her to accept him again. He will be relieved if she does that. She will, but in her deathbed.
>
> [PD-sad RC-illicit FC-reject ESB-shame NDB-goods NSA-forgive FB-split]

> (Cm 29) Remorseful, his grandmother is offended. He is ashamed; the father of a child. She's disappointed. He's trying to apologize. She is not willing to listen or understand. For now she cannot accept apology. Caring for him she will eventually will see it wasn't such a big problem. He will be very guilty for a while. *She's stubborn*, will take a while.
>
> [RB-regret RC-ex-sex ESC-lessen RB-guilt RA-apology DDB-rigid]

In stories of wrongdoing a mother's forgiveness is important because is restores closeness. Confession can be an important part of it.

> (Cf 12) A mother concerned with her son. He seems to be confessing her something, and mother is astonished. She cannot even speak. She is very tense. He is a little far out, far from reality, only remembering his past. I believe his mother will embrace him and forgive him. He felt the need to tell something to his mother. He is afraid to face her.
>
> [RA-apology PD-shock PB-trouble DDA-pardon]

In contrast, for Venezuelans the mother can be a benevolent, forgiving figure; the son can count on her siding on his behalf. Her function is also to alleviate his sense of guilt as well as deal with a sense of shame.

(Vlf 19) You can see at mother's face that there is a problem, even if not a grave one. She is indignant and he feels guilty. In the past he was a good man (hombre de provecho—a useful man) and she was proud of him; looks like he has no father (le faltara lack of). At the present time, he did something that she is complaining about, but without vehemence, in the future you can see that she is an understanding woman and he loves her. They will not have problems anymore, and he will tell her that he will never do anything that could hurt her.

[DDA-scold RB-guilty EDA-praise FA-empathy FB-aware]

All in all, separation is a less frequent theme on Card 6BM for Canadian students (see below).

Mother as Dependent: Expressive Concerns with Nurture

A secondary theme appearing in 6 percent of the vertical stories of the present samples are themes that center on a mother needing care. It is the reversal of seeing the mother in an authority or nurturing role with a son. This theme also appears as a subsidiary concern is a few of the stories of a death in the family as we will illustrate below. It appears in three Canadian stories, but is absent or shows a single occurrence in the other groups.

It appears to be more important among the lower status Brazilians. A mother needing care appears in four of twenty-two (18 percent) of Portuguese and four of twenty-six (16 percent) of the Afro-Brazilian samples. This appearance suggests an underlying concern in the Favela with threats to health, especially as they may affect money needs and dependent emotional ties. Illness of a mother would necessitate a stressful rearrangement of caregiving functions.

One sees money questions.

(BPm 8) A boy who liked his grandmother very much, but no money. He earned not enough to give her what she wanted. He found an opportunity of a better job; got it. He was then able to give his grandmother everything she wanted.

[NDB-thwart AA-nurture NDA-goods]

One sees money questions and possible separation.

(Pf 7) A son without money. He has to pay the rent and bills. He is in big trouble: He wonders whether taking mother to a nursing home will be good or bad. He can't give her a better life. He has to work, he doesn't earn enough for himself. Will it be good to take mother to that home? She is afraid that he will leave her and will never more go to see her.

[NSD-goods NDB-thwart FB-apart]

There are problems of care related to illness.

(BPm 6) A ten-year-old boy had to go out of the State in order to play soccer. But he didn't want to leave his sick mother alone. Then he told his soccer mates to find another player.

[RA-o-duty NDA-family]

(ABm 26) A son who liked his mother who was sick very much. He was very sad because of her sickness and decided to stay home and stop working for a while to take care of her until she gets better. He used to clean the house, to cook for her and to give the right medicines. He liked her very much, that is why he quit his job to take care of her.

[FA-love NDA-devote]

(Mxf 36) It is a man whose grandmother is already very aged. He is worried because she is very ill. He doesn't know what to do, for she doesn't want to undergo any treatment. She says she doesn't like to take medical advice.

[KB-illness NSC-refuse]

There may appear a nurturant need to take care of those not even in the family.

(Mxf35) A man who has found an aged lady who had nobody to count on. He took her to his home, bathed her and introduced his family to her. Everybody liked her, and they decided to keep her with them.

[NDA-charity]

There are also conflicting motives about care. The nursing home is a possible way out.

(PABf21) An old woman lived with younger son. But her son wanted to take her to a nursing home, because he had no freedom to go out. There was nobody to stay with her. He said terrible things to her, insulted her. His mother was very sad about being taken to a nursing home, but she was resigned, for she had always lived with her son. Now time has passed. He wants to put her there. This is one more story of many aged people who get into trouble when living in the same house with children.

[HC-discord DSA-free HC-cruel EDC-insolent KA-resign NDC-desert]

To be noted in a few of these stories, as in the above one from Brazil, is the appearance of placement in a nursing home or senior residence as a possibility of what to do with the helpless elderly. This is a newer theme not found in previous samples from the 1950s or the 1960s. It is a recent theme appearing notably in some nurture stories, among this Canadian sample. Stories depict the long-term possibility that a son must face that care of an aging mother may involve placing her away in a nursing home or senior residence.

(Cf 58) He brought his mother to a nursing home. She has Alzheimers. Although he loves her, he just doesn't have the abilities to care for her properly. The decision

> was a long process. He loves mother so much. He wishes there were some way, but no. With time she meets friends and fits into the nursing home. Her son visits regularly. Everything works out.
>
> [KB-illness FA-love NDD-unable CA-endure FA-distant]

The Canadian mother can still be placed in her own home. this differs from the Latin American samples where care can be in the home of the son.

> (Cf 61) Mo told him that she's sick. He's quite concerned, she is worried too. He doesn't know what will happen. spend time talking will get advice from a doctor. Make a decision about treatment she will get. *Then he will take her to her house to look after her.*
>
> [KB-illness CB-worry NSB-help NDA-active]

Horizontal Relationships: Themes of Affiliation or Discord

Although the proportions vary, as we have been indicating, expressive concerns centering on reactions to a fateful events or issues of affiliation or nurture comprise over 50 percent of the stories in our groups. Only two of our samples are below 55 percent: the older Japanese (33 percent) and the lower status Venezuelans (42 percent). Depictions of reactions to a fateful event, frequently the death of a father, comprise close to 25 percent of all stories. Themes of possible separation and some themes of discord make up the majority of the remainder. While such stories are found across all groups, the nuances depicted show some notable differences.

Canadians

In the Canadian responses to Card 6BM, the most singular feature found uniquely in a variety of expressive contexts illustrated is how, presently, both male and female students focused so explicitly on the inability of a young man to communicate, or to gain satisfactory affiliative closeness with a maternal figure. There is, normatively, a sense of isolation, emotional alienation or an inability to express emotions openly.

Canadians of both sexes react to a fateful event such as a death with a concern about an inability to communicate one's feelings in fourteen (31 percent) of their stories. Additionally, an inability to be close is depicted in another three stories. Such ethnic nuances about lack of closeness appear also as a minor theme in other stories as well. In all, Negative Affiliation themes, mostly regarding mother-son relationship or a mother's isolation, are strikingly frequent (twenty stories).

In the context of a reaction to death, mutual sorrow does not easily lead to any affiliative coming together. Additionally, the older woman is depicted, as in no other group, needing to maintain self reliance or to endure alone. This theme appears in 10 percent of Canadian stories. In contrast to the Canadians, all the other samples in their expressive stories are more positively concerned in depicting emotional consequences and an anticipated dependency on the part of a mother.

Canadian stories of negative affiliation illustrate a son wants some closeness but doesn't know how to reach his mourning mother.

> (Cm 85) Son has come home because his father is dying. He doesn't know his mother very well and he feels he should be doing something to comfort her, but doesn't know how. . . . Her son knows she is upset but doesn't really understand how big a part his father was. He is also upset about his father's condition, but mostly he's concerned about his mother. Looks like she is going to fall apart once her husband dies. Son knows that, but feels there is nothing he can do. In this scene he wants to comfort her, hugs her, but feels out of place, as if he doesn't know her anymore. He will leave without doing anything for his mother. Before he leaves he'll quietly, and almost apologetically, say that he will be back tomorrow.
>
> [KD-ill-die FB-distant NDD-comfort FD-empathy NDB-welfare]

In this case, as in some other stories where the son doesn't know how to reach the mourning mother, there is also expressed a concern with proper behavior: the son *should* be able to console his mother. The following subject again refers very explicitly to a painful inability to express affect.

> (Cm 84) Mother is elderly and has a terminal illness like cancer. Obviously he is upset and grief and that sort of thing. He has never been an emotional kind of guy; maybe he is but doesn't show. . . . He didn't show many emotions. He worries about what people will think when she dies. That he might not care. This is a major problem for his whole life. His father was the same and he will pass it on to his kids. Maybe when on his deathbed he will at least understand why his children will not seem too upset.
>
> [KD-ill-die PD-sad FB-shy NDD-comfort ESB-appear KD-defect]

A distinctive note in some stories is the isolation, alienation, and emotional distance between mother and son, or from deceased father and/or husband.

> (Cm 83) Looks like someone died. The dad died. The mother and son are mourning. The funeral just ended. They aren't very close and not talking about it. They both want to get on, do their own thing. They both feel alone. That's about it. Not much exciting happening in this picture.
>
> [KD-death PD-sad FB-distant FB-alone]

> (Cm 80) A man and his mother. They have visions in completely different directions about their lives. She's despairing, and he doesn't know why. There is much space between them. They are not connecting. The scene ends without any emotional interaction that has substance. They'll shake hands when he leaves and

then continue on in the same mind set as before. Both are unwilling to give a little bit to break the detachment.

[PD-depress FB-empathy FB-distant FC-flee]

(Cf 6) When her husband died, it wasn't grief she felt, but resignation. She was to be alone and now everybody would know it, which was the only difference from the way it was before. Because she had always felt mentally and psychologically alone. Now she was physically alone too. The boy, now a man, was surprised and sad because he could no longer remember his father's face and yet he had seen it nearly every day all of his life until a few days ago, when he passed away. He was sad, not for the loss of a person close to him, but rather for the absence of that feeling of loss. He was confused.

[KD-resign FB-alone FD-affect PD-sad PB-trouble]

The following black humor story also reveals alienation and affective distance.

(Cf 46) I am sorry Mrs. Collins, your husband was eaten by an alligator. All that we could find was his leg and his band with his wedding band on. . . . "Oh well," said Mrs. Collins: "Jed always did love the swamp." And then she picked up and moved to Burnaby Hills with her son Lawrence.

[KD-death KA-accept]

In one story the son attempts to overcome distance in order to console or support a mother aware of loneliness.

(Cm 87) She wants his companionship. She is feeling lonely. . . . He wishes she would be able to just enjoy his visit and it's difficult for him to understand that. They were not that close before and she wants to make amends. He tries to understand her and he does care a lot for her. He's about to get married and eventually the mother will move in with him and his wife and it will work out well and he will be pleased to alleviate her loneliness.

[FB-longing FB-empathy FC-flee FA-mend FA-empathy]

Two subjects describe the son as not only alienated, but angry in the mourning situation, a very unusual feeling in reaction to this card. What can be depicted is a need to cope internally with one's emotions without interaction. In a number of the stories distance is symbolically represented by not making a mother son story, but one involving a more distant relative or an in-law.

(Cf 26) It is not a sure relationship between two. Bad news. It is an aunt, not a mother and a son because they don't look close enough. She is trying to deal with the situation by staring out, getting peace from scenery. He doesn't know what to do . . . yet he is still being respectful. He is also deeply hurt by news of the death. She leans on a chair and stares out. He will go for long walk. He has aggression and energy inside that has to get out.

[KD-death FB-distant PA-relief FB-aware PB-anger PA-relief]

(Cf 1) He is mourning the loss of his father. The wife is in denial, the son is more angry. A rocky relationship in the past but a turning point. For a short term conclusion, there is no change. If I were to be positive: in the long run they will become closer, not farther apart.

[KD-death PD-sad PB-denial PB-anger HB-split FA-mend]

Regarding defenses to the affective impact of the stimulus, some subjects, as in the above, refer directly to denial or lack of emotional expression. Above all they remain isolated.

(Cm 73) A mother and son. Somebody has died. A son-in-law comes to console. She is looking out, remembering her husband. He doesn't know really what to say. They might talk about the person over a cup of tea. He's sad and she's still in shock. She carries on the best she can. It is a sort of denial.

[KD-death NDA-comfort FB-distant PD-sad PB-denial]

(Cf 36) Both are in shock. Bad news. Mother and son. She told him the bad news. The father has died. They are in shock, staring into space. They can't believe it. They are not comforting each other. Each is in own world. He is thinking how to reach out. Should I touch her or hug her? She's spaced out. He turns away and leaves.

[KD-death PD-shock FB-distant FB-aware NDD-comfort]

(Cf 43) A man and his mother. Her husband has just passed away, and the son doesn't know how to comfort mother. She stares out thinking of her husband. There is no emotional embrace between mother and son. They just quietly think of their father/husband, each alone.

[KD-death NDD-comfort FB-distant]

(Cm 88) He would like to comfort. There is a strong emotional attachment. He is simply unable to express himself. There is an emotional gap. Uncle passes away. The nephew still cannot reach aunt and he leaves. She will deal with grief on her own.

[KD-death NDD-comfort FA-love FB-distant PA-endure]

Among these stories of alienation, distance and difficulty of affective expression could be included in the following wherein the need to cope independently is emphasized. Lack of any close relationship is again stressed. The story becomes more instrumental, as the older woman is described positively, as a stoic "tough lady" that will carry on alone busying herself with activities.

(Cm 39) He's come to tell her news. They are not related. He feels pain and confused. She's been expecting him. Just a matter of time. He told her that her husband passed away. She was prepared for it. She is sad but she will carry on with everything. She's keeping her grief inside. She's a tough lady. She knew she was going to lose him and has already accepted it. She'll never get over loss, but it will get easier. And she will keep herself busy.

[KD-death FB-aware PD-sad PA-endure KA-accept CA-endure]

In another story of this type, the normative expectation of mother solving the situation by herself is also described, even though there is a more salient concern for her solitude.

(Cm 65) Her husband had just died. The fellow has just brought the news. She turns away in shock and disbelief. The man feels sorry. He knew the couple. He's an acquaintance. It's very hard for him to tell her. She will break into tears and eventually he will put his arms around her. He offers to stay but she says no. She needs time to herself. To think. She probably knew it was coming. She feels a bit of guilt, wondering if she could have done anything to stop it. She also worries about her future and being alone.

[KD-death PD-shock FB-aware NDB-pity NSA-s-help RB-guilt FB-alone]

Some of the stories of interpersonal alienation and emotional distance may illustrate extreme individual adaptations to the Anglo-American socialization patterns of separation and independence training. Self-reliance, self-sufficiency, and self-control are virtues to be cultivated. Undue dependency is to be avoided. The above stories describe disconnected people, some of them taking this for granted, some of them concerned with being more connected.[1]

Venezuelans

In contrast to the Canadians, in seven (15 percent) of their stories, the Venezuelan samples (as is true for the Brazilians) react to a fateful happening with more feeling of pity or nurture (five of seven are female). There is no mention of any distance in relating emotionally.

---

[1]In this context, see the following quotations from McGoldrick (1989):

First, in regard to the intervention of choice for the unattached-young-adult phase of the life cycle: "In a WASP family, the need will be to reconnect, since disengagement has usually already occurred to a great extent and relationships may have already become superficial and ritualized."

Regarding ethnicity and death: "WASPs have tended to value a handling of death that involves 'no mess, no fuss,' a rational handling of the experience, with minimal expressions of feeling, carried out in the most pragmatic, practical way." As one friend put it when explaining why he had not attended the funeral of his twin sister, "What would have been the point of spending the money to go? She was already dead."

(Vlf 21) News is given to a mother of death by accident. He is concerned for her. It is difficult to face the situation and give hope to this mother. She feels depressed, tears, that pain that is carried inside when someone loved dies.

[KD-death NDB-pity NDB-unable PD-sad]

(Vhf 58) Something has happened before. A grandmother. He came to tell her his work problems; he is finished with his sweetheart or crashed the car or someone died in the family. She has a face of *susto*, in shock. He feels sorry to have to tell her. She needs time to recover. He will do anything to help. Someone very close died.

[FC-split KD-death PD-shock NDA-active]

(Vhf 61) Two people preoccupied about someone they have in common, a woman I suppose, that is sick. it is grave. and the women is thinking that it is not possible, that something like that happened to her. And he also preoccupied on how it is going to finish. that she would die soon, They both think on the way to help her so that she doesn't suffer and she is suffering (could be his sweetheart and her daughter).

[KD ill-die MTA-task NDA-comfort PD-suffer]

(Vhf 54) Mother and son, sad, death of sick husband and father. He consoles his mother. She is going to live with her children and take care of grandchildren. So times goes by and then she dies.

[KD-ill-die NDA-comfort NDA-family KD-death]

Others consider affiliative needs.

(Vhf 49) Something happened before. Bad news. Cannot believe what happened. They will embrace after that (they learned something; they lost money in the bank or a relative died).

[KD-loss PD-shock FA-share]

(Vlm 4) I see sadness in both personages. Maybe it is the death of a relative. The women is asking God peace for her relative who died. He looks at the body of a man, maybe his father, and remembers happy memories. He knows that he has to be resigned. She also remembers how both saw their children growing up, and that he is now better that he is with God. They both go ahead with a positive mind.

[KD-death PD-sad NSA-pray PA-memory KA-accept NSA-god KB-hope]

Afro-Brazilian and Portuguese

The news of death stories among the Brazilian samples are varied and unexceptional.

(ABf 34) He is sad about his wife's death. Neither he nor his mother knew how to tell his children the truth. Very nervous, he asked his mother for advice. mother, also nervous, was standing near window asked him to calm down and to keep cool: "When your children arrive we will tell them."

[KD-death FD-fate PB-trouble NSA advice NDA-teach]

(ABf33) This is a very aged lady. She has a son. Both are sad. He is her grandson. They are sad because they have lost her husband and his grandfather.

[KD-death FD-fate PD-sad]

(Pm 63) Jonathan's father had a car accident, and he took him to a doctor. After hours he came to tell his mother that his father had died. His mother said that he had been a good man. Life will go on the same, but there will be always something missing in order to complete them.

[KD-ac-die KA-endure PA-endure FB-alone]

Separation Themes

Card 6BM can evoke themes of parting or reunion as central to the story. We have already illustrated above some separation that occurs in contexts of a youth seeking achievement, independence, or autonomy. It's interesting to notice that in the four negative or unresolved separation stories given by Canadians, mother is upset with son's leaving (see above). He is not supported by her in his wishes to be independent, but the son seems to take for granted that he is exercising his rights. These mothers probably are not functioning according to the cultural normative expectations and are described negatively. Even in the most negative autonomy story—"mother dies of malnourishment because son went off"—the subject describes that mother "felt he needed his independence and to go on his own." The issue here is not so much presented as instrumental autonomy, but as the desire of the son to not have his mother depending on him. Also differently from two Venezuelan stories of a mother dying because of separation, there is a more affective distance in this story, where mother's dependent behavior is somehow described as somehow inappropriate.

There are other circumstances in which separation occurs, either due to outer necessity or inner discord. Such stories are scattered throughout the groups we are considering. The stories of discord we shall presently consider tend to show greater ethnic differences than a theme of necessary parting found in all the groups. Nevertheless, the higher status Venezuelans are most conscious of the necessity to have children leave home, possibly to travel to another country for educational purposes. It is a frequent occurrence in their society (see stories Vhf45, Vhf53, Vhf57, Vhm50 above).

Separation can be painful. There is strong affect expressed.

(Vhf62) He has to leave and both are sad. She is consoling him. The son has to go because the decision has already been made, but doesn't want to. At the end, I think they are going to embrace each other and they will understand that the trip is necessary.

[FB-apart PD-sad NDA-comfort FA-love KA-accept]

(Vhf 68) Son has to leave home because he found work not where he wanted but far from his natal city. Quite old mother is inconsolable. There are always news that inflicts pain. She is widowed, he is now fatherless. It was impossible for him to take mother with him or stay in touch frequently. Mother dies from sadness some months later. He knows the great pain that he is inflicting on her, but he thinks that mother has to understand that he has to leave.

[FB-wait KD-death NSD-sustain NDD-unable FB-aware]

The Venezuelans recognize the mother's need for nurture and affiliation as legitimate abiding concerns. There may be disagreements or complaints of not being understood by the mother, but none of them question the legitimacy of her demands or suggest efforts for an older person to become independent as in the Canadian stories.

The Japanese stories, similar to the Venezuelans, recognize necessity and the sadness faced by the mother. Moreover, a few stories suggest that a son must express his regret and ask for permission to leave.

(Jmy 1x) He is saying he is sorry he has to leave. She cared for him during his life and has been living with her. The mother is looking out the window.

[FB-apart NDA-nurture]

(Jmy 17) A son is asking mother because he will have to leave home and can't continue living with her. She is very sad because of the expression on her face. She does not like to understand.

[FB-apart DSA-permit PD-sad FB-split]

The few Italian and German separation stories manifest somewhat less affective concern.

(Im 2) The son is preparing to travel about, and the mother looks out of the window to see if the bus arrives. He used to help his mother before. He travels afterwards.

[FB-apart NDA-active PA-curious]

(Gm 3) He is obliged to travel. He will live away. He will be obliged to leave his grandma living alone. He lived with her before. Now he is going to travel. She will stay alone. There's nothing to do.

[KD-thwart RA-duty-o FD-fate]

There are some similar stories among Favela Brazilians.

(ABm 65) The boy told his grandmother that he was moving to another place. His grandmother was shocked and he, sort of pitying her, tried to convince her that everything would work out. His grandmother became calmer, but she was still sad because of her grandson's journey.

[FC-split PD-shock DDA-advice PD-sad]

Some Favela Portuguese and Afro-Brazilian stories depict negative attitudes or escape from a negative family situation.

(BPm 57) Dinora's son disappears from home without leaving any message. She and her husband Oscar remain nervously at the window, with some hope that Ricardo would come back. After some time passed, their hope vanished and they never saw their son again.

[FC-selfish FB-wait FD-split]

(BABm 70) A son and his mother. The son was already desperate because of the things his mother did; he wanted to leave but couldn't because he had lost his job. He decided to look for another job and got some money in order to buy a ticket. He managed to buy it and left.

[RC-wrong FC-flee KD-poor CA-able]

Themes of Discord

Direct dissension or discord as central to a story appears relatively infrequently on Card 6BM compared to previously discussed categories. In the present samples such stories appear in more than 10 percent of the records in four groups: Portuguese, three in twenty-two (14 percent); Venezuelan, five in forty-nine (10 percent); Japanese seven in fifty (14 percent). More specifically as to sex, two of twelve ethnic German males; three of twelve lower status Venezuelan men; three of twelve younger Japanese women; and two of twelve higher status Venezuelan women see conflict as a theme. The Canadians produced no confrontational stories.

Japanese themes of discord directly refer to generational conflict in a detached way.

(Jfy 9) This is the *obasan* (lady/aunt) and a grandson. There is a fight going on. The youth said something to the obasan and she is with a sad face or there is something sad going on. Someone has died.

[HC-discord PD-sad KD-death]

(Jmy 16) A conflict of generations. The older person has a different way of thinking—a different way of living. Each generation has different behaviors and modes . . . both are having difficulties uniting/connecting. One does not know who is right and who is wrong in such situations.

[HC-discord HB-role FD-empathy]

(Jfy 18) Here is a mother and son in another conflict. They are discussing something, but the mother thinks in a way that the son does not agree with. Parents always have ideas that sons or daughters do not agree with.

[HC-discord HB-role]

(Jms 62) The son is with his mother and they are talking to each other. But their way of thinking is different and they do not agree.

[HC-discord HB-role FD-empathy]

The varied Venezuelan conflict themes focus on sources of internal family conflict not so related to a change in generation. (In some, marriage choice is an issue, see Vlm24 above.)

(Vhf 67) He is already married, lives in other city. He came to visit his mother because he didn't see her for a long time. He is trying to talk but she remains angry. Later on they are going to get along (Woman was angry because he had almost forgotten her.)

[FC-neglect HB-resent HA-pacify FA-mend]

(Vlm 22) There was a discussion or surprise for he did something unexpected. The present is uncertain. There is confusion and even pain by the impression the man gives, by his hand, holding the hat. There may be also anger, and there could be an uncertain future between them, it is for the women to clarify and normalize the situation.

[PB-surprise PB-trouble HC-discord HB-role]

(Vlm 20) I see the two persons thinking about things that happened previously. I think they had problems between them, but afterward there would be a solution about what they think.

[HC-discord HA-mend]

(Vhf 55) Grandson and grandmother are afraid that his mother will not return because of some discordant problems they had. [Future?] They get to find her, but she will not come back. She stays living there.

[HC-discord FD-split]

The Brazilian groups depict a variety of domestic issues. Two of the three Portuguese stories depicts attitudes taken by patriarchal or exploitative males. The mother is seen wanting respect.

(BPf 1) He is tormented by his mother's leaving from his father's house. He didn't know reason, so asked the cook, about it. She answered parents' marriage wasn't very well. Then he left home and looked for his mother. He explained there would be a party for both her and her husband, and that she should accept the rules of his father. She accepted under the condition that he should treat her as a wife, not as a stranger.

[FC-apart HC-discord DSA-Family HB-role FA-mend]

> (BPm 5) A boss, a very bad man, had a very good maid. Once asked to bring coffee, but coffee warmed over . . . boss threw it on her face. She was so kind remained still. He swore badly at her and sent her away. The maid no place to go, no clothes. The boss then felt sorry for her, called her to the living room and said: "Never more over-warmed coffee, for I only drink fresh-made coffee." The maid was very happy and everything remained at peace.
>
> [DDC-exploit HC-injury PC-cruel HA-devote NSB-goods NDB-pity HC-pacify]

In one German story family quarrels are a reason for leaving home. In another, a quarrel is followed by proper apology.

> (BGm 14) A son telling his mother a sad story, and she became sad too. the mother is looking out of the window, and he looks to the ground as he tells story. The son tells the story that he wants to leave. He can't stay home any longer. And he leaves indeed, he is so determined. He leaves because of family quarrels.
>
> [PD-sad FD-split HC-discord]

> (BGm 22) It is a couple, having an argument. The man was guilty. He went there and apologized to the woman. They stayed at peace and happy.
>
> [HC-discord RC-wrong RA-apology HA-mend]

Even in this relatively small number of stories of discord it is possible to recognize some ethnic differences in content and nuance. Only the Japanese use a story of discord to didactically express a problem of change between generations. The Portuguese indirectly depict underlying social issues related to male behavior within families related to the exploitative treatment of women. The Canadians give no stories of direct confrontation. As noted above, they stress a lack of easy communication rather than depicting any scenes of direct confrontation.

Conclusion

The above illustrations should amply demonstrate the relative emphases in the interpersonal concerns of small samples of male and female stories of Canadian college students, Venezuelan youth from two different social class strata, Brazilian high school youth from different socioeconomic and ethnic groups and age differences in Japanese Brazilians. Comparing samples of age, sex, class, ethnicity, and minority status cross-nationally on the TAT should demonstrate the validity of cross cultural comparisons of the TAT even by using a single card, 6BM of the Murray set. Reading these stories in organized clusters brings out differences in the lives experienced by individuals from different social settings.

The fact that in the scene presented the individuals are wearing clothes no longer found in the societies investigated does not prevent us from eliciting attitudes of a socially revealing nature. Some of these themes are found in each society we tested. For example, stories of reactions to bad news (usually someone's death) are universally present. Also found cross culturally are themes of separation and departure. They suggest certain human universals in social interaction and social perception. But what is most important is that they reveal manifest differences in salient normative emphasis between the groups considered. Nuances of interpersonal concern become apparent as related to the differing experiences encountered by individuals living within different social circumstances. These difference are also related to age and sex, as well as to national-cultural settings.

Though a card such as Murray 6BM appears to be limited in its period-specific clothes and racial appearance, the implied mother-adult son relationship is picked up by most individuals presented with the card. For example, the status position of a mother is seen to differ with age and cultural background. Problems of possible wrongdoing envisioned in the context of this relationship differ from group to group. For instance, repeated concerns with an inability to communicate are found singularly among Canadian students.

It is sometimes too facile to pursue only themes of specific interest to the investigator. Other contentions arise in narratives that are unanticipated by the investigator, but deserve attention. Without some objectifying notational system that forces consideration of all topics elicited, the possible complexity of human thought encountered could readily overwhelm those analyzing primary materials. The ICSS permits us to better differentiate systematically what is elicited. The categories and subcategories utilized forces us to attend to nuances of responses that could be neglected by a too direct recourse to interpretation arising out of preconceived hypotheses.

References

Caudill, William and De Vos, George. 1956. Achievement, Culture and Personality: The Case of the Japanese Americans. *American Anthropologist*, 58(6), 1102–1126.

Connor, John. 1977. *Tradition and Change in Three Generations of Japanese Americans*. Chicago: Nelson Hall.

De Vos, George A. 1973. *Socialization for Achievement: Essays on the Cultural Psychology of the Japanese*. Berkeley: University of California Press.

Henry, W.E. 1956. *The Analysis of Fantasy: The Thematic Apperception Technique in the Study of Personality*. New York: Wiley.

McGoldrick, Monica. 1989. Ethnicity and the Family Life Cycle. In Betty Carter and Monica McGoldrick (Eds.), *The Changing Family Life Cycle: A Framework for Family Therapy* (2nd edition). Boston: Allyn and Bacon.

Vaughn, Curtis. 1988. *Cognitive Independence, Social Independence and Achievement Orientation: A Comparison of Japanese and United States Students*. Dissertation. Dept. of Education, University of California at Berkeley.

Chapter 12

Living on the Amazon: Tukuna Indians and New Brazilian Settlers

Cicero Emidio Vaz[2]
George A. De Vos

As part of our collaborative research in Brazil comparing various ethnic groups we have also compared differences between a random sample of twenty-six Tukuna Indians and twenty-six Brazilian settlers who have migrated to the same vicinity of the Amazon River. Excerpts from this comparison illustrate how the TAT can be used on groups who lived in comparatively isolated native communities. The Murray TAT, a testing instrument with basically western culture dress and European facial features, can, nevertheless, elicit revealing salient interpersonal concerns in a native group that can be compared in instrumental and emotional content with groups from other cultures. Today, there is practically no place on earth so isolated that one is unable to obtain meaningful responses that characterize particular social groups.

The Tukuna people live on the border of the Javari River and High Solimbes, extending from the boundaries of Brazil, Peru, and Colombia to the town of Beruri in the state of Amazonas. They are considered to be one of the largest Brazilian Indian nations. The total Tukuna population comprises approximately 18,000

---

[2]Professor of the Pontifical Catholic University of Rio Grande do Sul (PUCRS), Brazil. Research Associate of the Institute of Personality Assessment (IPAR), 1989–1990, University of California at Berkeley.

inhabitants. They are distributed into sixty-nine small rural communities and also reside in the towns of Benjamin Constant, Tabatinga, Sao Paulo de Olivenga, Amatura, Santo Antonio do Iga, Tonantins, Jutal', and Beruri. Traveling through High Solimbes, besides the larger settlements, there are extensive rural areas with small nuclei of dwellings, some formed by the Tukuna, and others formed by non-Tukuna settlers from elsewhere in Brazil. There is practically no mixed social contact within the same neighboring dwelling sites. The dwellings located along the large river bank are predominantly non-Tukuna settlers, whereas the Tukuna live mostly along "igarapes," smaller streams, and within the forested areas.

Most of the larger Indian settlements visited had elementary schools. The teachers, ethnically Tukuna, had been trained by PUCRS, the Catholic university in which Vaz served on the Faculty of Psychology. During the psychological testing conducted by Vaz, when fourteen to seventeen-year-old teenagers were questioned, the following answer was frequent: "I don't know what to do after I finish elementary school." With a sad disenchanted look, some would say, "Neither do the others." They were referring to the teenagers from settler families living in their vicinity.

This TAT study was part of field research first carried out in 1988, which had as a basic goal to investigate to what extent the process of acculturation influences, if not so much the structure, at least the adaptive reactions of the indigenous Tukuna as they interact with Brazilian settlers from more technologically advanced areas in Brazil. The purpose was not ethnographic, but psychological in scope. The focus was on personality variables and on the psychological content of communication, not on cultural or behavioral data. A central concern was on the personality evaluation made possible by projective tests and by the direct observation of the behavior occurring in contact with a psychologist.

Vaz conducted his research project in two stages. The first step was the field research in the High Solimbes region of the state of Amazonas, carried out in November and December 1988 in the Tukuna and in settler communities. The groups were carefully matched. Both range from sixteen to sixty years of age. Both had some Catholic education. Vaz had the logistic support of the branch Campus of the Catholic University of Rio Grande do Sul (PUCRS), located in the nearby town of Benjamin Constant. The second stage, the study of the collected data, became part of a collaborative effort with De Vos at the Department of Anthropology of the University of California at Berkeley in 1989.

These samples were obtained prior to collaboration. As part of Vaz's 1988 field work, the Rorschach technique and Murray TAT Cards 1, 2, 3BM, 4, 6BM, 7BM, 8BM, and 13MF, were given to both the Tukuna and non-Tukuna male youth over seventeen years of age. Cards 1, 2, 3GF, 4, and 18GF were given to women. De Vos, in his work, has found it better to ignore the suggestion given in the Murray manual (followed by Vaz) to give some different cards to male and female subjects. Rather, for comparative purposes it is more useful to employ the same cards for all those tested regardless of age or sex.

In the present chapter we shall look only at the material obtained on Cards 1, 2, 3BM, 3GF, 4, 8BM, and 18GF. The material obtained on these seven cards is sufficient for the present purpose of illustrating how the TAT is a valid device to gain insight into the personal concerns of even relatively isolated groups with different cultural backgrounds.

Problems of anxiety were notably more frequent in the Tukuna sample than in the settlers. Although relative to other samples, neither group gave many stories concerning self-motivated achievement, the settlers overall showed more concerns with achievement than did the Tukuna. On all cards the Tukuna especially revealed an abiding fear about becoming victims of violence, hunger, and disease. Such concerns were not lacking in the settler group as well. Feelings of sorrow, sickness, death, anger, and problems encountered in sexual and love relationships were very similar for both groups, especially the women. Missionary activity was reflected in a number of the stories in each group. Overall, the Tukuna records were suggestive of a more passive attitudinal stance. Overall, the settlers are somewhat less pessimistic about their social relationships, but give evidence of concern about drunkenness and physical violence expressed within the family unit.

The Boy with the Violin on the Amazon

Contrary to those who doubt the ability to use the TAT cross culturally we had no difficulty in obtaining stories from Tukuna Indians that reflected their salient inner or interpersonal concerns.

Tukuna stories given to Card 1 are as directly interpretable as those obtained from samples elsewhere (De Vos, 1996; De Vos, Hauswald, and Borders, 1979; Helm, De Vos, and Carterette, 1960). They reveal, as does the material from other cards, that they experience a considerable sense of incapacity on an instrumental level. On an expressive level they reveal a prevailing concern with death, illness, and loneliness that intrudes even on this card. Such themes only appear very rarely in other groups (De Vos and Wagatsuma, 1959).

Themes of Achievement or Future Purpose

Themes about possible future achievement or concerns with competence are evoked by Card 1 among the youthful Tukuna Indians from eleven of twenty-six respondents and from thirteen of twenty-six of the children of settlers, but the distribution of positive and negative themes differ markedly. Among the Tukuna, there are only three that may be considered positive themes of capacity or achievement, while there are ten positive themes elicited from the settlers. The settlers' distribution of themes given to Card 1 do not differ significantly from what we obtained from the

Brazilian groups obtain in the more economically developed south (see chapter 8, volume II).

Table 12.1
Card 1—Boy with Violin: Tukuna and Settler Stories

	Tukuna		*Settlers*	
Total	*m 13*	*f 13*	*m 14*	*f 12*
Control-Authority	-	-	3	-
Achievement or Competence Concerns	7	4	6	7
Positive results	1	1	4	2
Capable	-	-	1	2
Thinking about the future	1	-	-	1
Uncertain about what to do	3	1	-	-
Incapable	2	3	1	2
Internal State	3	2	2	2
Positive pleasure	-	-	1	-
Tired	1	1	1	1
Hunger	1	-	-	1
Sorrow	1	1	-	-
Affiliative Concern	1	2	1	-
Positive	-	-	1	-
Negative	1	2	-	-
Entertaining Others	-	1	-	-
(Nurture)	-	1	-	-
Hostility	-	-	-	1
Concern with Objects	2	-	1	2
Illness or death	-	4	1	-

(TUK f 09) (age 17) Here is a boy. He is thinking. He wants to play bass viol. He's cheerful and likes to play cheerfully.

[PA-play AA-persist]

(TUK m 11) (19) This is an instrument. The person is thinking about the music. It (indefinite) would like to play a music. It (indefinite) would like to play a little more.

[CB-able AA-persist]

(BSet m 10) (17) He is holding a violin. He is looking at the one on the table violin and is thinking . . . he wants to play, but he doesn't know. . . . So he goes on to looking at the violin. [Q]: He is too young yet, he is 15 years old, he has a great deal. . . . He is thinking a lot; but he will play the violin, surely.

[CB-able AA persist]

(BSet m 11) (17) This is a kid; he would like to play violin but his mother did not allow him to do so. Sometime he hid himself; he has sat down on a table and began to play violin. Now he is playing violin.

[DDC-rigid AA-self]

(BSet m 14) (20) It's as boy with the hands holding his chin and looking at a musical instrument. The instrument is over the table. He is thinking . . . how to play the instrument. [Q]: The boy is 14 years old. He will play the instrument; after a period of thinking and training he will have success with this instrument.

[CB-able DDA-educate AA-persist]

The Tukuna stories feature no long-range career goals, with one exception. This single story expresses an interest in becoming a carpenter.

(TUK m 17) (40) This here is a person; he is thinking about future work; perhaps about mechanics or carpentry; he is thinking to be in the future perhaps an authority . . . that is what he would like to be (a smile).

[AB-think]

One settler gives a story of benevolent giving which instigates a need to achieve. This story also shows concern with social class in a self-conscious intellectual manner that is unusual in this Amazon sample.

(BSet m 13) (19) A boy who would like to receive a violin as a birthday gift! He has received the violin, and now he is asking himself how can he use it? He doesn't know the musical notes. He says: I don't know the musical notes! Why does he have instruments if he cannot use it? But he said: now I have the violin and I like music and so I will play the violin. To play violin is important to awake the emotions in persons and to change the sorrowful feelings into feelings of freedom. [Q]: His family belongs to the social medial class and he is 10 years old. He will play the violin. What is made with love brings happiness to the persons always.

[NDA-reward CB-difficult AA-persist NDA-charity DDA-lead]

The Tukuna stories emphasize uncertainty or incapacity in nine stories.

(TUK m 08) (age 16) Someone with hands on his face and on his ear. It's a boy. He doesn't know what he will do. He's 12 years old.

[CB-decide]

(TUK m 16) (31) This person here is sad, is thinking enough about his family. I think this way. How can I live (referring to life)? What am I going to do ? When he would grow up what would be with him?

[PA-sad NDB-welfare AB-decide]

(TUK f 10) (age 17) A boy is sitting down. He has put the bass viol on the table and is beginning to think what about to do? [Q]: The boy is 12 years old. He will not find what he can do.

[CB-decide]

(TUK f 02) (age 14) This person is trying to play violin . . . (please, would you develop a little more your story?). Nothing. [Q]: It's a boy. He's 15 years old. He will not succeed in violin.

[CB-difficult CC-failure]

(TUK f 12) (20) A boy looking at a little guitar. He is thinking about to play or not to play the guitar. [Q]: He is 12 years old. He likes that instrument, but he is thinking only, he cannot play.

[AB-inactive CD-unable]

Only three of the settlers stress incapacity.

(BSet f 03) (14) This here is sad because he cannot play violin. He is trying to learn but he cannot. So, he becomes sad. [Q]: I think that is a boy and he is 10 years old. He will go on trying to learn but he will cannot.

[PD-sad CD-unable]

(BSet f 05) (15) I think that he is sad. He wants to play violin, but he doesn't how. He has sat down at the table and is looking now. He has put a towel on the violin; so, the violin cannot become dirty. He's very thoughtful. [Q]: This is Jefferson, a 14 years old boy. He has covered the violin to protect it from scratches and dirties.

[PD-sad CD-unable OA-guard]

(BSet m 16) (23) This here is a kid; he is coming to a place where is a toy and he is thinking now how to play. He is looking to one side, is looking to another side . . . but he will cannot resolve anything. [Q]: The kid's toy is a gun (revolver, in Portuguese). He doesn't know how to use the gun; he is a kid; he is only 5 years old.

[CB-difficult CD-unable]

Punishment by a parent appears in two of the settler stories. There are *no* stories given by either group of a parent pushing a child's interest in accomplishment as found in the Brazilian Japanese (see chapter 6) or in many American stories.

(BSet m 19) (30) A boy is thinking. . . . No, he was thinking and now he is sleeping. He is putting one hand on his ear and the hand on the eye. He is a son of a "gaucho." He is a tall boy and is sitting down. [Q]: I don't know how old he is; I think that he is ten years old and that he has had a spanking from his mother.

[PB-tired DDA-punish]

(BSet m 26) (53) It's a little boy. He is thinking, he is *sad* . . . he is thoughtful. . . . He is thinking about his father or his mother. [Q]: It's a 12 or 13 years boy; his mother has reproached him because he has done something that he should not do.

[DDA-scold PD-sad RC-wrong]

The prevailing themes given by Tukuna Indian women (eight of thirteen) are negative in tone. They feature four stories of illness or death as a spontaneous response to this card and to the other cards as well.

(TUK f 01) (17) sick, taking medicine. has taken medicine and is better now. Vigorous now. [Q] Ah, it's a boy; he's 12 years old. The sickness he has had has transformed his skin to pale skin.

[KD-illness RA-duty-o OB-body]

(TUK f 03) (16) This person here is sad and is crying. He is sitting down and is feeling a great sorrow. [Q] It's a boy, he 17 years old. He is sad because of his sister's death. She was dead by sickness.

[PD-sad KD-ill-die]

(TUK f 18) (42) This seems someone . . . sleeping. It (undefined) is suffering headache (putting the hands on her head) . . . ah, he is suffering! [Q]: He is a boy and is 15 years old. He is suffering too much.

[PD-suffer KD-illness]

(TUK f22) (50) I don't know. (I repeated the instructions). No, this doesn't mean anything for me! [Q]: I think that this is a young boy looking at a dying man. This man is in a doorway.

[KD-death]

There are two female Tukuna themes with negative affiliative features.

(TUK f24) (58) This person here is longing for another person. One of them is feeling . . . homesickness; the other one respects the homesick person. [Q]: The homesick person is a man, he is an alone person. The other is not here but I am thinking that is a woman.

[FB-longing]

(TUK f26) (60) This person is telephoning to his family. [Q]: He is a boy, 4 years old. His family lives in Campo Alegre (a city and not a village). I think that he is talking with his uncle.

[HA-family]

There are two remaining themes of being tired or sorrowful in Tukuna women.

(TUK f 04) (18) The tired person is sleeping and is on a seat. [Q]: This is a boy; he is 16 years old; he is sitting on a table and is dreaming.

[PB-tired]

(TUK f 20) (49) I have nothing to tell you . . . (I repeated the rapport and the instructions). I cannot. [Q]: This person is sorrowful. I don't know . . . sorrow . . . sorrow.

[PD-sorrow]

This card and the others shows that the TAT picks up what is salient in a person's mind whether on the Amazon or in a New York inner-city area. The comparative presence of thematic material gives us a clue as the relative presence of future ambitions or present concerns. We have no difficulty concluding that a positive future time orientation is relatively lacking in the Amazon groups, especially in the Indian group, even though it is presently experiencing Catholic missionary experience in the public schools attended by its youth. That the presence of Christian education has arrived is evident in the results of testing with Card 2 a rural agricultural scene. Education has arrived, but as we shall present in what follows, it has as yet not produced any prevailing forms of long-range achievement motivation in most of the youth contacted.

A Rural Farm Scene: Responses to TAT Card 2

A picture of a farm scene, with a young woman carrying two books in the foreground, an older woman in working garb leaning against a tree in the right background, and a man directing a horse in the far center, has been by now been given to a number of individuals from a variety of cultural settings. In previous Chinese, Japanese, and Koreans samples this card brought out stories of poor farmers improving themselves by attempting more modern agriculture (De Vos, Hauswald, and Borders, 1979; De Vos and Kim, 1993; De Vos and Wagatsuma, 1961). A young girl in many stories goes to school either to escape rural poverty or to return with knowledge to improve the economic lot of her family. An additional theme that was given by several Koreans, but never by Japanese, was a religious one. It depicted how the source of change for the farmers was the Christian preaching of a young missionary (De Vos and Kim, 1993). We note that such religious themes appear with considerable frequency in the present sample. They reflect the recent activities of the Catholic church in setting up schools in this region of Brazil.

Very frequently in all groups tested, the stories simply depict daily labor activities that are the lot of farmers, while going to school is the role taken by the young girl. In every group so far tested there are also a few stories of sexual liaisons or triangular situations involving two women and a man.

All these themes appear in the Amazonian stories, but the proportions and nuances of the stories are quite different from what was found in previous samples. We shall illustrate how we categorized of all the stories obtained.

Table 12.2
Responses of Tukuna and Non-Tukuna to Card 2, the Farm Scene

	Tukuna		*Settlers*	
Total	*m 13*	*f 13*	*m 14*	*f 12*
School Achievement	1	1	-	1
Positive	1	1	-	-
Negative	-	-	-	1
Religious Themes	3	2	2	1
Career choice	1	-	-	-
The book, Mass	2	1	2	-
Forced to attend	-	-	-	1
Other	-	1	-	-
Role Description	2	1	6	5
Religious and work	1	-	2	-
Teaching and work	-	-	3	-
Studying and work	-	-	1	3
Work activities	1	1	-	-
Achievement theme to work	-	-	-	1
Harmonious future	-	-	-	1
Affiliative Concerns	1	3	-	4
Friendship or visiting (pos)	1	2	-	1
Negative situation	-	-	-	2
Love triangle	-	1	-	1
Fear of Attack, Fright	1	1	2	-
Sexual approach	1	-	1	-
Fear of attack	-	1	1	-
Pity and Compassion	2	2	3	1
Preaching	-	1	1	1
Religious compassion	1	-	2	-
Secular compassion	1	-	-	-
Illness	-	1	-	-
Internal Affective States	2	1	1	-
Sad not defined	1	-	-	-
Tired	1	-	1	-
Hunger	-	1	-	-

Table 12.2
Responses of Tukuna and Non-Tukuna to Card 2, the Farm Scene

	Tukuna		*Settlers*	
Total	*m 13*	*f 13*	*m 14*	*f 12*
Other	**1**	**2**	-	-
Horse used for travel	1	1	-	-
Card description	-	1	-	-

Achievement through Studying

The achievement theme found in some incidence in other cultural groups (De Vos, 1973; De Vos, Hauswald, and Borders, 1979; De Vos and Kim, 1993) and the southern Brazilian sample (this volume) was almost totally lacking in our Amazon samples. Of the sample of fifty-two records it appears in three records, two Tukuna and one settler.

> (TUK m 16) (Card 2) Two women and a man . . . on the horse. . . . The man is whipping the horse which is lazy and doesn't want to work. The woman is looking at the man and is intending to make something with man's horse. The other woman which is bringing two books is going to study. [Q] One of these women is the man's wife. The most important for me is the other woman, the unmarried teacher.
>
> [DDA-punish RA-work AA-self HA-depict]

> (TUK f 09) (Card 2) She is a girl and she is going to the school. She is thinking only about her studies. She is a teenager girl and she likes to study a lot. [Q]: She doesn't like to work on the land; she likes her teacher. Her teacher is a 22 years old woman.
>
> [AA-counter PA-satisfy FA-empathy]

> (Set f 01) (Card 2) That is a lady who lives in a farm. She is leaning on a tree and is very repentant. Sometimes she had the opportunity to study in the city . . . but now . . . she must work hard and has to face the suffering of this life. [Q]: She is a 42-year-old lady and she hadn't never gone to the city. She had the opportunity but she had not gone.
>
> [RB-guilt AD-refuse RA-work PD-suffer]

Religious Themes

Religious themes appear in several forms.[3] They certainly reflect the living presence of the Catholic church and the use of the bible as a symbol of literacy and attendance at mass and other activities as symbolizing social belonging. These stories are of some frequency both among the Tukuna (nine of twenty-six stories) and in the settlers (eight of twenty-six). One Tukuna story even suggests an interest in joining a religious order.

> (TUK m 17) (Card 2) These two persons here are thinking about a joint work for their life. They are showing them religious style of life. [Q]: There are two women wearing a long sleeve dresses*. They are religious and so they must be dressed. [*Long sleeves dresses are a requirement of the Religion of Da Cruz.]
>
> [RA-duty-s HA-devote RA-order]

The books in the hands of the young woman suggest religion to many of the informants. There may be little contact with other books. The book evokes thought of a religious setting or church attendance. Such a them is central to the plot in eleven stories.

> (TUK m 21) (Card 2) A woman is getting a bible; she was resting on a stick ("var-a" in Portuguese) and is standing up now. [Q]: The woman is thinking something. She will go to the mass. A man will go by horse. He is thinking about this woman. He will go, but he will think about the woman. This woman [by the tree] is also thinking about the man.
>
> [HA-rite RA-ritual FA-love FC-triangle]

> (TUK m 25) (Card 2) Here I can see a church. A woman and a man and a horse. The man is preparing the horse for walking. Here is one of his brothers; here is the priest's sexton. The sexton is getting something; I don't know what he is getting.
>
> [HA-depict RA-ritual]

> (Set m 24) (Card 2) Here is a chapel or a church. Near to this chapel there are two women and a man. There is also a horse. The man is holding the horse; a woman has a book in her hands and the other woman is on the side of the man. [Q]: The most important for me is the woman with the book.
>
> [HA-depict RA-ritual OA-awe]

> (Set m 26) (Card 2) That's a scene of an older [previous age], a scene of the old cities; a woman is holding a bible and is looking at the other woman who is on

---

[3]Such a theme appeared among Koreans both in Japan and elsewhere. Koreans have been influenced by missionary activities. See De Vos and Kim (1993).

back. A man is fishing. [Q]: The house, the clothes and the models are very similar to these one of the old days.

[PA-memory HA-rite HA-depict]

Not all the group is seen as equally positive about religion. In one Tukuna story there is reluctance.

(TUK f 10) (Card 2) A woman is picking up two books to go to the mass. Then, she has seen another woman and asked: what are you doing here? The other one said: and you, what are going to do? I'm going to the mass, she answered. [Q] The first woman is 22 years old, she likes to go to the mass. The other one doesn't like to.

[HA-rite RA-ritual PA-satisfy PB-dislike]

One settler sees parental insistence as necessary for attendance. It is a relatively rare instance of parental discipline expressed in the Amazon sample.

(Set f 09) (Card 2) She is going to the church and her mother is standing up and controlling her at the distance. She is decided to go back to church and now she is near to her mother. This man is working and seeing the horse. [Q]: I don't know why she gave up going to church. Man is her father who is preparing to go on a trip.

[RA-ritual DDC-rigid DSB-torn HA-depict]

One story is a fanciful one of the Jews as killers of Christ. One can imagine some anti-Semitic teaching about the history of Christianity must have occurred to produce this obviously distorted story by a disturbed young settler woman. This theme appears on other cards as well, mostly given by the same person.

(TUK f 18) (Card 2) Someone like God. The Jews have killed Jesus! The Jews always kill the persons. [Q]: God is on the right. The Jewish people are below but now they cannot kill Jesus, because Jesus has many friends. Jesus and his friends are above.

[DDA-god-punish HC-murder NSA-malice NSA-god]

Role Description of Daily Activities

The farm scene as work is far more characteristic of the settlers than for the Tukuna Indians. Of the twenty-six settler stories, eleven are centered on work activities. Such stories appear only in three of the twenty-six Tukuna. Some stories combine religious themes with descriptions of daily work.

(TUK m07) (Card 2) These here are two bibles in her arms. The other is a man; he's working. [Q]: She is bringing the bible to the other woman. The man is caring for the horse.

[OA-awe RA-work HA-depict]

(Set m 18) (Card 2) There are two women and one man. The man is working; one woman is standing up and the other is coming to her; the arriving woman has a book. A little before the woman with a book was going to the church, but when she saw the other woman [by the tree], she decided to go back to talk to her. [Q]: It is a family. The daughter is that woman with a book; she is talking with her mother.

[RA-work HA-rite HA-depict]

The presence of Protestant missionaries competing with the Catholics is suggested by one story.

(Set m25) (Card 2) Here this woman is going to the church, with a bible in her hands and there is another woman who is waiting for her. [Q]: The woman with the bible is Protestant and the other is a Catholic woman. The man is a worker man; he is struggling for life; the three persons are important for me, but . . . the most important is woman with the bible.

[HA-rite RA-duty-o EDA-status CA-endure]

The presence of teachers who are instructing working villagers is also evoked by seeing the books in the arms of the young woman. These stories are found among the settlers (nine instances), but not in the Tukuna. There are in the Amazon sample, as in other samples, a few who see the figure by the tree as pregnant.

(Set m 17) (Card 2) There are some people here. A man who is working, a teacher woman and another woman. The teacher has some books and the pregnant woman is leaning against a tree.

[HA-depict]

(Set m 11) (Card 2) Here is a woman; she has many books; there is also a working man. Ah, that's another woman looking at a man working on the ground. [Q]: The woman has 2 books; she was reading the books and stopped to observe the other woman. The other woman is that man's wife. The woman with the books is a teacher.

[HA-depict OA-pleas RA-work]

(Set m 22) (Card 2) A lady with two books! she is going to the classroom. The man is taking care of a little horse. There is another lady in front, on the first plane. This is a family which I cannot know. [Q]: The woman who is holding the books is a teacher; she likes the man and the wife of this man. The most important for me is the teacher.

[HA-depict RA-work HA-family FA-friend]

The role of student is sometimes contrasted or seen as complementary to the roles of a working family.

> (Set m 014) (Card 2) Two girls, a man, a horse, some houses and hills. One girl is a student, because she has some books. The other girl is pregnant. The houses are old and the man is working.
>
> [RA-work <u>HA-depict</u> OB-body]

> (Set f 20) (Card 2) Well, this here is a student girl, the other is a woman looking at the landscape, a farmer man taking care of a horse and a lot of rocks. The mother, the father and the daughter. The father is working, the daughter is going to the school and the mother is resting.
>
> [RA-work <u>HA-depict</u>]

> (Set f 12) (Card 2) I think that is a farm. A man is taking care of the horse and the woman is going to her studies. Another woman is leaning against a tree and is thinking about . . . she is a thoughtful woman. They are not relatives. The leaning one is the wife of this man; I don't know what she is thinking about.
>
> [RA-work <u>HA-depict</u> FB-alien]

Ethnic differences, interaction, or potential conflict between Tukuna and settlers do not generally appear as a theme in the Amazon TAT stories. The following is an exception.

> (Set f 23) (Card 2) An old village! this is not that village made only by the Tukuna Indians use for living, but one used by every kind of person. There are many houses made with clay; one girl is going to the classroom; this woman is her mother and she is appreciating the work of that man. The mother is thoughtful. She has an up-to-date face or appearance [girl with books]. There is another landscape behind. A little far from this village is another village; it is very similar to a place I saw on the side of the Tocantins river. This picture is wonderful . . . many hills. [Q]:This is a city near to Tocantins river. It is really a very nice city, a city with some villages. In this village here there are 3 persons: the mother with an hinterland woman face but at the same time she is a normal person, the girl and the father; the father is working in the farm and the girl is going to the school. The most important for me is the nature setting.
>
> [RA-work PA-nature <u>HA-group</u> EDA-praise HA-family]

Of the four stories centering only on work (two settlers, two Tukuna) work is related to future achievement or satisfaction only in the two settler stories. The Tukuna stories rather suggest others working being observed at a distance rather than evoking any direct identification with the work activities.

> (TUK m13) (Card 2) Here there are appearing two girls. There were two houses in the middle of the mountains. The houses were made with cement. This house proprietor is holding a horse. The girls don't know that he is the proprietor of the houses. One of the two girls has two books. Then, they ask: what are we doing with these books? [Q]: the girl who is on the left is 18 years and the other one on

the right is 19 years old. They can work and prepare the food. The man takes away the horse with the load.

[OA-wealth RA-work NDA-food]

(TUK f22) (Card 2) I am seeing a person and also an ox [the horse]. It seems like land. There are many people carrying out many things. [Q]: The people are working on the ground. The woman is not working; that's because she has a good life. The ox is eating on the ground.

[RA-work HA-depict KA-social PA-relief]

In the two Settler stories there is a direct relation to work and some sense of ambition.

(Set f 15) (Card 2) The boy . . . here . . . is ploughing the earth; the horse is dragging the plough. Ah, yes, the boy is preparing this earth to plant. He will succeed in this work; he is going to sow and will produce a good crop. [Q]: The boy, yes, but he is 35 years old! He is a man and the horse is very important for him.

[RA-work AA-persist CA-future]

(Set f 05) (Card 2) This is a farm. The woman is a teacher; and she [woman by tree] is pregnant. The man is working and is taking care of the horse, because the horse can help them on the working. The place is very beautiful; there is a river and many stones. . . . The woman is pregnant. The other woman is a teacher; she is coming from the school and is thinking . . . looking away. . . . [Q]: The pregnant woman is the working man's wife. The teacher woman is a student yet and she intends to be pregnant in the future. The horse is useful for working in the farm and for the persons going to the cities. The pregnant woman is thinking about her future infant. The most important for me is the teacher woman.

[HA-family PA-nature OB-body NDA-active]

Expressive Concerns

Positive expressive concerns with friendship, love, pity and compassion, or negative fears, are most prevalent in the Tukuna women. They appear in eleven of their thirteen stories. Tukuna thirteen men gave six basically expressive themes. Among the Settlers, basically expressive themes appear in five of twelve women, and six of fourteen men. Religious interests are combined with a sense of compassion in assisting others.

Affiliative concerns or sexual interest appear in a eight stories, seven by women. These are more positively toned among the Tukuna.

(TUK m14) (Card 2) This lady is coming and she needs to talk, she needs to come near to this person to talk about community concerns. That person lives in the village and the lady is going to talk to the person, which is a woman. [Q]: The lady is going to talk about the village people, because she wants to make the best for this community. They become friends (the lady and the village woman).

[MTA-group NDA-active FA-friend]

(TUK f04) (Card 2) The people are going for a walk. [Q]: That is a man who is preparing to walk to a very far road, to reach another house.

[FA-travel FA-distant]

(TUK f03) (Card 2) This is stand up. I think these people will walk by horse. There's another person on crossed arms. [Q]: She is a lady. The person who is walking by the horse is a man. He's going [to visit] with relatives. The lady will not go. The other lady on crossed arms is feeling cold.

[FA-friend PB-body]

In three settler women there is concern with parting, worry about pregnancy, or an unhappy family situation.

(Set f 03) (Card 2) Here is a girl. She is going to the school with another person. They are going on the street. I think that her mother is also here. Her mother is pregnant. That's all! [Q]: The girl is 15 years old; she is sad because her mother will be alone at home when she is in the school.

[RA-work OB-body FB-aware FB-parting]

(Set f 02) (Card 2) They are working. She has a bible. Other woman is pregnant; she has worried about bad possibilities to become sad. Other one is asking her: "what are you feeling?" [Q]: Farmers. We can see rice-plantation and some small houses. Woman is a sister of the pregnant one.

[OA-awe OB-body KB-events FA-empathy]

(Set f 08) (Card 2) A lady . . . she is walking; she is going to the school as a pupil or as a teacher. A little behind her there is another lady leaning against a tree; she is pregnant and is using a handkerchief; she is a little sad; the man who is in front of her is her husband. There are any houses, a path (vereda, in Portuguese) and a street, a small cart (carroca) and many hills. This is the place where this family is living; the girl is going to the school and the mother is standing up and thinking about . . . [Q]: The girl is a student and her mother is pregnant. The mother is thinking about the pregnancy and because the family is not so happy. This place is very far from the city. The cart and the horse are useful because the walking to the city becomes more rapid.

[PD-sad RA-work OB-body HB-family]

Love triangles are depicted by two women, one Tukuna and one settler. Such themes are more prevalent in other groups, especially in lower-class Americans.

(TUK f06) (Card 2) This woman is alone and she is married. I'm going to talk to her. I'm going to ask her about what she is thinking; why is she standing up? why is she alone? Where does she live? No, she will answer to me! Other people have abandoned my husband somewhere. I don't know where I am going to. [Q]: The husband of this woman has abandoned her to live with another woman.

[FB-alone HC-hostile FC-triangle FC-desert]

(Set f 07) (Card 2) A woman is looking at another woman. There is a tied horse. The woman is holding a book in her hand. What else? [Q]: The woman is looking at the other because that one is pregnant; the pregnant woman is 30 years old and the non pregnant is 35 years old. The older woman is admiring the pregnancy. Man is taking care of the horse. Man likes both women.

[OB-body FA-similar OA-awe FC-triangle]

Negative stories of fear of attack or unwanted sexual approach are found in four stories.

(TUK m11) (Card 2) This one is thinking about God. There are two women, one man and one horse near 3 houses. That one nearer the house is thinking that the man is a horse-trainer. The other woman with books on the hands and with the rolled up head is a nun. [Q]: The women are thinking that the man is trying to get them to his home.

[EDA-awe RA-work HB-f-attack]

(TUK f01) (Card 2) There, the person, the girl is studying: she's walking her horse. That girl is afraid of the horse and the woman is afraid of the horse too. [Q] The man attends to the horse in order to protect the woman and the girl.

[AA-self HB-f-attack NDA-secure]

(Set m 16) (Card 2) It is very similar to two sisters in front of a church; one has a bible and the other one is putting the hand on the waist. There is a man near to a horse. The women cannot know where they are going to and so they are looking and talking. [Q]: Sisters looking at the man; they have not seen the man before; now they are frightened by the man. One sister has a bible.

[OA-awe HB-f-attack]

(Set m 19) (Card 2) This person is going . . . he is alarmed. The other person is making physical movements; another who is playing is using a cloth on the head. The person is alarmed because of the movement. All these persons are alarmed (assustadas, in Portuguese). [Q]: They are frightened, yes. I don't know why. The husband, the wife and the daughter.

[PB-fright]

Seven stories have to do with worry, pity, or compassion directed toward others. There is a need to help others expressed in these stories, often in a religious context.

(TUK m15) (Card 2) Here is a lady getting a bible. She is in the city, there is a man holding a horse with a cord and one other . . . woman who is leaning against a tree. [Q]: Sometimes the lady gets one bible, sometimes she gets two bibles. She likes to help people. The other woman became sad because there are three houses for living. The people who are going to live in these houses are: the man and the two women. [Not clear as to meaning]

[NDA-charity PA-sad HA-depict]

(TUK f12) (Card 2) A woman with a book. There is a horse, a man looking at the water going down. There is a woman in back of the plants. [Q]: The woman is going to preach the gospel. The other woman is asking her for a book. The man is holding the horse and the water is going down through the brook within the forest.

[NDA-charity NSA-comfort PA-nature]

(Set m 06) (Card 2) I think that is a girl and she is preaching the gospel; she went to a city district to preaching the gospel to this lady. The lady didn't play attention to her; the men have begin to work and so the girl decided to go back. [Q]: She is a Catholic girl. The lady and the men don't believe in this religion. They didn't pay attention to the girl.

[NDA-charity NSC-refuse FB-thwart]

(Set m 13) (Card 2) This is a young and religious lady; she takes care of her home and likes to pray; she likes to relate with other persons. She feels sorrow for the ignorant, selfish and greedy persons of this world. There are other sad persons who think about what they can do to please God.

[FB-aware PA-sad RC-wrong DSA-soothe DSA-pray]

(Set f 04) (Card 2) Mary is going to the church for teaching to the children. She is just thinking about these children. [Q]: Mary is a girl who likes children. She is a teacher and she helps the children to pray.

[NDA-charity]

(Set m 10) (Card 2) This woman is coming from some place and is bringing some books. There is a man taking care of the horses and another woman; she is leaning back and is thinking. The woman with books stopped to observe the leaning woman. Meanwhile a man was working. [Q]: The most important for me is the woman who is bringing the books; she is worried about the leaning woman.

[HA-depict OA-pleasure FB-aware]

Two Tukuna express pity for old age or illness.

(TUK m 23) (Card 2) Here is appearing a horse. It seems . . . to be on working. The man is working with the horse. But this lady there. . . . That one there (pointing out to the other female fig.) is very sad; she is crying. [Q]: The man is 50 years old. The lady on the left has a bible. The other lady is crying because the man is too old for working.

[FB-aware RA-work OA-awe PA-sad KD-age]

(TUK f26) (Card 2) I can see . . . a daughter who is very sick; the man is holding her. The man is very sad, he is leaning his head down over the horse. [Q]: The man and his wife was walking and during the walking their daughter became sick. Then, he and his wife got down from the horse and are going now with their daughter.

[KD-illness NDB-pity]

Various internal affective states are expressed in four stories. Note that feeling tired or hungry never have appeared as stories given to this card in any previous samples. Such unusual stories certainly indicate the degree that such pressing bodily concerns can intrude on interpersonal experiences. Stories of hunger also appeared sporadically in Tukuna stories given to the other cards. Worry about hunger must be a pressing experience. Tiredness from arduous exertion must be a frequent experience.

(TUK f24) (Card 2) Here any persons . . . there are persons . . . they are walking jointly. That is all! [Q]: These persons are in a city, a lot of persons. I cannot know what they are looking for, perhaps they are looking for food.

[PB-hunger]

(TUK m05) (Card 2) There are a women looking. . . . This woman is getting two books. The other is looking at the horse; she is very sad. The man is securing the horse; he is a worker. He is looking, also.

[RA-work PD-sorrow]

(TUK m 19) (Card 2) A city! No? Isn't a city? Someone is sleeping . . . (looking at me, as he was looking for help. I said: you are at home, please talk about what you are feeling). Ah, he is sleeping [similar to his story given previously to Card 1].

[PB-tired]

(Set m 21) (Card 2) . . . two women, a man and a horse. They are stopped. They are tired because they have walked very much. [Q]: The women and the man are looking at the horse. I don't know why they are looking at the horse! I don't know where they are now. They are very tired and are coming from some place far from here.

[PB-tired]

In the following two stories and in others as well we can note that the horse is seen as a mode of travel in this remote setting on the Amazon.

(TUK f02) (Card 2) This person is holding the horse and *trying* to ride on it. [Q]: The person is a man; he's riding on the horse for a trip to the city.

[CB-able]

(TUK m08) (Card 2) A person holding the horse. This person is riding on a horse and he is *wishing* to travel. [Q]: This is a man. He is going through a path in the middle of a town.

[PA-play]

As on other cards, the informant may be evasive and resort to simple card description. One must note that, in general, the participants in Vaz's sample were cooperative and attempted to give genuine stories. There are relatively few stories as the following.

(TUK f 20) (Card 2) A persons. I think that they are . . . ah, they are a women. [Q]: Women, yes . . .but I don't know what they are doing.

[Card description]

Travails of a Distraught Figure: Cards 3BM, 3GF

Vaz gave Card 3BM, a picture of a slumped figure, who is most often seen as a young woman, but not infrequently as a young boy, only to males. Card 3GF which Vaz gave to the women in his sample is usually seen as a young woman leaning in a distraught manner against the jamb of an open door.

In the present instance we are combining the results on one table. It is noteworthy that the results are close enough to allow us to compare the male and female samples in terms of their positive or negative content or the type of stories elicited. The differences between Tukuna and settler groups are consistent across the sexes (see Table 12.3). For example, the slumped figure of Card 3BM or the distraught woman of 3GF evoked fewer stories of rejected love than are found in American groups. We shall illustrate some but not all the stories obtained.

Instrumental Stories of Authority or Responsibility

Among the male settlers seven of fourteen give responses related to instrumental control with authority or wrongdoing. Only two such stories appear in Tukuna males.

Among the settlers one finds punishing control of parents or authorities (three stories). No such story appears in the Tukuna. Their one authority story is about tiredness due to compliance to school homework. Themes of the beating of children appear among settlers (two stories), but none in the Indians.

(Set m 14) (3BM) I am seeing a prisoner. I don't know if it is a man or a woman. This person is crying and is sitting on the floor and is over his right leg. The person has the head on the bed and is using socks and shoes. He is of a higher class, because he is using socks and good quality shoes.

[DDA-police DSB-torn OA-status]

(Set m 16) (3BM) A woman came here; she leaned against a stick and began to sleep. [Q]: She was very tired. It was too late; it was at night. She was coming from a party and she had no time to sleep before, then she decided to sleep here; a young girl and was afraid of going back to home so late.

[PB-tired DSB-punish]

(Set m 6) (3BM) Here her mother has beaten her. She had not obeyed the mother and then the mother has beaten her hard. She is crying now, meanwhile she is sure that her mother is right. [Q]: She is 18 years and her mother is 37 years old. The girl is crying but at the same time she knows that her mother is right.

[DDC-punish DSC-disobey DDA-punish]

Table 12.3
Responses to Card 3BM, A Slumped Figure; 3GF, A Distraught Woman

	Tukuna		*Settlers*	
Total	*m 13*	*f 13*	*m 14*	*f 12*
Control-Authority	**1**	**1**	**3**	-
Legitimate order	1	1	-	-
Parental punishment	-	-	2	-
Police authority	-	-	1	-
Responsibility	**1**	-	**4**	**2**
Bad behavior of others	-	-	1	-
Wrongdoing (not specified)	-	-	1	-
Disobedient	-	-	-	2
Drunken state	1	-	2	-
Inner State	**5**	**3**	**3**	-
Physical activity	1	-	-	-
Tired	2	-	3	-
Sorrow	-	3	-	-
Physical discomfort	2	-	-	-
Affiliation	-	**3**	**1**	**1**
Positive love	-	1	-	-
Alone	-	1	-	-
Rejection or abandonment	-	1	1	1
Nurture	-	-	**1**	**1**
Esteem	-	**1**	-	-
Discord or Violence	**2**	**3**	-	**6**
Discord	-	1	-	2
Beating or rape	-	-	-	3
Murder (Biblical)	-	2	-	-
Incurred violence	2	-	-	1
Death, Illness, or Accident	**4**	**2**	**2**	**2**
Sick	1	-	-	2
Illness-death	1	1	1	-
Accident	2	1	1	-

In the settlers there are stories of wrongdoing or irresponsible drunkenness, in males (four), in females (two). There is one such story given by a Tukuna male.

> (TUK m 08) (3BM) Here she is dreaming, because it's night. She is a woman. [Q]: She is dreaming because she became a drunk woman.
>
> [RC-abuse PB-tired]

> (Set m 22) (3BM) This here is sleeping, he is over a bench; he is a *drunk* and is using a long sleeves shirt. [Q]: He is a drunk and is sleeping on a bench of that square shape.
>
> [RC-abuse PB-tired]

> (Set m 25) (3BM) She is crying or sleeping, or thinking. . . . It's one of these three things. Isn't right? [Q]: It's a woman; she is sleeping and leaning down . . . I think that she did something and now is sleeping and repentant.
>
> [RC-wrong PB-tired RB-guilt]

> (Set m 17) (3BM) Here is a boy or a woman; he is sleeping. I don't know what was happened; I think that he has drunk too much and became drunk. [Q]: I am not sure if boy or girl! I'm sure that he or she became drunk and that now he or she is sleeping.
>
> [RC-abuse PB-tired]

> (Set f 09) (3GF) That is happening something with this girl, because she is crying now. She is at her home and putting the hands on her face; is crying. [Q]: girl 12 years old. don't know what's happening. I think that she has did something that was not allowed.
>
> [RC-status]

Discord, Violence, or Death

Three negative categories are more frequent among the Tukuna. There are stories of discord or violence in five of twenty-six stories. There are stories of death, illness, or accident in six of twenty-six Tukuna. Additionally, there are five stories of sorrow or physical discomfort in five of twenty-six Tukuna. This is a total of sixteen of twenty-six stories among the Tukuna. These responses compare with ten of twenty-six such negative stories found among the settlers. There are six stories of discord or violence among settler women, none among the men. Death, illness, or accident appear in only two male and two female settlers. There are no stories of sorrow or physical discomfort.

Looking more specifically at the stories we note further differences. The Tukuna males give ten stories of incurred violence happening to a loved one. This suggests some underlying fear of attack from outside one's group.

(TUK m 11) (3BM) Here is a woman sitting down on . . . she has become sad and is sleeping on the table now. The clothes she uses has long sleeves and her hairs are smooth. [Q]: This woman is sad because her husband was *killed.*

[PD-sad HD-death]

(TUK m 15) (3BM) There is a person; somebody is crying nearly. She is thinking about a gun and a knife that is a little down there. [Q]: The woman is crying because some relative of hers was killed.

[PD-sad HD-death]

In the one story given by a female settler, the violence incurred was that suffered by a wife beaten by a husband.

(Set f 12) (3GF) A woman is coming in and is *crying* too much; she is opening the door; she is crying because someone beat at her face. Her head is leaning down. [Q]: Husband of this woman has beaten her; she likes him yet; a 30 years old woman.

[HD-injury DDC-punish]

Beatings and rape appear in another three settler women. The two stories of discord are between man and wife. We gain a general picture of women among the settlers who are afraid of their husbands.

(Set f 01) (3GF) A woman. She's crying and getting out home. The husband has beaten her and so she is going away. She is crying. She is leaving the room. [Q]: She is 22 years and her husband is 27 years old probably. There was no reason for the beatings but she will not go back.

[PD-suffer HD-injury FC-parting]

(Set f 04) (3GF) Charlie is her name. She is crying because her husband has beaten her. Her husband is a bad man. [Q]: Charlie has become angry and so she has not prepared the lunch for him! That's good!

[HC-injury DDC-punish]

(Set f 23) (3GF) This is the weeping woman. She is sad, I think so. The man has grasped her elsewhere; something was happened, because she is crying now. [Q]: She was grasped by some man; she didn't like it; she was grasped forcibly. Now she is repentant about being assaulted.

[HC-rape RC-guilty]

(Set f 08) (3GF) This is a lady. She is crying and holding herself at the door; she is putting her hands on her face and is suffering something. She is leaving her home. [Q:] The lady is 25 years. She is going away. I don't know if she is single or married. I think that she is married and that was happened a quarrel between her and her husband. She is leaving . . . she is going away.

[HC-discord FC-parting]

In the dead and illness stories there are some characteristic differences about the source of worry. The settler women see worry about one's children and falling ill with fever as the concerns. The Tukuna women see a man dying early and a sister bitten by a snake. Among the men, one sees a woman suffering a broken arm, and other woman suffering the loss of two children. The Tukuna men give stories of a friend returning with an illness after a visit to the city. Another sees a mother suffering the death of a child. Two stories are injuries incurred by falling from a tree. There are suggestions in these stories that there is concern about spousal abuse incurred by settler women. In these stories we also gain a brief glance at the possible accidents and illnesses envisioned by those living along the Amazon. In addition to the fear of family violence in the settlers there are numerous dangers connected with physical safety or illness that can be incurred despite precautions.

Affiliative Problems between a Man and a Woman Visualized on Card 4

Card 4 of the TAT depicts a young man turning away from a young woman who has him by the arm. There is a dim figure of another woman in the background that is sometime taken to be a poster on a wall. Very often it is ignored in making a story. There are a variety of themes given to this card from tender love relationships, to the scene of a quarrel, to a young woman restraining the man from quarreling or fighting with an outside figure not seen on the card.

The present samples vary among these themes, demonstrating that this card provokes similar stories to those evoked in other cultural settings. What is characteristic for the present groups, however, is a somewhat heavier concentration of stories involving sexual problems of infidelity related to love triangles involving another woman.

Expressions of Mutual Love or Positive Concern about Another

The Tukuna Indians display what we might consider ordinary positive expressions of love between a man and woman in six of twenty-six stories. There are four such stories in the settler males. There are no positive stories among the settler women. As on other cards, the women tend to depict more negative man-woman relationships.

> (TUK m 17) (Card 4) We can see how much a person loves her husband or his wife! It's the representation of an Adam and Eve's part of life. It is showing the family union. [Q]: Here is a man and a woman. The man is 25 and the woman is 18 years old. I have said Adam and Eve because they loved each other.
>
> [FA-love HA-family]

(TUK f 18) (Card 4) Ah, here they are in love (a big smile)! She has a dark and nice hair. [Q]: Yes, they are in love. He is 40 years and she is 20 years old. I was smiling because they are in love (another smile).

[FA-love]

(TUK m 19) (Card 4) A woman caressing to him, she is caressing her husband. [Q]: The wife is caressing her husband because he is a good man. Every woman likes the good man.

[FA-love RA-good]

(TUK f 04) (Card 4) There are persons holding each other. They are sitting and loving each other.

[FA-love]

(TUK m 25) (Card 4) Embracing his wife. She likes him. He is embracing her. Is she his wife or no (looking at me, asking for approval)? She is very beautiful; he is a very old man, like me.

[FA-love]

(Set m 16) (Card 4) Two sweethearts here! The girl is caressing him, but there is another woman behind them. This woman is looking at the man and seeing what they are doing. [Q]: The man is 30 years and the woman is 23 years old; the other woman is a friend of the 23 years old girl; she is looking what the sweethearts are doing; she intends to do the same thing in the future when she will be a sweetheart.

[FA-love FB-observe CA-future]

(Set m 19) (Card 4) Now, he is well; he is embracing a woman and another woman is looking at him. He is happy now. [Q]: He is 20 years and the embracing woman is 19 years old. The other woman is sitting down; she is a 30 years old woman; she is the mother of this boy; she likes the sweetheart of hers son.

[FA-love PA-vicar]

(Set m 21) (Card 4) There are three persons. I think that is a couple and a daughter . . . the daughter is very high and the woman too. The man is embracing his wife and the daughter is sitting down. [Q]: The second woman is the wife's man sister.

[FA-love HA-family]

There is a depiction of sexual attraction.

(TUK f 20) (Card 4) These persons are pleasing one another, that is like playing, do you know? They are pleasing one to another, like playing together. You know.

[PA-play FA-sex]

Table 12.4
Affiliative Problems between a Man and a Woman

	Tukuna		*Settlers*	
Total	*m 13*	*f 13*	*m 14*	*f 12*
Affiliative Concerns	**10**	**7**	**9**	**8**
Positive expression of love	3	2	3	-
Pity	-	-	1	-
Sexual attraction	-	1	-	-
Seduction	1	-	-	2
Betrayal	-	1	-	-
Rejection	-	2	-	3
Triangular situation resolved	1	1	1	2
Triangle unresolved or negative	5	-	4	1
Discord	**2**	**3**	**4**	**4**
In a triangular situation	2	1	1	2
Vengeful toward outside	-	-	2	-
Quarrel	-	-	1	2
Murder	-	2	-	-
Nurture	**1**	**1**	-	-
Food	1	-	-	-
Illness	-	1	-	-
Death, Illness, or Accident	-	**1**	**1**	-
Card Description	-	**1**	-	-

There is an expression of pity.

(Set m 18) (Card 4) The husband and his wife are standing up and are looking at that woman . . . [Q]: They are looking at that woman and are concerned with her sorrow.

[FB-aware]

Betrayal or Seduction

In five of their stories the settler young women reveal a distrustful attitude and fear of rejection in male-female relationships. Three such stories also appear in the Tukuna women. The settler women show fewer "love" stories.

(BSet f 03) (Card 4) This is a woman who is trying to make conquest of a boy, but he doesn't want it. Let me go away, he said and she answered: no! [Q]: The woman is 22 years and the boy is 20 years old. That is because he doesn't like her. She likes him. He will go away.

[FC-seduce FC-sex-rej FB-dislike]

(BSet f 12) (Card 4) Here is a sweetheart couple; she is trying to seduce him but he "is out" ("nao esta nem ai"). She is caressing his body, but he is covering his eyes; he doesn't look at her; he is angry. Both are in a little room. She is pleasing to him but he "is out." [Q]: This guy is angry but he is not right. He is thinking that she is immoral, but this is not true.

[FC-seduce PA-sensual HB-anger RC-ex-sex RA-sex]

Given the posture of the figures, betrayal or rejection is usually a male activity. Note these are stories given by women suggesting the fear about fickle men who may leave.

(TUK f 06) (Card 4) The woman is in love with this man. He has betrayed her. I don't like what you've done against me, but I like you, she said. Meanwhile I will remain with you! [Q]: She is embracing and kissing her husband. The most important for me is the woman.

[FA-love FC-betray]

(TUK f 09) (Card 4) This is the case of a man and a woman. She likes him, but he doesn't like her. She is asking him for an embrace, but he doesn't like her. [Q]: He doesn't want to embrace her because he doesn't like her; she is not his wife.

[FA-love FC-reject RA-duty-s]

(TUK f 02) (Card 4) This persons are in love. They are grasping each other. [Q]: She likes him a lot but he doesn't it so, he doesn't like any one. The most important for me is the woman.

[FA-love FD-affect]

(Set f 01) (Card 4) Ah, they were discussing and he decided to go away; she is embracing him, asking for staying with her. You must stay! [Q] He will go away. She is *sorrowful* and *angry* at the same time.

[FD-reject PD-sad HB-angry]

(Set f 07) (Card 4) A woman is embracing her husband; he is preparing to go out and she is wanting to talk to him. [Q]: She likes him; he doesn't like her. He is a handsome man. The most important for me is the man. I would be with him but not with her.

[FA-love FC-reject EDA-appear]

(Set f 08) (Card 4) Here is a married happy couple; the woman is embracing the husband; he is a little getting loose, but they are talking about their children. [Q]: He is a handsome man but I think that he is not a good person; she is a good person.

[FA-love NDA-family RC-wrong RA-duty-s]

Triangular Relationships

Triangular relationships are depicted both by the Tukuna (ten of twenty-six) and the settlers (eleven of twenty-six). The males are particularly prone to give such stories.

> (TUK m 14) (Card 4) This is the husband of this lady. She is pleasing him by talking. [Q]: There's another woman who is very interested on the other's husband; but the legitimate marriage gets the best.
>
> [FC-triangle RA-duty-s]

> (TUK m 05) (Card 4) This person here is a woman holding on her husband. The husband is only looking. [Q]: The husband likes her but he likes the other woman also.
>
> [FA-love FC-triangle]

> (TUK m 07) (Card 4) Someone looking at another man. [Q]: It's a woman looking at the man. She wants to talk to him. There's another woman wishing kisses from the man.
>
> [FC-triangle FB-thwart]

> (TUK m 15) (Card 4) This is a man with his sweetheart. There's another woman sitting down behind his sweetheart. [Q]: One of the women is trying to fondle the man. The other is controlling the man.
>
> [FA-love FC-triangle DDC-press]

> (TUK m 21) (Card 4) A person in love with the other one. [Q]: This is a man who is in love with two women.
>
> [FC-triangle]

> (TUK m 23) (Card 4) She is embracing her husband. He doesn't want it. There is another woman looking at him. [Q]: The woman who is looking at the man is his sister-in-law. He likes his sister-in-law; she is younger than the other woman. The most important for me is the man.
>
> [FC-triangle FC-reject]

> (TUK f 01) (Card 4) Here the person is in love. The man is seating and the woman is embracing him; but he doesn't like to look at the woman embracing him. The woman is trying to kiss him, but he doesn't want to kiss her. [Q]: There are 2 women and 1 man. The other woman likes the man too, but he will prefer the embracing woman for definitive love. The most important for me is the embracing woman.
>
> [FA-love FC-triangle FC-reject]

> (TUK m 13) (Card 4) Then, this is one man and two girls. One girl is looking at him; she is looking too much, she is embracing him. The man is saying with

himself: what will I do? Other people are photographing the things (the situation) . . . in a bedroom.

[FC-seduce ESB-shame]

(Set m 14) (Card 4) Two women and one man. One of the women is sitting down on the bed and is looking at the two. The other woman is holding the man not to go away; he is trying to go away. Both women very beautiful. [Q]: Woman sitting down the man's mistress; the other his wife; all are in the same home. He is leaving both women, because he became angry with the mistress. He likes better his wife; the real wife likes him too. I think that he will be with the real wife.

[FC-triangle FC-gone OA-Body HB-anger FA-mend]

(Set m 26) (Card 4) Now they are in love. She is worry with her love, with him, but he is not worry with his love, with her. The other woman is looking at this man. The man is worry with the sitting down woman and looking at her . . . [Q]: The man who is in love with her is his wife; he is worry with the other woman and the wife is brave . . . I think that the other woman is interested on this man.

[FA-love FC-triangle]

(Set f 04) (Card 4) Charlie is wanting to love her husband, but he doesn't want it. He loves the other woman; he is looking at her and her name is Antoinie. [Q]: Antoinie is behind them; she likes the Charlie's husband. Antoinie is more beautiful than Charlie, but I like better Charlie, the real wife.

[FB-thwart FC-triangle FC-reject OA-body]

(Set m 06) (Card 4) Here the boy is angry with his wife; he would like to love the girl who is behind. His wife doesn't want it! And so he has become angry and left her *alone*.

[HB-anger FC-triangle]

(Set m 24) (Card 4) Here is one man and two women. One of the women is embracing the man and the other is sitting down, crossing her legs and looking at the man. [Q]: The man likes the woman who is embracing him.

[FC-triangle FC-seduce]

(Set m 22) (Card 4) They are caressing each other. There is another person sitting down, it's a woman. This woman is looking at the embracing couple. But the embracing woman is only the mistress of this man. The real wife is that who is sitting down on the bench. [Q]: The man is 38 years and the mistress is 29 years old; the real wife is older than the mistress. The real wife is only looking at the man and the mistress.

[FA-love FC-triangle]

(Set f 02) (Card 4) Here the wife of this man is the one in the background. The other woman is embracing the man and he is looking only, she is wanting to love him, but he loves the other woman who is his wife. [Q]: The real wife is 34 years and the other woman is 38 years old. He is a handsome man and a good man for his wife. The woman who is trying to win him is a friend of the real wife, but she will not win the man.

[FC-triangle FC-betray FA-love]

(Set f 20) (Card 4) Ah, it's a picture. This is a sweetheart couple (smile)! The man was with his mistress (*amante*, in Portuguese) and his wife caught them red-handed. [Q]: This man neither likes his wife nor the mistress. The wife likes him; the mistress doesn't like him. The wife will pardon him. The most important for me is the man.

[FA-love FC-triangle FB-dislike FA-forgive]

Some of these triangular situations involve active discord.

(TUK m 08) (Card 4) He is holding his wife. He became drunk and is angry now. [Q]: She is not angry. There is another woman; this one is sitting down.

[RC-abuse HC-anger FC-triangle]

(TUK m 11) (Card 4) One man and two women. . . . One woman is holding the man and the other is looking at him. The first woman, that who is holding the man, is looking for talking to him; she is sure that the man is angry with the other woman. [Q]: The man likes the woman who is holding him. The most important for me is the man.

[HC-anger FA-love]

(TUK f 10) (Card 4) A woman has had a quarrel with her husband; but she has embraced and now is asking him: what is happening with you? Not at all, woman! he answered. She was needing to talk to him, but he was angry. The other woman is looking at the man. [Q]: The man likes the other woman. He will change, he will fall in love with the other woman.

[HC-discord HA-pacify FC-reject FC-triangle]

(Set m 17) (Card 4) Here a couple is appearing; it is a man and a woman; they are quarreling; he is very angry; she is trying to change him into a quiet man, to have a quiet mind, but he is turning his face to the other side. [Q]: The wife was out home and when she went back, her husband was with another woman at home; she didn't like it, and then the couple began to quarrel. Now, she is quiet but he is brave. He doesn't like her. The most important for me is the quiet woman.

[HC-discord HA-pacify HB-anger FC-triangle HB-jealous]

(Set f 05) (Card 4) A beautiful woman! The man I am seeing is her husband. They are in love. Suddenly they begin to discuss. He is wanting to turn away but the woman is holding his hands. She is trying to explain something to him. [Q]: The woman is very beautiful and he is a handsome man. He was out of home on a traveling business and when he was going back, he was suspecting something between her and another man. She is trying to explain that he was thinking badly about her feelings . . . that it was not true.

[OA-body FA-love HC-discord FB-jealous HA-pacify]

(Set f 23) (Card 4) A "macho" (*metido a macho*—smile!) man. This is a jealousy scene. A man is in a saloon (bar). A woman is coming and suddenly she can see his husband with another woman who is showing her legs to him. The man becomes angry. It seems a movie scene! [Q]: The man is 35 years; his wife is 30 years old; the showing legs woman is 25 years old. The man's wife didn't like to see him with another woman; the wife and the husband become angry.

[FB-jealous FC-triangle HB-anger]

In the present sample there are only two stories of a man angry with an outside adversary. These were given by settler men. Such stories that frequently include anger about a man who finds someone approaching his wife are much more frequent in American responses to this card.

(Set m 13) (Card 4) Here is an adventurous man; he likes life; he has high thoughts, is a sentimental man and likes reality. He drinks sportily and doesn't want his friends to scold ("chingar," in Portuguese) him; he becomes furious and nervous easily and is a revengeful man. His wife is embracing him lovingly; she is asking him for not to be nervous, for not go away, not to mind. But, he goes on worried, looks at her and his eyes are vengeful. [Q]: This man is a adventurer; he is like a owner of lottery ("Jogo do bicho," forbidden by law in Brazil). He is a man who goes away looking for what's best for himself.

[PA-curious RC-mores HB-revenge HA-pacify]

(Set m 11) (Card 4) Here is a man and a woman. He is wanting to quarrel with her but she is trying to avoid it. He is angry with another man; he wants to face him, but the woman is holding him to avoid it. Trying to change this idea of her husband; she will succeed: he will not face the other man. [Q]: She likes her husband and he likes her. He is angry because another man was trying to seduce his wife. They will be OK; the husband and his wife are living jointly and will live together.

[HC-discord HA-pacify HB-anger FC-seduce FA-love]

Quarrels between a man and woman are absent in the Tukuna stories. They appear in three settlers.

(Set m 10) (Card 4) Here they were talking; she said something; he didn't like it and then he has turned his face from her eyes. She was going on to talk, but he was not wanting never to listen never to see her. [Q]: I think that he will decide to look at her and their relationship will be well again.

[HC-discord HB-anger FA-mend]

(Set f 15) (Card 4) Here is a couple, a man and a woman; he is wanting to go out but she is holding him. She is in love with him (*esta apaixonada*, in Portuguese); she is looking at him. I don't know what is happening! [Q]: Man is 37 years and she is 28 years old; difference is not so big. That is because they have a quarrel. Now, he is trying to go out to avoid some discussion.

[HC-discord FB-parting]

(Set f 09) (Card 4) This woman is holding this man and is very *angry*. She was going to talk to him but he has turned his face; then she became angry. He doesn't want to talk to her. [Q]: Wife has done something that husband didn't like. Now, is trying to talk with him, but he wants not listen to her. He doesn't like her; she likes him; he is not a good husband.

[HB-anger FB-Thwart HC-discord FB-dislike RC-wrong]

Concern with food, death, or illness are not themes usually found given to this card. The fact that they appear in three Tukuna stories demonstrate how strong such preoccupations are for them.

(TUK m 16) (Card 4) She is pleasing her husband who was coming; she was expecting him, making a lot of food. [Q]: She is a good wife; she stays at home and works . . . her husband is a great teacher.

[NA-nurture NA-food CA-present]

(TUK f 03) (Card 4) Here the people are holding. There is a person with fever. One is dressing the fever person. This one is laying down. [Q]: The person who is dressing the other is his wife. She likes him and has fallen in love with him. Her husband is suffering fever. She's dressing a wound and loving him. The most important for me is the wife.

[KD-illness FA-love NDA-nurture]

(TUK f 22) (Card 4) Persons here. One of them is dead. The other . . . [Q]: I think that one of them is not dead, he will be dead. The other is a man; he is very sad.

[KD-death PD-sad]

Choice of Visualizing Surgery or Violence on Card 8BM

Card 8BM has a limited range of possibilities. With a young person in the forefront the background scene is interpreted usually as either an attack on a prone figure by two men or as two doctors performing a surgery. A rifle diagonal across the left forefront can suggest, perhaps, that a deliberate or accidental shooting may have occurred, either by the youthful figure or by someone not in the picture. The pensive appearance of the youth in the foreground can suggest a revelry or a dream of becoming a surgeon in the future. Another frequent theme is a hunting accident. Sometimes it is a son who has accidentally shot his father.

The card was given only to twenty-four males in these samples, ten Tukuna and fourteen settlers. The theme of incurred violence is the preferred theme given by seven of ten Tukuna and five of the fourteen settlers. There are no stories of dreaming about becoming a doctor.

Table 12.5
Card 8BM: Surgery and/or Violence

Total	*Tukuna* *m 10*	*Settlers* *m 14*
Nurture (surgery or care)	<u>3</u>	<u>5</u>
No cause mentioned for surgery	-	3
Illness-surgery	2	1
Accidental violence-care	1	1
Nurture after Violence	<u>0</u>	<u>3</u>
Violence and care	-	3
Assault on Prone Figure	<u>7</u>	<u>5</u>
No motive given	3	1
Within family	2	-
Sexual conflict	-	1
Revenge	-	1
Drunk	2	-
Banditry	-	1
Christ injured by Jews	-	1
Other	**-**	**1**

The Tukuna

What is apparent among the Tukuna is their fear of violence being inflicted on someone, possibly from the outside.

No motives for the violence are given by three Tukuna.

> (TUK m 11) (8BM) There is a man killing other man with a knife. The woman becomes sad because the dead man was her husband.
>
> [<u>HC-murder</u> FD-loss]

> (TUK m 19) (8BM) This man was cut, isn't that right? His belly is being cut now. Isn't it? The belly of this woman was cut; she has a cut on her belly.
>
> [<u>HC-injury</u>]

> (TUK m 23) (8BM) This looks some person . . . a person who is dead. The other is looking at the dead person and there's another person who is crying. [Q]: The man who is above has killed the man below: but the man who is below is not yet dead, because he is crying.
>
> [<u>HC-murder</u> FD-fate]

Drunkenness is involved in two Tukuna stories.

(TUK m 08) (8BM) Here is a person killing another person. [Q]: A person is . . . (he could not define the person). The person is killing because he's a drunk.

[HC-murder RC-abuse]

(TUK m 25) (8BM) This person is dead. He was killed; he was cut by a knife. It's possible to see the gun and the criminal. The father of this dead man is crying. [Q]: The criminal was angry and drunk; the drunk and the gun are from the city. Ah, he was cut by a knife also. The knife is also from the city. The dead man is not from the city.

[HC-murder FD-death HB-anger RC-abuse]

In two cases among the Tukuna the killings occur within family relations.

(TUK m 013) (8BM) Two men are over this other man. They are slitting and killing this man. Here's a rifle on the side. Men who are slitting the other doesn't appear so clearly. Men who are killing didn't know that the dead one is their brother.

[HC-murder FC-misc]

(TUK m 14) (8BM) There is nothing here! I think that is a woman or a man. Is a woman or a man? I think that is one man who is wanting to kill the woman. [Q]: Two men and both are killing the husband of some woman. One man has a knife, the other holds the man . . . the husband, was sleeping . . . before. The woman doesn't become indifferent on seeing her husband being killed.

[MTC-plot HC-murder FB-aware]

As throughout the TAT cards, sickness shows up as the major concern in two Tukuna stories.

(TUK m 07) (8BM) Here is a *sick* man. Someone is cutting to open his belly. There's a rifle also. The physician has cut his belly.

[KD-illness CA-repair]

(TUKm 16) (8BM) Here I can see a doctor treating a person. This person is suffering a sickness that is called hernia. There is also a nurse on the side. After the operation the person will be healthy alike another persons; he will become a 18 years old person and so will feel better. [Q]: This sickness man is 40 years old and he was sick since 3 years before.

[KD-illness CA-repair KA-recovery]

The frequent theme to this card of a hunting accident shows up in one Tukuna story.

(TUK m 17) (8BM) Here is a physician. He is making a surgery; ah, he is making a surgery. One man went to hunt and then there was an accident. maybe one other killed him? There is a rifle besides.

[CA-repair KD-accident HC-murder]

The Settlers' Stories

In nine of fourteen settler stories surgery or care is brought to mind. Deliberate violence occurs in six stories. They are more apt to give motives for the violence than are the Tukuna.

Only one violence story is seen without motive.

(Set m 26) (8BM) A case of surgery! No, it is not . . . I don't know . . . Ah, I think that they are cutting into the other boy really. They are in a house; the little boy is nervous. . . . Two boys are killing another boy. The youngest boy is very nervous, he is a brother of the killing boy.

[CA-repair HC-murder]

Banditry appears in one story.

(Set m 14) (8BM) Here are three men and one woman. The woman is wearing a coat and also a tie. One of the three men is leaning down and I think that he is being slit; he is a bandit. The woman has turned her back to the three men. [Q]: The woman is the wife of the leaning down man; she is nervous and is not liking what is going on. The two other men are killing this man. The woman is very nervous; she cannot do anything.

[OB-clothes AC-criminal HC-murder CB-difficult]

Revenge is the motive in two stories, one involving sexual conflict.

(Set m 25) (8BM) This is a criminal situation, isn't right? One person is punishing another, drawing out the viscera from the person. The woman is worried; she is being quiet but she is afraid. . . . [Q]: That man is killing another and so he is punishing him for something that this man did. The woman is the sister of the man who is being killed.

[HB-revenge HC-murder]

(Set m 06) (8BM) Woman is having a dream. In the dream she is seeing her husband. Two men are boring into her husband; both men are brothers; they are stabbing him, because he was intending to love the woman of one of these men.

[HC-injury HB-revenge RC-ex-sex]

A religious theme is evoked in one settler recalling the agony of Christ.

(Set m 16) (8BM) It is a scene at the time of Christ. The Jews are mocking Jesus Christ. They are boring into Jesus Christ's belly. [Q]: Jesus Christ is *dying* and there is a woman turning her back to the Jews; she is Our Lady. But she pardons the Jews.

[HC-murder DSA-god NDA-pardon]

Among the care or surgery stories, three are without reasons given for the surgery.

(Set m 19) (8BM) There are four persons here; three of them are standing up and one is laying down; one person is very alarmed; the other is making a surgery. [Q]: It is happening a surgery, yes. The person who is alarmed is the patient's brother.

[CA-repair FB-aware]

(Set m 22) (8BM) Here I'm seeing three persons. They are making a surgery or killing another person. I can see a rifle on this side. Ah, a surgery happening in a forest.

[KD-illness CA-repair HC-murder]

(Set m 24) (8BM) A man is laying down; the other man is boring into the belly of the laying down man and the other man is standing up, looking at. . . . There is also a rifle on the other side. I am joining all and concluding that this is a case of surgery. This patient will be safe. The most important for me is the man who is boring the belly of the patient. I think that he is a physician.

[CA-repair]

One settler story is of an accidental shooting.

(Set m 17) (8BM) A person was shot; someone is trying to extract the bullet from this person. This little boy I am seeing in front is a son of that person. The one who is trying to draw out the shot is a physician. They are in a forest; no, they are in a house, because it is a window here. The physician gets to draw out the bullet. The little boy is suffering and is very sad.

[HD-injury CA-repair FB-aware]

Three stories are about care given after some incurred violence.

(Set m 10) (8BM) Here someone was riddled with shots (crivou de balas) a man. This man is suffering strong pain. A third man is thinking about what he can do to draw out the bullets. He will draw out the shots. [Q]: The man will not die. The doctor will draw out the shots.

[HD-injury PD-suffer CA-repair]

(Set m 11) (8BM) Boy with a gun! Doctors are making a surgery; they are trying to draw out the shot; it is difficult for them. [Q]: A boy has shot at this man. . . . Doctors will save the patient. Boy is here and I think now repentant.

[CB-difficult HC-injury CA-repair RB-regret]

(Set m 13) (8BM) Three men and one woman! They are in a conflict. One of the three men was shot and the friends are trying to help him; they are trying to draw up the shot out of his belly. The true friend is also a friend in one's sad hour; the sad person needs to divide his problems with his friends. Q: They will draw out the shot. They are doctors. The sorrow will go.

[HD-injury NDA-active FB-aware]

These stories reflect the social world and concerns of both the settler and Tukuna Indian group. One noted a more passive form of concern with violence in the Indian group than among the settlers. Violent protagonists are apt to be drunk. A heavy concern with possible physical illness is also evident. The settlers attend more directly to various motives such as banditry or revenge that could stimulate violent acts. The need for good medical attention appears in several stories.

Crises of Affection Revealed on Card 18GF

In testing the present sample on the Amazon, the women were given Card 18GF, which depicts one woman with her hands on the neck of another figure, usually seen as a woman. This card alternatively evokes themes of care of an afflicted person or violence. In the present samples, negative interpersonal themes appeared in four of thirteen Tukuna women compared with five of twelve settlers. Of these latter, mother as disciplinarian appeared in two stories. Themes of active care-giving appeared in six of thirteen Tukuna compared with four of twelve settler women. A religious context appeared a part of several of the stories. Overall the stories of the Tukuna women tended toward less assertiveness and more concern with receiving care to a statistically nonsignificant degree in this small sample.

Stories of Maternal Control

Two maternal discipline stories appear among the settlers. Mother as a disciplinarian is almost absent in all the Tukuna Indians stories, but not among the settlers. On Card 18GF, there is one story of a mother made angry by the daughter for some unspecified reason.

(Set f 12) (18GF) (A big smile) I think that is a mother holding a woman. The mother is sad; she is holding the woman's neck to be able to look well at the face of this woman. They are near to the stairs. [Q]: The mother and her daughter! The daughter has made something that her mother has not liked and so the mother is angry now. They are now very sad.

[RC-wrong HB-anger PD-sad]

In the second story an angry sister chastises her brother for not telling his mother of his failure to do his homework.

> (Set f 05) (18GF) I think that there are two persons: two men, no, it is one woman and one man. She is angry with him. He was coming down the stairs, then she has holding him. He is asking her to set him free! She is going to set him free and then he will tell the truth to her. [Q]: Her brother. Did not do his work for the school and has not told the reasons to his mother. Sister angry because she thinks that he must tell truth to the mother. He was obliged to tell mother: he has not made his homework for the school.
>
> [HB-resent RC-wrong RD-work]

Stories of Violence

Of the six Amazonian stories depicting violence, only one is specified as aimed at another woman. In previous samples in the west, the person being attacked has usually been another woman. In Japan, however, the person attacked occasionally could be a husband or son, depended on the status background of the story teller.

In a low-status Japanese fishing village, for example, the person being attacked could be a drunken husband, whereas in a middle status farming village it could be a wayward or delinquent son. A mother's discipline could reach the extreme of violence, but among middle-class farmers, no woman would be depicted as acting violently toward her husband by informants of either sex (De Vos and Wagatsuma, 1961).

Women among the Tukuna and among the settlers gave stories of violence toward a man.

> (TUK f 09) (18GF) A woman has killed a man. She has twisted his neck. [Q]: She was liking him very much, but as he would not like her she has killed him. He is dead now. I think that she will repent.
>
> [FB-thwart HC-murder RB-guilt]

In one story, the victim is not specified as to sex.

> (Set f 08) (18GF) Here is a stairs. There is a woman who is severely hurting a person. The bruising person has joked with the feelings of that woman. I don't know if this person is a man or a woman. [Q]: The woman is angry; she is 50 or 42 years old. The bruised person is not a handsome person and cannot make any reaction.
>
> [HC-injury EDC-tease OD-body]

Table 12.6
Card 18GF: Crises with Care or Violence

	Tukuna	*Settlers*
Total	*f 13*	*f 12*
Control	**1**	-
God corrects	1	-
Wrongdoing	-	**2**
Offends mother	-	1
Fails to do homework	-	1
Violence	**3**	**3**
Not specified	-	1
Toward man	2	1
Toward other woman	-	1
Toward male child	1	-
Death, Illness, or Accident	**1**	**3**
Accident	-	1
Illness leads to death	1	2
Nurture	**6**	**4**
Religious context	3	-
Helping ill person	2	4
Unable to help	1	-
Abandonment	**1**	-
Inner State	**1**	-
Sorrow	1	-

In another, the violence is directed toward a husband.

(TUK f 03) (18GF) Here is another person laying down by his wife. She has beaten this man on the ears. She puts the man on her arms and is dressing a wound on his ears. [Q]: He likes her, but she doesn't like him. They are in love. The most important for me is the wife dressing a wound.

[HC-hurt NDA-nurture FA-love]

(Set f 23) (18GF) What is this? A woman is beating strongly ("*dando um samba de pau*," in Portuguese) this man! It is impossible! The woman is beating the man. Women (plural) are beating the men today, professor? Meanwhile this woman is beating with a "samba de pau" on this man. [Q]: This is a samba of beatings ("Samba de pau," in Portuguese). This man has made something that his wife has not liked and then she went into a *samba of beatings*.

[HC-injury]

In another, it is toward a male child to the point of killing him!

> (TUK f 10) (18GF) Woman has slapped a child! Child had cried at the same time; ah, don't make it with me, he cried. But she decided to kill him. [Q]: I think that the woman was right. The child could not defend himself. He was a terrible kid.
>
> [HC-viol <u>HC-murder</u> RC-wrong]

In another, it is toward other woman in a nonspecified situation.

> (Set f 09) (18GF) Here a woman is holding another woman. The woman who is being held has done something that the other has not liked . . . and so. . . . The woman is crying. [Q]: The crying of the holding woman is not a repentant crying.
>
> [<u>HB-revenge</u> HD-repent]

Themes of Illness, Accidents, and Nurture

Situations of illness or accident become the themes of several stories. Death can be the result.

> (Set f 01) (18GF) It is near to the school. A lady was coming down and then she has fallen. Another woman has tried to help her but is was too late, the lady was dead. The woman is crying and complaining now. [Q]: The older lady is 78 years old. She was forbidden to leave the room, but she was an obstinate woman. The other woman is *crying* now, and that is because she was a friend of the good old lady.
>
> [<u>KD-ac-die</u> DSC-disobey FD-fate]

> (Set f 03) (18GF) This person . . . her son is dead, perhaps. She sets him on the bed and starts to cry. [Q]: The woman's son is dead; he became dead after an illness. This was the unique son she had. She is a widow and an old woman.
>
> [<u>KD-ill-die</u> KD-death KD-age]

> (TUK f 01) (18GF) This lady and her friend are crying. That's because a friend male of this friend female (she used the feminine) is sick. The lady is crying. The friend is dying. [Q]: The friend is a man, but he doesn't appear here. The lady had liked him a lot, too; so, she is crying more then her friend.
>
> [PA-sad <u>KD-ill-die</u>]

In eleven of twenty-five stories the women envision some person's desire to supply succoring or nurturant care.

> (TUK f 02) (18GF) That's a person who is dressing a wound on someone. The person is a man. The other is a man suffering of fever.
>
> [KD-illness <u>NDA-nurture</u>]

(TUK f04) (18GF) He . . . is dreaming, no, he's extracting the tooth of this person here. [Q]: The man has extracted the tooth of the woman. She is his wife. She is feeling an ache.

[PB-body NDA-nurture]

(Set f07) (18GF) Woman is holding her son; he was going up the stairs and almost fell down. [Q]: He is a boy, 25 years old; the woman is 40 years old; she is the mother. She is holding him because he was almost fainting; he has fainted now.

[KD-accident NDA-nurture]

(Set f02) (18GF) Her son was playing; he has felt some aches and then his mother became sad and is *crying* now. [Q]: The son is 8 years old and is feeling colic. The mother provides medicines.

[KD-illness NDA-nurture]

(Set f04) (18GF) Here is Manoelie. She's attending to her mother who is suffering an illness. That's all! [Q]: Manoelie is 29 years and her mother is 57 years old. The illness is heart-disease. But she is not dead. Manoelie takes care of her and attends her on time.

[KD-illness NDA-nurture]

(Set f 15) (18GF) A mother is taking care of her son; he is *sick*; she is giving medicine to him. He will win back his health.

[KD-illness NDA-nurture]

(Set f 20) (18GF) Mother is holding her daughter; daughter is probably sick. Mother looks to be worried with her daughter's sickness. She is taking care of and caressing her. [Q]: The most important for me is the mother.

[KD-illness NDA-nurture]

Compared with the settler concern with responding to accident or illness, the Tukuna women's stories are more apt to be passive. Nevertheless, one is about simple nurture.

(TUK f 18) (18GF) Some person nursing a little child. Child is laying down in a net. [Q]: This woman is 40 years old. I have liked it [looking at the card for a long time] I am liking it. [Are you feeling anything?] I always feel . . . (looking at the interpreter and at me) . . . homesick [and lowers her eyes].

[NDA-nurture FB-longing]

Others distort the content of the picture, expressing a more passive experience of receiving nurture or being controlled in a religious context.

(TUK f 12) (18GF) Jesus here! Here is someone with a child on his arms; she is listening to the child. There is a lot of hanging "lianas" behind the child. It is a forest, I think so. [Q]: That is Jesus on the arms of a woman. The high woman is a Samaritan. Jesus is lying down . The Samaritan is a high woman.

[NDA-charity EDA-awe]

(TUK f 24) (18GF) This here is God. God would like to accept the people, formerly. Today all is different, people live without God. [Q]: God is Christ; he looks at us to care for ourselves.

[EDA-awe NDA-charity]

(TUK f 26) (18GF) My wife and me! We are going together. That how God corrects us! The black here is like the past time before God's world creation. That's because the man must go always with his wife.

[DDA-advice RA-duty-o FA-love]

One Tukuna describes experiencing an inability to help.

(TUK f22) (18GF) A woman with her son. She is putting her hand on the son's ears. I think that he is suffering an earache. [Q]: The woman is 40 years old. Her son is sick. She doesn't know what is necessary to do against the sickness.

[KD-illness NDD-unable]

One sees a woman seeking son's solace for being abandoned by one's man.

(TUK f 06) (18GF) My son, your father has abandoned me! Sometimes, perhaps you will help me. Now, you must stay with me to make a piece of arable land, in order to purchase our clothes. I love you, my son. When your father will go back he will like you. [Q]: the husband has abandoned his wife and now he is living with another woman.

[FD-desert NSB-help FC-triangle]

Another simply express an inner state of sorrow.

(TUK f 20) (18GF) I don't, know what this here means . . . I cannot . . . [Q]: No, only sorrow.

[PD-sorrow]

Discussion

The foregoing material should well illustrate how a scoring system that focuses on universal instrumental and expressive social and personal themes picks up meaningful material, regardless of the cultural context of the groups being investigated. The standard Murray cards may not evoke settings known to the subjects tested, but they can elicit material of a psychological nature that allows us glimpses into the relatively salient concerns of a positive or negative nature. The TAT can attest to common humanity as well as the peculiarities found in diverse cultural settings. This material is not to be considered in isolation of ethnographic observation. Rather it helps the investigation in exploring issues in their relative saliency. The material elicited is of an emic nature. Projective tests gain spontaneous responses that are of a concern to those contacted, rather than being of an a-priori concern of the psychologist or anthropologist conducting the research. The Tukuna Indians in this sample do reveal their inner concerns. The above stories reveal much of the personal lives of the other Brazilians who have come to practice agriculture on newly opened lands bordering the Amazon. The difficulties present in relationships experienced within the family certainly become apparent, as well as the relative lack of a future time orientation that may be more characteristic of other pioneer groups elsewhere.

References

Connor, John W. and George A. De Vos. 1989. Cultural Influences on Achievement Motivation and Orientation Toward Work in Japanese and American Youth. In David Stern and Dorothy Eichorn (Eds.), *Adolescence and Work: Influence of Social Structure, Labor Markets, and Culture*. Hillsdale, N.J.: Lawrence Erlbaum Associates.

De Vos, George. 1973. *Socialization for Achievement: Essays on the Cultural Psychology of the Japanese*. Berkeley: University of California Press.

———. 1996. Internalized Achievement or External Authority: Some Cultural Comparisons of Responses to TAT Card 1. In Irving B. Weiner (Ed.), *Rorschachiana XXI Yearbook of the International Rorschach Society*. Göttingen: Hogrefe & Huber.

De Vos, George, Lisabeth Hauswald, and Orin Borders. 1979. Cultural Differences in Family Socialization: A Psychocultural Comparison of Chinese and Japanese. In Albert M. Craig (Ed.), *Japan: A Comparative View* (pp. 214–269). Princeton, N.J.: Princeton University Press.

De Vos, George and Eun-Young Kim. 1993. Koreans in Japan: Problems with Achievement, Alienation Authority. In I. Light and P. Bhachu (Eds.), *California Immigrants in World Perspective*. New Brunswick, N.J.: Transaction Books.

De Vos, George and Eiji Murakami. 1974. Violence and Aggression in Fantasy: A Comparison of American and Japanese Lower Class Youth. In William P. Lebra (Ed.), *Youth, Socialization and Mental Health* (pp. 153–177). Honolulu: University Press of Hawaii.

De Vos, George and Hiroshi Wagatsuma. 1959. Psycho-Cultural Significance of Concern over Death and Illness Among Rural Japanese. *International Journal of Social Psychiatry*, **5**(1): 6–19.

———. 1961. Value Attitudes Toward Role Behavior of Women in Two Japanese Villages. *American Anthropologist*, **63**(6): 1204–1230.

———. 1970. Status and Role Behavior in Changing Japan: Psycho-Cultural Continuities. In Georgene H. Seward and Robert C. Williams (Eds.), *Sex Roles in Changing Society* (pp. 334–370). New York: Random House.

Helm, June, George A. De Vos, and Teresa Carterette. 1960. Variations in Personality and Ego Identification Within a Slavery Indian Kin-Community. National Museum of Canada Bulletin, No. 190, *Contributions to Anthropology*, Part II.

Chapter 13

A Taxonomy of Esteem Values in the Philippines

Robert F. Manlove

Introduction

While exploring Philippine urban values in connection with social inequality (Manlove, 1990), I discovered that many of the long-known Philippine values (*amor propio, hiya, pakikisama, utang na loob*, and others) are not independently defined or independently operative in the culture. Previous writers (e.g., Bulatao, 1964; Guthrie, 1968; Hollnsteiner, 1961; Kaut, 1961; Lynch, 1962, 1973) have presented these values as if they operate independently, each a separate pillar upon which the culture is built. On the contrary, as I analyzed the Thematic Apperception Test (TAT) and Sentence Completion Test (SCT) results from a random sample of urbanites, it became clear that there is a definite structure to this portion of the Philippine value system. Some values are subsumed by others, and that each value takes its social significance, i.e., its meaning, from its contrast with the other values in a hierarchical, interactive structure of values.

In the process of delineating this structure, I was able to establish that there exists in the Philippines a locus of thinking centered upon the concept of esteem, and in this way produce support for George De Vos's theory of universals in thematic concerns. The implications in this theory extend into the relationship between culture and biology. Consequently, in this paper, I will do three things: I will first set out the central ideas of the theory as it is pertinent to Philippine culture and explore briefly the implications of these ideas to the study of culture more generally. Secondly, I shall present data from my direct study of the Philippine value system and, using the TAT and SCT projective vehicles, demonstrate the existence of an interactive structure within the esteem values. Third, I will fold these two parts together, showing that the Philippine data helps verify and confirm De Vos's theory.

Theoretical Frame

The Mental Framework of Culture

Major strides have been made toward the consilience of culture and biology. From the biological side, the mapping of the human genome offers glimpses of the genetic basis of behavior. From the cultural side, De Vos (1973) has made a major watershed contribution in his exploration of relative cultural saliency among universal thematic concerns. Using data demonstrating variations in human responses to common stimuli in several cultures, De Vos has been able to show that the thought patterns and behavior of human beings everywhere can be understood and categorized in terms of twelve universal human concerns: five instrumental concerns and five expressive interpersonal concerns and two impersonal concerns which can be arranged in complementary pairs. This universality immediately suggests that there is a connection between these culturally represented foci and the general evolutionary development of human beings. No other scientific explanation adequately addresses this unity of human thought. Further, it suggests that the organization of the human brain may in some way reflect these twelve foci of human thought.[1] And, if this is shown true, we are beginning to understand the crossover between the functioning of human biology and the complexities of human culture.

The twelve universal concerns that De Vos has identified are shown diagrammatically in Figure 1. I have matched them from the perspective of polarities I have found operative in the Philippine cultural setting. In the Philippine

[1]Some evidence already exists that specific parts of the human brain govern specific human concerns which have evolutionary significance. Patients with very localized brain damage dramatically demonstrate De Vos's categories. The most famous of these cases is that of Phineas Gage, whose left frontal lobe was punctured by a three foot iron rod and who was subsequently entirely normal except that he had no sense of moral responsibility (Damasio, 1994). Equally interesting in the present context was Damasio's patient "Elliot" whose tumor-damaged brain was deficient in the opposing area of the brain in the right frontal lobe. This patient could make socially acceptable moral judgments but continuously made poor decisions because he did not care what others thought of him. He seems to have lost the capacity of self-esteem, i.e., a sense of personal worth in the eyes of others (Damasio, 1994). For further elaboration of these issues, please see Manlove (2001).

case, the data suggest that Fate is an expressive category, and interest in objects or possessions is basically instrumental in nature. Hence in Figure 1 below on the left are six instrumental concerns—control/power, mutuality, responsibility, achievement, competence, and possession—and on the right in my diagram I have located six expressive concerns—fate, harmony, esteem, nurturance, affiliation, and pleasure. That these twelve concerns are evolutionary in nature is seen on close inspection. Each category and each pair of categories represent a distinct evolutionary advantage to individuals whose mental capabilities are organized to efficiently analyze social and environmental data and to generate effective, self-preserving responses.

Figure 1

Universal Thematic Concerns

Instrumental	*Expressive*
Control/Power	Fate
Mutual Purpose	Harmony
Responsibility	Esteem
Achievement	Nurturance
Competence	Affiliation
Objects (Possession)	Pleasure

Control/power has an obvious evolutionary advantage in that an individual who utilizes effective dominance and submission strategies is likely to be well integrated into the social group. On the expressive side, there are situations in every individual's life in which personal control is not an option and in which one must operate within unexplained and frequently frightening outside forces. In these circumstances, one's equanimity, one's ability to function and to survive is tied to mental processes involving transference, usually the displacement of causal forces to a larger realm than the human society present. These I see as fate responses.

The mutual purpose concerns represent the ability to work with others for a common good; clearly, this generates responses of evolutionary value in the face of a variety of social and physical environmental problems. One need only imagine large predator animals and large game animals in early hunting and gathering circumstances to see the advantages of mutual instrumental behavior. Harmony, the expressive side of mutuality, refers to mechanisms needed to maintain peace and to mend the inevitable stresses and strains upon the social fabric. It promotes an individual's ability to get along with his/her social group and, hence, to survive with their support.

Next we see a locus of concern around responsibility paired with a locus for esteem. A well-developed mental organization for responsibility allows an individual to act instrumentally independent of the group while being able to predict the reaction of other members of the group. That is, group survival is promoted by a common belief system, a consistent mode of thinking about moral correctness. Esteem is also seen as a mechanism for maintaining group solidarity. Positively used, it is a recognition of an individual's support of the social group while, negatively used (as we shall see in the Philippine materials), it is a threat to membership and the support of the group.

Mental organization for achievement in the next pair reflects an individual's concern for personal improvement and advancement within the group. This would clearly have an evolutionary advantage in mate selection. Similarly, on the other side of this pair, being mentally adept at nurturing strategies has a distinct evolutionary advantage. Nurturance is here seen as expressive aid to others; in an evolutionary sense, it is an unguaranteed investment in future assistance.

The concern for competence or ability is evolutionary because it involves the recognition, organization, and development of skills designed for the individual's and the group's benefit. Its complementary concern, affiliation, is the mental foundation that allows us to form intense attachments with other individuals (friendship, love) and is evolutionary in its promotion of supportive relationships within the group. The pairing of competence and affiliation can be partially understood by the complementarity of abilities of attracted individuals.

Attention to manipulatable objects (possession) represents the mental recognition and organization of the implements and implement attributes that may be vital to survival in a particular environment. Such an organized locus in the brain would facilitate the manufacture and understanding of tool types. It may explain, for example, the incredible transmission of the Acheulean handax technology over thousands of generations. And, lastly, the pleasure concern is the mental ability to sense current and future conditions and trends in physical and social environments so as to seek change toward more comfortable and possibly more survivable conditions for the individual. For example, when a person is seriously ill, the individual will normally drop his or her interest in other concerns so as to maximize comfort and minimize pain. Seeking for new excitement and the development of curiosity are also of obvious adaptive value.

Predictions and Tests of the Theory

One might suggest that De Vos's scheme is merely a mechanism for analysis, that the observations he is making could be grouped into other categories. However, the past successful application of the twelve foci to cultures around the world demonstrates that this is not a mere analytical device but rather reflects a basic pattern in human thinking. In my own work (discussed below), thousands of responses showed that the respondents were first choosing one of the twelve concerns and then exploring it as one would a new object of interest. They would then connect the primary concern with secondary concerns in a manner that is understood in terms of the overall structure of the twelve concerns. The secondary concern is more likely to be the paired concern in Figure 1 than another concern, especially when the primary concern is one of great interest to the respondent. When this happens, I will refer to the secondary paired concern as a *crossover concern*. Other secondary concerns are also predictable on the basis of the knowledge of the twelve categories and the emerging of a frequently repeatable cultural pattern. Very basically, it is now understood that, when we go into an untested culture, we will know *a priori* the categories of their thought.

It is the broader implications of the theory, however, that are truly engaging. It provides the beginnings of a universal definition of mental health. As an investigator works with a body of responses, it soon becomes clear that, regardless of the culture, individuals who are well adjusted to their social situation are those who balance their attention to the twelve concerns and do not become fixated without cause upon one or another. There are social conditions that will call upon individuals to concentrate their thoughts and behaviors upon one concern: in a time of warfare, it may be the epitome of sanity to focus entirely upon control and power. In less dire circumstances, however, a person who focuses all of his or her attention on control and power and subjugates all harmony, nurturance, affiliation, etc., to the quest for control is internally poorly adjusted—perhaps—neurotic or psychotic. Another source of mental illness lies in conflicts between the universal concerns. When an individual must continuously address a conflict between achievement and affiliation, for example, the loss in equanimity can be quite devastating.

The theory also has several important implications for learning. To take one aspect in particular, numerous experiments have shown that learning is most effective when multiple concerns are engaged in the learner. If a teacher requires students to learn mathematics, for example, entirely in the context of achievement, the learning will be agonizing and ineffective. On the other hand, if a teacher presents mathematics in the context of possessions, affiliation, control, or some other concern, the learning will not only be easier and more pleasing but also more effective.

Of greatest importance for anthropology, the theory provides the basis for the comparison of value systems without ethnocentrism and provides the possibility of understanding the evolution of present-day cultures from ancestral cultures. Perhaps most significant, the epistemology of culture becomes a fruitful field shared by both anthropology and biology.

We must inevitably come to the question of how cultural variation develops in the context of universal human concerns. Here it becomes evident that De Vos's theory is capable of explaining and predicting several aspects of culture.

First, the theory proposes that an underlying mental framework, an organization of the brain, exists for the generation of basic social agreements. This does not mean that the social agreements are the same in all societies; it means only that culture is generated by universal concerns.

Second, the theory suggests that the world's cultures will have much more in common than they have in difference. In fact, any careful study would reveal that the underlying unity among cultures greatly outweighs the apparent uniqueness; anthropologists have been frequently guilty of exaggerating differences simply because the differences are more interesting than similarities.

Third, the theory proposes that every culture will have values or norms for all of the concerns. There is no culture, for example, so utopian that it lacks all concern about dominance and there is no culture that occupies so sweet a physical environment that it has no norms for maximizing physical comfort. A complete study of the values of a particular culture would ask for the rules for coping in *each* of the twelve areas.

Fourth, the theory proposes that each culture will emphasize some of the universal concerns at the expense of other concerns. Every anthropologist knows cultures that place a high premium on harmony (e.g., the Inuit cultures) and, in contrast, cultures that place little emphasis upon harmony (e.g., Reo Fortune's Dobuans). This situation is the result of the particular social and environmental problems that the society has faced and, of course, produces the uniqueness of the particular culture. Commonly, a society will develop multiple strategies or values for the emphasized concerns; in the evolutionary perspective, these take the form "if A happens or is desired,[2] do B to maximize the result." Also, we may add that the values for an emphasized concern are usually easier for the individuals to verbalize because the concern represents an area of mutual anxiety that is discussed or debated.

Fifth, the theory explains cultural relativity, i.e., the concept that different aspects of a culture are consistent and supportive of each other, by suggesting that the brain's activity is not long confined to any particular portion of the brain or to any particular concern. There is, consequently, internal consistency within each individual's thinking which translates to a consistency across the culture. Conclusions about how societal harmony is achieved, for example, are consistent with conclusions about how one becomes dominant or acquires tools.

Sixth, De Vos's theory predicts that the organization of values of a particular universal concern will be inherently taxonomic. If the values take the form "if A happens or is desired, do B," they represent choices that compete with each other in a particular situation. There could also be a value "if A happens or is desired, do C." Consequently, the values will be organized into a hierarchical structure and the significance and definition of each value are determined by its position in the hierarchy. This hierarchical nature of the values will also have some reference in the structure of the brain since there is survival value in being systematic in the solution of human problems. Under specific social or environmental conditions, a specific, learned (previously successful) response should be generated. We may note that it is already well known that many parts of cultures are structured and taxonomic. The

---

[2]In my view, it is not productive to differentiate between internal and external stimuli.

rules for choosing parts of speech (e.g., pronouns) fit into tidy taxonomies as do the rules for identifying different categories of kinship in a society. The same mental tendencies will apply to all rules governing behavior.

The Philippine Example

I turn next to the illustration of these ideas by my data from the Philippines, looking primarily at 7,500 TAT and SCT responses that I collected. I will first discuss briefly the data collection in order to demonstrate the nature and rigor of the process. Second, I will show how the TAT identifies the human concerns that are most important in the Philippine culture and, in particular, how it highlights the importance of esteem. Third, using both TAT and SCT data, I will show that there is a coherent structure of values within the esteem focus found specifically in the Philippine culture.

Sampling and the Data Base

A detailed description of the sampling and the use of the two projective tests is to be found in my Ph.D. dissertation for the University of California, Berkeley: *Ozamiz: A Case Study in Urban Anthropology*. However, I want to give a short description of the fieldwork here because it was somewhat unusual for anthropology. Instead of relying heavily upon participatory observation, a rigorous statistical sample was taken to ensure that the results represented the city as a whole.

After establishing myself in the community and learning the local language (Visayan) over a period of several months,[3] I interviewed a random sample of 10 percent of the households of the city of Ozamiz to obtain a detailed understanding of their economic and social characteristics. Since there were 4,942 households (35,800 persons) in the city, this procedure required the interviewing of the household heads of 494 households. To be sure that the households were randomly selected, I mapped the city, numbered the households by kitchen (multiple kitchens in a house meant multiple households), and then interviewed every tenth household. Although a few household heads declined to be interviewed (and caused me to move to the next household in the sequence), 99 percent of the households chosen by this method extended great hospitality and agreed to be interviewed.

On the basis of the interviewing, I accumulated a massive amount of socio-economic data on each household (including kinship relations, education, occupations, land ownership, income, forms of social participation, longevity in the

---

[3]I had served two years as a Peace Corps volunteer in an urban setting in the southern Philippines prior to the fieldwork here described.

community, godparenthood, and much more). This allowed me to determine that there are six social classes in the city as follows:

Class	*Principal Occupations*	*% of Households*
A	Tenant farmer, fisherman, tricycle driver, market vendor, cook, tailor, barber, auto mechanic, truck or bus driver	51%
B	Farmer (land-owning), teacher, policeman, soldier, fireman, government or store clerk, electrician, plumber, tinsmith	33%
C	Agent of a national firm, entrepreneur, small business owner	5%
D	Doctor, lawyer, dentist, engineer, optometrist, army officer, civil administrator	8%
E	Chinese merchant	2%
F	Landed elite (large copra and rice farm owner)	1%

I discovered that it is possible to identify a family's class standing by simply noticing the number and nature of the possessions in the household and the size of the house. Subsequently, I devised an economic index that measured these things and I used the definitive ranges in this index to identify the class standing of unusual households (e.g., a widow's household). This economic index proved invaluable in maintaining the randomness of later TAT and SCT sampling since it took the human factor out of the selection of household samples.

The TAT and SCT sample groups were constructed on the basis of the initial socioeconomic analysis. Knowing the range of the economic index for each class and identifying the modal value of the index for each class, we were able to choose individuals that most clearly represented each class. We drew fifty-one individuals from Class A whose households fell at the modal value of their index range and, similarly, thirty-three from Class B, five from Class C, eight from Class D, two from Class E, and one from Class F. In this way, we created a TAT sample of 100 individuals. A second drawing was done in similar fashion to produce a different group of 100 individuals for the SCT sample. All of the individuals were heads of households or their spouses. If the middle digit of the sample number was even, we chose a female respondent and, if it was odd, we chose a male respondent thus ensuring randomly that half were male and half were female.

Both test vehicles, the TAT card set and the list of sentence fragments in the SCT, went through extensive pre-testing before they were used with the chosen respondents. The faces and scenes in the Murray TAT pictures were redrawn to be

Filipino faces and scenes. (American movies are widely available in the Philippines and we found that when TAT pictures depicted what they saw as an American scene, it occasionally produced a response based upon their stereotypes of Americans and sometimes upon the story of the most recent American movie to visit the city.) However, the adjustments of the Murray pictures were minimized to preserve the comparability of our TAT results with those obtained in other cultures. All of the responses to the vehicles were collected in writing by well-known local Filipinos who had been hired and trained for the task so that the respondents would not be directly influenced by the American anthropologist. The respondents all came to a central, neutral locality in the city to write down their responses. Although approximately half of the population of Ozamiz is fluent in English, 80 percent of the respondents chose to write in Visayan. After experimenting with a translation/back-translation method, I found that translating into English was accomplished most accurately by using three independent translators in serial. A local college instructor, who had done social survey work herself, was chosen as the primary translator from the many individuals in Ozamiz who were fluent in both languages. The second and third translators reviewed her translation for completeness and accuracy, adding any overlooked nuances in the responses and correcting any slight, inadvertent bias. Due to the sensitivity to criticism in the Philippine culture, each translator worked without knowledge of the identity of the other translators.

Research Results: The Foci of Philippine Values as Shown by the TAT

The unique character of the Philippine culture emerges when we see that they respond differentially to standard stimuli. Rather than address all possible concerns, they concentrate their interests on particular concerns. And within these concentrations will lie the greatest development of values to guide individual behavior. That is, the topics that the Filipinos worry about most will logically generate the largest number of prescriptions for behavior.

Here I will review the results of five TATs, numbered 1, 2, 12, 16, and 19, obtained in a series of twenty. Three of these are derivative of the standard Murray set (1, 2, and 16) and two are special pictures made to reflect the Philippine cultural setting (12 and 19). In discussing the TAT data, however, it is important to understand a central aspect of the TAT pictures, namely, that, although they are constructed to be somewhat stimulus-free, they do nevertheless contain stimuli. With the exception of TAT No. 16, the blank card, each picture contains at least one stimulus bias that must be taken into account in the process of analyzing the responses.

TAT No. 1, shown with the other TATs in Appendix B, is a standard Murray picture redrawn slightly to show a Philippine face. This picture contained a clear achievement bias in the minds of the Filipinos; 95 percent felt compelled to account for the boy's achievement. This strong bias is indicative of the fact that the Filipinos are very much interested in achievement, a pattern that will emerge below. However, it would be inaccurate to suggest that they spend 95 percent of their time thinking about achievement. In fact, when they were writing about this card, all of the respondents went beyond the achievement theme to discuss another major concern as if to say, "Yes, the boy wants to achieve; now let's talk about something else." For this reason, I have tallied only the secondary concerns below to see the concerns that are the foci of the culture. Other TAT data will give us a picture of the importance of achievement.

There is another bias in the TAT No. 1 data that must be recognized. This is the bias toward nurturance which, at 39 percent, received considerably more attention in this TAT than it does in other TATs. This bias may be simply a result of the fact that there is a child in the picture. However, the theory leads to a different conclusion, namely, that there is an instrumental-expressive crossover phenomenon occurring in Filipino thought. That is, the strong achievement response is generating interest in its expressive counterpart, nurturance. There will be more evidence about these instrumental-expressive crossovers below.

Eliminating the achievement focus, TAT No. 1 generated the distribution of concerns shown in Table 13.1.

Table 13.1

Card 1: Distribution of Stories in ICSS Categories

Concern	*% of Responses*	*Concern*	*% of Responses*
Control	4	Fate	5
Mutual Purpose	1	Harmony	1
Responsibility	14	Esteem	20
Achievement	X	Nurturance	39
Competence	8	Affiliation	3
Possession	3	Pleasure	2

In the context of this card and its achievement bias, the respondents focused on responsibility, esteem and nurturance. The following story will illustrate how the respondents would first touch on achievement (e.g., decide to learn the violin) and then move to a concern such as esteem and build their response around it.

> (Card 1: class A female) The boy is thinking deeply in what to do. Then he decided that he should learn how to play with the violin very well. He should do it well so

that he will be praised by others. Finally he is happy for his decision because he became a famous musician.

[AA-self AA-status ESA-fame]

Other stories chose responsibility as the focus, typically with a strong emphasis on the temptations that exist in life and the importance of a strong moral code:

(Card 1: class A female) This picture shows a boy who is not happy about what he is studying. He is a son of a wealthy family who has everything he needed in life. His parents want him to learn how to play the violin, but he is not interested. He just likes to go with friends to the movies which are not good for teenagers. Until he learned about sex. He indulged in sex to satisfy him. He got married and met many problems. He does not know any job. His wealthy parents died broken-hearted because they have lost their wealth. They have all sold them just to pay for his wrong doings. Now he is a notorious robber, an enemy of the government. He wasn't able to give a good future to the family he left behind.

[KA-wealth AA-parent RC-indulge CD-unable RC-result PD-sad KD-poverty RC-illegal]

In the nurturance stories of Card 1, the dominant portrayal is that success is possible only with help, particularly parental help:

(Card 1: class A female) This child is sad because he wanted to go to school. But because they were poor and his parents cannot afford to let him study the violin, then he is very sad because it is his great desire that he would study but how could he when they are poor. He did not succeed in his ambition. Because his parents couldn't do anything.

[AA-self KD-poverty NDB-unable KD-hopeless]

Each of these stories represents a doorway into a thought pattern that the Filipinos use. In each case, it is possible to open the pattern for closer inspection and greater understanding.

Turning to TAT No. 2, the stimulus is the picture of a rural family. An adult male is shown plowing the field; a heavy-set woman, usually seen as pregnant, watches him; a young woman is turned away with books on her arm. Here there appears to be a bias toward achievement (the young woman is going out of the family to achieve) and nurturance (raising a family) and a bias away from esteem. Within the family, the respondents seem to be saying, one's honor is not at stake; as a result, there is no need to speak of esteem (i.e., honor or appreciation). The primary foci of the stories given for this TAT are tabulated in Table 13.2.

This TAT produced a large number of achievement-nurturance crossover stories. In these cases, it was analytically necessary to decide whether the emphasis was on achievement or on nurturance but, in general, this was not difficult. The following story, classified as a nurturance story, is typical of these crossover stories.

Table 13.2

Card 2: Distribution of Stories in ICSS Categories

Concern	*% of Responses*	*Concern*	*% of Responses*
Control	2	Fate	1
Mutual Purpose	0	Harmony	0
Responsibility	27	Esteem	3
Achievement	33	Nurturance	33
Competence	0	Affiliation	1
Possession	0	Pleasure	0

> (Card 2: class A female) This young girl at the start was just an ordinary girl who wished that she will be successful so that she can give comforts to her parents. She is just a daughter of a farmer and she thought that her father can't give her a bright future. So she thought of some ways that she can help her parents. She saved every centavo. She earned money by peddling. In this way, she is helping her parents. Then she was able to finish schooling. She became a teacher and little by little, she helped her parents and was able to save some money for their own good in the future.
>
> [AA-nurture NDB-unable RA-duty-s NDA-family AA-counter]

There were also several responsibility-esteem crossover stories; most of these were heavy with responsibility and relatively light on the esteem concern and were, consequently, classified most often as responsibility stories:

> (Card 2: class B female) The Student from the Country: In the small barrio of Labo, there's a couple with one daughter. Their daughter's name is Lumen. They were very happy, even if they are poor. They are understanding parents. Lumen is also respectful to her parents. Before the sun rises up, Lumen starts working in the kitchen to cook their breakfast early. After cooking, she will clean the house, the yard and afterwards, take a bath so that she will change her clothes, eat her breakfast and then go to school which is about 1 ½ kilometers away.
>
> [HA-family EDA-respect RA-duty-s]

Occasionally, a respondent would switch concerns in the middle of a story. In the case given below, the respondent started with an achievement-nurturance crossover story and then started a new paragraph with a responsibility-nurturance crossover story. Other concerns are subsumed to the principle concerns. Control/power ("obedient") as well as fate (God's judgment) provide the mental framework for the main concerns which nevertheless remain clear:

(Card 2: class A female) This is a picture of a happy family. The father is showing his diligence and the wife her support. The obedient child is also showing interest in her studies. The father is always industrious since the start because he wants to give a good future to his only daughter.

[HA-family RA-work DSA-comply NDA-active AA-nurture]

[changes story:] He has high hopes that in the future, he can see his daughter successful in her studies. But he was disappointed because his daughter fell into sin. So they are disappointed because their daughter wasted the time and effort they have given her. The father lost his interest and he got sick because of what had happened to his beloved daughter. The father is now waiting for God's judgment.

[NDA-active RC-wrong AD-motive KD-illness DDB-god]

The TAT No. 2 stories provide three pieces of evidence: First, they confirm the Philippine interest in responsibility, esteem, achievement, and nurturance over the other concerns. Second, they demonstrate the significance of the instrumental-expressive crossover phenomenon in general. And, third, they demonstrate the Philippine interest in particular types of crossovers.

In the next TAT, No. 12, two men are shown meeting in a public place, one man dressed well and the other dressed relatively poorly. The picture was drawn specifically to elicit stories about social inequality and therefore contains a bias toward control/power; a large portion of the respondents (92 percent) sought to explain the social inequality between the two men. They then went on to develop other thematic concerns and, since these lie beyond the stimulus, it is these other concerns that are tabulated in Table 13.3.

Table 13.3

Card 12: Distribution of Stories in ICSS Categories

Concern	*% of Responses*	*Concern*	*% of Responses*
Control	X	Fate	3
Mutual Purpose	0	Harmony	2
Responsibility	14	Esteem	19
Achievement	24	Nurturance	27
Competence	0	Affiliation	10
Possession	0	Pleasure	1

Once again we see concentrations in the responsibility, esteem, achievement, and nurturance concerns with a smaller concentration in affiliation. In the responsibility stories, there were two general types of stories. In one type, the well-dressed man was said to have a responsibility relative to the other man or to society in general. Although we might expect these stories to contain nurturance subthemes, stating that the well-dressed man had a responsibility to *help*, this is relatively unusual. Subthemes are more likely to focus on esteem. The following is an example of this:

> (Card 12P: class B female) We can see two men in this picture. One of them has a responsibility and we can see that the other is asking about experience because we can see that the other asked something from the educated. Because we have the courteous practice of helping those who ask for help. So in this part, we can see that the man is asking and the other answered.
>
> [RA-good NDA-active CA-aware CB-help EDA-respect]

The other type of responsibility story focuses on negative responsibility. Since Filipino families frequently send their sons and daughters away to school, the common story here is that the young person fails in his or her responsibility to attend school.

> (Card 12P:class B male) The weather was hot at that time. An old man went out to the city to find out if his son is studying because he heard talks that his son is no longer going to school but just roaming around. When he reached the gate of the school, he saw the teacher and there he learned that his child did not come to school for almost a week. His son is intelligent but why did he misbehave. The father was very angry because he has been sending money several times but it was just wasted by his son. So he let his son stop schooling and let him work in the rice field.
>
> [DDA-control RA-duty-s RC-wrong RC-waste DDA-punish]

The achievement stories for this TAT showed an interesting pattern relative to the class of the respondent. The stories that focused on achievement came almost entirely from the higher classes (classes B, C, D, E, and F). This is, of course, what we would expect; individuals who process the achievement motivation well are likely to be upwardly mobile in an open class system and, since this separates them from other people, it is likely to be a matter that activates worries (conflicts with other concerns). Interestingly, the achievement stories from the class B tended to be mixed with other concerns, i.e., they tend to be less purely focused on achievement. The following is an example of the class B response in which the focus is on achievement but responsibility also comes into play.

> (Card 12P: class B male) A man needs patience, even in his studies so that he will be successful in his ambitions. Study, goodness, uprightness and industry must be there. If laziness will prevail in man, poverty and hardship in life will engulf him;

especially those who have families. Hardships in his existence will lead a man to steal the properties of others. If we can find a job, we must serve our employer honestly so that we will be praised by our manager. Then our salary will increase because of the honesty we showed.

[RA-control AA-self RC-indulge KD-poverty RC-illegal DSA-author ESA-praise NDA-means]

The nurturance stories for TAT 12, on the other hand, came almost entirely from the lower class:

(Card 12P: class A male) These two persons meet on the road. One here is rich and the other is poor. This poor man asked something from the rich man and said, "Have pity on me. Help me find a job because I'm very poor and I have no one to go to except you." The rich man said, "Yes, I am looking for a worker to work at home," and the man was very happy.

[KB-status NSA-assist NDA-means]

Here again we see instrumental-expressive crossovers; the poor man is saying "please help me to achieve" (e.g., find a job).

The affiliation stories in TAT 12 may represent a stimulus bias. However, they were interesting because they contained a particular collection of subthemes. Some of the stories included the expected crossover to competence (ability) but the competence subtheme was not strongly developed:

(Card 12P: class E female) These two were classmates in high school before. After high school, the other one because he was rich was able to go to college but the one being poor wasn't able to study. So he was just working in the farm. He has no improvement until he married somebody who's their neighbor in the same barrio. He thought of going to town to look for another job. There he saw his classmate in high school who was also his close friend. He was happy and they engaged in a conversation. He asked the advice of his friend about a job, even as a janitor or a gardener, just as long as he can work. His friend pitied him. Because they were very close in high school, he was helped and given a job in his friend's shop.

[KB-status RA-duty-o FA-friend NDB-pity NDA-means]

Other affiliation stories started strongly on the theme of friendship but then switched to other concerns, such as the esteem subtheme in this example:

(Card 12P: class A male) Story of Two Friends: These two friends, during their first companionship, were more than brothers because anywhere they went, they were always together. Time came that one of the friends has to go to school because he was already thinking that he can succeed and his friend cultivated a farm and was also thinking of the future. His friend prospered and worked in an office and is already well dressed. His old friend called him because he became a well-known man in town. Thinking that the character of his friend has not changed, he approached him. But he was not met by his friend. Instead, he did not mind him because they are no longer of the same standards of living.

[FA-friend AA-self OB-clothes FD-rejected FC-reject EDC-status]

And yet other affiliation stories suggest but do not specify a mutual purpose subtheme, but remains focused on an expressive relationship:

(Card 12P: class A male) In a certain place there were two close friends. Anywhere they went, they always were together either to the party or going to church, they always went together. Most of the people who saw them said that they were very loving, even visiting or anywhere they don't separate. They are very happy. What I could say is that they are two very close friends and are very happy.

[FA-friend PA-joy]

Once again, we sense that we are analytically peering into an open door. More research would demonstrate the mental framework that the Filipinos use for affiliation and control-power.

TAT No. 19 elicited a somewhat different set of stories. This card showed two men, one Filipino and one Chinese, engaged in a purchase in a typical store and was designed to test ethnic relations between the Filipino and Chinese populations of the city. It was quite effective at doing this; 46 percent of the respondents dedicated part of their story to the description of Chinese-Filipino relations.[4] From our present perspective, this constitutes a mutual purpose bias which I have eliminated by tabulating below only the concerns that were given in addition to the mutuality concern. The harmony responses tabulated in Table 13.4 are probably also part of that bias and represent the instrumental-expressive crossover effect that we have seen above. Also there are an unusually large number of stories about possessions, generated no doubt by the commercial setting of the picture; such stories are rare elsewhere.

[4]For further information about these remarkably positive ethnic relations, readers may wish to refer to my dissertation (Manlove, 1990).

Table 13.4

Card 19: Distribution of Stories in ICSS Categories

Concern	*% of Responses*	*Concern*	*% of Responses*
Control	0	Fate	4
Mutual Purpose	X	Harmony	14
Responsibility	26	Esteem	9
Achievement	12	Nurturance	20
Competence	0	Affiliation	5
Possession	10	Pleasure	0

Typical of the responsibility stories is this story about an immoral customer.

> (Card 19P: class A male) This is a person who doesn't have a future in life because he is a drunkard and asked money from the stores. He is feared by the people in this town because he is one of those lawbreakers. He abandoned his wife and children and let them follow the wrong way. So this is the situation now because if you are the one to lose your way, you will fall into the road of darkness.
>
> [RC-Abuse NSC-demand RC-illegal ND-desert]

Almost all of the responsibility stories were negative ones, cataloging all the evils that young people can encounter. As mentioned above, the Filipinos are very concerned about the morality of young people who are away from home and, hence, away from the control of the family. It is not possible to criticize someone in public without very serious repercussions and the family must therefore be the source of a moral code for each offspring. These stories constitute a list of "thou shalt nots" such as smoking and drinking to excess, gambling, cheating, stealing, and general laziness. The Chinese merchant is never seen as irresponsible in these stories and, in fact, is praised for his support of the community.

The harmony stories tabulated for this TAT above are actually mutual purpose and harmony crossover stories that typically describe either the Chinese merchant's civic spirit or the Filipino customer's problems with credit:

> (Card 19P: class A male) To be a storekeeper is good if you know how to deal with customers. Even if he is a creditor, be good to him, even if you are already angry. Here you can measure how far is your patience to creditors. If they don't pay immediately, try to talk to them well so that their heart will be softened. Not that you will let them to pay immediately, even if they don't have money. A person who knows how to borrow also knows how to pay.
>
> [RA-work RA-control HA-depict OB-money HA-pacify MTA-interest]

The next example is a mutuality-harmony story which adds a nurturance subtheme and shows the general appreciation of the Chinese merchant as well as a fear of urban fire:[5]

> (Card 19P: class B female) An Alien Friend: Chiong is a Chinese who lives in our town and his character was almost similar to ours because he has been staying there for many years. He had helped plenty; for example, he will extend credit to the employees, especially to teachers who did not receive their salary yet. He will loan money without any interest as long as it will be returned. To the young men, he is very close because he will tell them what to do in order to help their parents. One day, there was a fire near the place where the store of the Chinese was situated and because the people pitied that the store of the Chinese will be burned, they helped to transfer the goods and stocks in the plaza while the others are fetching water to save the store which is next target of the fire. Even the firemen tried their best to stop the fire. Finally, the fire was stopped and the store of the Chinese was not burned.
>
> [EDA-ethnic FA-share MTA-interest NDA-advice KD-mishap NDA-active]

In the lower classes, achievement stories or stories of working for motives again tend to be nurturance crossovers with emphasis on financial need such as this one:

> (Card 19P: class A male) There was a young man who went inside a store and applied for a job. The Chinese was hesitant at first. But he pleaded, even if he won't be given a salary, as long as he can eat. The Chinese pitied him and he was accepted. He thanked God because he did not fail in looking for a job.
>
> [NSA assist NDB-pity NSA-grateful]

As with TAT 12 above, achievement stories from the upper class tend to be more purely focused on instrumental activities rather than need:

> (Card 19P: class E male) This child's dream wasn't useless. He graduated from commerce. Now he's applying for a job in a store. He has a profession so he was accepted. He worked hard until after several days he became the manager of a big store.
>
> [AA-self CB-help]

Lastly, we turn to TAT 16, the blank card. The absence of stimulus bias makes this card particularly interesting but, because it is totally open-ended in terms of possible responses, there are other analytical problems. The stories are frequently autobiographical and much longer than the responses to other cards. And, as might be expected in a long monologue, a respondent does not stay on a single concern but goes from one to another, linking the concerns in the context of the story. The

---

[5]One third of the city burned down six months after my research was complete.

most common pattern was to choose a single pair of concerns but, unlike responses to other cards, it was frequently not possible to determine which concern was most important.

To analyze these data, consequently, I made a judgment about which *pair* of concerns was most important to the respondent and scored each story in both categories. This led to 200 total data entries, and the number of times a particular concern was mentioned had to be divided by two to get the percent of the responses in which that concern was a major focus. (For example, control/power happened to be one of the foci in thirteen pairs so it is found in 6.5 percent of the responses.) The linkages are, of course, of prime interest here. Theoretically, there are sixty-six types of linkage possible if twelve concerns are taken two at a time. Of these, thirty-five were used by the Filipinos. The most popular linkages were instrumental-expressive linkages (63 percent) and one third of these (21 percent) were the instrumental-expressive crossovers predicted by the theory. Since the theory predicts a tendency to favor the six particular pairs shown in Figure 1 which constitute only 9 percent of the possible pairings, this 21 percent figure is too large to be explained by random chance and is therefore in support of the theory. Thirty-seven percent of the linkages were *not* instrumental-expressive; 22 percent were expressive-expressive and 15 percent were instrumental-instrumental.

Table 13.5 indicates how often each concern was a prime focus in a TAT 16 story.

Table 13.5

Card 16: Distribution of Stories in ICSS Categories

Concern	*% of Responses*	*Concern*	*% of Responses*
Control	6.5	Fate	15.5
Mutual Purpose	4.5	Harmony	4.0
Responsibility	17.0	Esteem	4.5
Achievement	14.5	Nurturance	21.5
Competence	2.5	Affiliation	7.0
Possession	1.5	Pleasure	1.0

Perhaps the most interesting aspects of these results are the decrease in esteem replies and the increase in fate and control replies compared to other cards. This is explained by the autobiographical nature of these stories. When a person is referring to himself or herself, there is, at least in the Philippines, a shift in the person's concerns away from personal honor and toward the larger frame of control or personal destiny in which one must operate. Here they are much more likely to credit their success or failure to outside forces such as the government, acts of nature, or God's will than in their responses to other cards. An example is this autobiographical story:

> (Card 16: class B male) A Poor Farmer—Before Masagana 99 [a government program] was implemented, Carlos, who was a farmer, has a regular standard of living. Now he owes a lot to the Masagana 99 and he has nothing to pay his debt. Before Masagana 99, he was very happy because he can borrow money from the bank and buy fertilizer. So his plants grew well but when harvest time comes, he has saved a little even if he has something to pay to the bank. The second year the system was still the same. Carlos borrowed money from the Masagana 99 but a time came when there was pestilence. The rats ate all the plants. Carlos found no other alternative; he sold his carabao to pay his debt and because he has nothing to eat, he leased his work to buy rice and other things. So Carlos, a farmer in Ozamiz City, said the condition before was better than today.
>
> [KD-poverty OB-money DDB-result KD-thwart]

Achievement-nurturance crossover stories, of which the following is an example, were the most abundant type of response to TAT 16.

> (Card 16: class A male) I have a story about my childhood. At 7 years of age, I studied at Banadero Elementary School. I was still a child and I kept on asking money from my mother to buy my snacks during vacant time. At my sixth grade in elementary, I was no longer given money because there were already three of us going to school and my parents were hard up. I can have pocket money. I said to my father, I will shine shoes and my father agreed. From Monday until Friday I go to school. Saturdays and Sundays I shine shoes. After elementary, I said to my father, I will study but he said he has no money. I said to my father not to worry because I will find money so that I can study. I sell newspapers and I study at night until I finished 2nd year high school. Then I looked for another job as helper in a certain company in Ozamiz City. Until now, this is my work.
>
> [AA-self NSA-means KD-poverty AA-counter]

The second most common type of story was a crossover story that pulled in all four of the dominant concerns—responsibility, esteem, achievement, and nurturance. Typically, responsibility and nurturance were the most emphasized as in the following two stories.

> (Card 16: class A male) My story is that I have happiness in my life, especially that I was taught by my parents good manners and right conduct. Because for me, I do not regret my life because of the advice of my parents, especially when I taught how to manage business. And I know that even my parents are happy because it is their pride to have a good son.
>
> [NDA-advice RA-duty-s EDA-praise PA-joy]

> (Card 16: class A male) The Life of a Tricycle Driver: A tricycle driver sacrifices day and night so that he will live. But even though he is just a tricycle driver,

> behind his sacrifices he receives something. A person who labors will receive something. A person who labors will receive the fruit of his labors. This driver does not expect greatness or glory but who knows if your occupation is honest, God will reward you. In this earth, we are from God. If we behave, we will be blessed by Him, because God knows everything, what do we do here either good or bad. So a tricycle driver can still expect something good if he will be good.
>
> [PA-endure NSA-god NSA-reward]

This example shows the responsibility-esteem crossover which appeared in five of the 100 stories:

> (Card 16: class A male) If you have a pure heart, you will not be ashamed to your fellow men, even if you are lower than them. You can be proud of yourself facing people. Those who have black consciences will not be at ease, they are uneasy facing the society. It seems somebody will pinpoint at them and they cannot understand their feelings. But those who have pure hearts will not be ashamed to face, no matter how many misfortunes will come to life.
>
> [RA-good ESA-worth ESB-status PA-endure]

In summary, the data of the five TATs we have reviewed support the theory in two principal ways. First, the data have shown that there are four major concerns—responsibility, achievement, esteem, and nurturance—which absorb the attention of the Filipinos to the exclusion of other concerns.

It remains an open question whether all cultures would respond to these stimuli with these concentrations. Certainly, the ethnographic literature would tend to deny that conclusion. What the theory suggests, and what I hope to show in the next sections, is that these concentrations of concern are unique to the Philippines in their internal structure. In other words, they represent concentrations of values that address the particular concern and that are uniquely Philippine in their nature.[6]

The second way in which the TAT data support the theory lies in the prevalence of instrumental-expressive crossovers of the types that are predicted. When they are talking about control or power, they have a tendency to also speak in terms of fate; when they discuss responsibility, they also speak of esteem; when they focus on achievement, they tie it into nurturance, and so forth.

---

[6]It is my intention here to show only that these concerns are foci for values in the Philippine culture. The relative amount of interest in individual concerns is not to be implied in the numbers in the preceding table in any rigorous manner and, indeed, will no doubt vary depending upon the social circumstances.

Table 13.6

Distribution of Stories in ICSS Categories in Five TAT Cards

Concern	*Average % of Responses in Five TATs*	*Concern*	*Average % of Responses in Five TATs*
Control	3	Fate	6
Mutual Purpose	1	Harmony	4
Responsibility	20	Esteem	11
Achievement	21	Nurturance	28
Competence	2	Affiliation	5
Possession	3	Pleasure	1

This may at first seem like a series of truisms, to say, for example, that if they are speaking of responsibility, the "thou shalt nots" of the society, they will also feel obligated to account for the edicts of esteem, i.e., honor and shame. However, I would point out that responsibility could just as easily be tied to harmony (getting along with each other), control (who should say how correct behavior is defined), or the other concerns. Responsibility might therefore be found to be uniformly associated with all of the other concerns. But instead we find a distinct tendency for informants to associate it with esteem. This marked consistency of the linkages between complementary concerns is one of the main proofs of the theory.

Esteem Values in the TAT Data—Hints of a Taxonomy

There are, of course, values in all twelve of the concerns. However, the emotional emphasis upon the four areas makes it most productive to look specifically at the dominant concerns. In addition, the values of other lesser concerns will prove to be brought under the four dominant concerns and thought of by the respondents as needed to resolve problems in the dominant areas. Consequently, the next step, both in terms of understanding the Philippine value system and in terms of confirming the theory, is to demonstrate that the four dominant concerns are internally structured and cohesive, that is, that they represent modes of thinking for the respondents in which clear and contrasting decisions are made. In this paper, however, I will confine my attention to one area, namely, esteem.

Esteem is a strong force in the Philippines. Two of the most important and most publicized Philippine values, shame (*hiya*) and self-esteem (*amor propio*), lie in this part of the Philippine taxonomy. It is not possible to live in the Philippines for long without running into esteem-driven behavior. Social clubs, such as Rotary or Lions, go to great lengths to bestow honor on their own members, and club members take great umbrage if not publicly recognized periodically. Social classes operate primarily on the basis of esteem mechanisms that have little to do with power, achievement, competence, and other factors. The opposite side of honor, shame, is also a major factor in Philippine life. Scolding outside of the family, for example, is absolutely taboo since it directly activates shame.

The TAT stories demonstrate the importance of esteem and its use as a focus of thinking. The following stories are vivid examples of this. First we see esteem as defined by honors:

> (Card 12P: Class B male) This is a picture of a poor man talking to an honorable (distinguished) man. Maybe he is a man who holds a high position. Although he is a distinguished man, he still greets the other man who I think is a mere laborer. This poor man has respect toward the distinguished man. Even in his poverty, he has a distinct honor. The distinguished man is not proud. He paid attention to his fellowmen. So our character should not be changed in spite of our being honorable.
> [ESB-status <u>EDA-respect</u>]

> (Card 1: Class B female) The boy is thinking deeply in what to do. Then he decided that he should learn how to play with the violin very well. He should do it well so that he will be praised by others. Finally he is happy for his decision because he became a famous musician.
> [AA-self AA-status PA-joy <u>ESA-praised</u>]

> (Card 12P: Class A male) This person, who is well dressed, works in the bank. He receives a big salary. The other man is a farmer. The farmer greeted the professional but he was told to go away because he smells like mud. The farmer was deeply hurt, but he bore everything. Then time came that this person got sick and was fired from his work. All his savings were consumed. One day, he met the farmer. Instead that the farmer didn't harbor a grudge, he approached the man and gave him food.
> [OA-clothes OA-wealth <u>EDC-disdain</u> KD-illness <u>NDA-nurture</u>]

And then we see esteem as defined by shame:

> (Card 16: Class A male) If you have a pure heart, you will not be ashamed to your fellow men, even if you are lower than them. You can be proud of yourself facing people. Those who have black consciences will not be at ease, they are uneasy facing the society. It seems somebody will pinpoint at them and they cannot understand their feelings. But those who have pure hearts will not be ashamed to face, no matter how many misfortunes will come to life.
> [<u>RA-good</u> <u>ESA-worth</u> ESB-esteem KD-mishap ESA-worth]

> (Card 12P: Class A male) While this man who approached the other man who is perhaps his master, and when he approached, he was hesitant because, before, when he approached for help, he was not attended to. And now, as he approached the man, he felt shy but he thought that his problem will never be solved if he will

not go on with his intention to his master. And so he was happy, maybe because God helped him. He did not fail in his request.

[ESB-ignore FB-shy NSA-assist NSA-god]

Now we begin to look for the underlying principles. In the stories above, the general principle can be seen to be that if one's honor is challenged or in doubt, the best reaction is to simply be patient and humble. That is, the respondents believe that their personal worth as individuals will eventually be recognized and their honor restored.

In other stories, we see a somewhat different principle. The following stories are typical of many esteem stories, stories that also evoke concerns regarding proper authority.

(Card 12P: Class A male) One day while he was going to school, his father met him and told him that his mother is very sick. But he told his father not to see him in school because he is ashamed of him, being a farmer only. He asked him just to write to him if ever he wants to give a message. Immediately his father left hurt. Then his parents died, broken-hearted, because of their son whom they hoped would alleviate them from poverty.

[KD-illness ESB-shame HB-hurt HD-withheld KD-death]

(Card 1: Class B female) One day, a little boy was in a very deep thought thinking how to play the guitar. He is very much eager to know how to do it, but he just can't because he is afraid he might get scolded by his father or else he might break it.

[AA-self DSB-punish CB-able OB-break]

In these stories, the respondents are saying that if you have had or expect a direct challenge to your honor or face unfair punishment it is better to suffer in silence than to risk further dishonor. The difference between this and the previous principle is that here they do not expect the suffering to end. Nevertheless, it is seen as better to suffer than to challenge the system or social relationship on which honor or authority is based.

Yet other respondents wrote stories in which a more proactive reaction is possible. When a person's honor or authority is challenged, the appropriate response is to analyze the situation and find instrumental and expressive ways to receive recognition or redeem one's honor:

(Card 16: Class E male) This is a story of a teacher. Before, while she was still a student, if the teacher gave her an assignment, she won't listen to her and she won't do it. Now that she is a teacher, she experienced the same thing. Her students won't listen to her, no respect for her. She was hurt, but she remembered the time when she was only a student. She now realized that it's not easy to be a teacher, especially if nobody respects and listens to you. Now she was thinking of how to discipline her students. She will be firm but still friendly.

[DSC-disobey EDC-insolent HB-hurt ESB-status DDA-control EDA-respect]

The general principle illustrated here is that, if an individual is dishonored, he/she should go directly to the responsible person(s) and rectify the situation. Also notice that, although this story's focus is esteem, the respondent seeks resolution to the problem by going over to control/power ("discipline") and affiliation ("friendly"). This is, of course, an important feature of the value system: the most important values confirm and are consistent with values that lie in different concerns than the one being addressed. Another example of this principle is this story linking esteem with mutual purpose:

> (Card 12P: Class A male) This man goes out of his house and met a man and he asks, "Where are you going?" And the other man said, "I will go to your home because I want something from you but I am ashamed, so I'll just tell you that I will borrow your carabao because I will load it with bananas." And the owner said, "Just get it at the mudhole yourself because I have to go."
>
> [ESB-status NSA-assist MTA-task]

Lastly, there is a small group of esteem stories that have a dark side to them. In these stories, the respondent states that, if someone dishonors you, you should attack the person, either physically or verbally, as in this story:

> (Card 19P: Class A male) A Storekeeper: In a certain place in the city, a businessman established a store. Then a man wanted to buy and the storekeeper asked him where his money was, but the man got angry and told the storekeeper he would box him. Then he sat down and later on, somebody asked what was the reason why the man was angry. The storekeeper told him he was not given because he had no money.
>
> [MTB-distrust HB-resent ESB-shame]

In sum, the esteem stories in the TAT can be seen to suggest a limited variety of socially acceptable mechanisms to gain esteem or to regain it if lost. The stories thus hint at a taxonomy of choices that an individual will utilize in particular situations. There are, however, several questions unanswered by the TAT data. Are all possible choices represented? Do the choices reflect a mental hierarchy or taxonomy that represents the population as a whole? If so, how is the taxonomy used? What social conditions dictate or influence the choices? To answer these questions, we must leave the TAT and go to the data of the Sentence Completion Test (SCT) which can be structured to address specific questions and issues.

The Curious Absence of *Pakikisama*

Before going to the SCT data on esteem, however, it is productive to take two short detours to other sections of the overall Philippine value structure in order to fully understand the esteem category in particular. First, I was quite surprised by the weak response in the harmony category in the TAT data. *Pakikisama*, or smooth interpersonal relations, is said to be an important Philippine value but very few harmony stories were written for the TAT. Second, another widely known Philippine trait is *utang na loob* or debt of the heart. This describes the obligation that an individual continues to feel toward a benefactor after a debt has been repaid. If this sentiment is strong, we would expect to hear much about it in stories which involved a gift or assistance. There were several examples of this type of story but *utang na loob* is mentioned only in a few particular instances.

Let us look at the *pakikisama* puzzle first. More than any other individual, Frank Lynch of the Ateneo de Manila has devoted great energy to gathering data in support of *pakikisama* as a major Philippine value. He has repeatedly published data from several sources (1962, 1964, 1968, 1973) to build a case for this value. Filipinos will sacrifice their own interests, he believed, to maintain harmonious relations. They will shun people who are too blunt or who otherwise disturb smooth relations. They will hide their own feelings for the same reason.

However, the TAT results showed a notable absence of such sentiments in isolation. That is, they value smooth interpersonal relations but only in the context of other considerations. In the few stories in which they were focusing on harmony, the Filipinos typically said that they did not sacrifice their own interests for smooth interpersonal relations but that they should:

> (Card 16: Class A female) A woman quarreled with her neighbor because her child was hit by a child with a stone. When the mother knew this and the head of her child was already bloody, she went to the house of the child who threw the stone. She whipped the child. The mother of the child she whipped was surprised. She shouted at the woman whipping her child. The woman was very angry because she did not know the real cause why her child was whipped. The mother of the child hit by a stone quarreled. A police passed by and they were settled. The mother of the child hit by the stone was mistaken because she did not talk to the other mother first. So we should not hurry up in whatever we do. We should think over and talk with the mother so that the incident will not become big.
>
> [HC-discord HC-beat HC-verbal HA-pacify]

Turning to the SCT data, some of the sentence fragments were devised to specifically elicit a *pakikisama* response. The respondents were asked, for example, to complete the sentence "After he/she won the sweepstakes, he/she used the money for . . ." The expected *pakikisama* reaction would be "for friends, coworkers and neighbors" or "for a neighborhood party, a blowout." However, only 1 percent of all the uses mentioned by the respondents could be said to be at all supportive of *pakikisama*. The majority of the responses were self- or family-centered and decidedly disharmonious: 46 percent indicated they would use the money for private business, personal education, or land, 25 percent indicated they would pay for the children's education or buy things the family needs, 3 percent suggested spending the money on personal amusement and 24 percent proposed giving to charity. The *pakikisama* response was essentially absent.

In another SCT item, they were asked to finish the sentence "He/she is successful because he/she . . ." If *pakikisama* were an important norm, we would expect them to say "because he/she gets along well with others" or "works well with others." But neither of these reasons was suggested by even a single informant. Successful people are industrious, helpful, and virtuous, but not necessarily harmonious.

A third sentence fragment was worded in a more general manner, namely, "His/her most important activity is . . ." In this case, the *pakikisama* reply would be "to get along with others" and this type of reply did in fact appear. But only 3 percent gave this specifically *pakikisama* reply and 2 percent gave related mutual purpose replies, e.g., "to help others." Most of the answers focused away from interpersonal relations: earning a living had 38 percent of the answers; providing for the family, 22 percent; being virtuous, 20 percent; and being charitable to the (anonymous) poor, 10 percent. So, once again, *pakikisama* appears to be relatively unimportant.

At this point, we might ask, where *is* the *pakikisama*? Is it a figment of the anthropologists' imagination? If we look at one more SCT item, we get a clue to the puzzle. When they finished the sentence fragment "In his/her relations with other people, the thing that he/she is most careful of is . . . ," most of their answers (65 percent) lay in the esteem area. The most popular answer was "his/her honor" (34 percent) and the second most popular answer was "respecting them" (31 percent). In third place, with 19 percent of the answers, was an expression of their desire to be moral or proper (i.e., responsibility). But the fourth answer, with 13 percent response, was the *pakikisama* (harmony) answer, namely, that he/she would take care to get along with them and not cause any trouble. And the remainder of the answers (3 percent) was in the mutual purpose category, the instrumental counterpart of harmony.

So here is the answer to the question of the missing *pakikisama*. Certainly, the Filipinos value harmony as do all the world's societies. However, it does not appear as a strong, independent value or set of values. Rather it appears only when the concern for esteem is strong. Thus I suggest that *pakikisama* is primarily related to esteem rather than harmony and will appear as a subcategory of esteem. Smooth interpersonal relations are more a product of their desire for respect and honor than their desire for an orderly, peaceful community.

The Asymmetry of *Utang na Loob*

Setting *pakikisama* aside for now, we turn to a second puzzle in the data that will also help us understand esteem. This centers upon another of the four widely known Philippine values, *utang na loob*. Mary Hollnsteiner (1961, 1963) and Charles Kaut (1961) have written important articles about this Philippine value. As mentioned above, it refers to the residual emotional attachment or obligation that is associated with a gift or assistance but which goes beyond the repayment of the gift or assistance. For example, if a poor man is given money or a job, he presumably has *utang na loob* for his benefactor that would link the poor man to the business, political, and social interests of his benefactor. The poor man would, in theory, feel obligated to support the benefactor regardless of his personal feelings about an issue. And he would continue to feel obligated after the debt was repaid.

The data from my study, however, suggest that *utang na loob* does not function exactly that way. First, the responses to TAT Card 12 mentioned above included several stories in which the well-dressed individual was identified as the benefactor of the poor man. These stories fell into a clear pattern: When the story was written by a lower class individual, the recipient simply accepted the help of the benefactor and went on his or her way. There was no mention of *utang na loob*. The gift or assistance was explained in these stories by saying either that upper class people enjoy helping people (nurturance) or that the upper class was morally obligated to help the poor (responsibility). Some upper class respondents also wrote stories that fit this pattern. In contrast to these stories, a small portion of the upper class respondents wrote about a gift or assistance as obligating the lower class person in the future, i.e., as generating *utang na loob*.

The same pattern emerged with a SCT item that read, "His/her friend loaned him/her a large amount of money that he/she needed very much. After he/she repaid the money, he/she felt that . . ." Most of the respondents, 63 percent, said that the individual simply felt relieved of his or her debt, giving no indication of *utang na loob*. The remaining 37 percent was divided into two groups: 4 percent said that friendship continued after the debt was paid, implying *utang na loob*, and 33 percent said explicitly that there was *utang na loob* thereafter. But, significantly, of these thirty-seven responses, 62 percent are from the *upper* classes, compared to 49 percent of the sample. That is to say, the *utang na loob* value is held predominantly by those who are more likely to be benefactors than recipients.

Thus, my data suggest that *utang na loob* exists mainly, if not entirely, in the mind of the benefactor and is a product of his/her desire for recognition and respect. It is an asymmetrical value in that it operates primarily downward, i.e., from someone of higher status toward someone of lower status. The recipient would deny or ignore any *utang na loob*; he/she has been recognized and honored directly by the gift or assistance and his/her need for recognition has been sated. *Utang na loob* is, therefore, primarily an esteem value, rather than a responsibility value which, in the form of a "thou shalt not" rule, would be applicable to all. It is also not a nurturance value because it relates to the aftermath of a gift more than to the gift itself. In other words, nurturance and responsibility situations will generate *utang na loob* only if the honor or esteem of a participant is in question.

The Taxonomy of Esteem

Now we are ready to look at the data of esteem and to show how the Filipinos sort out the values in the form of a taxonomy for personal decisions. First, esteem is logically subdivided into two categories: esteem that is self-directed and esteem that is other-directed. Both of these categories are important in the Philippines. However, it is in the self-esteem category that we find the most important values and, in particular, it is here that we find the last two of the four most publicized and studied Philippine values, namely, *hiya* (shame) and *amor propio*.

Figure 2

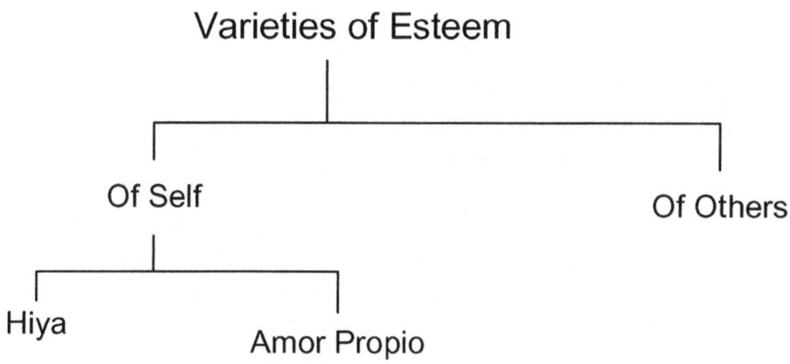

Looking first at *hiya* or shame, Western analysts would define this concept by contrasting it with guilt. Both shame and guilt are forms of self-censure on the basis of an internalized moral code; however, guilt is self-activated whereas shame is activated by the perception of *external* censure. Shame is activated only if you are caught. This perspective, however, misses the fundamental point that the two concepts serve the individual in different ways, that one concept is instrumental and the other expressive. In practice, people understand shame by contrasting it with other potential expressive reactions to specific situations, not by contrasting it with instrumental reactions. An individual can be ashamed and guilty at the same time. Filipinos, in particular, would understand shame by contrasting it with *amor propio* as diagramed in Figure 2. *Amor propio*, like shame, is a set of values dealing with the fear of being unnoticed, disrespected, or criticized by others. The contrast that the Filipinos would use to distinguish and understand the two concepts lies in the perceived validity of the external censure. A shame reaction in a person is based on the belief that the external censure is valid whereas an *amor propio* reaction is based on the belief that the external censure is invalid. Shame can be defined as negative honor. However, if the taxonomic model of mental processes is correct, it should be placed in contrast with self-esteem, *amor propio*, since there is a conscious or subconscious decision regarding the validity of the censure.

Next, setting shame aside, let us explore the way that the Filipinos think about *amor propio* with data from the SCT. Two of the sentence fragments in the SCT were specifically designed to elicit *amor propio* responses. In the first, I asked for appropriate reactions when someone is criticized by an inferior, a social situation always characterized by *amor propio* in the Philippines. This SCT item is summarized in Figure 3 with samples of their individual responses given under the numbered response types.

Putting the Filipinos in this awkward situation generated five types of responses although, as we shall see, the second and fifth are two forms of the same response. The first response in Figure 3, interestingly, is that of hostility and resentment; when criticized, they would get angry, retaliate, sever the relationship. This reaction, called *magalit* in Tagalog, is judged appropriate in many *amor propio* cases, and the fact that this rather strong reaction was the response of so many of the Filipinos is a clear indication of the great importance of *amor propio*. The second type of answer that the Filipinos gave was a mixture of responsibility and harmony; they said that the inferior should not criticize and was morally wrong to do so. From the responsibility perspective, they are commenting in effect that it is wrong to question one's superiors but, from the harmony perspective, they are supporting the status quo or smooth interpersonal relations. In other words, this is a *pakikisama* answer with moral overtones. The pure *pakakisama* response is the fifth most common reply in which the superior individual goes to great lengths to maintain good will and harmony. Thus, combining the two, we see that *pakikisama* is a more common response of the Filipinos than *magalit*, accounting as it does for 36 percent of the answers. The third type of response that the Filipinos gave to this situation was a humility response; this constitutes a value that we have already seen, namely, that if criticized, it is best to be humble; the critic will realize his mistake sooner or later. This "just be humble" approach is called *pagtiti-is* in Tagalog. The fourth type of response in Figure 3 is also one that we have seen above: when criticized by an inferior, an appropriate reaction is to be hurt without doing anything, that is, to endure sufferings silently. This is an unstudied Filipino value, which, in Tagalog, is called *pagtitimpi* and which may be related to concepts of suffering in Catholicism. In some ways, *pagtitimpi* might be considered a passive form of *pakikisama*. Both act to maintain the *status quo*. However, their responses to the projective tests make it clear that they regard *pagtitimpi* as a distinct response separate from *pakikisama*.

Figure 3

"When he was criticized by his inferior, he . . ."

General Response		Mental Focus and Representative Responses	Class A	Classes B to F	Total
quarreled, quit the job	1.	**Harmony** (negative) Got angry, retaliated, quit the job, quarreled with her, flared up	19 (10M 9F)	13 (9M, 4F)	32
said "do not criticize"	2.	**Responsibility-Harmony** Said "do not criticize, you are only an inferior," ignored him, said "he does not understand the plan," said he is wrong	11 (7M, 4F)	12 (4M, 8F)	23
felt shy, ashamed	3.	**Esteem** (positive-passive) Feels shy, humbles himself, feels ashamed	13 (4M, 9F)	5 (1M, 4F)	18
feels hurt	4.	**Esteem** (negative) Was belittled, feels insulted, became a snob, was hurt	5 (2M, 3F)	9 (3M, 6F)	14
accepted the criticism	5.	**Harmony** (positive) Accepted the criticism and considered whether it was right or wrong, thanked them for telling him so, will not get sore	3 (2M, 1F)	10 (8M, 2F)	13

Since these four reactions constitute the only responses given by the Filipinos to this *amor propio* situation, we may conclude that *amor propio* generates four values that guide their behavior in different situations: *pakikisama, magalit, pagtiti-is*, and *pagtitimpi.* This conclusion is confirmed by the data of another SCT item which, in the male version, was phrased "When he found out that his best friend spoke against him, he . . ." The reactions to this sentence fragment are shown in Figure 4.

The *pakikisama* response in Figure 4 is the first one, namely, to ignore the friend's remark or to go to see the friend, find out what the problem is, and smooth it over. The *magalit* response is the second one, to become irate and to retaliate against your friend if he speaks against you. We see the *pagtitimpi* response in the third response as a self-inflicted psychological wound; the person passively accuses himself or herself of fault. And the *pagtiti-is* response is seen in the fourth response, a positive but still passive approach to the situation. Further, we see in Figure 4 that the relative popularity of the four values when we are dealing with relationships between peers is the same in the upper classes as it is in the lower class. *Pakikisama* is the strongest followed by *magalit*, *patitimpi* and *pagtiti-is*. That is, when a peer censures or criticizes an individual, the most probable response is to act to smooth out the difficulties in some way. A substantial number would react with anger or resentment and lesser numbers would adopt either a position of quiet suffering or the attitude of humility.

Figure 4

"When he found out that his best friend spoke against him, he . . ."

General Response		Mental Focus and Representative Responses	Class A	Classes B to F	Total
sought out his friend to find out why	1.	**Harmony-Affiliation** (pos.) Tried to find out why, listen and forget, had a dialogue with the friend, ignored the gossip, forgave him	20 (11M 9F)	19 (12M, 7F)	39
became angry, avoided him	2.	**Harmony-Affiliation** (neg.) Became angry, avoided him, retaliated, quarreled with her	18 (8M, 10F)	16 (9M, 7F)	34
felt hurt	3.	**Esteem** (negative) Cried, was hurt, was saddened and asked herself "what are my mistakes?"	7 (5M, 2F)	8 (2M, 6F)	15
was patient	4.	**Esteem** (positive-passive) Was patient, just bore it, humbled herself	6 (1M, 5F)	6 (2M, 4F)	12

Now we have the tentative subdivision of *amor propio* as shown in Figure 5.

This taxonomy would, in all likelihood, be used by different people in different ways. In particular, it would be used differently by different classes. The data of Figure 3 and Figure 4 tell us that the upper classes would tend to choose *pakikisama* and *magalit* rather than *pagtitimpi* or *pagtiti-is* in their relations with inferiors and in their relations with their peers. Unfortunately, the data of Figure 3 does not tell us how the lower class would utilize the taxonomy but only how they anticipate the upper class would use it. It is likely, however, considering the nature of the values we are discussing, that the lower class would tend to choose *pagtitimpi* and *pagtiti-is* more often than the upper classes. The data of Figure 4 nevertheless suggest that *pakikisama* and *magalit* would remain the dominant responses even in the lower class.

Figure 5

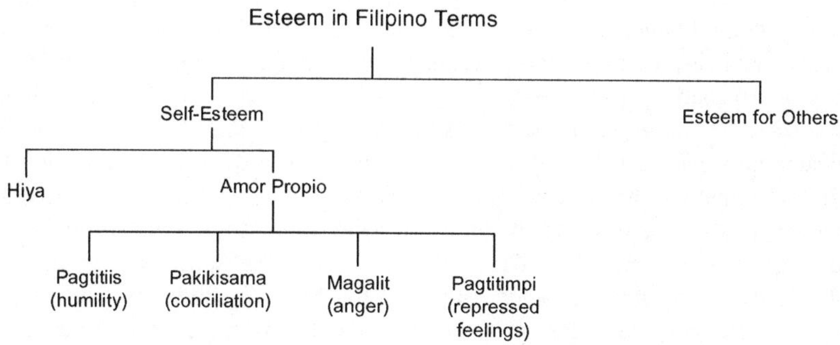

Finally, to complete the taxonomy, we need only find room for *utang na loob* which has been shown to be a product of *amor propio* and therefore derivative of this value set. This is accomplished by acknowledging that the taxonomy will change slightly if there is a gift or assistance involved and if the person using the taxonomy sees himself in a superior status. In this case, the taxonomy becomes what is represented in Figure 6.

Figure 6

Downward Amor Proprio Responses When a Gift or Assistance Is Involved

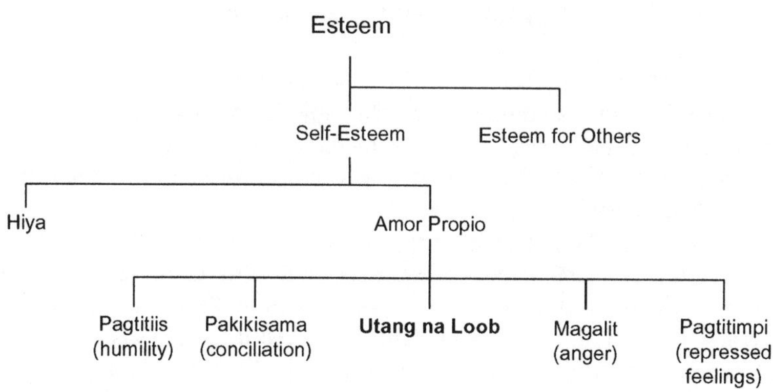

Now it is important to note, as implied by the taxonomy, that the choices under *amor propio*, are *mutually exclusive*. If a benefactor interprets a situation as generating *utang na loob*, he or she will *not* act to ensure harmony (*pakikisama*), for example. Reactions of anger, humility or repression (*magalit*, *pagtitiis*, and *pagtitimpi*) are also precluded when *utang na loob* is invoked, even when the requests for recognition are unfulfilled by the recipient. This taxonomy is therefore crucial to understanding how *utang na loob* works in the Philippines. Like *pagtitiis* and *pagtitimpi*, *utang na loob* is a class-maintaining and class-building value. It can be used explicitly or implicitly to validate the unequal distribution of social and economic resources and, hence, to justify the position of the elite classes. *Pakikisama* and *magalit*, on the other hand, act against classes. They are primarily activated between peers but, if there is an element of inequality in the relationship, *pakikisama* and the threat of *magalit* will lessen its importance. Unequal access to resources tends to be obviated by these two values. One could say that *pakikisama* and *magalit* occupy one side of the scales of justice and *utang na loob*, *pagtitiis*, and *pagtitimpi* occupy the other side of the scales. At different times and in different situations, the scales tip in one direction or the other. As long as a balance of some sort is maintained, the society is stable.

Social classes are maintained by several mechanisms but, in the Philippines, *utang na loob* is one of the most important mechanisms. For example, it is impossible to understand the highly exploitive practice of *prenda* in the Philippines without *utang na loob*. In *prenda*, a peasant farmer's land is used as collateral for a loan and all of the land's produce must be paid as interest for the loan, leaving nothing for the repayment of the principal and making foreclosure inevitable. The upper class elite see the transfer of the property to themselves as a proper result of the gift of a loan. The fact that *utnag na loob*, *pakikisama* and *magalit* are mutually exclusive choices in the taxonomy of values explains why this practice continues without wholesale rioting and revolution.

Summary and Conclusions

Now returning to the underlying theory, we can see that De Vos's theory provides a mechanism for us to see through the seemingly cacophonous voices of a culture and to discern the underlying unity and structure. Still stronger, the theory points the way to an understanding of all cultures and an understanding of the fundamental patterns in human thought.

The data from the Philippines support De Vos's theory in three fundamental ways. *First*, the data confirms the completeness of the theoretical framework. There is nothing in the data that does not find representation in De Vos's twelve universal concerns. This is an important point. Had there been data elements that were not found everywhere else, the most basic tenets of the theory would have been challenged. *Second*, the data from the projective tests was modularized by the respondents in a manner that could be identified with the twelve concerns. That is, from an analytical point of view, the responses were focused upon the concerns rather than presented in the manner of a spectrum. Specifically, the Filipinos responded to the tests by choosing one of the concerns as their main theme of a story and then explained the primary concern with reference to other concerns. It is this thematic approach that demonstrates the modularity of their thought. *Third*, the respondents frequently complimented the main concern with a secondary concern that was predicted in De Vos's theory. An achievement story, for example, was most likely to be complimented with a nurturance subtheme. This type of response, involving crossover pairs, occurred considerably more often than could be explained by chance, and therefore constitutes a confirmation of the theory.

The Philippine data also develops the theory by demonstrating the manner in which a given society addresses the twelve concerns. Certainly, one major function of society, i.e., one major outcome of living together, is the harmonizing of concerns. They select certain concerns as the focal points of the culture while de-emphasizing others and, within the emphasized concerns, they harmonize their responses. In the present case, the Filipinos showed special interest in four concerns—responsibility, esteem, achievement, and nurturance—and showed less interest in the other eight concerns. When the stimulus biases of particular TAT cards were accounted for, more than half of the responses fell in the four major concerns.

As a corollary to this concentration of interest in certain concerns, the data demonstrates the manner in which some of the de-emphasized universal concerns are addressed in the context of the emphasized concerns. A strong harmony value, *pakikisama*, is shown to be subsumed in the concern for esteem. Another value, *utang na loob*, defined as an obligation to cooperate after a gift or assistance, is disclosed to be a mutual purpose value but it, too, appears as a subdivision of esteem.

An important contribution of this work lies in the demonstration of the taxonomic structure within a concern. Each of the concerns is believed to contain a series of values that are hierarchically arranged to allow individuals to react to social circumstances such as to maximize individual benefit in socially acceptable ways. This was confirmed by looking at the esteem category and examining the respondents' reactions to situations that question a person's self-worth. It was found that self-esteem is subdivided first into two conditions, in one of which the individual feels at fault, generating shame, and, in the other, the individual feels unjustly accused or criticized. Partly as the result of their social history, the Filipinos are very interested in and sensitive to the latter situations. Their responses to these unwarranted challenges to personal dignity have come to be known as *amor propio*.

Amor propio, in turn, is found to be subdivided primarily into four different values, *pagtiti-is* (humility), *pagtitimpi* (repression), *pakikisama* (harmony), and *magalit* (aggression). In a special social circumstance, when the person using the hierarchy has given a gift or assistance, a fifth value, *utang na loob* (obligatory mutual purpose), is added to the structure at the same level as the other four. Further, by studying the responses and observing the Filipinos using the taxonomy in day-to-day situations, it becomes clear that these five values are mutually exclusive responses, as we would expect if they are on the same level of the taxonomy. For example, when a benefactor feels that the *utang na loob* response is appropriate, he feels no need to build community harmony, *pakikisama*, or to respond with other amor propio values because these values are defined by their contrast with *utang na loob* and by their contrast with each other.

Each value in the taxonomy is a unique node or locus of thought that can be explored in terms of its social and individual consequences. The little-studied value, *pagti-timpi*, for example, is frequently found in family situations in which any effort to correct or explain an unjust accusation will undermine the family statuses involved. Family life is characterized by episodes of *pagti-timpi*, episodes that are resolved by the accusing party receiving additional information or simply by changing circumstances.

Each value in the taxonomy can also be studied in terms of larger social dynamics. I have pointed out that three of the amor propio values build social inequality and two values lessen or destroy social inequality. The balance in the usage of these values may play a pivotal role in understanding the evolution of the society. For example, between 1945 and the election of Marcos in 1966, marriages between people of different classes were increasing; Marcos stressed the right of the elite families to rule and the number of marriages between people of different classes began to decrease (Manlove, 1990: 235–244).

But, more fundamentally, the taxonomy of esteem and its values represent the modularization of Filipino thought and demonstrate the validity of characterizing all human thought in this manner. If we take a step back and translate the Philippine taxonomy completely, as I have done in Figure 7, we find ourselves looking at ourselves. We recognize, not too comfortably, our own reactions to questions about our self-worth. We find our culture represented, not in the exact expression of the categories, but in the categories themselves.

Figure 7

A Modular Approach to Self-Esteem

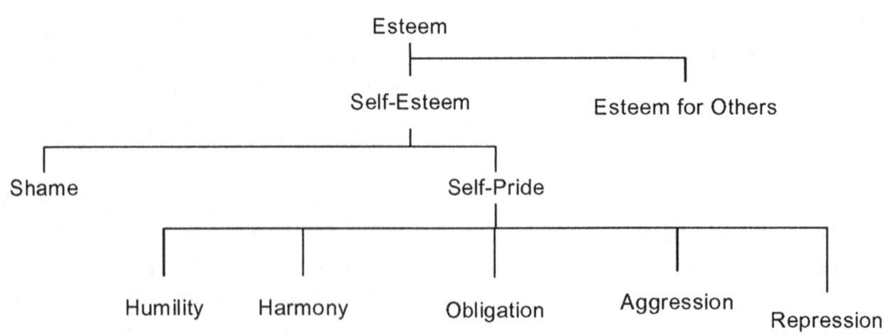

We come then to the realization that the Philippine data, with the help of De Vos's theory, has given us a glimpse into how cultures are built in the mind and hence how biology and culture interface. The human brain is wired, not just for language, but for culture as a whole. These data join other research in cognitive science that, as Michael Gazzaniga has put it recently, have "directed attention to the idea that brain and mind are built from discrete units—or modules—that carry out specific functions. According to this theory, the brain is not a general problem-solving device whose every part is capable of any function. Rather it is a collection of devices that assist the mind's information-processing demands" (*Scientific American*, July 1998, p. 53).

The data here presented demonstrate specifically the cerebral modularity with reference to esteem in the Philippines. But it points toward an underlying taxonomic structure to the human brain built out of eons of biological evolution in the context of social living. While much remains unknown about the relationship between the taxonomic organization and the physical structure of the brain, we are clearly moving toward a significant understanding of the culture-biology interface.

References

Bulatao, Jaime. 1962. Philippine Values I: Manileno's Mainsprings. *Philippine Studies*, **10**: 32–44.

Damasio, A.R. 1994. *Descartes Error: Emotion, Reason and the Human Brain*. New York: Avon Books Inc.

De Vos, George. 1973. *Socialization for Achievement: Essays on the Cultural Psychology of the Japanese*. Berkeley: University of California Press.

Gazzaniga, Michael S. 1998. The Split Brain Revisited. *Scientific American*, **279**: 50–55.

Guthrie, George M. 1968. The Philippine Temperament. In George M. Guthrie (Ed.), *Six Perspectives on the Philippines*. Manila: The Bookmark Co., Inc.

Hollnsteiner, Mary R. 1961. Reciprocity in the Lowland Philippines. *Philippine Studies*, **9**: 387–413.

———. 1963. *The Dynamics of Power in a Philippine Municipality*. Quezon City: University of the Philippines Community Development Research Council.

Kaut, Charles. 1961. Utang na Loob: A System of Contractual Obligations Among Tagalogs. *Southwestern Journal of Anthropology*, **17**: 256–272.

Lynch, Frank. 1962. Philippine Values II: Social Acceptance. *Philippine Studies*, **10**: 82–99.

———. 1964. Social Acceptance. In *Four Readings on Philippine Values*. Quezon City: Ateneo de Manila University Press.

———. 1968. Social Acceptance. In *Four Readings on Philippine Values*, revised edition. Quezon City: Ateneo de Manila University Press.

———. 1973. Social Acceptance Reconsidered. In *Four Readings on Philippine Values*, revised edition. Quezon City: Ateneo de Manila University Press.

Manlove, Robert F. 1990. *Ozamiz: A Case Study in Urban Anthropology*. Unpublished Ph.D. Dissertation. Berkeley: University of California.

———. 2001. Patterns of Universal Brain Function in Cross-Cultural Data. *World Cultures*, **12**: 107–125.

Wilson, Edward O. 1997. *Consilience: The Unity of Knowledge*. New York: Alfred A. Knopf, Inc.

Chapter 14

Climbing on the Tree of Gold: Fate and Nurturance in Tibetan Youth

Dorsh Marie de Voe

This chapter examines TAT narratives given by Tibetan refugee youth in India in 1989. For this discussion, Tibetan stories from Card 17BM (the rope card) were scored using the Interpersonal Concerns Scoring System (ICSS). The analysis of this collection of TAT narratives demonstrates that projective tests are capable of evoking patterns of responses that reveal consistencies in Tibetan cultural emphasis, thus confirming the utility of narrative materials as a fieldwork tool.

Since 1977, I have conducted periodic fieldwork with Tibetan refugees in India. In 1980–1982, I collected a small number of TAT narratives from Tibetan refugee youth in India. In 1989, I collected 468 TAT stories from Tibetan refugee youth between the ages of eight and nineteen years old living in various Tibetan refugee camps and Tibetan children's villages in India. I used a partial set of the original Murray Cards: 1, 2, 3BM, 6BM, 7BM, 7GF, 18GF, 13MF, 17BM. In this chapter, I present only findings from narratives obtained on one card, 17BM, depicting a lightly clad man either ascending or descending a rope. I plan for a more complete reporting of my results and findings at a later date.

Forty-nine individuals responded to TAT Card 17BM. Their responses provide strong evidence of the inner needs and motivations of Tibetan refugee youth and corroborate observations from my fieldwork about Tibetan beliefs, behavior, and motivations. In this chapter, the centrality of fate and recurrent themes of nurturance and responsibility are dramatically illustrated. Their stories directly reflect the general values and beliefs found evident among Tibetans everywhere.

Background to Tibetans as Refugees

Tibet, situated due north of India, was a theocratic Buddhist society historically governed by a series of reincarnate Dalai Lamas. Relations with the Chinese had for centuries been delicate. As early as 1910, the Dalai Lama, anticipating dangerous Chinese encroachment, sought temporary refuge in India. Since 1949, when the People's Republic of China was established, Tibetans experienced innumerable incursive acts by the Chinese intending to establish control over all of Tibet, which, it was claimed, had always been part of China.

In March 1959, after an unusually dramatic demonstration by Tibetans, fearing that he would be kidnapped, the Fourteenth Dalai Lama and a small group of advisors clandestinely fled, risking the arduous Trans-Himalayan journey for shelter in neighboring India. Nearly 90,000 Tibetans followed suit in the next several months.[7] Initially, Tibetan refugees stayed in border area transit camps, and within months, they were transferred to roadwork sites in the mountainous Himalayan region of northern India. Living in tents and shanty towns which skirted the road beds they laid, Tibetans remember that even then they thought asylum was only temporary, and that it would be a matter of weeks before they could return to their homes in Tibet.

But, by December 1960, plans were made for more permanent Tibetan resettlement throughout India. Lying deep in southern India, Karnataka State was one of the first states to respond with an offer of arable land. By 1980, there were thirteen farming settlements, nine industrial settlements, and over one hundred monasteries, nunneries, and temples. The Tibetan government in exile was firmly established in Dharamsala, a hill station in the north Indian State of Himachel Pradesh. Cultural preservation was a priority and, with the blessing of the Indian government, a Tibetan medical school, Tibetan library and archives, Tibetan music, dance and drama school, and several Tibetan children's schools were set up in India.[8] Thus, while Tibetans were living in the context of a predominantly Hindu society, they were able to educate their youth in Tibetan language, art and letters, customs, and religion. Theirs has been a very successful story of cultural conservation in the attendant condition of refugee life.

---

[7]Estimates on the number of Tibetan who fled into exile in 1959–1960 vary. This is in part due to the difficulties of census-taking in India and Nepal, as well as questions of interpretation as to which Tibetans to include in the refugee count, i.e., Tibetan Muslims, Gyagar Khampas who had settled in India prior to the refugee event, etc.

[8]For greater detail on the early development of the Tibetan refugee settlements and cultural preservation endeavors in India, see *Tibetans in Exile: 1959–1980*, Dharamsala: Information Office of His Holiness the Dalai Lama, 1981.

Previous TAT Studies among Tibetans

It must be noted that two anthropologists have reported earlier collections of projective tests. It would be fascinating to interpret their stories using the Interpersonal Concerns Scoring System, but that project must wait for another time.

Prince Peter of Greece and Denmark (1965) was an anthropologist who spent seven years among Tibetans in Kalimpong, India. This was in 1950–1957, prior to the Tibetan refugee movement, which began in March 1959 when the Dalai Lama fled Tibet due to the Chinese invasion. Prince Peter had psychoanalytic interests and thus used both the Rorschach and twelve Thematic Apperception type cards with three Tibetan adults. In his published paper on this topic, Prince Peter provided the actual texts of the narratives he received, and briefly commented on the "aggressive" content of the stories.

In 1970–1972, anthropologist Beatrice Miller was able to obtain ninety-one narratives from modified TAT cards, which were given to Tibetan refugee youth in India (see Miller, 1978, pp. 365–393). Miller's paper did not report actual texts of the collected narratives. However, Miller described several significant themes in the collected narratives including content about Tibet, the importance of the harmonious and cooperative family, mutual responsibility, and the possibility of change. It appears that Miller too found discord in her collection of TAT narratives, but she noted that tensions were usually resolved positively. Miller concluded her analysis on a positive note, painting a picture of people who have a sense of fair play, of justice, resilience, family responsibility, and optimism about the future.

The Present Study

Generally, the TATs of Tibetan youth provide fascinating reading, reminiscent of the great oral traditions of this historically nomadic people whose gift as storytellers entertained and informed family, friends, and strangers in their travels and encampments in old Tibet. Their stories do not conform to common topics, but rather, their subject matter is highly varied, unconventional, and sometimes extraordinary. Tibetan stories typically have a beginning, middle, and ending. They go through time. They are rich with introduced characters, animals, and events which are often more important than, and completely different from, the immediate figures depicted on the TAT card itself.

Often, family members not illustrated on the card are discussed and have critical roles in the story, confirming the central importance of the family group in Tibetan society. While Tibetan stories are multifarious and diversified in content, common themes of interpersonal concerns emerge. Sometimes there is apparent caprice and fantasy in their stories, but, from a Tibetan perspective, unpredictable sequences of events and fantastic interventions are real and illustrative of possible experiences in life. Further, a variety of sentient beings from spiders to elephants have pivotal roles in Tibetan TAT stories. While many would assume that the appearance of such creatures in Tibetan youth TATs is due to the developmental stage of the storytellers, this assumption is erroneous. In fact, animals, bugs, serpents, and fairies appear in adult stories, in folktales, and in stories about the life of Buddha. Storytelling is still an important pastime among Tibetans.

In response solely to the man-on-a-rope card herein considered, elaborate stories were told about family life in Tibet, the invasion of the Chinese, the flight from Tibet, and the struggle to survive when they walked over the Himalayan mountains and arrived in India, a land they had already revered because of the Buddha's past presence.

The specific TATs reported herein were gathered in 1989 from Tibetan refugee youth in India who lived in Dharamsala, Delhi, or in other Tibetan refugee settlements. All these youth attended Tibetan schools, either as residential or day students. The age range of these youth was ten to nineteen years. There were twenty-eight females and twenty-one males. The TATs were collected with the help of Tibetans who taught in these schools in Dharamsala, Dalhousie, Delhi, Manali, and Mainpat.

Of the total of 467 narratives collected in 1989, forty-nine narratives from youth were given in response to the man-on-a-rope card. Forty narratives were from youth whose families had come to India during the main refugee flight of 1959–1960. Though these youth were born in India, they identify themselves as Tibetan refugees, the children of parents who fled Tibet in 1959–1960.

Additionally, nine narratives on Card 17BM were given by youth who were newcomers to India. These are youth who clandestinely fled Chinese-occupied Tibet by walking across the border into Nepal. When these newcomers reach India, they are processed through the Tibetan government and placed in Tibetan schools. There, they meet not only the standard requirements of the Indian school system, but moreover, they are exposed to a thoroughly Tibetan education that is not available now in Tibet. In this review of these TAT narratives, I found similar themes in the stories of these youth born in Tibet and those born in exile in India.

Tibetan culture is really shaped by its Buddhist religion, which the Chinese have attempted to eradicate. The inclusion in this sample of Tibetan youth who were born in Tibet and only recently had escaped to India is illuminating in that, despite the fact that they grew up in Chinese communist-controlled Tibet, they still think, act, and feel like their Tibetan counterparts who were born and raised in the context of Indian exile. There is strong evidence of Tibetan cultural continuity despite Chinese efforts to change it. There remains a dominance of Buddhism in Tibetan life, with its emphasis on the ethics of compassion, the moral virtues of family life and duty, and a repudiation of individualistic deviant behavior. As we shall see, these elements of concern are reflected in the man-on-a-rope card narratives of Tibetan youth.

Tibetan Concepts of Fate and the Importance of Giving

In many cultures, fate is viewed simply as lucky or unlucky events. Tibetans, as Buddhists, have a more complex understanding of fate. For Tibetans, fate is the consequence of one's own actions committed in past lives or in earlier stages of one's present existence. Such actions follow us and affect our every rebirth. It is important to grasp the Tibetan understanding of fate prior to embarking on a review of their TAT narratives because this perception is perhaps the most fundamental guide into the world view of Tibetans.

Thus, one of the most substantial concepts in understanding the Tibetan personality is commonly referred to in its Sanskrit version, "karma." To Tibetans, this concept is called *Las*, which refers to any action, deed, or work and also means the net effect of actions in one life as transmitted to and exemplified in the next life. There may be more accuracy in using the word in its compound form, las-rGyu-hBras, which literally means "work-cause-effect." These are not archaic words in the ancient Tibetan language. Rather, they express a concept that guides Tibetans in daily life activities (see Chandra Das, 1993, pp. 1210–1212, and also, Ekvall, 1978, pp. 251–262). Evans-Wentz, renowned translator, editor, and annotator of Tibetan religious texts, explains the Tibetan Buddhist view: karma cannot possibly be escaped; it must be faced eventually and no matter how terrible, experienced, if not in one lifetime, then in another. There is no place to which one can go to get away from oneself or from the results of one's actions (Evans-Wentz, 1969, p. 206). Everyone has karma, which causes and regulates the accumulation of tendencies residing in the present mind of an individual. These tendencies have been gathering from time immemorial, during untold past lives. Like waves upon the ocean, they rise on the mind, one after another (HH the Dalai Lama, 1984, p. 90).

In the Tibetan world view, the law of the universe is that every result, regardless of the judgment placed on it, must have a cause, and every action its own consequence. One's actions are the result of one's karma; one's karma orchestrates the course of one's life. That is, the present scheme of daily life is dependent on the individual's accumulated actions in previous lives. Believing in karma as the basic truth about the nature of life, Tibetans tend to accept with humility the way they are, the way others around them act and think, as well as the circumstances they are in. "The consequences of karma are definite: negative actions always bring about suffering and positive actions always bring happiness. If you do good, you will have happiness; if you do bad, you yourself will suffer."[9]

It is one's karma that ascribes a man's position in this life, delineates, concentrates, or dilutes his struggles and sufferings. In his teachings about karma, the Dalai Lama suggests the importance of accepting one's position and role in life.

---

[9]HH the Dalai Lama, *The Way to Freedom*, New York: HarperCollins Publishers, 1994, p. 90.

One who can protect should harbor another who needs help and seeks refuge.[10] The strong must help and provide for the weak. Notice that being strong or weak is neutral: one is not better than the other is, for they both are as such due to karma.

Tibetans understand the meaning and manner of giving, receiving, and returning, for theirs is a historic culture steeped in the principles of exchange. As refugees, Tibetans have been in the recipient role vis-à-vis aid agencies.[11] Many Westerners who visit India remark on how happy Tibetans appear with their lot, even though they are refugees without a country. Their acceptance of life as refugees, as recipients, stems from acceptance of karma. Even if it is "bad" karma, it is the Tibetan tryst with destiny. Visitors to Tibetan refugee communities also note a passivity that is appreciated as politeness, a live and let live attitude. Indeed, in my early years of fieldwork among Tibetan refugees, I too noticed that the lay usage of Las or karma often appeared as an apology, an excuse, or rationalization for sickness, disease, unemployment, poverty, or the general malaise of the refugee condition. But such discussions inevitably turned to the topic of happiness and acceptance of worldly circumstances with an insightful view of the past, present, and future. For Tibetans, the right attitude is reflected in the moral "I take life as it comes" rather than "I take from life what I can," an approach more familiar to Westerners. Despite their circumstances as displaced people, as refugees living in camps and performing menial labor Tibetans seem "happy" to outsiders. The Tibetan understanding of fate is the underpinning of this contentment or inner peace which others so readily notice. With this basic instruction, even the youngest Tibetan child appears to be mindful of the fateful consequences of his actions. While American children share the experience of bottling bugs, pinning up butterflies, and squishing snails and worms, Tibetan children take great care to rescue and protect such helpless creatures. They, as their parents, happily ransom fish and other animals headed to market, giving these creatures another chance to live, and earning good merit in the process. Saving, sustaining, and protecting life are thus consequential activities for Tibetans.

In old Tibet, there were other versions of ransom, including saving humans from revenge killings through payment. This practice of paying life money to atone for the killing of a person was called Mi sTong (see Ekvall, 1954, pp. 136–145). It is pertinent to note that such payments were not given by the murderer and his family only: each member of his entire community or tribe had to contribute to the cost that was determined through arbitration. Thus, the social group as a whole was held accountable for an individual's actions. Buying of life through Mi sTong was an important Tibetan practice for restoration of peace between communities, and

---

[10]HH the Dalai Lama, *An Introduction to Buddhism*, New Delhi: Statesman Press, no date, p. 18.

[11]For further discussion on this topic, see Dorsh de Voe, *Survival of a Refugee Culture: The Long-Term Gift Exchange Between Tibetan Refugees and Donors in India*. Ann Arbor: University Dissertation Microfilms International, 1983.

it was another way in which one could obtain merit toward future, more favorable rebirth.

In the Tibetan belief system, the ethic of compassionate giving creates merit, which governs Tibetan motivation in daily life activities. Thus, from the Tibetan cultural context, it is not surprising that the vast majority of the Tibetan youth TAT narratives examined for this chapter are stories about helping, rescuing, giving, supporting, protecting, encouraging, or sustaining others. Indeed, even Tibetan achievement stories conclude with recognition of the accomplishment as worthy only in the context of a larger community. That is, while personal achievement may bring wealth, status, and happiness, its value rests only in the context of society at large and what the achievement had done to help others.

For Tibetan youth, the man-on-a-rope TAT card scene frequently elicits stories in which a fateful condition or event has occurred, such as poverty, an accident, or death. There is some kind of loss or negative event. In fact, fate was present in 73 percent of the man-on-a-rope TAT narratives.

The strength of family ties can be illustrated, most poignantly, in the following story told by a twelve-year-old recent arrival from Tibet:

> This is a story of a long time ago. There lived a small family. They have a son named Dhondup. One day, the parents went to the market and Dhondup was left alone at home. Then a big monkey came and took Dhondup to the forest. When the parents got home, they could not find Dhondup. They felt very sad. But the boy has become like a monkey. After many years, the mother saw a child that looked like Dhondup. She called him but he does not understand her words at all. The mother became so sad and she could not do anything. After two years, the poor mother died. She could not live without her son.
>
> [FB-apart KD-animal FD-thought FD-death]

This story begins with the temporary absence of the parents (FB-apart), an ominous situation for the son because, without any explanation, a monkey (KD-animal) suddenly abducts the son. One feels the passage of time as the boy becomes like the monkey and cannot communicate with her (FD-thought). Mother and son are estranged. The mother dies, as she cannot live without her son (FD-death). The family bond is pivotal and the mother cannot survive the loss of her son, in effect, dying of sorrow.

In the following narrative, the poor family's situation (KD-poverty) changes after their son, wrongly accused of theft and jailed (DDC-unfair), escapes (DSA-free). He does not run away alone, however, but rather he takes his parents with him, he gets work, and they live happily ever after. For an American youth telling this story, there might be wrongful accusation and imprisonment and escape, but it is most unlikely that the accused would come back and move his parents with him as he runs away to a new place to start over and providing for them (NDA-family), establishes a harmonious, happy life (HA-family). It is also unlikely, I might add, that the American parents would wish to move away with their child. Thus, in contrast, one can see the strength of the Tibetan view of family that is not broken by life events. In Tibetan society, there is an expectation that family members stay together, each working for the betterment of the others:

> Long ago, there lived a very poor family in a small village. The father whose name was Nicob worked in the garden of a very rich man in the same village. One day the wife of his master found that her golden ring with a diamond on it was missing. She blamed the poor man and had him arrested and put into prison. As Nicob hadn't done anything wrong, and also was very worried about his small family, he planned to run away from the prison but found no way. But, unexpectedly, one day Nicob found a rope in a corner of the dark prison and he made a big hole with the help of his pocket knife which he always kept with him. Then he fled to his own family and there, when he reached home, they all fled quietly away from their village to a city. There in the city, Nicob got a very good job, much better than previously. He earned a lot of money. From then on, he and his family lived happily.
>
> [KD-poverty RA-work OB-theft DDC-unfair DSA-free NDA-family HA-family]

Achievement after Deprivation and Loss

Often, as illustrated in the following three narratives, it is a son who comes forth to rescue, help, succor, or take care of his family or a larger community (N). Responsible behavior is sometimes overtly discussed, and obligation or duty is sometimes implied in the stories (R). We see that very young children are capable of taking on immense responsibility for the sake of the family. This parallels my observations in Tibetan refugee settlements in India and also, I must add, in eastern Tibet where, in 1991, I noticed very young Khampa children fetch water, wash clothes, find and carry firewood, and herd unruly yak. They not only diligently labored alongside their parents, but they also performed such tasks alone while their parents were busy with other chores. In Tibetan society, there is clearly a belief that the young are capable of hard work and can shoulder responsibilities that are critical for survival.

Tibetan youth view their parents, especially their mothers, as benefactors who gave them life and nourishment. These gifts are not given without suffering. Tibetans acknowledge the suffering of women in carrying the unborn, in labor and delivery, and in raising children. The mother is the ultimate benefactress. It is quite natural, therefore, that Tibetan youth not only feel obliged to help their parents, but moreover, look forward to opportunities to repay parental kindness. Tibetan youth express their gratitude, or drin-lan,[12] for their parents through compliant, socially acceptable behaviors which help to alleviate the hardships and suffering that their parents and others endure. This concern to repay parents and other adult caregivers

---

[12]Chandra Das, p. 654. It is interesting to note that the Tibetan definition of gratitude combines English concepts of kindness, benevolence, and obligation.

for their suffering and sacrifice emerges as a salient subject in Tibetan youth narratives. It is not unusual for the narrative to end on a positive note that the son has been able to achieve enough so that he can help his parents or community. Achievement is meaningful, valued, and esteemed only when the achiever takes responsibility to nurture others.

I found that achievement was a recurrent concern in Tibetan youth narratives on the man-on-a-rope TAT card as it appeared in 61 percent of the narratives. When achievement was a concern on the card, it usually was inspired by another (AA-inspire), a result of reform (RA-reform), or to nurture others (AA-nurture). There were few instances wherein achievement was motivated by the sheer desire to gain personal fortune or fame, although favorable changes in one's circumstances often occurred. Typically, Tibetan youth gave narratives in which situations of deprivation or loss were first described and later overcome. In the following narrative, the twelve-year-old child is described as hard working (RA-work), clever in persisting and achieving his goal (Ca-endure AA-duty) of getting firewood for his poor, old parents (KD-poverty NDA-nurture) despite the obstacles he encounters along the way:

> Here the boy is climbing on the tree. He was living in a small village near the forest. He was a hardworking boy of twelve years. There was no firewood to cook food. His parents were too old to work. He was the only boy of his parents. It was not easy to go, as there were many forest officers in this forest. It is a very thick forest. He had to go alone in the forest. By the time of cutting a tree, he saw many forest officers coming toward him. At once a trick came to mind. He tied his rope to the branch and climbed with the help of the rope. After the forest officers went back, he climbed down and went back home with plenty of wood.
>
> [RA-work KD-poverty CA-endure AA-duty NDA-family]

In another example, the narrative begins with the circumstances of poverty, old age, and death. The only son grows up with a desire to make his mother's life comfortable (RA-duty) and he achieves this through hard work (AA-persist; AA-nurture):

> Once there was an old woman and a son. Her husband dies when her son was at the age of ten (KD-death). Everything was earned by the father when he was alive, but unfortunately the mother has now got to do everything though she can't (NDD-unable). They led life in a miserable condition (KD-poverty). The years went by and the son became quite grow up and he always used to think about his mother to keep her happy for the rest of her life (NDB-welfare). One day, he received a letter from his friend who was a weight lifter. In the letter, he was informing that they needed a new weight lifter within two weeks. So, his joy doubled and he ran toward his mother to tell that he was going to join that club (KA-luck). He always used to practice climbing on the rope to build up his muscles strong (CA-improve), since he wanted to be very strong and the best weight lifter in that club so that he can fulfill his wishes to make his mother's life very comfortable as well as his life. As a result everything went successfully according to his plan (AA-persist AA-

> nurture). Later he became a very famous weight lifter (ESA-fame) in the club and both of them lived happily for the rest of their lives.
>
> [KD-death NDD-unable KD-poverty NBA-welfare KA-luck CA-improve AA-persist AA-nurture ESA-fame]

In a third example, given by a thirteen-year-old girl who was a recent arrival from Tibet, the narrative again begins with deprivation, poverty, and old age (KD-poverty). The importance Tibetans give to the obligation of the oldest son for family responsibility is openly stated. The son is successful in his job search and is able to send money (AA-nurture). Then, while it appears that the son is avoiding his duty to help his parents by running away, instead, we find he runs in order to study and become a scholar (AA-persist). In the end, the boy is not only able to help his parents but also many others as well (RA-duty-others; AA-nurture).

> According to this picture, I would like to tell you a brief story. This boy is from a small family. The parents have three children. This family does not have clothes to wear and food to eat (KD-poverty). Therefore, the boy went to search for a job. Since he is the oldest child from this family, he has to take the responsibility (RA-work). His parents are old and therefore the boy will do any job he finds (NDA-family). He never finds a good job because he never had the chance to go to school when he was young (KD-unjust). One day, the boy went to become a servant in a home. As soon as he got his salary, he sent it to his parents (NDA-family). One day, he saw many children studying nearby a road. Immediately, he jumped from the window with a rope and ran away. He went with those children. Then the boy studied really hard (CA-improve). Later the boy became a scholar (AA-persist). And he went to his home. He not only made his family happy but also helped other people too (AA-nurture NDA-social).

Sometimes, it is the parent that rescues the child and restores tranquility to the family. The following narrative begins with the fateful circumstance of poverty (KD-poverty) and, also, anxiety about natural danger (KB-natural). Despite the parents' protests, the son goes into the forest for firewood (NDA-family). Concerns about harmony/discord come up in the boy's fear of attack (HB-f-attack), but he is rescued by his father (NDA-rescue) and their closeness is expressed (FA-happen):

> Once there was a poor family who had got only one son (KD-poverty). They sent him every day to fetch wood in the forest which was quite far from their house (RA-work). One day, the weather became terrible with the wind blowing and rain falling heavily. Unfortunately, on that same day, there was not even a single wood left in their house. So, the boy went into the forest though his parents insisted that he not go (NDA-family). On the way back to the house, the weather became worse as well as it became dark (KD-nature). Finally, he lost his way and all of a sudden, he saw someone coming after him (HB-f-attack). Then he started running as fast as his legs could carry him and he found an old high tower with a rope hanging. Without looking back, he started climbing it and when he was in the middle of it, he looked down to se who it was. At the same time, there came lightening and he

saw his father searching for him (HDB-welfare). With a smile on his face, he started climbing down and the rain also stopped suddenly. His father clung to him as soon as he was down, and they returned home happily (FA-happen).

Harmony through Active Nurturance

A Tibetan theme of giving and helping for the benefit of the family, community, or nation not only illustrates the Tibetan preoccupation with giving but also highlights the importance of living in harmony (H) with all sentient beings. Tibetan youth gave several TAT rope card narratives that had an expressive concern about harmony. In their stories, group reconciliation, cohesion, protection, or sustenance was achieved through nurturing activities.

Tibetan youth narratives often contain the appearance of some other type of sentient being, such as a bug or animal, that plays a key role in the twist of fate. Many old Tibetan folk tales also include animals that provide instruction and guidance to man.[13] In the following story, given by a seventeen-year-old boy, the spider is an intentional being that inspires the king (AA-inspire) to persist and finally free his country. According to Tibetan friends, this narrative is a retelling of the "King Bruce" tale that Tibetans in India read in fifth or sixth grade. They are taught that the moral of the King Bruce story is failure as the key to success. This narrative starts with conflict (HA-combat), but harmony is restored as the king succeeds in freeing his country (NDA-active).

For this storyteller, the rope evokes memory of the King Bruce tale, a tale of competition and triumph for a legitimate purpose, the country. Note that the king does not achieve on his own; he is helped by the spider's message. And, when the king is victorious, it again is not for his personal gain but rather for his countrymen who are now free. This story, and several others I collected, reveals political content related to Tibetan youth concern about the Chinese takeover of Tibet. Certainly the vision of Tibetan youth is that Tibet will one day be free and that they will have a role in its freedom:

> Once there was a king. He wanted to free his country from the other country, which conquered them (HA-combat). He fought many battles against the enemy, but was defeated every time (MVA-war). Finally he gave up the attempt and went into the forest and hid himself in a deep cave (MVD-quit). One day, he was sitting in a sad mood. Suddenly, he saw a spider fall from its cobweb in the ceiling. It hung on a fine silk thread. It tried again and again to climb up and reach its web (CA-endure). But every time it fell down and hung lower than before. The king became interested in it. The spider lay faint for a while. He thought that the poor creature

[13]See, for example, the story of *The Umbrella Tree*, and the story of *The Frog*, in Fredrick and Audrey Hyde-Chambers, *Tibetan Folk Tales*, Boulder: Shambala Press, 1981, pp. 156–163 and pp.169–186.

> would try no more, but surprisingly, it began to crawl up slowly again till it was very near its home. Finally the spider succeeded in weaving its web (AA-persist). So the king jumped with joy. He thought that if a small creature like the spider could succeed after many failures, why could he not? So, he came down from the cave with strong ropes and fought several attempts against the enemy and this time he succeeded in freeing his country (MVA-war AA-nurture).

This is a purposeful, instrumental story in which active achievement to nurture is attained. For the Tibetans, the ultimate act of giving is helping to free the country. It is this singularly focused perspective that Tibetans hope will help them achieve their ultimate goal of freedom.

In this narrative, one is reminded of the Tibetan refugee plight and their leader's response to this situation. The Dalai Lama has indicated that living as a refugee has been an extremely important, even beneficial, experience: "Being a refugee has been very useful. You are much closer to reality. I became a refugee. Very good. So there was a good opportunity to gain experience, and also determination or inner strength."[14]

The Dalai Lama has also said, "The main reason we are in exile is our concern for the welfare of six million Tibetans in Tibet" (see *The Tibet Society Newsletter*, No. 7, Spring, 1979, p. 1). In the sociological sense, a refugee is dislodged from one's natural or native habitat, displaced. In Buddhist teachings, however, one seeks and takes refuge. Thus, for example, the Sanskrit term for refugee, anagarika, means homeless, a spiritual seeker. So, with the heady pragmatism Tibetans are well known for, life in refuge has, somehow, a philosophical quality to it. It is a time for gathering inner strength, for greater wisdom and reflection, and a time for contribution to the cause, alleviating the suffering of those left behind in Tibet.

It is understood by Tibetan youth everywhere that the role of parents and other adults is to guide and support them. In the 1970s and 1980s, Tibetan youth in India clearly had another reason to view not only their parents but also other adult community members with great respect (E) for, as refugees, they survived. Tibetan youth TAT rope card narratives display respect for adult authority especially parental—and reform or achievement in order to help family, community, or country. The love and commitment that Tibetan children feel to their parents is illustrated time and again in their TAT stories. In the following story, told by a thirteen-year-old boy who lives in the Delhi Tibetan refugee camp, the son responds to his parents' poverty by trying to steal food for them.

> Once there was a family. This family does not have a single penny to buy food (KD-poverty). They have a son and his name is Ramesh. One day, for the sake of food to support his parents, Ramesh threw a rope to a high building and started to climb to steal. But people near the building saw him and handed him over to the

---

[14]See John Avedon, *An Interview with the Dalai Lama*. New York: Littlebird Publications, 1980, p. 21.

> police (NDA-means AC-theft DDA-police). He was put in jail for 6 mos. After coming out from the prison, he went to his parents to ask their forgiveness (DSA-forgive) and he promised that he would never do this kind of act again. So, he joined the army and wanted to help his country (RA-reform NDA-social).

This story begins with a fateful statement of poverty (KD-poverty). The son's theft is double-scored as achievement and nurturance (AC-theft; NDA-means) as he is stealing the food for an honorable cause to feed his parents. Control themes arise as the son is caught and jailed by police. Then, he asks his parents' forgiveness (DSA-forgive). Finally, he takes a responsible step and joins the army to help his society (RA-reform; NDA-social).

Unlike most other groups wherein this would be the end of the story, the Tibetan story goes on to say, "and he wanted to help his country." Again, the Tibetan story moves from the individual to the larger group, in this case, the country. And again, the achievement of the youth and the responsibility he takes on are not just for him alone, but rather for the larger cause of family and country. This narrative was given by a thirteen-year-old boy whose family left Kham, Tibet in 1959 and, as refugees, settled in India. In 1989 when this narrative was given, this youth lived in a Tibetan refugee camp, Majuna ka Tilak, on the outskirts of old Delhi. Despite some degree of assimilation of this youth who told his story in Hindi, this boy clearly illustrates a Tibetan theme of responsible, nurturing behavior for the sake of others. Even though this boy was born in exile, the loss of country is still meaningful to him and becomes the goal of his activities.

Another example of this appears in the following narrative given by a twelve-year-old Tibetan boy from Manali:

> To me this man looks like a great inspector (EDA-fame), because such people have the courage to sacrifice their own life for the country's prestige and honor. I think this inspector in the picture too is risking his own life for his country (NDA-devote). Such people are very fortunate and they are very rare in this world. We should immortalize their names in glittering letters (EDA-praise), for our country has very few people like them.

In this narrative, the esteemed inspector (EDA-fame) is risking his life for his country (NDA-devote) and should be publicly acclaimed (EDA-praise). There is then a moralistic statement that suggests he is a hero to the young storyteller. Note the respect and admiration shown for the adult in this narrative. Here, we clearly see the esteem (E) accorded by Tibetans to those who nurture him this case, sacrificing to the point of risking his life for his country.

Dynamic Forms of Nurturance in Tibetan Culture

Giving or nurturing is an essential Tibetan preoccupation and is a dominant subject in Tibetan Buddhist teachings. For Tibetans, every act in life should be kind and compassionate and done with proper motivation. Giving is to be done selflessly to reduce the misery and suffering of other sentient beings. sGam.po.pa's discussion of benevolence and compassion as a remedy against attachment to self-complacency offers a philosophical explanation of the primacy of working for the benefit of others.[15] It is said that the root of benevolence lies in the memory of benefits received from our greatest benefactor in this life, our mother.[16] If we work for the benefit of others, we may obtain enlightenment. Generosity, or liberality, is a highly valued quality in a person and it is believed that ìa liberal person will be rich in all existences and attain happiness.[17] There is considerable discussion about the proper motivation and manner of giving.

In classical Tibetan language, a gift, alms, or offering is expressed in the same word, sByin-Pa. A charitable person, the one who distributes gifts to large numbers of people, is called a sByin-gTon. In Chandra Das's Tibetan dictionary (1979, pp. 939–940), all of the meanings ascribed to gifts are religious. That is, gifts and the process of giving fall within the realm of teachings of the Buddhist dharma and hence, for Tibetans, are endowed with religious value. Gifts, Das tells us, are therefore never to include arms, wine, women, or poisons. Historical social structures for gift giving in old Tibet included the patron-priest system. The basic gift-giver, the sByin-bDag or patron, was typically a layman who showed his piety and reverence by giving gifts to those in the priesthood. Gifts sustained and nurtured the monasteries in old Tibet as well as in the Tibetan refugee communities in India. For Tibetans, the act of giving implies sacrifice and status is accorded to gift-givers for this reason.

It is interesting to note that a new use for the ancient term sByin-bDag developed in the Tibetan refugee community. A sByin-bDag is the word most popularly used for westerners who in any way help Tibetans. Thus, in exile, a sByin-bDag is a sponsor who pays or provides in-kind support for Tibetan refugee community or individual Tibetan endeavors.

Being in the donor position puts one in the position to give, to help, to rescue, to provide for, or to take care of other sentient beings. This is the fantasy, the goal for Tibetans and it comes across clearly in man-on-a-rope card TAT narratives of their youth. Nurture appears in 57 percent or twenty-eight of forty-nine of the man-on-a-rope TAT card narratives. Several Tibetan youth narratives on the rope card depict positive self esteem and fame gained through competence. Normally, these achievement stories are not just about one individual's personal success. Families, friends, colleagues, community, cause, or country are typically the recipient of some benefit because of the individual's achievement. In the end, the achiever takes on

---

[15]See especially Chapter 7 and Chapter 12 in *The Jewel Ornament of Liberation* by sGam.po.pa. Translated and annotated by Herbert V. Guenther. Berkeley: Shambala Press, 1971.

[16]Ibid., pp. 92.

[17]Ibid., p. 152.

responsibilities to help someone other than himself. Some examples of these narratives are provided below:

> Once there lived a poor family in a village near Bhuppur (KD-poverty). They have four children, two boys and two girls. The eldest son named Raju was very bad and always fighting, stealing and doing bad things (RC-status). The other three were quite good (RA-good). So, the poor father and mother advised Raju to avoid bad manners but he did not listen to the advice of his father. The poor mother and father are both working in the field to get little profit every year. They had to feed their four children (NDA-means). Thus, many years passed. His father and mother became old and could not do any work (KD-age). So, the responsibilities of his family fell on the eldest son. He always tried to get a job everywhere, but all the people knew he was very bad. Finally, he told his father and mother of his wishes to join the army and they were very glad to learn this (RA-duty-o PA-joy). Raju went to the army and started sending money to his poor father and mother every month (NDA-means). A few months went by and he learned all the necessities of the army and there is shown a snapshot when he was studying how to climb up ropes (CA-persist). After many years, he was married (FA-sex) and the poor family lived happily (HA-family).

> Once upon a time, there was a village near Mysore which was surrounded by many trees (PA-nature). In this village there is one boy who was naughty and lazy (RC-indulge). His name was Tom and he was 17. When he was young, he had not gone to any school because his parents belonged to a poor family (KD-deprive). So when his friends were going to school, he used to take a rope and climb the tree. He will also not do the fieldwork due to his laziness. Later on when he became quite old, he was remembering what he had done during his younger days. He also remembers that he was not standing on his feet and was totally dependent on his parents (NSC-demand). Now he thought it was too late to join the school. So he wants to earn his living. He went to his neighbour's house to borrow some money and later he bought some material and sold it at very high rates and got much profit (AA-counter). Now he became a rich person in the village and he used to give food whenever beggars come to him (NDA-social). Later he became a good person and all the people of the village respected him (ESA-praised).

The following story was given in 1989 by a fifteen-year-old Tibetan boy who was at that time a recent arrival in India. He reported that his parents were still in Tibet. He is one of thousands of Tibetan youth and young adults who, since the mid-1980s, braved mountains and Chinese border militia to escape Chinese-occupied Tibet.[18]

---

[18]The Tibetan Centre for Democracy reported that, in 1998 alone, 1,190 Tibetan children are known to have escaped from Tibet. The harrowing stories of youth who have attempted to escape are periodically documented by news media. Many Tibetans do not make it out. Recently, for example, the press reported the rape of three Tibetan youth by China's border police. These young women were caught as they tried to escape across the border into Nepal.

> Look here you people, this powerful man (CA-body) is jumping on the roof of a house by a rope. Isn't he a great person? His name is Tenzin Sherpa. His original birthplace is Tibet and he left Tibet in 1949 and went to settle in the Sherpa region, because the Chinese took over Tibet, Since he stayed in the Sherpa region as their citizen and took his name Tenzin Sherpa. He was a very good sport and has good athletic capability and I am sure you all know about this man (EDA-fame). He is an expert in sports. He was the first man in the world to climb Everest and this picture shows it (AA-self). He was a brave man, because he could climb the world's highest mountain. The mountain is covered by snow all year round. It is very difficult and risky to take such a journey (CB-arduous). Therefore, he became a very famous person, as we all know.

Several of the Tibetan stories I collected in 1988–1989 contain explicit references to the Chinese takeover of Tibet and show pride in Tibetan identity. Here, the storyteller describes the world-famous mountain climber as a refugee: his original birthplace is Tibet and he left Tibet in 1949 because the Chinese took over Tibet. The story goes on to extol Tenzin Sherpa's athletic capabilities and depicts him as a brave and famous man. What is interesting about this story is that it picks up not only the theme of achievement but also that of ethnic purpose. Among the Tibetans, Tenzin Sherpa is in fact a hero. In this story, there is an implicit instrumental aspect of doing something for Tibetans as a group. That is, it is suggested that climbing the mountain for individual fame or fortune is not the salient feature. There is the pride that Tenzin Sherpa as a Tibetan has climbed the world's highest mountain. Thus, while the rope card stimulates some competition, it is the esteemed achievement of Tenzin Sherpa as a Tibetan that is important.

Here is another climbing narrative, told in Hindi by a fifteen-year-old Tibetan girl from Nepal who attends school at the Tibetan Children's Village in Dharamsala, India:

> Long, long ago, there lived a boy called Suraj. He was very nice and kind-hearted boy. He always helped the poor and destitute (NDA-charity). His only aim in life was to climb Mt. Everest (AA-purpose). In the beginning, he started climbing small mountains (CA-improve). Then one day, he got the chance to join the army. This inspired him more to climb Mt. Everest (AA-inspire). Suraj was ready to work with ropes and other necessary articles. When they started the expedition, Suraj was leading everyone, leaving behind all others (MVA-game). His fellow climbers also followed him. But Suraj succeeded in reaching the peak first and he hoisted the national flag on it (ESA-ethnic).

See "Tibetan girls raped by police," *Tibetan Bulletin*, 3(2), March-April 1999, p. 6. Tibetans who do escape to Nepal face persecution if caught by Nepalese police. See, for example, Jenna Ziman, "Police Brutality in the Himalayas: The Price of Being Tibetan Refugees," *Tibetan Review*, December 1996, pp. 21–22.

In this story, Suraj is depicted as nurturing (NDA-charity) as he always helps the poor and destitute. He has a singular aim in life (AA-purpose), however, and that is to climb Mt. Everest. Suraj joins the army and leads the Everest expedition, thus achieving his goal. This story alternates between competition and cooperation with a predominant theme of ethnic purpose. While Suraj is first among his peers in reaching the peak, the overall effect of the story is one of harmony rather than cutthroat competition. In the end, the telltale Tibetan theme of personal achievement for the benefit of others comes into focus when Suraj succeeded in reaching the peak first and he hoisted the national flag on it. For Tibetans, the ultimate value is not on getting there first or being number one. In this example, the importance of Suraj's achievement is that it puts him in the position to display the nation's flag. Displaying the Tibetan flag is, of course, a defiant statement of independence and nationhood, and in China, it is illegal not only to display it but also even to own it.

Perhaps, then, the most prominent theme in Tibetan narratives is nurture for family, for kingdom, for country. Competition and achievement are rarely depicted as satisfying for oneself only. What is satisfying for Tibetans is having the compassion to help others by alleviating their misery and affliction. Personal success has no value unless such success is helpful to the community at large. While there are situations of hard work and competition, winning and achieving are usually for the legitimate purpose of saving or helping another. Time and again, the Tibetan teen population tells stories about fighting for or saving their country. Though most of these narratives were collected from Tibetan youth born in India, they are acutely aware of their refugee status and share unshakeable pride in their Tibetan identity. They tell immensely sorrowful tales of Tibetan losses to the Chinese. They share political awareness about Tibet's situation and express it in their narratives.

A fifteen-year-old boy whose family lives in Delhi told the following fate-nurturance narrative in Hindi. In this narrative, heroic deeds of three brothers are acknowledged by a grateful king who generously repays them:

> This is a story of a long time ago. There lived three brothers in a village called Ramgard. The 3 brothers are Ram, Sham, and Dara. Ram is very good in reading and writing (CA-present). Sham is very shy (FB-shy) and Dara is very wise and he is also good at climbing trees (CA-present CA-body). The king of this village is Chandrasan. Chandrasan is a powerful (DDA-control) and kind king (NDA-charity). He has one daughter and her name is Chanda. The princess loves to play in the garden (PA-play) and one-day when she was playing, a big devil flew from the sky and kidnapped the princess (DDC-capture). After this news, the king was very upset (PB-trouble) and told his people that whoever can bring the daughter back will get a large sum of presents and half of his kingdom (NSA-assist). On hearing this news, the three brothers decided to fight the devil. Sham made a big arrow and a bow. Dara made a big and strong rope and he climbed up the big rocky mountain where the devil hides. Dara fought with the devil and killed him (HA-combat NDA-rescue). Dara took the princess to the palace. The king was very pleased and gave lots of presents for these three brave brothers and half the

> kingdom too (NDA-reward). All three brothers got married and lived happily ever after (HA-harmony).

This is a story about the rescue of an abducted princess. It is typically Tibetan that each of the brothers has a different strength or competence. Another Tibetan belief surfaces in that the family is strong as a cohesive unit. Together, they are able to save the princess who has been abducted by a devil flying down from the sky. In doing so, they restore happiness to the king and harmony to the kingdom. There is not one hero but, rather, three. It is through their united efforts and combined talents that harmony is restored. They are in turn amply rewarded by the king and are given half the kingdom. The reference to their marriage may suggest a marriage to the princess by the three brothers in a polyandrous arrangement that still occurs among Tibetans in exile.[19] The affiliative relationship between the brothers makes it possible for them to rescue (NDA-rescue) the princess. Their nurturing act begets gratitude from the king who amply rewards them (NDA-reward). This story again illustrates a fundamental Tibetan belief that personal happiness is achieved through helpful, benevolent, and compassionate actions.

Conversely, in the Tibetan worldview, negative actions in this life can affect one's future rebirths, as aptly illustrated in this narrative:

> Long ago, there lived a husband, his wife. They had two children. The husband used to go to the jungle daily to collect firewood (NDA-secure). One day, as the husband went to the jungle as usual to collect wood, he lost his way and could not find his way back home (CB-help). Suddenly, an elephant passed by. The elephant was Lord Buddha's follower. Due to a certain curse, he was made to live as an elephant. The elephant heard the man's voice and went to help. When the elephant came towards, him, the man was frightened and started running away (HB-f-attack). The elephant ran after him. But when the elephant realized that the man was scared of him, the elephant said, "oh good human being! Why are you running away from me? I have come to help you." The man stopped but wondered how an elephant can speak human language. He went toward the elephant and asked, do you really want to help me? Then please tell me the way to Rampur Village. The elephant told the man to ride on his back. So the two went towards Rampur village (NDA-rescue). When they reached Rampur village, the man thanked the elephant for his help (NSA-grateful). But the elephant said, you don't have to thank a friend (FA-friend). It was my duty (RA-duty-o). The elephant and man talked a while and both went to their respective homes. The wife of the man was overjoyed to see her husband back home (PA-joy). She asked him what happened and the husband told the whole story. The wife's heart was overcome with greed and avarice (OC-greed). She told her husband that if the elephant wanted to help us, why not ask for his tusk? We can sell it now and become rich overnight. The husband's heart too

[19]Melvyn Goldstein, the anthropologist, has written extensively about Tibetan polyandry. See, for example, "Stratification, Polyandry, and Family Structure in Tibet," *Southwestern Journal of Anthropology*, 27, 64–74.

> was afflicted with greed. The very next morning, he left toward the forest and met the elephant and said, I'm very poor (KD-poverty). Please give me your tusk (NSC-demand). The elephant took pity and gave his tusk (NDB-pity). He returned home. Many people saw him taking home the tusk and they set their minds on it (NSB-envy). Among them, Kalu Dada was most determined to steal the tusk. One night, he went and stole the tusk (AC-theft). The next day, the husband and wife came to know the tusk was stolen and they despaired and cried. But suddenly another idea came into the wife's mind. Both went to the elephant and told him about the theft and begged for his skin. The elephant was merciful (NDB-welfare). He told then that they can kill him and take away the skin. The husband axed the elephant and killed him (RC-property HC-selfish). The Buddha was annoyed with the greedy couple and he destroyed them with fire (DDA-curse). In their next life, the husband and wife were born as a boar and a sow. They lived on leftovers. The elephant was born in a royal family and lived happily ever after (DDA-give HA-family).

This story is rich in its texture of fate and nurture. It begins with the father going into the jungle for firewood (NDA-secure). When he gets lost, an elephant appears. For Tibetans, an elephant is considered a wise and compassionate sentient being. So, in this story, the elephant offers to help the father find his way home (NDA-rescue), explaining to the father that it is his "duty" to do so (RA-duty-o). Then, the narrative depicts many negative actions that are the subject of Tibetan Buddhist teachings.[20] Greed consumes the wife and inflicts the husband like a disease. Finally, after killing the elephant for his skin, fate takes its course. Buddha destroys the couple with fire and they are born as pigs in their next lives. The helpful, compassionate elephant, however, is reborn in a royal family and lives happily ever after.

This story reminds us of the tale of how the young Buddha offered himself to the hungry tigress who needed sustenance to feed her starving cubs. He sacrificed his own life to alleviate the hunger of the starving tigress and her cubs. This story is often told in Tibetan circles as a reminder of the worthiness of such an absolute gift. In this elephant story, the Tibetan youth depicts the importance of giving in Tibetan culture. The ultimate sacrifice is that of one's own body. There are several ways in which this belief is played out in Tibetan society. In 1998, for example, the Tibetan Youth Congress organized a Tibetan hunger-strike-unto-death in Delhi, India in order to publicize the Tibetan freedom struggle. After several days, as the hunger strikers were getting weaker and international attention was growing, the

---

[20]See Patrul Rinpoche's *The Words of My Perfect Teacher* (translated by the Padmakara Translation Group) San Francisco: HarperCollins Publishers, 1994, especially Chapter 4, Part I, *Negative Actions to be Abandoned,* pp. 101–117.

Indian police moved in. Rather than be forcibly removed, one of the hunger strikers, Thupten Ngodup, doused himself with petrol and died in the flames.[21]

Another completely different story of sacrifice through organ donation is widely told among Tibetans. Upon learning of his aunt's terminal illness due to kidney failure, a young Tibetan boy in India insisted that he be allowed to donate one of his kidneys to her. His desire to help her was so persistent and strong that he was finally allowed to undergo the surgery. The operation was successful and the aunt has recovered her health. Another Tibetan living in the United States recently donated his kidney to his ailing sibling in Asia. When discussing these events, Tibetans reflect that the donors made the supreme sacrifice by giving a piece of their own body to save other human beings. Furthermore, Tibetans state that even if these donors do not reap the benefits from their sacrifice in this lifetime, they will certainly experience favorable conditions in subsequent rebirths, a direct reference to Buddhist teachings on compassion and the accumulation of merit. Indeed, it is said that giving of one's own flesh is one of the ten possessions a Buddhist should be ready to bestow.

Climbing on the Tree of Gold

Perhaps the most imaginative and poignant rope card narrative was given by a sixteen-year-old female whose parents fled from Kham, Tibet in 1960 and who was attending the Central School of Tibetans in Dalhousie, India at the time. Her way of telling this story reminds us of the great oral traditions of Tibetans and reads like a folktale:

> The name of this story is a farmer who became a king. There lived a poor farmer (KD-poverty). His name is Hariya. One day when Hariya returned from town to village, he lost his way. After roaming here and there, he reached a very thick jungle. He was very tired so he lay down under one tree (NSB-help). Suddenly, he saw a rope hanging on the tree (NDA-magic). He ran and climbed up on the tree. There he saw that all the branches and leaves are of gold (OA-wealth). He quickly plucked all the leaves and put them in the bag and went to find shelter far away when he saw a beautiful place (PA-esthetic). He ran happily and reached the place. He saw that there were many tents and cattle. He was surprised that he didn't see any man. He asked himself who built this tent and who looked after the cattle? Suddenly, he heard some men talking. He went to the place where the voices were coming. He saw that there was a meeting about their king because they haven't got any king (MTA-task). The country without a king is like a man without education. They declared that any strange man who came to this country would be the king.

[21]For a complete account of Thupten Ngodup's life and circumstances of his death, see Jamyang Norbu's "The Life and Sacrifice of Thupten Ngodup" in *Tibetan Review*, 33(8), August 1998, pp. 15–19.

After dismissing their meeting, they saw that Hariya was standing near. They asked "are you a strange man in this country?" "Yes," he replied. They happily put a garland on his neck and put a crown on his head. On that night they all danced and enjoyed eating and drinking. In this way, Hariya became the king of that country (KA-luck DDA-control). He was very wise and brave (CA-present). He spent all the gold on the people to build houses and improved all things in the country (NDA-social). He married a poor woman. She is named Basanti. Basanti was very beautiful (OA-body) and simple woman. After she married King Hariya, she became queen and God gave them one sweet prince (NDA-god). This way, they led a very happy life with their people (HA-group). The tree of gold was useful to Hariya (KA-luck) and he improved the country (NDA-social). Hariya's life started when he climbed on the tree of gold that is showing in the picture. He is climbing on the tree of gold; he gets the tree of gold; he became a king with the help of the tree of gold.

The circumstantial appearance of the stranger who is subsequently appointed king reminds us of the legendary account of how an Indian prince, a "skygod," became the first king of Tibet. He came down from the peak of a sacred mountain that was pictured as a ladder linking heaven and earth, a Tibetan ladder, that is to say, a tree trunk with notches cut into it for footholds. Twelve chieftains who had come to pay religious homage to the mountain met this being from on high and took him as their king.[22]

Note how fate weaves its way throughout this Tibetan story. The first sentence says that this is the story about a farmer who becomes king, a fateful change of status. Next we are told that the farmer is also poor, a negatively incurred situation of fate. After the farmer loses his way in the jungle, there is a magical appearance of an object, the rope, which takes him up a tree to the leaves of gold. One must view this as miraculous intervention of great consequence. The story moves on as the farmer again wanders toward a distant, beautiful place and comes across a gathering of people. Hariya, a stranger, is crowned king of this country, a destiny that Hariya readily accepts. He is of good character for he is wise and brave. Great happiness comes to all.

Of course, the king has bliss too, for as noted above, it is the Tibetan belief that positive actions and good deeds result in personal happiness. The new king marries a poor girl and her fate changes to one of wealth and a new status of queen. Twice, the narrator tells us that the king spends the gold from the tree to improve life for the people he now serves. Hariya, with his recently acquired authority (DDA-control), sets about to improve the lot of his new countrymen. There is an expressive quality to his helpfulness as his activities sustain and improve the country. Thus, through a series of fateful events, the poor farmer moves to a

---

[22]For a complete account of Thupten Ngodup's life and circumstances of his death, see Jamyang Norbu's "The Life and Sacrifice of Thupten Ngodup," in *Tibetan Review*, 33(8), August 1998, pp. 15–19.

position of authority. What is good about this is that he is now in a position to help others. He embraces his new role not for personal power and glory but, rather, for the betterment of the community. For the Tibetan, the donor position is an ideal one, for one is then in a position to alleviate suffering by helping others, ultimately giving contentment to both donor and recipient. Here is a modern-day version of the Gesar tale, the legendary wise and benevolent warrior-king of Tibet who protected the poor, took care of the kingdom, and defended the land from evil. The epic of Gesar has become the national story of Tibet, but to the people of the Land of Snows, it is not just past history: it contains many prophecies of Gesar's return to Tibet, so the epic is also a guarantee to Tibetans that once again their land will know the rule of a just king in a free realm (Hyde-Chambers, 1981, p. 29).

Concluding Remarks

It is interesting to note that in my fieldwork among Tibetan refugees in India in 1977–1978, 1980–1982, and 1988–1989, I found that legitimate success stories were typically ones that portrayed achievement and work endeavors as sacrifice for the Tibetan community or nation. Hence, in exile, status could be achieved through careers such as teaching in Tibetan refugee schools, performing in the Tibetan Music, Dance, and Drama Society (now known as TIPA, the Tibetan Institute of Performing Arts), nursing in Tibetan refugee camps, and holding positions of any kind in the Tibetan government-in-exile. The fact that Tibetans were working for the betterment of their group was key in evaluating the job and the person in it. The element of sacrifice was common to all these positions, as salaries were usually lower than those in Indian schools and offices. Further, they were working for their own unrecognized, exiled government, and ultimately, working for the cause, the eventual freedom of Tibet.

In traditional Tibetan society, inter-community cooperation (M) was necessary. The land of old Tibet was harsh and unyielding. Exchange and reciprocity were vital elements of both feudalism and the patronage system that supported the monastic system. Essentially, these systems were forms of exchange that guaranteed connections between individuals and institutions of all ranks and regions. Exchange linked, for instance, laymen seeking to garner religious merit with lamas who, bestowed with spiritual power, could give blessings and advice (N) in exchange for offerings. Cooperation was necessary for individuals to survive. From a fundamental point of view, the bonds of harmonious relationships (H) were requisite for Tibetan survival. For Tibetans, the social order is predicated on unfaltering belief in and commitment to the Buddhist faith, which teaches individual control in action (R) and thought, and emphasizes compassion and giving (N). As we have seen, these concerns were emphasized in the Tibetan refugee youth TAT narratives.

For Tibetans, the resolution of conflict (HC-discord), while often problematic, is desirable. In these TAT stories, there is a sense of relief when conflict is absent, avoided, or settled. Deviant behavior (RC-mores) is rare, and when it appears, it is short-lived for the dominance of Buddhist precepts in the Tibetan culture prevail. Family matters appear to be a central preoccupation. As Beatrice Miller had noted in her Tibetan TAT study, most highly approved is the image of a family as a harmonious and cooperative enterprise. This harmony and cooperation is supposed to be based on love, respect, and understanding between the spouses (regardless of their number), between parents and their children, and between siblings, whether they be actually full or half or stepsiblings (Miller, 1972, pp. 387–388). Tibetan emphasis is placed on the value of the good family.

In my analysis of the Tibetan youth responses on the man-on-a-rope TAT card, I note several expressions of loss (FD-death). In many narratives, one or two parents were deceased. There was poverty and hunger as a negative fateful circumstance. In Tibetan youth TATs, the immense sense of deprivation and loss may be displayed as the psychological wound from the refugee event. However, one must remember the harsh environmental circumstances of old Tibet in which the basic struggle for survival was a daily preoccupation for the ordinary man. What is most poignant in these narratives is the resilience, the forward-striving efforts to improve not only one's personal circumstances, but also those of others.

Indeed, similar interpersonal and family concerns have been found in other refugee groups such as the Central American refugees in the United States. Marcelo Suárez-Orozco (1989) has documented the violence these refugees experienced prior to flight as well as the fear, deprivation, and loss they experience post-flight, as students in an inner-city school setting in California. As with Tibetan refugee youth in India, family and self-sacrifice appear as pivotal concerns for Central American refugees. A pattern of mutuality and interdependence emerges that exhibits a basic continuity: as their parents had helped their own folks, so now many informants feel it was their turn to help their parents achieve a better future (Suárez-Orozco, 1989, p. 85). (See also the next chapter.) For Tibetan youth, their comprehension of the refugee event in their families' lives and their response to it are grounded in their Buddhist worldview.

Perhaps it is not surprising to see the negative hand of fate in Tibetan youth narratives, for they are, after all, refugees who feel very strongly the loss of their country. In these stories, there is poverty, deprivation, separation, estrangement, and death. However, in almost every story, there is recovery and success. Tibetan youth narratives clearly illustrate that, for Tibetans, the consequence of loss is a question of nurture. That is, poverty, for example, while causing inordinate suffering, is viewed as a context for achievement, responsibility, and nurturance, for expression of true sacrifice and love. Suffering and loss can be transcended through virtuous simplicity, godliness, and diligent industriousness. In Tibetan youth narratives, resolution favors community harmony and family unity, the fulfillment of the child's obligation to his family, and a commitment from the child to protect and provide for his parents. The overwhelming response of Tibetan refugee youth on the rope card is that of a benevolent fate and nurture, with a harmonious, happy ending.

References

Avedon, John. 1980. *An Interview with the Dalai Lama*. New York: Littlebird Publications.

Dalai Lama. 1979. Statement of His Holiness the Dalai Lama on the 20th Anniversary of the Tibetan National Uprising of March 10, 1959. *The Tibet Society Newsletter*, **7**(spring): 1.

———. 1994. *The Way to Freedom*. New York: HarperCollins Publishers.

———. 1999. Statement of His Holiness the Dalai Lama on the 20th Anniversary of the Tibetan National Uprising of March 10, 1959." *The Tibet Society Newsletter*, **7**.

———. no date. *An Introduction to Buddhism*. New Delhi: Statesman Press.

Das, Chandra. 1993. *Tibetan-English Dictionary*. Kyoto: Rinsen Book Company. Reprint, originally published: Calcutta: Bengal Secretariat Book Depot, 1902.

de Voe, Dorsh. 1983. *Survival of a Refugee Culture: The Long-Term Gift Exchange Between Tibetan Refugees and Donors in India*. Ann Arbor: University Dissertation Microfilms International.

Ekvall, Robert B. 1954. Mi sTong: The Tibetan Custom of Life Indemnity. *Sociologus*, **4**(2): 136–145.

Ekvall, R.B. 1978. Correlation of Contradictions: A Tibetan Semantic Device. In James Fisher (Ed.), *Himalayan Anthropology* (pp. 251–262). The Hague.

Evans-Wentz, Walter Yeeling. 1969. (Editor and Translator) *The Tibetan Book of Great Liberation*. New York: Oxford University Press.

Goldstein, Melvyn. 1971. Stratification, Polyandry, and Family Structure in Tibet. *Southwestern Journal of Anthropology*, **27**: 64–74.

Hyde-Chambers, Fredrick and Audrey Hyde-Chambers. 1981. The Umbrella Tree, and The Frog. In *Tibetan Folk Tales* (pp. 156–163 and pp.169-186). Boulder: Shambala Press.

Information Office of HH the Dalai Lama. 1981. Tibetans in Exile: 1959–1980. Dharamsala, India.

Miller, Beatrice. 1978. Tibetan Culture and Personality: Refugee Responses to a Culture-Bound TAT. In James F. Fisher (Ed.), *Himalayan Anthropology* (pp. 365–393). The Hague: Mouton Publishers.

Norbu, Jamyang. 1998. The Life and Sacrifice of Thupten Ngodup. In *Tibetan Review*, **33**(8)(August): 15–19.

Patrul, Rinpoche. 1994. *The Words of My Perfect Teacher*. Translated by the Padmakara Translation Group. San Francisco: HarperCollins Publishers, especially Chapter 4, Part I, *Negative Actions to be Abandoned* (pp. 101–117).

Prince Peter of Greece and Denmark. 1965. The Psychological Testing of Todas and Tibetans. In Max Schur (Ed.), *Drives, Affects, Behavior*, Vol. 2 (pp. 418–502). New York: International Universities Press, Inc.

sGam.po.pa. 1971. *The Jewel Ornament of Liberation*. Translated and annotated by Herbert V. Guenther. Berkeley, Calif.: Shambala Press.

Stein, Rolf Alfred. 1972. *Tibetan Civilization*. Stanford: Stanford University Press.

Suárez-Orozco, Marcelo M. 1989. *Central American Refugees and US High School: A Psychosocial Study of Motivation and Achievement*. Palo Alto: Stanford U. Press.

"Tibetan Girls Raped by Police," *2000 Tibetan Bulletin*, **3**(2).

Tibetans in Exile: 1959–1980. Dharamsala: Information Office of His Holiness the Dalai Lama, 1981.

Ziman, Jenna. 1996. Police Brutality in the Himalayas: The Price of Being Tibetan Refugees. *Tibetan Review*, December, pp. 21–22.

Chapter 15

Wandering Souls: The Interpersonal Concerns of Adolescent Immigrants

Carola Suárez-Orozco
Marcelo Suárez-Orozco
Irina Todorova

In recent years, there has been a resurgence of social science and policy work in the area of immigration. This new work can be related to the intensification of globalization, transnationalisim, and large-scale immigration in the dawn of the new century. Indeed, worldwide, we are witnessing unprecedented patterns of large-scale immigration involving literally hundreds of millions of individuals (Suárez-Orozco and Suárez-Orozco, 2001). The new immigrants originate in countless urban and rural centers throughout Latin America, Asia, the Caribbean, and Africa and their journeys typically take them to wealthier developed countries in the Northern Hemisphere (Suárez-Orozco, 1996).

The new corpus of scholarship represents continuity to pioneering work conducted in the 1950s and 1960s on the social and psychological consequences of migration. George De Vos, in collaboration with a cadre of psychologists, sociologists, and anthropologists, conducted a series of innovative, interdisciplinary studies of immigration and its impact on family life, community dynamics, and individual development (Kleinberg and De Vos, 1973). While immigrants come from myriad cultural backgrounds and face distinct social realities that defy broad generalizations, they do share certain aspirations and ambitions as well as anxieties about the future. Immigration involves not only the possibility of significant gains but also a number of losses—some minor, some ambiguous, and some irreparable (Ainslie, 1998; Boss, 1999).

As previous chapters suggest, the TAT has been used in an impressive variety of cultural settings to engage a host of interpersonal concerns and psychocultural dynamics. Various studies as illustrated in this volume have demonstrated the value of the TAT as a tool for narrative analysis in revealing cultural values, social attitudes, and interpersonal expectations. In this chapter, we reflect upon the strengths and limitations of this specialized technique for cross-cultural research based upon our own work with this instrument over a period of two decades with immigrants and refugees.

First, we explore how the TAT enabled us to identify a pattern of nurturant achievement motivation among a sample of Central American refugee youth. These data led us to investigate whether this was related to cultural values originating in the county of origin or rather from the losses, uncertainty, and self-doubt engendered by migration.

In a subsequent study, we compared three groups of Mexican origin adolescents (residing in Mexico, first-generation immigrants in the United States, and second-generation Mexican Americans) to a sample of white American adolescents. These data also revealed patterns of affiliative or nurturant achievement for the youth of Mexican origin. Furthermore, among immigrant youth we encountered narratives laced with a disorienting sense of anxiety and loss.

These findings led to a third major study, currently under way, designed to more broadly examine the effect of recent migration on youth originating from a variety of sending centers—the Dominican Republic, Haiti, Mexico, Central America, and China. This design allows us to consider the nature of achievement motivation in the context of losses secondary to migration as well as distinct psychocultural patterns, unique to each cultural group under consideration. In this chapter, we report on preliminary findings from this most recent study demonstrating how the TAT can be used as a highly effective tool in revealing the dominant interpersonal preoccupations associated with immigration.

Individualistic vs. Affiliative/Nurturant Achievement

In the 1950s, David McClelland and his associates at Harvard conducted a series of pioneer studies on achievement motivation among white American students (McClelland, Atkinson, Clark, and Lowell, 1953). They defined achievement motivation as the need for "competition with a standard of excellence" (1953: 161). These studies suggested that achievement motivation flourishes when youngsters are trained to become independent from their families. Concretely, this work attempted to document achievement concerns under various experimental conditions through the use of projective tests, including the Thematic Apperception Test.

McClelland and his associates found that among white American middle-class samples, TAT narratives of achievement-oriented individuals captured an ethos in which achievement themes emerged in the context of attempting to gain independence from the family. According to this model, achievement motivation and individualism were highly correlated. This postulated relationship between achievement motivation and individualism was then extended to other cultural groups (McClelland, 1961). According to McClelland "need Achievement" in various settings ought to flourish in an atmosphere of individualism. Children who are taught to solve problems at an early age *by themselves*, and who are encouraged to think of themselves as independent of their caretakers are said to have higher levels of achievement motivation as adults (McClelland, 1961).

By extension, some theorists argued that among ethnic minorities, including Latinos, a cultural framework orienting individuals heavily to the family might be responsible for thwarting achievement motivation. For example, Heller claimed that Latino families hinder mobility "by stressing . . . [such values as] family ties, honor, masculinity . . . and by neglecting values that are conductive to it, achievement, independence and deferred gratification" (Heller, 1966). In the same vein, Carter and Segura (Carter and Segura, 1979) reviewed a number of studies suggesting that Latino children are not sufficiently trained in "independence" patterns, and consequently remain caught in a family web of values that are said to hinder achievement motivation. But do Latino families indeed neglect the values conducive to achievement? In order to achieve, must Latino youth break their interdependence on family ties? Or, can an ethos of familistic affiliation and mutual nurture be a key ingredient in the making of achievement motivation?

In this chapter, we argue that much of the foundational scholarship on the study of achievement motivation is based on the erroneous supposition that independence training is a *sine qua non* for achievement motivation and that various ethnic traditions of interdependence, cooperation, and mutual nurturance are impediments to its growth. While the early work may correctly address self-oriented achievement motivation themes among white middle-class Americans, the achievement-individualism cluster does not fit the motivational dynamics encountered among a variety of ethnic groups including the Japanese (De Vos, 1973), Central American refugees (Suárez-Orozco, 1989), Mexican origin adolescents (Suárez-Orozco and Suárez-Orozco, 1995), or, as we will also report in this chapter, immigrants from Mexico, Central America, Haiti, the Dominican Republic, and China.

Central American Adolescent Refugees

In the early to mid-1980s, Marcelo Suárez-Orozco conducted an interdisciplinary study of fifty recent arrivals from war-torn Central America.[1] These youngsters had undergone considerable upheaval in their journey to a West Coast urban center. Most of the immigrant youth were keenly aware of the continuities in a cultural chain of mutual nurturance and affiliation. Many youngsters reported that their parents had to face hard work at a premature age in Latin America to help their own parents and siblings make ends meet. They perceived that their parents had made tremendous sacrifices in order to settle them in the safety of the United States (Suárez-Orozco, 1989).

As part of the study, Marcelo Suárez-Orozco collected a sample of TAT stories from these informants. Their narratives tended to reflect high levels of achievement motivation coupled with affiliative or nurturant concerns. Their narratives spoke very directly of a drive to work hard to "become a somebody" as well as of a desire to help out the parents who had sacrificed for them. To Card 2 for example,[2] the protagonist of the Central American refugee stories commonly strives to achieve in order to take care of her poor parents and to end their hardship with the fruit of her studies. These stories stood in sharp contrast to the stories commonly told by more independent and individualistic North Americans (De Vos, 1983). Indeed, in 56 percent of the Central American narratives to Card 2, themes of nurturant achievement emerged. For example:

> She is looking at her poor parents working hard on the land so she can study, so she can become somebody. She wants to achieve something so that her parents do not continue to live in poverty, always working so hard. The mother is thinking that one day her daughter will do something for them. And that is why they give her the possibility to study hard. They work hard so that in the future their daughter may become someone, so she won't have to live what they had to live through. The daughter will get them out of poverty. She will get them out of their misery. She will study hard, she will become a good, educated person. She goes to school to become somebody.

> She has books. Her parents work the land. She wants to study to become somebody. She wants a career. Her parents are very poor. She wants a career to help her poor parents, so they do not have to suffer so much. She studies hard and becomes somebody. Her parents are so proud of her. With their help she is able to become a professional. Whenever they need help, she is there for them.

---

[1]Twenty females and thirty males, ages fourteen to nineteen.

[2]TAT Card 2 depicts a young woman in the foreground clutching books to her chest with a man working in a field in the background.

To Card 1, the boy with a violin, a similar theme emerges. In 36 percent of the stories, nurturant tales of achievement emerge:

> This is a boy from a very poor family. He thinks a great deal about his poor family. He thinks that playing the violin will bring his family many benefits. He thinks about his younger siblings, he wants to be an example to them. He will become an example to all. He will play the violin very well to make money to help his family. In the future, the violin will help them a great deal.

Among the Central American refugees, the theme of "nurturant achievement" was related to ongoing feelings of responsibility based on guilt over the sacrifices parents had made (Suárez-Orozco, 1989). "Becoming a somebody" was viewed as a reparative act to alleviate parental hardships. The interpersonal concerns running through the lives of most of the Central American refugees involved a strong wish to achieve in order to be able to help one's parents, relatives, and other less fortunate folk left in war-torn Central America.

Another theme that emerged in 30 percent of these stories is one that involves concerns about instrumental competence, or the lack of the requisite knowledge to achieve the task at hand. In such cases, the protagonist typically searches for help from others:

> The boy did not know how to play the violin. He looks for an older man to teach him. He finds help. He practices the violin and eventually gets ahead in life by playing the violin. He then teaches other children to play.

> He is bored. He would love to play the violin. An older friend takes him to school with him. The older friend teaches him. They study hard together. After some time, he becomes a star.

The Central American data do not fit the white middle-class American paradigm for achievement motivation. The most motivated of these youth were not individualists searching for self-advancement and independence. The research with Central Americans captured an altogether different achievement pattern. Their narratives typically revealed two types of nurturant achievement—one in which the protagonist is driven to achieve in order to help others and another where others are called upon to help the protagonist reach his or her goals. This form of achievement cluster revealed in TAT narratives was consistent with the findings from the ethnographic data and structured interviews. The ethnographic work demonstrated that older, more experienced youth aided the younger or more recent arrivals in order to help them find work, to tutor them, and to otherwise aid them in their first steps in the new land. Additionally, of the 68 percent of Central American youth who worked while attending school full time, *all* reported sending money back home on a regular basis (Suárez-Orozco, 1989). Thus, the concerns reflected in the TAT narratives were acted upon in everyday practices.

A Comparative View of Mexican and White American Youth

In the Central American case, rather than encountering a pattern of individualism and independence, we find the emergence of a worldview that orients the self to others in the context of resettling in the new land. Whether or not the Central American case would hold true for other Latino youth was a theoretical question of some interest. Previous research that considered the psychocultural patterning of achievement motivation among Latinos, however, tended to explore these issues focusing in on the experiences of migrants and subsequent United States-born generations. Previous studies did not distinguish migrants and their descendants from their compatriots in the various countries of origin. Such research confounds cultural issues such as the patterning of Latino family values with issues related to immigration and minority status. Many concerns—loss, culture shock, disorientation, discrimination, and economic pressures to help the family—associated with migration and minority status surely also influence achievement patterns. We asked ourselves: does achievement *for the family* emerge as a motivator for other Latino groups? And is this interdependent nurturant achievement cluster related to cultural patterns originating in the country of origin or rather does it emerge (or is it magnified) in the process of migration?

To examine these questions, we conducted a three-year interdisciplinary (anthropological, psychological, and educational) research project in an area of high emigration in central Mexico and in an immigrant-receiving area of southern California. We addressed some normative patterns in cultural psychology among two groups of non-immigrants (Mexicans in Mexico and white Americans in the United States) and then systematically compared them to Mexican immigrant and United States-born Mexican Americans. With a sample of 189 informants[3] we considered school dynamics, family relations, and achievement concerns using a number of assessment strategies including ethnographic observations, structured interviews, and "objective" as well as projective tests (such as the TAT, Sentence Completion Tasks, and Problem Situation Tasks).

It is beyond the scope of this paper to report all of the major findings of this study. Rather, in this chapter, we focus on the patterns revealed by TAT narratives and a sampling of other projective data.[4] We asked all of our informants to respond with a yes or no to the sentence "To me school is the most important thing." Mexican youth were significantly more likely to respond with a "yes" to this sentence. The immigrant youth were even more likely to do so. The Mexican

[3]There were forty-seven informants in the Mexican, Mexican Immigrant, and White American group and forty-eight informants in the second-generation Mexican American group.

[4]This research was made possible by funding from the Spencer Foundation. For more detail, please refer to *Transformations: Migration, Family Life, and Achievement Motivation Among Latino Adolescents* (Suárez-Orozco and Suárez-Orozco, 1995). The original data is on file at the Radcliffe Center for Advanced Studies.

American second generation fell between the white Americans and Mexicans in their responses.[5]

Table 15.1

Responses to "To me school is the most important thing."

	White	*Mexican*	*Mexican Immigrant*	*Mexican American*
Yes	40%	75%	84%	55%
No	60%	25%	16%	45%

*Chi-Square *p < .01*

In a particularly revealing Sentence Completion Task, we asked all our informants to complete the following: "My school is _______." For analytical purposes, we divided student responses into three categories—positive, neutral, and negative associations. White American students were most likely to complete the sentence with negative responses—fully 42 percent of their responses were negative (such as "boring," "the worst," "junky," "stupid," "terrible," "hell"). Only 20 percent of the white American youths completed the sentence with positive terms (including "cool," "fun," "pretty nice"). The rest completed the sentence with neutral terms (such as "a place to go on a daily basis").

Table 15.2

Group Differences in Responses to "My school is ____"

Theme	*White*	*Mexican*	*Mexican Immigrant*	*Mexican American*
Positive	20%	84%	81%	66%
Neutral	38%	16%	17%	14%
Negative	42%	0%	2%	20%

*Chi-Square *p < .01*

Mexican youngsters living in Mexico completed the sentence very differently. Fully 84 percent of them had positive associations. Their responses included: "a great place with great teachers," "a happy place," "the key to my success." Not a single Mexican student completed the sentence with a negative term. Among immigrant students (who were attending *the same school* as the white Americans) the pattern of response was quite similar to the group in Mexico. Eighty-one

[5]For analytical purposes we coded student responses into three categories: positive, neutral, and negative associations. We detected significant group differences using Chi-square analyses.

percent of the immigrant students completed the sentence with a term revealing positive affect such as: "My school is the greatest thing I ever had," "pretty, I can study a lot here," "the most beautiful school in the county," and "fabulous." Mexican American students (also attending the same school as their white American and Mexican immigrant peers) were less positive than their Mexico-born peers but more positive than their white American peers. Sixty-six percent of them completed the sentence with a positive association such as: "My school is great," "my school is the best," and "my school is cool." Yet 20 percent of them had negative associations such as: "my school is 'ugly,' 'cheap,' 'boring.'" Note that among United States-born students—both white Americans and second generation—boredom was a typical complaint.

A number of other Sentence Completion Tasks as well as Problem Situation Tasks revealed a similar pattern. The youth from different groups varied in their attitudes towards school and school authorities. American white students tended to display highly ambivalent attitudes towards school and, particularly, school authorities. These students understood that they had to go to school to ensure a good future but they were more likely to say they did not like school than students from any of the other groups. They are also much more likely to have negative associations to school and school authorities. Many of these students seem to experience school as "boring" and school authorities as "unfair." Some of these students just want to graduate and "get out of here."

On the other hand, both Mexican and Mexican immigrant students tended to articulate much more positive associations towards school and school authorities. These students were not bored and alienated but were appreciative of the opportunity to pursue an education. Likewise, their attitudes towards school authorities were overall positive. There is a *respect for authority figures*—teacher and principal—and a feeling that they exercise authority in a legitimate and fair manner. Mexican American students, the children of two worlds, shared attitudes of both groups.

Our interview data also revealed some of the special issues facing newly arrived immigrants. Immigrant students were less likely to turn to parents for help with school-related tasks—instead, they tended to rely more on siblings. They were also more likely to think about going to work full time when they finish high school. Among these students, we found a sense of *obligation* to help the family by working full time to earn money. This is quite in keeping with the results of our projective TAT materials.[6] In the TAT data rather than achieving for self-

---

[6]All of the stories were grouped by subsample (i.e., white American, Mexican, Mexican immigrant, and Mexican American) and all of the responses for each group were read separately. In reading through the TAT responses to Card 1, it became evident that different themes seemed to be prominent for each group. A list of recurring themes was compiled. All of the stories for Card 1 were then placed together randomly. The stories were read, analyzed, and discussed by two raters who were blind to the group membership of the storyteller. Each story

advancement, immigrants—and Latinos more generally—achieve in order to help others.

Table 15.3

Group Differences in Themes Emerging from TAT Card 2

Theme	*White*	*Mexican*	*Mexican Immigrant*	*Mexican American*
Pursuit of Education	32%	56%	52%	36%
Wanting to Help Others	14%	28%	38%	24%

*Chi-Square *p < .05*

To TAT Card 2, 32 percent of the white Americans told narratives around a theme of pursuing an education. However, their stories tended to represent education as means to gain independence. A typical story:

> She is living on a farm, and she hates living there. She wants to live somewhere where there are people within 200 miles. Her parents are working really hard. She decides to move by herself. She goes away to school, gets an education, and gets a job. Then she goes back to visit her parents. Finally, she feels that she's doing something with her life. So she keeps visiting her parents but stays at her job away from the farm.

Fifty-six percent of the Mexican adolescents told self-motivated achievement stories focused on pursuing an education. In half of these achievement stories, the protagonist was specifically motivated to help others:

> This girl is going to school to help her parents buy machinery to seed the fields more easily. The father works hard to give the daughter the opportunity to go to school. She completes her studies with the help of her family. She becomes a professional, and she in turn helps her parents.

Second-generation Mexican American youths revealed preoccupations that were similar to the other Mexican origin youth. Wanting to help others occurred in 24 percent of the stories (in contrast to 14 percent of their white American peers). However, they were similar to their white American peers in that they were less

---

was rated for the presence or absence of each of the themes under consideration. The incidence of each theme was tallied for each group. Chi square analyses were then conducted to check for significant differences between groups. The table below illustrates statistically significant group differences at p<.01.

likely to tell stories of pursuing an education. Often the second generation told stories of feeling torn between pursuing an education and helping their parents:

> This is a girl, and she is watching her parents working so hard. She is trying to study and she doesn't know what to do to help her parents. She feels like they have a big problem. She tries to help her parents, but she also has to study. In the end she tries to help them.

> This girl is coming home from school. She sees them working very hard, and she feels bad because she is going to school and they are working so hard. Then, she thinks she has to go to school and she feels like a traitor she is not home helping. She helps them after she goes to school.

Mexican immigrant youth, like their peers in Mexico were likely to tell narratives focused upon themes of achievement. They were the most likely of all of the groups to tell stories of protagonists focused upon helping others. As with the earlier Central American data, the TAT narratives did not frame achievement as an individualistic enterprise; rather, achievement was the product of social interdependence. Reciprocity is a unifying principal in many of these stories. The parents are depicted as working hard to support the family; the protagonist pursues schooling in order to help her sacrificing parents:

> These parents are working the fields, pursuing as much as they can from the earth. This seems to be the wife, and she is pregnant. I think the girl is going to school to receive an education. They continue cultivating the earth and the girl goes to get an education to help her parents. I say that she gets an education, and when she gets a good job they are all going to leave the countryside and go to live with her. She is going to give them a house to help them.

The point of achievement is not to gain independence from the family but rather for reciprocal nurturing. Like the Mexican American second generation, the protagonist in about a quarter of the stories is torn between pursuing education and the need to work to help the family:

> Her parents want her to work, but she wants to study. Her mom wants her to help at home, but she would rather study. She talks with them about what she wants to study and explains that in the long run she can find a better job if she studies. They agree and let her study. She does well and gets a good job and helps them buy a house. She feels happy.

It is particularly instructive to delve into the most significant themes that emerged from Card 1 of the TAT. The predominant theme, in the TAT stories told by white American adolescents, is that of frustration. Fully 50 percent of the white American youths told stories in which the protagonist expressed frustration (or anger in 16 percent of the stories) with performing the task at hand. This is particularly striking when one considers the relative absence of this theme among the other subsamples; only 2 percent of the Mexican sample told stories of frustration.

In the majority of the narratives, frustration seems to be the outcome of either the difficulties or challenges presented by the task at hand (playing the violin) or as a result of the pressures of a parental figure imposing the task on an unwilling child (in 36 percent of the narratives). The theme running through these stories is that of motivational ambivalence and tension. The narratives told by the white American adolescent narratives reflected concerns with autonomy and gave some indication that, with these youths, adolescence is a period of significant turmoil that is particularly revealed by tensions with parental figures. Themes of individuation and independence are prominent within this group.

The concern here is not with "he wants to play the violin" but rather "they are making him play the violin." Indeed, the theme of embracing the task as a result of an internalized wish to learn to play is expressed in only 14 percent of the stories told by this white American subsample. It should be noted that this finding of tension resulting from perceived parental pressure is highly consistent with findings from earlier TAT samples of white Americans collected by Banfield (1958), De Vos (1973), Connor and De Vos (1989), and Vaughn (1988) (see chapter 6, volume II, above).

In many of the stories told by the white Americans, the child is depicted as being pressured to play the violin and responds in a variety of ways. In some stories, the child succumbs to parental will and eventually achieves mastery over a demanding task:

> He is thinking. His parents are forcing him to take violin lessons. He is looking at the violin, thinking that maybe it won't be so hard. He takes the lessons and turns out to like them and turns into the next Mozart. Right now, he is wondering why his parents want him to do it and then afterwards he understands that his parents just want him to be a well-rounded person.

In other stories the child simply refuses to succumb to the parental pressure. In these stories, the child angrily refuses to do what the parents want him to do and chooses instead to follow his own path:

> The boy is in a music class. He is at home; his parents are making him practice the violin. He doesn't want to practice. He feels angry that his parents are making him do something that he doesn't want to do. He is refusing to play. His parents end up letting him quit since he doesn't like the violin. He joins something else that he does like.

In the most extreme cases, the child actively resists the parents' pressures by destroying the violin. In 10 percent of the stories of our 1998 sample, the child is depicted as responding to parental pressure by purposefully destroying the violin! This stands in contrast to the fact that none of the Mexican or immigrant adolescents told stories of a purposefully broken violin and only 2 percent of the Mexican American youth did so:

> The boy is sad because his parents want him to play the violin. He wants to be something else. He is sitting there and is looking at the violin and is trying to think about what to say to his parents. He throws his violin and breaks it. His parents get mad and so he tells them he wants to play baseball. He is sad and angry and he feels forced into something. He gets mad and they finally realize that it is his life and they encourage him to do what he wants.

Turning to the Mexican sample, the dominant theme running through the stories told by these informants is that of self-initiated achievement. In 54 percent of these stories—versus 14 percent of white American students—the protagonist is depicted as achievement-oriented in a self-motivated fashion. In these stories, the boy wants to play the violin and there is no concern over unwillingly taking on a task imposed by the parents:

> This boy, since he was very small, liked the violin. He believes that in the future he will be able to become a good violinist and musician, so he works hard and concentrates on achieving his goal.

Rather than entering into a battle of wills with an imposing adult, an important preoccupation of the protagonist in this subsample is a concern with overcoming inadequacy in achieving the arduous but self-imposed task. The boy wants to play the violin, the question is: *Can* he do it? And, perhaps more importantly, will he be good at it? In 22 percent of these stories, there is an explicit concern with adequacy. How are these concerns with adequacy resolved? In 34 percent of the Mexican stories, the boy is depicted as working hard to achieve his self-imposed desire to succeed. In these stories, achieving success is the product of long hours of diligent work:

> There was a boy that wanted to learn to play the violin but he did not know how. He is sitting there thinking and contemplating about the future. He's thinking about whether he will be able to learn to play and become a great violinist. Just now he is imagining that he is in a concert hall giving a concert. After thinking about it he tells himself that he needs to put a lot of effort and enthusiasm into learning so that he will be able to achieve his dreams in the future.

In the Mexican subsample, the theme of frustration is not prevalent; in only 2 percent of the stories is the theme of frustration brought up. Likewise, not a single story in the Mexican subsample expresses concerns with anger in the boy learning to play the violin. It is, of course, impossible to determine from these data whether Mexican adolescents are less prone to anger and frustration than white American youths. We can say that in our sample Mexican youths are much less likely to voice anger towards their parents than white American adolescents.

In contrast to the white American subsample, in which the parental figures were typically depicted as pressuring, in the Mexican stories, there is a large number of narratives in which the parental *dramatis personae* are depicted as nurturing, warm, and supportive (16 percent of the stories).

> This boy is looking at his violin that he inherited from his father. He doesn't have anyone to help him learn to play the violin. He is very sad and he realizes that he doesn't know how to play the violin. His mother is going to help him find someone to help him learn to play. His family doesn't have any money to get anyone to help. She manages anyway and when he gets to be older, he has learned how to play. He learns to play very well. He learned when he was 15 years old and he began working and with the money that he earned, he took more and more lessons in order to become a better musician.

A related concern in the Mexican subsample is actively searching for help from a competent person to aid the protagonist to accomplish the difficult task at hand (in 12 percent of the stories):

> He is thinking of the instrument that he sees before him. He is thinking that he wants to play it and he is thinking of whom he knows who might teach him to play it since he doesn't know how to play it. After someone teaches him, he will become a star and will earn a lot of money and will be able to buy anything he wants.

Another theme expressed in this subsample is the sense of pleasure, joy, and happiness that is derived from the activity (occurring in 18 percent of the Mexican stories). In these stories, the task may be depicted as difficult and challenging, but it is intrinsically pleasurable:

> The boy is sad because he doesn't know how to play the violin. But he works at it until he becomes excellent at it. He learns how to play and he gives concerts and demonstrations at schools. He helps to teach other students how to play. He gets a lot of satisfaction from the help that he gives others as well as of his success.

In the case of the second-generation Mexican Americans, we encountered an overlap with the other subsamples. The percentage of stories in which the predominant theme is self-motivated achievement orientation is comparable to the American subsample (14 percent and 18 percent respectively). As with the white American sample, an important feature of the narratives articulated by the second-generation youths is one of parental figures (including teachers and other authority figures in society) pressuring the protagonist to perform the task (in 30 percent of the stories). On the other hand, there are themes expressed in the second-generation narratives, which clearly overlap with the concerns articulated by Mexican and immigrant youths (such as in searching out help from others and in being motivated to achieve in order to help others).

A very striking theme found in the second-generation narratives is a concern with *failure.* In 28 percent of the Mexican American stories, there is reference to a concern with threatened failure to achieve the task at hand. This contrasts with 2 percent among the Mexican and Mexican immigrant groups and 4 percent among white Americans. Whereas in many of the stories told by the Mexican and the immigrant subsamples, concerns with adequacy are voiced, there is a strong sense of hope and optimism for the future (i.e., the initial inadequacy is overcome and through hard work, success is finally achieved). In a number of the stories told by the second generation, however, a disturbing preoccupation with failure and a sense of hopelessness is revealed. In many such stories, the future looks bleak:

> The child was very interested in playing the violin in the beginning. Now he doesn't know what to do without any help. Now he is going through stages where he puts too much effort and nothing is happening. So he is feeling depressed. He loses his interest in music and now has a mental block. He can't solve other problems. He gives up all interest in music and has a mental block. He loses confidence in solving problems.

> There was this little boy who wanted to play the violin. He had the violin but no money to take classes. He got a job and worked and worked for days. Finally, he got money but he couldn't find where to go to take classes. He looked and looked and found some place to go and learn. He took classes but couldn't learn how to play it. One day, he was playing in the park with some friends and he kicked a ball and broke a window. He went to his parents and told them and asked them to pay for the window. They said "no." He either would have to work or sell his violin, they told him. He went to his room and sat down and stared at it and though about it. He decided to sell it. He feels sad because he was starting to learn to play it and let it go.

In some of these stories the protagonist attempts to engage with the task; he tries to play the violin but he eventually quits, realizing that he is not competent. In others, the protagonist cannot learn without help or simply tries but is unable to play adequately and is disheartened by this. In yet other narratives, the concern with failure is more specifically related to obstacles in the environment, which prevent the protagonist from taking on the challenge. In these stories, the boy is trying to learn the violin but must give it up due to factors outside his control. In some cases, though the protagonist struggles with the threat of failure, he eventually finds a solution by asking for help from others.

A sense of frustration is found in 14 percent of the stories told by the second-generation Mexican Americans. This is a higher number than either the stories told by Mexicans in Mexico or by Mexican immigrants in the United States. However, it is lower than the percentage of frustration stories related by the white American sample (50 percent). A sense of anger is revealed in fully 20 percent of the stories told by the Mexican American subsample. This is significantly higher than in the Mexican or immigrant subsamples (0 percent and 6 percent respectively). On the other hand, the theme of anger was found in 14 percent of the white American stories. It is recognized that anger and frustration may be related. It is interesting to note that American adolescents chose to use the word "frustration" more frequently while the Mexican American adolescents chose the words "mad" or "angry."

It is particularly poignant to note the discontinuities in the narratives told by the Mexicans in Mexico, the Mexican immigrants, and the second-generation Mexican Americans. Whereas native Mexicans and immigrant students revealed a faith that through hard work success was possible, too many of the second-generation youths told stories in which failure was a significant preoccupation. The energy and faith in "making it" that are characteristic of the Mexican and immigrant students seem to have significantly diminished by the second generation.

We relate these findings to the vicissitudes in the path from immigration into minority status. Typically, immigrants endure their affective losses by concentrating on the material gains to be made by exploiting the new opportunities in a host country. Members of the second generation, on the other hand, do not measure their current state in terms of life back in Mexico. Rather, they use as their standard the ideals and expectations of the majority society (Suárez-Orozco and Suárez-Orozco, 1993). Using this standard, many Mexican Americans may fall short of their aspirations. Racism, disparagement, and lack of equal opportunity may compromise the faith of at-risk youths in their ability to make it. This may well be related to the disturbingly high dropout rates from schools among second- and third-generation Mexican American youths (Bean, 1991; Chapa, 1988; Kantrowitz and Rosado, 1991).

Turning to the immigrant subsample, the most striking feature of the narratives articulated by the youngsters is that of a sense of sadness attributed to the protagonist of the story. Sixty-six percent of the stories depict the boy as "feeling sad," "feeling low," or "feeling bad." It should be noted that many TAT cards (including Card 1) tend to "pull" for such concerns (Bellak, 1986). What is of significance is the *relative* occurrence of such themes across groups. While only 16 percent of the Mexican sample attributed sadness to the protagonist, and 32 and 34 percent (respectively) of the white American and Mexican American informants told stories with such themes, the percentage nearly doubles for the Mexican immigrant subsample:

> He's very sad because he doesn't know how to play the violin. But if somebody helps him, he can learn it and he can become a great musician. No one helps him. He will try to play it until he can do it. He succeeds.

> He is sad because he is not able to play the violin and he doesn't know whom he can ask to help him. He is trying to figure out how he might be able to play it. His mom is sad also because she asked him if he could play and he said no. She decided that he needed to get someone to help him. She finds someone to help him and teach him how to play and he learns how to play and he feels really happy about it.

The pervasive sadness found in the stories told by this subsample of immigrant youngsters is consistent with the general pattern of normative reactive depression found in other studies of recent immigrants (Antokoletz, 1993; Kaminsky, 1993; Padillo, 1993; Espin, 1987; Grinberg and Grinberg, 1990; Garza-Guerrero, 1974; Suárez-Orozco, 2000). These immigrant youth are coping with the multiple tangible as well as ambiguous losses (Boss, 1999) of immigration as well as with culture shock. Many of their parents may be relatively unavailable to them either physically (because of long work hours) or emotionally (because of their own depressions triggered by the stresses of immigration).

As with the Mexican sample, the immigrants articulate a preoccupation with self-initiated achievement orientation (in 32 percent of the stories) often laced with concerns with adequacy (occurring in 36 percent of the stories). Again, the protagonist has internalized a desire to play the violin. The question of greatest concern is whether or not he will be able to master the task:

> He is looking at it, trying to use it—what parts it has. He feels worried and preoccupied because he is still unable to use it well. He will find out how to play this. He doesn't have help. He does it alone. He feels sad and thinks that he needs someone who can help him, show him how to use it. He will be happy when he knows how to use it.

> This boy wants to learn to play the violin but he does not know how. He is thinking about how he will learn to play. He feels very sad because he is not able to play the violin. The violin is his father's. In the end he learns how to play it and he feels good.

Overall, the resolution with regard to the tension caused by the challenge tends to be favorable. Only in 2 percent of the stories does the initial concern with inadequacy lead to failure. In 8 percent of the stories, the outcome remains unresolved. In 26 percent of the stories the resolution is favorable. Note, however, that many of these stories appear to be about small victories. Rather than achieving the important large-scale successes and notoriety told in the stories of the Mexican informants, many stories told by immigrant adolescents reveal a much smaller scale of success. Rather than playing in orchestras all over the world or being applauded by many, the protagonist of the immigrant stories, when he succeeds, merely learns how to play. Hence, the expected successes seem to be significantly scaled back:

> This is a boy that liked to play the violin but he didn't know how. He is sad but he takes classes on how to learn. After a time he learns to play and he is content.

In the immigrant stories told in which the violin is broken (14 percent), it is always the case that the breakage is as a result of an accident rather than resulting from a purposeful act (as is the case with some white American narratives). The breakage imposes an obstacle that the protagonist anxiously must somehow overcome:

> This boy was trying to play the violin, and he accidentally broke a string. He feels sad because he has to finish an assignment and now he can't. He can't finish it until his parents arrive and buy him a new string. And he won't be able to finish one of his assignments that his music teacher gave him. His parents arrive, and they scold him because he hasn't finished his homework and because he'd been playing a lot with the strings, and broke it.

An important theme emerging in the immigrant sample is that of actively searching for help from others. In order to master the task, 26 percent of the immigrant sample turns to a family member, friend, or teacher for help—versus 12 percent of Mexican and Mexican American youths. This propensity to turn to others for help occurred only rarely (in only four cases) in the white American stories:

> He is thinking about the fact that he cannot play the violin even though he really wants to. It is because he does not know how and he feels desperate about this. So, he tells his parents that he does not know how to play the violin and they tell him that he needs to take a class to learn how. So he goes to his teacher and the teacher helps him and little by little he learns how to play.

> He feels really sad because he was practicing the violin but he can't play a song that he had heard and wanted to play. Later, he asks a friend to help. He gets help and he practices a lot and his friends help him to learn to play well.

Based on findings from this comparative study we draw the following conclusions. Clearly, the achievement stories narrated by Latino youths tend to be quite different from those narrated by white American students. The achievement stories told by Mexican origin youth are largely self-initiated—the protagonist works hard to achieve the goal of success rather than having the task imposed upon him by his parents. Furthermore, white American students articulate narratives in which achieving success is a means for independence from the family; Latinos typically offer stories in which achieving success or "becoming somebody" means giving back to the family.

Data from this study suggested several important issues in reference to earlier work on achievement motivation. A key point emerging from our data is that Mexican and Mexican immigrant youth were more positive toward schooling and expressed more achievement narratives. Many white American students experience education more ambivalently—as a necessary frustration—to ensure a good job and the good life.

That Mexican-born youths (both Mexicans in Mexico and Mexican immigrants) revealed more concerns with self-initiated achievement and less ambivalence about school and school authorities than did the white American youths is a finding that is neither in keeping with cultural stereotypes nor with expectations based on the literature. As noted earlier, some researchers had suggested that characteristics of the cultural background are somehow responsible for the relatively high levels of school failure and dropout (Carter and Segura, 1979;

Heller, 1966). The findings of our study do not support these contentions. Our findings suggest that the Mexican cultural background does indeed emphasize self-initiated achievement, as well as the notion that hard work is critical for success though interdependence (Delgado-Gaitan and Trueba, 1991; Trueba, 1989).

The achievement-individualism cluster identified among white Americans in the classic studies of McClelland and his associates do not explain achievement motivation among Latinos—or, for that matter, other ethnic groups (De Vos, 1973). Among Latinos and other samples, achievement motivation flourishes in an atmosphere of nurture and interdependence. Our data suggest that Latino families, indeed Latino culture in more general terms, do indeed foster the values and behaviors, which are conducive to achieving in schools. Therefore, whatever problems Latinos face in U.S. schools cannot be the consequence of so-called cultural or motivational deficits related to the culture of origin.

While our data reveal that Mexican youths in Mexico and Mexican immigrants maintain the conviction that school is the key to a better future, among more acculturated Latinos, we found diminished expectations. The more acculturated students are, the more skeptical and ambivalent they become about schools. Mexican American youths may be assimilating to the American adolescent paradigm of ambivalence towards authority and schools. In addition, other factors such as the stresses of minority status, discrimination, alienating schools, peer group patterns, economic hardships, and pressures to work may all contribute to the high school dropout rate in this population.

Our data also pointed to an interesting pattern that seemed to be related to the vicissitudes of migration. Overall, the Mexican immigrant sample like their Mexican peers were likely to relate narratives in which the protagonist is motivated to play the violin for self-initiated reasons rather than because the task is imposed upon him. However, they expressed the greatest concern with inadequacy worrying about whether they were up to the task. Of all groups they were also the most likely to have the protagonist search out help from others. This turning to others for help is a characteristic that is more evident in all of the Latino subgroups under consideration (including the Central Americans) than in the white American informants. Furthermore, in Mexican immigrant narratives, the protagonist was also significantly more likely to be portrayed as being sad.

We hypothesized that these themes may be related to the disorienting anxiety (Grinberg and Grinberg, 1990) and ambiguous losses (Boss, 1999) experienced by immigrants. Considered in this light, the need for a cultural interpreter to assist them in understanding the new culture and accomplishing difficult tasks in a new setting is obvious. Immigration imposes particular stresses and losses that propel individuals to turn to one another for advice and help—a tendency that is illuminated in TAT narratives.

A Comparative View of Recent Immigrant Youth

In our subsequent study, currently underway, we have turned our focus to immigrant youth from a variety of countries.[7] Immigrants are among the fastest growing population of children in American schools. Currently, one in five children in this country is a child of immigrants—the majority of them of Latino, Asian, and Caribbean origin. Although there is a significant body of literature on a variety of aspects of immigration, the research on the adaptation of the children of immigrants is quite limited. While issues of variability in school adaptations and outcomes among immigrant students have been considered, there is to date no systematic study examining psychocultural changes over time as different groups of immigrant youth adapt to American schools.

While many immigrant children perform brilliantly in school, recent data from a variety of sources suggest an unsettling pattern: among some immigrant groups today, length of residence in the United States is associated with *declining* health (Rumbaut and Cornelius, 1995; Hernandez and Charney, 1998), school achievement, and aspirations (Suárez-Orozco, 2000; Waters, 1999). While this pattern has been established through cross-sectional research, such matters as changes over time and psychosocial risk factors (including incoming factors and host context factors) have not been established. In order to examine these issues, we developed a longitudinal, interdisciplinary, and comparative study to document continuities and discontinuities in immigrant educational attitudes and social adaptations over time.

For the Longitudinal Immigrant Student Adaptation Project (L.I.S.A.), we recruited recent immigrant youth representative of some of the most significant groups coming into the United States today (Central American, Chinese, Dominican, Haitian, and Mexican immigrants) from Boston area and San Francisco area schools. A total of 400 students, aged nine to fourteen at the beginning of the study, are being followed for a period of five years by thirty bicultural and bilingual graduate research assistants. This project was initiated in the fall of 1997.

In this study, we are considering a series of research questions: What is the nature of immigrant students' academic engagement? How does this change over time? What are the immigrants' "cultural models" of schooling and how do such models relate to schooling behaviors, experiences, and outcomes? How do these models change over time? How does immigration affect the family system, including culturally constructed role expectations, patterns of familial cohesion, authority and discipline, linguistic and literacy patterns, and sibling relations? How does the school context impact adjustment? How do social relations (including extended family, peers, teachers, mentors, community and religious leaders) influence academic achievement? With each of these areas of inquiry, we are

---

[7]The National Science Foundation, the W.T. Grant Foundation, and the Spencer Foundation have funded this project.

interested in establishing a baseline of "between" group differences. Changes over time are then considered.

We deploy research anthropology strategies to gain perspectives on immigrant "cultural models" of schooling and to document the social contexts of changing attitudes and behaviors. The youth are observed and interviewed in their schools, their communities, and their homes. Research psychology strategies are used to document changes in school attitudes and behaviors over time. Our data are triangulated using a variety of assessment strategies: ethnographic participant observations; structured interviews of students, school personnel, and parents; psychosocial measures (including projective measures such as Cards 1 and 2 of the TAT and Sentence Completion Tasks); individually administered bilingual verbal ability and achievement assessments; and academic records. The same kind of data (demographic, psychological, and cultural) is systematically collected for each group.

In the remaining section of this chapter, we report on preliminary findings focusing on the TAT narratives to Card 1 of 388 informants.[8] The card was computer scanned and modified to depict a phenotypically ambiguous child. The responses were dictated in the native language to a trained research assistant who wrote down the story and later translated it. Two raters (Carola Suárez-Orozco and Irina Todorova) read through approximately fifty stories and compiled lists of themes that emerged from the data.[9]

Table 15.4 summarizes the emerging themes.

---

[8]Seventy-five Central Americans; seventy-nine Chinese; seventy-nine Dominicans; seventy-one Haitians; and eighty-four Mexican adolescents gave responses to TAT Card 1.

[9]The list was narrowed to conceptual categories that were noted on a rating form; each category was defined in a first draft of scoring procedures. The raters scored twenty-five stories together, discussing the rationale for why each scale was scored in a specific manner for each story. When there was disagreement, the item was discussed until a consensus was obtained. The rationale was articulated and noted in the emerging scoring procedures. Once these first twenty stories were scored, the raters each received a copy of the draft of the scoring procedures and they scored another twenty stories separately. The inter-rater reliability was calculated for each scale. The inter-rater reliability for the fourteen subscales ranged from .80 to 1.0; the average inter-rater reliability for the combined scales was .90. The remaining stories were then coded by raters trained to this assessment tool. After all stories were scored, the incidence of each theme was tallied for each group under consideration. Chi-square analyses were conducted to check for significant differences between groups.

Table 15.4

L.I.S.A. Group Differences in Themes Emerging from TAT Card 1

Theme	*Total*	*Chinese*	*Dominican*	*Central American*	*Haitian*	*Mexican*	*Chi-Square*
Outside Parental Pressure	10.9%	26.6%	7.6%	4.0%	11.3%	4.8%	*
Academic Pressures	16.2%	7.6%	15.2%	18.7%	19.7%	20.2%	*
Fame	7.7%	17.7%	8.9%	1.3%	7.04%	3.57%	*
Situational Success	30.6%	25.3%	36.7%	30.7%	28.2%	32.1%	ns
Mastering Task	31.4%	34.2%	24.1%	32.0%	32.4%	34.5%	ns
Personal Effort	32.9%	44.3%	30.4%	18.7%	38.0%	33.3%	*
Help from Others	25.0%	25.3%	30.4%	32.0%	14.1%	23.4%	*
Successful Resolution	55.1%	70.9%	69.6%	52.0%	29.6%	53.6%	*
Failure	9.1%	6.3%	7.6%	4.0%	16.9%	10.7%	*
Concerns with Adequacy	41.7%	27.8%	41.7%	44.0%	52.1%	42.9%	*
Lacking Knowledge	43.8%	40.5%	38.0%	45.3%	53.5%	42.9%	ns
Broken Violin	19.3%	26.6%	20.3%	13.3%	16.9%	19.1%	ns
Boredom/Unfocused	19.8%	17.7%	20.3%	22.7%	19.7%	19.1%	ns
Sadness	45.6%	22.8%	45.6%	62.7%	47.9%	48.8%	*

Unlike the white American youth described above, pressure from parents was not a dominant concern for the immigrants in this sample. Indeed, only 10.9 percent of this sample voiced this type of concern (in contrast to the 36 percent white American adolescents reported above). However, for this particular theme, there was a significant difference between groups. This story captures this concern:

> A boy is sitting. His mother asked him to play the violin. He does not like it. When he practiced, he does not play it well. His mother asked him to play another instrument. He chose the drum. His mother did not like the drum. He stopped playing the drum. He started playing the violin again and he likes it. [Haitian girl]

Chinese youth were more likely to tell narratives of feeling pressured by parents (26.6 percent):

> There is a boy who has a hearing problem. His whole family plays music. His parents are musicians. He is idiotic to music. He is a good baseball player. He is great in playing baseball. However, his parents do not like him to play sports and have him play music. He played music at home and he played very bad (the tone

> of the music is awful). He did not know what to do. He stared blankly at the violin. He chose to play baseball in the end. [Chinese boy]

In several Chinese narratives (7.6 percent) there is an interesting twist on the pressure theme; when the parents exert pressure it is *not* to play the violin as it is viewed as a frivolous activity. This theme is usually coupled with a great internal certainty about the importance of playing the violin and a strong resolve to continue. When quitting is considered, it is temporary and the child plans to come back to the activity when economic conditions for the family improve. In tune with the other examples of self-initiated achievement, these narratives point to a determination to succeed, to follow a dream, or to strive toward an ideal in spite of external barriers. This determination, however, is in the context of a sensitive consideration of the opinions of parents and the needs of the family as a whole. For example:

> There was a boy, he really liked, hoped he could play violin and play well. But his family didn't let him play. Because, because [his family] felt that, that is, felt that violin did not, did not quite fit him. Then he thought for a long time in front of the violin. He felt that he should listen to his parents, or fulfill his own ideal. Then he himself, that is, the violin, he himself has saved up a lot of money. That is, he saved up money to buy this violin. Then he thought in front of the violin . . . I feel that in the picture his decision will be putting away his violin, then he will obey his parents. After that, maybe later, when he has more money, by then he can fulfill his own dream—telling his parents that in fact learning to do, play violin can be successful. [Chinese boy]

Among white American students, when the boy feels an outside pressure, it almost always comes from parents. In immigrant narratives on the other hand, the protagonist in the story typically feels pressure due to academic concerns over being able to do homework adequately or performing in a forthcoming test (16.2 percent). Here is a typical story that reflects this concern:

> The boy had taken violin lessons in the afternoon schools for a long time. One day he had to withdraw from the violin class because he had too much homework. He did not want to give up the opportunity of studying violin. He was pondering while sitting by the table. He was very worried. If he continued to study violin he wouldn't be able to catch up with his homework. But he had made big progress in his violin skills and his violin teacher wanted him to continue to study at advanced levels. He was so worried. He finally decided to give up the violin study to do his homework. [Chinese boy]

In our previous research, we noticed that the immigrant youth were less likely than the other groups to tell stories where fame was the outcome. Instead, they tended to recount stories that reflected successes—but on a small scale. In coding, we considered what was the narrator's definition of success (whether or not the resolution of the story was successful). Only 7.7 percent of the stories reflected an outcome of fame. When such stories occurred, they were more likely to be told by a Chinese participant (17.7 percent). For example:

> It was in 1964, this boy was very poor, he only had a violin at home. His house was merely a dilapidated one, and he made a living by playing some tunes on his violin at streets, begging for money from by-passers. He could hardly get some money because his tune was bad. Now he was cracking his brain for making a good tune. He hoped that he would play a very sad tune, which was so sad. While he played all the by-passers who heard this tune would come up to give him money. Later there was a very rich couple that adopted him. Through hard work, finally be became a very famous violinist. [Chinese boy]

> He looks sad. Maybe it was his birthday and he wanted a guitar but (his parents) got him a violin. His parents told him there's nothing they could do because they couldn't return the violin. The boy doesn't like it but his parents got him a violin teacher. The boy feels bad and doesn't know what to do. If he does what he likes (playing the guitar) or if he does what his parents want. In the end, the boy becomes a great violin player. [Mexican girl]

Instead, stories often defined success with a more constricted successful resolution of a particular one-time event such as a concert or solving a particular problem. These kinds of stories were evenly distributed between groups and accounted for 30.6 percent of all narratives:

> He feels sad because he is going to study and because he does not want to play the violin. Later he played the violin and he played it well. And the next day he had a concert. When he played, everyone clapped. And the boy ended up being happy. [Dominican boy]

> A boy is taking classes after school to learn to play the guitar. He doesn't know how to play it but he is thinking about it and trying to concentrate. Then he plays at a concert in front of a group of people. [Haitian boy]

Mastering a task such as learning to play the violin, learning a language, or tackling a particular subject matter was the other frequently recounted definition of success. In 31.4 percent of these stories, evenly distributed across groups, mastering a new skill was the standard of success. For example:

> One day, Ming's mother asked Ming to learn the violin. He promised to do so. His mother invited a violin teacher home to teach Ming how to play violin. Ming finished the lesson and practiced afterwards. But he could not play the violin. He was frustrated. His mother saw his frustration. She came to him, "I know that you are getting frustrated, but I believe that you have read Shan Gi Jin [a Chinese traditional literature which teaches children moral lessons]. One of the sayings states, 'If you have a persistent heart, you can grind a metal rod into a needle.' Do you know what this statement means? This statement means if you work on

something persistently, you can solve any problem." After listening to his mother, Ming gathered his thought and continued to practice. At the end, he could play the violin. [Chinese girl]

The boy doesn't know how to play the violin and he wants to learn. And his friends don't know how to play and he is sad. Then he practiced a lot and he learned how to play and his friends saw that he could play. [Dominican boy]

For achievement stories, we were also were interested in assessing to what the storyteller attributed the success or failure. Was the success a result of personal effort, innate talent, or obtaining the help of others? In the group of immigrant children as a whole, the storyteller attributed a successful outcome to hard work, effort, and practice in 32.9 percent of the narratives. The Chinese participants were most likely to attribute success to personal effort; Central Americans were least likely to do so.

There was a child; his interest is music. He realized that he didn't know what kind of music he would like to work on. He just played around. Now he was thinking: how can I make a piece of good music? Finally, he gradually tried and saw that he could do it. At some point he was really focused. He made something and it is sort of like music. Then he continued to play music. After a while, he made a piece of good music. He practiced everyday; he practiced other songs. He wrote a lot of touching songs. Finally, he became a musician. [Chinese boy]

A boy was getting ready for a big concert. And he was practicing and he thought . . . and they said everybody had to pick an instrument they liked. And he picked that instrument because that was the closest one to where he was. So he actually went home and practiced and practiced and he couldn't get. He just keeps practicing until he got it. One day, he found out what was wrong and he finally got it. And he made it to play the violin. He was proud of himself. [Haitian boy]

When the protagonist succeeded because a family member, teacher, or other person provided support and assistance, "Help from Others" was coded. In 25 percent of the stories, the protagonist sought help from others. Haitians were least likely to turn to others for help (14.1 percent). Interestingly, Chinese youth were most likely to turn to peers, while Dominicans were most likely to turn to their father, and Mexicans were most likely to seek help from their mother. Chinese children also frequently turned for help in solving the problem to an older teacher or other non-parental figure. They would look for a person from the older generation who has the reputation of wisdom and skill, exemplifying the place of respect that they hold in the culture.

Xiao Ming bought a violin one day. He looked at the violin feeling that the violin was so beautiful, so he wanted to learn how to play it. One day, he carried his violin and went to look for teachers all over the place. Three years later, he ran into an old man who knew how to play the violin. The old man taught him. The boy

> learned how to play violin and later became a famous violinist. He shared half of his wealth with the old man. He loved his violin very much and he felt that the old man was very likable.

In the group of white American students discussed in the previous section, success was attributed to personal (individualized) effort in 51.1 percent of the stories. In contrast to that, help from others was sought in only 8.9 percent of the narratives from this group. These differences are significant, with the first figure being greater, and the second one being lower than that in any of the immigrant groups. These findings further illustrate the saliency of the relational aspects of the meanings of achievement for children who have recently immigrated to the United States. Below are some representative stories from the immigrant children:

> The boy is a very good violinist and he plays the violin very well. But there is something that blocks him suddenly. He feels very upset. He thinks "whom should I ask for help?" He thinks of one person who is suitable to help him and he goes to see him. The person helps him solve the problem. He feels very happy. He has a very capable, understanding, and loving person around him. [Chinese girl]

> A long time ago, there was a boy who learned how to play violin. He did not play well. His teacher told him to go home to practice. He was upset. His good friend asked him to go out to play. He did not. He stayed home to play violin. One of his good friends taught him how to play violin, and gave him [the gift of] music. The friend taught him how to play well. Finally, he played the violin. [Chinese girl]

> The story is about a boy who wants to learn to play the violin. But he doesn't have anyone to teach him and he is sad. He feels sad because he wants to learn this. He has a violin but he does not know how to play it. He does not play it. And he feels bored and very sad. The boy's father sends him to school to learn how to play the violin and the boy gets happy. [Dominican boy]

> The boy is sad because he can't play the violin. He keeps looking at the violin and feeling sad. He asks his mom to help. She does and he's happy. [Mexican boy]

Of interest was whether or not the tension in the story was successfully resolved. The narratives tended to reflect the general optimism of immigrants (Suárez-Orozco and Suárez-Orozco, 2001). Fully 55.1 percent of the immigrant stories were successfully resolved. However, the Chinese and Dominicans were most likely to relate successful outcomes (70.9 percent and 69.6 percent respectively).

> This person is working on something here. He is doing experiments or stuff like that. Maybe he has come across some minor difficulties. He doesn't know what it is about. He is thinking. He thinks very hard. He has to find a scientific way to solve this problem. He will get the solution. Because, from the picture one can tell that he is very focused. He looks at it . . . he just thinks, he finally gets it and he is

> very happy, "I finally succeed." [Chinese girl] [Note that in switching to the first person, the informant projects herself into the boy's role.]

> There was kid who wanted to learn music but he didn't know how. He would try, try, and try and he couldn't. He was poor and wanted an instrument and his mother worked and worked to buy him the instrument and then 2 years later his mother gave him one for Christmas and then the kid was registered at a music school and then he learned. [Dominican boy]

Haitians were least likely to provide successful resolutions to their stories and were most likely to narrate stories that ended in failure. These stories reflect the particularly adverse conditions recent immigrants from Haiti are leaving (intensification of violence, great poverty, lack of adequate educational services for all) as well as the less than optimal contexts they are entering (violent neighborhoods, segregation, low teacher expectations, and social discrimination). For many, the future (as well as the past) appears bleak. These stories reflect this pessimism born of experience.

> The boy wants to be a musician and he has to play in front of a lot of people. And he went there. He didn't play well, so he's mad and sad. [Haitian boy]

Stories resulting in failure are told by other immigrant youth as well:

> A boy wanted to take violin classes to go to a contest and then he practiced and practiced and he went to a theater competition and he thought he would win but he lost and he was sad. [Dominican boy]

As we saw in the previous section of this chapter, immigrant youth were more likely than any of the groups to voice concern with whether or not the protagonist could accomplish a task. In many such stories, the protagonist was worried about whether or not he had the necessary skills and talents to succeed. The new study confirms the earlier findings. Fully 41.7 percent of the stories in the L.I.S.A. sample reflected concerns over adequacy. There were significant group differences on this theme of "concerns with adequacy." Chinese youth were least likely to cite such concerns and Haitian participants were most likely to do so (27.8 percent and 52.1 percent respectively).

> The boy is lonely and sad because nobody's home and don't know how to play the violin. And there's a big recital in 2 weeks. He's thinking maybe he should quit playing the violin since he doesn't want to mess up in the recital. [Haitian girl]

> The boy feels sad. He can't do his homework. He tries to play the violin. He can't do it. He leaves it alone because he can't do it. [Mexican boy]

There's a person in the picture. He just came to the United States from China as well. When he was in China, he liked to play violin, and he played well. People liked to listen to him play. But after he came to the United States he doesn't know how to read the music. That is why he hates American English and he doesn't play the violin anymore. [Chinese girl]

Like he's really sad. He's looking at some homework. He's thinking about what he has to do. It looks like he has to do some job, homework—sad and thinking about what he has to do. It appears that he doesn't know what he has to do because he's unmotivated. He doesn't want this—the homework. At the end he'll be able to work fine without any problems. It appears as if he's at school except that there's nobody else there, only him. It appears like it's music class; like he wants to learn music. It appears as if he has a violin but he doesn't know how. He wants to learn to play but he's sad because he doesn't know what he has to do. When he gets to school, he starts playing the violin because he learned to play the violin. He learned how to play the violin thinking, practicing a lot, watching musicals with a textbook and things like this. [Dominican boy]

The boy is feeling bad. Perhaps he doesn't understand the homework or the drawings and he is thinking about if the homework will come out—good or bad. Perhaps the boy's teacher could punish him because he doesn't do his homework or exams right. His mom could come to school to see what's happening with him. If he doesn't pass the exams, they punish him or send him to another school. He wants to be at this one. They send him to an English school and he can't do the homework. Little by little he learns English and gets the homework right. [Central American girl]

It is poignant to see how in such narratives, we can detect a direct projection onto the protagonist in the story of the informant's preoccupation with learning English as a *sine qua non* for mastering an academic task. This is a major preoccupation among immigrants not found in other populations sampled with the TAT. Our findings indicate that playing the violin is a metaphor for mastering an arduous task—learning English, passing a test, doing well on an assignment.

In many narratives there is some tension around impediments to completing the task at hand. Among immigrants, not having the requisite knowledge to complete the task at hand was the most frequently cited impediment presented in the narrative. In the overall immigrant sample, 43.8 percent of the narratives reflected this theme:

A boy was looking at a violin and he didn't know how to play and he thought, "What do I do with this if I don't know how to play?" [Dominican boy]

He feels sad because he can't play the violin. He does not know how to play. He wants a music teacher to give him lessons so he can learn and not feel sad. In the end he learns to play and is happy. [Central American girl]

The story is about a boy that does not know how to play the violin. He is sad because he does not know how to play. The solution would be that somebody would help him by showing him how to play. The boy then would know how to play. The story would end well. [Mexican boy]

In many immigrant stories, the impediment presented is that the violin is broken. It is psychologically significant whether an angry protagonist purposefully breaks the violin or whether it is accidentally broken and the protagonist is searching for a way to fix it. Unlike the white American stories in our earlier research where the boy in the story purposefully breaks the violin (in 10 percent of the stories), only one violin was purposefully broken by the protagonist in all of the 388 immigrant stories we collected for the L.I.S.A. project. However, in 19.3 percent of these stories, evenly distributed among the immigrant groups, the violin is broken either *accidentally* by the protagonist, or accidentally or purposefully by others. These stories create a crisis to be overcome and reflect an anxious quality as well as despair about the externally imposed hardships of life. The cases in which others purposefully break the violin are few; however, they are important to note, since they reflect a tense interpersonal environment. These are frequently stories involving broken trust in friends.

Table 15.5

Broken Violin—Types of Stories among the Immigrant Groups

Immigrant Group	*Purposefully by Self*		*Accidentally by Self or Other*		*Purposefully by Other*		*Total Broken Violin*	
	N	*%*	*N*	*%*	*N*	*%*	*N*	*%*
Chinese	1	1.2%	18	22.8%	2	2.5%	21	26.5%
Dominican	0	0	14	17.7%	2	2.5%	16	20.3%
Central American	0	0	10	13.3%	0	0	10	13.3%
Haitian	0	0	10	14.0%	2	2.8%	12	16.9%
Mexican	0	0	12	14.2%	4	4.8%	16	19.1%

Whether the breakage of the violin has occurred purposefully or accidentally, there is a concern about being scolded, and more poignantly, concern about saving money to pay for the repair and regret about causing additional financial burdens for the family. Almost always, these are stories of immense sadness, since the love for the violin is quite palpable. Generally, in the presence of a broken violin the process of repair—and thus metaphorically of healing and making things better—is very central. The repair is also frequently a relational process, as the child would seek out friends or parent to help with mending the broken instrument.

At the beginning, she really wanted to be a female musician. But her musical instrument was broken. She couldn't play it. When the instrument was fixed, she

> didn't play it. She borrowed money to repay her loan. Her friends didn't play with her—they didn't lend her money. She felt sad, very sad. Because she wanted to be a musician; she wanted to play the instrument, yet the instrument was broken. And her friends didn't want to loan her any money to fix the instrument. That's why she was troubled. Then she worked very, very hard. After she began worrying, she made some money to fix the instrument. Then her music gets better. Then she became a musician. [Chinese girl]

> Before, the violin string broke. Now the boy is pensive and thinking about how to fix it because he has to give it to the professor to play a piece. The boy was thinking. Then he went to find a piece of wire. He tried to fix it. The result is that he put it on and the wire worked out. And he played the violin to see if it worked. The boy was happy to play the violin. It was obvious that the violin was broken. He became desperate because he didn't know what to do. A friend came. He lends him a string that he kept. [Dominican girl]

> One day, Xiao Ming bought a violin with his own saved money. He saved for a long time because he really loved playing the violin. But one day his violin was broken by another person. Xiao Ming didn't blame the person, but he went home and sat by the table feeling unhappy and very sad. He thought of all the ideas to fix the violin, but he couldn't fix it. He then pulled one string to here. After a while the violin could make many different notes. He could play the violin again. Consequently, he felt relaxed and happy. [Chinese boy]

A more internalized impediment to engaging the task at hand occurs in stories where the protagonist is unfocused or bored. This lack of focus on the task at hand is reflected in 19.8 percent of the stories.

> I think this person has a problem and is thinking about it and cannot concentrate well in what he is doing. It could be a family problem that he is sad because something happened. He feels too sad and he cannot stop thinking about it; he is exhausted. I think that after thinking about it, he can resolve it. [Dominican boy]

> The boy is doing something important and he's not going to do well because he is not paying attention. He's thinking about something else. He feels sad. If this is a test, he's not to earn points or make the grade. [Mexican Central American girl]

> The kid does not like to play the violin because he thinks it's boring. Nothing more. He stays sitting and looking at the music sheets. The story ends when he gets up and leaves. [Mexican boy]

In this sample, as with our previous research with immigrants, the dominant affect is that of sadness. In 45.6 percent of the stories, the protagonist is portrayed as sad. The significant losses and anxieties of immigrant youth are clearly reflected in the narratives they recount.

It seems like the boy is sad because he doesn't know how to play the guitar. It seems that there is no one that can help him with the problem. Nobody could help him and he continued to be a sad boy. [Dominican girl]

He feels sad because the violin is ruined and he doesn't know how to fix it or perhaps he doesn't know how to play it. He asks a friend to come and play it or tells his dad to fix the violin. [Central American boy]

This story is about a boy. He's sad because he can't learn things or the word his teacher dictated to him. He's nervous because he has an exam tomorrow. So he practiced a lot and did well on the exam. [Mexican boy]

Concluding Thoughts

Our interdisciplinary studies of refugee and immigrant youth have identified a series of broad interpersonal concerns emerging in the context of the upheaval of uprooting and resettling in the new country. The TAT narratives analyzed in this chapter reflect a variety of such concerns. First, immigration requires a great deal of energy and a faith that the future will bring better instrumental opportunities in the new land. The narratives recounted by immigrants capture this spirit. They are replete with reference to hard work, sacrifice, and faith in the future.

Our data have allowed us to identify the subtle configurations of an achievement motivation pattern among recent immigrants that seem to be quite distinct from the achievement narratives of non-immigrant white American youth. Immigrant youth, as a rule, create narratives imagining success as an internally motivated project, not a project imposed by parents or other authority figures. More importantly perhaps, immigrant narratives tend to be laced with what we have termed nurturant achievement—*for* others and *with the help of* others. Our data suggest that the independent self-oriented achievement cluster is almost non-existent in this sample of youth originating from such diverse regions of the world as the Caribbean, Asia, and Latin America. Our findings suggest that nurturant achievement is a more prevalent cluster than independent achievement.

These narratives also reveal the great travails that go into the making of the immigrant journey. Immigrants struggle hard to overcome disorientation and the feelings of *inadequacy* involved in moving to another country and successfully operating in a new cultural code. Learning the new "rules of engagement" requires hard work. Perhaps the dominant instrumental concern about competence among all new immigrants is the ability to master the new language. A number of the TAT narratives beautifully capture this concern in stories where the main theme was the boy struggling to learn English.

A most prevalent expressive affiliative theme in immigrant narratives is that of prevailing sadness. We interpret this in the context of the multiple losses that are attendant upon immigration. Immigrants leave behind relatives and friends, social roles, language competencies, and a whole array of social and cultural attributes. These losses are normative and almost inevitable in the context of immigration. Although a great deal of the sociological literature focuses on immigrant gains (better jobs, better status for women, better schooling for children), the psychological literature has long ago identified a pattern of normative reactive depression secondary to migration. While these psychological studies have tended to focus on clinical populations, the non-clinical samples reported upon in this chapter suggest that sadness and concern with loss is indeed a prevalent issue in the lives of immigrants.

Two decades of basic interdisciplinary research have taught us that the TAT can be a powerful tool when carefully used in the context of other ethnographic and sociological data. It is most useful when it allows informants to delve into interpersonal concerns that have affective valence. In such cases, it can be less intrusive than direct interviewing and subtler than ethnographic observations. We are convinced that it is best used along with other data after achieving the kind of ethnographic trust and rapport that can only be gained after months of ongoing research. Otherwise, informants tend to tell mechanical stories that lack the imaginative complexity and affective loading needed for meaningful psychocultural interpretation. Those envisioning using the TAT in their psychocultural research tool kit must proceed with caution. It is a labor-intensive technique requiring discipline in translation, coding, and interpretation. Failure to place findings in their proper social and cultural context can be dangerous, leading to cultural caricatures, psychological reductionism, and misrepresentation of social complexity. However, used properly, the TAT can generate empirical nuggets that beautifully capture cultural themes not easily revealed otherwise.

References

Ainslie, R. 1998. Cultural Mourning, Immigration, and Engagement: Vignettes from the Mexican Experience. In M. M. Suárez-Orozco (Ed.), *Crossings: Mexican Immigration in Interdisciplinary Perspectives*. Cambridge, Mass.: David Rockefeller Center for Latin American Studies/Harvard University Press.

Antokoletz, J. 1993. A Psychoanalytic View of Cross-Cultural Passages. *The American Journal of Psychoanalysis*, **53**(1): 35–54.

Banfield, E.C. 1958. *The Moral Basis of a Backward Society*. New York: Free Press.

Bean. 1991 (June 17-18, 1991). *Educational and Sociodemographic Incorporation Among Hispanic Immigrants to the United States.* Paper presented at the Conference on Immigration, Ethnicity and the Integration of America's Newest Immigrants, The Urban Institute.

Bellak, L. 1986. *The Thematic Apperception Test, the Children's Apperception Test and the Senior Apperception Technique in Clinical Use* (Fourth ed.). New York: Grune and Stratton Inc.

Boss, P. 1999. *Ambiguous Losses*. Cambridge, Mass.: Harvard University Press.

Carter, T.P. and R.D. Segura. 1979. *Mexican Americans in School: Decade of Change*. New York: College Entrance Examination.

Chapa, J. 1988. *The Question of Mexican-American Assimilation: Socioeconomic Parity or Underclass Formation?* Austin: Lyndon B. Johnson School of Public Affairs, University of Texas at Austin.

Connor, John W. and George A. De Vos. 1989. Cultural Influences on Achievement Motivation and Orientation Toward Work in Japanese and American Youth. In David Stern and Dorothy Eichorn (Eds.), *Adolescence and Work: Influence of Social Structure, Labor Markets, and Culture* (pp. 291–326). Hillsdale, N.J.: Lawrence Erlbaum Associates.

Delgado-Gaitan, C. and H.T. Trueba. 1991. *Crossing Cultural Borders: Education for Immigrant Families in America*. London: The Falmer Press.

De Vos, George. 1973. *Socialization for Achievement: Essays on the Cultural Psychology of the Japanese*. Berkeley: University of California Press.

De Vos, George. 1983. Achievement Motivation and Intra-family Attitudes in Immigrant Koreans. *Journal of Psychoanalytic Anthropology*, **6**: 25–71.

Espin, O.M. 1987. Psychological Impact of Migration on Latinas: Implications for Psychotherapeutic Practice. *Psychology of Women Quarterly*, **11**(4): 489–503.

Garza-Guerrero, A. 1974. Culture Shock: Its Mourning and Vicissitudes of Identity. *Journal of the Psychoanalytic Association*, **22**: 408–429.

Grinberg, L. and R. Grinberg. 1990. *Psychoanalytic Perspectives on Migration and Exile*. New Haven: Yale University Press.

Heller, C. 1966. *Mexican American Youth: The Forgotten Youth at the Crossroads*. New York: Random Press.

Hernandez, D. and E. Charney. (Eds.). 1998. *From Generation to Generation: the Health and Well-Being of Children of Immigrant Families*. Washington, D.C.: National Academy Press.

Kaminsky, M. 1993. On the Site of Loss: A Response to Antokeletz's Paper on Cross-cultural Transformation. *The American Journal of Psychoanalysis*, **52**(3): 103–108S.

Kantrowitz, B. and L. Rosado. 1991. (August 19). Falling further behind. *Newsweek*, 60.

Kleinberg, O. and G. De Vos. 1973. *Migration: Report of the Research Conference Migration, Ethnic Minority Status, and Social Adaptation*. Rome: United Nations Social Defense Research Institute.

McClelland, D. 1961. *The Achieving Society*. Princeton, N.J.: Van Nostrand.

McClelland, D.J., J.W. Atkinson, R.H. Clark, and E.L. Lowell. 1953. *The Achievement Motive*. New York: Appleton-Century-Crofts.

Padillo, A. 1993. (January 22–23). *The Psychological Dimensions in Understanding Immigrant Students: The Missing Link*. Paper presented at the the Conference on Immigrant Students in California Schools: Empirical Research and, Center for United States-Mexican Studies, University of California, San Diego.

Rumbaut, R. and W. Cornelius. 1995. *California's Immigrant Children: Theory, Research, and Implications for Policy*. La Jolla, Calif.: Center for United States-Mexican Studies.

Suárez-Orozco, C. 2000. Identities Under Siege: Immigration Stress and Social Mirroring Among the Children of Immigrants. In A. Robben and M. Suárez-Orozco (Eds.), *Cultures Under Siege: Social Violence and Trauma*. Cambridge: Cambridge University Press.

Suárez-Orozco, C. and M. Suárez-Orozco. 2001. *Children of Immigration*. Cambridge, Mass.: Harvard University Press.

Suárez-Orozco, C. and M. Suárez-Orozco. 1995. *Transformations: Migration, Family Life, and Achievement Motivation Among Latino Adolescents*. Palo Alto, Calif.: Stanford University Press.

Suárez-Orozco, C. and M. Suárez-Orozco. 1995. *Transformations: Immigration, Family Life, and Achievement Motivation among Latino Adolescents*. Stanford, Calif.: Stanford University Press.

Suárez-Orozco, M. 1989. *Central American Refugees and United States High Schools: A Psychosocial Study of Motivation and Achievement*. Stanford, Calif.: Stanford University Press.

Suárez-Orozco, M. 1996. Unwelcome Mats. *Harvard Magazine*, **98**: 32–35.

Suárez-Orozco, M. and C. Suárez-Orozco. 1993. Hispanic Cultural Psychology: Implications for Education Theory and Research. In P. a. A. L. D. Phelan (Ed.), *Renegotiating Cultural Diversity in American Schools* (pp. 108–138). New York City: Teachers College Press.

Trueba, H.T. 1989. *Raising Silent Voices: Educating the Linguistic Minorities for the 21st Century*. Cambridge, Mass.: Newbury House.

Vaughn, Curtis. 1988. *Cognitive Independence, Social Independence, and Achievement Orientation: A Comparison of Japanese and US Students*. Unpublished Ph.D. Dissertation, University of California, Berkeley.

Waters, M. 1999. *Black Identities: West Indian Dreams and American Realities*. Cambridge: Harvard University Press.

Index

Appendixes

Appendix A
Basic Interpersonal Concerns, Part 1
Emotional or Expressive Behavior

Pleasure: P

Self-Oriented, Internal Emotional States [S]

Sensation, Curiosity, Elation, Serenity, Satisfaction/Pain, Boredom, Depression, Anxiety, Frustration

A. Subjective Inner States

Physical Pleasure

PA-body	Physical or sensual—food, drink, bodily functions
PA-sensual	Sensuality in sexual or other bodily functions

Curiosity; Surprise, Exploratory Excitement, Ecstasy

PA-curious	Curiosity and discovery
PA-surprise	Positive unanticipated event or discovery; new experiences, sudden waking from a dream
PA-joke	Joking or the unexpected in humor
PA-excite	A positive sense of excitement
PA-ecstasy	Ecstasy, religious state or altered consciousness

Elation; Happiness, Joy, Play

PA-joy	Emotional pleasure, happiness, joy, mirth
PA-play	Play, recreation or relaxation
PA-memory	Happy memories

Serenity—Quietude

PA-relief	Relief, relaxation, or restorative feeling after an ordeal or difficulty
PA-meditate	Meditation—peace, quietude

Satisfaction—Contentment

PA-satisfy	Pleasure in productivity accomplishment, in music or work, etc.
PA-order	Sense of order, composition or harmony
PA-vicar	Vicarious pleasure in the happiness of others
PA-purge	Activity to relieve strong feelings; catharsis
PA-endure	Satisfaction while enduring through ordeal

Mixed

PA-esthetic	Aesthetic pleasure: (a) aesthetic, (b) graphic, (c) plastic, (d) music, etc.
PA-nature	Pleasure in nature or in the environment
PA-god	Happiness in god or religion
PA-hope	Feeling of hope and optimism

B. Unresolved Concerns with Pleasure and Pain

Unresolved Physical Discomfort

PB-tired	Tired or sleeping
PB-body	Physical discomfort
PB-hunger	Hungry or thirsty
PB-rage	Inner impulse of anger not specified

Disinterest; Boredom

PB-surprise	Surprised
PB-bored	Boredom, indifference, ennui
PB-sated	To be sated or jaded

Unresolved Emotional States

PB-denial	A directly expressed denial of emotional expression

Anxious Condition

PB-trouble	Troubled or disturbed
PB-anxiety	Unspecified general anxiety
PB-exist	Existential anxiety about human mortality

Frustration; Discontent, Dissatisfaction

PB-satisfy	Lack of resolved pleasure or satisfaction
PB-dislike	Expression of dislike or discontent; dislike of situation or circumstance
PB-sulk	Sulking; in a pout
PB-work	Displeasure in relation with the work situation or occupation
PB-defer	Deferred pleasure

Mixed

PB-torn	Ambivalent or uncertain emotional state
PB-stress	Internally stressed condition

C. Negative Categories Related to Arousal

Undue Active Physical State

PC-sensual	Nonspecified undue sensuality, overindulgence of the senses
PC-lust	Out of control, nonfocused sexual experiences, a negative perception of one's lustful nature

Crazed State

PC-crazed	Crazed state caused by unusual mental reactions to external events

Negatively Judged Elation

PC-cruel	Pleasure in cruelty; sadism
PC-evil	"Sinful" or evil pleasure (to be double scored when context makes it necessary)

Agitation

PC-unrest	Continually agitated, unable to attain serenity

Frustration; Dissatisfaction

PC-anger	Diffuse unfocused experiences of anger
PC-unsated	Insatiability or overindulgence (i.e., gluttony, avarice)

Mixed

PC-pain	Self-inflicted punishment or suffering
PC-suicide	Injurious or suicidal acts or thoughts

D. Passive States of Malaise

Pain; Bodily Sensations; Physical Suffering

PD-sex	Sexual activity viewed as unpleasant
PD-suffer	Suffering
Passive State of Negative Excitement	
PD-shock	Reaction of shock to events
PD-sloth	Sense of an incapacity to mobilize effort or interest
Depression	
PD-denial	Denial of emotions, incapacity to feel (acute or chronic)
PD-sad	Sad over specified situation
PD-submit	Masochistic pleasure in submission
PD-sorrow	General or unspecified grief or sorrow (crying, etc.)
PD-depress	Depression, despair
PD-suicide	Suicidal despair
PD-witness	Witnessed or imagined present or past unpleasantness
Pervasive Anxiety	
PD-anxiety	Diffuse sense of anxiety
Frustration; Dissatisfaction	
PD-thwart	Unspecified frustration or discontent
Mixed	
PD-mad	Madness caused by possible internal personality factors
PD-disorder	A sense of disorder or disarray
PD-disgust	Disgust in contact with unaesthetic people, objects, or behavior
PD-lost	Wistful over lost innocence

Nurturance: N

Vertical, Donor-Recipient, Status Positions [V]

Care, Succor, Protection/Withholding, Deprivation

From the Donor Position (ND)

A. Positive Nurture, Succor, Protection

NDA-nurture	Love, nurture; physical care
NDA-reward	Rewards, gifts, etc.
NDA-means	Material, educational, or economic assistance
NDA-comfort	Emotional comforting
NDA-nurse	Nurturant feeding or restorative care
NDA-secure	Giving or attempting protection and security
NDA-advice	Advice, instruction, guidance
NDA-active	Helpful activities on behalf of someone or group
NDA-family	General familial (acts done for the family); adoption
NDA-social	Acts done for community, society
NDA-rescue	Rescue or saving someone
NDA-devote	To be devoted to acts of sacrifice as an act of nurturance
NDA-charity	Benevolent act (often in religious context)
NDA-god	Rewarding deity; God's help, magical protection
NDA-prayer	Prayer for another
NDA-ritual	Protective or beneficial rituals
NDA-magic	Benevolent use of magic
NDA-help-s	Self-remedial or self-helping behavior
NDA-memory	Nostalgic nurture or care for others
NDA-disown	Denial of support from undeserving recipient

B. Concerns or Worry Over Giving or Helping

NDB-pity	Sense of pity, compassion for another's need or travail
NDB-welfare	Concern with another's well-being
NDB-body	Concern with bodily problems of another
NDB-means	Concern with material problems of others
NDB-lack	Lack of another to nurture (childless)
NDB-unable	Wanting to help unresolved (presently lacking resources or knowledge to be helpful)
NDB-thwart	Frustrated or rebuffed desire to help
NDB-reject	Fear or having one's nurturant acts rejected

C. Withholding, Abandonment

NDC-hard	Hard and ungiving, stern, unapproachable
NDC-selfish	Selfish lack of concern for others' needs
NDC-deprive	To withhold materially or educationally
NDC-comfort	To withhold or deprive emotionally
NDC-succor	Refusal of help or succor
NDC-desert	Abandonment of a needy one
NDC-protect	Refusal to protect
NDC-legal	Withholding of assistance due to a legal technicality
NDC-repay	Provide something to force repayment later
NDC-indulge	Overprotection, indulge, inducing dependency

D. Omission, Inability, Ineptitude

NDD-neglect	Deprivation through neglect or omission
NDD-unable	Inept and unable to help or take care of someone
NDD-comfort	Unable to provide emotional support
NDD-means	Unable to support financially

From the Recipient or Dependent Position (NS)

A. Receiving Nurture, Succor, Protection

NSA-trust	Trust in receiving care or protection
NSA-assist	Actively seeks assistance or help
NSA-reward	Given rewards, gifts, etc.
NSA-means	Given material, educational or economic aid
NSA-comfort	Given emotional aid
NSA-nurse	Given bodily succor
NSA-secure	Given security, protection, or blessing
NSA-edified	Given advice, intellectual or educational aid
NSA-grateful	Grateful behavior or feeling
NSA-forgive	Seeks forgiveness for past action or omission
NSA-god	Being taken care of by God
NSA-prayer	Seeking for protection or care of a deity, magic
NSA-malice	Counterprotection from malevolence
NSA-s-help	Becomes independent, needs no help
NSA-memory	Memory of being taken care of

B. Insecurity, Unresolved Worry Over Sustenance

NSB-help	Needs help, succor, or support
NSB-depend	Uncertain about emotional dependency
NSB-insecure	Fear of withdrawal or absence of care or protection
NSB-means	Fear of economic want
NSB-social	General uncertainty about security
NSB-other	Wants other than what given
NSB-deprive	Fear of deprivation by another
NSB-loss	Fear of losing something, or being stolen from
NSB-distrust	Distrust about receiving
NSB-envy	Unresolved envy over what another receives
NSB-jealous	Jealous and uncertain about one's dependency, related to rivalry about receiving nurture
NSB-god	Questions or distrust of God's goodness
NSB-bless	Uncertain about receiving blessing as support

C. Undue Demands, Covetousness

NSC-rivalry	Rivalrous over getting nurturance
NSC-envy	Active envy, coveting another's nurture
NSC-demand	Improperly dependent, demanding, wanting
NSC-refuse	Refusal to receive nurture, gift, etc.
NSC-injury	Injurious act to self or others' sense of deprivation
NSC-suicide	Injurious act (self or other) to force nurture

D. Passive Sense of Deprivation, Abandonment

NSD-lack	Insufficient help
NSD-comfort	Being emotionally deprived
NSD-means	Being economically or materially deprived
NSD-parent	No parents; homeless
NSD-deserted	Being or having been, abandoned
NSD-no-help	No help possible
NSD-sustain	Incapacity to sustain oneself; helplessness
NSD-suicide	Despair; lack of economic and or emotional support
NSD-intake	Inability to accept assistance or help

Affiliation: F

Horizontal-Reciprocal Relationships [H]

Closeness, Reunion, Good Communication/Loss or Lack of Relationship, Poor Communication

A. Positive Contact, Communication, or Reunion

Closeness

FA-empathy	Resonance, sympathy, empathy, understanding
FA-inform	Seeking closeness through communication
FA-friend	Friendship
FA-love	Love and warmth in a relationship; Physical closeness
FA-sex	Sexual relationships reviewed positively
FA-trust	Emphasis on trust in an affiliative relationship
FA-similar	Affiliation through a sense of similarity (Kinship, ethnicity, gender, class physical appearance)
FA-share	Affiliation through a sense of shared experiences or similarity in past experiences
FA-ties	Affiliation valued more than concern with objects or other activities
FA-injury	Injurious act to self or others as an act of love (includes euthanasia)

Positive Coping with Separation or Reunion

FA-distant	Contact despite distance
FA-solitude	Hermetic solitude viewed positively
FA-travel	Travel for a friendly visit
FA-console	Self-consoling, coping with separation
FA-happen	Reestablishment of contact broken due to external circumstances
FA-mend	Reestablishment of relationship broken due to discord, etc.
FA-rite	Ritual of amity or restoration of relationship
FA-death	Dyadic reunion in death
FA-mystic	Closeness to the ineffable or merger with the sacred
FA-casual	Casual relationship, nontraumatic

B. Unresolved Problems Related to Affiliation

Felt Need; Wanting Better Contact or Expressions of Warmth

FB-aware	Awareness of the sorrow or discomfort of another
FB-shy	Shyness
FB-isolate	Frustrated affiliation; inability to communicate
FB-alone	A deep sense of unresolved isolation or aloneness
FB-longing	Loneliness or longing for someone, homesick
FB-apart	Concern with possible or actual separation, temporary or not (due to circumstances)
FB-wait	Waiting for someone
FB-reach	Worry about getting close or communicating

Problematic Relationship

FB-problem	Undefined problem in relationship
FB-thwart	Thwarted in establishing a desired relation
FB-unruly	Passionately involved, helplessly in love
FB-accord	Lack of mutual understanding; unfamiliarity
FB-cry	Crying after a falling out
FB-distant	Unresolved feeling of emotional or attitudinal distance
FB-separate	Separation required by other purpose
FB-neglect	Sense of being neglected in a relationship
FB-envy	Envy of the closeness of others
FB-jealousy	Fear of being replaced; rivalry about attention or regard
FB-distrust	Distrust, anxieties about sincerity
FB-unmet	Discontent, dissatisfaction in a relation
FB-unsuited	Incompatibility in a relationship
FB-commit	Unresolved commitment
FB-split	Unresolved after attempt at split
FB-result	Negative influence of lover or peers
FB-observe	Observing without contact
FB-alien	No relationship depicted among the characters in a story
FB-identity	Problem about social identity

C. Negative Acts in an Affiliative Context

FC-split	Separation (sometimes not explained); flight from contact; withdrawal
FC-drift	Loss of feelings or closeness of another with time
FC-reveal	Reveal an uncomfortable secret
FC-neglect	Neglect of another
FC-deceit	Deception of a spouse or family member
FC-desert	Abandon friend or lover
FC-reject	Rejection and divorce
FC-triangle	Triangular relationship
FC-sex-rej	Sexual rejection of a partner
FC-betray	Deception or betrayal of a friend, lover
FC-seduce	Seduction of a sexual or nonsexual nature, also impersonal lust
FC-impose	An imposed continuance of a relationship
FC-selfish	Disregard of another, incapacity to be sensitive to another
FC-demand	Excessive demand or excessive focus (emotional or physical)
FC-affect	Inability to accept affection
FC-union	Suicide with another to create union (double score with HC-injury)
FC-injure-s	Injury to self and other due to loss of a relationship (double score with HC-injury)
FC-suicide	Injurious act to self after the hurt of a love object (Double score with HC-injury or HC-murder)
FC-pact	An affiliative pact leading to injury of both for self motives

D. Incurred Loss, Separation, or Isolation

FD-fate	Loss of love or friend due to circumstances, including death or a need to choose between loved ones
FD-death	Death following a loss of affiliation
FD-social	Loss of love due to social obedience
FD-split	Final separation (double score when necessary as due to discord, punishment)
FD-cold	Indifferent coldness or neglect of other person
FD-affect	Inability to feel affection or other feeling
FD-rejected	Loss due to rejection or divorce
FD-autonomy	Loss of love object or friendship due to another's assumption of an independent life or autonomy
FD-isolate	Experience an isolate, lonely existence
FD-no-one	No-one; homeless, bereft of companionship
FD-seduced	Seduced into a negative relationship
FD-thought	Inability to share thoughts or comprehend another
FD-shunned	A person may be shunned by one's social group
FD-retreat	Retreat from others due to feeling hurt

Esteem: E

Vertical, Horizontal, and Self-Oriented [V, H, S]

Appreciation/Denigration; Self-Respect/Shame

According Esteem or Evaluating Others (ED)

A. Positive Evaluative Attitudes

EDA-respect	According respect
EDA-awe	According awe and reverence
EDA-holy	Appreciation of another's holiness or purity (related to religion)
EDA-status	Positively perceived status
EDA-family	Appreciation of another's family or lineage
EDA-ethnic	Appreciation of another ethnic group
EDA-praise	Appreciation or praise of another
EDA-fame	Famous or recognized person
EDA-appear	Physical appreciation of another (beauty, strength, etc.)
EDA-reclean	Reestablishment of another's status after degradation or pollution

B. Unresolved Evaluative Attitudes

EDB-lessen	Disappointment in another
EDB-appear	Concern with the appearance of another
EDB-evaluate	Uncertain or undisclosed evaluation
EDB-torn	Unresolved respect toward another
EDB-envy	Envy of the regard or status afforded another
EDB-status	Concern with social status of another

C. Negative Evaluation of Others

EDC-disdain	Pride, arrogance, disdain, humiliation, degradation of another
EDC-group	Depreciation or degradation of a group
EDC-contempt	Expressing contempt despising another
EDC-sarcasm	Sarcasm, teasing; verbal dueling
EDC-insolent	Rude or insolent behavior toward a superior
EDC-brash	Brash, no respect for others' feelings or opinions
EDC-status	Defensive use of status against other/others, chauvinism, sexism, etc.
EDC-moral	Moral self righteous toward another
EDC-expect	Devaluating expectations of another
EDC-disgust	Finding another repulsive, ugly, or disgusting
EDC-slander	Slander, calumny
EDC-lessen	General disparaging of society, disillusionment

D. Ineffectual or Unseemly Evaluation

EDD-withhold	Withholding of recognition
EDD-unable	Incapable of giving recognition
EDD-awe	Excessive regard for another
EDD-praise	Excessive praise, flattery or adulation

Esteem: E

Vertical, Horizontal, and Self-Oriented [V, H, S]

Appreciation/Denigration; Self-Respect/Shame

Subject to Evaluation of Others
or Self-Directed Concerns About Acceptance *(ES)*

A. Positive Evaluative Attitudes

ESA-status	Positively perceived social-professional status
ESA-family	Pride in one's family or lineage
ESA-ethnic	Ethnic pride as self-appreciation
ESA-worth	Self-respect, sense of worth or acceptability
ESA-praised	Appreciated
ESA-loved	Loved, popular
ESA-approved	Approval of an audience, authority
ESA-appear	Approved appearance; physical characteristic
ESA-pride	Others are proud of self
ESA-demure	Self-effacing, modest, "shy" as a virtue opposite of self-forwarding
ESA-fame	Recognition of achieved status (fame)
ESA-heroic	Recognized as heroic in deeds
ESA-awe	Receiving awe or deference
ESA-restore	Restoration of honor by sacrificial act
ESA-pure	Pure or purified, in religious terms

B. Unresolved Evaluative Attitudes

ESB-esteem	Insecure self-respect or self-esteem
ESB-praised	Worry about being appreciated
ESB-shamed	Worry about negative evaluation of others; embarrassment
ESB-appear	Worry about appearance
ESB-accepted	Worry about being accepted
ESB-regard	Unresolved regard or recognition of peers
ESB-ignored	Worry about being ignored
ESB-teased	Concerned with being teased
ESB-unworthy	Concern about unworthiness
ESB-status	Doubt about social acceptance or status
ESB-expose	Worry about compromising exposure

C. Negative Active Evaluation Related to Self

ESC-conceit	Narcissistic preoccupation or pride
ESC-exhibit	"Showing off" unduly exhibitionistic
ESC-lessen	Disappointment someone loses others' esteem
ESC-detract-s	Self-depreciation (general)
ESC-group	Self-depreciation related to one's group
ESC-appear-s	Active self-depreciative sense of ugliness
ESC-hate-*s*	Sense of active self-hatred
ESC-abase-s	Self-abasement before others
ESC-disgrace	Behavior brings disgrace on family or group
ESC-injury	Hurt to self or others due to loss of status
ESC-suicide	Suicide due to loss of social regard
ESC-honor	Vengeance related to personal or family honor (Double score with HD-revenge)

D. Negatively Incurred Evaluations

ESD-unfair	Unfairly unappreciated
ESD-shamed	Feeling of being shamed, humiliated, mortified
ESD-shunned	Being shunned for one's behavior
ESD-disgraced	Family or group shamed by another member
ESD-exposed	Exposed or revealed for bad behavior
ESD-infamy	Considered notorious or infamous
ESD-base	Sense of worthlessness
ESD-impure	Sense of impurity or defilement
ESD-illusory	Disillusionment with the self

Harmony: H

Vertical and Horizontal [V, H]

Harmoniousness, Conciliation/Discord, Destruction (Hostility)

A. Positive Harmony, Cohesion, Reconciliation; Group Maintenance or Protection

Internal Harmony

HA-depict	Descriptive appropriate role behavior
HA-family	Expressions of harmonious family relationships
HA-group	Harmonious interaction or group concordance
HA-conform	Conformity to preserve group harmony
HA-agree	Agreeable, congenial, good-natured disarming role behavior
HA-pacify	Attempted mollification, mediation, or conciliation of discord
HA-forgive	Forgiveness to reestablish group or mutual togetherness
HA-mend	Reestablishment of harmony
HA-reunite	Group reunion occasioned by death, usually a family member
HA-symbol	Symbolic peace
HA-rite	Group ceremony or ritual; religious activity, attendance
HA-god	Belief in the harmony of God's world or in a divinely or perfectly ordered cosmos

Positive Defensive Postures

HA-courage	Courage enabling one to face personal adversaries or opponents
HA-secure	A sense of harmonious within-group security
HA-combat	Righteous combativeness or defense aggression, or protest to preserve group
HA-engulf	Dedication, loss of self in political or religious group; engulfed in a movement as an expression of role dedication toward group maintenance, including self sacrifice

B. Unresolved or Potential Discord; Fear of Malice

Unresolved Anger

HB-dislike	Unresolved dislike
HB-anger	Anger (sometimes nonspecified)
HB-inhibit	Repressed, inhibited physical violence
HB-revenge	Desire for vengeance
HB-envy	Envy
HB-jealous	Jealous of one's love
HB-hurt	Hurt feelings
HB-resent	Unresolved resentment, real or imagined deception, or injury
HB-family	Concern about family cohesion
HB-group	Concern about group cohesion
HB-unrest	Condition of social unrest
HB-split	Concern about potential removal from family
HB-control	Unresolved anger, irritation over being pressured or controlled
HB-torn	Ambivalence about expected social role participation
HB-break	"Fed up" with a social or personal situation; desire to break ties
HB-role	Possible conflict between role expectations
HB-deceit	Deceit to avoid anger or preserve harmony

Impending Fears

HB-fright	Frightened, not specified as to source
HB-f-attack	Feared attack (animal or human)
HB-f-anger	Feared anger of another
HB-f-fury	Fear of potential violence
HB-f-repay	Fear of possible vengeance
HB-f-envy	Fear of envious behavior
HB-f-super	Fear of malevolent supernatural
HB-f-magic	Fear of magic
HB-god	Questions about religious harmony

C. Negative Active Discord, Destruction, Violence

HC-discord	Anger, quarrel or discord
HC-hostile	Some form of specified or nonspecified hostility toward others to make them suffer
HC-verbal	Abusive verbal attack; Excessive nagging
HC-beat	Physical expression of violence, beating
HC-injure	Physical injury of another
HC-cruel	Cruelty, sadism, inflicting psychological trauma
HC-rape	Rape; force used in sexual situation
HC-murder	Homicide
HC-elder	Generational animosity
HC-triangle	Discord in triangular relationship
HC-faction	Factional behavior; also excluding a group member
HC-selfish	Inconsiderate behavior causes hurt
HC-revenge	Revenge (when with physical violence double score)
HC-control	Dominance as a gratification of power at the expense of another (double score with DDC)
HC-contempt	Expression of repugnancy or contempt causing hurt (double score with EDC-contempt)
HC-vandal	Vandalism, arson, wanton destruction
HC-rake	Dissolute or self-destructive behavior
HC-suicide	Suicide anger directed toward self
HC-magic	Malevolent magic

D. Passively Incurred Discord or Dissolution

HD-hurt	To feel hurt by another or others
HD-injured	To be physically injured by others, to be made ill
HD-crime	Victim of an assaultive crime
HD-death	To incur the violent death of someone
HD-withheld	To feel hurt by destructively intended withdrawal or withholding (double score)
HD-maligned	Victim of malice, or being maligned
HD-vilified	To be hurt by derogation or disparagement, or social injury (double score)
HD-decay	Dissolution, decay, or decomposition of an individual, group, family, or society
HD-paranoia	Delusions of persecution
HD-bedeviled	Taken or captured by supernatural being
HD-bewitched	Bewitched, or injured supernaturally

Basic Interpersonal Concerns, Part 2

Instrumental, Purposeful, Regulatory Behavior

Achievement: A
Self-Oriented [S]

Purpose/Anomy, Alienation

A. Positive Active Achievement or Purpose

AA-self	Self-initiated activities toward the attainment of a goal
AA-persist	Persistence toward a goal, hard work-endurance
AA-inspire	Inspired by person or idealized achievement (including religious thought)
AA-counter	Compensatory achievement; overcoming the past, or avoiding future negative circumstances
AA-else	Alternative goal
AA-status	Achievement for status
AA-duty	Achievement as responsibility or duty
AA-nurture	Achievement to nurture others
AA-repay	Achievement as repayment for past nurture, etc.
AA-parent	Parent- or mentor-initiated activities toward the attainment of a goal
AA-peer	Peer group–initiated activities toward the attainment of a goal
AA-moral	Moralistic statement about achievement
AA-purpose	Existential meaning; self-defined positive purpose of life
AA-divine	A sense of divine purpose inspiring or guiding behavior

B. Passive Inactive or Unresolved Commitment

AB-inactive	Inactivity but interested in a task
AB-dream	Daydreaming about achievement (unrealistic ambition)
AB-think	Thinking about the future
AB-decide	Undecided future goal or contradiction or ambivalence about alternative goals
AB-torn	Alternative goal as possibility unresolved
AB-waver	Vacillation or inability to arrive at a commitment
AB-endure	Questions about endurance or frustration tolerance toward the realization of a goal
AB-purpose	Worry over possible loss of purpose or meaning of life

C. Anomic or Lawless Behavior

AC-illicit	Achieving through questionable activities
AC-crime	Direct criminal oriented activity toward a goal
AC-chance	Looking for opportunity for negative behavior
AC-bribe	Bribery to achieve
AC-plot	Plotting to achieve goal
AC-theft	Thefts and crime against property
AC-gang	Organized illegal activities
AC-motive	Dysfunctional activity due to insufficient motivation
AC-hurry	Impatience leading to abandonment of a proper long-range goal
AC-asocial	Success at the expense of relationships with others
AC-injury	Injurious action to self or others due to alienation

D. Alienation; Social Withdrawal or Lack of Purpose

AD-motive	Lack of motivation
AD-mediocre	Mediocre attainment due to lack of strong purpose
AD-lack	Give up ambition due to lack of funds, proper education, opportunity
AD-bias	Give up ambition due to discrimination, unfair treatment
AD-refuse	Refusal of proffered opportunity
AD-withdraw	An alienated withdrawal from a task or goal
AD-purpose	Expressed alienated sense of lack of social purpose
AD-endure	Incapacity to endure or tolerate frustration necessary toward attainment of a goal
AD-dream	Escapist daydreaming (so seen by the storyteller)
AD-irony	Ironic form of distancing from social goals
AD-meaning	Attenuation of social meaning
AD-regress	Psychological withdrawal can result in a regressive psychotic state

Competence: C

Self-Oriented Internalized Judgment of Performance [S]

Mastery/Failure, Incapacity

A. Realization of Mastery and Adequacy in Problem-Solving Behavior

CA-present	Expression of present mastery, capacity, ability, or adequacy, including awareness of aging
CA-past	Expression of past mastery, capacity, ability, or adequacy
CA-future	Expression of future mastery, capacity, ability, or adequacy
CA-test	Demonstration of competence (passing a test or ordeal)
CA-endure	Capacity to endure or survive tribulations or difficulties in life
CA-body	Reference to one's capable body
CA-defect	Overcoming a handicap
CA-comic	Success despite inadequacy (the comic-comedy)
CA-repair	Capacity to repair
CA-improve	Self-improvement through persistence or hard work; mastery
CA-open	Open minded and adaptive to circumstance
CA-expert	Capacity through experience
CA-able	Positive actualization of one's own occupation or destined role
CA-create	Positive sense of capacity to be creative
CA-model	Copy or use model to emulate, learn, or gain proficiency
CA-aware	Scientific causality and awareness to solve problems
CA-help-s	Self-help, self-improvement by internal reordering (meditation)
CA-relief	Internally achieved confidence as a relief from anxiety
CA-affirm	Affirmation of an achieved status
CA-know-s	Knowledge, perception (insight) into oneself
CA-know-o	Knowledge, perception (insight) into others
CA-magic	Supernatural or magical ability
CA-trance	Empowerment through a supernatural entity by entering a trance state

B. Unresolved Issues of Personal Ability

CB-help	Needs help to solve problem—outside assistance
CB-worry	General or unspecified worry, doubt, or anxiety
CB-arduous	Difficulty with a task, or emergency situation; need to solve a problem or enigma
CB-able	Worry, doubt about capacity, ability
CB-blind	Innocence or ignorance preventing adequate behavior
CB-age	Concern about diminishing ability with aging
CB-inferior	Worry, doubt about inferiority
CB-decide	Vacillation in a decision; making a decision with great difficulty
CB-chafing	Impatient, chafing, to complete task
CB-else	Secondary or compensatory goal of which one is capable rather than primary objective
CB-hope	Hope for the future capacity of another
CB-defect	Difficulty in repairing or overcoming a defect
CB-status	Worry about the capacity to realize a desired social status
CB-delay	Procrastination, put off starting
CB-weak	Concern about weakness in self-assertion
CB-prayer	Seeks supernatural assistance in a task

C. Ineptitude in Attempted Performance

CC-inept	Ineptitude in proper performance of a task
CC-fake	Fraudulent or faked competence
CC-mental	Frustrated or bungled action due to internal factors of an intellectual order (lack of intelligence, or knowledge)
CC-body	Frustrated or bungled action due to internal factors of a physical order
CC-artist	Frustrated or bungled action due to lack of artistic capacity
CC-tragic	Failed action due to tragic flaw; tragedy
CC-loss	Injurious action to self or others due to failing professional, mental, physical, or sexual capacity
CC-break	Inept inadvertent breakage
CC-grand	Grandiosity

D. Withdrawal from Tasks Due to Ineptitude or Sense of Inner Incapacity

CD-inept	Judged to be inept by others or by self
CD-mediocre	Mediocre attainment due to inability, not lack of purpose
CD-unable	Inability to initiate or do task
CD-finish	Inability to realize a task that has been started
CD-weak	Feelings of weakness, powerlessness, helplessness
CD-inferior	Sense of inferiority in relation to others
CD-sex	Sexual incapacity or ineptitude
CD-chagrin	Chagrin or a sense of mortification over one's incapacity or lack of mastery
CD-aide	A helpless incapacity to aid or ameliorate the conditions of others
CD-psycho	Psychotic withdrawal due to incapacity to solve problems
CD-belief	Inability to perform or protect due to countering beliefs or convictions
CD-age	Loss of ability due to age

Control: D

Vertical, Superordinate-Subordinate Status Positions [V]

Influence, Power, Domination/Autonomy, Rebellion, Submission

From the Superordinate or Influential Position (DD)

A. Positive Control, Compliance or Autonomy

DDA-control	Legitimate power, authority including family control
DDA-scold	Parental scolding, disapproval, censure
DDA-punish	Parental punishment
DDA-reject	Rejection of family membership as punishment
DDA-group	Group or peer pressure
DDA-lead	Lead or seek to influence peers (score with MVA)
DDA-educate	Educational directives, or supervisory control
DDA-advice	Advice or persuasion (either peer or authority); mentorship
DDA-author	Exercise of proper civil authority or interdiction
DDA-police	Punitive community authority or surveillance
DDA-censure	Censure or disapproval from authorities
DDA-pardon	Pardon, absolution tolerance, or approval
DDA-mediate	Intervention or mediation in an authority context
DDA-trust	Put trust in or delegate to a subordinate
DDA-patient	Be patient or understanding with a subordinate
DDA-give	Instrumental giving used positively
DDA-free	Permission for another to assume autonomy
DDA-gambit	Instrumental sacrifice to induce behavior
DDA-curse	Supernatural punishment by legitimate authority
DDA-create	Creative act used to influence others
DDA-model	Influence others by serving as role model

B. Unresolved Legitimacy or Uncertainty About Authority

DDB-result	Doubting consequences of authority to others
DDB-torn	Ambivalent about assuming authority
DDB-worry	Worry about how to exercise authority
DDB-rigid	Uncertain about rigidity in enforcing regulations
DDB-free	Uncertain or insecure over autonomy of another
DDB-licit	Ambiguity of the legitimacy of one's actions
DDB-order	Fear of chaos or disorder, a need for social control
DDB-jealousy	Jealous about one's authority
DDB-example	Fear of influence of one's past or present behavior as negative example
DDB-patient	Unresolved patience or understanding with subordinate

C. Negative or Illicit Control or Resistance

DDC-unfair	Unfairness or discriminatory authority
DDC-press	Undue pressure, or punishment
DDC-rigid	Undue inflexibility or rigidity in enforcing control
DDC-despot	Undue dominance or the exercise of power for its own sake (political or religious)
DDC-exploit	Exploitation of vulnerability
DDC-corrupt	Corrupt authorities
DDC-punish	Overexertion of punishment or destructiveness
DDC-result	Negative consequence to others (may be due to poor judgment)
DDC-capture	Capture of another person
DDC-manage	Manipulative control
DDC-give	Manipulative giving, or reward inducing behavior
DDC-provoke	Provocative teasing
DDC-suicide	Threat or act of injury, suicide against subordinate
DDC-watch	Undue surveillance spying (police, etc.)
DDC-magic	Exercise magical control over another

D. Excessive Passivity in Exercising Control

DDD-lax	Lax and too indulgent in training role; lack of proper supervision
DDD-neglect	Irresponsibility or neglect
DDD-inept	Inept or ineffective exercise of power
DDD-weak	Failure to punish others when expected
DDD-helpless	Failure to respond to rebellion, or a sense of helplessness about attack by subordinates
DDD-deluded	Paranoid delusions in respect to subordinates

From the Subordinate or Autonomous Position (DS)

A. Positive Compliance or Exertion of Autonomy

DSA-permit	Asks permission of authority
DSA-assert	Autonomy or self-assertion from authority, family, peer pressure
DSA-mutiny	Overthrow of despotic authority
DSA-free	Escape from a status discrimination or from wrong scolding or punishment (family or authority)
DSA-free-s	Self-liberation; freeing self from excessive self-control or super-ego
DSA-comply	Proper compliance to family authority
DSA-author	Compliance conform with legitimate authority
DSA-trust	Trust in authority or superior
DSA-soothe	Supplication acts to please another
DSA-forgive	Supplicating forgiveness
DSA-appease	Instrumental donation or propitiation
DSA-persuade	Induced positive action by authority due to subordinate's persuasion or instigation
DSA-disobey	Disobedience as ultimate respect for authority
DSA-god	Belief in being subject to divine control
DSA-ritual	Ritual of supplication of the supernatural
DSA-prayer	Use of prayer

B. Unresolved Legitimacy or Uncertainty About Authority

DSB-punish	Fear of punishment by authority
DSB-torn	Ambivalent about legitimacy of authority
DSB-rebel	Concern with legitimacy of rebellion
DSB-obey	Reluctant obedience
DSB-ignore	Ignore or disregard authority
DSB-control	Uncertain of how to overcome dominance
DSB-advice	Uncertain about advice or guidance
DSB-envy	Envy of the greater influence of another
DSB-pardon	Concerns with pardon or absolution
DSB-approve	Need for approval
DSB-god	Awaiting God's judgment

C. Illicit Resistance or Manipulation

DSC-accuse	False accusations against a superior or authority
DSC-disobey	Defiant, self-willed, lacking proper humility
DSC-family	Resistance or rebel against family authority
DSC-resist	Resist or rebel against tutoring or social authority
DSC-escape	Escape from family, jail; violation of interdiction
DSC-rude	Rude, disrespectful behavior
DSC-tantrum	Emotional blackmail (temper tantrums)
DSC-seduce	Seductive or "Amaeru" behavior to influence others
DSC-manage	Manipulative to avoid any control
DSC-amaeru	Submissive to either gain instrumental goals or gain expressive gratification
DSC-give	Manipulative giving to please controller
DSC-injury	Injury to self to induce action of a superior

D. Excessive Passivity or Submissiveness

DSD-family	Excessive submission to family control
DSD-submit	Excessive submission to social authority
DSD-peer	Excessive submission to peer group
DSD-captive	Remain captive to a person or to a system of external or ideological control
DSD-fawning	Excessive fawning, obsequiousness, to gain instrumental ends

Responsibility: R

Self-Oriented Internalized Social Status and Self-Judgment [S]

Duty, Role, Fulfillment/Dereliction, Transgression (Guilt)

A. Active, Responsible Behavior

RA-work	Work; daily tasks as a responsibility
RA-good	A "good" person; responsible products or activities or unspecified as to nature of "goodness"
RA-example	Behavior as an example for guidance or training of others
RA-duty-s	Assumption of self-oriented or self-defined obligations or duties
RA-duty-o	Assumption of externally or socially defined obligations or duties
RA-order	Proper exercise of propriety, regularity, a positive sense of order
RA-control	Self-control in order to accomplish goals or duties
RA-stoic	Stoic reactions to adversity
RA-sex	Responsible in sexual behavior
RA-reform	Taking responsibility for previous behavior by reform, or reparation, resolution of guilt
RA-apology	Taking responsibility by apology, confession
RA-expiate	To give oneself up for punishment as a means of expiation
RA-hurt-s	Self-punishment or injurious behavior as an act of taking responsibility for negative behavior
RA-buck-o	Taking responsibility for the behavior of another, e.g., family members, subordinates, etc.
RA-injure	Injurious behavior to self or others in taking responsibility for the negative behavior of others
RA-repay	Obligatory reciprocity; necessary gifts (Japanese "giri" relationships)
RA-ritual	Ritual or ceremonial obligations
RA-suicide	Suicide as an act of duty or responsibility

B. Inner Concerns About Responsibility (Feelings Rather Than Actions)

RB-guilt	Guilt; unresolved repentance for present or past acts
RB-regret	Regret; ruefulness
RB-omit	To experience guilt or negative feelings for not having done something; guilt of omission
RB-duty	Unresolved duty or uncertain about how to be responsible
RB-resign	Unresolved resignation to the role behavior expected by others
RB-torn	Ambivalence about accepting responsibility
RB-role	Conflict between role responsibilities
RB-ideals	Internal conflict over social values or ideals
RB-legit	Ambivalent activities; questions of legitimacy

C. Excessive Irresponsible or Forbidden Behavior

RC-wrong	Wrongdoing unspecified; a "bad" person, unspecified
RC-group	Irresponsible group activities
RC-duty	To violate one's duty; corrupt authority
RC-rigid	Excessively rigid and inflexible
RC-control	Loss or lack of self-control
RC-indulge	General or unspecified acts of indulgence; sins of gluttony, laziness (sloth), lust with prostitutes, etc.
RC-messy	Messy or disorderly behavior; lack of inner or outer regularity, impropriety
RC-abuse	Self-indulgence, substance abuse (drink, narcotics, etc.)
RC-waste	Wasteful with money (gambling, etc.)
RC-rash	Rash, heedless, irresponsible acts
RC-illegal	Illicit or illegal acts
RC-ex-sex	Extramarital or prohibited sexual behavior (violating rights of legitimate partner)
RC-pre-sex	Premarital or nonmarital sexual behavior (with socially prohibited partner)
RC-perverse	Acts perceived as socially perverse; homosexuality, incest, fetishes, etc.
RC-mores	Violation of norms or customs, e.g., gossip, impoliteness, and improprieties of behavior
RC-status	Status violation, such as wife or husband neglect duties; children behave badly against family expectations; rowdiness; etc.
RC-property	Irresponsible or invasive use of another's property or social space
RC-hurt-s	Excessive self-punishment due to guilt
RC-example	Setting a bad example for others
RC-evade	Use of role or authority for evasion of responsibility
RC-sacred	Religious sacrilege

D. Avoidance; Refusal to Internalize Social Obligations

RD-weak	Inability to overcome addiction or resist temptation
RD-fail	Failure to take responsibility or be responsible for other's action
RD-wrong	Avoidance, escape of consequences of wrong behavior
RD-personal	Avoidance, escape or denial of personal obligations
RD-social	Avoidance, escape or denial of social obligations
RD-work	Avoidance, escape or denial of school or work duties, laziness, being (ne'er do well) deadly sin of sloth
RD-ignorant	Ignorance as destructive
RD-control	Escape from the expected obligations of an authority position demanding action influencing others
RD-environ	Escape or denial of responsibility for negative influence on social or environmental conditions

Mutual Purpose: M

Horizontal Reciprocal or Peer Relationships [H]

Competition/Cheating; Cooperation/Defection

Competition or Adversarial Conflict (Versus-MV)

A. Positively Perceived Rivalry or Competition

MVA-game	Regulated competition (games, contests, etc.)
MVA-work	Successful business or work competition
MVA-vie	Maneuvering for advantage or first among peers
MVA-smart	To outwit an opponent or win an argument
MVA-regard	Seeks competitive recognition
MVA-profess	Physical, artistic, academic competitive excellence
MVA-means	Competitive success in economic ventures
MVA-gambit	Acts of giving or concession to enhance, own competitive position
MVA-faction	Constructive factional in-group competition
MVA-war	Instrumental war waged against an enemy

B. Unresolved Competitive Situations

MVB-deal	Unresolved negotiation or deal
MVB-differ	Differ about how to compete
MVB-distrust	Distrust about fair play of competitors
MVB-envy	Envy of competitor's ability
MVB-jealousy	Jealous fear of the competence of another; fear of encroachment
MVB-anger	Anger over failure to win out or prevail
MVB-elders	Generational conflict in instrumental coping
MVB-against	Intergroup competitive emphasis (double score with other appropriate categories)

C. Unethical or Destructive Methods

MVC-war	Instrumental war seen negatively
MVC-faction	Divisive factional in-group competition
MVC-cheat	Unethical business behavior; lying, trickery, cheating
MVC-slander	Calumny, slander, etc. for competitive advantage
MVC-bribe	Comparative self-enhancement or status through gift exchange or bribery
MVC-remove	Removal of an opponent even by murder
MVC-magic	Use of magic to gain unfair advantage over rival

D. Withdrawal or Victimization

MVD-yield	Admission of defeat or capitulation to adversary; refugee flight
MVD-quit	Withdrawal from competition
MVD-refuse	Refusal to compete
MVD-cheated	Victim of unfair competition

Cooperation (Together-MT)

A. Concerted Behavior

MTA-interest	Sharing common interest
MTA-task	Cooperation in a task for a goal
MTA-family	Family action for a goal, specific or not
MTA-trust	Trust in others regarding tasks
MTA-union	Organizational affiliation trade unions, etc.
MTA-contract	Contract relationship (organic solidarity)
MTA-group	Group maintenance or enhancement
MTA-allied	Intergroup cooperative emphasis (double score with other appropriate categories)
MTA-defense	Cooperation in group defense (double score with Harmony categories if necessary)
MTA-devote	Subordination or sacrifice for group goals
MTA-repay	Reciprocal behavior to facilitate common behavior (including gifts)

B. Inactive or Unresolved Cooperative Situations

MTB-worry	Worry about the success or failure of a cooperative effort
MTB-join	Doubt about desire to join group effort
MTB-differ	Disagreement not specified
MTB-means	Disagreement about the means used
MTB-ends	Disagreement about the goal
MTB-rapport	Difficulties in communicating
MTB-distrust	Mutual distrust within one's own group
MTB-secret	Secretive activity going on not defined
MTB-allied	Unresolved intergroup cooperative emphasis (double score with other appropriate categories)

C. Negative Group Activities

MTC-crime	Group criminal behavior
MTC-plot	Plotting or political conspiracy
MTC-ethic	Unethical behavior
MTC-selfish	Selfish interests stronger than group's goals
MTC-false	Hypocritical, untrustworthy behavior
MTC-failure	Failure to fulfill one's part in group activities
MTC-betray	Betrayal or deception of an ally or colleague
MTC-injury	Injury to others for group ends
MTC-allied	Intergroup cooperative emphasis seen negatively (double score with other appropriate categories)

D. Betrayed or Exploited

MTD-victim	Being the victim of a conspiracy
MTD-exploited	Being exploited by others
MTD-cheated	Being cheated by others
MTD-accord	Suffer lack of coordination between parts of a group
MTD-failure	A sense of failure of a group effort

Basic Interpersonal Concerns
Objects and Fate

Objects: O

Attention to Objects, Possessions, the Environment, or the Body

A. Positive Use, Acquisition, or Possession

OA-body	Positive about the body
OA-clothes	Attention to clothes
OA-own	Positive about acquisition or possession of an object
OA-wealth	General concern with possessions or wealth
OA-please	Pleasurable use of objects
OA-esthetic	The aesthetic pleasure derived from object
OA-reward	Object as reward
OA-gift	Gift of an object to others or gift exchange
OA-pet	Having a pet as an object
OA-job	Job providing a sense of financial security
OA-status	Concern with status or ethnic symbols
OA-pride	Pride or attention to, beauty, or possessions
OA-guard	Protection of objects from harm; conservation
OA-create	Construction or creation of an object
OA-free	Indifference toward objects or possessions, viewed as a positive attribute
OA-collect	Collection of objects
OA-order	Arranging objects, order
OA-awe	Awe or reverence toward an object
OA-magic	Magical acquisition of an object
OA-spell	Magical use of an object
OA-symbol	Object or objects symbolizing the social self
OA-alive	Object as animate (pets)

B. Unresolved Concerns About Objects

OB-think	Thinking about an object
OB-want	Desire for an object
OB-torn	Ambivalence about possession of an object
OB-body	Preoccupied with body; attention to pregnancy
OB-care	Care of body, exercise
OB-clothes	Concern with clothes
OB-money	Concern with earning money, having a job
OB-compare	Concern with relative wealth or poverty
OB-baby	Concern with pregnancy or about the baby
OB-loss	Fear of losing something
OB-theft	Fear of theft
OB-break	Fear of breakage; fear of injury or destruction of object
OB-defect	Concern with bodily defect
OB-repair	Concern with repair of object
OB-jealous	Jealous fear of losing something to another
OB-envy	Fear of having an object envied
OB-dislike	Dislike or disinterest in an object
OB-worth	Indifference toward objects or possessions
OB-nature	Story switched to attention to physical surroundings or nature
OB-depict	Deflection into card description; description of physique, etc.

C. Negative Attitudes or Activities in Respect to Objects

OC-display	Excessive concern with display, exhibition; physical appearance or clothes
OC-clothes	Negative appearance of other's clothes
OC-body	Negative appearance of body
OC-greed	Excessive concern with money; greed; avarice
OC-wealth	Objects or impersonal ambition (wealth) given priority over a personal relationship (double score)
OC-revere	Excessive reverence for objects; idolatry
OC-hate	Hate of an object or objects
OC-discard	Abandonment or discarding of an object
OC-debase	Depreciation of an object
OC-destroy	Hate or destruction or injury of an object or aspects of our ecosystem
OC-indulge	Destructive use of the body (e.g., gluttony, or use of drugs)
OC-self-hurt	Bodily self-injury
OC-vandal	Destruction or injury of an object as a means of hurting a person or group (double score)
OC-rob	Robbery or theft
OC-control	Using objects to control people
OC-possess	Keeping an animal or person as a possession; psychic control or depersonalization of people into objects
OC-deceit	Acquisition by threat or deceit (double score)
OC-envy	Envy of the possession of others (double score)
OC-magic	Magical use of an object

D. Negative Incurred Experience in Respect to Material Objects

OD-body	Negative body image
OD-suffer	Body as object of suffering or negative depersonalized state experienced by body (including hunger)
OD-neglect	Neglectfulness toward an object or one's body as an object
OD-money	Without money
OD-loss	Loss of an object or possession
OD-robbed	Robbed
OD-broken	Suffering destruction of an object
OD-symbol	Symbolic destruction of an object
OD-taken	Being obsessed or possessed by objects
OD-used	Used as an object or kept as a possession (including slavery)
OD-psychic	Being possessed or used psychically

Kismet, Fate: K

Fortune, Fate, Circumstances, Inadvertencies, Accidents

A. Good Fortune

KA-luck	Good fortune, good luck
KA-social	Good social circumstances
KA-wealth	Good economic circumstances
KA-status	Inherited status or propitiously received status
KA-able	Inherited aptitude
KA-hardy	Hardiness, resiliency, courage, adaptive traits
KA-know	Chance acquisition of knowledge
KA-results	Inadvertent behavior leading to good consequences for self or another
KA-recovery	Recovery
KA-dream	Recovery from a bad dream; bad circumstance but a dream
KA-accept	Recognition or acceptance of one's fate
KA-magic	Magical intervention
KA-karma	Good fortune due to karmic inheritance from the past

B. Unresolved Karmic Conditions: Concerns About External Events and Superstitious Fears

KB-crisis	A social, environmental or medical crisis
KB-chance	Chance situation as yet not resolved
KB-events	Concern or anxiety in reaction to external events
KB-status	Concern with relative status
KB-want	Concern or fear of economic want
KB-mishap-s	Accident or fear or accident to self
KB-mishap-o	Accident or fear of accident involving another
KB-illness	Fear of illness or aging
KB-survive	Worries about physical survival
KB-nature	Concern or fear of natural dangers darkness
KB-hurt	Fear of behavior accidentally causing or allowing negative consequences
KB-magic	Superstitious fears (including the evil eye)
KB-hope	Hope in future good fortune
KB-karma	Uncertain fortune due to karmic inheritance from the past

C. Unfortunate Acts Releasing Negative Agents or Magical Consequences

KC-break	Accidental braking of an object
KC-hurt-o	Accidentally producing negative circumstances for others
KC-hurt-s	Behavior accidentally causing fateful consequences to the self
KC-taboo	Inadvertent breaking of a proscription or taboo with negative consequences
KC-evil eye	Trait accidentally causing or allowing negative consequences for another (evil eye)
KC-karma	Ill fortunate due to karmic inheritance from the past

D. Negatively Incurred Fate

KD-luck	Bad fortune, bad luck, or failure due to unspecified external events
KD-hopeless	Hopeless or irremediable situation
KD-news	Receiving bad news, unspecified
KD-loss	Loss of someone due to inadvertent circumstances
KD-poverty	Bad conditions or consequences of bad economic conditions
KD-deprive	Depriving, ungiving environment
KD-unjust	Unjust or unfair life conditions
KD-thwart	Frustrating life situation or occupation
KD-war	War
KD-animal	Suffers animal attack
KD-mishap	Accidents; inadvertent frustration of plans by unexpected presence or absence of another
KD-ac-die	Accidents leading to death; death in war
KD-illness	Illness
KD-ill-die	Illness leading to death
KD-death	Death (natural or unspecified)
KD-age	Old age, pity about age
KD-defect	Birth defect, handicap, crippling, inherited mental or personality defect
KD-mental	Insanity or neurosis, congenital mental damage
KD-resign	Resignation or succumbing to one's fate
KD-karma	Negative destiny due to karmic inheritance from the past

Appendix B

Japanese Cards

J-1: Boy with violin

J-2: Farm scene

J-6BM: Mother-Son

J-7BM: Mentor

J-8BM: Surgery

Japanese Cards

J-9: Family crisis

J-12F: Mother-in-law

J-13MF: Sex scene

J-18GF: Hand on neck

J-22: Family dispute

Kenyan and Filipino Cards

K-1: Boy with violin

P-1: Boy with violin

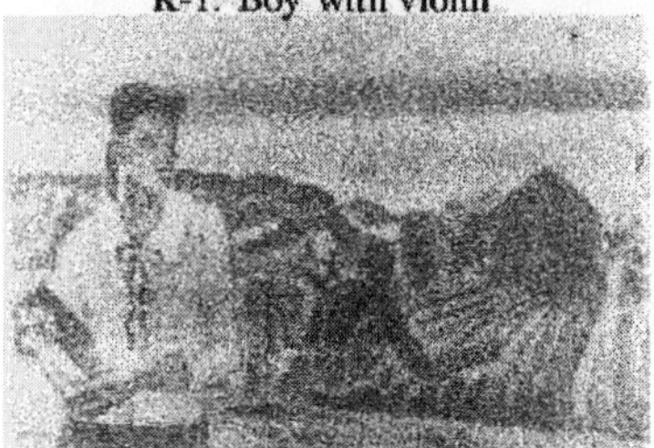

K-2: Farm scene

P-2: Farm scene

K-17BM: Man on rope

P-17BM: Man on rope

Additional Examples from Filipino Set

P-4: Man and woman

P-12: Two men

P-13B: Boy in doorway

P-19: In a store

About the Authors

George A. De Vos is both a psychologist and an anthropologist. He was trained at The University of Chicago and is now emeritus professor of anthropology at the University of California, Berkeley. His integrative social-sciences perspective is reflected in more than fifty years of field research in the United States, East Asia, and Western Europe. His twenty books and 180 articles have addressed topics such as delinquency, status inequality, ethnic identity, and the use of psychological tests in cross-cultural research.

Eric De Vos earned his doctorate in psychology at The University of Chicago's Committee on Human Development. He is currently professor of psychology at Saginaw Valley State University. His interests include thematic analysis of narratives as a cultural psychology methodology; the development of "self," self-regulation, and moral responsibility in cultural contexts; psychosocial factors in pregnancy outcome and infant development; Tibetan culture and Tibetan Buddhist psychology; and philosophical and psychological perspectives on consciousness and causality.